FROM PROGRESSIVE
to NEW DEALER

FROM PROGRESSIVE to NEW DEALER

Frederic C. Howe and American Liberalism

Kenneth E. Miller

THE PENNSYLVANIA STATE UNIVERSITY PRESS
UNIVERSITY PARK, PENNSYLVANIA

Library of Congress Cataloging-in-Publication Data
Miller, Kenneth E., 1926–
From progressive to New Dealer : Frederic C. Howe and American liberalism / Kenneth E. Miller.
    p. cm.
Includes bibliographical references and index.
Summary: "A biography of Frederic C. Howe, a reformer and political activist in Cleveland, New York, and Washington, D.C., in the Progressive and New Deal eras (1890s to 1930s)"—Provided by publisher.
    ISBN 978-0-271-03742-4 (cloth : alk. paper)
    ISBN 978-0-271-03743-1 (pbk : alk. paper)
    1. Howe, Frederic Clemson, 1867–1940.
    2. Social reformers—United States—Biography.
    3. Political activists—United States—Biography.
    4. United States—Social conditions—20th century.
    5. United States—Politics and government—20th century.
        I. Title.

H59.H6M55   2010
362.92—dc22
[B]
                        2010018246

Copyright © 2010 The Pennsylvania State University
All rights reserved
Printed in the United States of America
Published by The Pennsylvania State University Press,
University Park, PA 16802-1003

The Pennsylvania State University Press is a member of the
Association of American University Presses.

It is the policy of The Pennsylvania State University Press to use acid-free paper. Publications on uncoated stock satisfy the minimum requirements of American National Standard for Information Sciences—Permanence of Paper for Printed Library Material, ANSI Z39.48-1992.

*For Marilyn, Harold, Lisa, Susan,
and Connor, the youngest of the Millers*

CONTENTS

List of Illustrations   viii
Acknowledgments   ix
Abbreviations   xii

Introduction   1
1   A Comfortable Little World   4
2   The Truth Will Make You Free   17
3   Hanging on the Ragged Edge   30
4   Vistas of Political Possibilities   43
5   The City on a Hill   63
6   The Hope of Democracy   86
7   Writing and Politicking   114
8   Uprising and Uplifting   140
9   Marie Howe and the Heterodites   164
10   A Happy Interim   179
11   The Island of Tears   212
12   Liberals and the Great War   246
13   Peacemaking and Red Baiting   276
14   Searching for a New Party   302
15   Searching for Wisdom   334
16   Fred and Marie   362
17   Protecting the Consumer   377
18   From Washington to Manila   406

Bibliography   445
Index   467

ILLUSTRATIONS

FIG 1   Frederic C. Howe, rising thirty-three-year-old lawyer and soon-to-be Cleveland city councilman, ca. 1900 (Ferdinand Hamburger Archives of the Johns Hopkins University)   62

FIG 2   Rev. Marie H. Jenney, age thirty, assistant pastor, First Unitarian Church, Des Moines, Iowa, ca. 1900 (the Schlesinger Library, Radcliffe Institute, Harvard University)   87

FIG 3   An authors' meeting for woman suffrage, Cooper Union, January 12, 1914 (History Image, Portland, Ore.)   170

FIG 4   Frederic C. Howe, commissioner of immigration, Port of New York, Ellis Island, ca. 1914 (Prints and Photographs Division, Library of Congress)   208

FIG 5/6   Frederic C. Howe, consumers counsel and New Dealer, 1934: sketch and text by Peggy Bacon (Chesler Collection, Drew University, Special Collections, Madison, N.J.)   414

ACKNOWLEDGMENTS

This book has been a long time in the making. Neither Frederic C. Howe nor Marie Jenney Howe left collections of letters or other papers—indeed, they sought to have their correspondence destroyed. This meant that the search for their lives became something of a detective story in which clues had to be uncovered in the papers of many other people. Fortunately, Fred Howe was the friend or acquaintance of, or corresponded with, most of those who were engaged in politics or reform movements from the 1890s into the 1930s, and *their* papers have mostly been saved. Unfortunately, nearly all of Marie Howe's correspondence, except for a number of letters exchanged with Lincoln Steffens, is lost.

I am very grateful to those people who knew Frederic Howe and provided me with useful information through interviews and correspondence: Thomas C. Blaisdell Jr., Thomas H. Eliot, Arthur Goldschmidt, Alger Hiss, Gardner Means, Philip Morris, Edouard Stackpole, Grace Tugwell, and Caroline Ware. The late Warren Kliewer made it possible for me to hear Michele LaRue's stirring rendition of Marie Howe's "Anti-Suffrage Monologue." Jane Northshield, the Village Historian of Croton-on-Hudson, not only provided information but also took my wife and me on a tour of the community, including the house where the Howes once lived. My student assistant, Suzanne Mirenda, ably undertook the tedious but essential task of tracking down Fred Howe's numerous articles. My wife, Marilyn, read the manuscript and offered many helpful and judicious comments both on style and content. My daughter Susan not only usefully criticized the manuscript but also came to my rescue whenever I ran into computer problems. My brother, Glenn H. Miller Jr., discovered several useful pieces of information for me. For the Penn State University Press, Sandy Thatcher has been a helpful and encouraging editor.

The Kent State University Press, which now holds the copyright, has generously given me permission to use extended quotations from Howe's autobiography. *The Confessions of a Reformer* has been published in three editions: first by Charles Scribner's Sons in 1925, then by Quadrangle/New York Times in 1967, with an introduction by John Braeman, and most recently by the Kent State University Press in 1988, with an introduction by James F. Richardson. The layout and pagination are the same for all three books. A paperback edition is available from the Kent State University Press.

For assistance in searching for materials on the Howes, I am greatly indebted to the staffs of numerous libraries and archives throughout the nation. I appreciate the help of the staff of the Library of Congress's Manuscript Division with materials from their collections: the James A. Garfield Papers, the Harry Garfield Papers, the William Gibbs McAdoo Papers, the William Allen White Papers, the Louis F. Post Papers, the A. J. McKelway Papers, the Ray Stannard Baker Papers, the Gutzon Borglum Papers, Papers Relating to the Ford Peace Plan, the Benjamin B. Lindsey Papers, the John Purroy Mitchel Papers, the La Follette Family Papers, the Amos Pinchot Papers, the Gifford Pinchot Papers, and the Newton D. Baker Papers. The staff of the Franklin D. Roosevelt Library was also very helpful with materials from the New Deal. Information on Frederic Howe as consumers counsel comes from the National Archives.

I want to thank the Manuscript and Archives Division of the New York Public Library (Astor, Lennox and Tilden Foundations) for permission to quote from the Frank P. Walsh Papers, the John H. Finley Papers, the Bolton Hall Papers, the National Civic Federation Papers, the National Board of Review of Motion Pictures Records, and the Peoples Institute Records.

I have quoted with permission from the Forget-Me-Not Files of the Survey Associate Records, Social Welfare History Archives, University of Minnesota Libraries; from the Herbert Baxter Adams Papers, MS 4, and the Isaiah Bowman Papers, MS 58, both in Special Collections, Sheridan Libraries, the Johns Hopkins University; and from the Inez Haynes Irwin Papers, Schlesinger Library, Radcliffe Institute, Harvard University.

I am grateful for permission to quote from correspondence between Frederic Howe and Colonel House in the Edward Mandell House Papers, Manuscripts and Archives, Yale University Library; between Howe and Henry L. Stimson in the Henry Lewis Stimson Papers, Manuscripts and Archives, Yale University Library; and between Howe and William Kent in the William Kent Family Papers, Manuscripts and Archives, Yale University Library. I appreciate the permission of the Wisconsin Historical Society to publish quotations from the Richard T. Ely Papers, the Charles McCarthy Papers, the Morris Hillquit Papers, and the Edward A. Ross Papers. I have also had permission to quote from correspondence between Howe and A. M. Molter in the Records of the New York Peace Society, Swarthmore College Peace Collection; and from correspondence of Howe and L. Hollingsworth Wood in the Haverford College Library, Haverford, Pa., Quaker Collection, L. Hollingsworth Wood Papers, Coll. No. 1175,

Boxes 1 and 2, American Commission on Conditions in Ireland, February 2, 1921, and September 28, 1921.

I have quoted with permission from the correspondence of Frederic Howe with W. E. Brownell and Maxwell Perkins in the Archives of Charles Scribner's Sons, Manuscript Division, Department of Rare Books and Special Collections, Princeton University Library; and from correspondence between Howe and President Wilson, in Arthur S. Link, *The Papers of Woodrow Wilson,* reprinted by permission of the Princeton University Press. I thank the Oral History Research Office of Columbia University for permission to quote from its interviews. I have also quoted with permission from the Lincoln Steffens Papers, Rare Book and Manuscript Library, Columbia University.

My research was materially aided by grants from the Rutgers Research Council, a National Endowment for the Humanities Travel to Collections Grant, and a Beeke-Levy Research Fellowship from the Franklin D. Roosevelt Four Freedoms Foundation.

My thanks to all those who have helped with the book. The responsibility for errors is mine, not theirs.

ABBREVIATIONS

FCH	Frederic C. Howe
MJH	Marie Jenney Howe
AAA	Agricultural Adjustment Administration
ACLU	American Civil Liberties Union
AUAM	American Union Against Militarism
CUOHROC	Columbia University Oral History Research Office Collection
CPPA	Conference for Progressive Political Action
FDR Library	Franklin D. Roosevelt Library
HCL	High cost of living
NAWSA	National American Woman Suffrage Association
NCF	National Civic Federation
NPRL	National Progressive Republican League
NSL	National Security League
NWP	National Woman's Party
WPP	Woman's Peace Party
WSP	Woman Suffrage Party

INTRODUCTION

Fred Howe was an unabashed liberal. "All of my activities have been part of a lifelong interest in the changing and improving of conditions that result in suffering or injustice," he wrote. "I hesitate to give a name to something that has been instinctive in me; whether it should be called the spirit of reform, or humanitarianism, or sentimentality, or the dreaming of dreams, or the seeing of visions depends entirely on the way one looks at life."[1] His beliefs and convictions led him to join in nearly every movement for political and economic change during the period Richard Hofstadter called the "age of reform"—from about 1890 to the Second World War—when the quest for reform largely dominated American politics.[2]

In the course of reform battles over more than fifty years, Howe's path crossed those of the leading men and women of his time. As a graduate student at the Johns Hopkins University, he learned from Woodrow Wilson, Richard Ely, Albert Shaw, Herbert Baxter Adams, and Lord Bryce. He fought for municipal reform alongside Tom Johnson, Newton Baker, Brand Whitlock, and Lincoln Steffens. He was immersed in the politics of Progressivism with Bob La Follette, Louis Brandeis, William Allen White, Walter Lippmann, Amos Pinchot, and Ben Lindsey. He served as Wilson's commissioner of immigration at Ellis Island in wartime, was present for the peacemaking at Versailles, and during the postwar "Red Scare" was harried by hostile congressmen and spied on by the minions of J. Edgar Hoover. A stalwart defender of freedom of speech (though himself involved in movie censorship), he worked with Roger Baldwin and Oswald Garrison Villard and was in on the founding of the American Civil

---

1. *Confessions of a Reformer*, 252–53. Howe's autobiography has been reprinted twice: by Quadrangle Books in 1967, with an introduction by John Braeman, and by Kent State University Press in 1988, with an introduction by James F. Richardson. The layout and pagination are the same for all three printings.
2. Hofstadter, *Age of Reform*, 3.

Liberties Union. He was a strong and tenacious defender of the rights of alien radicals detained without trial at Ellis Island, especially of their right to a fair hearing on the charges against them.

Howe was in the midst of the battles in the presidential campaigns of Wilson, La Follette, Al Smith, and Franklin D. Roosevelt. Fighting for mainstream feminist causes alongside Charlotte Perkins Gilman, Jane Addams, Lillian Wald, and Crystal Eastman, Howe also worked with those who were further to the left, like Emma Goldman and Elizabeth Gurley Flynn. In the 1920s his School of Opinion on Nantucket acquainted him not only with the nation's leading social scientists but also with such writers and artists as Sinclair Lewis and Gutzon Borglum. In the 1930s he defended consumers as the AAA's first consumer counsel; served with Henry Wallace, Rexford Tugwell, Jerome Frank, Pat Jackson, and Alger Hiss; and came to admire, and occasionally advise, such disparate figures as Franklin and Eleanor Roosevelt, on the one hand, and Douglas MacArthur, on the other.

Frederic Howe was no Roosevelt, La Follette, or Wilson. His own ambitions did not reach toward the higher offices in the land, and his attempts at winning lesser elective offices for himself were limited and not very successful. Much of his work was done behind the scenes: organizing, advising, helping in campaigns, raising money, building networks, lobbying, publicizing and promoting policies. People like Howe have sometimes been called "second-line" Progressives, but, as Eugene M. Tobin has pointed out, "they should more accurately and deservedly be placed in the front line because they were the heart, soul, and conscience of political liberalism."[3] Wherever there was a major movement for reform from the 1890s through the 1930s, there was Fred Howe, in the vanguard of the battle.

Howe was not always a liberal (a word he tended to use interchangeably with "Progressive" and, sometimes, with "radical"). He grew up in a small town in northwestern Pennsylvania, which he described as "Republican in politics, careful in conduct, Methodist in religion," where "watchful eyes observed us in all we did. There was a sense of being clamped down, stiff in a mould made for one."[4] He thought he had been liberated from the "small-town herd" and its "evangelistic morality" by his studies at Johns Hopkins, but he worried at various stages of his life that he had only substituted one set of authorities for another. Only when he had learned really to think for himself and to follow his own instinctive desires did he consider that he was truly free. In a lifelong process of what he called "unlearning," Howe moved from a simple faith in the

---

3. Tobin, *Organize or Perish*, 250.
4. *Confessions of a Reformer*, 10, 12.

regeneration of politics by the entry of good men to an advocacy of government action at all levels against the forces of privilege, and from a trust in the enlightened businessman to an embrace of labor, co-operatives, and a mixed economy with large doses of public ownership. Unlike other Progressives who fell by the wayside in the 1920s and 1930s, he remained a reformer, despite a growing disillusion with the course of the American system. His wife, Marie Jenney Howe, was also a reformer, considered by some to be more radical in her beliefs than her husband. After a brief career as a Unitarian minister prior to their marriage, she devoted her Cleveland years to work for consumers, women trade unionists, and social settlements, and her New York years to the woman suffrage movement. In New York City she founded, and for many years led, Heterodoxy, "a consciousness-raising group before the term was invented," a center of prewar feminism.[5] In the 1920s Marie withdrew from the political scene and turned her attention to French literature and especially to the life and writings of George Sand. Her story is an integral part of Fred's.

Howe was a figure of importance and stature among liberals during the age of reform. He was one of those who moved beyond muckraking and developed, in Robert Wiebe's words, "a more sophisticated, interpretive literature." Men like Howe encouraged local Progressives to see themselves as part of one great cause.[6] Combining his political activism with his scholarly interests, he wrote 17 books and at least 120 articles, pamphlets, and reports on subjects that included city government, municipal reform, town planning, tax policy, cooperatives, reform of the political structure, international relations, immigration, agriculture, war and imperialism, the League of Nations, woman suffrage, and consumer protection. Familiar with local and national governments in Europe, he helped bring knowledge of their economic and social policies to American reformers and to the general public through his many writings about developments in Britain, Germany, Denmark, Switzerland, and France. "In the Old World, Frederic Howe and his friends beheld a vision of the future—and it worked."[7] His work exemplified the wide-ranging interests of the reformer's mind, as well as the problems and dilemmas of those who seek change. His life revealed the variety of choices that reformers of his time had to make, as well as the outcomes and ramifications of some of those choices.

Howe was in the mainstream of American reform for half a century. His intellectual and political pilgrimage through two of the great periods of change in America—the Progressive Era and the New Deal—shows one man's efforts to answer the important and continuing questions of policy and politics.

5. Cott, *Grounding of Modern Feminism*, 39.
6. Wiebe, *Search for Order*, 199.
7. Morgan, "Future at Work," 269.

1

A COMFORTABLE LITTLE WORLD

Fred Howe liked to say that he had been born twice—not in any theological sense, one must hasten to add. His first birth was in Meadville, Pennsylvania, on November 21, 1867. The second, he said, took place about two decades later at Johns Hopkins University. The values and prejudices learned in Meadville had to be discarded, or modified and reintegrated into his outlook, in Baltimore. Such rebirths also occurred at other times in a long political career that would take him from the struggles of Progressivism to the battles of the New Deal.

Meadville, Howe's "first" birthplace, lies in the western foothills of the Alleghenies, ninety miles north of Pittsburgh. Founded in 1793, the town became the county seat of Crawford County in 1800 and grew in population from about 500 in 1820 to 7,103 by 1870. Though not among the earliest settlers in Meadville, the Howes and the Clemsons were well established in the community by the time of Frederic Clemson Howe's birth. John D. Clemson, Fred's maternal grandfather, was a grocer with a store on Arch Street near the family residence. Andrew Jackson Howe, who came to Meadville as a young man, married John Clemson's daughter, Jane. Their first child and only son, Frederic, was later joined by three daughters, Marian, Gertrude (called by her middle name, Isabel), and Josephine.

Andrew Howe had a furniture store and a small furniture factory. The firm appears to have been profitable for some time but then began to decline. Fred realized as he grew older that Andrew was a poor businessman. His father trusted everyone, he concluded, and everyone loved him, but affection did not mean that people paid their bills. Some summers, weekends, and holidays, Fred worked in the furniture factory, doing successively the jobs of finisher, cabinetmaker, and upholsterer. He was more interested in practical jokes than in learning the trade, but his fellow workers were not amused. They thought he was lazy or that he was spying on them for his father or that he might take away one of their jobs.[1]

Jane Howe, Fred's mother, had a gentle Quaker tolerance and kindliness that her son learned to appreciate. She managed a household whose worries centered mainly on money. The children learned to avoid extravagance as a cardinal sin, and the maxim "Take care of the pennies and the dollars will take care of themselves" was more deeply engraved in Fred's mind than any of the Ten Commandments. He knew that a spendthrift child was headed for the poorhouse. Right living meant living carefully, avoiding debt, and saving for the privations of sickness and old age. He and his sisters got "a money measure of life and a fear of prodigality from which I, for one, have never escaped."[2]

Neither parent was a reformer; neither wanted to change the world. "It was a comfortable little world," Howe recalled, but what he later emphasized about Meadville was the heavy hand of conformity in religion, in politics, and in life generally. Religion to young Fred meant going to the Methodist church, hearing long, boring sermons, wasting time at church sociables and prayer meetings. Older Methodists found the Presbyterians acceptable, but the Unitarians were "beyond some pale." In a rare departure from traditional patterns, the Howe children were allowed to attend church or not as they chose. Fred became a regular at Sunday school when he fell in love with his teacher. He tried to sit next to her at Sunday lessons and at parties she arranged with the girls in another class, taught by Ida M. Tarbell.[3]

Fred attended the Wednesday night prayer meetings more regularly than he did the Sunday services. He understood that salvation was "a catastrophic experience that changed a person in the twinkling of an eye." It should come to you when you were young; and if it did not, you would be eternally damned. "To experience religion seemed to me like a great climacteric; a tremendous personal drama that miraculously changed sinful nature." He drifted about the outskirts of the meetings, "getting hints of the drama, glimpses of the invisible scene where it was staged."

Politics in Meadville was simple and Republican. The Andrews brothers, followers of the state's Republican boss, Matthew Quay, decided on candidates and

---

1. In Howe's *Confessions of a Monopolist,* the narrator's description of his father seems drawn from the life of Andrew Howe: "When he departed the world at sixty he left his family the possession of his good name, a shining black 'strong box' filled with the promissory notes of his neighbors, and a declining business ruined by the more energetic competition of a younger and more easily satisfied generation" (1). Many of the early pages in this book appear autobiographical.

2. FCH to Newton D. Baker, April 29, 1935, Newton D. Baker Papers, Library of Congress. Unless otherwise indicated, quotations in this chapter are from Howe's *Confessions of a Reformer,* chaps. 1 and 2.

3. Ida Tarbell became a journalist, probably best known for her nineteen-part exposé (later a book) of the Standard Oil Company in *McClure's Magazine.*

advised higher-ups on local patronage. Fred shared the common opinion that those who criticized Matt Quay were malcontents who had failed to get the job or the contract they wanted. After all, Quay was a good organizer, a man of his word, a church member, an authority to be respected—"that was political morality enough for Meadville." After the Civil War, Crawford County was heavily Republican; no Democratic presidential candidate carried it between 1856 and 1916. For Fred, "there was something unthinkable to me about being a Democrat—Democrats, Copperheads, and atheists were persons whom one did not know socially." He did not play with the children of Democrats. The Republican Party and the Methodist Church were "the guardians of morality, respectability, and standing." Politics, religion, the daily activities of small-town life—in all these, there was the feeling that one's neighbors were always watching, always evaluating one's behavior. "And I rebelled against espionage, hated it, chafed under it," Howe wrote.

There were ways to escape, however, and Fred found some of them in the company of his father, who did not entirely fit the Meadville mold. Andrew Howe was president of his church's board of trustees, but this did not prevent him from shocking his fellow Methodists by crossing the public square on Sunday evenings to hear the preaching of a Unitarian minister and, what was worse, a Unitarian who had formerly been a Methodist clergyman. "The apostasy of Doctor Townsend had been in the nature of a public disgrace, hardly less than a crime. Lifelong friends shunned him. Yet my father, without discussion or defense of his action, forsook his own pew of a Sunday evening and went to hear strange doctrine." Fred realized, too, that his father never gave "testimony" at the prayer meetings and never talked about religion at home. Torn between conformity and rebellion, the son wondered if this was proper behavior for the president of the board of trustees. "In his consistent silence, when other brethren and sisters discussed their souls' salvation, he failed to live up to my conception of him, as he failed to live up to what the neighbors expected when he went to the Unitarian church."

Not only that but as Fred grew older, Andrew involved him in his sins. Meadville, a theatrical center for Crawford County and environs, had an Academy of Music, and to it came dramas, minstrel shows, vaudeville, and extravaganzas, starring the greats of the stage and even of pugilism: Otis Skinner, James O'Neill, Edwin Forrest, Joe Jefferson, Buffalo Bill Cody, John L. Sullivan, James J. Corbett. Russell Conwell delivered his famous "Acres of Diamonds" address there in October 1888 and again in January 1889. The churches frowned upon the theater, but the Howe men had a secret. After a meaningful exchange of glances during supper, father and son would meet casually in the yard. "After a little banter he would say: 'Like to go to the Opera House to-night to see Booth?' Or it might be Barrett, Joe Jefferson, Florence, Modjeska, or Lotta." They watched the performances from inconspicuous seats in the upper gallery. This was their only concession to the prying eyes of their fellow townspeople.

As time went by, Fred grew to understand his father better and to appreciate his qualities. He began to see in him "a person of distinction," distinguished not in honor or wealth but in his way of life and his treatment of his children. "He had a quiet independence of judgment and a humorous and tolerant quality that did not fit into the intellectual pattern of Meadville."

Fred found other "purple spots of freedom," as he called them. One was the French Creek canal, now fallen into disuse. "Wild, delightful Irish boys" lived along its banks, but he was forbidden to play with them. He envied their free and easy life—they didn't have to worry about keeping their clothes clean, and they lived in the midst of adventures. "I thought them happier than kings, and ran away whenever I could to play along the banks of that tempting waterway, which spelled romance to me. It went on and on, far down the valley to other towns.... It was the big world that some time I might see." After a fall into the canal, he received his first and only whipping.

Another escape was the firehouse and Taylor Hose Company No. 1. The volunteer firemen had a baseball team, sponsored a minstrel show, and held dances in their hall, which Fred sneaked away to attend. Sometimes he played cards secretly "with a colored driver in the barn." He loved the public library and devoured books of adventure. His favorite refuge was the printing office of the *Crawford Democrat* (interestingly enough, not the *Meadville Tribune*, the Republican newspaper). He skipped school to watch the presses, made friends with the printers and pressmen, got his hands black with printer's ink as he played with typesetting. When other boys went swimming, Fred slipped away to the newspaper office. If he failed to come home at night, his father knew where to look for him and would sometimes find him asleep behind the printing presses. Despite the tensions between conformity and rebellion, he later recalled these days of boyhood "through a haze, as of a tranquil, bright September day. There was no sharpness, no struggle, little reproof."

In the fall of 1885, Fred Howe began his studies at the local college. Seventy years before, a group of the leading men of Meadville—then a village of about four hundred inhabitants—had met and resolved to establish a "Collegiate Institution" to offer a classical education. After successful fundraising by Timothy Alden, its first president, and local businessmen, Allegheny College admitted its first freshman class in 1816, with a total faculty and administration of two, the president and a professor of "logick, metaphysicks, and ethicks." President Alden was also professor of Oriental languages, ecclesiastical history, and theology. His long and festive inauguration on July 28, 1817, featured addresses and replies in Latin, prayers, orations, and dialogues by students in Hebrew, Latin, Greek, and English. Since the proceedings were held at the courthouse, a truly captive audience of the county's prisoners had a great opportunity to extend their linguistic horizons. As one writer put it, "Mr. Alden was inaugurated amid an astonishing display of dead languages."[4]

The cornerstone of the college's first new building, Bentley Hall, was laid on July 5, 1820. It contained a remarkable set of items: a fragment of Plymouth Rock, marble from Dido's temple in Carthage, mortar from Virgil's tomb, and a piece of brick from the Tower of Babel. History records neither the authenticity nor the method of acquisition of these memorabilia. During Alden's sixteen years as president, the struggling institution generally had fewer than 10 students a year and often graduated no more than 1 of them. Slowly the number of students increased, by 1860 reaching 113 in the college and 119 in its preparatory department. In 1870 women began to be admitted as regular students on the same footing as men, but their numbers remained small for some time.

When Fred Howe entered the college's preparatory department in the fall of 1884, the whole campus needed a facelift. In rainy weather, he and his classmates had to slog their way from building to building in seas of mud and to attend classes in rooms that were often wet and cold. In a column he wrote for the school newspaper during his junior year, Howe observed: "The fact that the mud around the college buildings is something less than a foot deep, can hardly be considered as a sign of the coming of spring, as that has been the condition of the walks all winter." He also complained frequently of the poor ventilation in most of the college rooms and informed the faculty: "If some of the Professors would keep their recitation rooms better ventilated, there would not be so many sleepy recitations as there are. This would apply also to many of the churches of the city." By 1888, however, swampy areas had been drained, campus roads graded, boardwalks laid, and both Bentley and Hulings Hall, the women's residence, renovated inside and out.

Fred Howe entered Allegheny College's preparatory department in the fall term of 1884. For admission to the college proper, students had to pass an entrance examination in Latin, Greek, French, mathematics, history, English, and science. Deficiencies in some of those fields could be remedied by up to three years' study in the preparatory department, in which classes were taught by the regular faculty of the college. Howe spent a year—three terms—in the department, taking a variety of courses. His grades were good, especially in Greek, algebra and trigonometry, and zoology. He was weaker in Latin and

---

4. Bates, *Our County and Its People,* 258. On the history of the college, see E. Smith, *Allegheny—A Century of Education.*

geography. By the end of the spring term of 1885, he was ready to enter the college as a regular freshman.

Howe later wrote that he and his sisters went to Allegheny College "not because we had any love of learning but because it was the proper thing to do." Attendance there was also convenient and cheap. Tuition was ten dollars a term. Textbooks cost about nine dollars a year. Women students could live in Hulings Hall, but men had to find rooms in private homes for about fifty cents a week. The College estimated that fifty dollars a term would cover necessary expenditures. "The unnecessary expenses for sweetmeats, oyster suppers, concerts, etc., may be indefinitely greater." A poor student would suffer "no social disparagement. The only *caste* in the College is based on good conduct and good work."[5] Since Howe lived at home, his bill each term for tuition and books came to around thirteen dollars, and his father was able to stretch his income to provide a college education for all of his children.

Allegheny students found themselves in a restrictive academic world, with a prescribed and rigid curriculum. Most of them took nearly the same courses, regardless of their choice among classical, scientific, or Latin and modern languages tracks. All had fifteen or more courses in science and mathematics; all had six required English essays in each of their first three years; all took courses in evidences of Christianity, moral philosophy, political economy, the Constitution of the United States, logic, international and municipal law, and surveying. As might be expected, students in the classical department, like Frederic Howe, had many more courses in Greek and Latin, as well as nine lectures each term during both freshman and sophomore years on Greek mythology, art, and literature. A student ordinarily took three or four courses in each of the three terms of the academic year. The college emphasized the values of a classical education and also encouraged the study of modern languages, giving a student the option of substituting language courses for a few of the required subjects.

A faculty of seventeen professors, instructors, and tutors (including a "lady principal" to watch over the Hulings girls, and a regular army officer for military training) provided the instruction during Howe's attendance at Allegheny. The professors who taught English, the social sciences, philosophy, and classics were clergymen. Howe later complained about the dominance of the clergy, "who knew none too much about their subjects." In his autobiography, Howe barely refers to the faculty, except to say that at the time "they seemed tremendously wise" but "disagreeable, prone to be critical of me in the classroom." The only one he mentioned by name was President David H. Wheeler.

Fred followed the classical track but had some flexibility in his choice of subjects. Aside from his preparatory courses, by the time he finished his senior

---

5. Allegheny College catalogue, 1885–86, 19.

year he had had eight courses in Latin and Greek, nine in modern languages (six in French, three in German—he also had three in German in the preparatory department), eleven in science and mathematics, two in religion (evidences of Christianity, the Bible), eleven in history and the social sciences (including Francis Lieber's civil liberty, international law, two terms of municipal law, and two of political economy), four in English, and three in philosophy (counting moral philosophy here, rather than in religion), plus the required English essays and the lectures on life and letters in Greece. The only contemporary reference to Howe in the classroom was a bit of college humor in the college annual, the *Kaldron:*

> In Geology class—"Howe, in what kind of rocks is copper found?"
> Senior Howe—"In copper-bearing rocks."[6]

During Howe's college days, the Allegheny administration encouraged male students to join the College Corps of Cadets "since this is the most perfect way of obtaining necessary exercise, and at the same time they receive valuable instruction. The drill gives ease of bearing and promotes gentlemanly manners." Directed by a regular army officer (who bore the title of professor of military science and tactics), the four companies met weekly for three hours of drill and three hours of lectures and recitations. Shouldering old Springfield rifles furnished by the army and seldom if ever fired, the cadets drilled in pleasant weather on the Diamond in downtown Meadville, to the delight of local high school girls and boys. Their navy-blue uniforms, adorned with gold cord on the trousers and gold lace chevrons on the sleeves, had to be worn on all military occasions and could be worn for church and classes if the cadet chose. The highlight of the training program for many cadets was ten days each summer at Camp Ayer on Lake Conneaut.

Fred Howe must have been a good soldier, since he became first lieutenant and adjutant of the battalion in 1887 and attained the highest rank, captain, in April 1888. Both posts required the approval of the faculty. The commanding officer of the Corps reported that the battalion was in "passably good condition." Its members were, "with few exceptions, faithful to and interested in their work. The discipline is good, and the Cadets are gaining some idea of a soldier's first duty, obedience to and respect for his superiors."[7] Whatever Howe may have gained from his military training at Allegheny, it was hardly unquestioning obedience and respect for his superiors.

---

6. *Kaldron* (1890), 122.
7. Allegheny College catalogue 1885–86, 47; J. F. Kreps, "Military Department of Allegheny," *Kaldron* (1890), 91, 92.

Howe's recollections of Allegheny emphasized its extracurricular life and the institution's narrow sectarianism, rather than his academic experiences. For him, the centers of college life were the Allegheny Literary Society, the school paper and the yearbook, and Phi Gamma Delta fraternity.

The college catalogue observed that the four literary societies, through their public literary exercises and prize contests in the chapel, "render the College efficient services in the literary and forensic training of students and the society friendships are valuable to their members." The student newspaper also underscored the value of these and other organizations, pointing out that rather than spending all his time at his books, a student would be far better served by becoming "an active member of at least two or three of our various fraternities and societies, physical and intellectual, and so [acquiring] that breadth of culture and knowledge that always mark the highly educated man."[8]

Fred threw himself into his Allegheny Society's activities. He held numerous offices: critic in 1887, sergeant-at-arms, executive committee member, and speaker (president) in 1889. He captained his society's baseball team and played second base and center field.

Howe also busied himself with student publications; indeed, he found his journalistic endeavors the most rewarding of his college experiences. During his junior year, he was one of the editors of *Campus,* the student newspaper, and he wrote its "Locals" column, filling it with items on college news, school spirit, and brief comments on fellow students. In the fall of 1887, the junior class decided to publish a college annual, the *Kaldron,* and Fred became one of its editors and business managers. The work took up a great deal of his time. "The first thrill of my academic life came from getting out the commencement edition of the college weekly. I worked on it day and night. I could hardly wait for the summer vacation to end to take up the work again. The furtive and forbidden amusements of theatre-going, card-playing, and dancing were but slightly diverting as compared with the joy of working over an editorial column." Along with serious discussions of the college, *Kaldron* abounded in inside jokes about the editorial staff. The minutes of a mock editorial board meeting, dated May 1, 1889, reported "an interview with Howe who was very uneasy lest any allusions be made in the *Kaldron* detrimental to his moral character. Committee instructed to inform Howe that the *Kaldron* board did not deal with subjects of so dubious a nature."[9]

Fraternities were very important in Allegheny life, and in Fred Howe's. His uncle, Frank P. Ray, had been a member of Phi Gamma Delta, and Fred was

---

8. Allegheny college catalogue, 1885–86, 21; *Campus,* October 8, 1886, 5; *Kaldron* (1890), 62–63.

9. *Campus,* December 14, 1887, 56; April 14, 1888, 129; *Kaldron* (1890), 118. Howe says "weekly," but it seems clear that it was *Kaldron* he was referring to.

initiated as a member of Pi chapter in February 1885. Until 1888 the chapter leased rooms in a variety of Meadville locations. In the intervals between studies and chapter meetings (in which members were sometimes called upon to deliver serious or humorous impromptu speeches), "whist, the old-fashioned kind that keeps all the hands concealed, absorbed leisure hours. While the saloons thrived, it was not from Pi's patronage. A glass or two of beer appeased the thirst of the two or three that ever entered them." When chapter meetings were held on Saturday nights, attendance suffered, as some members preferred the attractions of Hulings to "the more lasting rewards of the fraternal assembly." In one meeting, "Fred Howe thundered against the practice in a speech on 'Fools, d—d fools, and those who go to Hulings Hall.'"[10]

Fred quickly became a leader in his fraternity. He held the main chapter offices: corresponding secretary in 1886–87, treasurer in 1887–88, and president in his senior year, 1888–89. He captained and played right field on its baseball team. On occasional trips away from Meadville, he looked in on other Phi Gam chapters, enjoying the hospitality of the Yale frat in the spring of 1889, when he celebrated Centennial week by visiting New Haven and New York City.

Fraternity membership also brought Howe additional experience in journalism. The national Phi Gamma Delta journal, the *Quarterly*, had been in financial straits since its founding in 1879. In early 1889, the national organization offered its Allegheny chapter the opportunity to assume the burden of the magazine. After much discussion, and after a committee chaired by Howe had interviewed printers about costs, the chapter voted to publish volume 11 of the *Quarterly*. It elected Howe editor-in-chief. He and some of his fraternity brothers wrote and laid out the stories, read the proofs, addressed each copy by hand, and wrapped it for mailing. It was hard but satisfying work. The first issue of the *Quarterly* from Allegheny appeared in March 1889. Two other issues followed, and the fraternity's national convention happily turned the magazine over to Howe and two other chapter members. The three served as joint editors until 1891 and even turned a profit of about $750 for their labors. Fred took over as sole editor in 1891 and retained that post until 1901, receiving a salary of $200 a year.

As Howe's continued tenure as editor of the *Quarterly* suggests, his ties with his fraternity had become deep and enduring. He regularly attended Phi Gamma Delta's national convention, missing only three of them from 1887 to 1902 and serving often on committees. He returned to the Allegheny campus on at least eight occasions between 1890 and 1915 to give talks at chapter "conviviums." In 1913 he was on the finance committee that raised funds for a new chapter house. He helped found a Phi Gam chapter at Johns Hopkins in 1891, and he persuaded Newton Baker, who became a lifelong friend, to join it.

10. Mattern, *Pi Chapter of Phi Gamma Delta*, 101–2, 120, 124.

Howe and Baker worked closely together to democratize the national fraternity and to limit the powers of its governing body, the Grand Chapter. Their correspondence in the 1890s is full of proposals and plots for reform. In these battles they saw themselves as "Progressives" (though Baker sometimes argued that they were really the true conservatives) combating an "oligarchy" of "conservatives." As Baker's term as president of the national organization neared an end in 1906, he launched a campaign for Howe as his successor. He urged his friend to accept the post, but Howe declined, apparently preferring that it go to another of his fraternity brothers.[11]

The fraternity men occasionally entertained their "lady friends" in staid parties with refreshments and piano playing, but the college enforced 11 p.m. closing hours for the women of Hulings Hall and kept a watchful eye on fraternity doings. Dancing was forbidden, and the college expected its students to behave like ladies and gentlemen. The student paper often noted the blossoming of romance, noting in March 1887, for example: "The heavens these evenings are very attractive to lovesick lads and lassies, and they can be found loose, or rather tied in a bow-knot, on all the walks around the College." How lovesick Fred ever became at Allegheny is unknown, though he did observe: "I never got stuck on a girl until she was engaged to someone else."[12]

For students at Allegheny College, fraternity politics, club politics, and class politics were all intertwined. Comments in the *Campus* showed that some students were interested in national politics. But this was neither the time nor the place for political activism. According to contemporary references, students much preferred *Punch* and *Judge* to more serious reading and found many pursuits more pleasurable than politics. There was no intercollegiate athletic competition until 1891, but the fraternity baseball teams and the college team, on which Howe played shortstop in his junior year, frequently engaged the town nines. Male students much enjoyed croquet with the Hulings girls. Fred belonged to the tennis club, the bicycle club, the fencing club, and the camera club—he did not join the YMCA.

As he looked back at Allegheny College after thirty-five years, Howe's heaviest condemnation fell on its narrow sectarianism and its pressures for religious conformity. The college was financially dependent on several Methodist conferences; its president was always a clergyman, as were many of the faculty; it encouraged male students to enter the ministry; it kept religion as part of the

---

11. See ibid., 135–38; Newton Baker to FCH, August 9, 1898; Baker to FCH, August 16, 1898. A more detailed account of the efforts by Howe, Baker, and others to reform the fraternity can be found in Chamberlin, *History of Phi Gamma Delta*, 2:75–86.

12. *Campus*, March 7, 1887, 104; *Kaldron* (1890), 47.

curriculum. Chapel services were held daily, and student attendance was compulsory. Regular attendance at a church chosen by student or parents was also required, and five unexcused absences from either church or chapel were grounds for a student's suspension. Prayer meetings were held every Wednesday evening. Fred tried to evade religion's restrictive embrace as much as possible. He skipped chapel enough to make it a matter of comment in his senior year. The *Campus* "locals" editor suggested: "Ask Fred Howe why he has become an habitual chapel-absentee." The annual, in a "College A, B, C, Book," made the same point:

> X—Stands for X, a quantity unknown;
> His name's Fred Howe, and to skipping is prone.[13]

Prayer and revival meetings were difficult to evade, according to Howe's account. He wrote that he was "inwardly rebellious, outwardly passive." Freshmen and sophomores were assigned to seniors, who took them on long walks and inquired about their souls. Revivalists prayed for them and worked on their fears that they would be eternally damned if they failed to accept the preachers' brand of religion. "Under the influence of Moody and Sankey hymns I went to the mourners' bench the second winter. I crept forward to be prayed for by strangers for sins of which I was ignorant and for a salvation that seemed at best dreary." He had conformed to the pressure of relatives, friends, and other students, but he had "no conviction of sin, no sense of guilt, or of being abandoned."

Worst of all, the great change that had been promised failed to occur. "I had gone through the ordeal of being prayed for, of confessing a desire for regeneration, and had found no relief; no heavenly manna had fallen my way."

Resenting religion, he refused thereafter to attend revival meetings, "scandalizing and grieving my teachers and friends." He summed up: "I conformed, but departed when I dared. In town and at college I resisted claims made upon me; decisions made by others; the dulness [sic] of classrooms, of chapel exercises, of conformity. I did not fit in as other boys did, and was conscious of questionings on the part of neighbors, my college professors, most of whom were friends of my family." He reflected later that neither outward conformity nor physical escape from religion meant that he had escaped from it morally.

In his autobiography, Howe recounts that as graduation neared, "various professors made unfavorable comments in faculty meeting on my scholarship and attendance. President David H. Wheeler asked how long I had been at

---

13. *Confessions of a Monopolist*, 8–9; *Kaldron* (1890), 122.

Allegheny. 'Five years,' he commented, on hearing the secretary's reply. 'Well, any one who can stay at this institution for five years deserves a degree.' And to that estimate of the worth of sectarian education pronounced by a man of genuine culture who was oddly out of place in it, I owe perhaps my bachelor's degree." This makes a good story, but it is probably largely inaccurate. Howe had completed forty-eight courses (not counting those in the preparatory department), all with satisfactory grades. Since the classical curriculum listed forty-six as required, his work certainly met the college's expectations for a degree, though there no doubt had been faculty complaints about the regularity of his class attendance.

On June 27, 1889, Howe received his diploma as Bachelor of Arts in ceremonies at the Methodist Stone Church. Upon payment of a fee of five dollars, the College would grant an M.A. to B.A.'s of three years' standing who had been engaged since graduation in a literary occupation and who possessed a good moral character. Howe somehow speeded up the timetable and received an M.A. from Allegheny in 1890.

Howe's five years at Allegheny College had been full ones and probably happier than he was subsequently willing to admit. He was what would later be called a big man on campus—he had been president of his class and his fraternity, an officer in his literary society, captain in the Cadet Corps, and a member of baseball teams (college, fraternity, literary society) and of most student organizations. He had gained journalistic experience by writing for and editing *Campus* and *Kaldron,* and he was continuing as editor of his fraternity's national quarterly. His classmates wrote humorously of his present and future. *Campus* suggested an oration topic for him: "Mendacious Schemes Evolved from my Pipe." *Kaldron* found him a role in a drama: "The Senior Election; Or, Who Pulled the Wires. Dramatis Personae: Mr. Didn't Know It Was Loaded . . . Howe." The yearbook also gave him a place in the senior orchestra ("Horse-fiddle") and predicted next year's occupation ("Bill-Poster for Ten Cent Museum, Philadelphia").[14] His academic work had not been brilliant, but his record was satisfactory enough to enable him to move on to graduate study.

Yet, when he looked back at Allegheny more than three decades later, Howe's evaluation of his undergraduate years was a gloomy one. He had submitted to college as "a tedious experience that had to be gotten through." Study was a bore. None of the subjects interested him much, and he cut classes as often as he dared. "I was never able to make head or tail of the sciences, mathematics, Latin, and Greek. As far as I can recall, I went through college without having an enthusiasm awakened, yet I wanted to know things, to be admitted to the

14. *Campus,* May 2, 1889, 141; *Kaldron* (1890), 107, 115, 130.

secrets of life.... What was offered was not what I wanted. It was not what any one wanted. College created no strength within me with which to face the world." His real life, he wrote, was outside the classroom, in politics, his fraternity, journalism, and "ephemeral college activities."

Howe wrote this evaluation in a period of disillusion, and his comments are somewhat belied by his continuing links with the College. He remained in touch with the Phi Gamma Delta chapter and returned frequently for visits and talks. When in later years the College acquired a chapter of Phi Beta Kappa, he was elected a member on the basis of his achievements. He was happy to accept an honorary Doctor of Laws degree in 1915. In the 1930s he enjoyed entertaining Allegheny College presidents at the Cosmos Club in Washington, D.C. On his death he bequeathed his books to the College library. If he was not completely satisfied with his education when he graduated in 1889, he was nonetheless ready to move on to new academic experiences. The school newspaper reported in the fall of 1889: "Fred C. Howe has gone to Johns Hopkins University to pursue a journalistic course."[15]

---

15. *Campus,* October 8, 1889, 7.

2

THE TRUTH WILL MAKE YOU FREE

As he was growing up in Meadville, Frederic Howe had no clear picture of the future he wanted, only romantic dreams. Perhaps he could go west, take up a homestead, and return home, wealthy, to live in a big brick residence like those owned by oilmen who had struck it rich. His ambition was "to make money and to enjoy the pleasures that possessors of wealth enjoyed." The post of county judge sounded appealing, though out of reach. What terrified him most was the prospect of being forced into the ministry, a calling urged on him by "maiden aunts and Sunday School teachers."[1]

His ideas began to change when, during the summer of his junior year at Allegheny College, he found a job as night clerk in a hotel at Lake Chautauqua. Although the hours were long—from six at night to nine or ten in the morning—he felt a sense of liberation in being on his own. The job had its adventures. One night the hotel owner gave him a heavy-caliber revolver and instructed him to defend the hotel against a drunken cook who had threatened to murder the kitchen help with a meat cleaver. Howe spent the night pacing up and down the kitchen, frightened by every noise; but the cook failed to return. Part of his job was to balance the hotel books, and he spent hours agonizing over them. Falling asleep with them one night, he was suddenly awakened about three o'clock by his employer's hand on his back. Thousands of dollars lay on the desk in front of him, and he had negligently left the hotel safe open, with the jewels of guests there for the taking. The previous morning Fred had gone out walking with a girl. They had not returned until evening, so he had had no sleep. "I expected sharp justice to be meted out. But it was tempered—

---

1. Unless otherwise indicated, quotations are from Howe's *Confessions of a Reformer*, chaps. 1–5.

possibly because I danced well." The proprietor overlooked his lapse, and he kept the hotel job for several summers.

Even more important than the summer's freedom from the prying eyes of Meadville was the chance to discover horizons broader than Allegheny College provided. Fred found time to attend lectures at the Chautauqua Institution, that unique center of popular education and culture. The summer faculty included two rising young academic stars from the Johns Hopkins University, Herbert Baxter Adams and Richard T. Ely. During Howe's first summer at Chautauqua in 1888, Adams offered courses on primitive culture and the origin of civilization, Hebrew culture and the origin of Christianity, and the revival of learning and the Protestant Reformation. Ely gave two series of lectures, one on political economy and the other on the modern state. Howe was mightily impressed by the lectures. "They made me want to know more about the big world outside of my little home town."

These stimuli were reinforced by new personal ties. Fred had doubtless kept up an acquaintance with Ida Tarbell, who had found a job with the *Chautauquan* two years after her graduation from Allegheny in 1880. During Howe's college days, she was working in Meadville, where the paper was published from September through June. In July and August the staff all moved to Chautauqua and put out the daily *Assembly Herald.* Ida had begun as a part-time assistant, researching and answering questions from readers, but soon was writing articles and editorials and assuming a variety of responsibilities with the paper.

Probably through Ida, Fred met and became friends with John H. Finley, a graduate student at Johns Hopkins who had a summer job as a proofreader for the *Herald.* Talking with Finley about journalism and the university, Howe suddenly realized what he wanted to do: he would become an editorial writer on a city newspaper. To succeed in that, he would need to know more about economics, history, and politics, and Johns Hopkins was apparently the place to study them. After he finished at Allegheny, he would go to Hopkins and work his way through. "For the first time in my life I had a definite, serious desire to do something, not because somebody expected me to do it or because it was there to do, but because I genuinely wanted it." He also dreamed of the "glamour" of a Ph.D. degree. "It seemed to me a hallmark of intellectual power. It might open doors to wealth and distinction." In Meadville, men lived comfortable lives on nine hundred dollars a year; few made more than twelve hundred. With the magical Ph.D., he might in time earn the "princely income" of fifteen hundred a year.

When Howe arrived in Baltimore in the fall of 1889, he found a university that, little more than a decade old, had already established itself as a center of scholarship and graduate education. Along with its growing academic reputation, the absence of ties to any church must have appealed to the young rebel against Methodism. Also attractive were the goals for its students advanced by the Johns Hopkins president, Daniel Coit Gilman: "There is a call for men who have been trained by other agencies than the caucus for the discussion of public affairs; men who know what the experience of the world has been in the development of institutions, and are prepared by intellectual and moral discipline to advance the public interests, irrespective of party, and indifferent to the attainment of official stations."[2] To students like Howe, such a call offered evangelism without religion and uplift without sanctimony.

The university's intellectual attractions more than compensated for its deficiencies in physical plant, a few buildings in downtown Baltimore. President Gilman had recruited an outstanding faculty. Unsuccessful in securing the international scholars he wanted to head the department of history and political science, he had to make do with a younger man, Herbert Baxter Adams, and several assistants on temporary appointments. Richard Ely fell into that category but soon was established on a more permanent basis. The department attracted graduate students from throughout the United States and abroad. Their quality was high—through the department's doors in the 1880s passed such future luminaries as Woodrow Wilson, Albert Shaw, Albion Small, J. Franklin Jameson, Frederick Jackson Turner, James S. Bassett, Edward A. Ross, and John R. Commons, to mention only a few.

Fred Howe felt ill-prepared to join such a brilliant group. Though not penniless, he had only meager financial resources for university study. Half his funds came from his summer earnings and half from his father, who could ill afford to give him anything. He had three years of study ahead of him, and only three hundred dollars in his pocket. "The struggle that was in store for me seems now, as I look back on it, one of the best things that ever happened to me. It forced me to be resourceful and to stand on my own feet." His father had also arranged for the best tailor in Meadville to outfit him in an expensive cutaway suit, made of broadcloth with broad satin stripes running up and down it. "This kindness of my father's caused me more unhappiness than any unkindness I ever experienced at his hands. The striped suit made me a marked man. In classrooms and on the street it proclaimed the small town from which I came." But the suit had to be worn; throwing it away would not be thrifty and would show a lack of regard for his father. "It was my first hair-shirt."

Impecunious and feeling like a country bumpkin, Fred at first found Johns Hopkins and Baltimore strange and unfriendly places. As a student from a sectarian college, he found it confusing "to be permitted to come and go as I

2. Inaugural address, quoted in Hawkins, *Pioneer,* 68.

willed. Informal methods of study without recitation were new, and I was badly prepared for study. I had done no real work at college." At Allegheny he had had only a smattering of courses in history and the social sciences. He considered himself unscholarly but found himself surrounded by students of ability.

He had no friends, and to forget his loneliness, he resorted to one of his Meadville escapes, the theater. Sitting in the top gallery one night, he saw Julia Marlowe in a Shakespearean role and was immediately infatuated ("desperately in love with her," as he put it). "I had never cared much about girls; at college I felt uncomfortable with them. But I was ready to sacrifice everything to be near Julia Marlowe." He thought about a job as a "super" and got as far as the stage door before his courage failed. Ignoring his classes, he attended every performance of the play in Baltimore and then followed it to Philadelphia for a week. "I would have gone farther, but the hopelessness of it and my rapidly failing bank-account sent me back to Baltimore, where I was lonelier and poorer than ever."

Howe's financial situation soon improved, however. He got a job writing about university sports for the *Baltimore American.* He sold to the Baltimore and Philadelphia newspapers articles on economics, written in a popular form. A piece on prison reform brought him a check for fifteen dollars from the *Christian Union,* plus the encouraging realization that things he wrote could be published in a form more permanent than a newspaper story.[3] His money troubles were further eased ("in a way that I was rather ashamed of," he recalled) when a traveling salesman for Heinz's pickles asked him to write a speech for him to deliver at a company meeting. Howe produced an oration, "full of mock-serious flourishes," that began by praising all the distinguished men and events of Pennsylvania history and ended by extolling the state's most eminent son, H. J. Heinz. The speech was a great success, and the grateful salesman paid Howe $50. News of his ghostwriting ability leaked out, and he wrote speeches "for greengrocers, for traveling men, for food conventions of divers sorts. And my finances flourished more than my self-esteem." The bedrock of his income remained his newswriting, however. He expanded his coverage from sports to university activities generally; he took topics from his instructors' lectures and rewrote them for the Baltimore and Philadelphia papers; he continued to edit the Phi Gamma Delta *Quarterly.* "During my second and third years I earned enough to feel free from worry. In fact, I earned more than I did years after graduation."

---

3. FCH, "Two Decades of Penological Progress," 67–69. In this article Howe praises the Elmira Reformatory as "the final crowning triumph of enlightened criminal legislation." In his autobiography he mistakenly calls the journal the *Christian Herald.*

Academically, Howe's insecurity continued. Judging from the emphasis he placed in his autobiography on his lack of scholarly interests, he must have had a feeling of great inferiority among the forty to fifty graduate students in history and political economy, at least in his first year at Hopkins. In the midst of these budding scholars, his journalistic ambitions may have seemed a lower calling. In his application for admission to Johns Hopkins, to a question inviting him to state his purpose in attending and the studies he wished to pursue, he had tersely replied, "History, Political Science and Modern Languages," eschewing any statement of high intent.[4] With his need for outside employment and with the limited preparation in history and economics that Allegheny College had provided, he found his studies a heavy load—he had fifteen courses in his first year, sixteen in his second, and twelve plus a thesis in his third.

During the fall term of his first academic year at Hopkins, 1889–90, Howe took six courses, a special series of lectures, and the history seminar. He was enrolled in the Department of History and Politics, headed by Herbert Baxter Adams. Talented as a scholar, Adams—educated in history, economics, and political science—was even more important as an enthusiastic teacher, an energetic director of research, and a continuing friend to his students.[5] He accepted the "germ theory of politics" and set his students to work researching the origins of governmental bodies and tracing the evolution of modern institutions from their ancient roots in a Teutonic or Saxon past.

Adams sometimes minced no words in his critique of student papers, but he believed in "refined criticism" and had an ability to encourage and to motivate the novice scholars. Howe praised him as a great teacher who was free from intellectual prejudices and who encouraged his students to discover their own enthusiasms in their own way. "We knew that he respected our choices; we learned to share in his scorn of stupid conventions, and caught from him a sense of education as a pleasurable thing, full of drama and excitement." Fred had more courses with Adams than with any other faculty member.

Richard T. Ely directed the department's work in political economy. Like Adams, he was influenced by the German scholarship of the day. Both men had received their Ph.D.s at Heidelberg. Unlike Adams, he found it difficult to establish himself and secure the professorship he desired at Hopkins, and he departed in 1892 for the University of Wisconsin. Ely challenged the dominant Manchester school of classical economics and argued that the "new economics" could not acknowledge laissez-faire as "an excuse for doing nothing while people

---

4. Application for admission to Johns Hopkins University, October 2, 1889, Ferdinand Hamburger Archives of the Johns Hopkins University.
5. See Vincent, "Herbert B. Adams."

starve." There was room in political economy for love, generosity, and recognition of the common good. The compatibility of this view with the message of the Social Gospel was clear, and he was deeply involved in that movement.

Ely insisted that the study of economics begin with statistical and historical examinations of actual conditions, rather than with a "standard of orthodoxy" that determined what the researcher would see. He wanted his students to be aware of modern problems, and in his lectures and writings he brought them topics not usually covered in economics courses: the labor movement, cooperatives, utopian societies, the economics of municipal governments. He did not hesitate to listen to radical speakers like the anarchist Johann Most when they visited the city, and he took his students to hear Henry George when the single taxer spoke at a rally in Baltimore in 1888. The views of the unorthodox became the basis for discussion and analysis in his classes. His critics, of whom there were many, branded him a "socialist," but he spurned the label, although he advocated public ownership of natural monopolies and accepted the need for government intervention against injustices in the economic system.

Ely's lectures, Howe wrote, presented the world as it was, not, as the classical economists did, "the world as it had been in the days of our grandfathers, when there were no railroads, when large-scale industry was not known, huge aggregations of capital had not appeared, and the industrial revolution had just begun." Where the orthodox texts pictured a society of competition, Ely showed his students "a world of monopoly, an economic feudalism that was fast taking the place of the theoretical world of freedom and equal opportunity. Under his teaching I found myself wrenched loose from the economic theories current in Meadville. Men who came under his influence learned to look at the world with inquiring minds and to challenge the finality of established things." Ely liked his Ph.D. students to avoid theory in their dissertations and to find topics that were historical and descriptive. Under his tutelage, Howe began work on a thesis on the history of the internal revenue system in the United States. Though the relationship between the two men was to have its ups and downs, they provided a great deal of help and support to each other over nearly forty years.[6]

Of great importance to Howe's intellectual development and future careers were three visiting lecturers, James Bryce, Albert Shaw, and Woodrow Wilson. Bryce, then Regius professor of civil law at Oxford, had close ties with Adams and the history and politics department and came to lecture at Hopkins on several occasions. Howe had a brief but significant exposure to the English scholar. He and other history and political science students found the *American*

---

6. On Ely's economic views and his days at Johns Hopkins, see Rader, *Academic Mind and Reform*, 16–53; Barber, "Political Economy"; Hawkins, *Pioneer*, 177–86; Goldman, *Rendezvous with Destiny*, 86–87; as well as Ely's *Ground Under Our Feet*.

Commonwealth, which appeared in 1888, "a work of Biblical authority." Howe recalled hearing him speak at Hopkins in October 1890 about democracy's failures and the need for the scholar in politics. Bryce's critique brought home to him the complacency with which the people of Meadville accepted their political system and their failure to take part in governing themselves. Bryce spoke as an authority. "When he visited our seminar on politics, professors and students accepted his opinions as beyond and above question. He talked about the spoils system, about the corruption of cities, and the decay of a sense of responsibility among the kind of people whom I knew. That was what impressed me most: the kind of people I knew had neglected their duties." Bryce dwelt on the evils of party politics and argued that America, lacking Britain's advantage of a leisure class involved in statecraft, had to find salvation in its scholars. "Unthrilled by eloquence—for Mr. Bryce was a dull lecturer—I accepted his creed of responsibility and service." Democracy had to be saved from the politicians and spoilsmen, from the like of the Andrews brothers and Senator Quay.[7]

Albert Shaw and his lectures were important to Fred in a different way. After graduating from Iowa College (now Grinnell) in 1879, Shaw had gone to work for an Iowa newspaper. Tiring of its routine aspects and feeling a need to know more about contemporary political and economic problems, he took a leave of absence from the paper in 1882 and entered the Johns Hopkins program in history and politics. He completed his graduate studies in a remarkably short time and received his doctorate two years later. He returned to the newspaper world but kept up his scholarly interests, contributing a section to a book planned by Ely and edited by Adams, writing articles and reviews, and editing a book, *The National Revenues,* that included selections from a number of prestigious contributors. Tiring once more of the newspaper routine, he left the *Minneapolis Tribune* and spent a good part of 1888 touring European cities, both for relaxation and for a study of their governmental institutions. After returning to the *Tribune* for a while, in 1890 he accepted the position of American editor of a British journal, the *Review of Reviews.*[8]

Throughout this period, Shaw had maintained his links with Johns Hopkins. He corresponded with Ely and Adams and worked with them in scholarly endeavors, and he was a charter member of the American Economic Association, which Ely was instrumental in founding. On Adams's invitation he returned to Hopkins in November 1889 to deliver eight lectures to graduate students on European cities, and he came back in October and November 1891

---

7. On Bryce's two earlier visits and lectures at Johns Hopkins, see Ions, *James Bryce and American Democracy,* 100–101, 118–22.

8. Graybar, *Albert Shaw,* 16–45.

to give ten more lectures on their economic and social problems. Howe was enrolled in both courses.

In his lectures Shaw covered a broad field. He examined history, organization, and municipal reform in Glasgow, London, Paris, Rome, Berlin, Vienna, and Budapest in the first series, and urban economic, social, and labor problems in the second. Fred found the lectures inspiring and wrote that Shaw stirred his imagination in a way that none of his other professors could. He painted pictures of cities that Howe could visualize—"cities that I wanted to take part in in America; cities managed as business enterprises; cities that were big business enterprises, that owned things and did things for people. There was order and beauty in the cities he described. They owned their own tramways and gas and electric lighting plants, and they made great successes of them. Good men ran them, business men, who gave up their business interests to do so." Howe could understand this kind of "objective politics" much more easily than he could grasp the economic abstractions he found in other courses. "It was about the only academic subject that fitted in with my background, to which something inside of me responded."[9]

Shaw turned his lectures into periodical articles and then into two books, *Municipal Government in Great Britain* and *Municipal Government in Continental Europe* (both published in 1895). Howe read the books "with zest," and they gave him his "first political enthusiasm." Shaw seemed to epitomize the scholar in journalism, the very role that Howe dreamed of. "I desired to be an editor and a writer, as was he, so that I could further the ideas I had gotten from him. I wanted to go to Europe and see for myself the cities he had described, to study their machinery, their municipal enterprises, their splendid streets, parks, and public buildings." The first of his books to gain Howe national attention was to be entitled *The City: The Hope of Democracy*.

If Shaw provided an example of one vocational road Howe might take, Woodrow Wilson over his lifetime offered several others. Wilson was a contemporary of Shaw at Johns Hopkins, receiving his Ph.D. two years after Shaw, in 1886, and the two were friends both at the university and in later years. While teaching at Wesleyan and Princeton, Wilson supplemented his income, continued the interest in public administration that Ely had stimulated, and gained the opportunity to teach graduate students (he had mainly undergraduates in his regular courses) by offering a series of lectures at Johns Hopkins. Adams liked to bring back successful alumni like Wilson and Shaw, both to enrich the offerings in the department and to display as role models to its graduate students.

9. *Fifteenth Annual Report*, 55; *Seventeenth Annual Report*, 56–57; *University Circular*, December 1889, 17–19, and July 1891, 143; Graybar, *Albert Shaw*, 70–90.

Wilson's lectures were given in the spring term, five days a week over a five-week period, beginning in 1889, in Howe's first year at Hopkins, and continuing annually until 1898. He defined "administration" broadly to include not only the "science of administration" but also municipal government (both American and European), public law, and democracy and the state generally. Howe eagerly attended the lectures all three of his years at Hopkins and found them inspiring, as did other graduate students.[10]

If Albert Shaw stirred Frederic Howe's imagination, Woodrow Wilson appealed to him for his vision and his idealism. Still unsure of his own beliefs, Howe gained from Wilson's lectures the feeling that Americans had departed from the ideals of the Founding Fathers and had betrayed the high calling of politics. "Great men had departed from Capitol Hill; the Senate no longer reverberated to the high morality of earlier days. Democracy was not concerned over issues of great constitutional import. Politics had become a struggle of vulgar interests, of ignoble motive, of untrained men." As with Bryce, the message was clear. The spoilsmen and the politicians had taken over the government of America. It must be reclaimed from them.

For a five-week period every spring, Wilson resided in Baltimore at Jane and Hannah Ashton's boardinghouse on McCullough Street, where he had lived as a graduate student. Fred Howe lived there for several years, too, and so had the opportunity to know Wilson personally, as well as through his lectures. Knowing Wilson was difficult, however—"austere, never inviting intimacies, he kept quite by himself at the university." In the boardinghouse he unbent occasionally and was not unfriendly; he "fraternized absently with the half a dozen men who lived there. He was a raconteur of good stories and a brilliant conversationalist. But he spent most of his time in his room by himself preparing his lectures and writing."

Like Shaw, Wilson became an early model for Fred Howe, a dual model of the possibilities of the scholar as academician and the scholar as political leader. Howe let nothing interfere with Wilson's courses, and he read "religiously" the books the professor suggested. "What he had achieved I might also achieve if I were diligent enough. I absorbed his conceptions of disinterested statesmanship, of government by *noblesse oblige*. That early discipleship gave me, years later, clews to the understanding of the powerful, baffled, lonely personality who took us into the Great War." He kept in touch with Wilson after leaving Hopkins, received from him an appointment as commissioner of immigration for the Port of New York, worked very actively in New York for Wilson's reelection in

---

10. For general discussions of the Hopkins lectures, see Bragdon, *Woodrow Wilson*, 188–201, and Mulder, *Woodrow Wilson*, 116–21. The lectures are briefly summarized in the *Annual Reports of the President of the Johns Hopkins University* and the *University Circulars* for the years involved.

1916, and offered much unsolicited advice on domestic and foreign policies during Wilson's presidential years.

Fred Howe's contemporaries among the graduate students in history, politics, and political economy were a remarkable group. The growing prestige of the university and the attractive fellowships that were offered brought in men who were to make their mark in American intellectual and political life.[11] Fred's friendship with many of these talented men continued throughout his lifetime. Especially close to him was a younger contemporary, Newton Baker. Baker entered Johns Hopkins as an undergraduate in 1889, received his B.A. in 1892, and stayed on for a year of graduate study in jurisprudence and Roman law. He and Howe were together in some classes and lived in the same boardinghouse for several years, the one where Woodrow Wilson also resided. Howe helped organize the Hopkins chapter of Phi Gamma Delta in 1891, and Baker became an ardent member. After securing his law degree from Washington and Lee University in 1894, he began a practice in Martinsburg, West Virginia, his hometown. He and Howe would soon be together again in Cleveland and in the federal government. Baker was to be mayor of Cleveland, secretary of war during World War I, and a potential nominee for the presidency.

Howe recalled that all the graduate students were "very serious minded." On Sunday, the only day they felt they could take off, they slept late and then went for long tramps in the country. "There was little to distract us from the great adventure of education on which we were engaged; an occasional dance in the gymnasium, an evening in the comfortable beer saloons around the university, glimpses of the charming hospitality of the city, were incidents in the great business of making ourselves scholars. Our own relationships and interests sufficed us, and the outside world seemed very far away." Their instructors stimulated in them "a spirit of courage and restless inquiry." The university's gifts, Howe later wrote, were "open-mindedness, a willingness to make sacrifices for the truth, a passion for change. Johns Hopkins taught men to think, not what to think." Its motto summed up this goal: *Veritas vos liberabit*—The truth shall make you free.

11. Howe's Chautauqua friend John Finley moved on from Hopkins to a career in journalism and education that included college presidencies and the editorship of the *New York Times*. Charles Homer Haskins, a Meadville native, became a full professor of history at the University of Wisconsin before he was twenty-two years old. After gaining his doctorate, Westel Woodbury Willoughby returned to Hopkins as an instructor and then a professor of political science. He became chair of the department when it gained independence from the history department and was instrumental in forming the American Political Science Association. Charles D. Hazen, also from Meadville and Allegheny College, became a professor of history at Columbia. David Kinley moved to the University of Wisconsin when Ely did and earned his doctorate there. He had an illustrious career at the University of Illinois, culminating in its presidency. After receiving his Ph.D., Edward A. Ross secured teaching positions at Indiana, Cornell, and Stanford and became a major figure in American sociology.

Ely held German scholarship in high esteem and expected his best students to study in Germany. Probably for that reason Howe and a fellow student, Westel Willoughby, spent part of the spring and summer of 1891 in Europe. A news item in the *Meadville Republican,* which bears the earmarks of Howe's tongue-in-cheek authorship, reported that he was going to Europe for "a special study of anthropopathy in England, with special reference to the education of criminal classes."[12] In later years he always recorded that he had engaged in graduate study at the University of Halle, but according to his account in his autobiography, he and Willoughby went first to Oxford. Finding it inhospitable, they went to Berlin and took lectures in history and political economy from von Treitschke and others. By living in student rooms, eating in student restaurants, sitting in the cheapest theater seats, and walking rather than riding, they managed to subsist on less than a dollar a day. When the summer semester ended, they were broke, but they tramped through Germany, Italy, and Switzerland before heading for Liverpool and the boat home. Prudently, they had paid for their return passage before they left the United States.

On June 14, 1892, Frederic Clemson Howe received his Ph.D. degree from the Johns Hopkins University. Despite his doubts, his dissertation, entitled "A History of the Internal Revenue System," had proved acceptable. The degree did not make him feel scholarly, and that concerned him. "I worried not a little over my lack of scholarly enthusiasms. I had none. I worked hard and read diligently what was assigned, but it was a good deal of a grind. Neither history, economics, nor jurisprudence gave me half the thrill that came from an assignment to write up a football game for one of the Baltimore papers." He was always more excited by the practical aspects of his studies than by the theoretical. "I had not been able to master the abstractions of political economy, I was not soaked in history as were some of my associates. And I had never had any great enthusiasm for any of my subjects." But the degree itself was most valuable, he was sure. "It would open doors, command friends, assure a job; of that there was no question. . . . A Hopkins Ph.D. was a distinction of which I was infinitely proud."

Evidence from Howe's academic record indicates that his self-assessment as a nonscholar was probably accurate. His course work was evidently satisfactory—it cannot be compared with that of others since Hopkins at that time recorded no grades for graduate students. His application for a fellowship in December 1890 was turned down (he felt "somewhat wronged" but comforted himself with the explanation that "my failure was due to having to work my

---

12. *Meadville Republican,* May 25, 1891. See also H. B. Adams to President Gilman, May 22, 1891, Hamburger Archives.

way through the university"). Unlike Willoughby and other students in the department, he was not recognized by name in the president's *Annual Report* for any paper he presented in the history or economics seminars. His dissertation was not published in the prestigious *Johns Hopkins University Studies in Historical and Political Science.* His teachers thought well of him, however, and they formed a network that aided and supported him in subsequent years. He saw Adams and Ely at Chautauqua in the summers; he corresponded with them about employment, his and their intellectual and professional pursuits, his writings, and his reform activities. But in his graduate school days they did not perceive him as one of their academic stars.

Yet his utilitarian assessment of what he had gained from Johns Hopkins—a trade union card, a certificate that would open doors—was too limited, as he himself admitted from time to time. He had had the experience of working in an invigorating intellectual environment, one in which faculty and students were free to pursue ideas without worries of religious taboos or community censure. His professors were not much older than many of their students, and they created a climate for joint efforts and inquiry. "As I gradually became accustomed to this new freedom, I myself pioneered into new fields of thought. I learned how to work, how to use books. I met men who were not afraid to use their minds, not afraid of what they might find if they looked for the truth." Unscholarly he might be, but he "came to love Johns Hopkins with a peculiar affection, as did other men of my time." They compared it to the medieval universities, where aspiring pupils journeyed for miles to sit at the feet of great teachers. "We too were masters and pupils, living simply, badly housed, indifferently fed; just a group of enthusiasts interested in a rediscovery of the mind."

Johns Hopkins, especially through the lectures of Albert Shaw and, to a lesser extent, those of Ely, Wilson, and Bryce, gave Howe a deep interest in the city and in municipal reform. He was not sure why this was the topic that gripped him most. "I cared about beauty and order in cities—cities that chose for their rulers university men, trained as I was being trained. Possibly because I was disorderly myself, I wanted order. And I hated waste. That I had been taught to esteem a cardinal sin, and American cities, I was told, were wasteful because they were ruled by politicians, whose only interest was jobs." Although Howe was to retreat temporarily to Meadville and to find a summer refuge on Nantucket, most of the rest of his life was to be spent in large cities: Cleveland, New York, Washington, D.C.

Looking back, Howe concluded that the "herd-mind" of Meadville and Allegheny College had been displaced by new external authorities rather than by independence of thought. He continued to think as others did, but his guides now were "wise men, men who paid little attention to the church, but who had a worshipful veneration for some scientist or teacher under whose influence they had fallen. I accepted these new authorities as quite natural. Acceptance fell in with my earlier assumption that authority was proper, necessary, probably the first of the moralities." Freedom—an independent freedom based on his own authority and will—had yet to be discovered.

Along with new authorities came "new moralities, the moralities of educated men, of scholars, of intellectual reformers." America's evils must be corrected by new leaders. Without their help, democracy would fail. "The people were hungry for guidance; of that we were clear—guidance which we, the scholars, alone could provide. To this brotherhood of service I belonged. I was one of the chosen. . . . The purple robe of doctor of philosophy dedicated me to this service, as it gave me a distinction which seemed rare in my world." The Johns Hopkins men of the 1890s were the Atlases who would bear the world's burdens on their shoulders. "And I rather enjoyed the burden that I was to carry. I accepted it with conscious satisfaction, though without any clear idea of just how to go about it." The old moralities, whatever they were, had been lost. "The new ones were only less uncertain."

The Ph.D. thus brought both responsibility and opportunity. Howe had now found, he later concluded, the salvation that had escaped him in the Allegheny revival meetings. He was now one of the saved, one of the elect, and he had a mission to pass on what he had learned to others. He must fight the evils that had been disclosed to him. "The political boss must be exiled, the spoilsmen must be replaced by trained men. The business man must be awakened to responsibility and led to take a disinterested part in municipal politics; he must bring his experience to the administration of the city as did the business men of England. The trusts, which were then rising to power, must be curbed or destroyed, while the public-utility corporations of the cities must be either owned or regulated in the interest of the public."

How much of this Howe really felt in 1892, and how deeply he felt it, is uncertain. His interest in reform did not immediately translate into political activism. The abstractions had not yet been made flesh through firsthand encounters with politicians, businessmen, monopolists, and street-railway magnates. He had a number of roads to try before the word "reformer" and the name Frederic Howe became synonymous. Meanwhile, he had a living to make, and a vocation (in a narrower sense) to choose. A "priesthood of service" puts little bread on the table.

3

HANGING ON THE RAGGED EDGE

A career in journalism had remained Fred Howe's goal, and throughout his Hopkins days he believed that he was preparing himself for that calling.[1] But there were other options. If necessity required, he could teach. He believed that his Johns Hopkins education would ensure easy entrance into the academic world. "Journalism was my goal, but I was not unwilling to consider a good academic post as a stop-gap." He and others in the department at Hopkins were "hanging on the ragged edge of expectancy," he wrote Edward A. Ross, and "have our eyes peeled for a job." Despite help from Ross and Ely, however, Howe could not find the academic berth he desired. By December 1892 his mentor was peevish at Howe's procrastination. "What he wants is some position as lecturer with a small salary, and not a great deal of work," Ely observed to Ross.[2]

Another possible choice for Howe was the law, which several Hopkins contemporaries were planning to pursue. This was a profession that he did not rate very highly, however, and it was at the bottom of his list of options.

Howe's choice turned back to journalism. He left Baltimore to seek a newspaper job in New York City, where he found lodgings on West Tenth Street near Sixth Avenue, in "a cheap and crowded boarding-house." There he shared a room with three other men from Allegheny College who had also come to the metropolis for newspaper work or to study. The city seemed full of unemployed men, many of them newspapermen, who spent the days fruitlessly looking for jobs. The nation was in the midst of a depression, and times were hard.

1. Unless otherwise indicated, quotations are from Howe's *Confessions of a Reformer*, chaps. 7 and 8.
2. FCH to Edward A. Ross, March 20, 1892, and April 15, 1892; FCH to Ross, April 15, 1892; Richard T. Ely to Edward A. Ross, April 20, 1892, September 15, 1892, and December 12, 1892. Ross Papers, Wisconsin Historical Society.

Howe was undaunted by either the economic downturn or the misfortunes of others. After all, he had worked his way through Johns Hopkins and earned substantial amounts of money without a great deal of effort. "I would quickly rise, as other Johns Hopkins men had done." He preferred a position on a paper edited by intellectual liberals, perhaps the *Nation* or the *Evening Post*. Since they might be beyond his immediate reach, he would give the *New York Times* (which appealed to him as a free-trade paper) the first opportunity to hire him. After a few days of waiting, he was able to talk to the city editor and to inform him about his special qualifications for editorial writing. "I had studied history and political economy. I was familiar with historical jurisprudence. I had traveled abroad; had been editor of several college publications. Very few men were as well equipped as I was." Moreover, he had a program: a new deal in politics, destruction of trusts and monopolies, perhaps public ownership of the railroads, treatment of labor with more consideration. He was sure that the *Times* was "the best of all mediums for the propagation of my ideas," and he was eager to begin work.

After listening patiently and tolerantly, the editor explained to the young man the facts of newspaper life. One did not begin at the top as an editorial writer. One had to become familiar with the city and with the paper's traditions, and to work his way up from a reporter's job. At last he agreed that Howe could sit around the office, without salary, and that he would be sent out on any assignment that the regular staff could not cover. For days Fred came faithfully to the newsroom, but no one paid any attention to him. Finally the editor sent him out to cover a fire, and Fred wrote "a remarkable bit of literature. It was at least a column long. That meant four dollars." The next morning he searched the *Times* for his masterpiece and finally found a few lines in an obscure corner, rewritten to eliminate all his fine language. He was so angry that in a few weeks he resigned from the *Times*—"rather, I just stayed at home. My weekly earnings scarcely paid car-fare."

Fred had no more luck at other newspapers than he had had at the *Times*. It was not his poverty that began to depress him, however. As a last resort, he could always go home. "That, however, seemed too humiliating to consider. In my case, going home meant adding another mouth for my father to feed." Far worse than poverty was his sense of failure. He had been preparing for journalism for eight years; he had been a success in Baltimore, earning enough from his newspaper work for an adequate living; he was ready for his opportunity. Now his Ph.D. seemed a liability, not an asset, and he soon stopped referring to it. He was willing to start at the bottom, but there were no jobs.

By Christmas 1892 Howe had to surrender to reality and abandon journalism. He came to fear building his future "on the capriciousness of journalism, on its uncertainties, on the apparently inevitable failure at forty or fifty which seemed to have been the fate of the men I met that winter. It was too precarious, too hard getting started." Reflecting on his decision in later years, Howe concluded that he might have done better to stick to the work that he wanted most to do. The Meadville lessons of thrift and responsibility were too strong in his mind, however. He had to establish himself quickly, to justify the years of preparation, to act on the assumption that suffering was good for one's character.

So he convinced himself that turning to law was the proper thing to do. It would offer security; it would open the door to politics; it would provide independence and a chance to do some writing. "Through it, too, I could get into reform work, for the lawyer speaks with authority and can devote himself to outside matters without injury to his profession." He enrolled in the New York Law School and planned to speed through its two-year course and take his examination in June 1894.[3] Through the secretary of the school, he found a part-time job in a lawyer's office. After working from nine till three, he attended lectures and then "studied listlessly until midnight."

During these trying months in New York City, Fred sought to maintain his academic interests and contacts. He kept in touch with Adams and Ely and attended meetings of the local Hopkins alumni association. His first professional publication, an article entitled "The Federal Revenues and the Income Tax," appeared in the *Annals of the American Academy of Political and Social Science* in January 1894. In it, he considered the desirability of reviving a federal income tax to meet the national budget deficit. He concluded that, although theoretically it was "the most equitable of taxes," in practice it had many defects, most notably its unpopularity with the American people. The best remedy for the deficit was an increase in taxes on whiskey, malt liquors, and tobacco, "articles usually held to be superfluous, and by many harmful luxuries."[4] Nothing in the article foreshadowed Howe's later thinking about the most desirable kind of tax.

Preparing for a career in the law failed to dissipate Fred's gloomy feelings of failure. "I wondered if I could ever crawl back to a place among the men I revered." Johns Hopkins had entrusted him with a mission to change the world, but here he was, living in a cheap rooming house, trapped in a menial job, "spending my days making collections in saloons, or pounding a typewriter in the office of a lawyer who knew nothing about jurisprudence, mediaeval texts, or Roman law." He needed to work for a cause, to do something to fulfill his obligation to society, and he soon found an opportunity.

3. No information on Howe's work at the New York Law School is available. The school has moved several times, and during one of the moves lost almost all its early records and materials. Marie S. Newman, Librarian, New York Law School, letter to author, July 1, 1987.

4. FCH, "Federal Revenues and the Income Tax." In the summer of 1893 Howe had written six articles on taxation in Pennsylvania for the *Pittsburgh Dispatch*.

A friend introduced him to Dr. Charles H. Parkhurst, pastor of the Madison Square Presbyterian Church. In February 1892 Parkhurst had startled his parishioners and greatly perturbed Tammany Hall with a biting sermon on New York City's corruption and vice. He called the Tammany machine "a lying, perjured, rum-soaked, and libidinous lot." When the press publicized his charges, the mayor and other public officials denounced him, and the minister, his belligerency aroused, set to work to prove his case. Parkhurst was president of the Society for the Prevention of Crime, a body of high-minded, well-to-do citizens. Using that organization and a new one he created, the City Vigilance League, the clergyman recruited a corps of young men to help his investigations into graft and sin. Each League member pledged himself "to study the municipal interests of this city, and to do everything in my power to promote the purity and honesty of its government."[5]

Fred took the pledge and was appointed captain of the state assembly district that included Greenwich Village. He was supposed to keep an eye on the saloons, report violations of the Sunday-closing law and the sale of liquor after hours, and watch for other breaches of state and local regulations. Though he later realized that he was "not really interested in this sort of work, in regulating people's habits, or putting them into jail," at the time he was "zealous about enforcing the laws." He was especially concerned with the saloons. In Meadville he had learned that the saloon was "the symbol of everything bad, the cause of the downfall of some of our relatives. If one went into saloons, one became a printer or a tramp; one associated with disreputable women." At Johns Hopkins he had acquired the abstract knowledge that the saloon was a source of political power. It was the boss's training school, it collected tribute from the underworld, it was a club for the immigrant leaders who controlled the city. "The saloon was the root of our political evils, that was clear. I must understand it; possibly I could aid in correcting its abuses if not in putting it out of business altogether."

He possessed a special qualification for his investigations—he knew "almost every saloon from the Battery to the old Hoffman House." As he walked back and forth to the law school, he often succumbed to the lure of the free lunch that came with a five-cent glass of beer. Sharing his room with three other men who often provided temporary lodging in it for unemployed acquaintances, he found the saloon across the street a refuge where he could study his law books. It was the only friendly place he had found in New York. "It was my club, where I had a comfortable warm corner to myself. I could study there better than in

---

5. Parkhurst, *Our Fight with Tammany*, 18, 111; Werner, *Tammany Hall*, 348. Parkhurst and his crusade are colorfully described in L. Morris, *Incredible New York*, 215–33.

the law library. The barkeeper, an Irish lad, listened patiently to everybody's troubles, including my own, and seemed to be really interested in them."

In his role as vigilante, he asked Jerry, the bartender, why his saloon stayed open beyond the legal hours, why it sold whiskey to women, why it had rooms upstairs for immoral purposes. Jerry explained that taxes and payoffs were so high that they had to do these things in order to stay in business. "If we keep the laws, we have to go out of business. If we break them, we have to pay the police to let us do it." There was no way out, he argued.

Fred pondered Jerry's words. Finding the analysis convincing, he wrote a letter to Dr. Parkhurst. We're after the wrong man, he explained. The people who make the laws and are responsible for the high taxes are "our kind of people," people like those in your congregation. "They take millions out of the saloon-keeper, and he in turn takes these millions out of the poor. He ruins women and children. He ruins homes. Finally he corrupts the politics of the city as well. And you and I profit out of the ruin. We don't have to pay as much taxes as we otherwise would. . . . If we had started out to make the saloon as bad as it could be made, we could not have made a better job of it." With his letter to Dr. Parkhurst he enclosed his resignation as a captain in the City Vigilance League. He received no reply.

Howe admitted that his thinking about the saloon may have been colored by his own poverty and by his liking for Jerry. But, as he later noted, his early judgment about the stupidity of regulation became stronger with time, "as has my contempt for the hypocrisy that is identified with it. We are not on the level in our moral crusades; worse still, of their hidden effects we are crudely ignorant. Possibly this is another by-product of the evangelical-mindedness that seeks a moralistic explanation of social problems and a religious solution for most of them."

As Howe sat around the saloons, he found a new view of life, "a world of political reality." Politics was not an abstraction but "part of everyday life, part of the family, of religion, of race"—"a real thing, a city block, a voting precinct, or a ward." To the graduate students at Hopkins, politics meant disinterested service, fulfillment of a duty to the state. "To the people of the East Side it meant getting something for themselves and their friends. . . . Government meant the district leader, the policeman, the local boss." Fred learned about the hierarchy of politics, about city jobs and the ethical code of rewards and punishments that applied to party service. "To be loyal to one's friends, to stand by the gang, to do as you were told, until you were in turn selected to tell others what to do, was all that the Constitution, the Bill of Rights, and the government of the United States meant to the average man in lower New York twenty-five years ago."

As Fred watched, he learned to appreciate the East Side's Irish politicians, a clan whose concept of politics was quite alien to the cold, negative, aristocratic English view praised in the university. The Irish "warmed the state into a human thing, made frank demands on it for things they could not get for themselves. They provided an amalgam to extreme Anglo-Saxon individualism, which had an aversion to the state and a resentment of any extension of its activities beyond routine things." Looking back on the years after his first New York sojourn, Howe concluded that from then on, he had never ceased liking the Irish. "I should not like to think of America with them left out." By wanting things and getting them, they had made New York a great city.

Perhaps politics had a human side, Howe speculated. "Perhaps the state should do things for the happiness of its people instead of being merely a policeman. And perhaps things had to be gotten by the people who needed them most, not for them by some scholar or leader." He began to take an interest in people and to lose his distrust of the poor and the uneducated. "Some priggishness I think went out of me, unwillingly, through my schooling on the streets of lower New York."

Howe's unlearning was continuing, but despite his heresies he had not yet escaped the "new authorities" and "new moralities" acquired at the university. "My confidence in my own kind was not impaired. I still believed that America would be aroused only through disinterested service. But this faith was strangely confused by new human equations, by the warmer point of view of the Tammany leader and his followers in the tenements of the lower East Side."

In the midst of these new experiences and new questionings, Fred continued to prepare for the bar examination, looking forward confidently to taking it in June 1894. Then, in April, the Board changed the rules to require at least two years of legal studies before admission to the bar. Howe found the prospect of six more months in law school impossible to contemplate. He had little money and was far behind in his rent. The only solution was to retreat to Meadville.

Howe used the word "humiliating" three or four times in his autobiography to describe his return to Meadville. He had left the town with high ambitions five years earlier, after five years as a campus leader at Allegheny College. He had attended a prestigious university and attained its highest mark of scholarship, the Ph.D. degree. Now he was home again, penniless, unemployed, a financial drain on an impecunious family, and little closer to a profession than when he had departed in 1889. "At twenty-five [actually twenty-seven], with no money, no profession, no outlook, and a disinclination for the law, the future seemed pretty hopeless. I had no liking for teaching, had failed at journalism, and was marooned in a small town where my university training was worse than useless."

Continuing the study of law, despite his lack of interest in it, seemed the only thing he could do. In most states, it was still possible to take the bar exam after studying—"reading law"—with an established attorney. He began to read law with his uncle, Frank P. Ray, in his office on Chestnut Street. Ray had a great deal of legal and political experience to share with his nephew, but Fred was scarcely interested. "I pored over dusty law-books that failed to awaken the slightest response in me." Most of the time he sat with his feet on the desk, "peering into a future that contained not a suggestion of hope or allurement."

Then one afternoon, as Fred walked in the country, he passed a girl he had not seen before. He kept his eyes on her until she was out of sight. "There was something about her that held me. I wanted to follow and speak with her. She did not live in Meadville. Perhaps she belonged to a theatrical company. She wore a wide, sweeping hat, her feet were unusually small, and her ankles were in keeping with her trim body. It was her eyes that held me. They were big and brown and warm." Inquiry among his sisters revealed that her name was Marie Jenney and that she was a student at the Meadville Theological Seminary.

Marie Hoffendahl Jenney was born in Syracuse, New York, on December 26, 1870. She came from a family described as "distinguished for brainy women and able lawyers."[6] Her paternal grandfather, William Jenney, was a Baptist minister and educator. Her maternal grandfather, George F. Saul, was pastor of a schismatic German Evangelical church in Syracuse for three years, had a book and music store, and founded in 1852 a German newspaper, the *Onondaga Demokrat*, later the *Syracuse Union*. Her maternal grandmother, Julia Regula Hoffendahl, was a painter. Marie's father, Edwin Sherman Jenney, gave up reading law in Syracuse at the outbreak of the Civil War, raised his own company of troops, and served until near the end of the war, leaving the army with the rank of colonel. He completed his legal studies, was admitted to the bar in 1865, and a few years later established the firm of Jenney and Jenney, made up of the colonel, his sons Alexander and William, and his daughter Julie Regula Jenney. The colonel was a lifelong Democrat, sometimes at odds with the party organization.

Marie's mother, Marie Regula Jenney, was a major figure in the life of Syracuse. The list of her philanthropic and civic activities is impressive: founder and president for eighteen terms of the Ka-na-te-nah Club of 350 women; president of the Syracuse Council of Women's Clubs; president for thirteen years of the Syracuse Morning Musicals; cofounder with her husband of the Charity Ball; organizer of the Women's Unitarian Alliance; member of the Consumers League and the Fortnightly Club. She was as politically active as it was possible for a

---

6. *New York World*, July 14, 1922. Information on the Jenney family is drawn from a number of newspaper clippings provided by the Onondaga Historical Association and the Onondaga County Public Library, collected in Obituaries and Biographical Clippings, vol. 11.

woman to be in the last decades of the nineteenth century and the first years of the twentieth: a director of the Syracuse Political Equality Club; first vice president of the New York State Federation of Women's Clubs and chair of its Committee on Suffrage; president of the Onondaga County Suffrage Association; founder of the Women's Democratic Club. On her death in 1922, the *Syracuse Post-Standard* observed that "strong convictions, clear intellect and a large store of gentleness never mistaken long for weakness, made her a personage."

Marie's older sister, Julie Regula Jenney, was at first interested in the stage but abandoned that ambition and earned a law degree from the University of Michigan. She became the first practicing woman lawyer in Syracuse; one of the first woman lawyers to argue before New York's highest court, the Court of Appeals; and, in the 1920s, the first woman to be appointed an assistant attorney general of New York State. A Unitarian in religion, in politics she adopted many of the same causes as her mother, held offices in the Political Equality Club and the Woman Suffrage Association, and spoke at national and state conventions of the National American Woman Suffrage Association.[7]

Marie, four years younger than Julie, was the third oldest of the four Jenney children (a fifth, Edwin, had died in infancy) and the only one who did not seek a career in the law. She was educated in several private schools, including Parsons School in Greenfield, Massachusetts. She was also a student for several years in the Misses Masters' Boarding and Day School for Young Ladies and Children (now the Masters School) in Dobbs Ferry, New York. Miss Eliza B. (Lillie) Masters, for many years the dominant force in the institution, objected to the label "finishing school," since the curriculum was broader, more academic, and more demanding than that in "finishing schools." The Misses Masters School offered a variety of subjects: English, French, Latin, music, art, the Bible and moral philosophy, history, elementary astronomy and botany, mathematics, domestic science, etiquette. The school was nonsectarian but had a high moral and religious tone.[8]

Her schooling completed, Marie made her debut in Syracuse society and in the late 1880s became a leader in the Cooking Club, an organization of young women. "It is a funny thing," she said several decades later, "that club turned out young women in almost every profession but cooking. There is not a cook

---

7. Along with the scrapbook cited above, see Leonard, *Woman's Who's Who of America*, 431; Harper, *History of Woman Suffrage*, 4:255, 483.

8. "In its first quarter-century, Dobbs had established its reputation as a first-rate boarding school for girls. Its nature was that of a secure family, protected from the world (although interested in it) much like the firmly rooted Victorian families of those times, and propelled by the strength and personality of its founder." Vose, *Masters School: 1877/1977*, 15. The dates of Marie's attendance are unknown, since the sketchy early records of the school are silent about her. Nancy McKenzie, Alumnae Director, the Masters School, letter to author, August 7, 1990.

among us." She recalled that when she was a young girl her desire for a career was stimulated by the example of Susan B. Anthony. When some of the women who were asked to join the local suffrage association replied that they first had to go home and ask their husbands, Marie vowed that she would never marry.[9] Interested in religion, she turned to Unitarianism rather than to law and studied for a time with Dr. S. R. Calthrop, a Unitarian minister and the author of several theological works. In the fall of 1893 she enrolled in the Meadville Theological School.

The school had no connection with Allegheny College, and the two institutions offered quite a contrast. The college was sectarian and heavily Methodist in governance and outlook. The school had been founded in 1844 by a combination of Unitarians, independent Congregationalists, and Campbellite Christians. The second nonsectarian theological seminary in America (Harvard's Divinity School was the first), it stressed freedom of conscience and opened its doors not only to Christians of all denominations but also to students of any faith. Its enrollment of twenty-five to forty students included Jews, Hindus, Buddhists, and other non-Christians. The school admitted women from 1868 on and had its first woman graduate in 1873. Marie was the only woman among the five associate editors (the editor was a seminary professor) of the rather serious *Meadville Portfolio*, which began bimonthly publication in her first year of study.

She and her classmates found themselves in a school whose president and faculty believed in keeping up with changing times. After the appearance of Charles Darwin's *Origin of Species*, the faculty supplemented the teaching of natural theology with courses in zoology and botany, "though they were naturally not of an advanced type."[10] Courses in comparative religion were introduced in the 1870s, and visiting scholars in the history of religions were brought in. In the 1880s courses in political economy and sociology entered the curriculum; Professor Henry Hervey Berber maintained that the study of sociology was essential preparation for a minister's career. In 1892 the school established a lectureship on Christian sociology, which became the forum for wide-ranging discussion of social reforms. President George Lovell Cary and other faculty members pursued the "higher criticism" in analyzing and interpreting the Gospels and their authors. The curricular differences between the Meadville Theological School and its neighbor across the way, Allegheny College, could hardly have been greater.

It was in the spring of Marie's first year at the school that Fred Howe saw her and made it his immediate business to find out who she was. His sisters told

---

9. Obituaries and Biographical Clippings. The clipping is dated October 19, 1906, and is probably from the *Syracuse Journal*.

10. Christie, *Makers of the Meadville Theological School*, 121.

him all they had heard. People in town wondered about her. "She was too beautiful to be a minister. People insisted that she could not be serious. They argued that there was probably a man at the seminary who had brought her there. Only a man could explain such a beautiful girl, with good clothes and evidences of wealth, at a theological seminary."[11]

Several days later, Fred noticed an announcement that a group called the "Footlights" would perform several comedies at the Unitarian chapel, and he saw Marie listed as a member of the cast. From his front-row seat, hating throughout the evening all the male actors in the plays, he found her acting "extraordinary." He had to invent a way to meet her.

The next Sunday, he waited outside the Unitarian church and wangled a dinner invitation from the people with whom Marie was staying. She came to dinner late, her arms filled with flowers, and Fred "fell quite dumb at the introduction." She seemed scarcely to notice him and ignored him at dinner. He hardly knew how to talk to her. "Why should such a woman want to be a minister, I thought; why should she be studying Hebrew, Greek, and the early church fathers? It was all very stupid. I had never heard of such a thing. She could not be serious. All girls got married if they could; certainly all good-looking girls did." He tried a joke that fell flat, and then he blustered that Johns Hopkins did not admit women and he hoped it never would. After the meal, he tried to redeem himself in a discussion with Marie about political economy. She was especially interested in socialism and other advanced ideas. Fred tried to show off his Hopkins-acquired wisdom. "But the afternoon was a dismal failure. She seemed quite willing to see me go."

Nevertheless, he persevered, and soon the two were taking walks, picnicking at the lake, and reading together books on economics. Most of the time Fred found himself "preoccupied and silent." He realized that he knew a great deal about economics and politics from books, but nothing about women. His idea of a woman's role stemmed from his childhood observations of family and neighbors. "Men and women fell in love, they married, had children; the wife cooked the meals, kept the house clean, entertained relatives and friends, spent as little as possible, asked for what she got on Saturday evening with the weekly expense-account in her hands. She cared for the family when sick, got the children ready for school and church, arranged the men's clothes, on Sundays went on a buggy ride, and during the winter made cakes and pies for the church sociables." A good wife was careful in her conduct and expressed her opinions only in a whisper. All in all, women were conveniences of men. "Men were kind

---

11. Everything we know about Fred's and Marie's early acquaintanceship and courtship comes from his autobiography.

to them; they did not swear in their presence, they cleaned their boots before entering the house, gave them as good a home as they could, and were true to their marital vows. That was the most binding obligation of all."

Some day, Howe had assumed, he would have a wife who fit the Meadville pattern. He had been so absorbed in other things in college that he had not thought much about women. "I had a kind of fear of them; certainly a bashfulness that I had never outgrown. They were outside of my life, but when they entered they would enter on my terms, the terms of my boyhood conceptions as to the proprieties of things." Marie was totally different from the stereotype he had created, and this disturbed him, "especially as I was so greatly attracted to the disturber." Women ought to agree with men, but "she had ideas of her own; they were better than my own, more logical, more consistent too with my democratic ideas on other things." She believed women should have the right to vote; Fred snorted at this. She thought women should go to college, have careers, be economically independent, treat marriage as an equal partnership. Life was something to be enjoyed by both men and women. "There should be equality in all things, not in the ballot alone but in the mind, in work, in a career. Men and women were different in some ways, they were alike in more."

Fred had not found it difficult to shed his small-town credos of politics and economics and to replace them with the beliefs of his new authorities at Johns Hopkins. But "giving up my masculine authority meant giving up of one eminence I felt sure of." In his conversations with Marie, he tried to evade the disagreeable topic of men and women. After marriage, there would be time enough to discuss them. But they could not be evaded and kept coming up as Fred and Marie talked about life and about each other. On one level, Fred realized that he wanted Marie's independence of mind. "I would get courage from a woman who saw things as she saw them; could rely on a woman who faced me when other women would have smiled assent. She has courage as well as beauty, I thought." But he could not square his ideas about marriage with hers—"I could not give up the belief that a woman's place was where other women were."

Then came the chance for a job that would take Fred away to Pittsburgh. He was "tortured with indecision. . . . I had no right to be in love as I was, I had no money, no prospects, no chance apparently to get started inside of ten years at least. And I might never get started at all." His last day in town, the couple took a long walk that he wanted to go on forever. He finally tried to tell her how he felt. She seemed to understand. "But she wanted her career; she wanted to do something for the world. She loved her work and I hated mine. And I was twenty-five [actually twenty-seven] and was just where I had been four years before when I left Meadville with high hopes for the conquest of the world. We parted agreeing to write to each other." His letters were alternately hopeful and despairing; hers were "full of the work she planned to do."

By the end of the summer of 1894, Howe had accepted the position in Pittsburgh as secretary of the Pennsylvania Tax Commission. Before that came the bar examination, for which he felt totally unprepared, especially on Pennsylvania law and trial procedure. Fortunately, his first oral examiner was "a man of learning" who asked only two questions, one on equity jurisprudence and the other on the feudal system. Howe had mastered those subjects at Johns Hopkins and proceeded to snow his inquisitor under, killing as much time as possible. When his second examiner appeared, the first lawyer told him, "You don't need to bother about this man. He's all right. He knows more about the history of real property, about equity, than we do." Neither could know that Howe would have failed almost any question on a legal topic more recent than the eighteenth century. "For the law was still a confused maze of irrelevant things to me."

Nevertheless, he passed the examination. The *Crawford Journal* announced on September 13: "Fred C. Howe, of this city, was on Monday admitted to practice at the bar of Crawford County. Mr. Howe is a well-read young man, and will doubtless make his mark in his chosen profession."[12]

Fred may have been well read, but he remained completely unsure about both his new profession and his new job. Despite his membership in the bar and the knowledge of public finance gained in Hopkins classes and his dissertation research, he felt unprepared for his work with the Tax Commission. He despised the spoils system that he saw in state government, loathed the political corruption that he associated with the Quay machine, was outraged by the control of government by business interests. The members of the Tax Commission seemed indifferent to political conditions and friendly to Boss Quay. He concluded that the commission had been set up to produce a report favorable to the big corporations and that his own work was being twisted to serve that purpose.

Although he needed the money, he resigned after a few weeks and reluctantly began to consider practicing law. He thought about Pittsburgh as a place to start—he had college friends there and could make "advantageous connections." But the city was dirty and so badly governed that the streets were poorly paved and the public buildings unsightly. Orthodoxy was sovereign, and life was dull. "On Sunday the heads of its respectable families talked about religion; after six o'clock on Sunday, and from then on until Saturday night, they talked business and baseball." Ruling out Pittsburgh, he decided first to find a place where he would like to live and then to adjust his professional life to it. After visits to

12. *Crawford Journal,* September 13, 1894, 5.

Buffalo, Detroit, Chicago, and Cleveland, he decided on the Ohio city. "It had possibilities of beauty. It stretched for miles along the lake front and still kept some of the quality of a small town." By October 1894 he was ready to put his unhappiness in Meadville and Pittsburgh behind him and to see what Cleveland had to offer an unemployed lawyer.

4

VISTAS OF POLITICAL POSSIBILITIES

Cleveland in 1894 was already in the midst of planning the celebration of its 1896 centennial. Favorably located on Lake Erie at the mouth of the Cuyahoga River, the city had begun to evolve from a New England–like village to a shipping and commercial center after the Ohio and Erie Canal was completed in 1832. The Civil War and the ensuing decades brought rapid industrial development. The iron-and-steel industry flourished, and the city became the nation's oil capital after John D. Rockefeller established Standard Oil in 1870. Its population grew from less than 80,000 in 1860 to more than 261,000 in 1890, making it the tenth-largest American city. By 1894, when Fred Howe arrived, the rapidly growing metropolis had 381,760 people.[1] The early homogeneity of its people had been altered by the arrival of Irish and German settlers in the 1820s and 1830s, and after the Civil War a massive influx of immigrants from southern and eastern Europe helped meet the needs of industry for cheap labor. Between 1890 and 1900, foreign-born residents became nearly a third of the population.

Politically, Ohio was Republican territory (the party had carried it in every presidential election and most state elections since the Civil War), and so were Cleveland and Cuyahoga County. Statewide, Republican politics was dominated by two powerful rivals, Senator Joseph Benson Foraker and Marcus Alonzo Hanna, the Cleveland millionaire. In the winter of 1894–95, Hanna set aside his extensive business interests and began to devote his time fully to promoting the presidential candidacy of the Republican governor, William McKinley. In Cleveland a Republican mayor, Robert S. McKisson, had been able to strengthen both the mayor's power and his own personal position, operating under the new charter of 1891.

---

1. Van Tassel and Grabowski, eds., *Cleveland*, 30. On Cleveland's history, see Condon, *Cleveland*; Rose, *Cleveland*; J. Whipple, "Cleveland in Conflict."

Fred Howe arrived in Cleveland in the fall of 1894, unemployed and with no immediate prospects for a job. He found temporary quarters with a college friend in an apartment "on the edge of the red-light district, where half a dozen of us lived, sleeping two in a bed and knowing no privacy. A colored woman cooked our meals, and one of the boys who was out of a job served as bartender. We drank and played cards; our amusements were boisterous and distasteful to me." He made the rounds of lawyers' offices, seeking a position but finding no opening and becoming increasingly discouraged. One day he entered the office of Garfield and Garfield, met Harry Garfield, told him his situation, and made him a proposition:

> "If you don't mind, I will sit in your outer office here and do anything you want done. I like this place better than any office in town and I want to stay."
>
> "But we have no need of another clerk," he said. "We have only started at the law ourselves. There isn't anything for you to do."
>
> "That's all right," I answered," but if you don't mind, I would like very much to stay."[2]

The Garfields surprised themselves by agreeing to Howe's proposal. On November 22, 1894, James Garfield recorded in his diary: "We have taken a student into our office—F. C. Howe from Meadville, Penn. He expects to be admitted to the bar next January. I think we will like him and he will be of benefit to us. It seems rather curious that our office should be desirable for a young man to enter—it is only a few years since we were in his condition."[3] In age, the three were practically contemporaries: in November 1894 Fred was twenty-seven, James twenty-nine, and Harry thirty-one.

Harry A. Garfield and James R. Garfield were sons of the late president of the United States (assassinated in 1881). Both had received undergraduate educations at Williams College, studied law at Columbia, and been admitted to the Ohio bar in 1888. They established the firm of Garfield and Garfield in July 1888 and began a practice whose main elements were estate, corporate, and railroad law.

Writing some years later, Howe depicted himself as essentially unhappy, uninterested, and uninvolved in the legal practice that he entered in 1894. "I sat for years rather idly around the outer office, picking up small collection fees, busied with unimportant matters." He spent hours looking out over Lake Erie,

---

2. *Confessions of a Reformer*, 74.
3. James R. Garfield, diary (1894), entry of November 22, 1894, James R. Garfield Papers.

thinking about himself as a failure. "I disliked the law, had a fear of the judges, and most of all shrank from the experienced practitioners with whom I felt I could never cope. My university training gave me little comfort, it made me no friends, it did not aid me in trial work. At times it impeded me." It had been a mistake to think he could escape Meadville; he should have remained there, helping save his father's store. On the other hand, business seemed commonplace, "and I wanted to be back in the university library, where there was no conflict, no failure."[4]

One must guard against assuming that such later observations and generalizations represent an accurate portrayal of Howe's opinions and feelings at the time. His autobiography, *Confessions of a Reformer,* was written in a time of political defeat and disillusion, when the hopes and dreams of earlier years seemed lost. Certainly the law had not been his first choice as a profession. Yet, though the law failed to excite him or ultimately to satisfy him, he was a more than adequate lawyer, and even found many aspects of the work interesting and challenging, judging both from his own comments and those of his partners. He must have been doing more than sitting around the office, working listlessly. "I am glad to have Mr. Howe with us—things can safely be left in his charge," wrote James Garfield in July 1895, less than eight months after Fred entered the office. About the only complaint the Garfields had was that Howe was not a very capable accountant: "Howe is a good lawyer but does not know how to keep books orderly."[5] That Howe's performance was satisfactory is plainly indicated by the fact that, less than three years from the day he began sitting in their outer office, the Garfields made him a partner in the firm. On New Year's Day 1898 James wrote in his diary: "Frederic C. Howe became a member of our law firm today—our name is now Garfield, Garfield & Howe: he is a good lawyer and a gentleman."[6]

Garfield, Garfield and Howe prospered. In 1902 the partnership account showed $56,314.44 for Harry Garfield, $25,060.63 for James Garfield, and $23,964.80 for Fred Howe; in 1907 the corresponding figures (at a time when none of the three were very active in the firm) were $59,891.28, $26,555.76, and $26,236.63. They added another lawyer, David Westenhaver, to the office, and

---

4. *Confessions of a Reformer,* 74, 75. See also *Confessions of a Monopolist,* 14–15.
5. James R. Garfield, diary (1895), entries of July 6, 1895, and November 17, 1897. Howe cheerfully admitted the charge, writing Harry Garfield in 1908 about a financial statement: "It seems to be all right, although I did not go into it very minutely as I am not much good when it comes to bookkeeping." FCH to Harry A. Garfield, April 4, 1908, Harry A. Garfield Papers, Library of Congress.
6. James R. Garfield, diary (1898), entry of January 1, 1898.

in 1904 made him a partner, so that the firm became Garfield, Garfield, Howe and Westenhaver.[7]

All in all, the records of Garfield, Garfield and Howe, and the correspondence and other papers of the partners, do not show Fred Howe to be an inept and discontented lawyer. Perhaps his comment in a 1906 letter to Harry Garfield best expresses his feelings about his legal career at a time when it was drawing to an end: "Yes, I am out of the law and have no regrets. It did me much good and put me on my feet and was a fine, happy experience in many ways, but it never satisfied me."[8]

In the midst of his new law practice, Howe found time to continue his scholarly life. In 1892 Richard Ely had become editor of a new series of books, the Crowell Library of Economics and Politics. In December 1894 Fred wrote his professor that he would like to submit his revised doctoral dissertation for publication in the series. Ely apparently encouraged him to proceed, and about a month later Howe sent him the manuscript.

Ely discussed publication with T. Y. Crowell but almost immediately ran into a roadblock. Discovering that Houghton Mifflin planned to publish a book on the internal revenue system, Crowell thought it would be hardly worthwhile to bring out a similar book. Ely worked with Howe to make additional revisions in the manuscript and was able to overcome Crowell's doubts. On November 6, 1895, the publisher informed his editor that he would take "the Internal Revenue book" on the usual terms: a royalty of 10 percent after the first thousand copies were sold. On February 20, 1896, Crowell could announce that the ninth volume in the Library of Economics and Politics would be *Taxation in the United States Under the Internal Revenue System* by Dr. Frederic C. Howe of Cleveland, Ohio. The cost would be $1.75, postpaid.[9]

The book's subtitle described its scope: "An Historical Sketch of the Organization, Development, and Later Modification of Direct and Excise Taxation Under the Constitution." In a straightforward account, in unexciting prose, it traced this history from the beginnings of the republic to the 1890s, devoting

---

7. Ibid., entry of December 7, 1898; diary (1900), entry of January 1, 1900; diary (1901), entry of January 15, 1901; statement, Partnership Account of Garfield, Garfield and Howe; FCH to James R. Garfield, December 23, 1903. A West Virginia friend of Newton Baker, Westenhaver had come to Cleveland in 1903. He became a federal judge in 1917.

8. FCH to Harry A. Garfield, October 19, 1906.

9. FCH to Richard T. Ely, December 11, 1894, January 26, 1895; T. Y. Crowell to Richard T. Ely, February 4, 1895, February 26, 1895; FCH to Richard T. Ely, February 13, 1895, March 15, 1895, July 6, 1895, August 10, 1895; Crowell to Ely, October 9, 1895; FCH to Ely, October 18, 1895; Crowell to Ely, November 6, 1895; FCH to Ely, November 14, 1895, November 23, 1895, December 19, 1895, January 13, 1896, January 31, 1896, March 12, 1896; general letter from Crowell, February 20, 1896. The book actually appeared as volume 11 in the series under a slightly different title, *Taxation and Taxes in the United States Under the Internal Revenue System, 1791–1895*.

about half its coverage to the Civil War period. There were hints of Howe, the future reformer, in only a few places. He was critical of the spoils system, and he suggested the possibility of using graduated income and inheritance taxes "as a means for the readjustment of the inequalities in the distribution of wealth."[10]

Howe must have been pleased with the reviews of his first book. The reviewer for the *Dial* called it an "excellent account" that was "peculiarly timely." The *American Historical Review* found the book's historical treatment "distinctly fresh and interesting" and thought the criticisms "handled with skill and independence." There might be "a certain deficiency in the author's general knowledge of taxation and the literature of taxation, rather than any want of familiarity with his immediate subject. There he is always at home." For the *Annals,* Francis Walker, a leading economist of the day, declared that the book would "undoubtedly be welcomed as a valuable account of this important subject." The *Political Science Quarterly* thought that Howe, despite an "occasional slip," had "done the work well."[11]

Fred soon made friends in Cleveland, and several of those friendships were to lead directly to his involvement in local politics. His relations with the Garfields quickly became close and warm. One of the first comments on Fred in James's diary was dated February 28, 1895: "Home on the first train—Mr. Howe, who is in our office, with me. A pleasant evening talking of various things—we were at Mothers for an hour or so. . . . Mr. Howe is interested in political and economic questions, has studied them. I enjoy talking with him." And he repeated in his entry the next day: "I enjoyed Mr. Howe's visit." The formalities of *Mr.* Howe and *Mr.* Garfield rapidly gave way to Fred, Jim, and Harry. Howe often lunched with one or both of the partners. They enjoyed his conversation and his sociability and frequently invited him for dinner or to spend the weekend. Fred reciprocated in so far as his bachelordom permitted: "Mr. Howe is keeping house—we all dined with him very pleasantly." They played golf, bowled, coasted in the wintertime, went to dances at the country club, attended vaudeville ("spent the afternoon at the new Empire theatre—a good time—vaudeville—some excellent juggling by a chinaman"). Fred liked fishing, but he was hardly a dedicated angler: "As a matter of fact the only fishing I have ever done or ever expect to do has been with a bottle of scotch and soda and a brier-wood pipe, which according to my way of thinking is the only proper way of going fishing."[12]

10. Ibid., 239–40, v, 237.
11. *Dial* 21 (September 16, 1896): 154; *American Historical Review* 2 (July 1897): 744–45; *Annals of the American Academy of Political and Social Science* 8 (November 1896), 530; *Political Science Quarterly* 11 (September 1896): 567.
12. James R. Garfield, diary (1895), entries of February 28 and March 1, 1895; FCH to H. B. Adams, August 22, 1900, Adams Papers, Johns Hopkins University. James Garfield kept a diary regularly and Harry did not, so there is more specific information on James and Fred than on Harry and Fred.

Howe's mother and sisters (his father died in 1897) often shared in the Garfield hospitality. In 1898 and 1899 his mother and Isabel were living in Youngstown, and Fred was helping to support them by sending fifty dollars from time to time. The Garfields kept an eye on Fred's heart and his health. James noted what he thought was a budding romance with Mary E. Parsons of the Goodrich settlement house, and recorded in his diary: "Miss Parsons, Fred Howe, Stanley and Max dined and spent the afternoon with us. We are wondered [sic] if Fred and Miss Parsons are growing interested in one another."[13] When Fred was at the Homestead in Hot Springs for his health in the fall of 1900, Harry wrote solicitously: "I hope you are having a lovely time. Give your liver a good bit of exercise, and come home refreshed." Howe replied: "I am having a fine time here. It's a beautiful place, and we spend most of the days pursuing profane golf balls. My liver refuses to be boiled, I am sorry to say, and I shall go to Baltimore tonight where I can play golf and ride horseback and at the same time see my friends."[14]

Fred and the Garfield brothers were more than legal associates—they were friends and allies who consulted each other on personal and political matters. The Garfields brought Howe into the work of the Municipal Association, backed his candidacy for political office, respected his political ideas even when they disagreed with them, and stood up to his critics in Cleveland and elsewhere. Howe wrote later that his intimate association with them was the only thing that made the early years in Cleveland tolerable. They stood by him, even when he deserted the Republican party, became associated with Tom Johnson, and espoused ideas and causes that were bad for the firm's business. "I undoubtedly offended substantial clients, yet my partners never protested against my choices; they never sought to dissuade me from any decision, and never in an association of a dozen years alluded to financial considerations as a reason for keeping silent or changing my course. I realized at the time how generous this was. And I have realized it more fully since." He thought that the "herd instinct" was strong in all people, punishing desertions from the ranks and departures from creeds; but the Garfields never succumbed to that instinct.[15]

Fred's political activity in Cleveland was stimulated by his friendship with Morris Black. Two years younger than Howe, Black was a member of a well-established Hungarian family, a Harvard graduate, and, like Howe, a fledgling lawyer just beginning in practice. The two met at a dance, where "we drifted

13. James R. Garfield, diary (1896), entries of May 31, 1896, July 22, 1896; (1900) entry of February 22, 1900; (1899), entry of March 19, 1899. Another visit by Howe and Miss Parsons was noted on June 11.
14. Harry A. Garfield to FCH, October 6, 1900; FCH to Harry A. Garfield, October 9, 1900.
15. *Confessions of a Reformer*, 198.

into talk, told one another what we thought of our dirt-begrimed law-books, how we hated the petty things we were doing in the justice of the peace courts, laughed over the stupidities of our practice. . . . He was emotional, moody, full of vital energy, a musician. I was reserved and undemonstrative." The two became inseparable. "We dined and drank and tramped together. His home became my own."

Morris and Fred organized the Beer and Skittles Club, an informal group of young lawyers, newspapermen, and others interested in talking about political and social questions in a convivial setting. The club met weekly for dinner and talk, usually on Thursday evenings, in a Hungarian restaurant, Volls Jardinierre, near the lake front. Club members concocted their own special drink, which they called Slivowitz punch. "It seemed as harmless as lemonade, but as the dinner progressed it worked wonders. It was our delight to invite men of substantial reputation to our dinners and later tuck them tenderly into a cab, with instructions to the driver to take them to their homes."[16]

There was more to the club than food and drink, however. Fine dining was accompanied by conversation and discussions of a wide range of topics. The development of Cleveland's downtown lakeshore was a by-product of the club's existence. James Garfield, who was elected a member in December 1896, wrote of his first meeting: "We discussed socialism, municipal politics, etc. This club . . . is small, informal & jolly—through it we may be able to learn much of labor & social conditions." Not all the discussions were serious ones. Garfield records the entertainment of "a newspaper man who is walking from N.Y. to San Francisco—an interesting, pleasant evening."[17]

Fred and Morris talked frequently about local politics and agreed that boss control of their district was a disgrace. Each tried to convince the other to run for the city council as an antiboss Republican. They flipped a coin, and Black won. They began their campaign that very night by barging in on a Republican rally presided over by the organization leader, Bill Crawford. When Crawford was about to introduce his candidate for councilman, they pushed their way through the crowd to the platform, and Black announced his intention to run as an anti-Crawford candidate. The campaign soon began in earnest. "We spent night after night on the streets and in saloons. We organized committees and called on people at their homes. We covered nearly every street in the district. We had to drink a good deal—or thought we did. Black's father was rich and he spent a good deal of money. The campaign was unconventional and spectacular; all the newspapers featured it." In the primary on March 20, 1896, Black

16. Ibid., 80–81.
17. James R. Garfield, Diary (1896), entry of December 3, 1896; diary (1897), entries of February 12 and 17, 1897.

carried three of four wards and captured the Republican nomination. The *Plain Dealer* spoke favorably of his candidacy, and in the general election on April 6 he won easily over his Democratic rival. Howe found the outcome a justification of his Johns Hopkins creed. "A scholar could break into politics. I had helped to elect one to office. Morris Black and I had made a beginning at providing democracy in Cleveland with the leadership of men who served not from hope of personal gain but from a desire to improve the world."[18]

Black became an active member of the city council and, as its only antimachine Republican, a vigorous opponent of the McKisson administration. His career was cut short by his sudden death from appendicitis in March 1898. The funeral was held on March 20 at his father's residence. The streets around the house were crowded with people and carriages; many people could not get in for the simple secular service. Howe delivered the main address, described in the press as "an eloquent eulogy and fraught with deepest feeling." Black's life had been brief, he said, but it had made an indelible imprint on the community. "His thoughts, aspirations, and achievements will continue to blossom in the city in which he lived in an awakened public spirit, in a deepened civic responsibility and an elevated municipal consciousness."

For Howe the loss was desolating, and he considered abandoning the political world that was beginning to open to him. "My interest in life seemed pretty much ended with his death." When they were together, the law and its drudgery appeared unimportant, as did the odds that were stacked against them. "Adventuring together, we had dethroned a city boss. Like a couple of Don Quixotes, we had attacked windmills, and the windmills fell. I grieved over the loss of a friend and over the closing of vistas of political possibilities."[19] The Beer and Skittles Club soon faded away. New battles loomed, however, and the "vistas of political possibilities" did not remain closed.

Except for his venture into Republican politics with Black, Fred Howe kept to a largely nonpartisan path in his first years in Cleveland. The record is silent on his choice in the 1896 presidential election, but it is likely that he shared the Garfields' worries about William Jennings Bryan's economic policies.[20] He and the Garfields were Republicans with an independent, reformist bent. Howe's political adventures with Black had reinforced his belief in the Johns Hopkins creed of politics. H. B. Adams's advice was to start action in one's own community—general reform would follow from constant improvements of the local

18. *Confessions of a Reformer*, 83; *Cleveland Plain Dealer*, March 21, 1896, 1; April 1, 1896, 4; April 7, 1896, 1.
19. *Cleveland Plain Dealer*, March 19, 1898, 6; March 21, 1898, 1; *Confessions of a Reformer*, 84.
20. James Garfield wrote on the day after the election: "Our victory is overwhelming: our nation is saved & prosperity must come. Repudiation & revolution have been destroyed by the peaceful ballot." Diary (1896), entry of November 4, 1896.

situation. This "brighten the corner where you are" philosophy led Howe to the Municipal Association and the Goodrich settlement house.

Formation of the Municipal Association stemmed from a growing concern among leading business and professional men of Cleveland about the problems of their city government. In 1891 the state legislature had reorganized that government and created what was called a "Federal Plan" for its similarity to the presidential/congressional form. The mayor, previously a figurehead, now could appoint department heads with the council's approval and had the power to veto legislation. Robert E. McKisson, identified with the Foraker faction of the Republican Party, won nomination for mayor over Mark Hanna's choice, and was elected in 1895 and reelected in 1897. During his four years in office, he attempted to build up his own political machine, using the substantial patronage at his disposal and his powers under the new form of city government.[21]

In the fall of 1896, Howe joined with Harry Garfield and other community leaders to form the Municipal Association. After a preliminary meeting on November 14, the group held its first official meeting in Room 502 of the Garfield Building on December 5. Garfield was temporary chair and Howe temporary secretary. The gathering adopted a constitution that declared the organization's purposes. It would "induce citizens and tax payers to take a more active and earnest part in municipal affairs," "disseminate instructive information relative to the government of the City of Cleveland," "devise and advocate plans for its improvement," "promote businesslike, honest and efficient conduct in municipal affairs," "secure the choice of competent officials," and "encourage faithful performance of public duty to secure the enactment and enforcement of laws for the economic, intelligent and progressive management of the affairs of the City government." Membership was open to any Cleveland citizen or taxpayer who pledged himself to the purposes of the Association and paid dues of a dollar a year.[22] The initial membership of more than a hundred was composed mainly of businessmen and attorneys.

Those present at the first meeting elected a General Committee of Fifty (including both Howe and Garfield) to serve as the Association's governing body, and those at the second meeting on December 12 elected Harry Garfield president and Frederic C. Howe temporary secretary (pending election of a permanent one—a full-time salaried appointment was anticipated). The Association's slogan became "Citizens who want good government should vote for

---

21. See Finegold, *Experts and Politicians*, 73–81; J. Whipple, "Cleveland in Conflict," 355–65; Suman, *Radical Urban Politics*.

22. Constitution of the Municipal Association of Cleveland, Article II, Western Reserve Historical Society; *Cleveland Plain Dealer*, December 6, 1896.

good men." It scrutinized municipal expenditures, kept an eye on state legislation affecting Cleveland, and provided information on candidates for local office. It did not endorse any of them until the mayoral election of 1897, in which it became deeply involved.

Fred served as the Municipal Association's secretary for about a year and was a member of its Committee of Fifty from 1896 to 1899 and of its executive committee from 1897 to 1900. Probably his most important, and most controversial, contribution to its work was a pamphlet, "The City of Cleveland in Relation to the Street Railway Question," endorsed by the Association and published in its *Bulletin* on October 15, 1897. The occasion was an ordinance pending before the city council that would extend the franchises and set the fares for the Cleveland City Railway and the Cleveland Electric Railway Companies. Howe pointed out that the ordinance would bind the city to those companies for twenty-five years at a five-cent fare, at a time when other municipalities had three-cent fares and garnered more in taxes from their companies. This was not a good business proposition, he argued, and prudence would dictate waiting until current charters expired in 1905. If action were to be taken now, at least the city should require full information from the companies on their earnings, expenses, and finances before making a decision. Howe suggested that franchises be open for reappraisal every eight to ten years and that the city have the possibility of acquiring the companies.

Publication and distribution of the pamphlet under the aegis of the Municipal Association caused a stir. The vice president of the Cleveland Electric Railway Company found it inaccurate and unfair. Garfield replied that the company did not understand the Association's position. "It was . . . the intention to state the city's side of the question fairly and without hostility, with the expectation that the railroads would thereupon present . . . the street railway's side of the controversy." Both he and Howe pointed out that any inaccuracies in the pamphlet's figures resulted from the company's failure to supply basic information. Garfield commented in his diary on public reaction to the pamphlet: "The Municipal Assoc. bulletin has caused great discussion. Railroad men do not like it—they say it is unfair—but it will be found to be a wise move for it will call forth the true facts of the situation. It is not pleasant to have our friends think us unfair—but I believe that only those who are interested for or in railroads will think so: they have not read the bulletin carefully."[23]

Some members of the Association thought the pamphlet too radical. Howe wrote: "Our office telephone was busy with protests. But Harry and James Garfield stood by me, as they did on all other questions involving freedom of opinion." After the controversy had subsided, he mused about it:

23. *Cleveland Plain Dealer*, December 12, 1897, 22; January 19, 1898, 8; December 12, 1897, 6; James R. Garfield, diary (1897), entry of November 18, 1897.

Some times . . . I find my pecuniary advantage in conflict with my convictions and utterances and as a result I am not in as good repute with certain classes of clients as I would be otherwise. However, the men I am associated with are of a like mind with me and I found in the little tilt we had last fall that public opinion shifted around to our point of view when given time to collect itself. I am told by people here that our railway bulletin defeated the ordinance then pending for an extension of franchise and I think this is probably true.[24]

In the election of 1899 the Municipal Association abandoned its policy of nonendorsement of candidates and overtly opposed Mayor McKisson. Its *Bulletin* declared that Cleveland was "a wide open town," with saloons open on Sunday, gambling houses flourishing, and houses of ill fame enjoying immunity from police raids. "If Mayor McKisson is not the candidate of the saloon interests, and the keepers of gambling hells and brothels, he has their unquestioned and undivided support." McKisson retorted that the "so-called" Municipal Association was frantically trying to turn the city over to "a conscienceless gang of franchise grabbers" led by Mark Hanna. The Association had abandoned its laudable purposes and become an appendage of the Democratic Party and the corporations.[25] The Association endorsed Carlos M. Stone, the mayor's main opponent in the primary, but McKisson trounced him by a vote of 20,680 to 14,163.

The Association then sought pledges from "Honest John" Farley, the Democratic candidate, that he would not build up a political machine of his own and that he would oppose renewal of the street railway franchises. Farley agreed and won the Municipal Association's endorsement. Howe was busy in the campaign, collecting information and helping draft the anti-McKisson bulletins disseminated by the Association. Backed not only by the Association and the Democratic Party but also by the Hanna faction of the Republicans, Farley won the election handily.

The new mayor soon reneged on his promises and tried to push through the council a franchise ordinance opposed by the Association. Still learning about practical politics, Fred then understood a remark that a Farley supporter made confidentially to him on election night: "Of course we were glad to have the support of the Municipal Association, but you know that didn't elect us. We should have been beaten but for Mark Hanna's contribution of twenty thousand dollars to the campaign."[26] The election of 1899 virtually ended Howe's role in

24. FCH to Richard T. Ely, February 18, 1898.
25. *Cleveland Plain Dealer*, February 18, 1899, 10.
26. *Confessions of a Reformer*, 86.

the Municipal Association. By the time the next election rolled around, he had himself become a candidate for municipal office and could no longer participate in its affairs.

At the same time that Howe was working with the Association, he also busied himself with charitable and social settlement activities. Several of his Johns Hopkins professors had pointed him in this direction. Herbert Adams had been much impressed with Toynbee Hall, the pioneering settlement house in East London, and he had encouraged students in the History Seminary to help the Charity Organization Society's work among the needy of Baltimore, thus engaging in "the practical study of social science." Richard Ely had written extensively about diminishing class conflict through applied Christianity and social ethics, and had become a leading lay figure in the Social Gospel movement.[27] It was natural for a student imbued as Howe was with the Hopkins ideal of service and responsibility to turn his attention to good works in the community.

His first involvement was with the Bethel Associated Charities (later the Cleveland Associated Charities), the major private charitable organization in the city. Its declared objectives were reduction of pauperism and vagrancy and determination of their true causes, prevention of indiscriminate and duplicate giving, proper relief for all "deserving" cases of destitution, and assistance to applicants in finding employment. Its methods included registration of the needy to prevent imposture, investigation of each case, provision of help from existing agencies, and personal visitation so as to induce "self-respect, habits of thrift, and better living."[28] How direct a role Howe took in such activities is unknown—one would think that the distaste he developed from the Parkhurst vigilantism in New York City would have led him to emphasize research on poverty rather than investigation of individuals. Elected to Bethel's board of trustees in November 1893, he served on it for nearly a decade. Marie Howe became a member of the board after her husband left it.

More important than Fred's connections with Bethel were his associations with Goodrich House. The movement to establish social settlements expanded greatly in the 1890s as the foreign-born population of America's cities grew rapidly. Most of these new Americans lived in the worst sections of the city and had the poorest housing and the fewest services, both public and private. Compassion for them was obviously a principal factor in the establishment of social settlements. Beyond this, many middle-class Americans strongly believed

---

27. Especially significant among Ely's writings in this field were *The Social Aspects of Christianity* (1889) and *The Social Law of Service* (1896). See Rader, *Academic Mind and Reform*, 60–66; C. Hopkins, *Rise of the Social Gospel*; Frederick, *Knights of the Golden Rule*.

28. *Constitution of the Bethel Associated Charities for 1893–1894*, Articles II and III; Family Services Association of Cleveland Records 1857–1976, Western Reserve Historical Society.

that the new arrivals had to be Americanized, had to be brought into the American community and the American consensus. Otherwise they might well become a threat to its stability and its values. Social justice and the amelioration of gross inequities were necessities for both humane and defensive reasons.

The social settlement movement rested on the belief that the best way to provide help was by being a real neighbor, not an occasional visitor. The settlement house had to be located in the midst of the community it served, and it should have a corps of residents who lived and worked there. Besides the broader factors of compassion, social justice, and social order, the settlement house brought personal and psychological rewards to its residents. Like Fred Howe, they felt a need—in some cases almost a compulsion—to do something to benefit society and to solve its problems. The middle-class residents of the settlement house were there as exemplars for the poor, sharing with them their superior education, their greater knowledge, and their success in the American way of life. In the early years they were "practical idealists." By no means all of them were social or political reformers, but for many who became reformers, the settlement house was a first step along the road to political or governmental activism.[29]

The first social settlement in Cleveland was Hiram House, established in July 1896 by a group of Hiram College graduates. The second was Goodrich House, which grew out of the boys' clubs and classes that met in one of the city's prominent churches, the First Presbyterian (Old Stone) Church. The activities there attracted children from the populous and dilapidated area around the church, and the success of the gatherings was not lost on a member of the church, Flora Stone Mather. The wife of the wealthy financier Samuel Mather, she had become interested in social settlements, had perceived real needs to be met in Cleveland, and had begun the process that culminated in the decision to erect a settlement house in the vicinity of the church. She paid for the building, set up an endowment fund, and subsidized the operations of the house for many years. She defined it as a "Christian Social Settlement," and there were personal ties with the Old Stone Church through members of its congregation, but the settlement was separate from the church and nondenominational in its organization and activities.[30]

---

29. The term "practical idealists" is taken from May, *End of American Innocence,* 14–19. On the settlement houses and Progressivism, see A. Davis, *Spearheads of Reform.* In his first major book, *The City: The Hope of Democracy,* Howe wrote: "The settlement promotes order, it lessens crime, it reduces petty misdemeanors, and organizes the life and energy of the slum and turns it into good channels. The uniform testimony of police officials is to the effect that a settlement or a playground is as good as a half-dozen policemen" (283).

30. On the history of Cleveland social settlements generally, see Grabowski, "Social Reform and Philanthropic Order." On the history and development of Goodrich House, see Goodrich

Work on the building at St. Clair Avenue and East Sixth Street began in July 1896 and was completed in June 1897. Named after Dr. William H. Goodrich, who had been Flora Mather's pastor for twenty-five years, it housed baths, a laundry, a library, meeting rooms for clubs and neighborhood groups, and a gymnasium that could be converted into an auditorium with stage. The third floor had quarters for residents, as well as additional club rooms. The settlement's first director or headworker, Starr Cadwallader, began work several months before the building officially opened.

Goodrich House first served an Irish and German, and later an Eastern European, population. It acquired a reputation for liberalism or radicalism when it opened its meeting rooms to a variety of groups (including a socialist club) and provided a forum for discussion of political and social issues. Meetings at Goodrich led to formation of the Legal Aid Society in 1897 and the Consumers League of Ohio in 1900. The club for older boys at the Old Stone Church became part of Goodrich as the Lincoln Club. The house offered a full range of social clubs, crafts programs, adult education classes, gymnasium classes, choral singing, day nursery facilities, and summer camp programs.

The residents—numbering eleven in 1900—governed themselves under a code they had adopted. Prospective residents had a six-week trial period, and "if they enjoy the life of the House and are found useful they are asked to remain until the close of the settlement year." They were expected to devote at least eight hours a week of service to the house. Cadwallader's annual report for 1900 quoted an unnamed observer's characterization of the residents: "They are men and women who have the capacity of true democratic intercourse, who really enjoy the boys and girls, the men and women with whom they come in contact; who, without loss of dignity, forget that they are more favored of fortune than those they live among, and enter joyously and spontaneously, with true humor and comradeship, into all the functions of the house, whether of work or play."[31]

Fred Howe was one of the first residents of Goodrich House, but whether he became a resident in its initial year is uncertain. He was elected a member of the board of trustees on September 26, 1898, and he was certainly living in the house in early 1899. He lived at Goodrich for about two years, probably in 1899 and 1900. In his autobiography he offered three reasons why he had decided to become a resident. In the first place, it provided a pleasant place to live, "an escape from the life I was living in the crowded apartment on the lake front. Residents at the settlement had good food and comfortable rooms." Second,

---

Social Settlement, Records 1870–1960, Western Reserve Historical Society; Bourne, *First Four Decades;* Millicent Olmsted, "Where Good Citizens of the Future Are Being Trained," *Cleveland Plain Dealer,* March 25, 1900, pt. II, 8.

31. Bourne, *First Four Decades,* 19, 21.

living and working in a settlement house represented a fulfillment of the obligation of service to the community that he so strongly felt. "Here was my opportunity to justify my training, my sense of responsibility to the world." Third, one gained a kind of cachet by living there. Paradoxically, by working with the poor, one improved one's social standing. Residents enjoyed "a certain distinction because of their good works. Having joined the group of young men and women who lived there, I soon found myself invited out to dinners, asked to make speeches about immigrants, on politics, on cleaning up the city. I acquired a standing I had not had before. I was climbing."[32]

The first reason Howe offered, or the recollections on which it was based, can be questioned, and there are several other possible explanations for his decision to reside at Goodrich. The "crowded room" that he referred to was probably his first residence in Cleveland, in the Lakeview Flats, shared with three or more other men in his early months in the city when he was seeking a position. In 1898 he had become a partner in a prospering law firm, and there would have been no need to live in a "crowded room." By 1899, according to city telephone directories, he had already moved several times. Perhaps his memory in the 1920s confused his earliest days in Cleveland with his situation after he had resided in the city for five years.

Two other reasons that might have brought him to Goodrich House are undocumented but possible. One was his continuing interest in the city and its problems, stimulated at Johns Hopkins by Albert Shaw and James Bryce and whetted by his experiences in Cleveland. Living in a settlement house provided access to another piece of the urban condition. It brought one face to face with realities of poverty and hardship not to be discovered in the middle-class household or the ordinary law practice. The other likely factor was that life at Goodrich filled, for a time, a need for companionship that Howe felt deeply after Morris Black's death in 1898. From his own account, the loss hit him hard. The friendship of the Garfields may not have been sufficient to overcome his loneliness, which was perhaps assuaged by an active involvement in the "family" of Goodrich. It was undoubtedly relieved by the move to Cleveland, and to the settlement house, of his college friend Newton Baker.

After securing his undergraduate degree at Johns Hopkins and his law degree at Washington and Lee, Baker had opened a law office in 1894 in his hometown of Martinsburg, West Virginia. Clients were far from plentiful, and in 1896 he left the law temporarily to accept a position as private secretary to William L. Wilson, a West Virginia Democrat who was postmaster general in Grover Cleveland's cabinet. He enjoyed his brief stay in Washington, but his job ended

---

32. James R. Garfield, diary (1899), entry of February 6, 1899; *Confessions of a Reformer*, 75–76.

in 1897 with the change in the national administration, and he returned to Martinsburg. After several years of practice that brought little more reward than had his first law office, Baker began to look around for a city that might offer greater opportunity.

Fred and Newt had kept in touch through correspondence and visits in the years after their paths diverged in Baltimore. As fraternity brothers, they continued to plot together on Phi Gamma Delta matters. Baker relied on Howe to help him find a more satisfactory locale for the practice of law, and their thoughts turned to Cleveland. The West Virginian visited both Pittsburgh and Cleveland in 1897 but was discouraged by the prospects in both cities. Cleveland was still recovering from the Panic of 1893, and jobs were scarce. He was impressed by its civic spirit, however, and wrote a friend that the Ohio metropolis would be an "inspiring atmosphere to live in—but for the smoke of innumerable black-belching iron furnaces, which overhang the city like a hurricane cloud." By 1898 he was again ready to think about Cleveland, and he wrote Howe that he would be coming to the city soon and would "ask you to present me to some lawyers, with a view of attaching myself to some one there, if possible. Business here is drying up with the cutting off of the town's revenue from the railroad and before many years I should have to move to prevent starving. I admit I fret to see the strong and active years of my life passing and leaving me without even a start."[33]

A fortuitous event helped make the decision for Baker. In 1899 a Cleveland lawyer, Martin Foran, asked Howe if he knew an able young lawyer who might help in Foran's office. Howe immediately replied that the most capable lawyer he knew was Newton D. Baker of Martinsburg, West Virginia. Foran then recalled that he had actually met Baker on a return voyage from Europe in 1897—the young man had umpired a dispute on the Irish question between Foran and another traveler, and then had played chess with Foran throughout the rest of the voyage. He immediately invited Baker to join his office in Cleveland, and before long the firm became Foran, McTighe and Baker. Foran quickly introduced Baker into Democratic politics.[34]

Baker joined Howe as a resident in Goodrich House, and the two, along with James Garfield, who became a trustee in March 1900, served as the adult leaders of the Lincoln Club for older boys. Their own profession perhaps affected some of their activities with the club—at least, a contemporary recalled that "they naturally turned the minds of those boys toward study, and especially toward the study of law." Both Howe and Baker were on the Goodrich board of trustees

33. Quoted in Cramer, *Newton D. Baker*, 30; Newton D. Baker to FCH, November 22, 1898, Baker Papers.
34. Palmer, *Newton D. Baker*, 1:75; Cramer, *Newton D. Baker*, 30–31.

and the executive committee during their period of residence and after they had moved from the house. They were also members of an informal planning committee that met with Cadwallader and a few others and "smoked their pipes over projects of community welfare."[35]

While a resident at Goodrich House and afterward, Fred also participated in the study of social problems in the Cleveland Council of Sociology. That organization had been founded in 1893 by a number of local religious, business, and professional leaders, with the encouragement of the American Institute of Christian Sociology. Richard Ely was the Institute's president, and John R. Commons its secretary. Commons had written to a Cleveland minister in August 1893 of the Institute's hopes "to organize in every locality a local Institute to hold meetings weekly or fortnightly, the members to read and discuss in common the subjects of Sociology from the standpoint of Christ's teachings. . . . It is not numbers that are wanted but a small body of earnest, harmonious students, who can thereby train themselves for leadership." The Cleveland group was organized by the fall. The council, which frequently met at Goodrich House, was once described by its secretary as "a group of professional and businessmen . . . composed mainly of the more notorious cranks of the city."[36]

Howe was on the council from at least 1899 on. He served on its membership committee and on the "outing" committee for its annual excursions, helped get speakers for its meetings, and spoke himself a number of times. Other invited speakers included Richard Ely, Tom Johnson, and Peter Witt. The council provided another forum for critical discussion of the problems of Cleveland and of cities generally.

Frederic Howe left Goodrich House after two years of residence. In his autobiography he explained that his activities at the settlement had been "anything but fruitful." He was uncomfortable as a tenement visitor; he felt that he had little in common with the boys in the clubs; he did not enjoy dancing with "the heavy-footed mothers of many children who were lured from the tenements to our parties." When he gave talks on politics, he remembered his New York experiences and "felt that my philosophy was somehow out of joint." He found himself making "meaningless charts which nobody read but which we exhibited from time to time at meetings of the board of trustees." He was even more unhappy with the Bethel Associated Charities, he recalled, and especially with its cold bureaucracy and its stress on efficiency and "stamping out indiscriminate giving."

---

35. Bourne, *First Four Decades*, 30.
36. John R. Commons to Rev. E. Lyman Hood, August 21, 1893; Frederick C. Green to Elbert Hubbard, September 2, 1910, Cleveland Council of Sociology Records 1893–1914, both at Western Reserve Historical Society.

He did enjoy "the monthly meetings with men and women whose names appeared in the papers and who were known as the best people in the city."[37]

Then one day he received a letter from Dr. Lawrence Bryant Tuckerman. Tuckerman was a Cleveland gadfly, a radical who had run for mayor several times as an independent in the 1880s, a physician who contributed his medical services to the needy without charge. His letter, which for some reason reached Howe rather than the Bethel secretary, was an attack on organized charity. "Charity cannot be organized like the Steel Trust, or run by paid clerks," he wrote. "Charity means love; it is a personal thing, one of the beautiful things that Christ gave the world. When you do away with personal charity, you do away with love." If the organization were really interested in charity, it would end the twelve-hour day, increase wages, and eliminate the cruel killing and maiming of men.

The letter upset Howe. He realized that there was little talk about love or kindness in the monthly board meetings he attended. Wasn't Dr. Tuckerman right when he argued that charitable organizations had become business enterprises that sought to make poverty invisible and to make life more comfortable for the wealthy? Would there be any need for charity if workers received decent wages and if their safety on the job was protected? Howe's fellow trustees spoke indignantly of workers' demands but refused to provide adequate pay. Women who came to board meetings in their carriages talked of the need for thrift, but the harassed mothers of the tenements needed no instruction in being thrifty. "I began to have a dislike for our complacent reports and statistics of unworthy cases. Investigations into men's habits irritated me. I knew quite well that if I put in twelve hours in the rolling mills I should more likely than not drop into a saloon afterward." As Howe pondered these questions, he became more and more uncomfortable in board meetings, and he felt more and more dishonest in appealing to the public for money. "I ceased attending meetings of the trustees; then I resigned, and soon after left the settlement."[38]

Howe's account of his departure from Bethel Associated Charities and Goodrich House is probably more accurate as a reflection of his beliefs in the 1920s than as a statement of his feelings and actions at the turn of the century. It appears that his autobiography mixes up chronology and events and overdramatizes his break with charity organizations and social settlements. In *Confessions of a Reformer*, Goodrich House precedes Howe's meeting with Black and their involvement in politics. In actuality, his work at the settlement house came three years after Black's death. He may have been uncomfortable at Goodrich,

---

37. *Confessions of a Reformer*, 75–76.
38. Ibid., 78–79.

and he may have been led to reconsider his attitude toward organized charity by the Tuckerman letter, but, contrary to his autobiographical statement, he remained associated with both Bethel and Goodrich for some time. There were no immediate resignations. He stayed on the Bethel board until 1903, and his resignation then was probably as much due to his entry into party politics as to anything else—a governing principle of the society was its separation from "all political and sectarian influence."[39]

Fred continued to participate in Goodrich activities after he ceased being a resident, and he remained on its board of trustees until his resignation in January 1910, when he was about to leave Cleveland. He joined in the annual banquet of the Lincoln Club in February 1901, for example, and gave the toast "Cleveland and the Lincoln Club." The Club endorsed him when he ran for the city council in 1903. He served on Goodrich committees. In 1904 the trustees appointed him to confer with the president of the board of health on appointment of a district physician, and in 1905 and 1906 he was on a committee to investigate the management and finance of the city hospital. There was no sharp break with Goodrich, nor any apparent rejection of the settlement house, after Howe ceased to be a resident.

He and Baker moved from Goodrich into an apartment on Prospect Street and lived the cluttered life of bachelordom. "We were both absent-minded, absorbed in our work, indifferent to domestic comforts, but his mind was more orderly than mine, and I think that I was a trial to him now and then." Sometimes Fred forgot to leave notice that he would not be home for the dinners that a cook prepared for them from canned goods. "Once intrusted with moving our goods from one apartment to another, I forgot to give the keys of the new apartment to the expressman, and when we arrived at night eager to fit up our new home, we found our household belongings, including books, out on the front lawn, soaked with rain."[40] Their bachelor lives were soon to be disrupted, however. Baker was increasingly involved in Democratic politics (Mayor Tom Johnson appointed him legal adviser to the City Board of Equalization in May 1901), and he gave up the single life for marriage in the summer of 1902. Howe, still courting Marie Jenney mainly by correspondence, was ready to take the political, if not the marital, plunge. In January 1901 a group of residents of Morris Black's old ward called on him and urged him to seek the Republican nomination for the city council.

---

39. *Constitution of the Bethel Associated Charities,* article IV. Marie Howe became a life member of Bethel in 1905 and served on its board of trustees from 1905 to 1907.

40. *Confessions of a Reformer,* 190.

Fig 1 Frederic C. Howe, rising thirty-three-year-old lawyer and soon-to-be Cleveland city councilman, ca. 1900

5

THE CITY ON A HILL

By 1900 more than 25 million Americans—nearly a third of the nation's population—lived in cities of more than eight thousand people. Between 1880 and 1910 the urban population grew almost threefold, while that of rural and small-town America increased by only a third. Some cities doubled or tripled their populations in a decade or two. Cleveland, for example, grew by more than 50 percent in the 1870s and again in the 1880s.[1]

With the increase of urban population came an increase of urban problems, as growth outpaced the ability of municipalities to provide services and amenities for their citizens. Unpaved streets swirled with dust in the summer heat, oozed with quagmires after a rain, became too slippery with ice for safe transit in wintertime, and were contaminated always by horse droppings. Garbage and sewage disposal were practically nonexistent, left, as one writer notes, "to accident and time."[2] The water supply was polluted. Housing for most of the population was cheaply made and dilapidated, especially for the growing number of immigrants who settled in ethnic colonies in the congested, poorer areas of the city. Building codes remained the dream of a few visionaries. Saloons outnumbered schools. Crime rates rose as law enforcement was lax, badly organized, and often "on the take." Parks, playgrounds, and other public recreational facilities were scarce.

Not every urban dweller suffered from the ills of poverty, overcrowding, and inadequate housing, of course. As centers of commerce and industry, the cities had a growing middle class of small and large entrepreneurs and professionals. Besides expanding in population, urban centers were spreading geographically

---

1. Griffith, *History of American City Government*, 3:149–50. For a good general survey of urban development, see McKelvey, *Urbanization of America*.
2. Faulkner, *Politics, Reform and Expansion*, 23.

into what had been the countryside. Street railways had extended to the hinterlands, enabling thousands of better-off people to leave the central city, find homes on its fringes or in the developing suburbs, and commute by streetcar to jobs or business premises.

The rapid growth of the cities, the changes in urban life, and their accompanying problems placed a heavy strain on municipal governments, most of which had been designed for quieter, less troublesome times. Limited in their powers, divided institutionally, and often trammeled by the tight controls of state laws and legislatures, these governments reacted slowly and sluggishly to the new problems. Even when they tried to grapple with urban ills, they found action hindered by the absence of expert, nonpartisan civil servants. Some of the inadequacies in leadership and coordination were partly overcome by the political machine, which stepped in to organize and operate the political and governmental processes. But the bosses and their henchmen soon became the targets of reformers who found in the excesses of Tweed and Tammany only the most egregious example of municipal corruption, the spoils system, and irresponsible rule.

The decade of the 1890s saw major reform efforts in New York, in Boston, in Chicago—in fact, in nearly every large city and some middle-sized ones. Elected mayor of Detroit in 1889, Hazen S. Pingree fought valiant battles against corruption and privilege, brought a businesslike administration to the city, and became a convert to municipal ownership of public utilities. Toledo elected Samuel "Golden Rule" Jones mayor in 1897. He instituted the merit system, built playgrounds and parks, reformed the police, and sought to apply the principles of Christianity and Tolstoyan anarchism. Upon Jones's death in 1904, his secretary, Brand Whitlock, became mayor and continued the reform movement.

Urban reformers often differed on the most appropriate remedies for the ills of the city. For some, all that was needed was to throw the rascals out and elect good men to municipal office. Limited reforms might be desirable to restore efficiency in government and to improve law enforcement, but the chief remedy lay in replacing the bosses with leaders drawn from the capable, respectable, honest members of the community. Other reformers thought more was needed than good people and urged the adoption of improved governmental structures and processes. They found their remedies in the merit system and the unbiased expert, strong mayors, nonpartisan elections, and financial controls. A third set of reformers, smaller in number but increasing in strength throughout the Progressive Era, held that more was needed than changes in governmental structure or process. Measures of social justice—including better housing and elimination of the slums, child welfare services, and extension of public health facilities—were essential. Natural monopolies like street railways, gasworks, and electrical power had to be strictly regulated or brought under municipal ownership.

Differences among urban reformers were not as clear-cut as attempts to categorize them may suggest. An individual reformer might accept all these positions, advocating good men, changed institutions, and some social and economic reforms, but his emphasis among them would very likely change in the course of his lifetime. Fred Howe, for example, shared in all these outlooks at one time or another. His Johns Hopkins education and the influence of such mentors as James Bryce, Albert Shaw, and Woodrow Wilson led him first to accept the mission of good men and the educated elite. As his political experience broadened and his thinking progressed, he moved toward other solutions.

Cleveland, Howe's adopted city, shared in the nation's urban problems. By 1900 its population of nearly three hundred and eighty-two thousand had made it the seventh-largest American city. Nearly three-quarters of its people were foreign born or children of the foreign born. Italians, Poles, Hungarians, Russians, Czechs, and other new immigrants found homes among their compatriots in a series of "ethnic villages." The city's economy had a diverse industrial base. While the iron-and-steel industry continued to flourish, manufacturing became the most rapidly developing sector of the economy. The overhanging smoke and soot signaled the presence of numerous factories in the downtown area.[3]

Cleveland's municipal government still operated under the federal plan of 1891. With the help of the Municipal Association, "Honest John" Farley had defeated the McKisson machine in 1899, but leading Association members soon became concerned with the new mayor's failure to keep his campaign promises. Even at the time of Farley's election, James Garfield had despaired of the state of local politics: "We need a political hurricane to clean away the rubbish & purify the air."[4]

A few months later, a small gale from that hoped-for hurricane struck Fred Howe when a group of businessmen asked him run as a Republican candidate for the city council from the same ward that had elected Morris Black. They promised him everything he would need for the race—support, campaign management, money. Feeling that he could ill afford the expense and the distractions of campaigning, Howe postponed a decision for a day while he consulted with his law partners. They backed his candidacy, and when the delegation reappeared the next evening, he consented to run. "I liked being called from my law practice as Cincinnatus was called from the fields by the old Romans, liked being thought 'a good citizen.' And I was eager again to take part in the renaissance of

---

3. James F. Richardson, in Van Tassel and Grabowski, *Cleveland*, 171.
4. James R. Garfield, diary (1900), entry of April 11, 1900, Garfield Papers.

politics which I felt was coming; the renaissance started by Morris Black and myself."⁵

As Howe began his first campaign for public office, he became increasingly intrigued by the personality and ideas of the Democrats' candidate for mayor, Tom Johnson. Johnson was no ordinary office seeker. He had become rich through steel mills and street railways, freely admitting later that much of his wealth had come from special privileges, "acquired . . . by perfectly legitimate methods according to my own standards." In 1883, after a chance reading of Henry George's *Social Problems* and then a fuller study of *Progress and Poverty*, he became a convert to the single-tax philosophy.⁶ Retaining his business interests, though no longer taking pleasure in making money from them, Johnson became one of George's leading disciples and a close friend. He gave financial support to George's political campaigns and to single-tax newspapers such as Louis Post's *Recorder* in Cleveland and then his *Public* in Chicago.

George urged Johnson to get into politics, and in 1888 the millionaire ran as the Democratic candidate for the House of Representatives in Ohio's 21st district. He lost but carried the city of Cleveland. Trying again in 1890, he was elected and then reelected in 1892. He used the House as a forum to publicize the single tax and to press for free trade. He was defeated for reelection in 1894 when the Republicans captured control of the House in that depression year. Johnson supported William Jennings Bryan for the presidency in 1896, though he was not much interested in the silver issue. Rather, he considered Bryan's campaign "the first great protest of the American people against monopoly— the first great struggle of the masses in our country against the privileged classes."⁷

After Henry George's death in 1897, Johnson abandoned his business interests, disposed of his steel mills and street railways, and returned to Cleveland. As a well-known businessman, a former congressman from the Cleveland district, and a handsome contributor to Democratic candidates, he was obviously an attractive candidate for state or local office. He indicated his availability in a fighting speech to the Democrats' Jackson Day dinner in Cleveland in January 1901. On February 6, 1901, members of the Cuyahoga County Association of Democratic Clubs marched to Johnson's Euclid Avenue mansion with a petition bearing fifteen thousand signatures and a request that he make the race for

---

5. *Confessions of a Reformer*, 91.
6. T. Johnson, *My Story*, 48, 51; *Public*, May 17, 1902, quoted in Murdock, "Life of Tom L. Johnson," 32. An interesting discussion of Henry George's ideas can be found in Lustig, *Corporate Liberalism*, 57–77.
7. T. Johnson, *My Story*, xxxv, 109.

mayor. Johnson read a prepared statement of acceptance and agreed that he would be their nominee if Democratic voters endorsed him in the primary.[8]

Tom Johnson's mind was quick, inventive, practical, and open to new ideas. He was not a deep thinker, but he held firmly to certain principles. To him, the greatest battle in the modern world was that of the people against privilege. Privilege was the advantage conferred by law on some people, the advantage that denied others the opportunity to compete. Of all its monopoly powers, the greatest evil was land monopoly, made possible by the exemption of land values from taxation. The solution to the problem of privilege must come from an economic change to "remove the prizes which Privilege now secures from the People." In this fight against great odds, the people ultimately would prevail.[9]

For Johnson, the answer to the problem of privilege was a tax on the unearned increment of land, the recapture for the people of values that were socially created. Eliminating all other taxes, this single tax would liberate both the economy and the individual. All needed land would be forced into immediate use, enabling anyone who wanted profitable work to find it. "There could be no oppressive organization of capital, because capital would have no privileges. There could be no coercive labor unions because every worker would be his own all-sufficient union. And there would be no tyrannical government because all the people would be economically free, a condition that makes tyranny, either economic or political, impossible."

Conversion of the public would be a long-term proposition, he realized, but interim steps could bring society closer to the ultimate goal. When he ran for mayor, his program included a three-cent fare on the street railways; equal treatment in tax assessments; public improvements (including cleaner and brighter streets, more parks, and lakefront development); home rule; and honest government and the elimination of "franchise grabbers and contractors" who looted the city treasury.[10] To the hustings he brought a personality that was warm and friendly and a political style that was open and informal, delighting in debates and question-and-answer sessions, rather than the set orations that characterized much of the politics of the time.

To the neophyte candidate for city council, Tom Johnson was a riddle. Howe knew only what every Clevelander knew about the general outlines of the millionaire's career. "Although he was an intimate friend of many of the rich people of Cleveland, he was distrusted because of his unusual opinions and the apparent discrepancy between his social position and the things he advocated." He had a devoted following, especially among the poor, who found him generous.

---

8. Ibid., 107; *Cleveland Plain Dealer*, February 7, 1901.
9. T. Johnson, *My Story*, xxxv, xxxix.
10. Ibid., 154–55, 112.

"Waiters, doorkeepers, cab-drivers knew him as the man whose smallest change was a dollar bill."[11]

Intrigued by these contradictions, Howe went to a public meeting at which Johnson announced his candidacy for mayor. The puzzle continued. Here was "a short, pudgy man," who "stood round and smiling, hands in his pockets, he looked like a boy out for a lark." Surely, thought Howe, a man of wealth and position ought not to be so undignified. Johnson's words were "all very simple, very winning. But I could see why my friends distrusted him. Was he as candid and honest as he appeared, or was he using his frankness merely as a political blind? I was at sea." His approach seemed wrong. He wasn't indignant enough; he said nothing about corruption and the spoils system; he made no personal attacks. "He held a cigar in his hand, while he spoke and went away with a crowd of riotous politicians. He was not at all like my picture of the business man who was to redeem politics." Howe left the meeting, still pondering the Johnson enigma.

Fred's own campaign was run on traditional lines. He plunged into it wholeheartedly, spoke every night in the saloons, and went from house to house as he had done in Morris Black's campaign. He spent more money than he could afford, though he realized that "some one else" was spending much more on his behalf. "I had my photograph taken in a frock coat, and liked to see it on telegraph-poles, in shops, and in the windows of private homes. I looked thoroughly the good citizen." He discovered, to his surprise, that many of the ward politicians were distributing his literature and arranging meetings. They never asked him for money. They must not know I am a civil service reformer, he thought, and that I aim to put their type of politicians out of business. "Although I took the support of the politicians, I did not disguise my opinions. In fact, I emphasized them. When I talked about these things, they smiled. I remembered that afterward." Besides civil service reform, Howe urged the need to clean up the council and to take city government out of politics. "The principal issue in my mind . . . was corruption. The old gang should be cleaned out, a new kind of men put in. The kind of men I had in mind were business men, trained, university men. They were my friends."

When Howe could spare time from his own campaign, he kept an eye on Johnson's rallies. He heard the Democrat talk about poverty and argue that society should be changed not by electing good men to office but by making it possible for all men to be good. Most people would be reasonably good if they had a chance, he suggested. Social conditions, not people, were the problem,

---

11. These and subsequent quotations about Howe's first meetings with Johnson are from *Confessions of a Reformer*, 87–99.

and only politics could change those conditions. This line of argument bothered Howe. His own classifications were quite simple: there were good people, like members of the University Club, the Chamber of Commerce, and the Municipal Association, and bad people, like McKisson and other politicians. "It was all quite clear to me and very simple. It was the choice between the good and the bad."

Fred resented Johnson's speeches—they made his work in the Municipal Association seem false. "It hurt my ego, my self-respect, to be told that I was really not much better than the politician and that my class was not as important as I thought it was." In spite of his resentment, he became more and more drawn to Johnson, kept dropping in on his meetings, continued to ponder the paradox of a rich man advocating policies harmful to his own class, and began to discover truth in much of what Johnson said. "I fluttered about him mentally, accepting, withdrawing, irresistibly attracted."

Johnson frequently referred to *Progress and Poverty*. Howe had a passing acquaintance with Henry George's writings. He had read *Progress and Poverty* and had found its arguments interesting, almost convincing but probably false, both because they were simple and because, if they were true, the single tax would have been adopted long ago. He had perhaps been among the Hopkins students whom Ely had taken to hear George speak in 1888, and he was aware of the importance of Georgist influence on municipal reform in England. At last, Howe nerved himself to visit Johnson in his office, and the two men talked for a long time. After recounting his conversion to Georgism, Johnson explained why he was running for mayor. The place to begin was the city. If one city adopted the single tax, others would have to follow suit. If Cleveland were the first to take taxes off houses, factories, and machinery, it would gain a tremendous advantage. "With cheap land on the one hand and cheap houses, factories, and goods on the other, Cleveland will be the most attractive city in America." Convinced by Johnson's sincerity, Howe had a final question: why not reject the politicians and appeal to the "good" elements of the community—the businessmen, the young men, the educated classes? They will never support me, Johnson replied. "This fight cuts too deep. It touches too many interests, banks, business, preachers, doctors, lawyers, clubs, newspapers. They have to be on one side. And it isn't my side. They will be against me. The only people who can be for me are the poor people and the politicians who will have to follow the poor people when they get started."

Howe hesitated, still uncertain, still questioning in his mind whether poverty could be ended through political action, still reluctant to abandon the businessmen he trusted. But suddenly he found himself saying, "I think I will withdraw from the Republican ticket and come out and support you. I can't do it and remain a candidate. And you can do things I never could do." Parties don't matter, Johnson replied. Get elected as a Republican, and we'll work together. "As we shook hands he looked at me closely. 'You know you will have to pay,' he said, 'for siding with me.' He was wondering, he later confessed to me, if I would be willing to pay the price."

Neither Howe nor Johnson had any difficulty in winning their nominations in the primaries in February 1901. Howe carried his district by 1,269 votes to 465. As the general election neared, both the Municipal Association and the *Plain Dealer* endorsed him. On April 1 the voters of the Fourth District gave Howe a substantial majority. He carried all four wards in the district by sizable margins and the district as a whole by 2,197 to 958. In the mayoralty election Tom Johnson had a notable triumph. He won the Democratic wards of the immigrant West Side and did very well in the Republican East End wards, gaining a city-wide plurality of 6,000 votes.[12]

The new city council (half of whose members were holdovers who had not had to face the voters in 1901) still had a slim Republican majority, but this quickly disappeared when two Republicans—Frederic Howe and William J. Springborn—threw their support to Mayor Johnson's program. Central to that program was the street railway question. The railways needed franchises from the city in order to operate. As monopoly grants for a term of years, the franchises were attractive and profitable to business interests, and their acquisition and retention opened up possibilities of payoffs and graft.

In Cleveland, Marcus A. Hanna had brought together a number of street railway lines in a profitable venture that became known as the "Little Consolidated" or the "Little Con." Tom Johnson had also been active in the street railway business in Cleveland. He had purchased a number of lines and combined them as the "Big Consolidated" or the "Big Con," but he disposed of his holdings in the 1890s when he abandoned his business interests. The two railway systems were eventually combined as the Cleveland Electric Railway Company or "ConCon." The battle between Hanna and Johnson continued and expanded from municipal issues to state and national politics.

Hanna and his colleagues fought to keep the street railway system under private ownership, to maintain it as a profitable enterprise, and to restrict government regulation to a minimum. Johnson and his followers wanted, as a first step, closer regulation by the city and a three-cent fare. His ultimate goal was public ownership and free service. The battle for Johnson and his followers was thus more than a fight for low fares—it was the first step toward municipal

---

12. The Fourth District, in which Howe ran, was Republican territory. Morris Black had carried it by better than three to one in 1896.

ownership of natural monopolies. Furthermore, a victory in the Cleveland battle would become a beacon to other municipalities from the "city on the hill."

Street railway issues were nothing new to Fred Howe. In the spring of 1896 he had testified against fifty-year franchises before a state legislative committee. In 1897 his pamphlet for the Municipal Association had opposed early franchise extensions and the five-cent fare, advocated franchise reappraisal at eight- to ten-year intervals, and kept open the possibility of city acquisition of the companies. Concern with Mayor McKisson's policies on the franchises had led him to work with the Association to defeat McKisson and elect Farley in 1899, and to oppose Farley when the new mayor reneged on his preelection promises. Now, as councilman, he could take a direct part in the battle. On behalf of Mayor Johnson, he introduced a three-cent ordinance on December 9, 1901. The franchise grant would be for twenty years, but the city would have the right to purchase the line whenever Ohio law permitted.

In a council discussion of franchises a few months later, Howe indicated that he had moved toward Johnson's position. "It is the moral side of this question, more than the commercial side, which interests me," he declared. "I am not so much interested in making money for the city as in freeing it from these influences which trammel it and retard its progress." Howe began to feel that his council actions, and his association with Johnson, were affecting his relations with clients of his law firm and with others whose economic interests were involved. "I was conscious of increasing social alienation. At the club I was made to feel uncomfortable."[13]

The council accepted the only bid on the new franchise, made by a former associate of Johnson. But after a taxpayer suit was instituted, the Circuit Court, in June 1902, found the grant invalid. A few days later, the state Supreme Court, acting on a suit widely believed to have been sponsored by Republicans and anti-Johnson Democrats, found the Cleveland charter of 1891 to be unconstitutional, as a violation of the constitutional prohibition against special legislation. A little later, the court enjoined the Cleveland city council from granting any new franchises.

Besides postponing any immediate action on the street railway question, the court's action also emphasized to reformers the need for home rule for Ohio's cities. Under existing laws the state legislature decided both the form of government and the powers of municipal corporations. Reformers sought greater local autonomy. They wanted, through home rule, to acquire for the city the right to determine its own system of government and to decide for itself such questions as the municipal ownership of public utilities.

---

13. *Cleveland Plain Dealer*, March 4, 1902, 4; *Confessions of a Reformer*, 108.

Probably the most exciting event that Howe became involved in as a councilman was a controversy over a natural gas ordinance that granted the East Ohio Gas Company a franchise to supply Cleveland with natural gas from West Virginia. The importation of natural gas met vehement opposition from coal dealers and from the two companies that already supplied artificial gas.

When the council met to vote on the ordinance, a member declared that he had been offered five thousand dollars for his vote. When Mayor Johnson suggested that other councilmen might also have received payoffs from the gas companies, denials and acrimony filled the chamber. Outraged, Howe jumped up and "blazed out" against bribery and graft. He had heard complaints about anarchists speaking on the public square and advocating the destruction of organized government. "What is bribery but the destruction of government?" he asked. "It means substituting money for honest discussion. It means an end to democracy." The council voted unanimously to investigate the bribery charges, and then proceeded to pass the gas ordinance by a fifteen to six vote. Its investigation proved inconclusive.[14]

The bribery controversy was another important step in Fred Howe's political education. As he left the council chamber after the vote on the natural gas ordinance, he felt "exalted" in the certainty that people would now understand the need to put good men in office, men who were courageous enough to defend the city's interest and denounce corruption and bribery, no matter what its source. Several angry machine councilmen roughly accosted him and accused him of "double-crossing" the gas company. They told him that his nomination and election had been backed by the company and its contribution of two thousand dollars. Fred soon realized that this was true. "I was terribly confused. I began to understand much that had been mysterious. I understood where the army of men came from who had been set to work the day my name was entered in the primaries. They were gas-company employees.... I understood the anger of Mike and Johnny as they left the council-chamber. We were all gas-company men. The same men that had financed them had financed me. They had delivered the goods, but I had not."[15] From their point of view, he was the traitor, and they were the ones who had been loyal to their friends.

There was worse to come. The next day, a delegation of businessmen and bankers called on Howe. Their spokesman, a trustee of the Charity Organization Society, a friend of almost every good cause in Cleveland, a man whom Howe respected, condemned the councilman's comparison of bribers to anarchists.

14. *Confessions of a Reformer*, 103–4. For a summary of the natural gas controversy, see Murdock, "Life of Tom L. Johnson," 163–68.
15. *Confessions of a Reformer*, 104, 105.

Bribery, though deplorable, was often needed to protect the investments of public utility corporations from bad legislation. "Do you mean," Howe asked, "that a gas or electric lighting or street-railway company can live only by bribery and corruption? Can private individuals carry on business of this kind only by what we all know are criminal means?" They agreed that this was the case. Well, said Howe, if a private business can live only by bribery, the logical conclusion is that we can't have that type of private business. "We can fight the spoils system, bad as it is, in the open; it is not nearly so dangerous to democracy as is corruption. For corruption . . . will destroy responsible government. You gentlemen have made the most convincing argument that could be made for public ownership."[16]

Analyzing this conversation later, Howe concluded that his actions had touched something deep—a herd instinct. "The herd was not organized, but subconsciously all its members thought alike. It was afraid. I had justified my election pledges and I expected approval. I was rather eager for it. But I won no approval. Indeed, the reverse was true. I sustained myself by reflecting that some one had to pay in the cleaning-up process. It was rather fine that I was permitted to make the sacrifice." Still, it hurt that his friends at the club, the respectable members of his own class, failed to congratulate him on his stand against bribery.[17]

Howe's interest in public ownership continued as the council turned its attention to the possibility of a municipal electric lighting plant. As a member of the finance committee, he took the lead in advocating a city-owned facility. The plan ran into difficulties outside the council, however, and a municipal electric plant was not built until 1914.

Howe found himself working closely with Tom Johnson on other problems and policies besides street railways, natural gas, and electricity. Both shared an interest in the development of Cleveland's downtown and its lakefront. In the 1890s, inspired by their knowledge of German city planning and by Chicago's Columbian Exposition, Howe and Morris Black concluded that a number of new public buildings should be planned and located together as a group, as a center for Cleveland's civic life. They had worked behind the scenes through their Beer and Skittles Club to get stories in the newspapers on city planning and public buildings in Vienna, Paris, Dresden, and other European cities, as well as editorials favorable to a Cleveland project. They had also had a hand in persuading the local chapter of the American Institute of Architects to hold a competition for plans. Many Clevelanders had attended the Columbian Exposition in 1893 and had seen the "White City," a grouping of Beaux Arts–style

16. Ibid., 107
17. Ibid, 107–8.

buildings around a central mall, the Court of Honor. They had come home impressed by the vision of how a city might look.[18] By fortunate coincidence, Cleveland would shortly need to construct new buildings for federal, county, and city governments.

The Chamber of Commerce soon gave the "Group Plan" its backing. Tom Johnson also became a strong advocate and made the plan a part of his program after his election in 1901. The state legislature in the spring of 1902 enacted a statute authorizing the governor, at the request of a city council, to appoint a board of experts to plan the location, style, and size of public buildings. Howe introduced the necessary ordinance, and the council approved it in June 1902. On Johnson's recommendation, the governor picked a commission of three distinguished architects: Daniel H. Burnham, the architect of the Columbian Exposition; John M. Carrère, the architect of the Pan-American Exposition; and Arnold R. Brunner, already designated as the architect for a new federal building.[19]

The commission's first report, in August 1903, proposed a grouping of neoclassical buildings (city hall, county courthouse, public library, federal building, union station) around a grand mall. Its basic ideas were accepted (except that the union station was not built in the location proposed), and construction began during Johnson's first administration. The Group Plan was also a slum clearance project, ridding downtown Cleveland near Lake Erie of a hundred acres of rundown housing, saloons, and brothels. The final result—called "the first great city-planning project of the twentieth century"—was a harmonious, symmetrical group of public buildings united by the open space of the mall. It won high praise from architects, developers, and artists. Herbert Croly concluded: "There is no other city in the country where the local aspiration toward cleanliness, comeliness, and wholesomeness of municipal life has received abler and more varied expression."[20] Howe backed the Group Plan strongly and publicized it nationally in articles in *Harper's Weekly* and *Charities and the Commons*.[21]

Making the city a good place to live in meant more than providing civic space and fine buildings. One of Johnson's first acts as mayor was to order all

---

18. See Rydell, *All the World's a Fair*, 38–71.
19. *Confessions of a Reformer*, 80–82; *Cleveland Plain Dealer*, June 15, 1902, 10.
20. Rarick, *Progressive Vision*, 26; Croly, quoted in Hines, *Burnham of Chicago*, 171. On the Group Plan and its development, see Hines, *Burnham*, 158–73; Hines, "Paradox of 'Progressive' Architecture"; Rarick, *Progressive Vision*, 12–34; Johannesen, *Cleveland Architecture*, 71–76.
21. "Plans for a City Beautiful" and "Cleveland Group Plan." Howe got to know the architects for the Group Plan, kept an eye on them, and talked with them about the projects' problems, including those of political interference. See, for example, his letter to James R. Garfield, July 6, 1903.

the "Keep Off the Grass" signs removed from city parks. He opened the parks for picnics, sunbathing, games, and other pleasant activities, and he built more playgrounds. Howe approved wholeheartedly and sponsored legislation for play areas, parks, and public baths, arguing that other cities' experience showed "crime had been reduced where children were taken from the streets and given a place to play, with trained instructors to help them do so."[22]

He expected his business friends to endorse these measures but found that many of them seemed to put the tax rate, and their fear of increasing the mayor's popularity, ahead of human concerns. To his surprise, it was the machine councilmen, not the reformers, who helped him get the bills passed. "Cleveland became a play city, and this generous provision for play has declared dividends." One of those dividends was economic: workers liked to live in Cleveland, and so it was a good site for factories. "The growth of Cleveland in the last decade is partly traceable to the policy of making the city an attractive place in which to live."[23]

To help children who were dependent, neglected, or delinquent, Howe joined in a pioneering effort to establish juvenile courts in Ohio. In February 1902 he drafted a bill for submission to the state legislature. He explained that its chief object was "to remove juvenile offenders from the contaminating influence of the police station and the police court. A boy who may not be very bad is now arrested for some petty offense and confined in such an atmosphere of vice as would tend rather to make a criminal of him than to reform him." A juvenile court would have ample time to consider each case carefully and to "deal with the child as may seem best for his interests and future welfare." Howe thought that many citizens would volunteer to help the court as unpaid probation officers—"I myself would not hesitate to accept the duties of a probation officer." In May 1902 the legislature authorized juvenile courts, and Cuyahoga County set up the first one in Ohio. Outside government, Howe joined others concerned with child health to establish Cleveland's Visiting Nurse Association.[24]

Although kept busy by his work as a councilman and by his law practice, Howe did not abandon the Hopkins ideal of the scholar in politics. His first publications after leaving Hopkins dealt with taxation and were largely derived from his doctoral studies: the *Annals* article of 1894 and the *Taxation* book of 1896. He wrote two more tax articles in 1899, one for the *Annals* on the taxation

---

22. *Confessions of a Reformer*, 109. Howe ran into some problems with Jewish residents of the Sixteenth Ward who, although approving the councilman's advocacy of playgrounds, felt that some of his remarks had suggested that their children were criminals living in filth and squalor. This they emphatically denied. *Cleveland Plain Dealer*, June 15, 1901, 10.

23. *Confessions of a Reformer*, 109–10.

24. *Cleveland Plain Dealer*, February 16, 1902, 10; Rose, *Cleveland*, 630–31.

of quasi-public corporations in Ohio and the franchise tax and the other for the *American Law Review* on possible reforms in state and local taxes. In December 1900 he read a paper on the franchise tax and quasi-public corporations at the annual meeting of the American Economic Association in Detroit. He also presented a paper on interstate corporations at a tax conference in Buffalo in May 1901. Writing in the *Atlantic Monthly* in 1902, he argued that modern economic development had changed international trading relations, so that the time was ripe for a scientific readjustment of tariffs.[25]

These literary efforts were largely directed at economists, tax experts, lawyers, and other professionals, and were couched in heavy academic prose. Howe was to return very occasionally to such writings in later years, but by the turn of the century it was clear that he was beginning to seek a broader, less professionally oriented audience. He conceived the idea of editing a series of volumes on five chief justices of the Supreme Court (Jay, Marshall, Taney, Chase, Waite), but nothing came of this project.

Howe's interest in European cities had been captured by Albert Shaw's lectures at Johns Hopkins, and now, a decade later, he began his own research on them with a trip to England and Scotland. He explained to Ely that he wanted to meet "as many men doing work in sociology and economics as I can. . . . I find my work occupies my time so completely and as I am very much interested in municipal matters, I want to know what is going on the other side of the water. . . . Great Britian [*sic*] has solved so many of the problems that we are in the midst of, that it seems the duty of one who would keep in line with contemporary matters to know just what is being done there and how they are doing it."[26] Armed with letters of introduction from Ely and Adams, he hoped to meet Sidney Webb, George Bernard Shaw, John Burns, and others. He was in the British Isles from mid-May to mid-July in 1898 and returned there in the summer of 1902.

What he learned in British cities was not immediately reflected in his writings. Instead, he turned to the American city and, for the first time, began to speak to a national audience. His first article for the general, nonprofessional reader appeared in *World's Work* in February 1901. A hymn of praise to industrial development generally, and to economic growth in the Great Lakes region particularly, it could almost have been written by a Social Darwinist except for its approving references to Sam Jones and Hazen Pingree. Two other articles

---

25. "Taxation of Quasi-Public Corporations"; "Some Possible Reforms in State and Local Taxation"; FCH to Ely, March 9, 1900; Ely to FCH, September 7, 1900; Ely to FCH, September 14, 1900; Richard Ely to Charles H. Hull, January 23, 1901; Ely to FCH, January 23, 1901; "End of an Economic Cycle." The earlier *Annals* article and the book are discussed in chapter 4, above.

26. FCH to Ely, April 18, 1898, Ely Papers.

soon followed in the same journal: in February 1902 a paean to Tom Johnson and his work in Cleveland; and in March 1903 a look at the achievements of reformers in Chicago. For *Cosmopolitan,* he wrote a detailed description of the 1904 World's Fair and a straightforward account of Joseph W. Folk and reform in St. Louis. In another article for *World's Work,* he returned to the topic of reform in Cleveland.[27]

All these articles were essentially descriptive. They contained little that was analytical or that reflected a definite political or theoretical viewpoint in the author, save for a mildly reformist tinge. They were important for Howe in several ways, however. For the first time, he was speaking to a general audience in the mass media of the day, the magazine. He was learning that he could be successful in that kind of writing, that he could sell his articles to leading publications. And he was, slowly and peripherally in these pieces, beginning to develop ideas and themes that would appear in a finished form a few years later in his book, *The City.*

The years 1902 and 1903 were important in Fred Howe's political and intellectual development. By the end of his term as councilman, he had accepted Tom Johnson as his political leader and his mentor. He had not only spearheaded the fight in the city council for many of the mayor's measures, but he had also publicized him, his aims, and his achievements in articles for a national audience. He had begun to accept Johnson's basic ideas: that politics was a struggle of the people against privilege and that the single tax was the means to victory in that struggle. He was shedding some of his own old ideas, especially the beliefs that "good men" were the principal answer to municipal problems and that politics and the politician were shady elements to be avoided. He was coming to see the need for reforms on a broad scale, even though some might call them "revolutionary." "The cultivated and well-to-do classes have ever been as fearful of catching revolution as an old woman of catching cold." His political experiences and his academic learning were combining to bring a focus on the city as the principal arena of reform, the locus of the battle between people and privilege. He agreed with Johnson that "the great field of present political endeavor lies in our cities; that this is the weakest part of our political system; and that in this arena the greatest good can be achieved and the surest political preferment secured."[28]

In the process Howe came to love Cleveland and even the problems it presented. The city appealed to him as a social agency of great possibilities, he said.

---

27. "Great Empire by the Lakes"; "'Best Governed Community in the World'"; "The Municipal Character and Achievements of Chicago"; "World's Fair at St. Louis, 1904"; "Joseph W. Folk"; "Cleveland—A City Finding Itself."

28. "'Best Governed Community in the World,'" 1726, 1728.

No longer was it the economy or the political structure of the metropolis that interested him; it was the city as community enterprise. "I saw the city as an architect sees a skyscraper, as a commission of experts plans a world's fair exposition. It was a unit, a thing with a mind, with a conscious purpose, seeing far in advance of the present and taking precautions for the future. . . . The city was the enthusiasm of my life." Looking back more than twenty years later on his Cleveland days, he wrote: "I have never gotten over this enthusiasm. I never grow tired of city-building, of city enthusiasms, city ideals. And with all of its crudities and failures I have never lost faith that the American city will become a thing of beauty and an agency of social service as yet unplumbed."[29]

Howe realized, somewhat sadly, that his new course meant a break with many of his "respectable" friends. He felt increasingly isolated from them, shrank from their disapproval, kept away from the clubs, withdrew more and more into himself. As Tom Johnson had pointed out, there was a price reformers had to pay. He felt marginal, "caught between two herds"—the herd of his old friends and the herd of the politicians. The latter he had come to like and to get along with—they were "human, generous, kindly," but they were "not my kind." "I missed friendliness, approval, a herd, that satisfied my university picture of the role I should play."[30]

As his two-year term on the city council neared its end, Howe had a decision to make. He enjoyed being a councilman and was quite willing to continue, but it was clear that the Republicans would not endorse him. He had become closely identified with the Democratic administration, and he had alienated the Republican businessmen who had supported him in 1901. Tom Johnson hoped to find a place for him on the Democratic ticket but met some party opposition, and Howe was not yet ready to make that leap anyway. Instead, he decided to run as an independent, confident that he would be reelected. "The district was an intelligent one, the issues were clear, and the regular party candidates were obviously unfit."[31]

The Municipal Association once again endorsed Howe but could not bring itself to support Johnson, whom it considered too lax in his treatment of the saloons and the midnight and Sunday closing ordinances. In a backhanded compliment to the mayor, it declared: "When machine builders and political bosses seek election to office they should, in the judgment of the Association, be opposed, even though as men they bear good reputations. The greater their ability the greater the danger to the public."[32]

29. *Confessions of a Reformer*, 110, 113–14.
30. Ibid., 110–11.
31. FCH to James R. Garfield, June 9, 1902; *Confessions of a Reformer*, 111.
32. *Bulletin of the Municipal Association*, April 1903, 5.

Besides the endorsement of the Municipal Association, Howe received the backing of his friends in Goodrich House's Lincoln Club and the support of the *Plain Dealer,* which found his term in office "noteworthy for his independent, determined stand for honesty, and unflinching defense of the public interests." Despite these recommendations and despite the fact that the Democrats ran no candidate against him, Howe was soundly defeated when the Twelfth Ward voted on April 7, 1903. His total of 686 votes was far behind the Republican winner's 1,188. "People were not voting as my pattern of politics led me to believe they would. . . . From that time on I was identified frankly with Mr. Johnson and with the Democratic party."[33] Johnson led his party's ticket to victory, piling up a nearly six-thousand-vote plurality and carrying with him an absolute majority of Democrats in the city council.

Howe's defeat for a council seat did not send him back to the confines of a law practice. The month after the election, Mayor Johnson appointed him to the Board of Sinking Fund Trustees. New legislation had expanded the board's functions so that it not only managed Cleveland's municipal debt but also served as a tax commission with authority to approve the city's levies. Fred became chairman of the board and served on it for six years. He expanded his acquaintanceship with men of national prominence through work in the National Civic Federation. He had met the NCF's founder, Ralph W. Easley, at a conference of the organization, held on a steamer on Lake Erie. "There was plenty to eat, more to drink, and wolves and lambs were herded together in apparently peaceful fashion, the wolves being important business men, including Mr. Hanna, and the lambs John Mitchell, president of the Anthracite Coal Workers, Dan O'Keefe, of the Longshoremen's Union, and other labor leaders." Easley's goal was to bring capital and labor together to thrash out their differences. Howe later said he was "suspicious of the idea from the start," and thought it ultimately successful in weakening or destroying the "moral fibre" of the labor leaders who accepted it. Nevertheless, he participated in the NCF's work and became a member of its Commission on Public Ownership of Public Utilities. The Commission produced a long report in 1907, but by that time

33. *Cleveland Plain Dealer,* April 1, 1903, 4; *Confessions of a Reformer,* 111. Howe's own recollection of the election outcome was faulty. He wrote in *Confessions of a Reformer* that he had come in "a bad third" in his ward. Actually, he came in second, far ahead of another independent candidate who received only ninety-three votes.

Several sources indicate that in 1902 or early 1903 Howe declined an offer of appointment as "Secretary of Porto Rico," and one writer speculates that it was perhaps "an attempt by the national administration to lure a wayward Republican away from the 'corrupting' influence of the Democratic mayor." Huff, "Frederic C. Howe, Progressive," 43; Mattern, *Pi Chapter,* 350. It hardly seems likely that the national administration considered Howe politically important enough to warrant such an offer, and he makes no mention of it in his autobiography. The information in Mattern probably came from Howe, however.

Howe had moved beyond its rather innocuous conclusions. Work on the Commission at least gave him a chance to meet a variety of interesting people, including Mitchell; Louis Brandeis; Samuel Insull, the utilities executive; Jacob Riis; John P. Frey of the Iron Moulders Union; John G. Agar, the president of New York City's Reform Club; and Charles R. Crane, a Chicago millionaire who became a bankroller of Progressivism.[34]

Most important in Howe's political growth was his friendship and close association with Tom Johnson. In later years he wrote: "I had greater affection for Tom Johnson than for any man I have ever known. He was as dependent upon those he loved as he was indifferent to the hostility of his enemies. He had as much time for affection as he had for work, and he was greedy for both." The mayor believed that the main value of a social movement lay in the influence it exerted on those who took part in it and that "the greatest thing our Cleveland movement did was to make men." Johnson gathered around him a small group of these young men (attracted by both his personality and his program), who became his "kitchen cabinet" or brain trust. Its members included Howe and Newton Baker. The group (with their wives often included) met frequently at Johnson's mansion in "Millionaire's Row" on Euclid Avenue, sometimes at breakfast, lunch, or supper around the dining room table, sometimes near the fireplace in the main hall with Johnson in an enormous leather armchair his friends called the "throne-chair."

Over the years, many national figures were guests at the Johnson mansion, and Howe had an opportunity to meet and talk with them. He was present for a conversational sparring match between the mayor and William Jennings Bryan in which the single taxer tried unsuccessfully to convert Bryan to Georgism. Other notable guests included Sam Jones, Brand Whitlock, Clarence Darrow, Louis Post, Ida Tarbell, and Myron T. Herrick. Accompanying the mayor around Cleveland, Howe also had a chance to meet such visiting radicals as Emma Goldman and Elizabeth Gurley Flynn.[35]

Another visitor was Lincoln Steffens, with whom Fred Howe was to develop a lifelong friendship. The muckraker came to Cleveland in the spring of 1902, intending to expose Tom Johnson as "a demagogue and a dangerous man." He brought Howe a letter of introduction from Tarbell and quickly won entree into the mayor's circle. Howe told Steffens afterward that the mayor forbade them

---

34. Cleveland *Plain Dealer*, May 27, 1903, 1; December 16, 1903, 1, 2; J. Whipple, "Cleveland in Conflict," 237–40; *Confessions of a Reformer*, 149–50; Weinstein, *Corporate Ideal*, 24–25. See also Campbell and Miggins, *Birth of Modern Cleveland*, 142–43.

35. *Confessions of a Reformer*, 130–34, 138–39, 142. He may have heard Goldman earlier when she spoke on "The Basis of Morality" at the Franklin Club in March 1898. Franklin Club Records, 1895–1901, meeting of March 13, 1898.

to try to influence him and to give him any information he might want. After talking to many people and hearing only trivial complaints about Johnson and his administration, Steffens went away frustrated and skeptical, still convinced that there had to be something wrong and that the mayor eventually would be exposed. He returned a year later, when Johnson was running for governor, and scrutinized the Cleveland leader again. "My petty suspicions . . . vanished. . . . He was on 'our side,' the people's; that was why the other side, the plutogogues, called him a demagogue." He concluded that "Tom Johnson is the best Mayor of the best-governed city in the United States."[36]

Johnson shared both his work and his play with his friends, and his house became a social center for them and their wives and families. There were picnics, parties, masquerade balls, car rides (the Johnsons were among the first Clevelanders to own an automobile, and Tom loved to drive fast), and ice-skating on the family rink. Johnson bought a piece of land outside Cleveland, installed a trout farm, and worked for weeks on this playground to build a mechanical geyser like Yellowstone's Old Faithful. He loved to tinker and to invent, and his basement was his workshop. In his business career he had made money from inventions like a streetcar fare box, but his model for an electric railway without wheels, which he demonstrated with great pride to the Howes and other friends, proved less successful.

Fred's tasks as a member of Johnson's brain trust were many and varied. Besides serving on the Sinking Fund board, he was appointed by the council, on the mayor's recommendation, as one of the city's negotiators for the annexation of South Brooklyn, a village on Cleveland's southwestern border.[37] He often provided legal assistance to Johnson and to his friend Newton Baker, who had been elected city solicitor in 1903. He did a great deal of work on a new municipal code, to be submitted to the state legislature. His draft included most of the provisions pushed by municipal reformers of the time: a strong mayor who would appoint all executive officials except the auditor and the treasurer; abolition of most administrative boards; a merit system; reduction in the size of the council.

Howe stood by the mayor's side in the continuing battle over street railway franchises and fares. That controversy occupied all the Johnson years and was a

---

36. Steffens, *Autobiography*, 470–81; Steffens, *Struggle for Self-Government*, 183. Howe errs in his autobiography when he places the date of Steffen's first visit to Cleveland as 1903. *Confessions of a Reformer*, 182–84.

37. The annexation, which stirred up a considerable political battle, was important because South Brooklyn had its own municipal electric plant. Its annexation would give Cleveland its first step toward municipal ownership of that utility. See T. Johnson, *My Story*, 216–17; Murdock, "Life of Tom L. Johnson," 254–61.

central issue in every mayoralty campaign.[38] For the reformers, much more was at stake than a three-cent streetcar fare. To them, the exclusive franchises granted to street railway companies were a form of unearned increment. Their value increased as the city grew, and, through legally sanctioned monopolies, private individuals appropriated wealth that had been socially created. The effort to secure these gains led to bribery and corruption in municipal government. Besides providing the public with better service at lower fares, municipal ownership of the street railways would eliminate one of the rewards of privilege and strike a blow against political bossism and bad government.

Howe came to see the battle as a class struggle. "On the one side were men of property and influence; on the other the politicians, immigrants, workers, and persons of small means. This line of cleavage continued to the end." Once again, Howe regretted being on opposite sides with "friends, clients, my class," but he was "happy in the fight. It was always dramatic, and I had a passion for the thing we were fighting for."[39]

As old franchises expired, the city granted franchises to new companies that promised a three-cent fare. Since municipal ownership was impossible under Ohio law, Johnson hit upon another means to that end: the establishment of a holding company that would lease and manage street railway lines, guaranteeing a return of 6 percent to their stockholders. The profits earned would be used to maintain a three-cent fare, to purchase new equipment, and to expand services. The Municipal Traction Company was incorporated in June 1906 and began to lease and operate several of the street railway lines. Among the five friends of the mayor who held the stock of the company was Fred Howe, who became Municipal Traction's vice president.

ConCon struck back in the mayoral election of 1907, throwing its support to Congressman Theodore Burton, Johnson's old antagonist in congressional elections. To national Republican Party leaders, including Theodore Roosevelt, William Howard Taft, and James Garfield, the race offered a chance to defeat a leading Democrat in a pivotal state, and their pressure overcame Burton's reluctance to seek the mayor's office. Calling Burton's street railway proposal a "surrender" to ConCon, Johnson conducted his usual vigorous, down-to-earth campaign, while the congressman proved unfamiliar with local affairs and had great difficulty in reaching the average voter. Cleveland electors preferred the expert to the amateur and gave Johnson a 9,313-vote plurality.

38. Discussions of the complicated history of the street railway question in Cleveland may be found in D. Young, *Twentieth-Century Experience in Urban Transit*; Finegold, *Experts and Politicians*, 88–90; Bremner, "Street Railway Controversy"; T. Johnson, *My Story*; Lorenz, *Tom L. Johnson*, 139–65; Murdock, "Life of Tom L. Johnson," 331–61; Briggs, "Progressive Era in Cleveland," 11–36; Tarr, "From City to Suburb."

39. *Confessions of a Reformer*, 115, 116.

After this defeat, ConCon gave in and negotiated a settlement with Johnson in 1908. Municipal Traction took over all the street railway lines in Cleveland and began to run them with a three-cent fare. Howe continued as vice president and was optimistic that, despite some initial difficulties, the Municipal would give the city the best suburban service in the country.

Through all these activities, Howe learned more about politics and honed his own political skills. He not only saw what was going on from the inside but also had many opportunities to participate in the novel campaign methods that the mayor developed. During one of Johnson's congressional campaigns, he had been unable to rent a meeting hall and had used a canvas circus tent as a substitute. Thereafter, tent meetings were an integral and important part of all Johnson's campaigns. A tent (sometimes seating four thousand people) could be easily moved to any section of the city, obviating any concern about the availability of meeting halls or auditoriums. The meetings were democratic, open to all comers, including hecklers, whom Johnson delighted in dealing with. Between political speeches, stereopticon slide shows entertained and educated the audience on the accomplishments of the Johnson administration. For the mayor, the emphasis was on short speeches and plenty of interchange with his listeners; this was a political education for Fred. "I had had no training in public speaking, but standing before a crowd of people in the circus-tent, many of them hostile and ready to hurl questions at the speaker, taught me something of the art. The opposition hired men to heckle us, and we had to be ready with our answers or lose more than we gained by a speech."[40] Lincoln Steffens said Johnson's political meetings were "more like classes in economics and current (local) history than harangues."[41]

Another of Johnson's innovations was campaign by automobile. During his race for governor in 1903, he crisscrossed the state in his powerful (though not entirely reliable) Winton automobile, the "Red Devil." To conservative farmers, "his red car might have been a chariot of flame driven by an anarchist," but cars were still rare enough in Ohio to attract attention, and crowds came to see the car and to listen to its passengers. It was a campaign method that Fred would copy in a later presidential race.[42]

Howe and the other young men who followed the mayor were "proud of Tom Johnson's confidence; happy in the prominence he gave us. We threw ourselves into his fight, but knew little of the political game we were playing. At most we were lieutenants, giving unstinted affection to a leader who needed little else from us. . . . He gave us daily adventure, put us in the places where we

---

40. T. Campbell, "Mounting Crisis and Reform," 309; *Confessions of a Reformer*, 122.
41. Steffens, *Autobiography*, 477. See Bremner, "Political Techniques of the Progressives."
42. Whitlock, *Forty Years of It*, 167.

could do our best work, and we worked under him like players in a football squad."⁴³ Johnson backed Howe for the state senate, and in 1903 the county Democratic convention nominated him by acclamation. In the November election both Howe and Johnson, who was running for governor, went down to defeat in a statewide Republican landslide. Howe topped the Democratic slate for senator from Cuyahoga County (there were four seats to fill) with 37,349 votes, but his total was 5,523 votes fewer than the fourth Republican senatorial candidate received.⁴⁴

For Fred Howe, the friendship and close working relations with Tom Johnson gave him more than political adventure and governmental experience. They brought basic changes in his thinking about government and society. "I got the better part of my education from Tom Johnson. From him I acquired a simple, vivid picture of life. He cleaned up prejudices, swept away old habits of thought, old preconceptions." Political economy became a matter of a few principles, applicable to any problem. "The confusion of thinking which I had brought from the university was cleared up by his penetrating understanding, illustrated from his personal experience. My mind became receptive and retentive. History took on new meanings."⁴⁵

An acquaintance with Mark Hanna, and a close study of his economic and political power in Ohio and the nation, led Howe to conclude that Johnson's picture of politics as privilege versus the people was an accurate one. It was a class struggle. "Industry was war, with the employer and employee on opposite sides of the trenches. The no man's land of this warfare was occupied by liberals and reformers, deserters from their class, entitled, by its pitiless judgment, not even to the rules of humane warfare." The kind of men Howe had hoped to see in politics *were* in politics, but they were in politics for their own economic advantage. He still had mixed feelings about them: "I wanted to be part of this herd, even while I hated the things that it did. . . . I wanted approval from my crowd, and from myself as well." Fortunately, he wrote later, he did not have to resolve his conflict by choosing between his living and his convictions. "Largely by reason of the generosity of my law partners, the Garfields, I was never forced to make the choice."⁴⁶

---

43. *Confessions of a Reformer*, 128. Steffens made the same point about Johnson: "He knew the game. He could pick and lead a team; men loved to follow him; he made it fun." *Autobiography*, 478.

44. *Cleveland Plain Dealer*, November 5, 1903, 2

45. *Confessions of a Reformer*, 136. Lincoln Steffens put Johnson's influence more succinctly but in nearly identical language: "He cleared my head of a lot of rubbish, left there from my academic education and reform associations." *Autobiography*, 479. Newton Baker wrote: "The beauty of Tom's leadership was that he left us all free and taught us how to think straight and clear on public questions." Newton D. Baker to Dr. Harrison M. Noble, April 14, 1911, Baker Papers.

46. *Confessions of a Reformer*, 153–56.

Howe came to believe with Johnson that the single tax was the means by which the political and economic world could be changed, that it was "a fundamental plan for remaking society." He began to associate himself with the single-tax movement, endorsing in 1905 Louis Post's Georgist paper, the *Public* ("It sees straighter and thinks clearer than any other publication in America. It is a sort of chemical reagent that reduces life and politics to its true elements") and becoming one of its "corresponding editors" in 1907.[47] He spelled out his ideas and hopes for the single tax in his 1905 book *The City: The Hope for Democracy*.

Howe believed with Johnson that the city was the battleground between the people and the interests and that home rule, the direct primary, the short ballot, the initiative and the referendum, and municipal ownership of utilities were the people's weapons. He shared Johnson's vision for the city. "My passion for the city was also a passion for Tom Johnson. And I had come to love him as fervently as I loved the things he promised to achieve."[48]

It has been said that Johnson converted Frederic Howe to radicalism. This is too strong a statement. Ever since his days at Johns Hopkins, as his experience broadened, Fred had been questioning or abandoning many of the political and social ideas he had taken for granted in his early years, and he was ripe for conversion as he became increasingly involved in the political life of Cleveland. His friendship and close political association with Johnson sped up the process of change, and Johnson's influence in that process was certainly an important one. Howe always acknowledged his debt to Johnson. "The crusade of my youth, the greatest adventure of my life, as great a training school as a man could pass through—this the decade of struggle in Cleveland from 1901 to 1910 was to me."[49]

---

47. Bremner, "Single Tax Philosophy," 369; *The Public*, advertising brochure, November 1, 1905. See Candeloro, "Louis F. Post."
48. *Confessions of a Reformer*, 116.
49. Bremner, "Civic Revival in Ohio," 62; *Confessions of a Reformer*, 115.

6

THE HOPE OF DEMOCRACY

The Cleveland years were years of change for Fred Howe in his ideas, his politics, his profession, and his personal life. He had never lost his affection for Marie Jenney, despite the divergence of their paths in 1894. Marie completed her thesis on the social settlement movement and received a B.D. degree from the Meadville Theological School in 1897. Before graduation, she worked with Mary Safford as assistant pastor of the First Unitarian Church in Sioux City, Iowa, probably in the spring or fall of 1896.[1] After graduation, she continued in that post, taking the place of Eleanor Gordon, who had accepted a call to Iowa City. Thus Marie became linked with strong feminist leaders in an Iowa network of some twenty woman Unitarian ministers. The Iowa Sisterhood recruited, trained, and ordained its members and provided replacements for each other's churches when a member was ill or absent at a conference or on vacation. It came to dominate state and regional conference officers and to assume editorial control over *Old and New*, the Iowa liberals' monthly paper. For Marie, as for other woman pastors in Iowa, the Sisterhood was important as a "wide spread web," whose "little centers" were joined by a common thread spun out of women's "service and sympathy."[2] When she was ordained at the May Memorial Church in Syracuse on June 28, 1898, in a church crowded with childhood friends, three members of the Sisterhood—Safford, Florence Buck, and Marion E. Murdock—took part in the service.

---

1. Sources differ on whether Marie began her ministry in Sioux City in 1896 or 1897. I am using the dates provided in Snyder, "Unitarianism in Iowa," 364; and *Fifty Years of Unity Church*, 20. June 1896 seems the most likely date, since Gordon resigned in April 1896.

Apparently Marie's letters were nearly all destroyed after her death in 1934. Only a few have survived in the papers of other people. Fred's letters were also destroyed, but many can be found in other papers. We have only Fred's accounts and secondary sources for many of the events of their lives.

2. M. Jenney, "Women in the Ministry," 21. On the Iowa Sisterhood, see Tucker, *Prophetic Sisterhood*.

Fig 2 Rev. Marie H. Jenney, age thirty, assistant pastor, First Unitarian Church, Des Moines, Iowa, ca. 1900

At the time she started her full-time work in Sioux City, Marie already knew something of what to expect, both from her previous experience there and from a survey of women in the ministry she had undertaken in 1894. The Sioux City church's history describes her as "a beautiful young girl when she came to Sioux City, with a fine, highly developed mind. Out of her eyes shone the reflection of a loving heart and glowing soul."[3] Her concerns and interests in the first years of her ministry are best expressed in a long letter she wrote to Charlotte Perkins Gilman in 1899. Marie had finished reading Gilman's *Women and Economics* and was bubbling over with thoughts and ideas stimulated by it. It was a book she had waited all her life to read, one that justified "my most cherished convictions" and made her reconsider her views on marriage. She had long believed that women ought to be self-supporting but that the institutions of society made it impossible for married women to have economic independence. She had concluded that there was an "internecine warfare between this *ought* and this impossibility. The only hope I held was that of a radical change in the nature of men as husbands—a desperate hope indeed!"

But Gilman had proved that society itself had to alter and that this was possible. Marie was now ready to preach "Women and Economics" to her church's women's society and the Political Equality Club. Convincing a few women to care for political freedom would be hard—getting them to care about economic freedom would be even harder. "Even unmarried women, who may support themselves, do not seem to prize their independence. They are not born economically free, they do not achieve it, it is thrust upon them by the pressure of the society."

Her reading of Gilman's book convinced Marie that social customs could and would be adjusted to the economic freedom of women. "I tell you all this to show how much it means to me that the book has been written, and that you are in the world. It is solitary to hold these views, especially here in the west."[4]

When Mary Safford received a call from the First Unitarian Church in Des Moines in the spring of 1899, Marie chose to accompany her, and they began in their new church in the fall. Though still the assistant pastor, Marie found much of the work falling on her, as Safford was frequently absent because of her activities as secretary of the Iowa Conference. Marie's congregation affectionately called her "Our Little Minister." She combined social activism with her more strictly religious duties. "The sheer prophet who was content to talk about things" might influence people's minds and even restore their faith in progress,

---

3. *Fifty Years of Unity Church*, 20.
4. Marie Jenney to Charlotte Perkins Stetson, August 12, 1899, in Gilman, *The Living of Charlotte Perkins Gilman*, xx–xxii. I have quoted this letter at some length since it is the only personal statement—and the only letter I have found—from the period of Marie's Iowa ministry.

she argued, but only the "prophet in action" would spur people to change. She preached a series of sermons on "Reform, Leadership, and Christian Socialism" in the fall of 1900. In 1902 Marie attended the convention of the American League for Civic Improvement, heard an address by Jane Addams encouraging immigrants to use their artistic talents to beautify the cities, and learned of reform activities in St. Paul, St. Louis, and other cities.[5] At some point she was able to take a spring and summer off for a trip to Europe.

The Iowa Sisters were fighters for woman suffrage, and Marie joined gladly in that cause, both in Iowa and nationally. At the annual convention of the National American Woman Suffrage Association in New Orleans in March 1903, she discussed "Why Women Do Not Vote," comparing women to wild ducks, born in a farmyard and stepping timidly around the farmer who said, "Them ducks can fly, they can fly miles, but they don't know it." Women failed to vote because of "the entire self-effacement of many" and "the kindness of many men," she explained. "These are lovely traits but they may be misapplied. Women sometimes efface themselves to an extent that is bad for their men as well as themselves, and men out of mistaken kindness shield their women from responsibilities that it would be better for them to have." Marie also joined in the religious activities of the gathering, preaching in the Unitarian Church, assisting in Sunday services at the convention, and opening a memorial session with a prayer.[6]

Fred Howe had continued his courtship of Marie over the years, perhaps wavering briefly in his affections during his friendship with Mary Parsons in 1899. For Marie, as for many college-educated women of her time, the choice between marriage and a career was a most difficult one. Part of the unfairness of life was that men did not have to make that choice. She was certainly aware that marriage might end both her career and her independence. Society expected that after marriage a woman would be basically a homemaker, subordinate to her husband. Whether or not the husband behaved in a dominant manner, society recognized his superiority and expected the wife's deference. This conception was like the one Marie had criticized in her letter to Charlotte Perkins Gilman: woman was expected to cultivate the "feminine" virtues of self-sacrifice and gentleness, when the ideal should be the completed whole, "wherein no virtues are masculine and none are feminine."

    5. *Fifty Years of Unity Church,* 20; *Des Moines Leader,* June 6, 1900, quoted in Tucker, *Prophetic Sisterhood,* 169; M. Jenney, "American League for Civic Improvement." Marie published several other articles in *Old and New,* the monthly paper of the Unitarians' Western Conference: "Unselfishness and Resignation"; "The Young Women and the Church." The latter article was erroneously ascribed to Elizabeth Padgham.
    6. Harper, *History of Woman Suffrage,* 5:68–69, 72–73.

Why then did Marie break her vow never to marry? The answer can only be speculative, since specific evidence is virtually nonexistent and none of Fred's and Marie's letters to each other have survived. Perhaps, after seven years, she was beginning to find the ministry too confining as her interest in reform grew. Perhaps she was discouraged that her congregations did not fully share her more radical political and social beliefs. Perhaps a factor in her decision was the continuing discrimination she found against woman ministers. A few years later she spoke of the difficulties. Men and women did not have equal opportunities in the ministry. "In the very first place, you have to go to some little seminary. One could not go to Harvard or any of the crack places." The choice was limited to the Congregational, Universalist, and Unitarian churches. "You can't imagine a woman as a Catholic priest or as an Episcopal minister." After graduating from the seminary, the woman practically had to beg for a job. The only way a woman could ever get a church was "to take a wretched, forlorn one that no man would have under any circumstances. I found this one that had not had a minister for years and I took it at $400 a year, a salary no man would ever think of accepting. Well, I got on, and after starting it is easy. I built a church and built up my salary. You get applauded on all sides. You are one of the sights of the town, and every stranger is taken to see the little woman minister."

She had to live a quite different life than her male counterpart, however. All the young girls and the old maids flocked to him, but "if she receives a man at her house, married or single, if she is seen walking on the street with one, or if one happens to jump on the car in which she is riding she knows that she is going to receive a little note from the Trustees of the church, [that] will say: 'My dear young woman, don't you know that the one thing a young woman minister must do is to see that she is not talked about.'" She could not marry, or it was "good-by career." No one wanted a married woman minister. "The church wants all the woman minister's time—every bit of it. Oh, how it loves her! She must do a great deal more work than the man and for half the salary. Two women working together in a church will not make between them what would be given to one man in the same position."[7]

Marie's decision to marry Fred Howe troubled the Iowa Sisters. Many of them agreed that marriage ended both a woman's autonomy and her professional life. Only eight of twenty-one Iowa Sisters married. The Sisters feared that for Marie, marriage would mean a subversion of her independence and her growing radicalism. Fred noted that when they married, "there was a large protest from her friends," and he realized later that their fears were justified. "She

---

7. Tucker, *Prophetic Sisterhood*, 6, 235–40; *New York Times*, May 4, 1915, 9. The occasion for Marie's talk was the annual dinner of the Women Lawyers' Association in New York City.

was eager to continue her work, work which was life to her. But I wanted my old-fashioned picture of a wife rather than an equal partner."⁸ Whatever the reasons for her decision, and affection certainly must be counted one of them, Marie became more receptive to Fred's courting. He visited her several times in Des Moines, and on Christmas Day, 1902, she agreed to marry him.

On June 11, 1903, the Cleveland newspapers were filled with stories and pictures of the wedding that had taken place the previous day. The front page of the *Plain Dealer* exclaimed: "Euclid Avenue, though for years the center of social activity, has never been the setting for such a social pageant as was presented without and within St. Paul's yesterday morning." The wedding was that of Mark Hanna's daughter, Ruth, and Joseph Medill McCormick. The bride and groom had to compete for attention with a famous guest, President Theodore Roosevelt, and his daughter, Alice.

A much smaller news story on page 4 of the *Plain Dealer* chronicled the wedding on June 10, at the home of the bride's mother in Syracuse, of Marie Hoffendahl Jenney and Frederic C. Howe. Mary Safford officiated, assisted by Dr. S. R. Calthrop. "The wedding was one of the prettiest celebrated here this month. The flower decorations were gorgeous. . . . There were no ushers or bridesmaids. The bride was becomingly attired in a handsome gown of cream white silk crepe de chine trimmed with Brussels lace." Present were only relatives and a few close friends, including Harry Garfield and Newton Baker.⁹

The newlyweds lived at first in the Towers, an apartment house on Euclid Avenue. They started house hunting, and in December 1904 Fred wrote James Garfield that they had found "a very attractive place." They moved into the house at 4 Glen Park Place in May 1905, and Fred sent Garfield a description: "We have a very pretty little cottage, about ten acres of ground which another man keeps for us, and during the last six weeks I have been spending my spare time and spare money as well in trying to keep up an electric automobile." What with the cost of the house, the electric auto, and other expenses, Fred said that he felt like "the man who stopped at one of the leading hotels at Palm Beach. He went away for a rest and a change, and when he came back, and was asked by one of his friends whether he got it, he replied that he wasn't sure: He was under the impression that the bell boys got the change and the landlord got the rest." The electric car must not have proved satisfactory, because he soon was trying unsuccessfully to sell it to Newton Baker.¹⁰

---

8. Tucker, *Woman's Ministry*, 16–17; Tucker, *Prophetic Sisterhood*, 77–78; *Confessions of a Reformer*, 233.
9. *Cleveland Plain Dealer*, June 11, 1903, 1, 4.
10. FCH to James R. Garfield, December 19, 1904; May 15, 1905, Garfield Papers; FCH to Newton Baker, October 20, 1905, Baker Papers.

Marie was soon part of the social and intellectual circle that centered on the Johnson mansion. She and Fred joined in the parties and picnics and in the wide-ranging discussions around the dining room table and the fireplace. She liked Tom Johnson, and the Howes kept a room for him in their new house, a hideaway where he could come in the afternoon "to rest, to play a game of cards, or to think out his plans." The Newton Bakers were good friends, as were (to a lesser extent for Marie) the Garfields, though both James and Harry had left Cleveland before the Howes' marriage. Friendships deepened with Brand Whitlock and Lincoln Steffens. When the seventeen-year-old socialist Elizabeth Gurley Flynn spoke on socialism to an enthusiastic crowd in the public square in the fall of 1907, the Howes and Tom Johnson were in the audience. Johnson invited her for a ride in his car and a visit at the mansion. There are two versions of what happened next. According to a contemporary account in the *Plain Dealer*, Flynn's followers warned her against associating with capitalists, and she regretfully turned down the invitation. "I'm glad you liked my little talk," she said modestly to Mrs. Howe, as the two women clasped hands." In Flynn's own account, she liked Johnson at once and overruled those of her followers who thought that lunch would make her a traitor to the working class. Johnson whisked her off to the mansion in his big car, and there she met Marie and Fred, who "remained my good friends for years."[11]

The purchase of a house was a sign that Fred had gained a measure of financial security. He had attained that success by finding the secret of "wealth without labor."[12] Observing the clients of his law firm, he found that they fell into two groups: one that was always engaged in litigation and always in financial difficulties, and a second that seemed free from business worries and whose legal work was mainly consultative. Members of the latter group increased their wealth every year, they took life easy, they were prominent figures in the life of the community. Those in the first group seemed just as intelligent, but they had to work harder and were harassed, struggling, and often insolvent. How could the differences in wealth, power, and status be explained, Howe pondered. What was the key to social and financial success?

He ruled out the traditional virtues of hard work, thrift, saving, and sobriety that the rich preached to their employees and to the poor but themselves failed to practice. Rather, the wealth and power of the successful Cleveland businessmen came from ownership of land (and it helped if the land had iron ore or oil

---

11. *Confessions of a Reformer*, 137; *Cleveland Plain Dealer*, October 5, 1907, 1; Flynn, *Rebel Girl*, 79–81. Later, in mid-November 1915, after Flynn had been banned by the police from entry to Paterson, New Jersey, because of her activities in the 1913 textile strike, Marie Howe was one of several women who tried to smuggle Flynn into a Paterson meeting hall. Flynn was recognized by the police and denied an opportunity to speak. Ibid., 171–72.

12. The following account is drawn from *Confessions of a Reformer*, 213–24.

in it). Landowners derived substantial fortunes each year from ground rents. Next in importance to land ownership was banking, which gave the bankers control of other people's money and the opportunity to use it to direct or influence the political and economic life of the community.

The way to get rich, Howe decided, was "to have other people trust you, work for you, save for you. If you could use the money of other people, you need not have much money of your own." The seeker after wealth should "avoid competition—become a monopolist." The problem was how to make money without losing his soul. If he was to prosper, someone else would have to work and sacrifice. "Was there any compromise that justified me in enjoying privilege in the world in which I found myself? I wanted wealth, wanted the comforts and conveniences that wealth brings. I wanted to make a living as easily as possible. But there was no field of activity in which I could acquire wealth without violating some of my convictions." He believed in public ownership of public utilities; he felt the protective tariff immoral; he thought land speculation unsocial. Yet those were all avenues for the acquisition of wealth. "Must I refuse, I thought, to accept anything I did not myself produce?" His answer to his own queries was much like the advice Tom Johnson had received from Henry George. Change had to come through political action and the control of government by new groups, he thought, and not through individual abstentions from economic activity.

Until a better society existed, one could compromise. "I followed the manual in making investments, and kept away from competitive enterprises." An investment in land gained several hundred percent in a short time. Large profits came from a railroad and coal underwriting, from securities in a public utility corporation, and from investments in industries protected by patent rights. "'The world,' I said to myself, 'is topsyturvy; there is no personal wrong in taking advantage of its topsyturviness to make such money as one can. But I will keep my opinions straight. I will advocate municipal ownership, will be honest about the tariff, about land speculation, about special privileges of all kinds. I cannot escape the world into which I am born, but I will do what I can to change it.'"

Several investments required a great deal of attention from Howe and caused him many headaches. In 1899 he put money into the Long Arm System Company, a Cleveland corporation of which Harry Garfield was vice president. It manufactured and sold electrically controlled pneumatic doors for ships, which were expected to replace the old hydraulic doors. Fred found himself spending much time on the company's affairs, including a two-month sales trip to Europe in 1904. Long Arm had its problems in its early years, recovered, and was able to pay dividends of 8 percent to 10 percent in 1904–5, and then had labor troubles in 1907, from which it made a slow comeback.

Another company with which Howe was much involved was the Conneaut Water Works. When its bondholders brought suit in 1899 because of the utility's default on interest payments, the judge appointed him as receiver. The water works had a multiplicity of problems with its physical plant and was unable to resume paying dividends until 1905. The Garfield law firm held preferred stock in Conneaut, and Howe shared in the dividends, along with drawing his salary as receiver. Active with Conneaut for almost two decades, he ran it as a private enterprise while always advocating that it be publicly owned.[13] He suggested to H. B. Adams that his involvement in business was hardly unique in an America where the law was becoming a technical profession. He learned that he had to be "more or less conversant with ship building, electric telegraphy, hydraulic engineering as well as the ordinary branches of law." Lawyers, not philosophers, were the "modern encyclopedists," he concluded.[14]

Howe had other sources of income besides his investments. Even though he was devoting more and more time to political activity and to writing, he remained active in the law firm, receiving more than twenty-six thousand dollars from it in 1907. For several years, he drew a salary as director and vice president of the Municipal Traction Company. He also had earnings from his books and articles. By 1912 both *Harpers* and *Scribners* were paying him two or three hundred dollars an article. He was also prepared to take to the road under the auspices of the International Lecture Association of Chicago, whose stable of lecturers included cartoonists, an interpreter of Dickens, singers, and a necromancer. All in all, he became well off financially, able to maintain a summer home at Siasconset (Sconset) on Nantucket and, in the 1920s, an apartment in Paris, as well as his year-round home in Cleveland, and later on in New York.

Before their marriage, Fred and Marie must have had long talks about the opportunities for her to continue her activism in Cleveland. Despite Fred's traditional views on marriage, it could hardly have been expected that she would either want or agree to settle down as a housewife, Looking back from the 1920s, Fred realized that his outlook had restricted her sphere of activity in the Cleveland years. "Women did not take part in things in Cleveland; only a few had gone to college at that time; there were but few activities open to women. They did not earn their own living. That was a public admission of failure by the husband. I found reasons for deciding against each suggested activity in turn." It did not then occur to Fred that there was anything unjust, illogical, or contrary to his political principles in his attitude. "My mind simply held fast to

---

13. The Garfield Papers are full of correspondence between Howe and his law partners on both Long Arm and Conneaut. Howe's account of his problems with Conneaut may be found in his *Confessions of a Reformer*, 208–11.

14. FCH to H. B. Adams, February 16, 1900, Special Collections, Milton S. Eisenhower Library, Johns Hopkins University.

assumptions of my boyhood, which social prejudices seemed to justify. And as I look back over those years I realize that I never honestly faced what I was doing or the rightfulness of my wife's claims."[15]

So Marie's activities in Cleveland differed little from those of other college-educated women of her day. She continued to fight for woman suffrage, especially on the national level. She served on the executive committee of the National American Woman Suffrage Association (NAWSA) and attended its annual conventions. She had completed Fred's conversion to the cause (though he embraced it intellectually rather than emotionally), and both the Howes gave papers at the Association's 1906 convention. Marie spoke on "Woman's Municipal Vote" and Fred on "The City for the People."[16] Twenty years later, Howe perceived that "as to women, I followed the changing *mores*. I spoke for women's suffrage without much wanting it. And I urged freedom for women without liking it. My mind gave way, but not my instincts." Fred's postwar pessimism may have made him excessively critical of his role in the suffrage movement. One of Ohio's leaders for woman suffrage, Elizabeth Hauser, who was also the person Tom Johnson called on to help write his autobiography, praised Howe's part in the struggle.[17]

In 1906, at the New York state convention of the NAWSA, Marie gave one of the "tributes of reverence and appreciation" to Susan B. Anthony, who had died several months before. In 1910 she made a vigorous speech to the Thomas Paine National Historical Association in New York City. "American women are no better than they are because they are too fond of men," she declared. "If only some Pied Piper would lead off all the men, we would develop more in twenty years without them than in 200 years with them." She found Paine "the father of the woman's rights movement, and therefore the grandfather of the woman's suffrage movement." In Paine's time, she argued, women were believed to exist only to propagate the race. "Contrast this condition with that of today, when we have club women, bachelor girls, and even divorced women. . . . Things have changed gloriously. Paine held that the human species consisted of only the oppressors and the oppressed. Fortunately today it is hard to say which is which."[18]

Marie was much more involved in the national movement for woman suffrage than in Cleveland's, which had been late getting under way. By the time the movement began to assert itself in Cleveland, the Howes had departed for

---

15. *Confessions of a Reformer*, 233.
16. Harper, *History of Woman Suffrage*, 5:177, 21. NAWSA published an excerpt from his talk as a leaflet entitled *Frederic C. Howe on Suffrage*. Fred also spoke to the 1912 convention.
17. *Confessions of a Reformer*, 234; Hauser, "Woman Suffrage Movement in Ohio," 92.
18. *New York Times*, January 30, 1910, 8.

New York City. Probably Marie's greatest achievement for the cause on the local scene was her conversion of Tom Johnson. The mayor had not thought about the issue and had a traditional view of woman's role. Fred reports: "One evening my wife said to him: 'Mr. Johnson, you who are democratic in everything else, why are you not democratic about women? Why do you not believe in woman suffrage? Why do you think that men should decide questions for women?'" Johnson admitted that he had never thought of the question in that way. More conversations followed, and a few weeks later Johnson gave a ringing endorsement to equal rights for women. "From that time on, he lost no opportunity to speak for equal suffrage."[19]

Marie soon assumed a leading role in the Ohio Consumers League, for many years second only to New York among similar organizations throughout the country. The League had been founded in 1900 by the women of the Book and Thimble Club, who met at Goodrich House to discuss current issues. Its board included many of Cleveland's leading women, and Mary Parsons, Fred's old friend, held various offices over the years. The Ohio League kept an eye on the working conditions of women and children. It set minimum standards for hours, wages, and lunch periods and drew up a "White List" of firms and stores that met them. Those establishments were entitled to use the "White label" on their products. The League published its White List and urged its members, and consumers generally, to shop selectively, patronize stores on the List, and buy only goods with the White label. When selective boycotts proved ineffective, the League began in 1906 to endorse legislation as a remedy and set up a lobbying committee in 1909. Special campaigns sought to shorten the working hours and secure vacation time for women clerks in the retail stores. The standard work week at that time for the clerks was six days a week and often sixty to eighty hours.[20]

Marie quickly became an officer of the Ohio League, serving as a member of the executive committee (from 1904 to 1910) and then, successively, as state vice president and state president. Her position as president linked her with the National Consumers League, to which the Ohio group was affiliated, and she became an executive committee member and a vice president of the national group. She joined in the Ohio League's lobbying for legislation to protect child and woman workers. She was named to a committee of three to meet with the

19. Van Tassel, "Introduction: Cleveland and Reform," 9–10; *Confessions of a Reformer*, 137–38. See also Abbott, *History of Woman Suffrage*, 9–13. Nothing much was accomplished for woman suffrage in Cleveland until Elizabeth Hauser began to organize the campaign there in 1910. Earlier that year, Inez Milholland helped to start a local chapter of the National College Equal Suffrage League, and Marie was a charter member.

20. See Harrison, "Consumers' League of Ohio"; Wolfe, "Women, Consumerism, and the National Consumers' League."

Cuyahoga County state legislators and to present the need for woman inspectors to check on child labor. In 1908 she was a member of a large delegation that presented the case for a child labor law at a public hearing in the state senate. The senate, led by Fred Howe, then a state senator, passed the bill a few weeks later.[21] A bill setting limits of ten hours a day and fifty-four hours a week for woman workers finally passed in 1911.

Fred had ended his connection with the Bethel Associated Charities (later the Cleveland Associated Charities) in 1903, but his strictures on such organizations did not prevent Marie from serving on its board of trustees from 1905 to 1907. In September 1907 the Cleveland Board of Public Service appointed her and two other women as a visiting committee to "look after the interests of women and children in the city hospital, infirmary, workhouse and other similar institutions." The committee was to investigate at least every three months and to make recommendations about the administration of the services. Six weeks later, Marie and a fellow committee member visited the sanitarium at the Warrensville colony and gave its unqualified approval to what it found. Marie especially praised the new infirmary building as "the best planned and the best looking building of this kind in the United States."[22]

Marie's activities in these various fields were punctuated by periods of ill health. When Fred had to go to England and Germany on a lengthy business trip for Long Arm early in their marriage, she could not accompany him. "She dreads the voyage very much, and it now looks as though I would be travelling so much while there that there would be little comfort in the trip for her," he noted. Fred missed her very much during their two-month separation. "I have had a good but lonesome trip," he wrote James Garfield from the Hotel Russell in London. "It has been beastly lonesome and I never want to make such a trip again. In addition it has been very cold and I have hung about the fire trying to keep my temperature up to the living point." He had met some interesting people, he told Harry Garfield, and he "would have enjoyed myself greatly if Mrs. Howe had been with me." After he returned, he wrote Harry that he had "found Mrs. Howe very well on my return, really better than when I left home. I have had enough, however, of single travelling and do not fancy any more European trips alone." Fred was lonely again when Marie returned to Des Moines for several weeks in the fall because of Mary Safford's illness. "I am

---

21. Consumers' League of Ohio Report for the Year Ending February, 1906, 5, 6, 8 (microfilm edition, Western Reserve Historical Society); *Cleveland Plain Dealer*, December 7, 1905, 4; February 5, 1908, 8; February 26, 1908.

22. *Cleveland Plain Dealer*, September 22, 1907, 6; November 10, 1907, 3. The Warrensville Colony included the poorhouse, the workhouse, the tuberculosis sanatorium, and the municipal cemetery. See Bremner, "Harris R. Cooley." Marie also served as president of the Cleveland chapter of the National Women's Trade Union League and spoke to its national convention in 1910.

again thrown back on bachelordom, which I accept with far less satisfaction than I did before," he wrote James Garfield. She came back "very much worn out from the trip, but recovered in a few days time. She has so much recuperative capacity that she picks up very quickly, but unfortunately she gets tired almost as easily."[23]

Fred might not have fancied trips alone to Europe, but he was to make many more of them. In June 1905 he asked James Garfield, now commissioner of the federal Bureau of Corporations, to sponsor a trip for him to study English cities. He proposed to examine their indebtedness and its relation to municipal ownership, to examine their civil service and public attitudes toward it, and to compare English and American per capita expenditures for fire, police, health, and other services. The Bureau provided support, and Fred spent two months in England in the late summer and early fall of 1905. There is no indication in the extant correspondence that Marie accompanied him. The result of the trip was a long report entitled "Municipal Ownership in Great Britain."[24]

Fred also traveled alone to Europe in the spring of 1909, planning to spend four to six weeks collecting information for a series of articles on European social reforms for the *Outlook* and studying town planning for the Boston 1915 movement. Another purpose of the trip was to secure advice from European specialists about Marie's chronic ill health. Her American doctors had urged her to go to Carlsbad or Wildungen for their "water cures," but Marie did not want to make the trip until Fred had canvassed expert opinion in Europe on the efficacy of the treatments. He did so, and wrote James Garfield: "I have heard of so many successful cures of chronic gall and liver troubles that I cabled her to come." The two went to Carlsbad in early June. Marie had consulted "all kinds of experts in America and she has not been able to secure any relief for an enlargement." It was not a "vital matter," he told Garfield, "but she has been suffering so much lately that she could not travel and has been reduced to the sparsest kind of diet. I have been fearful that it would develop into something very serious."

After several weeks of treatment for Marie at Carlsbad, Fred was not sure whether she was better or worse, but he believed that the German doctors had at least found out what was wrong with her. "I have a long score to settle with the Cleveland doctors . . . who said that the trouble was nervous dyspepsia, then liver trouble and then her gall ducts. And we have been treating it for years on

---

23. FCH to Harry A. Garfield, March 12, 1904; May 24, 1904; May 31, 1904; FCH to James R. Garfield, May 10, 1904; November 21, 1904; December 19, 1904.

24. FCH to James R. Garfield, June 3, 1905; June 12, 1905; FCH to Frank Goodnow, October 19, 1905, Johns Hopkins University Library; FCH, "Municipal Ownership in Great Britain."

this theory." Her German doctor found it "much more serious and she has been in bed now for almost all of the time that she has been here. The doctor made an examination of her stomach and found that she had a stomach ulcer, which has really been bleeding for months. I can't tell how serious it is but it seems to be rather common here and the treatment well understood. But it worries me a good deal.... Aside from this I think the waters are doing Marie good and that the complaints which are more or less related to the main trouble are getting better."

When the Howes returned to the United States is not known. They stayed in Carlsbad at least until the end of July. Fred wrote Lincoln Steffens: "Marie and I are marooned here and have been for five weeks. The doctors discovered that she has something serious the matter with her stomach and will not let her sail. I do not know how long we will be kept.... How I wish you would drop in on us. God but we are lonely for some one we care for. Marie is able to do anything but get about and it chafes her to lie in bed." They summered, as usual, at Sconset, where Marie felt she benefited from the sea breezes. "I don't need them," wrote Fred, "but I am taking them daily nevertheless." By the fall he could write Steffens that Marie was "in fine health, the first time in years. Carlsbad nearly finished her but it put her in fine health as well."[25]

Marriage was not the only change in Howe's life. The law firm of Garfield, Garfield and Howe was breaking up as all three partners found other interests and challenges. The first to go was James Garfield. He had been active in Republican politics in Ohio, serving twice in the state senate but losing twice when he sought his party's nomination for the House of Representatives. His independence and reform proclivities had gained him the antagonism of Mark Hanna and many of the regular Republicans. In March 1902 President Theodore Roosevelt offered him an appointment to the federal Civil Service Commission. He thought long and hard about the position, consulted with his brother, Howe, and Newton Baker, and finally decided to accept. He left for Washington at the end of April and quickly became part of Roosevelt's "tennis cabinet," so quickly that Howe could write him in May: "I see by yesterday's paper that you have been playing 'Follow your leader' with the President. It sounded rather hazardous, but I think the entire country is inclined to adopt the same game, even

---

25. FCH to James R. Garfield, December 18, 1908; June 3, 1909; July 7, 1909; July 14, 1910; FCH to Lincoln Steffens, July 22, 1909; November 7, 1909; Steffens Papers. In the letter of June 3, Howe defined Marie's ailment as "enlargement of the ..." but omitted the next word. There are brief references to Marie's health and stay at Carlsbad in Newton D. Baker to FCH, June 23, 1909, and July 27, 1909. In the first of these letters, Baker wrote: "I am, myself, such a wife-baby that I can well understand how much her presence adds to your happiness."

though a few of those who have sat high in the councils of the party prefer the ferry boat of safety as adopted by one of your companions."[26]

In February 1903, over the opposition of some members of his own party, Roosevelt secured enactment of a law setting up a Department of Commerce and Labor, including a Bureau of Corporations to investigate the operations of interstate corporations. It was a sign of the president's closeness to Garfield that he appointed him as the Bureau's first commissioner. Howe sent him a congratulatory letter, saying that only his own approaching marriage gave him more pleasure than the appointment. Two weeks later, he passed on a further reflection: "I presume you are deluged and will be from now on with opinions, plans and suggestions of all the cranks in Christendom who have a panacea for all ills you have been made Chief Physician of. If it does not drive you mad, it should be a liberal education. I do not want to be a particeps criminum to the former alternative, and certainly have nothing to offer by way of contribution to the latter."

In 1906 Roosevelt appointed Garfield secretary of the interior. Howe considered this a post with one of the biggest of all possibilities, "for it deals with the physical underpinning of the nation and all of its physical resources and believing as I do that a people's life is largely measured by its economic opportunity and the freedom of access to nature."[27] As his term ended, Roosevelt urged his successor, William Howard Taft, to continue Garfield in the position. Garfield wanted to stay on, but Taft appointed Richard A. Ballinger. Garfield returned to Cleveland in 1909 and resumed the practice of law but remained close to Roosevelt.

Harry Garfield chose a different path. Less active in electoral politics than his brother, he, too, was an anti-Hanna reform Republican, one of the founders of the Municipal Association and its president from 1896 to 1899. On several occasions his name had been mentioned as a possible candidate for mayor of Cleveland. In June 1903 Woodrow Wilson, the president of Princeton, invited Garfield to hold the university's Chair of Politics, as a successor to John H. Finley, who had just been elected president of the College of the City of New York. It was a difficult decision. Fred was pleased that Harry had received the offer, but found it "hard to detach myself sufficiently from your constant kindness and goodness to me, not to speak of the fact that the practice of the law, without you being there would be a condition that my mind does not readily dwell upon." Self-realization was the important thing, however: "the finding of the *milieu* in

---

26. James R. Garfield, diary, March 29, 1902; FCH to James R. Garfield, May 26, 1902. The "tennis cabinet" was a group of Roosevelt's friends who joined him in tennis at the White House and in strenuous rambles in Rock Creek Park. The "Follow your leader" reference is to Garfield joining the president in rock climbing along the Potomac and in the park.

27. FCH to James R. Garfield, February 16, 1903; February 28, 1903; November 8, 1906.

which one's life lies, the expression of one's strongest bent in talent and the doing of that thing hard. That seems to me one of the few things one can be sure is right, for that is the giving back again to the world what nature has given to us. And I know you will not misunderstand me, or think I am not appreciative of your talents, achievements and all that if I say I think you have powers and messages which you have never yet given to the world."[28] After taking a month to think it over, Harry accepted. He left Cleveland in December 1903 and became professor of politics at Princeton in February 1904.

Fred's letters to Garfield at the time of his departure from Cleveland both show his affection for Harry and illuminate Howe's philosophy of life and his feelings about his own career. He explained to Harry: "I have never told you and cannot tell you how much and how greatly you have influenced my life during the past ten years. And you will never really learn, I presume one cannot, how the things you have been identified with have taken fire from you and bear the impress of your personality. You have saved many men from themselves and called out the desire to be as good as possible in this." The concrete achievements of life were always in a sense a disappointment, "but this is the sort of thing that is never a disappointment and somehow or other it does not soak into our consciousness and is only known to one's friends. . . . Let this 'buck you up' if you ever get the blue devils or feel as we all do, twenty-five past, thirty past, forty past and so little achieved." The most that any man has done "is to extend the circumference of himself so as to touch as many people with himself as possible. And if that circumference is both good and wide he can lie down in comfort to sweet dreams." He thought that Harry's decision to accept the Princeton professorship was a good one, noting that he knew of "no other teaching Chair in America of which I could say that, or which would suggest a larger field of action than does this."

Reflecting on his graduate student experiences at Johns Hopkins, he suggested that teaching ought to be "vivified. There is altogether too little dynamite in the College Professor." Out of all Fred's professors, only three or four, at most, had left any profound impression on him. He and other students disagreed completely with one, "and yet, he shocked the men into a mental alertness." The great virtue of Professor Adams was not his scholarship but his "way of inspiring the men who sat around his board with a belief in their own individuality that was unique." Adams used to spend "about half his time shaking the boys down with comments on contemporary matters, and the balance of the hour in suggestions about life and work, politics, religion and philosophy that in the end converted his students into living beings who were ready to try their hand at almost anything so long as it was an expression of themselves."

28. FCH to Harry A. Garfield, June 18, 1903.

That self-expression was, Howe repeated,

> the first obligation in life. . . . And I am not sure but that a man who finds himself, and then devotes all his joyous energy to the reexpression of himself, to the giving of himself to the world, has adopted a standard which satisfied his moral, mental and physical self better than any other. . . . I am not sure that the average man can do it until he reaches mature life. But when he reaches that point, the supreme moral obligation upon him is to follow his bent. I am inclined to think that he should sacrifice everything else to that end.

Fred apologized for parading his own view of life in a letter about Harry's decision. The idea that he was trying to suggest had been "a sort of pole-star" for him in settling troublesome personal problems and had "satisfied me better than any other considerations by which I have reached conclusions regarding my own life."[29]

Harry Garfield was professor of politics at Princeton until 1907, when he resigned to become president of Williams College, his alma mater. His predecessor in the Princeton professorship, John Finley, sent Woodrow Wilson a strong recommendation that he appoint Howe to the vacancy. Wilson probably gave Howe little, if any, consideration, since the Princeton president had his eye fixed on a more experienced and qualified person who already had a national reputation, Henry Jones Ford.[30]

A melancholy tone pervaded Fred's congratulatory letters to Harry Garfield. As the Garfield brothers were moving on in the world, he thought of himself as at a standstill. If self-realization meant "the expression of one's strongest bent in talent and the doing of that thing hard," where was Frederic Howe? What was his own "strongest bent in talent"? Certainly not in the law, a profession which he had chosen *faute de mieux*, and which he was gradually abandoning. Politics was still an option, but it was a bumpy road. There is no evidence that he was a strong contender for a Princeton professorship, but he had not abandoned the idea of an academic career. In 1897 he and some other lawyers organized the Baldwin University Law School, one of the precursors to Cleveland State University's present Cleveland-Marshall College of Law. From 1897 on, he was teaching courses in corporation and commercial law at the Cleveland Law

---

29. FCH to Harry A. Garfield, December 20, 1903; FCH to Harry A. Garfield, n.d., probably December, 1903.

30. FCH to Harry A. Garfield, July 5, 1907; John H. Finley to Woodrow Wilson, December 6, 1907, in Link, *The Papers of Woodrow Wilson*, 17:550; Wilson to Harry A. Garfield, April, 10, 1908, ibid., 18,:259, 287. Wilson offered Ford the appointment on May 5, 1908, and Ford accepted.

School (another precursor to Cleveland-Marshall) and lecturing on taxation at Western Reserve University.

His Hopkins professor, Richard Ely, was now at the University of Wisconsin, and the two formed a mutual-assistance society over the years. In their extensive correspondence, Ely asked Howe for suggestions for a response to a critical review of one of his books, for aid in raising money for various projects, for advice and help on a possible return to Johns Hopkins, for information needed in Ely's research—he even queried Howe about the possibility of their organizing a public utility company.[31] Howe provided information and suggestions for Ely's research and tried to raise money for it, asked for letters of introduction for his European trips, kept Ely informed about his political activities, and relied on his help in getting his early writings published.

Through Ely, he received in 1905 an appointment to give a series of lectures on his new book, *The City,* in the political science department at the University of Wisconsin. There is a suggestion that more was involved than the two weeks of lectures and a stipend of two hundred dollars. The visit would enable Howe "to become acquainted with us, and to let our people become acquainted with you," Ely wrote. Fred considered Wisconsin a university that was "willing to seek the truth irrespective of any other consideration than the truth," and was delighted at the prospect of teaching there. He gave his lectures in the winter of 1905 and enjoyed the ambience of the university: "In so far as I could judge, Madison seemed to me the most satisfactory University atmosphere I had ever been in. There was all the enthusiasm of Hopkins, together with an open-mindedness of students, professors and townspeople that was like balm to my soul." He told Edward Ross: "I came away feeling that I would rather live in Madison than in any place in America: There is such a fine atmosphere and so much that is delightful." He returned to lecture on European and American politics in the winter of 1909–10, spending a semester as a replacement for a political science professor who was on leave. Nothing developed in the way of a full-time position, if indeed Howe was being considered for one, but his teaching at Madison introduced him to Wisconsin Progressivism and its dynamic leader, Robert M. La Follette.[32]

If the road to self-realization through a university position seemed closed, the avenue through writing, and perhaps journalism, remained open. Amidst all his political, legal, and business activities, Fred still found time to write.

---

31. Richard T. Ely to FCH, February 26, 1902; FCH to Richard T. Ely, February 28, 1902, Ely Papers. Howe found the idea of a utility company interesting but pointed out some of its problems.

32. Richard T. Ely to FCH, November 19, 1904; FCH to Richard T. Ely, March 19, 1904; November 21, 1904; March 6, 1905; FCH to Edward A. Ross, January 18, 1906; *Confessions of a Reformer,* 237.

Although he continued to present his views occasionally for specialized audiences, after 1900 he turned his attention to a broader readership.[33] His first article for a major national magazine, "Great Empire by the Lakes," appeared in *World's Work* on February 1901. By 1905 he had published eight articles in *World's Work*, the *Atlantic Monthly, Cosmopolitan,* and *Harper's Weekly*.

In August 1904 he wrote the editors of the *Century Magazine* that he had completed a series of articles that he would eventually shape into a book on municipal conditions in America. It would not be a traditional academic treatment of organization and functions but "an attempt to portray in a broad way the city as the center of the new Twentieth Century civilization." The articles, which he considered "rather radical in their conclusions and proposals," drew on his experiences as a member of the Municipal Association and a city councilman and on "exhaustive reportorial study in the principal cities of America." Enclosing an abstract of the chapters, Howe explained that they were "an attempt to develop a program by which the cost which advancing civilization imposes upon society, and which is most acutely evidenced in our cities, may be paid by the municipality rather than by the individual."[34] The *Century* did not want the articles, but the publishing house of Charles Scribner's Sons became interested in the book. Howe's major work, *The City*, appeared in 1905 and almost immediately earned him a national reputation.

According to his autobiography, Fred's head was always full of ideas about books that he planned to write.[35] For some time, he had envisaged a series of ten volumes on democracy, to begin with one on the city. Cities, their problems and prospects, had fascinated him from the Johns Hopkins days when Albert Shaw's lectures aroused his first political enthusiasm and led him to dream of cities as they might be. In the ensuing years he had learned directly about urban life, and now he felt capable of writing the first book in his series, intended to show the practical, "business-minded," "parish-minded" American people the goal, the way to "build a city like a home." His book, he felt sure, would be "a manual of reform; it would hearten people and point out the steps to be taken. I put into it all my faith in the future of American cities, in the certainty of their redemption."

---

33. His more specialized writings included a paper on municipal ownership for a joint meeting of the American Political Science Association and the American Economic Association in December 1905, the report on municipal ownership in Britain for the Bureau of Labor in 1906, and a paper on the taxation of railroads and other public service corporations for the National Municipal League in 1907.

34. FCH to editors of *Century Magazine*, August 13, 1904, Century Collection, New York Public Library.

35. In his sixty-ninth year he was still bombarding Maxwell Perkins with proposals for several different books. FCH to Maxwell E. Perkins, February 26, 1936, Scribner Archives, Princeton University.

After Scribner's accepted *The City: The Hope of Democracy,* Howe soon began to receive the proofs, "interlined with helpful suggestions and humorous queries as to facts or arrangement." They were initialed W.C.B., and he quickly learned that the initials were those of William Crary Brownell, who has been described as "a formidable figure, for he was not just editor-in-chief but one of the most eminent literary critics in America." Fred found Brownell's assistance invaluable. "My sense of literary form was not commensurate with my zeal for the subject. There were exaggerations; I was frankly a propagandist disposed to repetition as a means of emphasis.... He gave me continued encouragement, along with illuminating suggestions as to style and manner of treatment that were never dogmatic and were always right."[36] Brownell was to continue as Howe's editor through ten other books, until Maxwell Perkins took over in 1919. Perkins was the editor for many famous writers, including Ernest Hemingway, F. Scott Fitzgerald, and Thomas Wolfe. Scribner's remained Howe's primary publisher throughout his life, publishing twelve of his seventeen books.

The City was a work of great importance for Fred's career. It immediately gave him national visibility and placed him in the first rank of writers on city life and urban reform. His optimism and hope for the city contrasted sharply with the perennial fear and dislike of the urban condition that had characterized American attitudes throughout the nineteenth century. The book gave him the opportunity to meld his ideas and his experiences and to work out and present his analysis of political life more systematically than ever before. The process of learning and unlearning that had been going on since Meadville days had produced a set of principles, many of which were to remain constant in Howe's political creed.

Fred began by rejecting all purely personal, political, and governmental interpretations of the city. They had produced inadequate remedies: charter reform, the merit system, limitation of the suffrage, improvement of the individual citizen and stimulation of his patriotism, government by businessmen, elimination of bosses and machines, charity, education. "We have been bailing water with a sieve." He adopted instead an economic interpretation, arguing that the economic environment created and controlled human action and attitudes.

Howe did not spare himself from his strictures on the mistaken ideas of urban reformers. "I have been forced by experience to a changed point of view, to a belief that democracy has not failed by its own inherent weakness so much as by virtue of the privileged interests which have taken possession of our institutions for their own enrichment." From a belief in a businessman's government, he had come to a belief in a people's government and from a conviction

---

36. Berg, *Max Perkins,* 15; *Confessions of a Reformer,* 237.

that we had too much democracy to a belief that we had too little. The study of history showed him that the progress of civilization had been a constant struggle of liberty against privilege. Urban reform was a class struggle in which "the few who enjoy privileges which they are seeking to retain" are pitted against "the millions awakening to the conviction of industrial democracy."[37]

Howe rejected all nostalgia for the rural past—there was no hope for return to a rural Eden. America was the city. "The city is El Dorado, the promised land which fires the imagination. Failure may come, it is true, but there is the chance, and life, movement, and recreation even in failure." For the first time in history, there was developing a really democratic city, a tremendous agency for human advancement.[38]

The city was both promise and problem. Its development had come with terrible costs: vice, crime, disease, a higher death rate, tenements and cheap lodging houses rather than homes, and the creation of a landless proletariat. That price had to continue to be paid, for the future of society was an urban future. "And to an ever-increasing extent the city will continue to take its hostages in poverty, disease, and crime, from those who brave her favor."[39]

The largely economic causes of these problems stemmed from the activities of the forces of privilege that looted and plundered the community. The "glittering prizes" of monopoly lure men from the paths of honest industry by enabling them to gain wealth without needing to work for it. To secure and defend such privileges, "the boss, the machine, and the system have become the virtual government of city and state all over the Union."[40]

The boss, the new feudal baron, was the link between the "criminal rich" and the "criminal poor," obtaining for the former "millions in grants, franchises, privileges, and immunity from the burdens of taxation," and dispensing to the latter, in payment for election services, "small gratuities in the form of protection from the police, in jobs, in staying the hand of justice, and in caring for the weak, sick, and helpless in time of need." The boss himself often graduated to the Senate of the United States, where he continued to protect the interests of the few against the many. The grasp of privilege thus extended to tariff protection, railroad monopoly, and the exemption of businesses from taxation, regulation, and competition. Its control was buttressed by the spoils system.[41]

The boss in the Senate was formidable but respectable. Citizens reserved their opprobrium for the boss on the ward level, who offended their sense of propriety. "For his graft is of another kind. It affects the poor, is a shelter to the

37. FCH, *City*, vii, ix–xi.
38. Ibid., 22, 25, 23.
39. Ibid., 32, 41–42.
40. Ibid., 70, 72.
41. Ibid., 96–98, 108, 110.

saloon-keeper, the gambler, the dive and policy-shop keeper. Apparently, he it is who blocks reform. He votes his precinct or his ward as advantage dictates. He deals in offices and in justice. He secures city contracts and distributes patronage. We do not see, or we will not see, that he is but a cog in the larger machine." His offenses were trivial compared to those of the boss in the Senate, and his machine would crumble if deprived of support from above.[42]

Although the system's strength may have appeared to make the situation hopeless for popular rule, there was "a spirit of revolt and a feeling of confidence in democracy that is demanding home rule for cities and a larger control of the machinery of government in the people . . . a belief that democracy can best work out its problems when government is responsible, as well as responsive, to the immediate community which it serves." American cities were becoming better. America already excelled in some municipal activities, as could be seen in fire departments, park administration, libraries, the public school system.[43] Much could be learned from British and German cities, but we were ahead of Europe in many respects.

How remedy the city's ills? First and foremost, eliminate the monopolistic and exploitative franchise system by the adoption of municipal ownership. Regulation had not worked. Reform would only come with removal of opportunities for a few to gain riches, power, and influence at the expense of the community. Natural monopolies had to be placed under public ownership. Operating under a merit system, municipally owned enterprises would be subject to the criticism of the citizen and the scrutiny of the press. "An enlarged public spirit will only come with enlarged public activity. . . . As has been well said, 'The cure for democracy is more democracy.'"[44]

To the charge that the extension of city activities was "socialistic," Howe replied, in language like Lester Ward's, that the history of civilization is a history of the emergence of society from savagery to social organization. "All of the present agencies of the state are an encroachment of society into the realm of private activities, and each, in turn, has given an added freedom to the individual and in no way threatened the liberty of initiative that those who challenge further activities fear." Monopoly and liberty could not coexist. "Either monopoly will control or seek to control the city, or the city must own the monopoly." Advocating municipal ownership of transportation, lighting, heat, power, and water, Howe added Henry George's argument that the growth of society enriched the private utility corporations and the landowners by a law "as resistless as the law of gravitation. The growth of the city and the necessity of a place

42. Ibid., 112.
43. Ibid., 159–60, 55, 56.
44. Ibid., 119, 122, 124.

on which to work and to stand involve the servitude to the franchise corporation and the land owner of all those who dwell therein."[45]

Other reforms were also needed. Decentralization and home rule would strengthen local democracy and create "city republics" like Athens and Rome. Cities would become democratic experiment stations in administration, taxation, and social improvement, to the benefit of the entire nation. Adoption of the initiative and the referendum would enhance popular rule.[46]

Howe welcomed the increased participation of women in city affairs, ascribed much of municipal "uplift" to their activities, and pointed out that "back of the settlement, the small park, the kindergarten, the crèche, the juvenile court, the schools, and the libraries; back of the Consumers' League, the movement for the abolition of child-labor; back of many a movement for bettering the conditions of life in home, shop, or factory, is the influence of woman." Man saw the city as an industrial center, while woman viewed it in the light of the home—"the vice, the saloon, the schools, the libraries, the water, gas, and transportation questions are to her questions of the family, of the child, questions of comfort, of happiness, of safety." As for woman suffrage, "probably no single reform would mean more for the ultimate, if not the immediate, betterment of conditions than the adding of woman's voice and counsel to the management of city affairs."[47]

Howe expressed little faith in charters or other paper forms, since bosses simply adjusted themselves to whatever political arrangements existed. He preferred a strong-mayor system of municipal government. The people should elect the mayor, comptroller, treasurer, and council. The mayor should appoint all other officers, who would hold office at his pleasure. A boss could appear under any form of government, but "under a system of centralized responsibility, the boss becomes responsible. Under any other system, the boss was an outside influence, responsible to no one, and inaccessible to the wrath or approval of the public. If our cities had to be governed by a boss, it was most desirable that he be an elective one."[48]

---

45. Ibid., 128, 129, 134, 156. Howe acknowledged his intellectual debt to Lester Ward in a letter to him a few years later: "Certainly the whole social philosophy of the present day is a formative expression of what you have said to be true. And I am but one of thousands who have had their mental mists cleared by your writings." FCH to Lester F. Ward, July 27, 1912, Ward Papers, Brown University Library.
46. *City*, 160, 165, 167, 174. More dubious about the direct primary, Howe preferred nomination of local officers by petition in order to eliminate the importance of the party label. But he did not oppose primaries. They "will not cure the ignorance of the voter, but they will free the game so that the popular will may express itself" (174)
47. Ibid., 175–76.
48. Ibid., 183, 185–86.

Thus strengthened and democratized, a city could tackle its social problems. A prime example was poor housing, which resulted from bad land policy. "In every community land values respond to the density of population, and it is the private enjoyment of land values that gives birth to the housing evil. There is, and can be, no other cause." The remedy was Henry George's: tax land values to capture the "unearned increment," and abandon taxes on buildings and improvements.[49]

Like the problems of housing, the causes of crime were largely economic. For many men, unemployment led to vagrancy and then to more serious offenses and incarceration in an archaic prison that "destroys self-respect, enfeebles the mind, and wrecks the body." Society was even more inhumane to juvenile offenders, both male and female, and to women. All this was done through an outdated and unchristian criminal law that "exposes the unfortunate, the child, the aged, and the helpless as did the Spartans of old. . . . Our attitude towards those who have offended against conventional morality is out of harmony with the teachings of twentieth-century Christianity." The emphasis was on punishment, not on rehabilitation or prevention. Hardly a dollar was spent "to protect and provide against the beginning of vice and crime. We make no effort to save self-respect before it is irretrievably lost." All the human wreckage was a price exacted by the present economic system. "There is no more cruel offence by the individual than that committed by society against the weak. There is no torture of the medieval code more pagan than the unnecessary destruction of self-respect by our jail and penal institutions or the brand that is placed on the forehead of the juvenile offender."

Experience in Cleveland and other cities pointed the way to change. Necessary reforms included juvenile courts; farm colonies for young offenders; more recreational activities in the slums; treatment and aid, rather than imprisonment, for drunks, vagrants, and prostitutes; a new spirit of helpfulness in police forces; work for the unemployed. There was "a right to labor, a right to employ God-given energy upon the boundless resources of the country. He who will work but cannot find it should not be forced to the alternative of vagrancy or outdoor relief." Economic opportunity was the best answer to the problems of crime and vice. "There must be an abandonment of the retributive ideas of the Old Testament and a substitution of the kindlier philosophy of the New."[50]

Improvements in the criminal justice systems were a sign of municipal progress. So was the increased interest of peoples and governments in beautification of their environs through municipal architecture, parks, and cleaner streets.

---

49. Ibid., 196, 208, 212.
50. Ibid., 214, 219–21, 225, 227–36, 237–38.

Modern democracy was coming to "demand and appreciate fitting monuments for the realization of its life, and splendid parks and structures as the embodiment of its ideals.... A determination has come to make the city a more beautiful as well as a more wholesome place of living." Cleveland was leading the way through its Group Plan.[51]

How could all these reforms be paid for? For Howe, the answer was simple: the single tax. The city itself produced wealth. Its treasure was "the constantly increasing value of urban land through the growth of the city." This revenue continually renewed itself and grew more rapidly than the city's needs. It was "a common treasure, a publicly created fund which rises in value with every dollar expended by the city. All men created this fund, and all should enjoy it. The rule of municipal life should be 'to the individual what he has created, to the city what it has created.'" Once the city took over this social treasure, it could provide education, health, protection, schools, kindergartens, libraries, art galleries, museums, parks, clubhouses, public music. Slums would be replaced by model tenements; rents would diminish; and vacant lots would give way to industry and to spacious homes. "The city industrial could then become the city beautiful, the city helpful, the city fraternal in the truest sense of the word.... Then life will be relieved of its most relentless punishments and the cost, the price, the vicarious suffering will be made good from out the common treasure of the city. Then opportunity will be enlarged and the plane of competition elevated; then higher education will become a possibility to all, while the poverty which is now the result of industrial causes will no longer impel man away from the good." All that was needed is legislation to permit each city to develop its own sources of revenue and its own methods of taxation.[52]

The new activities of the city "will enlarge our life, not limit it; will insure freedom, not destroy it; will give to the millions whose life goes to the city's upbuilding something more than ten hours of work, eight hours of sleep, a single room in a tenement for a home, and a few hours in the saloon as compensation for it all." As the city was divorced from state control, it would become "a centre of pride and patriotism. Here art and culture will flourish. The citizen will be attached to his community just as were the burghers of the medieval towns. Through direct legislation, the city will be democratized. Public opinion will be free to act." The tax on the unearned increment from land would relieve the economic burden on the populace and bring an end to poverty. "For poverty is an eradicable thing. It is not a dispensation of Providence, as we interpret the scriptural expression with which we justify our inaction."[53]

51. Ibid., 241, 239, 248, 243.
52. Ibid., 250, 263, 279.
53. Ibid., 287, 293, 295.

The reforms he advocated were no panaceas, Howe admitted, since the problems of popular government were "as complex as is our Protean civilization." But as the program of reforms was achieved in the city, democracy would end the class struggle between the privileged and the many. People would unite to improve the conditions of their lives. What the final agenda of the new city would be, we could not know, but that "it will be a programme making for a better civilization, a larger life, and increased comfort and opportunity, the gradual progression of society gives assurance."[54]

Howe hoped that his book would reach a wide audience. He wrote Edward A. Ross early in 1906: "I tried to do a somewhat hazardous thing, which was to preserve accuracy and at the same time make the book land. At the same time I was ready to sacrifice what might be termed the academic for the sake of reaching my audience." That he reached a member of that audience close at home is indicated by a comment of Lucretia Garfield, the mother of Harry and James: "By the way I have become a convert to the 'single-tax' idea so far as I understand it from reading Mr. Howe's book, *The City*."[55] Tom Johnson was so impressed with the book that he had a copy sent to each member of the Ohio legislature.

Reviews in leading magazines and newspapers brought the book to the attention of the national readership that Howe desired. Those in liberal and religious journals were quite favorable, even laudatory in most instances. The *Arena* declared, for example, that *City* was "a book so rich in vital truth, so instinct with the higher wisdom and statesmanship which is the hope and promise of the twentieth century, so luminous with the spirit of humanity or the new conscience, without which there can be no spiritual growth or permanent uplift, that we would urge every reader of *The Arena* to place it among the few books that he places on the list of works that he should purchase and study."[56] Other

---

54. Ibid., 176, 312–13, 301, 303, 305.
55. FCH to Edward A. Ross, January 18, 1906; Comer, *Harry Garfield's First Forty Years*, 249. Harry replied to his mother that some of the single-tax reasoning was based on false premises. "It is applicable and being applied to urban conditions, but unless gross injustice is to be done, it must be applied gradually. Fred Howe's other book, *The British City*, will throw additional light upon the subject—but don't mistake the shadows! Fred does sometimes." Ibid.
56. *Arena* 35 (May 1906): 544–53. "Every leader in city politics will find facts and arguments in this book to stimulate his hopes and to pilot his activities." *Independent* 59 (December 7, 1905): 1342–44. The book is "a frank discussion of municipal problems as they are actually encountered in the more typical of our American cities." *Review of Reviews* 32 (November 1905): 637. "Seldom does a writer so successfully justify an ambitious title; rarely is a sentiment, which to many must be a contradiction, so ably defended; and only at crucial epochs is it the privilege of a reformer to seize the psychological moment as Mr. Howe seems to have done in his critical and prophetic claim that the city, hitherto abused by all of its enemies and many of its friends, is the hope of democracy." *Dial* 40 (April 1, 1906): 230–32. Praise also came from several religious journals: *Congregationalist and Christian World* 90 (October 28, 1905): 601; *Churchman* 92 (November 25, 1905): 852; *Catholic World* 8 (March 6, 1906): 827.

periodicals gave mixed reviews, usually praising Howe's knowledge and sincere concern but disliking his remedies or his style. The *Nation* grumbled: "Human nature is not to be seriously altered by a change in the system of street-car management."[57] Newspaper notices were generally favorable, though the *New York Times* reviewer thought the author too much of a "theorist," offering more in the way of reforms than a "cautious reader" could accept.[58]

The City placed Fred Howe clearly and importantly within the Progressive Movement. For the first time, he had set down in a systematic way the principles and the lessons that he had derived from his studies, his political and governmental experiences, and his observations of community life in America and Europe. Many of these principles and conclusions remained constants in his political thought; some were to be modified by later experience. He had rejected both purely personal (good men) and purely political (good institutions) remedies for the ills of society and replaced them with an economic interpretation. He was now prepared to find a "system" of economic privilege at the root of modern problems and to seek economic remedies, most notably the single tax and public ownership of natural monopolies, for the evils produced by the forces of privilege. Changes in governmental structures and political processes were valuable but insufficient. He endorsed proposals for their reform, though he seemed less than enthusiastic about the direct primary and rather soft-spoken on woman suffrage, and he sometimes appeared to share the antiparty sentiments held by other reformers. Improvements in society required an active government, controlled by the people and not by privilege. His dream was the "city

---

57. *Nation* 83 (August 2, 1906): 105. "Much must be allowed to the fiery zeal of the reformer. We may not measure the vision of the prophet with the common yardstick. But while our fellow mortal has a perfect right to speak with unknown tongues, he must excuse the weary plodders amongst us who still use the alphabet, and must not ask us for belief, unless he supplies us with evidence." *Atlantic Monthly* 97 (June 1906): 845–46. *The City* is "a good work to place in the hands of advanced students. It is too strongly (although honestly and fairly) partisan to put in the hands of beginners. But for those who have acquired a balance and a viewpoint of their own it will prove of value and importance. . . . The work is interesting in style, stimulating in thought and treatment, hopeful in tone, and is well worth a careful reading by the student of municipal affairs." *Yale Review* 15 (February 1907): 463–65. Howe "weakened his case, from the viewpoint of persuasion, by the manner in which he has presented it. . . . None the less, the book is a really noteworthy contribution to a discussion of vital significance to all Americans." *Literary Digest* 32 (February 10, 1906): 215. The book was one-sided, but "this is not wholly without advantage, since extreme views often bring the various aspects of a subject into such bold relief as to make for clearness and, by stimulating argument in rebuttal, for ultimate truth." Nevertheless, *The City* was "a notable contribution to municipal literature." *Engineering News* 54 (December 14, 1905): 648.

58. *New York Times*, Saturday Review of Books, November 18, 1905, 773. Favorable notices appeared in the *Cleveland News*, the *Cleveland Plain Dealer*, the *Boston Advertiser*, the *Chicago Record-Herald*, and the *Memphis Commercial Appeal*.

In his influential book *The Promise of American Life* (1909), Herbert Croly embraced Howe's view of the contributions that cities might make (349).

republic," freed from state control and able to tackle a wide range of problems in housing, recreation, culture, unemployment, beautification, land use. Government should be more than a peacekeeper and a regulator—it should be a source of the good things of life for its citizens. Howe's vision of the city differed greatly from the hostile views of urban life that had generally prevailed in America. His passionate attachment to the city and his vision of its future were in sharp contrast to those gloomy assessments. Pervading *The City* is a spirit of hope and optimism and a faith in democracy that were to darken in his later years.

7

WRITING AND POLITICKING

Fred Howe's pen was busy in the years between *The City*'s publication in 1905 and his departure from Cleveland in 1910. In a number of articles, he reiterated the main points of his book: democracy, the fight against privilege, humane social policies, municipal ownership of natural monopolies, beautification, the single tax. He praised the reforms and the new "city sense" that had developed under Tom Johnson in Cleveland, where the battle was being won: "People talk city, and think city, and believe in their city in a way that is not to be found anywhere else in America. . . . The city has been elevated above party until today men are no longer proud to say that they vote a straight ticket." He lauded the penal reforms of Dr. Harris R. Cooley, Johnson's director of charities and corrections; the "Golden Rule" policies of Fred Kohler, his chief of police; the achievements of the Group Plan; and the supportive activities of the Cleveland Chamber of Commerce.[1]

Howe also turned his attention to the British city. His report on municipal ownership in Britain was published by the federal government's Bureau of Labor in 1906. Replete with facts and figures, it examined the criticisms and defenses of public ownership and surveyed its scope and workings in water supply, gas, tramways, electricity, and telephone service in England and Scotland, especially in the large cities of London, Glasgow, Liverpool, Manchester, Sheffield, and

---

1. "Tom Johnson and the City of Cleveland"; "A City in the Life-Saving Business"; "A Golden Rule Chief of Police"; "Cleveland Group Plan"; "Cleveland's Education"; "Milwaukee, a Socialist City." Hoyt Landon Warner has summed up Chief Kohler's "Golden Rule" policy: "Patrolmen were to be given large discretion in making arrests; only as a last resort were they to take offenders into custody; juveniles apprehended were to be sent home to their parents; intoxicated persons were escorted home, or retained, if necessary for their safety, and given a waiver of trial; those charged with a misdemeanor were to be released after signing the 'Golden Rule' book unless evidence indicated the crime was committed with malice aforethought or with the intent to injure property or persons." Warner, *Progressivism in Ohio*, 76.

Birmingham. Critics might call city ownership "municipal socialism," but Howe found it "not socialistic in intent, whatever its ultimate significance may be." Although backed by the fledgling Labour Party, the movement for municipalization of public utilities and services was "more largely a movement of the taxpaying and commercial classes, inspired by a belief in the city, a desire for better service and greater conveniences, as well as a zealous conviction that the city should own and operate all enterprises of a monopolistic character." Howe was also pleased to see the development of "a determined municipal movement for the taxation of land values, in order that the city may retake to itself the pecuniary returns of its own progressiveness." Backed by the solid middle class, workingmen, and "advanced liberals," the movement was bound to press on, despite the strength of its opponents, the franchise companies.[2]

Howe followed this document with a series of articles on British cities, fleshing out the prosaic statistics of the report.[3] His subsequent book, *The British City*, must have been easy to write since he could recycle materials from the articles and the municipal ownership report, and he frequently did so word for word. The book has two themes: the achievements of the British city (with due regard to its shortcomings) and the constraints on the cities imposed by the nation's privileged classes. As in *The City*, Howe sees political life as a battle between democracy and privilege, privilege being defined as the struggle of the few to live off the labor of the many. This conflict was the common element in the politics of all countries.[4]

The twentieth-century British city represented the beginnings of real democracy in the nation—it was a breakaway from control by the privileged minority. By expanding the number of municipal enterprises (discussed by Howe in some detail), British cities had taken over many natural monopolies and plan to provide additional services to their people. Municipal ownership should be judged by a moral, not a monetary, test. "An affectionate regard for the city, the absence of bulging dividends, the best possible service, and a fraternal sense between all classes of the community, are the returns of the British city from the public ownership of a public service." These were the only tests we should consider in evaluating the gains and losses of municipal ownership.[5]

In many ways, British cities were doing a better job than American ones, but the American cities were superior in some respects. Overly concerned with their

---

2. "Municipal Ownership in Great Britain," 1, 2, 4, 17–18, 56.
3. "Glasgow"; "London"; "American and the British City"; "Graft in England." To this list can also be added "Old London," a description of the city of London that appeared after *The British City*'s publication, and "Epoch-Making English Budget."
4. *British City*, 6.
5. Ibid., 10, 55–56, 123, 130.

taxpayers' purses, the British gave their cities a commercial, businesslike operation, less democratic than in America. The democracy of American cities was "more generous, more hospitable to new ideas, more ready to be liberal with its parks, its schools, its libraries, its provisions for the poor. . . . We are even willing to be wasteful in order to get the thing we want." But, Howe concluded, "the British city does the things it undertakes amazingly well. . . . The people care for the city and talk city in a way that we do not and cannot comprehend."[6]

All was not rosy in the British municipal future, however. The hand of the privileged classes still lay heavy upon the cities, which were "so limited by Parliament that every forward step has to pass the scrutiny of powerful vested interests who are jealous of the growing activities of the towns and in constant fear for the preservation of their privileges." A feudal oligarchy still ruled, and the resulting caste system had fostered servility and subservience in the middle and lower classes. The power of the upper class made itself felt in every important piece of legislation.[7]

The British city thus became the arena in which the democratic forces, spearheaded by socialists, advanced Progressives, and labor leaders, engaged the privileged interests. The democrats of the cities fought increasingly for the socialization of land values. The present tax system shifted the burden from land to labor and industry. "This, with the monopoly of the land, which is the inevitable result of its exemption from direct taxation, are the controlling influences in the life of the United Kingdom." The British city could only cure its economic diseases by opening the resources of the nation to all its people through adoption of the single tax. Howe hoped that the Liberal electoral victory in 1906 might presage the triumph of democracy over privilege but warned that "the task is a heavy one. . . . Democracy in Great Britain has a long way to go before it becomes articulate."[8]

The British City added little that was new to Howe's analyses and arguments in *The City*, but it presented them in a comparative dimension that enabled the reader to contrast the achievements and the problems of municipalities in Britain and America. It is less readable than *The City*, partly because of the minute detail offered on municipal enterprises and partly because Howe is often repetitive in his comments. He weakens his case by sweeping generalizations about the United Kingdom's ruling class, which he identifies solely as the landed gentry, paying little attention to other economic powers that exist in a commercial and industrial society. Somewhat inconsistent in his treatment of the class struggle he saw in Britain, he says sometimes that the movement toward democracy

---

6. Ibid., 233–34, 236, 240, 241–42.
7. Ibid., 64, 279–80, 286, 297.
8. Ibid., 251–52, 334–35, 302.

in the city has the support of all classes and sometimes that it is the product of the working class. He maintains the optimism of his earlier work, while arguing that the future lay with the American city rather than the British, unless the dominance of the feudal aristocracy in the British system could somehow be broken. The American city was the model for the world because it was free to choose its destiny.

Reviewers were somewhat more critical of *The British City* than they had been of *The City*, but they agreed that it was a book of merit and one that confirmed Howe's place in the front ranks of writers on urban problems and reforms. The editor of *The Arena* declared that Howe was "more than a critical, painstaking economic investigator. He has the broad vision of a true statesman and the faculty of getting at the foundation of any issue he discusses, that marks the philosopher." Even the more critical reviewers, who disliked the advocacy of municipal ownership, found the book valuable and useful.[9]

Howe did not limit himself to writing about American and British cities. He broadened his field of inquiry with six months of research on the European continent in 1909. Presenting his findings in five articles on industrial democracy in the *Outlook* in 1910, he focused on three of the smaller European states and on Germany. He sought to show the breakdown of "the old philosophy of individualism" and the need for the state to "protect the people and promote their common welfare." He was impressed with the changes that were occurring throughout Europe. "All Europe speaks of an irrepressible conflict between privilege and democracy. . . . It is not revolution, but evolution. It is not class war; it is class disintegration." Everywhere, old institutions were being challenged by the peasant, the writer, the artist, the statesman, even by members of the ruling classes. The "most positive gains" of social reform were in the smaller nations. In Switzerland, democracy, through extensive use of the initiative and referendum, had triumphed over privilege, and the state was developing the nation's waterpower for the benefit of all the people, instead of for private gain. Denmark was a "real democracy," resting on peasant proprietorship. Its successes stemmed from its land policies, the strength of the cooperative movement, and the political supremacy of the land-owning farmers. The economic and cultural life of Belgium—"in many ways the most poverty-stricken and ignorant country in western Europe"—was being altered by moderate socialists and the cooperative movement.[10]

---

9. Flower, "British City," 201–2, 208. Other reviews appeared in *Annals of the American Academy of Political and Social Science* 31 (June 1908): 196; *Journal of Political Economy* 15 (July 1907): 441; *Independent* 63 (October 10, 1907): 880–81; *Nation* 85 (July 25, 1907): 82–83. The *New York Times* summarized the book but gave no evaluation. September 14, 1907, 547.

10. "Commonwealth Ruled by Farmers," 450; "Peaceful Revolution," 115; "The White Coal of Switzerland"; "Conquering a Nation with Bread."

Howe lauded the outstanding achievements of Germany in social welfare, education, and city planning. Germany, more than any other European state, had entered on "a comprehensive programme of human salvage. She is devoting her thought and her energy to the making of people as well as of things." He could hardly ascribe these achievements to democracy, however, and pointed out that they had come by direction from above. "From the cradle to the grave the State has its finger on the pulse of the citizen. His education, his health, and his working efficiency are all a matter of constant concern.... The German boy must be a good soldier. The German girl must be a good mother. The State has a long vision of to-morrow. And it spends generously for the next generation." Supplementing the *Outlook* selection on Germany were two other articles, published at about the same time, that were overwhelming in their praise for the nation's municipal accomplishments. Düsseldorf came close to his dream of "a city whose ideals rose above mere business, a city that was built like a home, that had a communal bigness of vision, that was planned by city builders, and that served its people as a father might serve his children."[11]

The *Outlook* series and related articles offer interesting insights into Fred Howe's thought at this time in his life. Through these writings, he was becoming a source of information for American Progressives on successful reforms abroad that might be models for change at home: the initiative and referendum in Switzerland, city planning in Germany, public ownership of large-scale natural monopolies like waterpower in Switzerland, the value of cooperatives in Denmark and Belgium. He was clearly identified with the moderate Left, with Fabian socialism rather than Marxian, and he was selective in his advocacy of public ownership. He had moved beyond "gas and water socialism" and urban reform to advocacy of national policies for limited public ownership, social welfare, and land reform. He was convinced that change for the better was coming.

His enthusiasm for the changes he saw in Europe led him sometimes to uncritical praise. For example, he hailed German achievements in education, urban development, and social policy, yet his reporting indicated that these gains had come from the paternalism of the state, not from action by or through the people. Imperial Germany was far from a democracy, and he noted how individual freedom had to yield to the collective good, and how reforms were part of the state's efforts to enhance national power. "System, science, order"

---

11. "How Germany Cares for Her Working People," 940, 946; "City Building in Germany," 601, 602, 603; "Düsseldorf," 698, 705, 708; "German City Has Solved Problems," 7.

Fourteen years earlier, in one of his first published articles, Howe had been much more critical of Germany. He called the Kaiser "a firebrand in Germany's powder magazine and a thorn in the already sorely irritated side of Europe." His government still controlled speech and press, and "many years will probably elapse before Germany possesses the same degree of constitutional liberty as does England." "Imperial Germany."

were the watchwords. "In Germany, the aim is to make efficient people. 'The glory of the fatherland' is the motive, and the making of strong, healthy and competent citizens is the means."[12] Nowhere in these articles on Germany did he bemoan the lack of popular participation in policy making, and gone were the paeans for democracy that we find in his other writings. It was as if success were the only measure—accomplishment of the goals of *The City* was sufficient, even if done by state paternalism and nonpolitical experts.

His treatment of the basic theme of democracy itself was rather uncritical. He hailed the democracy of Switzerland and Denmark, yet ignored the fact that in both countries half the population—the nation's women—was excluded from full suffrage rights. In Denmark, women could vote in local elections but not in national elections until 1915. Switzerland did not give votes to women in federal elections until 1971. Apparently, though he expressed support for woman suffrage, it had not become an essential element in Howe's definition of democracy. Despite this omission, the battle of democracy against privilege remained a central part of his thinking. Writing Brand Whitlock, he noted, "There are many signs that the power of privelege [sic] is breaking down. If we only had the intelligence to steer the new forces we would be in a fair way to get something done."[13]

The European research trip of 1909 and the articles stemming from it represent the beginning of Howe's continuing interest in the cooperative movement, especially in Denmark. It was a subject to which he would return many times in his writings. More immediately, the articles produced from his journeys were to be recycled for a later book on European cities. The trip can also be seen as a manifestation of his growing concern with European affairs and with the two great power competitors and soon-to-be enemies Britain and Germany.

Howe also fixed his gaze more sharply on controversial domestic issues in the United States, as well as on the general problems of monopoly, privilege, and the land. He continued his support for woman suffrage but was hardly vehement about it. The National American Woman Suffrage Association (NAWSA) published excerpts from his talk to its 1906 convention in a leaflet in its Political Equality series. Interestingly, of its four pages, three dealt with municipal reform generally, and only one with votes for women.[14]

Howe's *City* had been quickly followed by *The Confessions of a Monopolist*, a didactic "autobiography" whose narrator, William Palmer, traces his path from childhood to a position of wealth and political power. This fictional life draws upon Howe's own youth, education, and practice of law; Tom Johnson's early

---

12. "Düsseldorf," 705.
13. FCH to Brand Whitlock, February 10, 1908, Brand Whitlock Papers, Library of Congress.
14. *Frederic C. Howe on Suffrage*.

experience with monopoly and his role as a reformer; and Mark Hanna's career as businessman and political leader. Palmer, educated in the law but unhappy in its practice, gains his riches through real estate speculation, street railway and gas franchises, coal, railroads, and Wall Street manipulations. Early in life he learns the way to economic success: monopoly. He soon finds that the quest for wealth and economic power leads inevitably to politics and corruption. One must "make a business of politics. The two things run together and cannot be separated. You cannot get very rich in any other way." It does not matter which party one controls, as long as it is the party in power.[15]

So Palmer becomes the Republican boss of his city, then his county, then his state, and finally, like Mark Hanna, he enters the United States Senate, "the refuge of monopoly," where members represent "the big business interests whose directors, attorneys and agents they are." His chief opponent along the way is the Democratic candidate for mayor of his city, clearly modeled after Tom Johnson.[16] Though the Democrat is elected, Palmer controls the council through bribery and economic pressure and, by splitting his rival's party, is able to defeat him in the next election.

Palmer concludes that he has discovered the secret of great wealth: "Make Society work for you. If you are big enough, make the whole world work for you. If you cannot do that, be content to have America work for you. If that is impossible, get some city. Even the latter is a big enough proposition to put millions in your purse." Get land, get a franchise, get a coal or a copper mine; then sit back, and while you sleep, society produces unearned wealth for you. The best of all businesses is politics, "for a legislative grant, franchise, subsidy or tax exemption is worth more than a Kimberly or Comstock lode, since it does not require any labor, either mental or physical, for its exploitation."[17]

Reviewers liked the book. The *Dial* thought it gave a vivid depiction of the intimate relation between political bosses and those dependent on them for favors. "It is not pleasant reading—it is too true to life, though possibly sometimes exaggerated or unnaturally concentrated either for artistic effect or for the sake of argument." The reviewer wondered why Howe had chosen fiction for his message, "for he is much more a master of straightforward argument and of the simple statement of facts. Perhaps he sought the widest possible audience for this exposition of his convictions, or can it be that he was not sure enough of his ground to state as a general condition what he has imagined as possibly an extreme case?" Heading its review "More Muck-Raking," the *New York*

---

15. *Confessions of a Monopolist*, 5, 143, 152. Several excerpts from the book appeared in the *World's Work* as "Confessions of a Commercial Senator."
16. *Confessions of a Monopolist*, vii, 47.
17. Ibid., 145, 155, 157.

Times called *The Confessions of a Monopolist* a "brightly written little book." The author would find the accumulation of a fortune easier in fiction than in fact, but "however that may be, the little volume is both interesting and instructive, whether regarded as a vade mecum for those desirous of practicing the new high finance, or as an addition to the horrors which our professional purifiers have revealed in order to reform them." The *Arena* judged the book "far and away the finest political satire on present-day American politics—a book that every thinking patriotic citizen should read."[18]

Howe's fictional autobiography of a monopolist was part of the growing critique of privilege in America. The single-tax movement is not generally given much credit as an active force in Progressivism; some historians fail to mention it at all. Yet it is amazing to see how many reformers in the pre–World War I period gave at least some support for the Georgist ideas. Men of some reputation who professed an attachment to the single tax or to land policies related to it included such reform stalwarts as Louis Post, Ben Lindsey, William S. U'Ren, Amos Pinchot, Bolton Hall, William Kent, Lincoln Steffens, and Frederic C. Howe.

That list does not include the major political figures—Theodore Roosevelt, Robert La Follette, Woodrow Wilson. They were after bigger game in the national arena, while the battles on the single tax nearly all occurred on the local level. In the first decades of the twentieth century, there were many elections involving land policy in such cities as Portland, Seattle, Cleveland, San Francisco, and many smaller municipalities. Some the single taxers won, some they lost. Their numbers remained small, however, and they failed to hold onto nearly all of their gains.[19] After the deaths of Henry George in 1897 and Tom Johnson in 1911, they had no national leaders of the first rank and no national political party like the Retsforbundet (Justice Party) in Denmark.

Many, if not most, of George's followers were true believers, avid disciples of his philosophy. For some, adoption of the single tax was their only aim. For others, it was the primary goal, but they were willing to join coalitions and work for other reforms as well, especially the instruments of direct democracy. Some of the single taxers worried about the ideological purity of those who involved themselves in reforms other than the single tax. What political organization the

---

18. *Dial* 43 (September 1, 1907): 121; *New York Times*, Saturday Review of Books, September 29, 1906, 595; *Arena* 36 (December 1906): 680.

19. See Johnston, *Radical Middle Class*, 159–76. In 2010 there were still a few communities that continued Henry George's idea: Fairhope, Alabama; Arden, Delaware; and Free Acres, Berkeley Heights, New Jersey. Organizations still promoting that idea include the Robert L. Schalkenbach Foundation, the Henry George Foundation, and the Henry George School of Social Science in New York City.

various Georgist adherents had came from the writings and speeches of a loose network of leading single taxers.

Fred Howe was one of those leaders. He continued his attacks on monopoly and his advocacy of the policies of Henry George in pamphlets for the National Single Tax League, as well as in periodical articles.[20] In a long letter to Daniel Kiefer in 1910, he related his belief in the single tax to his faith in democracy. Throughout the country, 90 percent of "the real radical and progressive work" was being done by single taxers. "They have started the fires for municipal ownership, for the Initiative and Referendum, for the recall, for free trade, for better conditions all around. And I think that the average man is right in thinking that there is no possible single thing that will cure all the troubles in society; and I am for the other forces that make for democracy almost as strongly as I am for the Single Tax." Georgists were "really founding all our hopes of success on democratic tools rather than on a straight out fight for the thing itself." When men get the "microbe" of the single tax, "they have a mental cholic [sic] for a while, but after awhile the microbe burrows into their prejudices to such an extent that they become radicals of one stamp or another. And there is no possible doubt but that socialist and insurgent will be single taxers when the psychological time comes for it."[21]

The quantity of Howe's literary output between 1901 and 1910 was amazing, especially when one recalls that he was a full-time politician and a part-time lawyer during that period. But though the literary life was promising, there was also a political road to self-realization that warranted further travel. In September 1905 the county Democratic convention, acting on the recommendation of Tom Johnson and other party leaders, unanimously nominated Howe for one of four state senate seats from Cuyahoga County. By that time, Johnson had become a kingpin in state Democratic politics, and he and other reformers had perceived control of the state government as a logical and necessary step for accomplishing their urban goals. In Ohio the state tightly controlled the cities, and, as the controversy over the federal plan and the municipal code had indicated, municipalities could find their structure and powers totally changed at the political whim of the state legislature or by a state court decision.

Howe summed up the problem as reformers saw it. With only the shadow of self-government, the city could not own or operate things or control private property. It was restricted in its ability to tax or borrow. The people could do "perfunctory things," but their hands were tied by the state constitution, the laws, the bosses, and the judges. "The city of Cleveland, like every other city in

---

20. *Taxation of Land Values*, 4–5; "Lure of the Land"; "Way Toward the Model City."
21. FCH to Daniel Kiefer, August 15, 1910, Bolton Hall Papers, New York Public Library.

the State, was ruled by the legislature; the fight for good government had to be carried to the State capital."[22]

Fred received the endorsement of the Municipal Association: "The county will be fortunate in securing as one of its representatives in the legislature a man of the type of Mr. Howe. He possesses mental ability of a high order and his character is above reproach." The Cuyahoga electorate agreed, and in November Howe led the Democratic senatorial ticket with 18,635 votes. All four Democratic candidates for the Senate won. The vote for the leading Republican candidate was 13,647. Fred commented to Harry Garfield that the results in Ohio were "a cross section of what is going on everywhere. It is an awakening preparatory to a new crystallization." He thought that crystallization would result "in the breaking of party lines all to pieces, and the ultimate reduction of partisanship to a mere organization for campaign purposes, with 20,000,000 independent voters ready to follow the square deal wherever it is presented."[23] Statewide, the Democrats elected their candidate for governor. In the Legislature the Senate had 18 Democrats, 18 Republicans, and an independent; the lower house had 62 Republicans, 57 Democrats, and 2 independents.

Senator Howe went to Columbus optimistic that the Democrats could work with Progressive Republicans to accomplish their program, which, after all, had received a mandate from the voters. The Democratic platform was clear: "it gave home rule to cities, gave them power to own and operate public-utility corporations, and do practically anything else that the people desired. It taxed railroads and public-utility corporations the same as other property. It committed us to a simple direct-primary law, to the initiative and referendum, and the recall." Fred saw no reason why this agenda could not be enacted in every detail. But when he expressed this belief to Ed Doty, the longtime clerk of the House, the response was a cynical laugh and the comment "You'll be lucky if you get one bill through."[24]

Howe quickly discovered the truth in that cynicism. Eager for the session to begin, he asked all the Democratic senators to meet in Columbus before the legislature convened, to work out the details of senate organization. At the conclave, he found that many of his colleagues were little concerned with legislation, had not read the party platform, and did not even understand the meaning of home rule, initiative and referendum, and direct primaries. What they were interested in was jobs. Mainly elderly farmers and small businessmen, "they were away from home for a good time. They did not want to be bothered about

22. *Confessions of a Reformer*, 157.
23. *Cleveland Plain Dealer*, November 2, 1905, 1; November 8, 1905, 2; FCH to Harry A. Garfield, November 13, 1905.
24. *Confessions of a Reformer*, 160–61.

ideals.... What they wanted was their share in the patronage—an insignificant job as stenographer, assistant, clerk, or messenger for a relative or friend."

After dividing up the jobs, they noticed that Fred had nothing. Asked what he wanted, he replied that he would like to be chairman of the committee on committees, a post that the others willingly gave him since it had no patronage connected with it. The Democrats organized the Senate and elected its officers, including Fred as chairman of the committee he wanted. Using this post, he packed the Senate committees. "I gave the reactionary senators unimportant assignments and put men who could be relied on in important positions."[25] The Republicans organized the House and practically ignored the reform Democrats in making assignments to the committees.

Howe soon found that the task of legislating was not easy. His own party was divided on many issues, as members from small towns and rural areas often disagreed with members from the cities and larger counties. On some measures, help could be expected from a few Republicans, as the movement for reform began to cut across party lines. Howe's bill to revise the real estate assessment laws was defeated in the Senate by a vote of twenty-three to eleven, despite "an earnest talk" by the senator. He tried to revive the bill on a motion to reconsider, but adjournment came before the Senate took it up.[26]

Defeat also came on a franchise tax bill introduced by Howe and strongly backed by Tom Johnson. It proposed a tax on the franchise value of public utilities, including railroads, the value to be based on the difference between the market value of their securities and the assessed valuation of their tangible property. Howe considered that the amount raised would be enough to free the counties from imposing any taxes for state purposes. Johnson laughingly said the measure's title should be "the bill to raise political h—l in Ohio." A majority in the Senate blocked action on the bill in the hurried final days before the session ended in March. At the same time, the House was defeating the Stockwell bill, a reform proposal designed to make it easier to grant franchises to new companies. Howe and the reformers blamed the blatant and vigorous opposition of lobbyists for the railroads and other corporations for the defeat of both measures.[27] Howe's bill to introduce the merit system into state government died in committee, as did another senator's proposal for the direct election of United States senators. Howe led the fight for a constitutional amendment providing for the initiative and the referendum, and the Senate approved it, but

---

25. Ibid., 161–62; FCH to Harry A. Garfield, January 13, 1906.

26. *Cleveland Plain Dealer*, January 19, 1906, 7; January 20, 1906, 226. *Cleveland Plain Dealer*, January 13, 1906; February 2, 1906; February 6, 1906; February 20, 1906.

27. Warner, *Progressivism in Ohio*, 177–78; *Cleveland Plain Dealer*, February 17, 1906, 4; March 30, 1906, 1.

the House failed to act. His bill to allow Cleveland and Cincinnati to keep their polling places open till 5:30 p.m. passed.

Most reformers were disappointed with the results of the 1906 legislative session. Fred Howe was more sanguine: some good legislation had passed, and the Legislature had at least done little harm. The measures that were pending on adjournment would come up again in the next session. "It is my great belief that in the present legislature great gain was made in preparatory work, there being open mindedness and comparatively little partisanship generally," he said. "All in all, it should be counted a satisfactory session."[28]

The legislature would not reconvene until January 1908, so Fred could turn his attention to other things. He had remained a partner in the Garfield law firm, even though his interest in practicing law had never been strong and his involvement had declined over the years. In the fall of 1906 an opportunity presented itself that took him finally away from the law. In September E. J. Ridgway, the publisher of *Everybody's Magazine,* announced plans for a new weekly magazine, to be published simultaneously in fourteen different cities. Each issue of *Ridgway's* would contain "telegraphic dispatches," articles, and fiction prepared centrally and distributed in advance to each city, plus a dozen pages of local material prepared by each city's editor. Thus the magazine, whose editorial policy would be "freedom from bias on any question, whether of politics, finance, religion, or statesmanship," would be both national and local in its content. Most of the local editors named by Ridgway were former newspaper editors or reporters. One of the few exceptions was Fred Howe, appointed as the Cleveland editor.[29]

His decision to accept the *Ridgway's* position meant his withdrawal from the law firm. The *Cleveland News* broke the story on October 8, 1906, in a brief parable entitled "Of Four Little Lawyers Only One Remains":

> Once upon a time there was a Law Firm that did slathers of soliciting and barristering for corporations and individuals and Waxed Well Off and added unto itself and called itself Garfield, Garfield, Howe & Westenhaver, or words to that effect, and inhabited a Great Pile called after itself, Garfield.
>
> Then one Garfield—he that was frontnamed Harry—was called hence and went and was a Professor of Political Polemics at Princeton. And that left only Garfield, Howe & Westenhaver.

---

28. *Cleveland Plain Dealer,* April 4, 1906, 6.
29. The other cities where *Ridgeway's* was to appear were New York, Boston, Washington, New Orleans, Chicago, Minneapolis, St. Louis, Pittsburgh, Denver, San Francisco, Seattle, Philadelphia, and Atlanta. *New York Times,* September 18, 1906, 4.

Then the other Garfield—for sake of contradistinction, Jimmy—journeyed down to the capital and got a Job in a department and arranged to work up. That left only Howe & Westenhaver.

Then Howe—which his full style and title is Frederic Copy—wearied of being a mere Lawyer, Legislator, Reformer and Author and got aboard as an Editor. That left only "& Westenhaver." When he goes, all that will be left of the law firm will be the "&."

In another item, the newspaper observed: "Editor Howe has unveiled his muck rake and expects to harrow deep the dirty pool of political stock jobbery, if he never mixes a metaphor." Max Rudolph, long associated with the law firm, confirmed Howe's departure in a letter to Harry Garfield: "Fred has withdrawn entirely from the firm; his resignation taking effect October 1st. His new work, as local editor of *Ridgway's*, a new publication, offers, we think, a splendid opportunity and as the position is quite lucrative we all think he is to be congratulated."[30]

"I did make a shift from the law to my first love very suddenly, without time to talk it over with anyone," Fred told Harry. "Yes, I am out of the law and have no regrets. It did me much good and put me on my feet and was a fine, happy experience in many ways, but it never satisfied me. I presume your philosophy that the things you want will come to you if you ought to have them is pretty nearly true, still I feel that it should be modified somewhat by saying that it comes quicker to those who hustle while they wait." Thus far, the editorial work had been "very arduous," and "beastly exacting to a man who has lived his own life as I have for so many years." He had been up all night and expected few holidays, but even a lot of work was play when a man enjoyed it. "I now feel that I am a producer as I have not been for a long time. Of course this is not fair to the law, but it is my feeling about it." Marie would help him edit the Cleveland magazine.[31]

Nearly twenty years later Howe appraised his legal career in Cleveland more harshly than he had in the October 1906 letter to Garfield. His early years at the bar had been made "tolerable" only through the close association with the two Garfields. He had never overcome his dislike for the law, and even the successes

---

30. *Cleveland News*, October 8, 1906; Max J. Rudolph to Harry A. Garfield, October 13, 1906. The process of winding up the affairs of Garfield, Howe and Westenhaver took until the summer of 1908. The library and the office furniture and fixtures had to be inventoried and appraised and the assets distributed among the partners. On July 1, 1908, D. C. Westenhaver, Max J. Rudolph, and two other attorneys announced their partnership, consolidating the business and law offices of Garfield, Howe and Westenhaver: Max J. Rudolph to Harry A. Garfield, March 6, 1908; FCH to Harry A. Garfield, April 4, 1908; announcement of new firm in Harry A. Garfield Papers.

31. FCH to Harry A. Garfield, October 19, 1906.

gave him little pleasure. He found trial work "distasteful" and was especially annoyed by the law's long delays. Personal-injury and workmen's compensation cases, in which the applicable law stemmed from medieval times, were particularly distasteful. Criminal cases were more interesting, and he was more successful with them. "I liked the personal problems involved, liked to go back into the life and experiences of men and women and find the thing that had started them wrong. Then having found the cause—it might be parental neglect, a chance escapade, some trouble with the police that marked them as suspect—I would make this the crux of my argument before the jury."[32]

The law as an institution aroused "a deep and fundamental protest" within him, Howe explained. He liked freedom, change, movement, the very things that the law—"a dead man's philosophy"—stood against. It was the dead hand of the past that made lawyers "peculiarly unfitted for public office. They resist change. They are instinctively hostile to anything new. They are inexperienced in constructive things. Their professional life and training is associated with the past. They want the past preserved." It was in their interest to retain as much complexity in the law as possible.[33]

Judges, too, were at fault, Howe argued. Tom Johnson would have nominated Howe to a judgeship if he had wanted it, but he had declined. "I wanted to take part in the affairs of the community. To be denied the right to express my own opinions was to be a man without a country. I resented the elevation of the courts above the people, their freedom from criticism, and the sanctity with which judges enveloped themselves." A judge should be as subject to criticism as any other public official. "He was merely an agent and as such no more sacrosanct than the mayor. The courts were agencies for administering one kind of justice, the city and the State agencies for administering another kind."[34] Courts had acquired their power to interfere with legislation outside the constitution, not as a constitutional empowerment. Reverence for them benefited the corporate interests that really picked the judges.

Howe believed that to work within the legal system, he had had to keep silent, challenge nothing, compromise with his conscience, become, in effect, part of the system.[35] Only financial independence and a determination to "keep

32. *Confessions of a Reformer*, 199, 200.
33. Ibid., 200–201.
34. Ibid., 202.
35. Ibid., 205, 211. Howe's thoughts on law and judges were more strongly expressed in his autobiography than at the time he left the law, but they are consistent with his opinions at that earlier time. In a letter to James Garfield in 1905, for example, he favored administrative rate making to judicial: "The power of review in the federal courts over a rate-making commission seems like an appeal from one doctor to another in case of emergency. As a matter of fact, it suggests an appeal from a skillful surgeon to an untrained lawyer, for the courts are lacking in just the special training which the Interstate Commerce Commission is supposed to have. Moreover, the latter commission

my opinions straight" and do what he could to change the world allowed him to break free from the system. The editorship of *Ridgway's* and his increasingly successful writing gave him the opportunity to do so.

The new magazine seemed likely to be both intellectually challenging and financially rewarding. "The whole thing was on a novel and extravagant scale. The magazine was advertised widely and we anticipated a great success," Howe wrote. Appearing in fourteen cities on October 6, the first issue resembled a newspaper except for its orange, green, and black covers and halftone illustrations. Throughout the country, its production had to contend with all sorts of glitches: paper or covers were not delivered on time, halftones arrived buckled, presses broke down, uniform type was not supplied to all offices, so that editorials and articles, carefully planned to fit certain spaces, proved too long in some cities and too short in others. Nevertheless, *Ridgway's Weekly* came out on schedule, and in most of its cities it had sold out by early afternoon.

With Marie's help, Fred had worked for weeks on the Cleveland edition, hardly leaving the printing office for the two days before the issue appeared. He recounts that when the magazine went to press, he fell asleep, only to be awakened by a man holding a copy of *Ridgway's* in his hand. "'Are you the editor of this sheet?' he asked. I proudly admitted that I was. 'Well, look at it,' he said. 'I could get out a better-looking thing than that down in Bucyrus.' I looked at the magazine. The first page was a blur. The second, third, and fourth pages were no better. It could hardly be read. The promoters in New York had failed to try out the idea of printing a magazine on a high-power newspaper press." He soon learned that editors in other cities had experienced a similar problem. They, like Howe, were in the "sloughs of discomfiture." The New York management seemed to shrug off the difficulties.

Weekly publication continued, and so did the blurring, and after six weeks the owner decided to end the fourteen-city plan. The magazine would appear in only four cities, and Cleveland was not to be one. The project had cost more than five hundred thousand dollars, and, as Howe pointed out, it "might have succeeded had a single printing been tried out before the enterprise was launched."[36] Its failure was a blow to Fred, and undoubtedly to Marie as well. It was certainly an important factor in their decision to leave Cleveland.

That decision was not to come for several years, however. In the meantime, Fred had his political and legislative work and his writing to occupy his time.

---

is a judicial body made up of lawyers of as high ability in the main as usually find their way to the courts." FCH to James R. Garfield, January 4, 1905. He told Garfield in another letter that he believed the courts "have usurped the functions and prerogatives which were never bestowed upon them." FCH to James R. Garfield, February 3, 1906.

36. *Confessions of a Reformer*, 231–32; *New York Times*, October 7, 1906, 9.

His sphere of activities expanded as he became a national figure in Progressivism. Through James Garfield, he had a channel to express his opinions on Teddy Roosevelt's policies, with the hope that they might be passed on to the president. He praised Garfield for the Bureau of Corporations' report on Standard Oil and told his friend his favorable opinion of Roosevelt's battle with Congress for reform legislation. He warned Garfield of the machinations of Mark Hanna and the opposition of financial and commercial interests to Roosevelt's renomination in 1904, and urged the president to take his case to the people, who liked Roosevelt's courage. "He never cried 'quits.' And they like a strong executive, and care very little for delicate conventionalities so long as the appeal is sincerely made in a straightforward way." Howe found much to admire in the president's policies, including his propensity for economic regulation by executive action, rather than reliance on the courts.[37]

Fred expanded his circle of acquaintances as he met or corresponded with a growing number of reformers across the country. He became a member of the executive committee of the National Municipal League, and in October 1906 he agreed to join the board of governors of the People's Lobby, a new nonpartisan watchdog group that planned both to supply national legislators with factual information and to keep an eye on their public activities. "Representatives and senators will be a little more careful how they act if they know that the folks at home will be made aware of their actions," Howe predicted. Fellow board members included Louis Brandeis, Samuel L. Clemens (Mark Twain), Judge Ben Lindsey, John Mitchell (president of the United Mine Workers), Steffens, Mark Sullivan, and William Allen White. Work with the People's Lobby began a long association between Howe and Benjamin Marsh.[38] He aided the Boston 1915 movement for planning that city's development. He spoke at Golden Rule Hall in Toledo at Whitlock's invitation and at New York City's Cooper Union in 1907 on nominations and ballot reform. He became prominent nationally in the single-tax movement, joining such people as Whitlock, Bolton Hall, Joseph Fels, and Henry George Jr. as an "advisory and contributing editor" of Louis Post's *Public*.[39]

As the second session of the legislature neared, Howe again tried to organize the Democratic senators. He proposed that they be bound by their caucus to united action on legislation recommended by their party platform. His colleagues voted this down but agreed to set up an advisory committee to inform

37. FCH to James A. Garfield, May 5, 1905; January 18, 1904; January 4, 1905.
38. *Cleveland Plain Dealer*, October 10, 1906, 7; December 24, 1906, 4. Benjamin Marsh was for many years the "people's lobbyist" for all sorts of good causes and remained the leader of the People's Lobby till his death in 1962. See his *Lobbyist for the People*.
39. Post, "Living A Long Life Over Again," 226a.

members about bills and to work for their passage. Fred and a few other reform senators opposed those in both parties who wanted to wipe the legislature's calendar clean and to begin anew on all the bills left over from the first session, but they lost after a bitter discussion. Fred blamed special interests for the defeat.[40]

Conservatives in both parties were ready to unite against any proposals backed by Tom Johnson. Howe's franchise tax bill, one of Johnson's favorites, again met fierce opposition from corporation lobbyists. Fred pointed out in vain that a billion dollars' worth of corporate property went untaxed in Ohio and that the tax burden fell upon the laboring man and the wage earner. But the senate proceeded to defeat his bill by a vote of twenty to fifteen. Howe reintroduced his tax assessment measure, which was adopted by the Senate after some maneuvering, only to be pigeonholed in the House. The Senate approved a proposal to amend the state constitution to introduce the initiative and the referendum, but opponents of direct legislation in the House adopted weakening changes, a conference committee could not work out a compromise, and the bill died. So did an initiative and referendum bill applying only to municipalities. Howe led the fight for both measures. In the parliamentary maneuvering on the local government bill, tempers ran high, and two senators "rushed at Howe as though they would tear him to pieces. The Cleveland senator not only stood his ground but drove his tormentors back. 'Kill the bill if you like, kill it I say,' cried Howe. 'But you have got to go on record. You cannot strangle the bill to death in the dark.'"[41] The Legislature managed to pass a bill providing for direct primaries to nominate county and local officers, but not state officers or members of Congress.

There were some victories interspersed with the defeats. The Legislature approved what the *Plain Dealer* called "Howe's pet measure," a law setting up a commission to investigate conditions in the state penitentiary. The legislature also adopted an act banning the employment of children under the age of fourteen and limiting their employment between the ages of fourteen and sixteen. Marie Howe and other representatives of the Consumers League, the state's women's clubs, and the labor unions had lobbied hard for passage, and Fred joined the bill's sponsor in beating off amendments to weaken the measure. Supported by the Legal Aid Society and the Associated Charities of Cleveland, he also worked for a bill to regulate interest rates charged by pawnbrokers, but

---

40. *Cleveland Plain Dealer*, January 7, 1908, 10. On these events, and the session generally, see Warner, *Progressivism in Ohio*, 192–202. The state constitution was amended in 1905 to provide for legislative elections in even, rather than odd, years, so the terms of legislators elected in 1905 extended to 1908, rather than 1907.

41. *Cleveland Plain Dealer*, January 31, 1908, 1; April 29, 1908, 8.

the measure failed to pass. Howe chaired a meeting of legislators, mayors, and charitable officials that called on the legislature to set up public works programs with jobs for the unemployed, but nothing came of this initiative.[42]

As in Howe's term on the city council, probably the most exciting event in his senatorial term was an investigation. For some time, it had been suspected that corruption existed in the state treasurer's office and that the treasurer was lining his own pockets with public funds. An investigation by the Republican-controlled house in 1902 failed to find any evidence of wrongdoing, but the Democrats remained unconvinced. The Cleveland legislative delegation revived the idea of an investigation in 1908, and when the Republican House failed to act, the job fell to the Senate Democrats, and to Howe, as chairman of the finance committee.

Accompanied by newspapermen, he visited the treasurer's office and asked to see the money in the vaults. When the treasurer, W. S. McKinnon, refused, Howe demanded the right as finance committee chairman and as a citizen to look at the books. "The treasurer lost his temper. 'It's none of your damn business,' he said, 'either as a senator or as a citizen where I keep the money or how I run my office.'" The remark made headlines all over the state, and the Senate immediately adopted a resolution, introduced by Howe, to appoint a three-man committee (two Democrats, one Republican, with Howe as chair) to investigate the state treasurer's office. The treasurer was uncooperative in the hearings that followed, but the investigation uncovered many irregularities, including the fact that McKinnon, the treasurer, had great difficulty in keeping state finances separate from those of McKinnon, the banker.[43] The Senate then expanded its investigation to include the state auditor and other officials, and the House got into the act by setting up its own investigation of the auditor. In April McKinnon left for a long trip for his "health." Republicans charged that the Senate probe was pure politics.

In May the majority of the Senate's investigating committee brought in its findings. For the two Democrats, Howe reported shoddy or nonexistent record keeping in the treasurer's and auditor's offices. Although they had discovered no graft, they had found evidence of favoritism in the deposit of state money and charged that "the office of treasurer has been administered with the grossest disregard of the public welfare." The Republican member of the investigating committee dissented, arguing that there was no evidence of dishonesty and that

---

42. Ibid., May 1, 1908, 1; FCH to Brand Whitlock, February 10, 1908, Whitlock Papers; *Cleveland Plain Dealer*, February 5, 1908, 8; February 26, 1908, 2; April 24, 1908, 9; February 28, 1908, 8.

43. *Confessions of a Reformer*, 164. "McKinnon, as treasurer, had used his position to favor McKinnon, as banker, placing state funds at low interest rates on deposit in banking institutions in which he held stock." Warner, *Progressivism in Ohio*, 201.

there had been no loss of public funds.⁴⁴ Like the investigation of bribery in the Cleveland city council, the investigation of corruption in the state treasurer's domain ended with no consensus, but the Democrats were pleased that they had exposed serious irregularities and developed a political issue.

Reformers were moderately happy with the results of the 1908 legislative session, but Frederic Howe was not. He came away from the Legislature with scant respect for the laws of the land. "I had seen how they were made. Some were frankly bought and paid for. Many were passed the last day. Only occasionally were bills in the public interest forced through by the pressure of public opinion. And these were so crippled with amendments that they were of little value. A great part of the laws was so much rubbish." He wrote Steffens that there were many times when "gloomy" would be "a correct mirror of my soul. There is nothing so calculated to drive the iron into one's system as a legislative assembly, for nowhere do all of the excesses of our money madness appear so constantly as here and nowhere are the motives which animate men in political life so apparent." Howe wished he could tell people the complete story "so that some at least might see how they are betrayed by institutions that they deem so sacred." He felt that he had sacrificed two years of his life to the Legislature when he should have been doing something more constructive. "For while I have done a good deal and have wakened many people in the state so that there may be an awakening in the near future, there is mighty little that is tangible to show for it and a loss of mental poise that I fear I can never get back."

All in all, he preferred the machine politician to the average reformer, he told Steffens. "For the vulgar grafter becomes so lovable and so harmless in comparison with his smug and highly respectable neighbor. The fellows who take money and who look you in the eye with a knowledge that you know they graft, but who have a ground wire with the soil and go straight on the great mass of questions on which they are not bought are so much less dangerous and cost the state so little in comparison with the fellows who go wrong on every question through class instinct or party expediency."⁴⁵

Yet there was much about the legislative life that attracted Fred. He worked hard but found time to enjoy dining and playing cards with the lobbyists. Brand Whitlock gives a picture of Howe as state senator: "Fred is a Doctor of Philosophy and when he was in the State Senate his opponents used to refer to him sedulously as 'Dr.' which, of course, did him a great deal of harm in politics. But I don't think he was as solemn as he looked or as you seem to think him. He was fond of a game of poker and a tot of whisky now and then." Howe

---

44. *Cleveland Plain Dealer*, May 10, 1908, 7; *Confessions of a Reformer*, 164–65. The investigation is examined in Warner, *Progressivism in Ohio*, 200–202.

45. *Confessions of a Reformer*, 166; FCH to Steffens, February 29, 1908.

wrote: "I liked the intimacy, the activity, the struggle. This was America. The legislature was a cross-section of the people. And I was so confident of the justice of our measures that I never lost hope."[46]

When all was said and done, he admitted at the end of the second session that Ed Doty had been right in his cynicism. Both the Democrats' political program and Howe's political creed had been defeated. By all the rules of popular government, the Democrats should have won a sweeping victory and enacted their entire program. They had the backing of the press and the support of the people, and there were intelligent legislators in both parties. But for some reason the government did not work. "It stalled, it did not function. Bosses remained unshaken in their power; our measures were buried in committees or crippled by amendment. . . . We could only win a skirmish, never a battle. We were defeated by the very instrument that was designed to insure popular government. The political machinery itself was at fault; that was the trouble."[47]

Nevertheless, Howe agreed to accept renomination to the Senate. He and other Cuyahoga County candidates campaigned in the usual tent meetings. He spoke frequently on state and national taxes. He was the stereopticon specialist for the Democrats, educating his listeners with "his picture talk in which he showed many street car buildings and commented upon the financial statements of the Municipal for the past five months." But it was mainly a Republican year in Ohio. The party's presidential candidate, William Howard Taft, carried the state, and the voters gave the Republicans a comfortable majority in the state legislature. All the Democratic candidates for the state senate from Cuyahoga County went down to defeat. Howe was second among the three Democratic losers with 41,840 votes, almost 11,000 fewer than the lowest Republican candidate's total.[48]

Still other Cleveland defeats lay ahead for Howe. The street railway controversy had not ended in the spring of 1908 with the agreement between the city and ConCon that Municipal Traction, the "Muny," should operate all lines with a three-cent fare. After a disastrous strike over job security and wages ended, disgruntled workers—backed by Republicans, the Cleveland Railway Company, some of the newspapers, and anti-Johnson business organizations—used a new law to force a referendum on the franchise grants. Things were not going well

---

46. Brand Whitlock to Julian Street, January 4, 1933, in Nevins, *Letters and Journal of Brand Whitlock*, 2:537; *Confessions of a Reformer*, 166.
47. *Confessions of a Reformer*, 168.
48. *Cleveland Plain Dealer*, October 10, 1908, 2; October 17, 1908, 12; October 18, 1908, 2; October 23, 1908, 2; November 5, 1908, 3. On the 1908 election in Ohio generally, see Warner, *Progressivism in Ohio*, 211–22.

for the Muny, which had had to raise fares and cut service and was near bankruptcy. The Johnson camp failed to run an effective campaign and lost the referendum in October 1908 by a small margin, 38,249 votes to 37,644. Howe saw the vote as a significant one. The people had spoken and turned the street railway lines back to the old companies. "Their victory was an empty one, for their dividends were limited to six per cent and could not exceed a fixed amount, while the rate of fare started at three cents and rose or fell as earnings might determine. But the city had lost. A great movement was ended. The dream of municipal ownership, of a free and sovereign city, was set back indefinitely." The Muny came to an end, the lines went into receivership, and the court directed a settlement that (modified after two referendums) returned the lines to the Cleveland Railway Company in March 1910. "This defeat was Tom Johnson's death-blow," Howe wrote. "For eight years he had given every bit of intelligence, every ounce of energy he possessed to the city. When victory was in his hand, the people turned against him."[49]

There was still one more campaign left in the mayor, however, and Fred was once again at his side. Despite his deteriorating health, Johnson sought reelection and won his party's nomination in September 1909, in the first direct primary in Cleveland's history. Howe was also a primary winner, this time as a candidate for the board of quadrennial assessors.

In March 1909 the legislature had finally enacted the changes on tax assessments that Howe had fought for during his term in the senate. Quadrennial assessments would replace decennial ones, and each city was to choose, in a nonpartisan election, five appraisers to serve four-year terms. As Howe had urged, the board was to publicize its appraisal list and to mail it to every resident. The choice of Cleveland's five appraisers was a matter of great concern to the city's newspapers, real estate interests and businessmen generally, and the parties, since the men elected would have power to make many changes in assessments. Although the names of the candidates were to appear on the ballot without party designations, numerous Republicans and Democrats sought nominations, and both parties made endorsements. The Municipal Association endorsed five Republicans and five Democrats. In its tepid recommendation of Howe as one of the Democrats, it said: "Mr. Howe's general knowledge of taxation matters would seem to qualify him for the office."[50] The Real Estate Board endorsed eight candidates, not including Howe.

49. Murdock, "Life of Tom L. Johnson," 407–12; *Confessions of a Reformer*, 126 See also D. Young, *Twentieth-Century Experience in Urban Transit*, 6–8, and, for a contemporary analysis by a Johnson supporter, Bemis, "Cleveland Referendum." Harry Garfield was critical of Johnson's methods in the street railway fight; see his "Private Rights in Street Railways."

50. Sidlo, "Ohio's First Step in Tax Reform"; *Cleveland Plain Dealer*, September 2, 1909, 1. The Association's bulletin gave more space to its Republican choices than to its Democratic recommendations.

In the primary voting Fred led the Democratic candidates with 8,383 votes (almost 2,000 more than the second Democrat) and was nominated. The *Plain Dealer* called for the election of four candidates (one Republican and three Democrats) recommended by the Real Estate Board; Howe did not receive the paper's endorsement. In November the voters elected four Democrats and one Republican to the board of quadrennial assessors. Howe was one of the successful Democrats. His 26,791 votes placed him fourth among the candidates, but 800 fewer votes would have meant another defeat.[51]

Tom Johnson lost his bid for a fifth term as mayor. Although he tried to make taxation the main issue in the campaign, the voters seemed still to focus on the street railway problems. Howe had been sure that Johnson would win, he wrote Lincoln Steffens, and there had been no reason to expect the defeat. Maybe the people were "tired of agitation that they did not share in and could not understand. It is so much easier to hold your crowd when you preach than it is when you do things especially when the things you are doing hurt so many people's predispositions about the sanctity of things. Maybe too the saying of some of the women really explained it better than any others and that was that the Mayor had been there long enough and they wanted a change, much as they wanted a new bonnet." The election was virtually a Republican sweep except for the victories of Newton Baker as city solicitor and the four Democrats as tax assessors.[52]

State law required the board of assessors to begin its work by January 15 and to finish by July 1. It lost no time in getting started. On November 20, less than three weeks after its election, Howe moved that the board hire a tax and land valuation expert, W. A. Somers, to put his system into effect in Cleveland, and the four Democrats passed the motion over the objections of the sole Republican member. The "Somers system" assessed land separately from improvements, used a committee of experts to appraise the land uniformly (making no distinction between vacant or underused land and fully built-up land), and assessed improvements on the basis of their reproduction value. In a number of large cities where the system had been used, the result had been an increase in assessments, greater uniformity, a reduction in land speculation, and a stimulation of improvements. Howe called it "the only scientific method known."[53] The board agreed that property should be assessed at full value.

Despite occasional difficulties, the board completed its work by the statutory deadline of July 1. It had supervised the appraisal of nearly one hundred and

---

51. Ibid., September 8, 1909, 8; November 4, 1909, 4.
52. FCH to Lincoln Steffens, Nov. 7, 1909. On the election, see Murdock, "Life of Tom L. Johnson," 423–29; Finegold, *Experts and Politicians*, 98–100; M. McCarthy, "Suburban Power."
53. *Cleveland Plain Dealer*, November 21, 1909, 9. The "Somers system" and the results of its use in a number of cities are summarized in Griffith, *History of American City Government*, 4:187–88.

fifty thousand parcels of land and one hundred thousand buildings and had increased the assessment of all property in Cleveland from less than 200 million dollars to 500 million dollars. It believed that it had produced more uniform and equitable assessments than ever before in Cleveland's history. It printed the assessments in pamphlet form and mailed them to all residents. Although the board was legally precluded from seeking a single-tax solution, Georgists were happy with its work as a first step. Howe found his work with the board "the most satisfying experience of my political life. It confirmed my belief in the results that would follow the taxation of land values and the exemption of improvements from taxation."[54]

Once the assessors' work was done, Fred and Marie escaped to their summer home in Sconset, where they must have spent a good part of their time considering their future. Fred wrote in his autobiography that he had thought things over when in Europe in the summer of 1909 and had decided on a move to New York. When he returned to Cleveland on primary election day (September 7, 1909), he "went directly to the voting-booth. There I discovered that I had been nominated by Mr. Johnson for the Tax Commission." He decided that he would postpone his departure since he could not pass up "the chance to do a piece of constructive work. It meant that I could try out our theories in practice."[55]

Except for his autobiographical account, written fifteen years later, there is no direct evidence on the Howes' decision to leave Cleveland, and there are reasons to doubt that the decision had been firmly made as early as the summer of 1909. It seems that Fred had been thinking about a break as early as the fall of 1908, when he told Steffens that he was planning a short trip to New York, apparently to look into his prospects there. "I want to get to work where I can do the most good," he wrote. "I don't know where that is. Do you? I have more liking for editorial work than for anything else and if I have any convictions about life at all it is that one's first obligation is to express himself." When he was teaching at Wisconsin in 1909, he indicated his ambivalence in another letter to Steffens: "I could drift into comfortable idleness in a University or back into the battle with almost equal ease. At least that has been my feeling for the past few weeks. But it is passing and by the first of the year I will be ready to follow the first sound of the Marseillaise that greets my ears."[56]

Fred and Marie may well have discussed the situation during 1908 and 1909 and reached some tentative conclusions. Fred went on with his activities in the spring of 1910, as if he planned a continuing career in Ohio politics and government. In May, for example, he helped write the Democratic county platform, a

54. FCH, *Confessions of a Reformer*, 230. See also Bremner, "Tax Equalization in Cleveland."
55. *Confessions of a Reformer*, 225–26.
56. FCH to Lincoln Steffens, November 15, 1908; November 24, 1909, Steffens Papers.

program that stood squarely for progressive reform. The county convention named him a delegate to the state Democratic convention and renominated him for the state senate.[57] He did not indicate in these actions any intent to abandon Ohio politics. Nothing in his extant correspondence for the period referred to a decision to do so until the fall of 1910.

So it is hard to say exactly when a conclusion was reached. Certainly the summer of 1910 must have been a time for serious reflection by the Howes on their future course. If a change was to be made, the moment seemed propitious. After her independence in Iowa, Marie undoubtedly found herself limited in her sphere of activities in Cleveland, even though her husband's view of their appropriate scope was altering. He wrote in his autobiography: "As I look back over those years I realize that I never honestly faced what I was doing or the rightfulness of my wife's claims. It was not until we came to New York, where the suffrage movement was claiming women of distinction, where no more notice was taken of a woman in work than a man, that I recast my prejudices. My mind did not do it, new standards did. Then I was as eager for her to find her work as I had been loath in Cleveland. And she rapidly found opportunities to her liking."[58]

With her health apparently improved, Marie was ready to plunge into New York's exciting battle for woman suffrage and its stimulating intellectual environment. She encouraged Fred to consider a change. There was no economic reason to keep them in Cleveland. The law firm was dissolved, and the local version of *Ridgway's* was defunct. They had a comfortable income from investments, and Fred's writing could be done anywhere. Their Cleveland ties had been weakened with the Garfields' departures, leaving only Newton Baker and the mortally ill Tom Johnson as close friends in the city.

A chance for a new start appealed to Fred. Despite many successes, he had experienced a string of disappointments: electoral rejections, legislative frustrations, the failure of *Ridgway's*, the defeats in the street railway battles. The people seemed to have turned their backs on Tom Johnson and on reform policies. He had found little satisfaction in his profession, the law, and gladly gave it up. At the same time, his horizons had been broadening. His books and articles were bringing national recognition; his political interests were extending beyond Cleveland and Columbus; and he was getting to know the national movers and

---

57. *Cleveland Plain Dealer*, May 22, 1910, 1. The county platform attacked the tariff and the trusts, called for "full and complete" government regulation of railways and public service corporations, urged extension of the initiative, the referendum, and the recall, advocated limitation of the working hours of women and children, and supported full home rule and the commission form of government for cities.

58. *Confessions of a Reformer*, 233.

shakers in what was becoming known as the Progressive Movement. For Fred, as for Marie, as for so many others over the years, New York City promised a new start, a new chapter, new beginnings in an exciting environment.

Tom Johnson tried to dissuade Fred. Though weak and gravely ill, the mayor undertook a tour of England (where he met leading single taxers and interested himself in their work) and the continent. In July 1910 he went to Sconset to summer with the Howes. Elizabeth Hauser, who completed Johnson's autobiography, wrote that he became a friend of every man, woman, and child with whom he came in contact. "Declining physical strength did not seem to lessen the charm of manner which gave him such a hold on the minds and hearts of all who came his way."[59] During that relaxing time at Sconset, he explored the Howes' plans with them and, according to Fred, did his best to persuade them to remain in Cleveland and take up the fight again. "But I wanted to be doing work of my own and wished to get away from the hatreds, the conflict, the ostracism which I professed not to mind. And I felt that Mr. Johnson only half believed that the fight could be renewed.[60] Though Howe felt guilty about leaving Johnson, he remained unpersuaded.

The existing correspondence seems to show that Fred and Marie had reached a final decision by September 1910. At that time, Newton Baker urged Fred (writing to him at the City Club in New York) to come back to Cleveland and make a few political speeches, but observed that when he mentioned this to Johnson, "he seemed a little impatient at any obligations being thrown on you in the matter." On October 5 Baker wrote Johnson: "I am inclined to believe that Fred's determination to withdraw from the ticket is wise, this particularly for the reason of Marie's decided preference for New York and also Fred's manifest fitness for the particular work he is now doing and the effectiveness of the work as compared with the distressingly small opportunities which the Ohio legislature is likely to afford with a reactionary governor and some other impediments upon progress." On October 13 the *Plain Dealer* reported Johnson's announcement of Howe's resignation as a candidate for the state senate and noted that "Howe resigned in order to live in New York, where he desires to follow literary pursuits." On October 17 Baker wrote Fred: "I am delighted that you are finally settled in New York and look forward with happy anticipation to your winter there. In this world's maladjustments it does give a distinct pleasure to find a man who not only realizes the thing he is best fitted for, but finds happiness in that work and is able to arrange his affairs so that he can do it under most favorable circumstances." Baker knew that he himself was not

---

59. T. Johnson, *My Story*, 303.
60. *Confessions of a Reformer*, 225.

adapted to that life but realized that "you and Marie are especially fitted for it and I know that you are going to be happy there."[61] The break with Cleveland was accomplished.

Tom Johnson had left Sconset in August and returned to Cleveland, where he worked on his autobiography with Elizabeth Hauser, who had been introduced to him by the Howes. He died in Cleveland in April 1911. Fred was one of the pallbearers who escorted the casket to Greenwood Cemetery in Brooklyn, where Johnson's grave was placed next to that of Henry George.[62]

---

61. Newton Baker to FCH, September 8, 1910; Baker to Tom Johnson, October 5, 1910; *Cleveland Plain Dealer*, October 13, 1910, 16; Baker to FCH, October 17, 1910, Baker Papers.

62. The last months of Johnson's life are described by Hauser in *My Story*, 295–313, and in Murdock, "Life of Tom L. Johnson," 439–49. A brief summary of Johnson's municipal achievements may be found in Griffith, *History of American City Government*, 4:146–48. Melvin G. Holli offers a brief biography in *American Mayor*, 52–58. In a ranking of big-city mayors in the period 1820–1993, a panel of experts put Johnson in second place among the "best" mayors, behind only Fiorello La Guardia of New York City. Holli, 5.

8

UPRISING AND UPLIFTING

The New York City Fred and Marie Howe found in the fall of 1910 was not the city Fred had known in 1894. It was larger, more sprawling, more congested. In 1898 it had tripled its area and doubled its population when Brooklyn, Queens, and Staten Island merged with Manhattan and the Bronx to create Greater New York. The composition of its population had changed as the last decades of the nineteenth century and the first of the twentieth brought a great influx of immigrants from southern and eastern Europe, mainly Italians and Russian Jews. The tide of immigrants overwhelmed Castle Garden, the old reception center at the Battery, and forced the federal government to transfer its immigration operations in 1890 to Ellis Island, near the Statue of Liberty. There it had constructed a complex of buildings to handle the admission or rejection of the aliens. A large proportion of the new arrivals remained in the city. By 1910 the city had almost 4.8 million people, nearly half of them living in Manhattan, and concern began to be expressed about the congestion of the metropolis.

The city was thronged not only with residents but also with thousands of commuters who arrived daily by train and ferry to work there. Fast and efficient transportation was now being provided by the subways (the fare, a nickel, not to be raised till after World War II), the first of which had begun operation in 1904. Most New Yorkers had seen the first horseless carriages on their streets in the 1896 Decoration Day races when a Duryea defeated two other Duryeas and a Benz, and many had attended the first automobile show at Madison Square Garden in 1900. By 1910 the streets were filled with cars.

New York City in the second decade of the century was a great place for anyone interested in politics, government, and reform. New York State was a crucial swing state in every presidential election, and the city, with its large electorate, had a decisive impact on state and national politics. The electoral demographics made local politics a matter of national attention. The municipal battle generally pitted a reform coalition against Tammany Hall, the Manhattan Democratic organization, which by 1910 had spread its influence to Brooklyn as well. To reformers, Tammany typified bossism, corruption, and machine rule. The mayor in 1910 was William J. Gaynor, who in 1909 had triumphed over a Republican candidate and an independent ticket led by William Randolph Hearst. Tammany had picked Gaynor as a politically respectable candidate, and the nominee had asserted his independence from the Democratic organization during the campaign. As mayor, he cut the municipal payroll and filled the top jobs with capable men. He and other mayors found the enlarged city difficult to govern and turned increasingly to experts and the new Bureau of Municipal Research (founded in 1907) for assistance in dealing with the varied and complicated municipal problems.[1] A reformer could hardly find a better or more exciting place to observe and to take part in local and national politics.

The Frederic Howe who took up residence in the bustling metropolis in 1910 was quite a different man from the Frederic Howe who had left it unhappily sixteen years before. Then, he was unemployed and discouraged, returning to Meadville in defeat to read law with his uncle. Now, at the age of forty-three, he was successful enough financially to leave the Garfield firm, and confident enough in himself to abandon the security of an established place in Cleveland for the uncertainties of life in New York. He had experienced electoral wins and losses, and, as part of Tom Johnson's inner circle for almost a decade, he had played an important role in Cleveland politics. He had gained governmental experience through service in the city council, the state senate, and the board of assessors. Through his books and articles, he had achieved national recognition as a student of the city and its problems and as a spokesman for municipal reform. Falling under Johnson's sway, he had become a Democrat, but a Democrat who understood the desirability of broad-based reform coalitions of Progressive Democrats, Republicans, and independents. He had embraced democracy and the single tax as the chief weapons in the war against privilege and monopoly. He saw the need for government to play a broader role and, Fabian-like, was moving beyond municipal ownership toward appreciation of the need for active intervention by the federal government in the nation's economic life. Recognizing the value of the instruments of direct democracy—the referendum, the initiative, the recall—he emphasized them less than did many

---

1. For a thumbnail sketch of Gaynor as mayor, see Sayre and Kaufman, *Governing New York City,* 694. On the independent Bureau of Municipal Research, see G. Hopkins, "New York Bureau of Municipal Research"; Dahlberg, *New York Bureau of Municipal Research;* Cerillo, *Reform in New York City,* 81–94.

other Progressives. He accepted woman suffrage intellectually, if not emotionally. He had become increasingly concerned with European affairs. His eyes there were fixed on Britain and Germany, with some attention to the attractiveness of the smaller democracies, especially Denmark and its cooperative movement. He realized that what he had seen in Cleveland and other American municipalities were not simply local matters but parts of a national and international picture.

The political and economic views he brought eastward with him had found their most recent crystallization in his new book, *Privilege and Democracy in America,* published by Scribner's in March of 1910. Howe argued that the open domain of the public lands of the West had made America free, and economic liberty had molded its political institutions. Surely our resources were intended for the people as a whole, but now those who owned the land owned the government. Control over economic, and hence also political, life had narrowed to domination by a small group of bankers. The power of those "Titans of finance" rested on monopolies created by statutes written by the ruling class. National, state, and local laws had created both the millionaire and the pauper, both the palace and the slum. "The line of division is not between the capitalist and the wage-earner; it is between those who are encamped within and those who are encamped without the citadel of laws which the ascendant class has erected for its own advantage."[2]

Consequently, feudalism—"the power of one class to live upon the labor of another class without giving any service in return"—still reigned in America. Democracy had abolished the appearances of class rule but not its substance. The cost of monopoly by a few had been poverty for the many, a more relentless struggle for existence, and a constantly falling standard of living.[3]

Why were the Astors, Rockefellers, Carnegies, and Morgans rich, while other men, equally talented, earned no more than a bare living, and millions lived in fear of sickness, industrial depression, or some other calamity that would disable the wage earner? The explanation lay in private ownership of land and its effects on society. The burden of rent strangled the production of wealth. No improvement in the well-being of humanity could be expected so long as private ownership of land prevailed. Though reforms might bring temporary relief, "so long as the private ownership of the land remains, wages and interest must tend to fall to the subsistence level, to the point where the wage-earner can only sustain life."[4]

2. *Privilege and Democracy in America,* 18, 44, 63, 203.
3. Ibid., 80, 82, 150–51.
4. Ibid., 186, 171, 200.

The forces of privilege escaped taxes, which were levied mainly on the things the poor consumed and not on wealth, income, or inheritance. Privilege "compels the consumer to maintain a government whose expenditures are largely devoted to the promotion of its interests, while, in addition, it compels him to pay excessive prices for all that monopoly produces and all of the services which it renders."[5]

The state had been perverted from its legitimate ends, Howe argued. Privilege had been exalted above liberty, and property rights above humanity. The nation's ideas of right and wrong reflected the ascendancy of privilege. The universities, the churches, and the learned professions were "all dependent upon those who have favors to grant." How, then, explain the recent attacks on big business? Howe's answer in 1910 is like Gabriel Kolko's some fifty years later. In order to preserve its dominant position, the ruling class must agree to restrain some excesses. Restrictive laws were designed to preserve privilege by checking the irresponsible offender. "By these means the public will be diverted from the fact that the institution itself is wrong, to the idea that it is the occasional offender who is at fault."[6]

Projecting a dismal future for America, Howe saw only two possibilities of salvation from the downward path of social and industrial decay. One was socialism, "based upon a society consciously organized, and controlling the agencies of production and distribution for the common welfare." The other was Henry George's ideal of "industrial freedom" and "the society which would result from the abolition of class-made laws and legalized privilege."[7]

It should come as no surprise that Howe chose the second alternative. The single-tax remedy was just, simple, and nonviolent. The state became the universal landlord and rent collector. When land became common property, opportunity would beckon, poverty would disappear, and the worker would receive "the full product of his toil." The public treasury would be enriched so that the activities of government could be increased and used for the benefit of the many, rather than the few. The Georgist remedy would restore the foundations of democracy and insure equality of opportunity. "It will usher in a social order in which men will be as free from the fear of want as they are from want itself. Then men will look forward not to diminishing, but to increasing opportunities, for freedom will not only continuously augment the wealth of the world, it will insure its just distribution to those who produce it."[8]

---

5. Ibid., 218, 223, 230.
6. Ibid., 231–32, 243, 249, 250. See Kolko, *Triumph of Conservatism*.
7. *Privilege and Democracy in America*, 240, 255.
8. Ibid., 256–57, 259, 302.

Neither in analysis nor in remedies did *Privilege and Democracy in America* depart in any significant way from Howe's previous writings, though its tone was more radical and its attack on privilege more direct. It struck a new theme, however, in its emphasis on national, rather than municipal, problems. While not abandoning the city as a center of interest, Howe was increasingly turning his attention to national affairs, both in his writings and in his political action.

The reviews of *Privilege and Democracy in America* were generally favorable but somewhat less enthusiastic than most of those for Howe's previous books. There were a number of good reviews. The *New York Times*, for example, called it "an important work on present-day problems in America," and found that Howe's "statement of certain conditions of modern industrial civilization is forceful and backed up by what is evidently a great deal of thorough and conscientious research."[9] Some reviewers saw value in the author's analysis but took issue with the remedies he proposed. The *Political Science Quarterly*'s conclusion was typical: "Dr. Howe is . . . more eloquent than convincing; for he does not show in the concrete how this simple remedy could work so marvelous a transformation in a society so infinitely complex as ours."[10] Nevertheless, despite the mixed reviews, *Privilege and Democracy* was a book that apparently satisfied both Howe and his publisher and kept his name prominent among reformers. It also helped him to enter state politics almost immediately upon his arrival in New York City.

With 1910 a gubernatorial election year, a fight was on for the control of the state Republican Party between ex-President Theodore Roosevelt and the Old Guard. Conservative Republicans in the Legislature had killed a direct primary bill in July 1910. Plunging into the fray, Roosevelt sought the post of temporary chairman of the convention that would write the party platform and nominate

---

9. *New York Times*, April 9, 1910, 195. *Survey* found the book "a lucid diagnosis of many of our social ailments" and thought that the author presented a cogent argument for taxing the unearned increment. *Survey* 24 (September 1910): 831. The *Annals* felt that the work presented "a good discussion of the facts regarding the altered status of land holding in the United States, and a passable analysis of the single tax theory." *Annals of the American Academy of Political and Social Science* 36 (July 1910): 236. The *Cleveland Plain Dealer* recognized *Privilege and Democracy* twice, observing in April 1910: "One does not have to be a single taxer to appreciate the excellence [of the book]. Any reader familiar with public affairs will agree with most of his facts and conclusions; and as for the rest, they are put forth with such plausibility and consistency that they compel attention." A month later, the paper printed excerpts from the volume in its Sunday magazine and observed: "It is a well written book, so clear in its statements that he who runs may read and when he is through he can have no doubt as to what the author means. . . . Anyone who reads the book and is not imbued with the idea that its proposed remedy is likely to be applied at once to the ailment of the state is likely to go forth with renewed determination to possess the earth." *Cleveland Plain Dealer*, April 2, 1910, 8, and "The Land, the Tariff, Other Big Questions, and a Cleveland Prophet," May 8, 1910, 5.

10. *Political Science Quarterly* 25 (September 1910): 573. Similar reviews appeared in the *American Journal of Sociology* 16 (July 1910): 123–24; the *Literary Digest* 40 (April 23, 1910): 825; and the *Independent* 69 (October 1910): 929–30.

its candidate for governor. At the convention in September, he triumphed on all fronts, gaining election as temporary chairman, getting a direct primary plank in the platform, and securing the gubernatorial nomination for his man, Henry L. Stimson.[11]

Stimson was a novice in electoral politics, though he had been involved in Republican politics in his assembly district and in various good government causes from the 1890s until his 1906 appointment by Roosevelt as United States attorney for the Southern District of New York. Roosevelt pushed him to become his party's nominee and persuaded him to accept despite the likelihood of Republican defeat in the November election.

After leaving the U.S. attorney's office, Stimson had taken time to read or renew his acquaintance with a number of authors who seemed to throw light on the problems of his time: Herbert Spencer, Henry George, Lord Bryce, Edward Bellamy—and Frederic C. Howe. He read *Privilege and Democracy* and found much that he could agree with in its treatment of monopoly and the financial manipulations of bankers. In a series of lectures given at the Harvard Business School in March 1910, he embraced the idea of strong government regulation of big business.[12]

Having learned from Raymond V. Ingersoll, chairman of the Congestion Committee's executive board, that Stimson had read his book and was interested in its ideas, Howe wrote the Republican candidate a long letter. He expressed his interest in Stimson's success and noted conditions favorable to his election. Stimson would gain Democratic votes upstate if he made it clear that "this is a movement of the new republicanism that is bent on eliminating special privelege [sic] from its own ranks." In his own travels throughout the country, Howe wrote, he had sensed that the temper of the people was "never as near freedom from party allegiance as it is today; it never was as hungry for constructive democracy, it never was as willing to follow courage to the ditch." The public had come to see the danger of merging business, pecuniary, and class interests with politics. He thought that "the unholy and criminal alliance of

---

11. According to a 1910 campaign ditty:

> If Stimson came from Africa
> If he was a Zulu Chief
> If he wore a feather in his hair
> And dressed in a fig leaf
> We'd vote for Henry just the same
> And carry out the plan
> Because he's Roosevelt's man.

Quoted in Morison, *Turmoil and Tradition*, 142.

12. For a summary of Stimson's political views, see ibid., 126–28; Gerber, *Limits of Liberalism*, 29–34, 95–96.

certain classes of corporations with both parties and through them the control of the state and the city" was something that "the people can be made to see and rally to as to no other issue."

Stimson could expect no support from Wall Street or its newspaper lackeys, but "for every man who owns an automobile there are three votes in his stable." He need not be dramatic in his statements nor say anything that he did not believe, but he must "be bold, be ever bold; be pregoressive [sic] to the limit of your convictions; and sear with a hot iron the corrupt alliances of parties, republican as well as democratic, with priveleged [sic] business." If Stimson could succeed in convincing the voters that he was a man of strong convictions who stood for "a new deal," and if he could make his campaign part of the reform movement that was sweeping America, Howe had no doubt that he would win.[13]

In another letter, Howe counseled the candidate to drive home his arguments by repetition, to raise suspicions about the Democratic nominee's associations with Wall Street, and to put his opponent on the spot by pointed questions about what he would do as governor and about his views on the direct primary and other reforms. "That puts your campaign at once on the aggressive and his on the defensive. Then if he does not answer coin some phrase that will stick as the crab candidate who moves backward, the retiring Mr. Dix who disappears into his shell. Pin to him the idea that he has no policy, that he has no program, that he dares not appear in the open." These tactics would put Stimson in "a positive aggressive position" that would suggest "faith, courage and conviction."[14]

Howe and Stimson soon met, and Howe began to play a role in the Republican's campaign, though it was minor compared with others in the entourage. Felix Frankfurter was the chief speechwriter, and he and George Carter handled most of the correspondence, finance, and logistics of the race. Howe made suggestions to Stimson and rode with him occasionally on his whistle-stop tours of the state. Some of the candidate's speeches show the influence, and even the language, of *Privilege and Democracy*. In his opening campaign address at Columbia University on October 12, 1910, Stimson pointed to the relation of free land and democracy. In a major speech at Buffalo on October 23, he emphasized his opposition to privilege and monopoly, including "the encroachment of our traction and gas companies, and our public service corporations." Howe

---

13. FCH to Henry L. Stimson, October 14, 1910, Henry L. Stimson Papers, Yale University Library. Fred could never seem to learn to spell "privilege" correctly. In the 1930s he was still spelling it "privelege," as in this letter to Stimson.

14. Letter to FCH, October 1910 (neither the sender nor the exact date is given in the letter); FCH to Henry L. Stimson, October 18, 1910.

and *Privilege and Democracy* can hardly be given sole credit for these themes, of course. Stimson had arrived at many of the ideas through his own reading and thinking, and many had become staples in the political vocabulary of American reform by 1910. As the campaign wore on, specific state and local issues tended to supplant the general ideas, though Stimson liked to talk about political theory.[15]

Neither Stimson nor Roosevelt had ever believed that the Republicans would capture the governor's office in 1910, and they were quite accurate in their prediction. Their party was deeply divided between adherents of Roosevelt and supporters of Taft and split over such issues as the direct primary. It was also burdened by graft and bribery scandals involving Republican legislators. Stimson was hardly the kind of candidate who could arouse enthusiasm among the party faithful and win converts from the Democrats. Though praising him for his honesty and ability, most of the newspapers portrayed him as cold, austere, and remote. When the votes were counted in November, he had lost by sixty-seven thousand votes to his Democratic opponent, John A. Dix Jr. It was the worst Republican defeat since 1892—all of the party's candidates for statewide office lost.

After the election, Stimson sent Howe a note of thanks for his "kind interest" in the campaign. "I had the pleasure last summer of reading your book 'Privilege and Democracy,' and it greatly helped me in crystallizing my own ideas on some of the important questions before the country," he wrote.[16] For Howe, the campaign and election had been educational. It had introduced him to New York politics, thus extending his experience beyond the politics of Ohio. It had broadened his circle of political acquaintances, introducing him to both Stimson and Frankfurter. It showed his continuing interest in the nuts and bolts of politics. Though he may have come to New York for a literary career, he was not ready to abandon the great game of politics—he could still hear the "Marseillaise." Indeed, his tactical advice to Stimson indicated that, on the basis of his experiences in Ohio and despite his relative lack of success as a candidate there, he considered himself a political pro, capable of advising others how to campaign and how to win elections. The Stimson campaign had also renewed his Republican contacts—though he remained a Democrat, he had signaled his willingness to work for and with Progressives in both parties.

In the Republican Party, the fight between President Taft and many of the Progressive Republicans was out in the open by the summer of 1910. "Fighting

15. *New York Times*, October 13, 1910, 4; October 23, 1910, 5. For brief accounts of the campaign, see Morrison, *Turmoil and Tradition*, 137–43; Hodgson, *The Colonel*, 70–72; Wesser, *Response to Progressivism*, 19–20, 38–41; Parrish, *Felix Frankfurter and His Times*, 35–37.

16. Henry L. Stimson to FCH, November 25, 1910.

Bob" La Follette stood in the forefront of the Republican "insurgents."[17] In three terms as governor of Wisconsin, and over the opposition of Republican "stalwarts," he had secured the adoption of an extensive program of reforms: a direct primary law, a presidential primary, increased taxation of corporations, antimonopoly legislation and regulation of public utilities and railroad rates, the merit system, regulation of campaign spending, workers' compensation, insurance of bank deposits, protection of women and children in the workforce, a state life insurance company. Elected to the United States Senate in 1905, he had worked for the Hepburn bill to strengthen the Interstate Commerce Commission's regulation of the railroads, and had fought against the Payne-Aldrich tariff bill, winning the enmity of President Taft in the process. Fiery, tireless, honest, serious, and eloquent, La Follette often seemed austere and chilly, intense and uncompromising. "In legislation *no bread* is better than *half a loaf*," he once said.[18] His name was being widely mentioned as a potential Republican presidential candidate, in 1916 if not in 1912.

Fred Howe admired La Follette's record in Wisconsin and had come to know him well. In November 1904, in probably his first letter to the then-governor, he had written: "Your work and your future command my admiration and sympathy, and may Providence give strength to you to see it through." He was able directly to observe Wisconsin Progressivism during his lecturing and teaching stints at the state university in the winter of 1905, the winter of 1908–9, and January 1910. Accompanied by Ida Tarbell, he first met La Follette in February 1907.

A close political and personal relationship soon developed between the Howes and La Follette and his family. Fred and Marie entertained Fola, the senator's daughter, when she visited Cleveland as a member of a touring theater company, and they brought Tom Johnson to the La Follette farm to meet Mrs. La Follette (the senator was then in California). Fola frequently visited the Howes in their summer home at Sconset, and her husband, George Middleton, called Marie "Fola's most intimate friend." Fred helped with *La Follette's Weekly Magazine*, and he praised the Progressive Republicans' platform for the 1910 election as the best political platform ever written. Beside the specifics in that program, La Follette's hostility to privilege, outspoken faith in democracy, and sympathy with Henry George's ideas fitted well with Howe's outlook. Fred and Marie were relieved and happy with the success of the senator's operation for gallstones in the fall of 1910. and Fred wrote him:

17. On the "insurgents," see Holt, *Congressional Insurgents and the Party System*; Hechler, *Insurgency*.
18. On La Follette, see La Follette, *La Follette's Autobiography*; La Follette and Fola La Follette, *Robert M. La Follette*; Doan, *La Follettes and the Wisconsin Idea*; Maxwell, *La Follette and the Rise of the Progressives*; Maxwell, *La Follette*.

I need not tell you how much we care for you and all of yours personally and how tremendous is the debt which America owes to you for the long and exhausting sacrifices you have made from the day you entered the fight. I shall be so happy to hear that you are out again and look forward to the next few years as the most satisfactory of your life. It is my hope that you will disprove the experience of almost all of the worlds Moses' [sic] and will be permitted to enter into the Promised Land of your hopes and desires.[19]

During 1910 La Follette and other insurgents had been discussing the formation of some sort of national Progressive organization. Whether Howe was aware of these conversations is unknown, but, if not informed of them, he was certainly thinking along a similar line. In early November 1910 he sent seventeen leading Progressives, including both Republicans and Democrats, a "plan for promoting the progressive movement in America and for focusing it on definite issues." A national organization, to be called For City and State, would be "a clearing house of approved legislation designed primarily to simplify the machinery and details of government through the Initiative, Referendum and Recall, Direct Primaries, Direct Nomination of United States Senators, Commission Form of City Government, the Short Ballot, and Home Rule for Cities." It might also work for passage of bills on conservation, railroad regulation, woman and child labor, industrial and accident insurance, and corrupt practices. The organization could prepare model bills and distribute them to governors and state legislators, and its press bureau could supply magazine and newspapers with publicity on the program. Funds to support the organization would come from thousands of small contributors. Howe hoped that his letter's recipients would approve the plan and that, early in 1911, a meeting in Washington might set up the organization. "If we can lay the foundations in our cities and states for the free expression of democracy through simple and workable tools, the larger federal questions will prove of easy solution. This I think is proven by those states that have simplified the tools of government and made them responsive to the popular will."[20]

Whether or not Fred's proposal was a direct stimulus to Senator La Follette, the Wisconsin insurgent proceeded in December to take the idea of a progressive organization out of the realm of discussion and into that of action. He must

---

19. FCH to Robert M. La Follette, November 21, 1904, Robert M. La Follette Papers, State Historical Society of Wisconsin, 1972; La Follette and La Follette, *Robert M. La Follette*, 1:224, 284, 306; Middleton, *These Things Are Mine*, 90; FCH to Robert M. La Follette, October 8, 1910, La Follette Family Papers, Library of Congress.

20. FCH to William Kent, November 11, 1910, Kent Papers, Yale University. The other letters were identical in content. I have found only Whitlock's favorable reply. Brand Whitlock to FCH, November 18, 1910, Whitlock Papers.

have broached his ideas to Howe early in the month, for Fred responded with a long letter of advice and suggestions on December 14. He indicated that his own partisan ties were weak. "Personally I have little faith in the democratic party. And I have no attachment to it. I believe the insurgent movement among the republicans is bound to capture that party and that when it comes it will leave the new organization so free of interests and influences that it can go on rapidly with its work." A new nonpartisan organization would receive an immediate and generous response from the American people, who were "inclined to be suspicious of any partisan organization." Enclosing practical suggestions for publicity and organization, Howe concluded with a reiteration of his own desire to be part of this reform movement: "I don't know in what way and care very little, but the improvement of the machinery of government seems to be the biggest job now before the American people and for that reason that is where I want to be working."[21]

Spurred on by the continuing antagonism between the insurgents and Taft, and perhaps by the suggestions of Howe and others, La Follette prepared his own ideas for a Progressive organization. Toward the end of December 1910, he sent them to insurgent members of Congress and leading Progressives throughout the country for endorsements and signatures. Meeting in La Follette's Washington residence on January 21, 1911, the leading Republican Progressives formally adopted the declaration of principles. The roster of adherents included nine senators, six governors, sixteen members of the House of Representatives, and twenty-one other nationally known Progressives.[22] The group chose Senator Jonathan Bourne of Oregon as president and Fred Howe as secretary. He now had his foot in the door in national politics.

The declaration of principles of the National Progressive Republican League (NPRL) differed in several respects from Howe's proposals of November 11 and December 14. He had advocated a nonpartisan association, embracing both Republican and Democratic Progressives. Some of the founders, including La Follette, preferred nonpartisanship but yielded to several members of Congress who feared that cooperation across party lines might hurt them in fights for renomination and reelection. The League had somewhat more limited goals than Howe had proposed. Emphasizing, as Howe's proposals had, power to the people through the extension of democracy, its declaration of principles advocated (1) the initiative, the recall, and the referendum; (2) direct primaries;

21. FCH to Robert M. La Follette, December 14, 1910.
22. For first-hand accounts on the founding of the League, see La Follette, *Autobiography*, 211–13; La Follette, "Beginning of a Great Movement," 7–9, 12; La Follette and La Follette, *Robert M. La Follette*, 314–19. The text of the declaration of principles, signed by the founders of the League, can be found in the Senator Robert M. La Follette Sr. Papers, Library of Congress.

(3) the direct election of United States senators; (4) presidential preference primaries; and (5) corrupt practices legislation. It omitted Howe's call for home rule and the commission form of government for the cities. It was not as specific as Howe had been in endorsing economic and social legislation. As in Howe's proposals, the declaration of principles affirmed that the League would assist in organizing state leagues, prepare bills for legislatures, and furnish speakers and literature in support of the five points in its program.

Conspicuously absent from the list of League adherents was the name of the man considered by many the most prominent Republican, Theodore Roosevelt. Despite pleas from La Follette, Bourne, and others, he declined membership in the League, although he publicly endorsed its principles save for the initiative, recall, and referendum. At this point, the ex-president was sure that Taft would be renominated and would go down to defeat to the Democratic candidate. Though fearing the influence of those he considered the "ultra radicals" in the Republican Party, he did not want to alienate the insurgents and handicap himself in a future role as savior of the party. In spite of pressure from his friends, Roosevelt refused to declare himself a candidate for the 1912 nomination.[23]

The former president's reluctance or coyness presented a difficulty for the League. Its declaration of principles said nothing about the approaching presidential election. According to its charter, its activities were to center on influencing state legislatures to adopt the reforms it espoused. But it was clear to nearly everyone that the League had an additional and, for many adherents, a much more important goal: denial of renomination to President Taft and acquisition of the nomination for a Progressive. La Follette and Bourne might announce that enactment of the measures in its declaration was the League's "sole aim and purpose," but there was general agreement that the group intended to stop Taft.

But who should the insurgent candidate be? Here was potentially a serious difficulty. A great many League members had Roosevelt as their first choice and continued to hope that he might be persuaded to run. In the interim, they would turn to another candidate, but for some of them—notably the Pinchots, James Garfield,[24] Gilson Gardner, perhaps William Allen White—this would be

---

23. Good discussions of Roosevelt's thinking and actions during this period can be found in Mowry, *Theodore Roosevelt and the Progressive Movement*, 174–82, and O'Toole, *When Trumpets Call*, 119–205.

24. Howe's old law partner had not been present at the League's organizational meeting, but Gifford Pinchot had added his name to the list of members. Garfield distrusted the League and took no active part in it, principally because Roosevelt, his presidential choice, was not a member. Pending a favorable decision by Roosevelt, he advocated a waiting policy and support for favorite sons. He did not believe La Follette a strong enough candidate. See J. M. Thompson, "James R. Garfield," 218–25.

a holding operation. If Teddy threw his hat into the ring, they would go to him. If not, then someone else would have to carry the insurgent banner. In the meantime, they would continue to try to persuade Roosevelt to make the race. Other League adherents were willing to take Roosevelt at his word and commit themselves to another candidate. Assuming that the former president was out of the running, they considered La Follette the strongest contender and were ready to back him. It was already apparent that the senator would soon announce his availability.

The goals of the League, both professed and covert, were not necessarily mutually exclusive, but concentration on presidential politics might come at the expense of legislative or programmatic activity, and vice versa. Those interested above all in stopping Taft might have little patience with time spent on developing model laws for state legislatures, and those concerned with organizing state leagues and persuading legislators to adopt reform laws might find their tasks complicated by the struggle for the nomination.

Fred Howe was in the midst of these conflicting elements. It was clear that in presidential politics his leanings were to La Follette, and he wrote the senator that the League might want to "throw all our energies" into the fight for the nomination.[25] But, as he was the only officer who could devote most of his time to League efforts, it fell to him as secretary to see to the practical details of organizing, propagandizing, and pushing for reform legislation in the states. Fred's credentials as a Progressive were strong, but his ties with Republican officeholders were weak. Perhaps this—and his Democratic affiliations—explains why he was not in the policy-making circle of the League. The secretary was the only officer who did not sit on the executive committee. His concentration on the organizational and legislative aspects of League work was likely to bring problems with those who saw the organization primarily as a vehicle to defeat Taft and secure the Republican nomination for their favored candidate.

Setting up state leagues in insurgent territory in the Middle West and West presented little difficulty, but establishing them in other parts of the country proved harder. Organizing took money, and Howe had to spend a fair amount of time trying to raise funds. The money came mainly from large contributors: William Kent gave ten thousand dollars, Amos Pinchot ten thousand dollars, Gifford Pinchot fifteen thousand dollars, Charles Crane one thousand dollars a month for a specified period. Howe's hope to raise money in small amounts from a large number of people had been dashed by League leaders. He wrote La Follette: "Anything like a popular appeal for funds was discouraged by the Executive Committee, it being decided to limit the appeal to selected names of men

25. FCH to Robert M. La Follette, December 14, 1910, Library of Congress.

known to approve of our program. However, the burden of carrying the work ought to be distributed as widely as possible so that it will not fall on the shoulders of a few men who are already contributing generously to reform movements in their respective cities and states." Despite Howe's feeling that there had been some neglect of the financial side, enough money was raised to employ fifty clerks to send out anti-Taft materials from the League's office in Washington.[26]

Howe wrote Kent that he found his League activities "the biggest work to which a man can contribute his time or money, for once our institutions are free, I am perfectly sanguine about the results." He busied himself promoting the League goal of extending direct democracy. Part of his time was spent securing information on how the initiative, the referendum, and the presidential primary worked in states that had adopted them. He corresponded extensively on these matters with Charles McCarthy, the chief of the Wisconsin Legislative Reference Library. He studied Oregon's initiative statute and compared it with a bill under consideration in Wisconsin. He analyzed state laws aimed at improving the machinery of government in the states and the cities.[27]

The results of this research were disseminated to state legislators, who were urged to adopt the necessary legislation. Howe offered the League's help to the state legislatures and concluded: "We believe the advancement of Popular Government, so that it will be responsive and responsible to the peoples will, is the greatest reform now before the American people. To the promotion of this reform we ask your aid and assistance." A similar letter went to all newspapers in states where legislatures were considering measures of direct democracy.[28]

The extant correspondence shows Howe happy with the development of the League and with the work he was doing for it in the early months of 1911. Not all League members perceived its activities in such a rosy light, however. Gifford Pinchot and others began to criticize what they considered the slow progress of the organization, and Howe received a good share of the blame. Pinchot started his litany of complaints almost before the League was off the drawing board. At its first meeting on January 21, 1911, the choice of Bourne as president displeased

---

26. See FCH to Louis D. Brandeis, January 31, 1911, February 9, 1911, February 14, 1911; FCH to Gifford Pinchot, February 1, 1911; Amos Pinchot to FCH, February 8, 1911, March 3, 1911; Louis D. Brandeis to FCH, February 13, 1911; Jonathan Bourne to Amos Pinchot, February 14, 1911; FCH to Amos Pinchot, March 6, 1911; FCH to William Kent, March 15, 1911; Pinchot, *History of the Progressive Party*, 23; FCH to Robert M. La Follette, March 15, 1911, La Follette Family Collection, NPRL Records, Library of Congress; Mowry, *Theodore Roosevelt and the Progressive Movement*, 185.

27. FCH to William Kent, March 15, 1911; FCH to Charles McCarthy, February 15, 1911, April 14, 1911, April 19, 1911; McCarthy to FCH, April 6, 1911, April 12, 1911, April 17, 1911, April 21, 1911, McCarthy Papers, State Historical Society of Wisconsin.

28. Form letters, February 24 and 25, 1911, La Follette Family Collection, NPRL Records.

him, and his animadversions soon extended to the choice of Howe as secretary. He wrote his brother: "Fred Howe of Cleveland, Jim Garfield's former partner, has been chosen Secretary of the Progressive League. I am not sure that the choice is a good one. It was made at the meeting of the Executive Committee while I was in New Haven." After a poorly attended League meeting in late February, he complained to Brandeis: "It was the most melancholy attempt at a meeting of a great movement I have happened to see. Bourne did not know what Howe had in mind, and Howe apparently did not know what he himself had in mind. The whole thing was desultory, ineffective, and pretty well useless." Pinchot did not try to conceal his feelings from Howe, writing him on March 3: "I feel very strongly that the League has got to do something more than it is doing now to maintain even a reasonable prospect of doing the work for which it was organized. There is a very clear-cut feeling among many men, whose opinion is worth while, that the League is falling down. It is evident that a great deal of hard work has got to be done if that opinion is to be prevented from spreading."[29]

Fred replied to Pinchot's criticisms both through a progress report submitted to the League executive committee on March 6, 1911, and in a lengthy letter to Pinchot on the same day. In his report, he pointed out that the organization had had a working existence of only about thirty days. In that short span of time, it had rented permanent offices in Washington, where its staff had been "swamped with requests for literature, enrollment blanks and for speakers, as well as for assistance in the drafting of bills in the various legislatures." The executive committee had decided to "concentrate immediate attention (1) on the promotion of legislation by working with Governors and members of State Assemblies, and (2) by organizing local and state leagues identified with the program and in sympathy with the purposes of the League." Much had been accomplished along these lines. Printed pamphlets and other literature had been sent to the governors of all the states. A personal letter, enrollment blanks for local leagues, a statement of the League's purposes, and resolution blanks for organizations to use in lobbying state legislatures had been sent to each of the fifteen hundred people who had written the League. This had been followed up by "a very active correspondence" with several hundred persons. Material had been submitted to magazines, and articles on the League, popular government, and the Oregon reforms would soon appear in the *American, Success, Hampton's, Munsey's*, and other journals. Despite the inability of members of

---

29. FCH to Louis D. Brandeis, February 14, 1911; Gifford Pinchot Diary, January 21, 1911, Gifford Pinchot Papers; Gifford Pinchot to Amos Pinchot, February 3, 1911, Amos Pinchot Papers; Gifford Pinchot to Louis D. Brandeis, March 1, 1911; Gifford Pinchot to FCH, March 3, 1911.

Congress to get away from Washington, speakers had been, or would be, provided for meetings in New York, Pennsylvania, New Jersey, Ohio, Massachusetts, Delaware, and Minnesota. Personal letters and League literature had been sent to state legislators and to newspaper editors. Leagues had been organized in eight states, and a large number of local units and college clubs had been formed. This year, state legislatures were enacting "more really fundamental legislation for popular government" than in the previous ten years. Above all, the organization of the League and the development of definite legislative proposals has "crystalized the progressive movement in all parties and in all sections of the country. It has offered a simple, rational, easy and convincing program of state legislation and has made this in a sense a creed of progressive Governors, legislatures and organizations all over the country. This sort of crystalization was most timely and the program of the League has become the working program of men all over the country."[30]

On the same day that he presented the progress report to the executive committee, Howe wrote directly to Gifford Pinchot to respond to his complaints. He asked his critic to "indicate just where you feel we are weak or falling down in the work." Howe had heard only two criticisms, one about the lack of a speakers program and the other about a lack of publicity. The pressures of congressional work had precluded insurgent senators and representatives from leaving Washington, but a half dozen members were now ready to accept speaking engagements. Publicity efforts had suffered from limitations set by the League constitution and the executive committee, as well as from a shortage of funds. Howe had hoped to develop a weekly newsletter, full of information that could be picked up by the press, but the committee had not approved the idea. However, stories about the League and the reform laws of Oregon would soon appear in at least five leading magazines, reaching a circulation of two million. "This is as substantial a piece of publicity work as any movement has ever achieved, and is secured at no expense."

Howe offered a strong defense of the League's accomplishments. "I would have preferred to have received your suggestions first, for I do not want to mitigate your criticisms in any way. We have been actively at work less than a month and have concentrated all our efforts on the legislatures now in session in order to secure the maximum of results before they adjourned." He pointed to the correspondence with governors, legislators, and newspapers and to the formation of local Leagues. "The real accomplishment, and it is a most substantial one, has been the crystalization of sentiment about the five articles in our

---

30. FCH, Report of Progress of the National Progressive Republican League, Submitted to the Executive Committee, March 6, 1911 (in Brandeis Papers, Murdock Papers)

creed. Men who were anxious to do something found in this a ready-made and reasonable program, and the idea of first perfecting our instrument of government has seized hold of state executives and assemblies." The actual achievement has been "colossal," Howe wrote. "I cannot claim that this is traceable to the League, but at least it has had the encouragement of concerted nation wide sympathy and has already resulted in more progressive legislation than has been achieved in the preceding twenty years." California, Nebraska, Michigan, Wisconsin, and North and South Dakota had adopted substantially the whole program, and Washington, Wyoming, Kansas, and Minnesota had adopted essential parts of it. Howe yielded no ground to Pinchot on the question of League achievements. "I am perfectly satisfied that we have achieved remarkable results," he concluded. "I am equally satisfied that a lot of things could be done that would contribute to the movement if we had the money to do so and were not subject to the limitations which are imposed upon the work of the League by its constitution.... If there is any way in which we can use the resources we have more effectively than we are doing, I surely want to do so. However, the results of our work are not to be measured by newspaper publicity but rather by the legislative results which have been obtained."[31] Unpersuaded by Howe's defense, Pinchot continued to believe that the League was failing in its efforts.

By mid-April, Charles McCarthy had entered the fray and expressed his misgivings about Howe and the League's work in two letters to Senator La Follette. "Frederick Howe is an excellent fellow, but I am afraid that the material sent around the country and the program which he is working out is not such as to last in this country," he observed. The League's propaganda in its present form was unlikely to be successful, since it did not appeal to the average man.

> Those connected with it are so enthusiastic and are such good fellows that it is hard for me to attack it in any way, but I fear that if it keeps on as it is it will meet with ridicule.... I cannot say it is not far seeing—indeed the trouble is that it is too far seeing—but it does not build as it goes along. There are too many fellows with "isms" getting on the band wagon. Now, they are all right, but some of them are singing "We don't know where we are going, but we are on the way."

Fred Howe fitted into this group, he suggested. "The movement cannot exist on such phrases as 'Trust the people', 'Put on the whole armor of God', etc. etc. They are very fine, but some good strong hard headed stuff which can't be picked to pieces must go with it." McCarthy asked La Follette to keep his comments confidential because "these men are friends of mine and I do not want

---

31. FCH to Gifford Pinchot, March 6, 1911.

to attack them. I am simply afraid of the movement as it is now going, and your name is too closely connected with it to take any chances."[32]

The letters from McCarthy, along with the continuing complaints of Gifford Pinchot, had their effect. Although McCarthy was not part of La Follette's inner circle, the senator respected him as "a man of marked originality and power" who had been the draftsman for the reform measures dubbed the "Wisconsin idea."[33] Pinchot had to be listened to as both a leading figure in the anti-Taft movement and a major financial contributor to the NPRL. No information is available on exactly what occurred, but by about May 1, Howe was no longer secretary of the League.[34] He was replaced by Anson W. Prescott, a former newspaperman who was a clerk to the Senate Committee on Fisheries.

Lacking inside information, we can only speculate on the reasons for the change. Gifford Pinchot and Fred Howe were not close. They had corresponded on minor items before formation of the League but had never worked together before. They developed no continuing political association, as did Howe and Amos Pinchot. Perhaps Gifford was wary about Fred's lack of solid Republican credentials. Certainly his own chief concern with the League was presidential politics—the defeat of Taft and the nomination of a Republican Progressive, preferably Roosevelt—while Howe as secretary, though not uninvolved in the nomination struggle, had to focus on the League's legislative program and on establishing and paying for an organization that had to be built from scratch. The differences in their perceptions of the League's primary goal were bound to bring discord into their working relationships. That those differences were at the root of their disagreements is indicated by Pinchot's continued criticism of the League's failures after Howe's departure, in much the same kind of language he had used before it. Thus, on May 29, 1911, he wrote his brother that he would "make a final attempt to stir up the animals. If that fails, I shall pull out with a clear conscience. At the present writing I am pretty mad, and worse disgusted."[35]

32. Charles McCarthy to Robert M. La Follette, two letters dated April 18, 1911, McCarthy Papers, Wisconsin Historical Society. Both letters have essentially the same message; one may be a draft that was not sent. McCarthy recommended to La Follette that he "get a few men, who understand some of the hard problems, together somewhere at once—on the quiet—a little committee of such men as yourself, Lenroot, Sanborn, Brandeis, Record, and Commons. I shall be glad to give what help I can if you want me. A scientific, harmonious, high grade programme must be worked out."

33. La Follette, *Autobiography*, 15.

34. "Your letter of the second brings me the first information I have had that Mr. Howe has been succeeded by Mr. Prescott as Secretary of the League." Louis D. Brandeis to Jonathan Bourne Jr., May 6, 1911, in Urofsky and Levy, *Letters of Louis D. Brandeis*, 2:432.

35. Gifford Pinchot to Amos Pinchot, May 29, 1911, Amos Pinchot Papers; Harold L. Ickes to Amos Pinchot, June 14, 1911, Amos Pinchot Papers. Harold Ickes had a similar complaint after talking with La Follette and Bourne in June: "I was not very strongly impressed that the Progressives in Washington had any very definite idea of what they proposed to do in the coming campaign.... The general impression that I get here since my return [to Chicago] is that nationally, the Insurgents are losing ground."

McCarthy's criticisms of Howe may be seen in part as a clash between a Wisconsin insider, who to an extent seemed to consider himself a proprietor of the "Wisconsin idea," and an outsider with a national reputation, who wanted to appropriate the Wisconsin reforms while giving as much praise or more to the Oregon version. The relationship of the two men was complicated by McCarthy's feeling that Howe had called him a "reactionary" (which Howe denied) and that Howe dealt in the generalities of uplift rather than the generation of constructive programs. There was also the complication that each was preparing a book on the Wisconsin experiment at the same time.

Nevertheless, some grounds existed for criticism of the job Howe was doing as secretary. As far back as his work in the Garfield law firm, there were indications that his talents were not in administration. Around the time Howe left his post, Senator Bourne found that he had done little to follow up on Brandeis's suggestions of men who might organize a league in Massachusetts.[36] It is quite likely that, given the numerous tasks set for the League in its early days, Howe neglected—probably had to neglect—following through on many such duties. It stood to his credit, however, that, in three months of operation, the League could make a good start with "effective work in advancing the principles to promote which it was organized" (La Follette's words).[37] Perhaps by the end of April Howe might even have welcomed a change in his role, if not such an abrupt end to it, as the usual attractions of Europe and a Sconset summer beckoned. The full-time job of League secretary may also have become a detriment to the writing that Fred had planned when he moved to New York City. Around the time when he was replaced by Prescott, he was negotiating for the job of director of the People's Institute, a post that would have required him to drop out of League activities.

At any rate, in the summer of 1911 Fred accompanied a group of about eighty American businessmen on a seven-week tour of Europe, sponsored by the Boston Chamber of Commerce. The purpose of the trip was to see how European municipalities were solving problems like those faced by American cities. He and Marie joined the group, which departed on June 27 and did not return until September 1. The trip and a stay in Sconset afterward kept him from involvement in the political machinations of the summer of 1911. Surviving letters indicate that, whatever the circumstances of his relinquishment of the post of NPRL secretary, he remained a friend and supporter of La Follette, and the ties between them became stronger. On April 26 he had sent the senator a list of eight issues he considered "ripe for presentation to the country" and that

---

36. Jonathan Bourne Jr. to Louis D. Brandeis, May 2, 1911, May 9, 1911.
37. La Follette, *Autobiography*, 213.

reflected "the present temper of public opinion. I do not pretend to know what the people are thinking about further than that they are in a state of angry unrest, with the stomach problem a very troublesome one." In June he forwarded a biographical sketch of La Follette that he had prepared, along with the senator's speeches arranged for publication. "I have enjoyed the work and fortunately had the time to do it. I wish I were free to do anything I can for your movement this summer, but hope to be able to be of some service in the fall when we return." In another letter, Fred spoke again of his willingness to help La Follette. He suggested that the senator might find useful campaign material in *Privilege and Democracy*.[38]

About the time when Fred and Marie sailed for Europe, opinions among Republican Progressives on their 1912 nominee had seemed to crystallize. As Roosevelt continued to indicate that he would not run, insurgent opinion swung to La Follette. Even those closest to the ex-president were willing to push the Wisconsin senator into the race, *faute de mieux,* and he required little coaxing, throwing his hat into the ring on June 17 and beginning a western speaking tour as soon as the congressional session was over. The Pinchots and others of the Roosevelt faithful continued in close touch with the Rough Rider, however, hoping for a change of mind.

By the fall of 1911, refreshed by a summer's relaxation, Howe was ready to reenter the political fray. He and Amos Pinchot had been working since March to arrange for a major speech by La Follette in New York City. Howe was president of the Insurgents Club, a supposedly nonpartisan organization but one composed mainly of Republican Progressives. The club had adopted the NPRL declaration of principles as part of its own program. Pinchot suggested to Howe that the club sponsor a large public meeting at Carnegie Hall with La Follette and a few other speakers. Pinchot was willing to put up the money to rent the Hall and suggested an array of possible speakers. "I think there is no question about filling the hall to overflowing if we make an organized campaign to get the interest of all the trade, social and political societies and guilds, university settlements, trade unions etc., from New York, Brooklyn and Jersey City. I feel particularly that it would be of advantage to La Follette to be seen and heard at this particular time. . . . I should say that without him the meeting would hardly be a go."[39]

After a little more consideration, Fred concluded that the speakers list should be narrowed down: "Senator La Follette is a rather long speaker, and yet I would suggest that we have him and Governor Wilson if possible for the speakers."

38. FCH to Robert M. La Follette, April 26, 1911; FCH to Robert M. La Follette, June 6, 1911; FCH to Robert M. La Follette, June 15, 1911, La Follette Family Collection, NPRL Records.
39. Amos Pinchot to FCH, March 3, 1911; March 6, 1911, Amos Pinchot Papers.

The New Jersey governor declined an invitation, though professing "warm sympathy with the objects of the [Insurgents] Club." Howe undertook to work out a date with La Follette for the New York City speech and, after some scheduling problems, he rented Carnegie Hall for the evening of January 22, 1912. He also suggested to the senator topics that would interest a New York audience.[40]

When La Follette arrived at Carnegie Hall, he found the building jammed. An overflow crowd filled several blocks on Seventh Avenue, and the senator could not pass through the throng until he made two impromptu speeches from his car. Seated on the stage were some two hundred members of the Insurgents Club, including Howe, Baker, Steffens, and Amos Pinchot. Gifford Pinchot introduced La Follette, whose speech was frequently interrupted by tumultuous applause. The *New York Times* reported: "It was the Wisconsin candidate's first appearance in New York, and the reception accorded him he himself said was as great as any he ever received in his own State. Carnegie Hall never held a bigger nor a more enthusiastic audience, and, although the Senator spoke for nearly two hours, it was not until near the close of his speech that anybody left the auditorium."[41]

Howe and Pinchot exchanged congratulations on the success of the meeting. Fred wrote: "I hope you feel properly proud of the Carnegie Hall meeting on Monday evening. It was a great achievement, thanks to your generosity and the work you did in the office." Amos replied: "I think you are more to be congratulated than anyone." Nothing came of Howe's idea that the speech might launch the Insurgents Club into a broad nonpartisan campaign for popular government, as the views of members were divided.[42]

The Carnegie Hall speech may well have been a success, but the La Follette candidacy was nevertheless in trouble. In the fall and winter of 1911, the signs had increased that Roosevelt might after all become a candidate. He had reacted vehemently against the Taft administration's antitrust suit against U.S. Steel, and many of his adherents, who had just about abandoned hope that he would seek the nomination, were again galvanized into action. Roosevelt allowed them to organize for his candidacy, and by December it appeared that he would be in the race. As the former president edged closer to an announcement, his supporters who had been backing La Follette started to look for an exit. Behind the scenes (and sometimes in front of them as well), they began to argue that the

---

40. Baker, *Woodrow Wilson*, 3:185; Woodrow Wilson to Ray Stannard Baker, February 8, 1911, in Link, *Papers of Woodrow Wilson*, 22:412; FCH to Belle Case La Follette, January 15, 1912, La Follette Family Collection, NPRL Records.

41. *New York Times*, January 22, 1912, 1. For other descriptions, see La Follette and La Follette, *Robert M. La Follette*, 1:387–90; La Follette, *Autobiography*, 253.

42. FCH to Amos Pinchot, January 24, 1912; Pinchot to FCH, January 27, 1912.

La Follette campaign had not taken fire, that the senator's appeal was limited and sectional, that he could not win against Taft, that his continued candidacy would split the Progressives. Roosevelt would be a stronger candidate, they suggested, and some of them took the position that their support for La Follette had always been intended as a holding action until Teddy made up his mind to enter the contest.[43]

The pro-Roosevelt Republicans soon found a reason—or an excuse—to abandon La Follette publicly. On February 2 the senator addressed the Periodical Publishers Association, meeting in Philadelphia. It was not a happy occasion for La Follette. His youngest daughter, Mary, had been taken to the hospital on January 29 and faced a very serious operation on February 3. He had not had time to prepare a speech specially for the occasion and spoke from a lengthy manuscript, which he tried to revise as he went along. He was tired, had suffered from indigestion during the day, and had had no dinner. The meeting was a long one, with other speakers (including Woodrow Wilson) preceding the senator, so that he did not begin his speech until 11:00 p.m. La Follette noted later: "I was not at my best and did not at once get hold of my audience. It was, I do not doubt, entirely my own fault—but I determined to make them hear me to the end. In my effort to do so I talked too long without realizing it."[44] Even his wife, describing his speech, used such words as "tactless," "aggressive," "strident in tone." George Middleton, his son-in-law, who was present at the meeting, recalled: "He got off on the wrong foot and he never got back. As an experienced speaker he intuitively knew he had lost control of the situation at the outset; had he been less fatigued he might even then have adapted himself and his material to the occasion. Instead he went doggedly ahead, determined to make the audience hear him though it was clear, as he went along, that he knew he was failing in a crisis." The result was a rambling discourse, sometimes a harangue, in which he lost both his audience and all sense of time—he spoke for nearly two hours. The La Follettes knew the speech was a disaster. His wife called it a "failure," and he referred to it as "my flunk at Philadelphia."[45]

The newspapers in the next few days were full of criticisms of La Follette's attacks on the press and of comments about the senator's "mental breakdown" or "collapse" or "illness." The stories were often accompanied by reports from

---

43. The maneuvers were often arcane and complicated. See, for the La Follette view of what transpired, La Follette, *Autobiography*, 211–64, and La Follette and La Follette, *Robert M. La Follette*, 1:313–35, 349–424. Other accounts of the events may be found in Mowry, *Theodore Roosevelt and the Progressive Movement*, 183–219; Broderick, *Progressivism at Risk*, 37–44.

44. La Follette, *Autobiography*, 259. The speech and the events surrounding it are described in ibid., 256–60, 322–42; La Follette and La Follette, *Robert M. La Follette*, 1:398–406; Pinchot, *History of the Progressive Party*, 134–39.

45. Quoted in La Follette and La Follette, *Robert M. La Follette*, 1:401, 405, 413.

ostensibly "authoritative sources" that La Follette was pulling out of the race. This was not true—he had no intention of quitting and had sanctioned no announcements to that effect. La Follette always believed that he had been betrayed. "The men who had already abandoned my candidacy, because I could not stand as a shield for another, or agree to any deals or combinations that would confuse the issue or mislead the people, seized upon what they were pleased to call my 'shattered health' as an excuse for their action."[46]

After two weeks of rest, the senator was back on the campaign trail, but the political damage was beyond repair. Many of his erstwhile supporters assumed his race was over and began to switch their fealty openly to Roosevelt. The list of Progressive Republicans announcing their allegiance to Roosevelt included the Pinchots, McCormick, William Allen White, Governors Stubbs of Kansas, Aldrich of Nebraska, and Hiram Johnson of California, Senator Cummins, Gilson Gardner. On February 25, responding to a carefully arranged open letter from seven Republican governors, Roosevelt announced that he would accept the Republican nomination for president.

Fred Howe stood by La Follette. That the senator considered him a loyal friend and adviser is indicated by his comment in a letter to Gilbert Roe four days after the ill-fated Philadelphia speech: "I have been in sore need of a few friends who were not in politics, and should have asked you and perhaps Fred and Steff to come over, but it seemed unreasonable to do it when I know how busy you are." He continued to provide La Follette with campaign materials, sending him information on the railroads, Alaska, and the tariff for use in his Middle West campaigning, for example.[47]

La Follette won America's first presidential preference primary in North Dakota in March 1912, and he also captured the Wisconsin primary in April. Those were his only victories, however, and he entered the Republican convention with just the thirty-six delegates from those two states. He received forty-one votes on the convention's only ballot for the nomination, picking up five from South Dakota. After the convention he refused to endorse any presidential candidate, although he gave various indications that he preferred Wilson to either Roosevelt or Taft. There is little direct evidence of Fred Howe's views during the 1912 presidential campaign. Given his loyalty to La Follette and his previous associations with and respect for Wilson, he doubtless agreed with the opinion Brandeis expressed to La Follette after Wilson's nomination: "It seems to me that those Progressives who do not consider themselves bound by party

---

46. Belle Case La Follette to Mrs. Charles Mayo, February 20, 1912, quoted in La Follette and La Follette, *Robert M. La Follette,* 1:407–8; La Follette, *Autobiography,* 260.

47. Robert M. La Follette to Gilbert Roe, February 6, 1912, quoted in Fola La Follette to FCH, May 12, 1936; FCH to Robert M. La Follette, February 7 and March 19, 1912.

affiliations ought to give Wilson thorough support, not only to insure his election, but to give him all the aid and comfort which he will need to maintain the Progressive position which he has assumed and to carry out the Progressive policies."[48]

In the only specific reference to Roosevelt's new party that has been found, Fred wrote Ben Lindsey (who was in Roosevelt's corner) that he was glad to see the breakup of the Republican Party. This would purge the reactionary influences, and "then we will be in for a period of real constructive statesmenship [sic] along social and economic lines." His feelings toward the new party would depend on its program. "Thus far there have been no declarations that made me feel that it had much more than an appeal against the bosses and machine control to justify it. Personally I passed through that stage about ten years ago and now I want a definite programme against privelege [sic]. We are wise enough to know what should be done." What was the new party going to say on the tariff, public ownership of the express business, the railroad monopoly? Would it be "a weasel worded platform that will win votes on the one hand and campaign contributions on the other? Such a platform cannot possibly win today. I think it will mean ignominious forfeiture of all claim to confidence if such a platform issues from the Chicago meeting no matter what the declarations may be on direct legislation, the recall and personal and political issues. We have moved on beyond that and I hope the Chicago meeting will break with the traditions of corporation alliance in fact as well as in word."[49]

It is doubtful that Howe found all that he wanted in the Progressive Party platform, and he had never had a close or direct relationship with Roosevelt. Many of his friends—Newton Baker, Brand Whitlock, Harry Garfield (James Garfield continued to be a Roosevelt man)—were enthusiastically backing Wilson. There is no reason to believe that Howe disagreed with them, and he cast his ballot for Woodrow Wilson in November.

---

48. Louis D. Brandeis to Robert M. La Follette, July 3, 1912, in Urofsky and Levy, *Letters of Louis D. Brandeis*, 638.
49. FCH to Ben Lindsey, July 18, 1912, Lindsey Papers, Library of Congress.

9

MARIE HOWE AND THE HETERODITES

When Fred and Marie Howe moved to New York, they lived first in the Chelsea Hotel, on West Twenty-third Street, between Seventh and Eighth avenues. That hostelry perhaps attracted them because of its literary associations. Its red-brick facade and lacy iron balconies had sheltered Mark Twain and O. Henry, as well as such stage luminaries as Sarah Bernhardt, Lillie Langtry, Lillian Russell, and Eva Tanguay in the days when the Chelsea area had been New York's theater district. Beginning life in 1884 as one of the city's first cooperative apartment houses, by 1905 it had become a hotel with a large proportion of permanent residents. The Howes stayed at the Chelsea until 1912.[1]

Amidst the stir of the La Follette campaign, the Howes found time to remain in touch with old friends—Baker, the Garfields, Steffens, Whitlock, Lindsey, among others—and to make new ones. Baker, elected mayor of Cleveland in 1911, kept them informed on developments there, as well as on Woodrow Wilson's quest for the Democratic nomination. He and Fred commented in their letters on Phi Gamma Delta affairs, exchanged materials for speeches and articles, and thought about joining forces to reform Pittsburgh. He summed up his friendship with Fred in glowing terms: "If there is any other fellow in the world as thoughtful and kind as you are, I would like to hear of him, although considerable proof would have to be taken on that subject before I could be induced

---

1. Among notable residents of the Chelsea over the years were Thomas Wolfe, Tennessee Williams, Edgar Lee Masters, John Sloan, Eugene O'Neill, James T. Farrell, Jackson Pollock, Arthur Miller, Hart Crane, Sherwood Anderson, Jessica Mitford, Virgil Thomson, Dylan Thomas, and Brendan Behan. Masters wrote a poem about the hotel, and it was the site of the Andy Warhol movie *Chelsea Girls,* as well as the locale for some scenes in Woody Allen's *Manhattan Murder Mystery.* For a description of the hotel in more recent times, see Turner, *At the Chelsea.* It is now officially a Manhattan landmark.

to render judgment in his favor."² Lincoln Steffens the Howes saw often, and he wrote frequently to Marie about his friends, his activities, the books he was reading, and his thoughts. Unfortunately, no letters of this period from Marie seem to have survived.

Among new friends were Walter Lippmann (whom the Howes met through Steffens), Amos Pinchot, and Theodore Dreiser. Fred and Amos first became acquainted in their work for the National Progressive Republican League, and by the time of La Follette's Carnegie Hall speech, which they had worked together to arrange, they were on a "Dear Fred" and "My dear Amos" basis in their correspondence. Fred came to know Dreiser as the editor of the Butterick Publishing Company's "Trio," three magazines with fairly large national circulations—the *Delineator,* the *Designer,* and the *New Idea Woman's Magazine.* Some of the novelist's friends made up a group called the Fantastic Toe Club, which got together for dancing at a hall on 125th Street, and Dreiser invited Fred and Marie to join in the frivolity. The Howes attended on various occasions. Fred wrote to Dreiser in December 1910: "Thank you for letting us know about the dancing party tonight. . . . We may get up late in the evening. I hope you will let us know of future affairs as we had a bully good time last week." A few weeks later he wrote again: "I shall be glad to be included in any plans you father for play."³

In late 1912 Fred and Marie moved from the Chelsea to an apartment in Greenwich Village, at 31 West Twelfth Street. The move opened the Bohemian literary and artistic world to them. Arriving in the Village at about the same time was Mabel Dodge, whose elegant brownstone at 23 Fifth Avenue was only three blocks from the Howe abode. Her famous "Evenings" brought together, in her words, "Socialists, Trade-Unionists, Anarchists, Suffragists, Poets, Relations, Lawyers, Murderers, 'Old Friends,' Psychoanalysts, I.W.W.'s, Single Taxers, Birth Controlists, Newspapermen, Artists, Modern-Artists, Clubwomen, Woman's-place-is-in-the-home Women, Clergymen, and just plain men [who] stammering in an unaccustomed freedom a kind of speech called Free, exchanged a variousness in vocabulary called, in euphemistic optimism, Opinions."⁴ In Mabel's salon, Fred and Marie not only encountered people they had already

---

2. See Newton D. Baker to FCH, September 22, 1913; October 2, 4, 18, 1913; November 6, 1913, Newton D. Baker Papers; Newton D. Baker to Tom Johnson, September 19, 1910; Baker to FCH, March 17, 1911.

3. FCH to Theodore Dreiser, October 8, December 7, and December 28, 1910, quoted with permission from the Theodore Dreiser Papers, Rare Book and Manuscript Library, University of Pennsylvania; Swanberg, *Dreiser,* 131.

4. Luhan, *Movers and Shakers,* 83. See Lasch, *New Radicalism in America,* 104–40; Stansell, *American Moderns,* 100–111; Lynn, "Rebels of Greenwich Village."

come to know—Elizabeth Gurley Flynn, Lippmann, Steffens, the Amos Pinchots, Emma Goldman, John Collier—but also rubbed shoulders and minds with a variety of other interesting persons—Max and Crystal Eastman, Hutchins Hapgood, Margaret Sanger, Mary Heaton Vorse, John Reed, Floyd Dell, Jo Davidson, Neith Boyce, John Sloan, Amy Lowell, Bill Haywood. Fred later described these Greenwich Village days.

> Brilliant young people, full of vitality, ardent about saving the world, floated in and out of our apartment. . . . Socialism was the vogue, also woman suffrage. Graduates of Harvard, Columbia, and Vassar, concerned for the well-being of society but not for its conventions, formed an American youth movement. They protested against industrial conditions, suffered vicariously with the poor, hated injustice. . . . Girls exchanged the dulness of social work in the settlements for something more fundamental. Young men challenged the stagnation of home and university. There was a splendid enthusiasm among these emotional rebels, a generous willingness to make sacrifices. And a demand for immediate change.[5]

Marie became close enough to Mabel Dodge to chastise her for betraying feminism by marrying Maurice Sterne. "You have *counted* so much for Women," she declared. "Your Example has stood for courage and strength! I wonder if you realize that hundreds of women and girls have been heartened and fortified by the position you took?" "Which one?" Mabel asked. "Why! By your life here!" Marie replied. "The fact that you had the nerve to live your own life openly and frankly—to take a lover if you wished, without hiding under the law. You have shown women they had the *right* to live as they chose to live and that they do not lose respect by assuming that right. But *now!* When I think of the *disappointment* in the whole woman's world today!" Marie was also close enough to Max Eastman to provide help to his friend and former lover, Florence Deshon, and to write him a long consoling letter after her suicide.[6]

With her health improved,[7] Marie could join with alacrity New York's world of feminist politics. Max Eastman described her then as looking "more like a

---

5. *Confessions of a Reformer*, 240–41. For a description of the Village at this time, see L. Morris, *Incredible New York*, 301–14, and Churchill, *Improper Bohemians*.
6. Luhan, *Movers and Shakers*, 526–27 (the italics are Mabel's); MJH to Max Eastman, February 6, 1922, in Eastman, *Love and Revolution*, 280–81.
7. Based on letter from Newton Baker to FCH (en route to Paris), June 14, 1911: "I am very much delighted to hear how great the improvement is in Marie's health. The sea part of your trip will doubtless be very helpful to her, and I share your feeling that she may now be entirely relieved of the difficulty that has for so many years been a constant annoyance and cause of anxiety to you both."

gypsy than a Presbyterian, being short of stature with gleaming dark eyes, arched black eyebrows and jewelly teeth."[8] Fred had come to understand the constraints that his traditionalist view of marriage had imposed upon Marie in Cleveland. Reflecting fifteen years later on the husband-wife relationship, he was justifiably critical of himself. "I had taken many years out of her life, had denied her the opportunity to pioneer, which she feared rather less than did I, and many of the enthusiasms that had been denied her in Cleveland could not be warmed into life again. . . . There was every reason why I should have allowed my wife any right which I enjoyed, should have given her every freedom which I took for myself, should have encouraged her to express her talents, which I recognized were of an unusual sort." He was proud of those qualities, and "my belief in freedom should have made me the first to insist that she use them as she willed. Instead, I discouraged them, because I preferred my early picture of a wife."

Society's view of women as property had fitted with his own instincts. "I hated privilege in the world of economics; I chose it in my own home. . . . There is something so jagged about our convictions; they do not run a hundred per cent true. My own unwillingness to abdicate masculine power made me better understand men's unwillingness to abdicate economic power." In the "woman movement," as in other social movements, equality had to be seized by the class that did not have it.[9] Information about the personal relationships of Fred and Marie is unfortunately lacking. There is, however, a brief but revealing comment in one of Fred's letters at this time. Writing to Senator La Follette, he observed: "I wish I could really tell you how much it has meant to Marie and me to have Fola [La Follette] coming back and forth in the house with her fresh, buoyant enthusiasms and interests this winter. We have been a family, instead of just two oft times rather lonely people."[10]

To Fred's intellectual and rational acceptance of woman suffrage, Marie counterpoised a commitment that was emotional and practical. In Cleveland, her role had been the accepted one of the educated, middle-class wife. She had worked in a social settlement and in the Consumers League. Now, in New York City, she could take on a much more vigorous and radical role.

The Howes arrived in the metropolis about the time when the suffrage movement there was heading in a new direction. Drawing on her own organizing experience in California and Idaho and on her observations of urban politics,

---

8. Eastman, *Love and Revolution*, 273. Eastman mistakenly thought Marie had been a Presbyterian minister, rather than a Unitarian. George Middleton, dramatist and husband of Fola La Follette, described Marie as "keen, eloquent, of deep feeling and rare beauty." Middleton, *These Things Are Mine*, 90.
9. *Confessions of a Reformer*, 233–35.
10. FCH to Robert M. La Follette, June 15, 1911.

Carrie Chapman Catt, the once and future president of the National American Woman Suffrage Association (NAWSA), had concluded that success would come only if the suffragists built up their own political machine. After studying Tammany Hall carefully, she and her co-workers decided in 1908 to create a new kind of organization for the New York City woman suffrage movement: a political party to push the campaign for votes for women. Each state senatorial and assembly district in the city would have a chairman. In October 1909 the chairmen and other delegates met in a city convention, which endorsed a popular vote on a woman suffrage amendment to the state constitution and a federal suffrage amendment and which approved a permanent organization for the new Woman Suffrage Party (WSP). The party soon had a city committee composed of chairmen elected from each of the five boroughs. In each assembly district, a leader appointed an election district captain for each precinct. By the fall of 1910, the party had acquired a four-room headquarters and claimed a membership of nearly twenty thousand.[11]

As one of Catt's devoted lieutenants, Marie became the WSP's leader in the 25th assembly district in Greenwich Village, coincidentally the same area in which Fred had been a captain for the Reverend Parkhurst's City Vigilance League twenty years before. Marie and her fellow activists did everything that their Tammany counterparts did, except that they put up no candidates for office and had no patronage to distribute. They held indoor and outdoor meetings, distributed leaflets, buttonholed voters, lobbied legislators, sent delegations to Albany, and appealed to churches and other organizations for support. Lincoln Steffens told Hutchins Hapgood that Marie had organized her district (which became known as the "Fighting Twenty-fifth" because of the women's activities there) more completely than any Tammany district leader ever had. She also served on the WSP's Organization Committee and on its Committee of Contributing Editors.[12]

A principal WSP aim was publicity for the suffrage movement, and to that end it sponsored street meetings, parades, lectures, and entertainments. Helping out, Marie wrote "An Anti-Suffrage Monologue," a witty ten-page parody of the arguments of the antisuffragists. The speaker's first argument against the suffrage was that "the women would not use it if they had it. You couldn't drive them to the polls." Her second argument was that "if the women were

---

11. See *Woman Voter*, no. 1 (February 1910); S. Graham, "Woman Suffrage," 122–26; Schaffer, "New York City Woman Suffrage Party"; Daniels, "Building a Winning Coalition"; National American Woman Suffrage Association, *Victory!* 108–12. I have followed the WSP usage of the word "chairman," rather than substituting the present-day "chair."

12. Peck, *Carrie Chapman Catt*, 222; H. Hapgood, *Victorian in the Modern World*, 332; Vorse, *Footnote to Folly*, 77–78. On the woman suffrage press, see Masel-Walters, "To Hustle with the Rowdies."

enfranchised they would neglect their homes, desert their families and spend all their time at the polls. You may tell me that the polls are only open once a year. But I know women. They are creatures of habit. If you let them go to the polls once a year, they will hang round the polls all the rest of the time."

She argued that she had proved the antisuffrage case "in a womanly way— that is, without stooping to the use of a single fact or argument or a single statistic." Warning of the terrible ordeal that the "delicate systems" of women voters would face, she concluded: "How shall I picture to you the terrors of the day after election? Divorce and death will rage unchecked, crime and contagious disease will stalk unbridled through the land. Oh, friends, on this subject I feel—I feel, so strongly that I can—not think!"[13] The Theatrical Committee arranged for the popular actress Marie Dressler to recite the monologue at one of their "general entertainments."

Work for WSP did not prevent continued participation by Marie in other forums. Catt had not tried to make WSP a national party—she realized that other suffragists might see it as a rival to the older organization. So, along with her vigorous leadership in WSP, Marie continued to work in NAWSA and held office as a vice president of the New York State Woman Suffrage Association, NAWSA's affiliate. In February 1914 she organized and chaired two "feminist mass meetings" at the People's Institute of Cooper Union. At the first of these, a dozen speakers gave ten-minute talks on "What Feminism Means to Me." At the second meeting, seven women spoke on "Breaking into the Human Race." Introducing the speakers, Marie proclaimed: "We're sick of being specialized to sex. We intend simply to be ourselves, not just our little female selves, but our whole, big, human selves. We have no intention of interfering with men, or telling them what they may do and what they may not do." Women put no fence around men, "but we insist that they shall not put any fence around us, either. We want to remove the fence they have put around us, and which is crumbling and decaying. But they object, because we might destroy the vines that have clambered over that rotten old fence, and the flowers and poems that grow on that vine. They do not see the human lives behind that fence." On Fola La Follette's topic, "The Right to Her Name," Marie noted the reason that she had been introduced as Marie Jenney Howe, and not as Mrs. Frederic Howe— she liked Frederic C., but not his name compared to hers.[14]

---

13. M. Howe, *Anti-suffrage Monologue*, 4, 6, 10. I am indebted to Michele LaRue and Warren Kliewer for the opportunity to hear Ms. LaRue's stirring rendition of Marie Howe's monologue at a presentation by the East Lynne Theatre Company in Cape May, New Jersey.

14. Middleton, *These Things Are Mine*, 129–31; Cott, *Grounding of Modern Feminism*, 12; *New York Times*, February 18, 1914, 2; February 21, 1914, 18. Marie was attacked by the National Association Opposed to Woman Suffrage as one who favored "free love," with her comments on pulling down the fences around women cited as the evidence. *New York Times*, May 25, 1914, 11.

Fig 3 An authors' meeting for woman suffrage, Cooper Union, January 12, 1914: (*seated, left to right*) Will Irwin (journalist, poet, novelist), Edwin Markham (poet, author of "The Man with the Hoe"), Lincoln Steffens (journalist, muckraker), Arturo Giovannitti (poet, labor leader), Percy MacKaye (playwright, poet), W. E. B. DuBois (civil rights leader); (*standing, left to right*) Flora Gaitlin, Ellis O. Jones (playwright), Elizabeth Freeman, William Hard (journalist), Paula Jakobi (playwright), Frederic C. Howe, Marie Jenney Howe

Marie joined the more militant wing of the suffrage movement in its fight for an amendment to the United States Constitution, associating herself with the Congressional Union for Woman Suffrage and the National Woman's Party. The Congressional Union, established in 1913 and led by Alice Paul and Lucy Burns, concentrated its efforts on the federal amendment and left state campaigns to NAWSA. After operating uneasily as a NAWSA affiliate, it took an independent course in 1914 and focused on lobbying Congress and the president for the amendment. Marie was named to the Union's first Advisory Council, along with such other luminaries as Mrs. John Dewey, Helen Keller, and Charlotte Perkins Gilman. She was also a member of the Advisory Council of the Union's New York state branch.

In 1917 the Congressional Union merged with the National Woman's Party (NWP), which had been formed at a convention called by Alice Paul in June 1916. The conclave decided that Union members would form its core, that it would be independent and unaligned with any existing political party, and that its only goal would be immediate passage of the federal woman suffrage amendment. Marie remained on its National Advisory Council into the 1920s. With 1916 a presidential election year, the NWP told the Democrats that unless they endorsed the federal amendment, it would campaign against them in the twelve western states where women already had the vote. Both the Democratic and the Republican conventions adopted states' rights planks on the suffrage, however. During the campaign, the Republican candidate, Charles Evans Hughes, came out for the federal amendment despite his party's platform. This delighted the NWP, which applauded Hughes without endorsing him or his party, concentrated its fire on Woodrow Wilson, and urged women voters to cast their ballots against the Democrats. To the administration's slogan, "He Kept Us out of War," they offered "He Kept Us out of Suffrage." The peace issue proved more important than the suffrage issue to the voters, and Wilson carried ten of the twelve states with woman suffrage, losing only Oregon and Illinois. Nevertheless, the NWP had demonstrated some political clout, and the election made both major parties aware of the importance of women voters.[15]

In January 1917 suffragists from the Congressional Union and the NWP began picketing the White House. After the United States entered the First World War, a split occurred between the party and NAWSA, as NAWSA decided to support the administration's war policies while continuing to work for woman suffrage. The NWP determined to place the suffrage ahead of the war effort. Picketing at the White House continued, but now there were confrontations and occasional acts of violence. In June the police began to arrest the pickets, and courts speedily convicted them of obstructing traffic. At first, judges released the arrested without penalty, but soon they began imposing fines. When the defendants refused to pay, they had to spend several days in jail. Upon their release they vowed to renew their picketing. Marie Howe spoke at a "jubilation breakfast" in Washington for freed suffragists on July 8, 1917. She could not understand, she said, why "this silent protest of women" met approval when used with state legislatures but was found "offensive to many" when applied to the national government. "I can't understand what there is about a state referendum that makes it dignified, while a national referendum is not. In regard to the pickets there is this same difficulty of our minds not being able to get beyond the symbolism." A few days later, on July 14, the court sentenced sixteen pickets

---

15. On the Congressional Union, the National Woman's Party, and the election of 1916, see Cott, *Grounding of Modern Feminism*, 53–59; Lunardini, *From Equal Suffrage to Equal Rights*, 85–103; I. Irwin, *Up Hill with Banners Flying*. How strongly Marie Howe participated in the NWP campaign against Woodrow Wilson is not known. Fred Howe obviously did not support it and was campaigning vigorously for Wilson in New York.

to sixty days in the workhouse, "a harsh and heavy-handed reaction on the part of the authorities." Present in the courtroom to lend moral support to the women on trial were a number of men, including Fred Howe, Dudley Field Malone, Frank Walsh, John A. H. Hopkins, and Amos Pinchot. Outraged at the sentence, both Malone, Collector of the Port of New York, and Hopkins, who had been Wilson's campaign coordinator in New Jersey, separately saw the president and urged that he intervene. On July 20 Wilson pardoned the suffragists in the workhouse.[16]

Fred Howe became a stalwart in the movement and spoke frequently at suffrage meetings. When Max Eastman organized the Men's League for Woman Suffrage, Fred became a member of its executive committee. The League held public meetings and joined the women in New York City suffrage parades. Fannie Hurst recalled participating in one of the parades:

> The next thing I knew, I was in formation, marching up [Fifth] Avenue, and helping my neighbor clutch the pole of a banner which read: Move Over, Gentlemen, We Have Come to Stay. . . . The woman with whom I shared the heavy pole was a brilliant-eyed, dark-haired mite who introduced herself, Marie Jenny [sic] Howe. Marching in the phalanx of men, I was later to discover, was her husband, Fred Howe, Commissioner of Immigration at Ellis Island. By happy chance they had read aloud one of my stories only the night before. It was thus I came to know a pair of fiery young liberals of the twenties.[17]

Fred lent his pen as well as his voice and his feet to the cause. His article "Why I Want Woman Suffrage" appeared in *Collier's* in March 1912 and was soon reprinted as a NAWSA pamphlet, *What the Ballot Will Do for Women and for Men*. "I want woman suffrage because it will free woman. It will also free man," he declared. Men would be able to correct the wrongs of society through the ballot, "but their correction will be hastened, it will come more surely, more wisely, by the cooperation of those who suffer most from the costs of the present

---

16. *New York Times*, July 9, 1917, 9; Lunardini, *From Equal Suffrage to Equal Rights*, 119–21; Stevens, *Jailed for Freedom*, 105, 158–63.

17. Hurst, *Anatomy of Me*, 246. On the Men's League, see Eastman, *Enjoyment of Living*, 306–8, 350–51; S. Graham, "Woman Suffrage," 147–48, 181. The male marchers in the suffrage parades often elicited laughter and ridicule from bystanders, especially, Will Irwin noted, from men who had been drinking. "One felt like an early Christian in the arena. Laughter began at my appearance and swelled to a roar at my rear—a roar punctuated by such unoriginal epithets as 'Sissy' and 'Nance' and such uninspired inquiries as 'Does your mother know you're out?' or 'Did your wife make you?' However, one original spirit broke through the police lines and marched for some time beside me, asking in a piercing falsetto: 'Oh, Lizzie! Do you wear lace on your drawers?'" W. Irwin, *Making of a Reporter*, 198–99.

system—by the votes of women."[18] Though from 1914 on he was serving in the Wilson administration as commissioner of immigration for the Port of New York, Howe did not allow the president's continued opposition to a federal amendment to weaken his adherence to the suffrage cause. His support for the women picketing the White House in 1917 has already been mentioned. "This is not the only time that truth has been on the scaffold," he observed.[19]

Many women engaged in the suffrage movement considered that battle only one aspect of a broader cause that by 1910 or thereabouts was beginning to be called feminism. For Marie Howe, feminism—"woman's struggle for freedom"—had three major components. "Its political phase is woman's will to vote. Its economic phase is woman's effort to pay her own way. Its social phase is woman's revaluation of outgrown customs and standards." There was no doubt that women were changing. They needed an appropriate word to register that fact, she wrote. "The term feminism has been foisted upon us. It will do as well as any other word to express woman's effort toward development." Feminism was not limited to any one cause or reform. "It strives for equal rights, equal laws, equal opportunity, equal wages, equal standards, and a whole new world of human equality." It meant more than a changed world. "It means a changed psychology, the creation of a new consciousness in women." The evolved feminist "does not adjust her life according to the masculine standard of what is womanly. She decides for herself what is womanly and what is natural. She thinks for herself. She lives according to her own convictions. If married, she retains her own identity. Underneath her wifehood and motherhood she knows herself a human being with human capacities for work, service and impersonal ideals." Freedom for women could not be won without the willingness of men ("many leading feminists are men"), who, by helping women to evolve, are also aiding their own evolution. "Feminism is woman's part of the struggle toward humanism. After feminism,—humanism."[20]

New York City had become the refuge of the independent, liberated woman, the "new woman" or "evolved feminist," who pursued a career along with, or instead of, marriage, who sought self-fulfillment and a lifestyle of her own choosing. For her, women's rights went beyond the right to vote, essential as that was. Many of these feminists had college degrees; most were from the middle or upper middle class. "They were young enough to work with the Elizabeth Gurley Flynns and old enough to be taken seriously by Mrs. Catt. They had already been to college, had worked for a while in New York City, and knew

18. FCH, "Why I Want Woman Suffrage." Howe used the same material for an article in *Public*.
19. Quoted in Lunardini, *From Equal Suffrage to Equal Rights*, 126.
20. M. Howe, "Feminism." On the origins and meanings of "feminism," see Cott, *Grounding of Modern Feminism*, 11–50.

something about living and working in the city. They had the enthusiasm of youth combined with the purpose and conviction that comes from personal experience."[21] Nearly all of them were caught up in the movement for reform, in the suffrage battle at least, if not in other causes as well. Inez Haynes Irwin captured the spirit of the day for reformers of both sexes. If she were asked to pick the most thrilling years of her life, she would choose the years between 1910 and 1914.

> Life was full of hope and freedom. Great movements were starting everywhere. In the United States, the loudest voice in the land was that of the liberal. Everyone was fighting for something. Everyone was sure of victory.... A speaker with a megaphone could go to the intersection of Forty-second Street, Broadway, and Sixth Avenue and announce, "I am here to gather recruits for a movement to free ..." and before he could state the object of his crusade, he would be in the center of a milling crowd of volunteers.

And New York City was the place to be. As Crystal Eastman wrote her brother Max: "I am sorry you don't like New York at all. I love it for the people there and the thousands of things they think and do ... especially the radicals, the reformers, the students—who really live to help, and yet get so much fun out of it." Max soon changed his mind about the city and also observed a difference between male and female reformers there: the women are "different from mere reformers—they're the people that want to live."[22]

To give these independent women a place where they could meet and talk about their lives and their problems, Marie organized the Heterodoxy club in 1912. "The only quality demanded of a member was that she should not be orthodox in her opinions," wrote Irwin.[23]

Included among the twenty-five original charter members were Irwin, Charlotte Perkins Gilman, Rheta Childe Dorr, Mary Heaton Vorse, Fola La Follette, Doris Stevens, and Susan Glaspell.[24] Of the members, about half were writers and/or journalists. Four were actresses, three were psychologists or psychiatrists, three were teachers, two were lawyers. Most were married. Their average age in 1912 was thirty-five. Gilman was the eldest, at fifty-two; Marie was forty-two. As others were invited to join, the membership reached sixty by 1920 and probably a maximum of seventy-five, with attendance usually running thirty-five to

---

21. Sochen, *New Woman*, 143–44. See also Kryder, "Self-Assertion and Social Commitment."
22. Eastman, *Enjoyment of Living*, 266, 316.
23. I. Irwin, "Adventures of Yesterday," 281.
24. Ibid., 413.

fifty.²⁵ Among later members were Marjorie Benton Cooke, a well-known novelist; Anna George De Mille, the daughter of Henry George, and her daughter, the famous dancer and choreographer Agnes De Mille; Mary Fels, the widow of Joseph Fels, a major benefactor of the American single-tax movement; Elizabeth Gurley Flynn; Freda Kirchway, later the editor and publisher of the *Nation;* Alice Duer Miller, writer and member of the famed Algonquin Round Table. There was one black member: Grace Johnson, married to the future secretary of the NAACP, James Weldon Johnson.

The marital and occupational profiles of the later members were much the same as those of the charter members. Along with the writers, journalists, and actresses, there were lawyers, stockbrokers, artists, social workers, teachers (high school and college), a printer, a physician, a nurse. Inez Haynes Irwin described the membership: "Among them were Democrats, Republicans, Prohibitionists, socialists, anarchists, liberals and radicals of all opinions. They possessed minds startlingly free of prejudice. They were at home with ideas. All could talk; all could argue; all could listen."²⁶ Regardless of occupation, women were in Heterodoxy not because of who their husbands were but because of who *they* were.

Judith Schwarz has observed that "the personal lives and relationships of the members ran the gamut from conventionally married heterosexual women (several of whom kept their maiden names after marriage), through scandalously divorced members and free-love advocates, to a rather large number of never married women, several of whom were lesbians involved in long-term relationships with each other or non-Heterodoxy women."²⁷ Their varied sexual preferences failed to disturb the harmony and the respect for each other that Heterodoxy embodied. One member, Florence Guy Woolston, wrote a tongue-in-cheek "scientific" study of the club, entitled "Marriage Customs and Taboo Among the Early Heterodites." Three types of sex relationships could be observed within the tribe, the monotonists, the varietists, and the resistants. "Most of the *monotonists* were mated young and by pressure of habit and circumstance have remained mated. The *varietists* have never been ceremonially mated but have preferred a succession of matings. The *resistants* have not mated at all." The tribe is without taboos. "There is the strongest taboo on taboo. Heterodites say that taboo is injurious to free development of mind and spirit.

25. I have found no complete list of charter members, but from various sources have compiled a list of twenty-nine who have been so identified. Obviously, several of these have been erroneously identified as charter members; Irwin, for example, named Elizabeth Gurley Flynn as a charter member, but Flynn indicates in her autobiography that she did not join until 1915.

26. Again, no complete list seems to be available. I have identified 108 women as members over the years, including the child of one member, considered an "honorary member."

27. I. Irwin, "Adventures of Yesterday," 414. For a fuller discussion of members' occupations and professions, see Schwarz, *Radical Feminists of Heterodoxy*, 44–54.

Members of the tribe suspected of a tendency to taboo are frequently disciplined. By preventing taboo the tribe has been able to preserve considerable unanimity of variety in opinion."[28]

Heterodoxy met fortnightly except during the summer months, at first in the Village and later at the Town Hall Club. Members paid dues of two dollars a year and also paid for their luncheons or dinners. The club avoided publicity and used its off-the-record meetings for free and untrammeled discussions of any and all issues. Speakers came both from inside and outside the group. They were mainly women but included some men.

After luncheon there were "two hours of talk, not mere clever conversation but informal discussion of some topic agreed upon at the last meeting."[29] The many and varied topics were usually new ideas and current problems: psychoanalysis, birth control, "twilight sleep" during childbirth, socialism, anarchism, pacifism, the IWW and its attempts to organize women workers in the textile industry, the conflict in Ireland, education, new plays, books, and art. One Heterodite, Caroline Singer, wrote of

> Loud talk and simple feasting: Discussion of philosophy,
> Investigation of subtleties. Tongues loosened
> And minds at one.
> Hearts refreshed
> By discharge of emotion!

If the postluncheon topic proved of "transcendent interest," there would be a husbands' evening and another discussion.[30]

At other times, Heterodoxy meetings turned on members' lives and experiences, a forerunner to women's consciousness-raising sessions in the 1960s and 1970s. The women called them "background talks." They must have helped break down barriers among the members, showing their common lot as women despite differences in occupation or lifestyle and providing a supportive and friendly audience for the revelations.

Marie was not only the founder of Heterodoxy but also its perpetual chair (until ill health forced her retirement), moderator, mediator, inspirer, and, one might almost say, mother-figure. She maintained peace, harmony, and good order among the articulate and frequently disputatious members. At Christmas

---

28. Schwarz, *Radical Feminists of Heterodoxy*, 1. She identifies 16 (about 15 per cent of the total membership) as lesbians or possible lesbians (67–72). See also Cott, *Grounding of Modern Feminism*, 45.

29. Woolston, "Marriage Customs and Taboo," 4, 6–7. The piece is dedicated to the Heterodite anthropologist Elsie Clews Parsons, and is a takeoff on her book *The Family*.

30. Dorr, *Woman of Fifty*, 271.

in 1920, the Heterodites presented her with an album of photographs and appreciations, and their affection for her permeated the tributes. The dedication spoke for all.

> What a Unity this group of free-willed, self-willed women has become; what a Fellowship you founded as you brought us and held us together; what a seamless shining robe the shuttle of Heterodoxy, moving through the warp and woof of us, has been weaving through these years, the garment of comradeship and loyalty, courage and charity, trust and faith and love. We have been scarcely aware of what has been happening to us in this little Order, so loosely held together, so casual, so free. Perhaps you have known and have kept wisely silent, biding the time when we too should know.[31]

Individual members added their praises. Paula Jacobi wrote:

Where was I? O yes. Marie
How we have nagged her because she hasn't signed her name
To a book, or a poem or a play or something.
What does she do anyway.
She has only a genius for friendship.
She only throws her great motherheart open
       To us all.

Inez Haynes Irwin toasted: "Here's to Marie who in the midst of this strange universe and this cold city created a little world for us: a little world in which we could laugh and play, talk and make friends."

By the early 1930s, Marie's health had forced her to give up active participation in Heterodoxy. One of the rare occasions when she attended was in February 1934, when the club heard a talk by Emma Goldman, whom Marie hailed: "We have missed our leader of unpopular causes, our defender of the persecuted and oppressed. We welcome you back and wish you could stay longer."[32]

Apparently Heterodoxy continued in existence until 1939 or 1940. Elizabeth Gurley Flynn said it endured until the late 1930s, "when its ranks were perceptibly thinned by the death of many of the older members." Irwin recalled that it "lasted until, in the Second World War, prices of food and meeting-places

    31. *Heterodoxy to Marie;* Dorr, *Woman of Fifty,* 271, 277–78.
    32. MJH to Emma Goldman, telegram, February 6, 1934; Goldman to FCH, February 17, 1934, Emma Goldman Papers, University of California–Berkeley, courtesy International Institute of Social History, Amsterdam.

became prohibitive." In later years, its surviving members continued to speak of what Heterodoxy had meant to them. Flynn's observation was typical. She considered that it was "good for my education and a broadening influence for me to come to know all these splendid 'Heterodoxy' members and to share in their enthusiasms. It made me conscious of women and their many accomplishments." For Freda Kirchwey, association with the feminists of Heterodoxy strengthened her commitment to her career. That must have been true for the other members as well.[33]

---

33. Flynn, *Rebel Girl*, 280; I. Irwin, "Adventures of Yesterday," 413. Irwin mentions that Heterodoxy lasted thirty-eight years, but she was obviously in error since that would put its end in 1950. Twenty-eight years is a more likely time span. Alpern, *Freda Kirchwey*, 42.

10

A HAPPY INTERIM

While Marie was embroiled with feminist causes, Fred was accompanying his excursions into national politics with single-tax activity and New York City politics. The single-tax movement was materially aided when, in January 1909, Joseph Fels, the manufacturer of Fels-Naptha soap, pledged to contribute twenty-five thousand dollars a year for five years to promote the cause in the United States. A Fels Fund Commission controlled and distributed the money. Fred Howe was a member of the commission from the beginning, along with friends like Lincoln Steffens, Daniel Kiefer, Tom Johnson, Carrie Chapman Catt, and Bolton Hall. The Commission used the money to spread the word about the single tax, to finance special campaigns in states where single-tax measures were on the ballot or before the legislature, and to promote the adoption of direct legislation (the theory being that people could then use the initiative and referendum to enact Georgist measures). The Fels Fund also financed annual single-tax conferences, the first in New York City in November 1910.[1]

Fred later observed that he had come to New York City intending to devote the rest of his life to writing but had found that "with leisure to write books, I could not write. I had won the prize of complete freedom from uncongenial work, and for some reason or other, I could not use it. The spur of contact with life was lacking. Apparently I needed to earn my freedom from day to day." Nevertheless, most authors would have gladly accepted the quantity of his output in 1911 and 1912: ten articles and a book, as well as several papers for professional meetings. Most of the articles dealt with the American city or compared

---

1. Fels's contribution called for American single-taxers to raise a matching amount, which they did. Fels, and after his death in February 1914 his widow, Mary Fels, actually gave the fund $173,000 between 1909 and 1915, and American single taxers contributed some $120,000. Mary Fels continued his single-tax work for a time, until her interests switched to the Zionist movement. See Dudden, *Joseph Fels and the Single-Tax Movement*, 199–202, 258–63.

it to the German or the English city. He also described progressive reforms in Oregon and examined Ohio's new constitution, inconsistently calling each state the most completely developed democracy in the world.[2] He presented a paper on municipal real estate policies to the Third National Conference on City Planning in May 1911, a paper on city planning to the annual meeting of the American Sociological Society in December 1911 (recycled as an article for the *American Journal of Sociology* in March 1912), and an address to the City Club of New York on "How the German City Cares for Its People" in December 1911.

Howe's book *Wisconsin: An Experiment in Democracy* grew out of his teaching stints at the University of Wisconsin, his work with the National Progressive Republican League, and his personal and political associations with Senator Robert M. La Follette. Although written and published during the senator's campaign for the Republican presidential nomination, it was not a traditional campaign biography but essentially a hymn of praise to the achievements of reform in Wisconsin. "Wisconsin is doing for America what Germany is doing for the world. It is an experiment station in politics, in social and industrial legislation, in the democratization of science and higher education. It is a state-wide laboratory in which popular government is being tested in its reaction on people, on the distribution of wealth, on social well-being." The book surveys the programs that had been adopted and gives special commendation to the role of the state university and its experts and to the work of Charles McCarthy and the legislative reference library. Fred wrote McCarthy that "the next few years will see people going to Madison to study democracy at work, much as we now go to Germany and Australia. And you have laid the foundations there so firmly in education and political democracy that there are no limits to the progress you can make. I very much envy you and the men who have had a hand in this programme of state building."[3]

Reviewers were not very critical of the work and tended to see it as the product of an enthusiast for the "Wisconsin idea." The *New York Times* found Howe part of a mutual admiration society, whose members were

> too modest to write books about themselves, but they have no reluctance to write books about each other, and ingenuous productions they are.... If the actors in the regeneration of Wisconsin had been content to do

---

2. *Confessions of a Reformer*, 238–39; "Land Values and Congestion"; "German and the American City"; "American City of To-Morrow"; "City as a Socializing Agency"; "In Defence of the American City"; "Garden Cities of England"; "Rule of the Expert"; "Cities That Think"; "Oregon"; "New Constitution of Ohio."

3. FCH, *Wisconsin*, 7, vii; Charles McCarthy to FCH, February 1, 1912; FCH to McCarthy, March 8, 1912, McCarthy Papers, Wisconsin Historical Society. McCarthy's book *The Wisconsin Idea* appeared at about the same time as Howe's.

good by stealth, and if then they had been detected and dragged blushing modestly before the world, the enthusiasm of their discoverers would have been understandable, and would have aroused sympathetic attention. But when the La Follette coterie ring up the curtain on their chorus of virtue, and claim the limelight, mutually pointing each at the other, weariness and wariness are inextricably mingled with the admiration so fiercely claimed.

Other reviewers also found the book interesting but one-sided.[4]

After nearly eighteen months in New York City, Fred must have felt himself somewhat marginalized politically. The leisure for writing that he expected the move from Cleveland to bring had not proved as productive as he had hoped. Although the quantity was acceptable, it had not taken him into new fields and had sustained rather than increased his reputation. Politically his activities had been interesting but unsuccessful. Stimson, his candidate for governor, had lost by a wide margin. The campaign for La Follette's nomination was going poorly, and Fred had had to relinquish his post in the National Progressive Republican League. In Cleveland, he had had solid bases to operate from—the Garfield law firm, Tom Johnson's "cabinet," the post of state senator. In New York City, he had no position that gave him continuing visibility and identity.

This was to alter in the spring of 1912. In his autobiography Howe makes the change appear almost a matter of chance. "Someone" heard him speak at the City Club on municipal administration in Germany in December 1911 and liked what he heard. "A short time after I was asked to become director of the People's Institute, a kind of popular university, which conducted a public forum at Cooper Union and carried on various educational activities south of Fourteenth Street."[5]

Actually, Howe's course to the job of director of the People's Institute was a bit more tortuous than his account indicated. The Institute was the brainchild

---

4. *New York Times*, May 12, 1912, pt. VI, 292. The *Nation*'s reviewer observed: "It is apparently as impossible to write about Wisconsin without indulging in superlatives, as it is, according to the story, to tell the truth about the Colorado climate without lying." In that respect Howe's book was like its predecessors—a "clear and interesting" but repetitious volume, whose author was "too enthusiastic over what has been accomplished to be well qualified to point out weaknesses, actual or potential." As a record the book was "highly valuable," but Howe's "comments and conclusions need modification." The *Survey* discovered nothing really new in the work—it consisted of "a personal eulogy of La Follette, plus unstinted commendation of the University of Wisconsin for democratizing learning." The *Literary Digest* called the book "bold and original," but considered it as "to some extent a manifesto of La Follette, and a fresh and striking exposition of what must be called 'La Follettism.'" *Nation* 94 (June 6, 1912): 569–70, and 94 (June 20, 1912): 606–7; *Survey* 28 (August 31, 1912): 686; *Literary Digest* 18 (May 18, 1912): 1066; *Independent* 72 (June 20, 1912): 1377–88.

5. *Confessions of a Reformer*, 240.

of Charles Sprague Smith, a member of a prominent New England family that had, among other worthy deeds, endowed Smith College for Women. Increasingly concerned about the gulf between the ivory tower of academe and the life of New York City and increasingly dissatisfied with the scholarly world, Smith resigned his professorship at Columbia in 1891. He explained in his autobiography that his life had been too sheltered, that he felt a need to do something to help the poor and weak in society. Possessing a real concern with the poverty, congestion, and morals of the city's lower classes, he also believed that overcoming class divisions would head off social revolution. How could this be done? By educating and uplifting the masses, especially the unassimilated immigrants of the Lower East Side. Education and reform were inextricably linked in his mind.[6]

Smith hit upon the idea of a new enterprise that would provide lectures and forums to the poor of the city. He took his plan to a group of prominent New Yorkers, who, after several meetings at the home of Abram S. Hewitt, established the People's Institute. According to its constitution, the Institute would furnish the people "continuous and ordered education in social science, history, literature, and such other subjects as time and the demand shall determine," and offer opportunity for "the interchange of thought upon topics of general interest between individuals of different occupations, thereby to assist in the solution of present problems." The enterprise would respect differences of opinion and be free of political or religious ties. It would "seek to unite all in a common effort for the advancement of the individual and of society."

As managing director and one of the trustees, Smith led and dominated the Institute from 1897 to 1910. The operations of the Institute depended on the largesse of a few wealthy individuals, including Andrew Carnegie, John D. Rockefeller, and J. P. Morgan. Hewitt was instrumental in arranging for the Institute to use Cooper Union as its home, and through his efforts its Great Hall became the site for lectures and meetings.

Under Smith's leadership, the People's Institute engaged in a wide range of activities. Its People's Forum provided a variety of lectures and debates, with half the time of each meeting reserved for the audience's questions, resolutions, and no-holds-barred discussions. Among the guest speakers were Charles Evans Hughes, Samuel Jones, Hazen Pingree, William Howard Taft, William Jennings Bryan, Booker T. Washington, W. E. B. Du Bois, Jane Addams, Sidney Webb, and even a then–state senator from Ohio, Frederic C. Howe. Heads of city departments reported on their agencies' activities at the Friday night meetings, "and in the heckling that follows [the department heads] have a unique opportunity of observing the state of the public barometer concerning their work."

6. C. Smith, *Working with the People,* ix–xiv.

From time to time the audience would take a stand on a public issue, and the People's Institute would lobby for it at City Hall or in Albany. On Sunday evenings the People's Church provided nonsectarian lectures and discussions on any and all religious and ethical beliefs. There were also evenings for drama and concerts, and the People's Institute arranged with the city's theaters to offer cut-rate tickets to workers and students. Concerned with wholesome entertainment for the masses, Smith helped organize the National Board of Censorship of Motion Pictures, which the Institute administered and staffed.

From the beginning, the Institute's offerings proved popular and drew a large attendance, mainly from Manhattan's East Side for the forums but from other parts of the city and from neighboring towns in New York and New Jersey for the People's Church. Smith was sensitive to critics' charges that these were assemblies of alien radicals, and, through crude surveys, he sought to show that the overwhelming majority of those who attended were citizens and registered voters. Robert Fisher concluded that "the people in the Institute audiences were aware, concerned, progressive democrats, not revolutionary socialists."[7]

Charles Sprague Smith's sudden death on March 30, 1910, removed from the People's Institute its founder, inspiration, and driving force. The board designated Lester F. Scott, the Institute's executive secretary, to be in charge temporarily, "to keep the work of the Institute intact." Scott was aided in this task by the civic secretary, John Collier.[8]

The hunt for a successor to Smith was to occupy the trustees for more than two years. A search committee considered a number of candidates, but no one seemed to fill the bill. Fred Howe's name apparently began to be mentioned in March and April 1912, and the chair of the search committee, Henry de Forest Baldwin, solicited recommendations for Howe from Louis Post and Newton Baker. Both of them enthusiastically endorsed their friend for the post of director. By April 18 he could report to Mrs. Charles Sprague Smith that Howe was ready to accept. Howe suggested a salary of four thousand dollars for his first year and five thousand dollars for his second, and these seemed reasonable amounts to Baldwin.[9] On May 9 the trustees unanimously approved Howe as

7. Fisher, "People's Institute," 81–84.
8. John Collier joined the People's Institute in 1908 as a "civic worker" and later became civic secretary and editor of its newspaper, the *Civic Journal*. He left the Institute in 1914 but returned a year later and worked there until 1919. He is best known as the reforming and controversial commissioner of Indian affairs, appointed by President Roosevelt in 1933 and serving until 1945. On Collier and the People's Institute, see his autobiography, *From Every Zenith*, 68–94; and Kelly, *Assault on Assimilation*, 23–38, 59–61.
9. Louis F. Post to Henry de Forest Baldwin, April 2, 1912; telegram, Post to Baldwin, April 3, 1912; Newton Baker to Baldwin, April 3, 1912; Baldwin to George McAneny, April 6, 1912; Baldwin to Mrs. Charles Sprague Smith, April 18, 1912; Baldwin to V. Everit Macy, May 7, 1912, Cooper Collection, People's Institute Papers, Cooper Union.

managing director of the People's Institute. He was at the meeting and presented a tentative program for the next year's Institute meetings, which was unanimously adopted.

As director of the People's Institute, Howe gained a number of advantages and opportunities. It provided him with a steady income—four or five thousand dollars a year was not an inconsiderable sum in the days before state and federal income taxes. As director, he would be in the midst of urban politics. Though the forums and other meetings had to be nonpartisan as far as candidates were concerned, their leaders and audiences did not have to ignore city problems. The Institute sponsored lectures by urban reformers in its Forum, and it organized mass meetings on specific issues, generally shortly before the city council or the state legislature was to act. A vote was usually taken after the discussion, and communication of the results brought pressure to bear on the appropriate governmental bodies. The Forum's legislative committee, made up of Institute trustees and lawyer volunteers, analyzed pending city and state legislation and provided information to Forum audiences. The Institute might not be able to endorse candidates, but it certainly could make its position clear on city and state issues and could pressure decision makers at both levels. So Howe found that the job of director gave him both a base from which to operate and the possibility of deeper involvement in the policies and politics of state and city.

Robert Fisher suggests that the change in leadership at the People's Institute came just at the point when the organization was beginning to seek scientific solutions to the city's problems. "Whereas prior to Smith's death the Institute was concerned with creating a virtuous and ethical citizenry which would reform society, in succeeding years it was more concerned with constructing a well-planned, efficient urban environment which would improve its residents."[10] Later on, Henry de Forest Baldwin, longtime chairman of the board of trustees, also observed that Howe had moved the Institute in a direction somewhat different from Smith's.[11] Yet the differences between the Smith approach and the Howe approach can be overstated. Though stressing education and moral uplift, Smith had involved the Institute in the problems of New York City. Howe's outlook led him to emphasize that political, social, and economic environments had to be altered if people's ideas were to be changed. But he shared many of Smith's beliefs and values, including that of the importance of education.

10. Fisher, "People's Institute," 255.
11. "Personally, I recognized that Dr. Howe's attitude toward social questions was from the point of view of an economist and a politician," Baldwin wrote in 1917. He made the same point a decade later in a memo on the Institute's history. Henry de Forest Baldwin to R. Fulton Cutting, March 23, 1917; memo, "The People's Institute of New York—Season 1928–1929—Thirty-first year," Cooper Collection, People's Institute Papers, courtesy of the Cooper Union.

There were, of course, differences in style. Smith was the founder—the inventor—of the People's Institute, and he was both its intellectual and its administrative leader. Howe had a great advantage in that he entered an institution that was already a going concern. He could leave the nuts and bolts of administration to the experienced hands of Scott and Collier, allowing himself time for other endeavors, including writing and politics. Especially pleasing to Howe was the freedom that the position afforded him. Since a substantial budget was assured and a proper environment for work provided, "the director was then free to do pretty much as he pleased." As he explained to Amos Pinchot, "we have an institution here that we can build in any way we want as a democratic agency for a lot of things. We are perfectly free. There is no inclination on the part of the trustees to restrain our ideas, and I believe we can build here a unique and affective [sic] institution for the city and state of New York."[12]

Much of the new director's time was taken up with planning meetings, arranging for speakers, presiding over sessions, and delivering his own lectures. After getting pro forma approval from the trustees on general themes, Howe chose both topics and participants. The coverage of topics was broad. In the winter of 1912–13, lectures and forums fell into four general categories: "The Political Needs of Greater New York," "The Awakening of Democracy Around the World," "Insurgency in Life," and "Mass Meetings on Measures of Urgent Public Concern." Although there was continuity with the programs of the Smith era, some topics began to receive greater attention: feminism, urban planning, and, after 1914, foreign policy. Howe called upon his network of friends and acquaintances as speakers, and his Institute correspondence is full of letters to people like Jane Addams, Charlotte Perkins Gilman, William Kent, Lincoln Steffens, Max Eastman, Louis Brandeis, Hutchins Hapgood, Oswald Villard, Joseph Fels, and Judge Ben Lindsey. Others of prominence with whom he was less well acquainted included Hilaire Belloc, Brooks Adams, Carrie Chapman Catt, Senator William Borah, William Jennings Bryan, Rev. John Haynes Holmes, Theodore Roosevelt, W. E. B. Du Bois, and Rabbi Stephen Wise.

Interestingly enough, in the light of their relationship in the 1930s, one of those whom the director pursued most assiduously as a speaker was William Wirt, educational reformer and superintendent of the Gary, Indiana, public schools. Howe explained to his various correspondents that he could not pay them well (only twenty-five dollars for an out-of town speaker), but they would be more than compensated by meeting "the most interesting audience in New York; Cooper Union has been identified with the promotion of new ideas for

---

12. *Confessions of a Reformer*, 240, 244–45; FCH to Amos Pinchot, November 25, 1912, Pinchot Papers.

more than fifty years, and the speakers who come to us seem to derive great pleasure from coming in contact with what is in many ways the most vital audience in the city of New York."[13]

Besides arranging and presiding over the numerous meetings, Howe himself delivered a dozen or more talks between March 1912 and April 1914 on topics ranging from "Recent American Municipal Programs" to "The Recreational Needs of New York." Audiences of up to sixteen hundred for forum meetings, and of fifteen hundred or more for the People's Church, listened to the various lectures, and many of the listeners pursued the speakers with penetrating questions. People attending were mostly serious, earnest, and open to consideration of the ideas presented to them. One of them, Benjamin Gitlow, destined for a more radical career than most of the other listeners, later described how the meetings affected him: "Attending the Cooper Union forum was like attending a living university. It was vibrant with the life of the times." After the meeting ended, "groups of intensely serious people discussed Philosophy, Religion, Politics, Socialism, Anarchism, Astronomy, Economics—there was no limit to the range of inquiry." Sometimes a group would hear from some itinerant worker about the wonders of the country and the world. "There, exchanging experiences and views, were tramps, hoboes, cranks, workers, students, and professional people, all representing numerous nationalities.... When I reached home and went to bed, I would turn over in my mind the things that left an impression upon me. I would try to fathom the problems confronting mankind."[14]

Charles Sprague Smith had been much concerned with problems of child welfare, and under his leadership the Institute had sponsored clubs, plays, musical events, and movies as "wholesome" recreation. Programs aimed at helping children and improving their neighborhoods expanded during Howe's tenure as director. With the backing of the board of education and the Institute, an independent citizens' group, the New York Social Center Committee, was formed in January 1912. Its goal was not only to provide constructive leisure-time activities for children but also to rebuild the neighborhood and restore the ties of the small community, sundered by metropolitan development.

In February 1912 the first of the new social centers was started at P.S. 63 on the congested Lower East Side. Workers from the People's Institute helped organize an elected local committee to run and partly pay for the center, though the

13. FCH to William Wirt, January 30, 1915, People's Institute Papers, New York Public Library; FCH to Wirt, October 27, 1915, Wirt Papers, courtesy of Lilly Library, Indiana University, Bloomington, IN; FCH to Edward A. Ross, September 30, 1915, Ross Papers, State Historical Society of Wisconsin.

14. Gitlow, *I Confess,* 7–8. Gitlow became a socialist, and then a communist. He was the Communist Party candidate for vice president of the United States in 1924 and 1928, and was a member of the Political Committee of the American Communist Party and the Presidium of the Comintern.

Institute continued to provide advice, general supervision, and financial aid. The aim, Howe reported, was "to develop a club house, town hall and democratic center for the life of the community, for the most part spent upon the streets, in the saloon and in the dance hall." The social center at P.S. 63 was a success and became a model for similar centers throughout the city. Activities included a weekly People's Forum on issues important to the neighborhood; projects directed by civic clubs; an information bureau to help with such things as citizenship, civil service exams, and jobs; social and literary clubs; pageants and festivals; educational movies; debates; plays; concerts; dances; athletics; and cooking classes.[15]

Howe could also report to the trustees in 1912 the establishment of the Educational Dramatic League and the People's Music League. Both proved quite successful in affording both entertainment and participation to children and adults. For the Music League, the Beethoven Musical Society and the Symphony Orchestra of the Cloak and Suit Makers' Union gave frequent concerts. A 1914 letter from Howe, soliciting the police commissioner's help in controlling crowds, indicates their appeal: "The attendance has been so great that we have had much difficulty in keeping the crowd from forcing their way into the hall after the seats were all occupied. . . . We find that the ushers are unable to hold the crowd back and must have police assistance."[16]

Howe's position as director of the People's Institute also involved him in censorship of a new and rapidly growing medium of entertainment, the movies. By 1909 there were some six hundred "nickelodeons" in New York City, mostly makeshift theaters set up by exhibitors who rented empty stores, installed projectors, and charged viewers five cents. Religious and civic organizations soon decried the crime, sex, and violence that were staples in many of the films, and there were also complaints about the dangers of fire and the sanitary conditions of the nickelodeons. Exhibitors and manufacturers found themselves threatened by city hall with censorship or a shutdown of the theaters. In self-defense, in March 1909 the New York State Association of Motion Picture Exhibitors asked the Institute to set up a bureau of censorship. They pledged themselves to submit all their films to the bureau and to abide by its decisions, no doubt hoping by this action to stave off state or city censorship by accepting instead review by a private organization that might be more sympathetic. Charles Sprague Smith, who saw the movies as a medium for both education and wholesome entertainment, quickly accepted the exhibitors' entreaty.

---

15. Sixteenth Annual Report, People's Institute, 1912–1913, 7.
16. FCH to Arthur Woods, December 28, 1914, People's Institute Papers, New York Public Library.

In March 1909, under the leadership of the People's Institute, the Board of Motion Picture Censorship of New York was created. In June the Board became nationwide in scope and changed its name to the National Board of Censorship of Motion Pictures. Overall direction came from its general committee, while an executive committee supervised day-to-day administration, acting through a general secretary whom it appointed. Until his death in 1909, Smith chaired the executive committee, as did all of his successors at the Institute. John Collier served as general secretary until 1914. Subcommittees of a censoring committee, made up of volunteers without ties to the movie industry, viewed films and, by majority vote, approved or condemned them or recommended cuts or changes. Censors were especially concerned with episodes dealing with "notorious characters," insanity, drugs, questionable morals, sacrilege and blasphemy, drinking, vulgarity, "prolonged passionate love scenes," marital infidelity, "costuming—tights and insufficient clothing," women smoking and drinking, underworld scenes, disrespect for the law and its officers, suicide, murder, and crime and violence generally.[17] The Board saw its relationship to movie manufacturers as cooperative, rather than hostile, and both the People's Institute and the movie industry were satisfied with the results. By 1914 the Board could report that it had viewed and censored 95 percent of the films presented in the seventeen thousand movie theaters in the United States. State and local governments throughout the nation followed the Board's recommendations.

When he became managing director of the People's Institute, Fred Howe also became chair of both the Board of Censorship's general committee and its executive committee. He apparently found little difficulty in resolving his views as a civil libertarian with his role as nominal head of movie censorship in the United States. The record indicates that he accepted the policies and standards worked out by Smith and the National Board prior to his appointment at the Institute.

In an article in the *Outlook,* Howe both upheld the work of the National Board and recognized the problems of censorship. He argued that the Board's most important work was "the gradual improvement of the quality of motion pictures and . . . the elimination from all the films of certain undesirable motives, which, in the opinion of the Board, should not be portrayed to audiences containing a considerable percentage of children. The Board also encourages films of an educational, civic, and seriously dramatic character." It had no legal power to ban or revise movies, he pointed out, and it worked only through moral coercion and the acquiescence of the producers. A voluntary system had

---

17. *Policy and Standards of the National Board of Censorship,* 10–23. On creation of the Board and its general operations, see Fisher, "People's Institute," 207–52.

its dangers, he admitted, and so a large and varied membership was provided in the censoring committee. Even under the wisest system, there would be mistakes of judgment, but none of these temporary evils compared in seriousness with "the danger to the art itself from the ascendency of a point of view which would stifle, or threaten to stifle, the freedom of this industry as a mirror of the everyday life, hopes, and aspirations of the people. For the motion-picture show is not only democracy's theater, it is a great educational agency, and it is likely to become a propagandist agency of unmeasured possibilities." Despite the risks of the voluntary system, Howe much preferred it to government censorship. Control of a governmental board would become a political prize well worth fighting for. And official censorship, if permitted, would set a precedent for control of the drama and the press as well.[18]

Though accepting censorship for the movies, Howe strongly opposed it in other forums. He defended a Broadway play, *The Fight*, which was under fire from the police and the city's chief magistrate for its treatment of "white slavery." He praised the play's realism and maintained that "the effect of every line, of every situation, is to arouse disgust and to awaken a sense of chivalry and honor in every man's soul. The second act is a twenty minute sermon in its repelling qualities." To compel the producers to cut the second act seemed "a travesty on censorship, in view of the suggestive, alluring, and vice-producing productions which are presented without protest, night after night, upon the stage of New York."[19] He also spoke up for the right of free discussion in the social centers that the People's Institute was creating in the public schools. When the *New York Times* opposed use of the centers by socialists or other radical agitators or for any partisan purposes, he wrote the paper that he heartily favored school use for "any orderly purposes." He could think of no better way to improve conditions in New York City than by opening five hundred school forums to discuss all manner of things all year long. "Wrong can only be corrected by liberty of speech, by liberty of the press, by liberty of discussion. That should be so axiomatic in America as to require no defense."[20]

Conservatives, who associated the People's Institute with rampant radicalism, could find ammunition in an event in 1914, when Fred and Marie Howe acted to support one of their Greenwich Village friends, Max Eastman. In the July

18. FCH, "What to Do with the Motion-Picture Show," 412–16.
19. *New York Times*, September 12, 1913, 3. The text of Howe's letter to Chief Magistrate McAdoo, defending *The Fight*, can be found in an article by the play's author, Bayard Veiller, in the *New York Times*, September 21, 1913, sec. 5, 4.
20. FCH, letter to *New York Times*, March 12, 1914, 8. The *Times* was unconvinced: "The doctrine of 'free speech' cannot be swung as a bludgeon over the heads of those who would keep out of the places of public education the teachers of anarchy and revolution." Editorial, "Free Speech," ibid. The *Times*'s original criticism is found in "Social Centres in Schools," March 8, 1914, 14.

1913 issue of *Masses*, Eastman had written an editorial indicting the Associated Press for failure to report the "military despotism" used against striking coal miners in West Virginia. Accompanying Eastman's words was a cartoon by Art Young depicting the head of the AP pouring "lies" from a bottle labeled "poison" into the reservoir that provided news to an American city. In December 1913 both men were indicted for criminal libel based on a complaint filed by the AP. A second indictment charged a libel of the AP president personally.

To many Progressives, the indictments were an assault on freedom of the press. Gilbert Roe agreed to be the defendants' legal counsel without fee, and Amos Pinchot put up their bail of two thousand dollars. A committee, of which both Fred and Marie were members, quickly arranged a mass "free speech, free press" meeting at Cooper Union. Inez Milholland presided, and speakers included Amos Pinchot, Lincoln Steffens, and Charlotte Perkins Gilman. Fred and Marie were listed in the program as "Patrons."[21] Eastman described the meeting as "packed full, with hundreds in the aisles and hundreds turned away," and the *Times* reported an attendance of more than 1,500.

The case against Eastman and Young never went to trial and after two years was dropped without explanation. Eastman's gratitude to Fred for his backing was evidenced in his reply to an invitation to speak at a People's Institute series on the War: "I hate to make speeches in New York where people know me and are on to my curves. But I can not very well refuse your request straight out after your generosity in helping me and *my* institution. Therefore, I shall have to say that on January 8th, if I can not find some absolutely perfect excuse, I will appear and talk on the subject of Internationalism and the War."[22]

Despite this and later battles in which he defended free speech and free press against government coercion and pressures, Howe continued to support the system of movie censorship that had been developed by the People's Institute. When he left the Institute to become Commissioner of Immigration in 1914, he agreed to continue as chairman of the National Board. In a press release, he reiterated his opposition both to state and federal censorship and to the abolition of censorship altogether, and argued for the "middle course: that there was some place for the disinterested public in connection with the motion picture show." Fred "would have the motion picture business as free as possible. I would send the man with the camera to the most inaccessible parts of the world. . . . It is because of the limitless possibilities of the motion picture that I want this agency to continue as free in the future as it has been in the past." He

---

21. FCH to Robert M. La Follette, January 19, 1914, La Follette Papers; *New York Times*, March 6, 1914, 20. Other patrons included John Dewey, Mr. and Mrs. Morris Hillquit, Norman Hapgood, and Fola La Follette.

22. Max Eastman to FCH, October 20, 1914, People's Institute Papers, New York Public Library.

believed that the existing system of censorship satisfactorily protected the public against immoral films.²³

Howe parted company with the majority of representatives of the "disinterested public" when they considered the time's most controversial, and some would say greatest, film, *The Birth of a Nation*. D. W. Griffith's classic work had had its premiere in Los Angeles in February 1915 and was slated to open in New York City in March. Its first showing had roused the vehement objections of the Los Angeles branch of the National Association for the Advancement of Colored People (NAACP). The group had unsuccessfully sought an injunction against the film's exhibition, arguing that its treatment of the Negro and its glorification of the Ku Klux Klan presented a threat to public safety and could lead to riots. The secretary of the NAACP's New York branch sent out thousands of pamphlets, alerting local chapters and friends of the organization to the film. The NAACP hoped that the National Board of Censorship would either condemn the movie or recommend substantial cuts in it. A subcommittee of the Board's censoring committee saw an advance screening in February 1915 and recommended the film's approval. There were reports that Fred Howe, still serving as chairman of the Board, was unhappy with the subcommittee's action. Because of the controversy about the film, a second screening was held for members of the general committee, the Board's governing body. That committee decided not to approve until it had viewed a re-edited version. Howe was said to want the entire second half of the film banned.²⁴

The New York premiere of *The Birth of a Nation* went off as scheduled. After Griffith had made several cuts in the film, the general committee of the Board viewed it again and voted fifteen to eight to approve. Fred Howe was one of those who voted no, and he refused the use of the Board's regular form of approval: "Passed by the National Board of Censorship of Motion Pictures, Frederic C. Howe, chairman." On March 30 Mayor Mitchel received a delegation from the NAACP and other organizations, who complained about the movie. It was denounced by W. E. B. Du Bois, Oswald Garrison Villard, Rabbi Stephen Wise, Lillian Wald, Fred Howe, members of the clergy, and others. Howe maintained that the film portrayed Negroes as "lustful" and "depraved." Its treatment of them was "cruel, vindictive, and untrue" and all black Americans, some 10 million people, were "degraded" by it. The mayor received the group sympathetically, but nothing much came of the meeting.²⁵

23. News release, sent by the National Board of Censorship of Motion Pictures to all New York newspapers, August 26, 1914, National Board of Review of Motion Pictures Papers, New York Public Library.

24. Schickel, *D. W. Griffith*, 272.

25. "Films and Births and Censorship," *Survey* 34 (April 3, 1915): 4; Schickel, *D. W. Griffith*, 285; *New York Times*, March 31, 1915, 9; FCH to W. D. McGuire Jr., April 1, 1915, National Board of Review of Motion Pictures Papers; W. D. McGuire Jr. to FCH, April 4, 1923, National Board of Review of Motion Pictures Papers.

The controversy over *The Birth of a Nation*, as well as the time required by his duties at Ellis Island, led Howe to press for acceptance of his resignation as chairman. "I presume the Board must feel embarrassed at my protest against 'The Birth of a Nation,'" he wrote, "and I hope the Board will feel free to elect my successor as Chairman of the Board as soon as possible. I am not doing this in a spirit of protest, as you know, for I tendered my resignation a long time ago and on subsequent occasions have urged upon you the desirability of finding someone who could give more time to the work than I can possibly give." The Board regretfully accepted his resignation but almost immediately elected him a member-at-large of its general committee. In 1916 the Board asked him to permit it to distribute to the press the text of a speech he had delivered when still chairman, and he agreed, on condition that it be reedited and approved. In it, he took the same position as in the earlier *Outlook* article and again praised the voluntary censorship system. In 1923 Howe went to Albany to lobby against censorship, and the Board published his speech as a pamphlet, *Why I Do Not Believe in Censorship of Motion Pictures*. He continued as a member of the Board's national advisory committee until 1921 and returned to it in 1924. In April 1930 he was unanimously elected to the executive committee, and he remained on the committee until 1940.[26]

His position at the People's Institute gave Howe not only a ringside seat in New York City politics but also a role as an actor in it. His acceptability to one of the elite groups of New York City was indicated by his speedy election to the Century Association in 1913. Described by Jan Morris as "a club of stylish tradition" and "one of the most distinguished and clubbable of Manhattan clubs," the Century was a men's club that had been founded in 1847 by a small group of artists and writers on art. It limited its membership to "authors, artists and amateurs of letters and the fine arts." Among New York clubs that served the "cultivated," it was considered the most exclusive. Its members were artists, writers, churchmen, businessmen, educators, and political leaders (including, in their time, presidents Cleveland, Theodore Roosevelt, Taft, Wilson, Hoover, and Franklin D. Roosevelt). To belong, one had to be nominated by a member or members, evaluated through supporting and opposing letters, assessed by a committee on admissions, and approved by a general membership meeting. Telling Howe in April 1913 that the admissions committee would soon recommend his membership, Henry de Forest Baldwin let him know of his good fortune. He had been proposed the previous summer, and the committee did

---

26. *New York Times*, January 26, 1929, 8; W.A.B., executive secretary, to FCH, April 3, 1930, National Board of Review of Motion Pictures Papers. The People's Institute's connection with the Board weakened after 1914 and was severed completely in 1922. See Fisher, "People's Institute," 249–52.

not often act on a name within a year. Once a member, Howe could rub shoulders with such notables as Ralph Adams Cram, Clarence Day Jr., Thomas W. Lamont, John Spencer Bassett, Charles Francis Adams, A. Lawrence Lowell, Harlan Fiske Stone, Dwight Morrow, Edward M. House, Oswald G. Villard, Augustus and Learned Hand, Brand Whitlock, W. L. Mackenzie King, William Gillette, Ray Stannard Baker, Henry Emerson Fosdick, and Frank Goodnow. The sociability and good talk that permeated the club's building on West Forty-third Street were doubtless enhanced by the meals and the bar available to Centurions—in 1917, cocktails or a carafe of gin, scotch, rum, or rye were a dime apiece, brandy went for fifteen cents a pony, and a julep or a Tom Collins for a quarter.[27]

Drawing upon his experience with franchises and urban transit in Cleveland, Howe became a voice for municipal ownership in New York City. He told the City Club: "I sometimes think that the transportation lines and the real estate dealers are in league to keep the people within a small radius. I think that every family is paying at least $100 a year more for land rent than they should. There isn't room on the surface to house all of the people, and so they are being housed up in the air." In the ongoing controversy over new subway construction, he joined those who advocated municipal ownership and operation of the lines. In this he was backed by the People's Institute's Forum, whose mass meetings passed numerous resolutions for public control. Among members of the Board of Estimate, only John Purroy Mitchel consistently supported public ownership. Howe applauded Mitchel's position, writing him: "I want to congratulate you on the statement of your alternative plan for the building of subways. It is very simple, direct and understandable, and seems to me very conclusive. I think you have done a splendid piece of work in meeting the situation as you have."[28]

Howe's visibility in controversies over public ownership was enhanced when he became president of the League for Municipal Ownership and Operation. In 1914 Ralph M. Easley, director of the National Civic Federation, asked him to speak to the NCF's annual meeting as an advocate of municipalization. "We are particularly anxious to have you make this address, because I know of no other pro who has made an examination of the matter on the ground," Easley wrote. "There are many other writers on the subject but they largely draw their views

27. J. Morris, *Manhattan*, 135, 137; Hammack, *Power and Society*, 73; Century Association, *Century, 1847–1946*, 233, 269; Henry de Forest Baldwin to FCH, April 25, 1913, Cooper Collection, People's Institute Papers, Cooper Union.

28. *New York Times*, January 28, 1912, 15; February 3, 1913, 1; *Confessions of a Reformer*, 245; Collier, *From Every Zenith*, 73–75; Fisher, "People's Institute," 129–35; Cerillo, *Reform in New York City*, 188–92; Lewinson, *John Purroy Mitchel*, 67–71; FCH to John Purroy Mitchel, February 18, 1913, Mitchel Papers, Library of Congress.

from you, and we would naturally rather draw them from their original source, and give them in their pristine purity." Howe was happy to accept and told the gathering that he had been led to support public ownership through experience, not statistics. Afterward, Easley wrote Howe: "I would give a million dollars if I could address an audience in as graceful and pleasing a manner as you did."[29]

Perhaps it was Howe's position on the subway issues that brought him to the attention of John Purroy Mitchel and led in the fall of 1913 to his appointment, along with Professor Frank Goodnow of Columbia, to study the organization of the New York City school system. Goodnow was an authority on public administration and the author of major works on municipal government. He was later to become president of Johns Hopkins. Mitchel and the other two members of the Board of Estimate's School Inquiry Committee asked Goodnow and Howe to inquire into "the organization and administration of the board of education and local school boards, and the relation of the department of education to the city government and to the state," and gave them a five-page list of topics that they might cover.[30]

The two municipal experts agreed in their general outlook on administration and apparently decided to divide the workload. Goodnow took primary responsibility for examining the legal and administrative status of the Board of Education, while Howe wrote a long supplementary report on educational and recreational uses of the public school plant. Their overall report (released in October 1913) found that confusion and conflict in organization had resulted in decreased efficiency and responsibility. A Board of Education of forty-six members was simply too large, and its committees were too numerous and their work too uncoordinated and unsupervised. Reorganization was clearly necessary both to improve efficiency and to focus responsibility for supervision of the school bureaucracy.[31]

Goodnow and Howe recommended a Board of eight members. The mayor would appoint three, each of the borough presidents would name a member, and there would be a system of weighted voting. An alternative arrangement would be mayoral appointment of all members, with a similar distribution of

29. Ralph M. Easley to FCH, November 19, 1914, National Civic Federation Papers, New York Public Library; *New York Times,* December 5, 1914, 9; Easley to FCH, December 10, 1914.

30. *New York Times,* November 15, 1912, 8; Frank J. Goodnow to John Purroy Mitchel, November 20, 1912, JHU; John Purroy Mitchel, William A. Prendergast, Cyrus E. Miller to Frank J. Goodnow and Frederick [sic] C. Howe, November 17, 1912. There are two letters of November 15 from Mitchel et al. Goodnow's ideas on administration and efficiency are summarized in Schiesl, *Politics of Efficiency,* 74–75. See also Lewinson, *John Purroy Mitchel,* 150–51. The Moore report was never printed as an official document but was published separately and nongovernmentally: Moore, *How New York City Administers Its Schools.*

31. Goodnow and Howe, "Organization, Status and Procedure," 18, 20.

borough representatives. The authors seemed to prefer the second plan since the mayor would become "the fountainhead of education in the city" and it would be easier to hold him accountable for the character and personnel of the Board. The state legislature should give the Board of Education wide power to experiment and to develop its own means of administration. Indeed, Goodnow and Howe would extend the principle to local school boards within the city. "Any change which would free the talent both of the teachers within and the people without the schools and promote that wholesome and healthy rivalry among superintendents and teachers, as well as among parents' associations and individuals interested in the subject, would probably be of as much value to the schools of New York as any reform that could be suggested. Without some competition schools are likely to become static and inert."[32] The report also made a number of specific recommendations on the staffing and functions of the bureaus and officers in the department of education.

Howe's lengthy supplementary report on recreational and leisure time needs of New York City suggested that greater efficiency be developed through "the voluntary organization of the community for the purpose of developing a leisure life through the wider use of the public schools." Notable throughout was Howe's emphasis on provision by the community for the leisure of its citizens. "Happiness is as normal and wholesome a want as is work. If it cannot be supplied by the individual it must be supplied by the community. And if commerce does not meet this need, or if the costs which commerce imposes make recreation prohibitive, then it is the duty of the community to add something other than toil to the lives of its people."[33]

Earlier, as the mayoral election of 1913 neared, Fred Howe took part in efforts to select a suitable candidate. Reformers were divided. The so-called good government people—from the City Club, the Citizens' Union, and the social settlements—wanted George McAneny, but local leaders of the Progressive Party and some followers of William Randolph Hearst preferred John Purroy Mitchel. A third possibility was the Republican-endorsed Charles Whitman, a popular district attorney. The names of all three candidates were presented to the 107 members of the Citizens' Municipal Committee, who on the ninth ballot gave a majority to Mitchel. As a member of the Committee, Howe cast his vote for

32. Ibid., 23–24, 33–34, 26, 27. When he became mayor, Mitchel sought the change to a smaller board of education that Goodnow and Howe had recommended. This aroused the opposition of teachers, parents, and school board incumbents, as did the mayor's tightfisted policy on school spending. Reformers finally convinced the state legislature in the spring of 1917 to set the membership of the New York City school board at seven, appointed by the mayor.

33. New York City, Board of Estimate and Apportionment, *Report of Committee on School Inquiry*, 385, 415. The report is listed separately as *The Economic Utilization of the Public School Plant for Educational and Recreational Purposes*, by Frederic C. Howe.

Mitchel. The candidate was acceptable to all the reform groups, won the endorsement of President Wilson, and headed a Fusion ticket backed by Republicans, Progressives, anti-Tammany Democrats, and independent reformers. The slate won handily in November, capturing not only the mayor's office but also the Board of Estimate and the Board of Aldermen.[34]

Howe was interested in the criminal justice and law enforcement systems and wrote the *New York Times* a long letter in opposition to the death penalty, arguing that capital punishment, as the deliberate act of society itself, turned him and all his fellow citizens into executioners. "Does it not involve an imperceptible loss to the best that is in us; is not civilization halted every time the death penalty is exacted; is not the evolution of goodness, of kindness, of the best that is in the world checked by the awakening of a sense of revenge, the desire for expiation, and a morbid interest in the gruesome details of the death penalty? Ought we not to take account of the unseen cost of it all and think in larger terms than that of retribution or revenge?" A jury may not only be mistaken in its verdict but also be incapable of judging the influences of birth, environment, social conditions, and suffering that lay behind the crime. It was time to abolish the death penalty and to protect ourselves from "the unseen, unmeasured, reaction upon all of us, . . . whose cost when repeated over and over again in the minds of a whole people is immeasurably more costly than any conceivable gain that can come from the retention of an institution which had its origin with the cave men, when vengeance was the universal law of life."[35]

In another letter to the *Times,* Howe supported Adolph Lewinsohn's protests against the New York state prison system and his argument that Sing Sing should be replaced by a "farm industrial prison." Howe agreed that the existing penal system was brutal and offered the Ohio prison farm as an alternative. "Harsh and cruel treatment, the isolated cell, and the general inhumanity of our prison systems cannot, and never has improved criminals; it must brutalize them," he argued. "For brutality must of necessity beget brutality. That is a law of life. It applies to those who are down and out just the same as it does to any

---

34. F. B. Shipley to John Purroy Mitchel, August 1, 1913, Mitchel Papers. Members of the Citizens' Municipal Committee included Andrew Carnegie, George W. Perkins, and John D. Rockefeller. Cerillo, *Reform in New York City,* 149. Norman Hapgood, the editor of *Collier's Weekly,* chaired the Committee. On Mitchel's nomination, see Lewinson, *John Purroy Mitchel,* 78–87.

Mitchel's single term of office was characterized by an emphasis on municipal effectiveness and efficiency, rather than on the attainment of new social or economic goals. In 1960 Wallace S. Sayre and Herbert Kaufman rated Mitchel as second only to Fiorello La Guardia among New York City mayors. On Mitchel and his administration, see Sayre and Kaufman, *Governing New York City,* 692–94; Cerillo, *Reform in New York City,* 149–54; Finegold, *Experts and Politicians,* 54–67; Schiesl, *Politics of Efficiency,* 165–69.

35. *New York Times,* November 1, 1912, 12.

one else."³⁶ Howe and the Forums of the People's Institute supported the warden of Sing Sing, Thomas Mott Osborne, in his fight against trumped-up charges of perjury and neglect of duty, fomented by enemies within the penal bureaucracy and backed by some newspapers. Like Howe, Osborne was a foe of capital punishment and a proponent of prison reform.³⁷

Fred Howe's writings during his tenure at the People's Institute for the most part covered familiar themes: the achievements of German cities, the desirability of city planning, the benefits of taxation of land values, the need for the community to provide opportunities for the proper use of leisure time. He praised the efforts of his friend Judge Ben Lindsey in juvenile justice, calling them "a live record of a big work, carried on unflaggingly in the face of harassing annoyances and ill health; a record of devotion and splendid achievement."³⁸

Several articles considered other aspects of social and economic policy. In the only article they published as joint authors, Fred and Marie advocated pensions for needy mothers, whether married, widowed, or unmarried. Marie probably supplied the structure—a lunchtime conversation among a teacher, a bachelor, a mother, a lawyer, a poet, a businessman, a social worker, and several other types—and the continuity, while Fred provided statistics and quotations from authorities. Mothers' pensions were presented as a matter of simple justice, as well as an economical policy. The mother observed: "It is a right. . . . I've raised four healthy children. It's been my business, just as much as my husband's factory has been his business. . . . And I consider my business as important to the state as his. . . . The government hasn't helped me to build my family, but it has helped my husband and his father before him to build their business. It has given them a tariff in favor of their infant industry. Why not give poor mothers an equivalent in favor of their infant kids?" By the end of the conversation, all the participants had pledged themselves to work for mothers' pensions in their own states.³⁹

In an article first presented to a national conference on unemployment, Fred found another right, the right to work. That right "ought to be included with those three fundamental rights of life, liberty and the pursuit of happiness. For of what possible value are those three rights of a man on the bread-line, to a man who has to go petitioning to a private charity for the right to live, when

36. Ibid., December 1, 1913, 8. Howe had expressed similar sentiments in 1893 in one of his earliest articles, "Two Decades of Penological Progress."
37. The charges against Osborne were soon thrown out of court or dropped. See *Confessions of a Reformer*, 242; R. Chamberlain, *There Is No Truce*, 283–364; Tannenbaum, *Osborne of Sing Sing*, 103–257.
38. FCH, "Where the Business Men Rule"; "Remaking of the American City"; "Leisure"; "Beast and a Boomerang."
39. Howe and Howe, "Pensioning the Widow and the Fatherless," 284–85.

his spirit craves for work?" He praised the German system of labor exchanges as a way of finding jobs for the unemployed. That system was by no means ideal, and America could do better. "But Germany has made a demonstration that to me is sufficient, just as Denmark has made a demonstration that to me is sufficient, that poverty can be cured, but that it can be cured only by law. We have already proceeded to exterminate disease by hygiene, and other legitimate methods. This is the next step in the social program: the cure and extermination of involuntary poverty by law."[40]

The only book written by Howe during his People's Institute period, *European Cities at Work*, appeared in the spring of 1913. In his preface, he presented it as a sequel to *The City: The Hope of Democracy*. Eight years later, one could detect some progress in America, but "we do not think in big community terms. We have not begun to plan and build with a vision of the whole. We do not appreciate the possibilities of city life." Some old-world cities justified our hope, however. "This book has been written with the hope that the achievements of European cities may aid in the solution of our problems."[41]

Fifteen of the following chapters deal with the German city, five treat aspects of the British municipality, and a final chapter offers a comparison of European and American cities. Again, as in earlier writings, the terrain is familiar and the descriptions often recycled from previous publications. He praises German cities for their planning, their use of experts, their concern with the city beautiful, their achievements in municipal ownership, social welfare, education, recreation, and housing. Howe's admiration for the Germany municipality is almost unbounded, although he notes inequalities in the electoral systems and domination by businessmen, and hints at the dangers of centralized power. He again finds that the accomplishments of British cities had been limited by excessive control from the national government, which stemmed from the class rule of the landed aristocracy.[42]

In conclusion, Howe points to the shortcomings of American cities and blames them on excessive individualism, lack of a sense of community, decision making by politicians rather than by experts, and such complications of American government as the system of checks and balances. He is not arguing that the United States had to copy German or British institutions, Howe asserts. Rather he is calling for Americans to reform their methods. America's virtue lay in its democracy. "We are raising a whole people to the art of self-government.... The cry of the almost disfranchised German is for democracy; of the British rate-payer for the American system of local taxation and more

40. FCH, "German System of Labor Exchanges," 300, 304.
41. FCH, *European Cities at Work*, vii, xi.
42. Ibid., 155, 319, 322–23.

generous concern for sweetness and light. The cry of the American city is for the things the German and English cities have already achieved." American cities already did many things better: our local tax system, our schools, our parks and playgrounds, our libraries, our fire departments. "We are beginning to see the city as a conscious, living organism which the architect and the engineer, the educator and the artist, the administrator and the dreamer, can build and plan for the comfort, convenience, and happiness of people, just as kings in an earlier age planned their cities for the gratification of their ambition and the glorification of their pride."[43]

The reviews of *European Cities at Work* were quite favorable. Most of the reviewers found Howe's descriptions of the activities of German cities not only interesting but also valuable as guides for American cities.[44] Several reviewers accepted the descriptions but were dissatisfied with Howe's analysis, finding too much acceptance of an undemocratic German paternalism.[45]

---

43. Ibid., 360, 361.
44. The reviewer for *Survey* thought the book "a stimulus to those practical citizens who always want to know whether a thing has ever been done before. It is a veritable compendium of facts presented in an illuminative and readable way." *Survey* 30 (July 12, 1913): 502. The *New York Times* praised Howe's "authoritative pen," and believed that the work was "bound to have a stimulating effect on the 'civic conscience.'" It listed the book among the year's one hundred best. *New York Times*, June 1, 1913, 336, and November 30, 1913, pt. 6, 678. The *Review of Reviews* found it "an authoritative presentation of the whole subject." *Review of Reviews* (August 1913): 246. The *Nation* suggested that one of the best ways to make urban progress in America was to "multiply such descriptions as he has given us. If we once acquire the zeal of the German cities, it will not be impossible to acquire the knowledge." *Nation* 96 (October 23, 1913): 389. The *Literary Digest*'s reviewer noted that the work was "full of . . . practical suggestions in all lines of city life," and the *Public*, agreeing that the German cities were marvels of efficiency, considered that it displayed not "the wild extravagances of an enthusiast" but the "cold analysis of the trained observer." *Literary Digest* 48 (January 3, 1914): 26; *Public* 17 (April 24, 1914): 402. Commented the reviewer for the *Political Science Quarterly*: "[Howe] writes with an authority which comes of practical experience with city affairs in this country and of a familiarity with European cities gained by many visits. . . . He writes also with a brightness and freedom which will make a wide appeal." *Political Science Quarterly* 28 (September 1913): 547.
45. Although John Fairlie noted in the *National Municipal Review* that the book was "written in an interesting style which should appeal to a wide circle of readers" and "should inspire Americans to raise their own standards and accomplishments," he thought that "Dr. Howe is distinctly less satisfactory . . . in attempting an explanation of German municipal success; and this phase of the subject calls for keener analysis than has yet been done." Howe had put too little emphasis on German centralization and had downplayed the lack of democracy in German and other municipalities. "A critic of democracy might suggest that municipal success in Europe appears to be in inverse ratio to the degree of political democracy." *National Municipal Review* 3 (January 1914): 184–85. *Survey*'s reviewer liked the book but faulted Howe's effort to explain why Germany's businessmen ruled for the general interest while America's did not: "His points are suggestive and interesting [but] they leave room for many questions and are not as satisfying as might be wished." *Survey* 30 (July 12, 1913): 502. The *Catholic World* thought Howe had given too little attention to American accomplishments but concluded that "in his interesting volume he has pointed out many things that our city fathers could study with profit, even if we do not want the paternalism of Germany to rule supreme in these free United States." *Catholic World* 97 (July 13, 1913): 541. Praising the descrip-

Looking back a dozen years later, Fred Howe found the years from 1911 to 1914 "a happy interim" in his life. Living in "a world that had confidence in literature and the power of ideas," and working with other college men and women who believed that the old order was crumbling, he was convinced that "a new dispensation was about to be ushered in." The evidence was plain. New magazines were prospering and exposing corruption and economic wrongdoing, and writers like Steffens, Tarbell, Ray Stannard Baker, and Charles Edward Russell were reaching the American audience. Churches were opening forums. "City reformers were springing up all over the country." A dozen insurgents sat in Congress. The instruments of direct democracy were being adopted, and reforms like municipal ownership, labor legislation, and woman suffrage were on the way. "It was good form to be a liberal," and even conservative lawyers and bankers were lending their names to radical movements. "The new freedom" would replace the old serfdom of bosses, and the younger generation would achieve the things that had been denied Howe's own.

A political renaissance was now surely coming, bringing with it "a rebirth of literature, art, music, and spirit. . . . It was to have the support of the more enlightened business men; it would call forth the impoverished talents of the immigrant and the poor. The spirit of this young America was generous, hospitable, brilliant; it was care-free and full of variety. The young people in whom it leaped to expression hated injustice. . . .They had supreme confidence in the mind. They believed, not less than I had always believed, that the truth would make us free." Thus Howe looked back, with a mixture of nostalgia and cynicism, at the prewar years.[46]

At that time, he would seem to have had a solid basis for happiness. As director of the People's Institute, he had a position of prestige and influence in New York City and access to those who counted in the municipality's political and economic life. His post was not a demanding one. He had stepped into an ongoing enterprise with an experienced and capable staff, and though he changed the Institute's emphasis a little, he had kept it going along Charles Sprague Smith's lines and had not invested time and energy in innovation. The work gave him plenty of time for writing and for politics. Yet he was not content, and less than a year after his appointment at the People's Institute, he was actively searching for another job. Indeed, he was engaged in that search during most of his incumbency as director.

---

tions of German and British cities, the *North American Review* found the book "fascinating reading" and praised the "thoroughly informed comments of the author upon municipal causes and effects." It thought the analysis rather general, however, and commented that the government of German cities seemed to be government by a plutocracy in the interest of the whole people. *North American Review* 198 (September 1913): 428, 429.

46. *Confessions of a Reformer*, 249–51.

His account in his autobiography is disingenuous. He fails to mention the fact that he had been busily looking for a different position but simply notes: "During the summer of 1914 I received a letter from President Wilson tendering me the position of United States Commissioner of Immigration at the port of New York."[47] He neglects to mention that within a month of Wilson's election in 1912, he was assiduously using his network of influential friends and acquaintances to help him find a place in the new administration. He did this both through direct canvassing and by sending information and advice to the appropriate people, thus bringing himself and his ideas to their attention.

Howe directed his efforts first to Senator La Follette. He wrote his friend on December 14, 1912, that he was thinking of enlisting in Wilson's administration. "Not that I want a job or desire to leave the work I am engaged on. But I feel that I would be of such substantial service to the things I believe in as well as to the President if I were his Secretary." He believed that he had had more kinds of experience as lawyer, politician, administrator, and writer than anyone else likely to seek the job. He wanted to organize a secretarial staff that would be the eyes and ears for the president, "a kind of secret and administrative efficiency staff that would reduce his fears and increase his powers; that would protect him from friend and foe, that could be sent on any kind of scouting expeditaion [sic], that could study bills, the qualifications of men and the thousands of problems that a single man cannot himself know and witout [sic] some such bureau cannot possibly know." Howe thought he had something to offer on the big problems of the next four years. "At least I would be a good foil for the shin plaster remedies that privelege [sic] is likely to offer as a substitute for real reform." He had already been through the experiences that would assail Wilson in the war against the interests. "We learned almost all of the devices of privelege [sic] in Cleveland, learned too the weight to be given to abuse."

For himself, duty came before personal preference. "I am quite honest when I say that I am very happy in my present work; honest when I say that I would prefer to remain here where I can build my own life. But at the same time I feel that I could be of service to the President as his secretary and probably of more service to the things I most believe in than in any other capacity that could be offered."[48]

In this letter, Howe displayed no small ambition. He apparently wanted to vault immediately into the new president's inner circle and to become, in effect, Wilson's chief of staff. There is no indication that he realized that several others, already closer to the president, had similar hopes and were in a better position to

47. Ibid., 252.
48. FCH to Robert M. La Follette, December 14, 1912, La Follette Papers.

fulfill them. Joseph P. Tumulty, the president's personal secretary, and Colonel Edward M. House, his closest adviser, were to provide a large part of the services that Howe suggested he could perform.

Throughout 1913 and into 1914, Howe continued to lobby La Follette, both with direct requests for aid in obtaining a position and with ideas on policies and appointments. We do not know what response the senator gave to Howe's importuning. Soon Howe went directly to the top. He sent Wilson a letter much like the one he had written to La Follette, although it waxed a bit more philosophic. It was "a time when men should enlist in a cause," he wrote, and he thought that he could serve better as Wilson's secretary than in any other place he knew. "Why? Because I believe so fully in the philosophy of industrial liberty that you awakened after fifty years of suppression and all that industrial liberty implies. I feel so confident that the worst of our social and industrial ills would disappear if we took the burden of privilege off the backs of the people and opened up opportunity to trade, to industry, to commerce and labor." He was aware of the difficulty of getting reliable and trusted assistants, he wrote, and he knew "something of the administrative loneliness and fear of imposition of those who are carrying executive responsibility." He could organize "an executive secretarial staff, a kind of bureau of research and efficiency," that would help lift "the burden of fear that always shadows one in the office of President, with the thousands of intrigues and ambitions that close the avenues of information against him." Thus the chief executive could "increase the number of his eyes and his ears in this way, by a corps of men who could examine into legislative and administrative problems, the claims of candidates for office and the thousands of questions which present themselves for consideration. I fancy no President has had such a service. Secretaries have been merely clerks. Even the Cabinet is usually streaked with ambitions, class instincts, traditions or political affiliations that introduce the element of unreliability."

Howe listed his qualifications for the position he had described: his experience with Tom Johnson; his practice of law and his service as city councilman and state senator; his experience with corporate law. He offered to come see Wilson in Princeton and suggested Senator La Follette, Charles R. Crane, Louis Brandeis, and Newton Baker as references.[49]

Howe's request for a post was only one of thousands that inundated the president-elect in the months after his election. No Democrat had occupied the White House in sixteen years, so there was a host of hungry office seekers. Some fifteen thousand letters poured into Princeton, and every Democrat of any stature seemed anxious to present his own list of party members deserving

---

49. FCH to Woodrow Wilson, December 18, 1912, Wilson Papers.

of a presidential appointment. Wilson announced that he would not be rushed in his choices and fled to Bermuda. His reply to Howe on December 23 offered no appointment but was not an explicit rebuff to his former student's ambitions. Howe wrote the president at once, making no mention of a job but making a number of suggestions on policy—reduction of the tariff, revision of the patent laws, strengthening local banks to check the power of Wall Street. Doubtless, Howe intended not merely to offer advice but to signal his expertise and his availability for an appointment in an economic or financial area.[50]

Having no immediate success with President Wilson or Senator La Follette in his job hunting, Howe turned for help to his old friend and fraternity brother Newton Baker. Still mayor of Cleveland, Baker had played an important part in winning the nomination for Wilson at the Democratic convention in Baltimore and had campaigned for him in Ohio and elsewhere. Wilson admired him as a rising young Progressive Democrat and had considered him for the post of private secretary that went to Tumulty. In 1913 Baker twice turned down the job of secretary of the interior but was to enter the Cabinet in 1916 as secretary of war. He wrote Howe in March 1913: "Ever since your letter of March 6th reached me I have been doing a lot of things suggested by it in the hope that in some way or another I could do the country a service by attaching you to some one of the departments in Washington, and I have no idea what if anything will come out of the suggestions I have been making." He thought Howe could be more useful to William Gibbs McAdoo, the new secretary of the Treasury, than to anyone else, and "as my relations with him are closer and more personal than to any of the others, I am doing whatever I can through him." He would continue his efforts for Howe, Baker promised, but "there is just one thing I am not willing to do, and that is to market your talents around from place to place. If you are to have an opportunity for service there it must come in a way befitting your dignity, and not as a mere concession of good will to somebody else."[51]

Howe already knew McAdoo slightly through the latter's activities in public affairs and New York politics. A wealthy lawyer and businessman, probably best known for organizing the company that built the Hudson tubes between New York and Jersey City, he had involved himself in politics as an anti-Tammany Democrat and an early supporter of Wilson for the presidential nomination. During the 1912 campaign, he served as vice chairman of the Democratic National Committee and became a key political adviser to the nominee. Fred had already been in touch with him to congratulate him on his appointment as secretary of the Treasury and to offer some thoughts and some flattery about

50. FCH to Woodrow Wilson, December 24, 1912, Wilson Papers.
51. Newton D. Baker to FCH, March 17, 1913

his cabinet position. He had been hoping against hope that McAdoo would be appointed, he wrote, "because it seemed almost too good to be true to have a man in that post free from the kind of entangling alliances that have ruled the Treasury portfolio ever since the Civil War. . . . It is good to have that post occupied by a man with a vision which transcends that of the banker."[52]

After Baker's suggestion in his letter of March 17 that McAdoo was the key to a federal job for Howe, Fred increased his efforts to keep himself in the Treasury secretary's mind. Rather than asking directly for help in getting an appointment, he again used the technique of reminding his correspondent of the extent of his own economic and financial knowledge and experience. In April he sent McAdoo a copy of his book *Taxation and Taxes in the United States Under the Internal Revenue System,* suggesting that it was still "accepted as authoritative by the colleges, and while it was written a good many years ago, I think I can still stand on the conclusions it offers. The book may possibly save you some work at some time when you have occasion to dig into the Internal Revenue System." The two men were on cordial terms and kept up their correspondence during 1913, but despite the friendly letters, nothing in the way of a federal job for Howe had emerged by the end of the year.[53]

Nor were Fred's efforts with Colonel House any more successful. He talked with the Texan about antitrust policy in December and then sent him a lengthy letter to clarify his views. After reviewing the various kinds of trusts, he concluded that the cure for monopoly was freedom from special privilege.[54] As in other letters of this period, Howe made no overt plea for a federal post. Rather, he indicated his ideas on an important issue sure to come before the Wilson administration and pointed, in his concluding paragraph, to the more than academic experience he had had with the problem. But, as with McAdoo, talks and letters produced no job offer from House. An attempt to get Howe the presidency of the College of the City of New York, spearheaded by Harry Garfield, also came to naught.

By then, Fred's opportunity for a federal position had at last come, although not the high-level post for which he had been angling. Finally Newton Baker's efforts with McAdoo paid off. On June 23, 1914, the secretary wrote the mayor: "I have always thought favorably of Frederic C. Howe, and I am thinking of

52. FCH to William Gibbs McAdoo, February 20, 1913, McAdoo Papers, Library of Congress. McAdoo acknowledged Howe's letter and expressed the hope that he could realize "the expectations of such fine friends as yourself in the great tasks that are ahead of me. You may be sure of one thing, that I have no other ambition or purpose than to serve the country with all the earnestness and sincerity and power that I possess." McAdoo to FCH, March 10, 1913.

53. FCH to McAdoo, April 9, 1913; McAdoo to FCH, August 15, 1913, November 16, 1913.

54. FCH to Colonel Edward M. House, December 19, 1913, House Papers, Yale University.

suggesting his name to the President for the position of Commissioner of Immigration at New York, for which it seems to me that he is admirably fitted. Won't you write me fully what you know about him and what you think of him?" Baker's enthusiastic response could hardly have come as a surprise. "His mind is one of the most subtle and well-stored that I have ever come in contact with. His character is not only above question, but sweet, and wholesome, and fine. . . . Fred's knowledge of the world and its peoples, his profound insight into American institutions, his devotion for better things for America and Americans, places him I think in the front rank of thinkers and doers in this country."

McAdoo endorsed Howe in a letter to President Wilson: "Do you know Frederick [sic] C. Howe, President of the People's Institute of New York? He is an exceedingly bright, energetic, and capable man, deeply interested in social work. He is a lawyer by profession, and I think is very highly regarded by Mayor Baker of Cleveland, Ohio. I know Mr. Howe myself and entertain the highest opinion of his character and ability. It just occurs to me that he would make a most admirable Commissioner of Immigration at New York, and I am taking the liberty of suggesting his name for your consideration." He enclosed Baker's letter or recommendation, "which confirms everything that I myself think of Mr. Howe."[55]

Woodrow Wilson's knowledge of Howe went back to their days at Johns Hopkins, and he had no hesitation in endorsing his former student and continuing correspondent for the position. Although McAdoo had a great deal of patronage at his disposal, he had been operating outside his jurisdiction in the Howe appointment, since the Bureau of Immigration fell under the new Department of Labor. The president brought the matter back into proper channels, writing Secretary of Labor William B. Wilson on July 10: "Here is a suggestion from the Secretary of the Treasury which strikes me very favorably indeed." Secretary Wilson at once replied that he would be "extremely well pleased" if Howe could be appointed. "He is a man of the type I have continuously had in mind for that position. If he could be selected it would be a happy solution to the problem." The president asked Wilson to find out whether Howe would accept the position and then to clear the appointment with James O'Gorman, the senator from New York. The post was subject to approval by the Senate. Senatorial courtesy therefore came into play, and the approval of the senator

---

55. William Gibbs McAdoo to Newton D. Baker, June 23, 1914, McAdoo Papers; Newton D. Baker to William Gibbs McAdoo, July 3, 1914, Baker Papers; Newton D. Baker to FCH, July 17, 1914, Baker Papers; William Gibbs McAdoo to Woodrow Wilson, July 8, 1914.

was essential, especially since O'Gorman felt he had been insufficiently consulted on other patronage.[56]

Secretary Wilson sounded out Howe, whose reply on July 19 was both receptive and hesitant. "I am deeply appreciative of the suggestion that I should permit my name to be considered for the post," he wrote, "and I am favorably disposed to it if the position is one, as I think it is, that justifies my giving up the work of the People's Institute of which I have been director for the past three years. But I am not familiar with the law or the powers and duties of the Commissioner and I cannot answer affirmatively until I know more about them." He asked Wilson to advise him "what you desire in the Commissioner, the attitude you wish observed in the conduct of the office and any specific program that you wish carried out." He concluded: "If the position is perfunctory and allows little opportunity for service I prefer to remain where I now am. If however the post is designed to provide, along with other things, a guide, counsellor and friend to the immigrant, for whom I have great sympathy and genuine respect and the law allows some executive latitude in the carrying out of such a program I should feel favorably disposed to its consideration."[57]

The two men met in Washington on August 8, and shortly thereafter Howe advised Wilson that he would accept the position. After a visit to Ellis Island, he found himself "strongly attracted to the place by the tremendous human appeal of the work." The secretary notified the president on August 18, passing on Senator O'Gorman's statement that the nomination was "very acceptable" to him. Wilson wrote in a formal memorandum to the president on the same date: "I have the honor to recommend to you for nomination as Commissioner of Immigration at the Port of New York, Mr. Frederic C. Howe, of New York City.... I feel satisfied that he is in every way qualified, and would make an efficient Commissioner of Immigration." The president made the appointment, and on August 26 the assistant secretary of labor, Louis F. Post, could inform his old friend that the Senate had given its approval.[58]

Fred understood that McAdoo had been chiefly responsible for his appointment and sent him his thanks "for the opportunity to do a piece of work that appeals to me very much." McAdoo replied: "I can't tell you how delighted I

---

56. Woodrow Wilson to William B. Wilson, July 10, 1914; William B. Wilson to Woodrow Wilson, July 13, 1914; Woodrow Wilson to William B. Wilson, July 14, 1914; General Records of the Department of Labor, 1907–1942, Chief Clerk's Files, File No. 2/288. See Broesamle, *William Gibbs McAdoo*, 86.

57. William B. Wilson to FCH, July 14, 1914; FCH to Wilson, July 29, 1914; General Records of the Department of Labor, 1907–1942, Chief Clerk's Files, File No. 2/288.

58. FCH to William B. Wilson, August 12, 1914; William B. Wilson to Woodrow Wilson, August 18, 1914 (letter and memorandum); Louis F. Post to FCH, August 16, 1914; General Records of the Department of Labor, 1907–1942, Chief Clerk's Files, File No. 2/288.

am with your nomination for the important position of Immigration Commissioner of New York. I hope you are going to accept and that when you come to Washington you will not fail to run in to me."[59]

Felicitations on the appointment as commissioner came from Fred's friends throughout the country. Amos Pinchot wrote that this was "one of the best things that Wilson has done, and I think he has done many." Colonel House declared: "Your acceptance of the Immigration Commissionership of New York has made me very happy for I know you will conduct the office in a way that will be a credit to the country, to the Administration and to your friends." John Finley was very pleased with the news: "My dear Fred Howe: I am delighted beyond measure to hear of your appointment as Immigration Commissioner. . . . This is better, after all, than a professorship at Princeton, which, except for the nobility and unselfishness of your own suggestion, you undoubtedly might have had from him who is now the President of the United States."[60]

Laudatory newspaper comments on Fred's appointment showed the general respect in which he was held. Among New York City papers, only the *Times*, which had its disagreements with the new commissioner, was editorially silent. Howe made sure that Secretary Wilson received the press clippings.[61]

Fred's replies to the congratulatory letters mingled pleasure at the prospect of a new challenge and regret at leaving the People's Institute. To Louis Post, he wrote that, after a visit to Ellis Island, he was "very enthusiastic over the opportunity." To Colonel House, he declared himself "very happy to know that you approve of the appointment. It is very hard for me to give up my present work but the lure of working with the present Administration and my affectionate feeling toward President Wilson overcame any hesitation on my part." He confided to Senator La Follette: "I am happy where I am and am making more money than I need for my daily fare so that my interest in a change is only in finding a place to use myself to better advantage. For the Institute does not call for the kind of radicalism that I feel and want to express in some way or other. . . . It isn't a job that I want but work." He told James Garfield that after his confirmation by the Senate, he would "start the Institute off on its winter's work and after that slide out although it is very hard for me to leave as I have

59. FCH to William Gibbs McAdoo, August 18, 1914; McAdoo to FCH, August 20, 1914. Howe continued to send suggestions to McAdoo during the time his appointment was being arranged, including a recommendation for an appointment to the Federal Reserve Board and some ideas on the development of American commerce. FCH to McAdoo, July 29, 1914; McAdoo to FCH, August 8, 1914.
60. Amos Pinchot to FCH, August 21, 1914, Amos Pinchot Papers, Library of Congress; Edward M. House to FCH, August 21, 1914, House Papers, Yale University; Benjamin B. Lindsey to FCH, September 18, 1914, Lindsey Papers; John H. Finley to FCH, September 22, 1914, John Huston Finley Papers, New York Public Library.
61. FCH to William B. Wilson, August 25, 1914.

Fig 4 Frederic C. Howe, commissioner of immigration, Port of New York, Ellis Island, ca. 1914

built up an institution that works like clock work and has a fine group of men and women interested in it."[62]

It is difficult to tell how satisfied Fred Howe really was with the appointment as Commissioner of Immigration for the Port of New York. His account in his

62. FCH to Louis Post, August 14, 1914; FCH to Edward M. House, August 29, 1914; FCH to Robert M. La Follette, July 29, 1914; FCH to Amos Pinchot, August 21, 1914, Amos Pinchot Papers; FCH to James R. Garfield, August 21, 1914.

autobiography, written a decade later, omitted any mention of his hunt for a federal position. He was happy in his work as director of the People's Institute, he wrote, and not very well informed about immigration. But Ellis Island attracted him as a "principality." The commissioner had a staff of six hundred to supervise, and, in normal times, as many as five thousand immigrants a day passed through the island. "The appointment made an appeal to something in me which has always been fundamental, something which stirred me in the university, led me into the social settlement, urged me into politics, impelled me to work for parks and playgrounds in Cleveland, and landed me in the People's Institute in New York. All of my activities have been part of a lifelong interest in the changing and improving of conditions that result in suffering or injustice." Whether this instinctive "something" should be called "the spirit of reform, or humanitarianism, or sentimentality, or the dreaming of dreams, or the seeing of visions," Howe did not know. It somehow related to "a better ordering of things; to freeing the individual so that he could achieve all that was in him." The position at Ellis Island offered an opportunity to "ameliorate the lot of several thousand human beings. It was also an opportunity to do the work I liked to do. No doubt I thought I wanted to do this work for the sake of the immigrants. Probably I wanted to do it to satisfy my own instincts. Here on a small scale was an environment to be changed and improved." He knew little about the island save that he had heard it called "the Island of Tears." Perhaps he could change and humanize it.[63]

Yet the commissionership was hardly the important post he had had in mind when he began his search for a federal appointment in December 1912. He had loftier ambitions—secretary or chief of staff to the president, undersecretary of the interior, perhaps an important economic or financial position in the Treasury, something worthy of his experience and talents that would take him near the center of power in Washington. The job of commissioner was a comedown from those hopes, and it was not one for which he had prepared himself. He had shown little interest in the field in which he would now have to function. Of course, he had displayed his sympathy with immigrants in his work at Goodrich House in Cleveland and the People's Institute in New York City. The Institute drew most of its audience from the foreign-born population and, along with its forums and meetings on topics of general interest, devoted many special efforts to working-class immigrants and their families. Its interest was what in the 1990s came to be called multiculturalism. Immigrants who came to the Institute or its neighborhood centers learned not only American ways but also the value of their own culture. Howe had made no special study of immigration policy or of immigrants, however, and his numerous writings had touched on

63. *Confessions of a Reformer*, 252–53.

them only through their inclusion among the weak and downtrodden whom society should protect.

And yet, did not the post as commissioner offer possibilities? McAdoo may well have had something else in mind besides doing a favor for Baker or for Howe. In distributing Treasury patronage in New York, the secretary had to meet some of the demands of Tammany Democrats, who controlled most of the state offices, and at the same time strengthen the independent and reform Democrats so that they might continue to challenge Tammany. This necessarily involved him in New York City politics, as did his own political ambitions and his desire for the image and the success of a reforming national administration. He and Colonel House had agreed in March 1913 on a general strategy that they hoped would win the mayor's office and the governorship for independent Democrats. These goals necessitated building coalitions among the diverse groups that opposed Tammany and the development of leaders to carry on the battles.[64] Fred Howe—a man already active and well known both in New York politics and nationally—must have seemed to McAdoo a good bet for one of those leaders. There is no evidence that McAdoo and Howe talked about this, but the appointment to Ellis Island kept Fred present on the New York scene and scarcely diminished his ability to be involved in politics there. And since he was now inside the administration and possessed the good will and friendship of the president, McAdoo, and House, the door to future advancement was not closed. In the meantime, he could continue to make policy proposals and to volunteer his services in fields other than immigration. A bit part it might be, but he was now a player on the national stage without leaving the local arena.

"Sliding out" of the work of the People's Institute took somewhat longer than Fred had anticipated. At the time of his resignation in September 1914, the Institute was facing a deficit, and the trustees were happy to delay paying the salary of a new director and to allow Fred to wear two hats for a while. As "honorary director," he arranged meetings and sought speakers, assisted in fund-raising, and aided in the leisurely search for his successor.

By the winter of 1914–15, he was apparently easing up on his Institute tasks, writing Gutzon Borglum (best known as the sculptor of Mount Rushmore) that "I have been so busy at Ellis Island that I have not kept the Cooper Union work up as well as in previous years." He was still arranging for speakers in the winter of 1915–16, however, and he found time to deliver for the Institute six lectures on "The Foundations of War" in November and December 1915. The Board elected him to the Forum Committee and the Finance Committee in 1915, and he continued as a somewhat inactive member of the Board of Trustees into the

---

64. Broesamle, *William Gibbs McAdoo*, 89–93.

1920s. Finally, in May 1916, the Board chose Edward F. Sanderson as his successor, and Fred could at last relinquish his responsibilities. Baldwin summed up Howe's tenure: "[He has] combined devotion, sympathy, education and intelligence. . . . His administration was notable for vigorous initiative and successful activities. Then the President of the United States drafted him to administer the Immigration Office. We have taken two years more before finding his successor and during those two years, Dr. Howe has been most generous in giving us his help and advice. He is entitled to the gratitude of all friends of the Institute."[65]

65. FCH to Gutzon Borglum, January 4, 1915, People's Institute Papers, New York Public Library; Lester F. Scott to Henry de Forest Baldwin, October 8, 1915, Cooper Collection; Henry de Forest Baldwin, notes for meeting of the People's Institute on November 11, 1916, Cooper Collection.

11

THE ISLAND OF TEARS

By September 1914 the new commissioner was on the job. As he had at the People's Institute, he had to determine how he would fit himself into an ongoing operation. The Bureau of Immigration, to whose commissioner general Howe would report, had been functioning for years, but it was now part of a new Department of Labor. Fittingly enough, the first secretary of labor was William B. Wilson, a former United Mine Workers organizer, who, as chairman of the House Labor Committee, had helped shape the law creating the new department. Not personally acquainted with his new secretary at the time of appointment, President Wilson developed great confidence in him during the eight years of their association. Fred Howe found in Secretary Wilson a sympathetic superior whose interest in reform was coupled with a sense of political feasibilities.

Fred had another friend in the department in Louis Post, the assistant secretary, whom he had known since their Cleveland days. Post had left Cleveland to settle in Chicago as founder, editor, and publisher of his single-tax paper, the *Public,* and Howe had become one of its contributing editors. Post quickly developed a close and cordial relationship with Secretary Wilson.

Fred was fortunate to have two friends and supporters at the top of the Labor Department hierarchy. He was less lucky with his immediate superior, Anthony Caminetti, the commissioner general of immigration. Caminetti had been a prosecuting attorney, a state legislator, and a congressman from California. His appointment was considered primarily a gesture to Italian Americans. There seemed to be general agreement that as commissioner general he avoided making decisions. Two later scholars found that "his inexpert administration of his office was nerveless to the point almost of paralysis." Howe wrote: "The Commissioner-General . . . was as untrained in administrative work as I was in higher mathematics, and his consciousness of his inexperience led him to refuse to take any action at all." Post and Wilson had the same complaint. The Bureau of Immigration, which Caminetti headed, had all but about two hundred of the department's two thousand employees in 1914 and consumed more than 70 percent of its budget. Post said that the bureau's administration of the immigration laws kept him "moving around in a cloud of gloom from the beginning to the end of my service in the Department of Labor."[1]

As commissioner of immigration for the Port of New York, Howe first needed to address humanizing conditions at Ellis Island. Upon being appointed, he perused press clippings and discovered that, so far as the newspapers were concerned, "there was an island out in the harbor which had no sympathy with the foreign-born, and whose function was to oppress, to find some means of excluding, arresting and deporting, and there was very little other impression of the station." It seemed to Howe that the attitude of the immigrant should be one of "love and confidence." He set himself the task of changing Ellis Island's reputation.[2]

Howe's goal was made easier by the decline in the number of immigrants arriving after the outbreak of the First World War. In the fiscal year before he became commissioner, more than 1,200,000 immigrants came to America, 878,052 of them arriving at Ellis Island. In Howe's first year (fiscal year 1914–15), the total dropped to 326,700, and only 178,416 came through Ellis Island. If the Ellis total had remained as high in his first year as it had been in the previous one, the staff and facilities of the island would have been fully engaged, seven days a week, in processing the new arrivals. There would have been little time, and the numbers would have been too large, for experiments in different treatment.

One of the first things that struck Howe was the strict segregation of those detained at the island. Men were kept apart from women and children, and husbands, wives, and families could be together only at mealtimes. He ordered the breaking of a doorway through the wall separating men and women and created common rooms where husbands and wives could intermingle. Neither men nor women had much to do from wakeup to lights-out, so he arranged for organized classes in knitting and sewing for the women and provided some of the men with work making doormats. Foreign-language newspapers were made available, as were toys for the children. He worked with the city board of education to provide classes for children and adults in "English, hygiene, motherhood, and other elementary subjects" and got the YMCA to furnish instructors

---

1. MacMahon and Millett, *Federal Administrators*, 424; FCH, *Confessions of a Reformer*, 255; Lombardi, *Labor's Voice in the Cabinet*, 128–29; Post, "Living a Long Life Over Again," 322; Ackerman, *Young J. Edgar*, 53–59.

2. FCH, *Confessions of a Reformer*, 256.

for the men in calisthenics and athletic games. He tried to beautify the station and make it as attractive as possible. The registry hall was lined with potted plants; flags were hung from the balcony; and large photographs of the presidents and historical events were placed upon the pillars.

Howe also tried to alleviate the dreariness of detention by opening up the island to its temporary residents. After a bureaucratic struggle of several weeks to "liberate" just one bench from the many stacked away in storage, he succeeded in getting that bench, and then others, placed on the lawn. Detainees were freed from the cheerless detention halls and allowed to sit outside and to walk around the grounds. "This aroused an indignant protest," Howe recorded. "The lawns had been made at great expense, the officials said. They made a beautiful approach to the island. I replied that live babies were more precious than live grass, and took a good deal of satisfaction in seeing the lawns trampled under foot." Howe worked with immigrant organizations to offer Sunday concerts by orchestras, bands, singing societies, and individual musicians. Many New Yorkers made the trip to Ellis Island to hear the fifty-piece band of the Hebrew Orphan Asylum on one Sunday afternoon, for example. Enrico Caruso sang on Italian Day. The Home Missions Council provided movies several times a week, and Howe bought a phonograph to play the dance music of the various groups on the island.[3]

For Howe, as for many Progressives before the First World War, immigrants and their assimilation into American life had not been a matter of great concern. Some reformers distrusted the immigrants, in part because they associated them with the big city, its vices, and its political machines. Others viewed them as victims of intolerance and economic exploitation. In the first decades of the century, settlement houses and social workers sought both to teach immigrants and to learn from them, to help them become good Americans and to preserve the diversity that made them "enriching additions to the whole culture."[4] The "best" in the alien tradition should be added to the American mix, though what was "best" often seemed to be defined in terms of folk dancing, quaint customs, handicrafts, music, and national holidays. Howe's experiences at Goodrich House and the People's Institute clearly disposed him to the humanitarian approach of the settlement house and the social worker.

---

3. Information and quotations concerning the changes Howe introduced at Ellis Island are taken from FCH to Commissioner General of Immigration, "Enumeration of Social Activities Inaugurated at Ellis Island," memorandum, February 14, 1915; *Confessions of a Reformer*, 256–57; "Turning Ellis Island Inside Out," *Survey* 33 (October 17, 1914): 63; FCH, "Turned Back in Time of War"; 147–56; Corsi, *In the Shadow of Liberty*, 281–82; *New York Times*, September 16, 1914, 11, and November 2, 1914, 9.

4. See Higham, *Strangers in the Land*, 116–22.

After the advent of the European war, attitudes toward immigrants began to change as concerns about national security and the potential disloyalty of "hyphenate Americans" roiled the public mind. In 1914 the federal Bureau of Naturalization started an active campaign to promote the Americanization of those aliens who had indicated their intention to become citizens. Soon joining the Bureau in these efforts was the Committee for Immigrants in America, which set up an auxiliary organization, the National Americanization Day Committee, to organize public receptions for new citizens on July 4, 1915, in cities throughout the nation.[5]

Fred Howe quickly became involved in the movement. In fact, in the autobiographical notes he submitted for his fraternity's history, he took credit for originating Americanization Day. Though this claim seems inaccurate, he was working hard for the idea in 1915. In May he sent letters to mayors throughout the country, urging them to arrange "Citizenship Receptions" or "New Voters' Days" on July 4, 1915. Mayors responded enthusiastically, and more than 100 cities had public meetings or receptions on Independence Day.[6]

Dropping the "Day" from its title, the National Americanization Committee continued to spearhead the movement, and Howe became a member of the Committee. At first the humanitarian impulses of the prewar era predominated, but increasingly the emphasis shifted to an "apprehensive nationalism" (John Higham's term). The Committee spoke less of the welfare of immigrants and more of a break with alien ties to the Old World, and promotion of loyalty to the United States. Indicative of the change was revision of the Committee's slogan: from "Many People, but One Nation," it became "America First." As the Committee altered its focus, Howe and other Progressives grew suspicious of its aims and activities. Frank Walsh's Committee on Industrial Relations, to which Howe belonged, told the National Americanization Committee in November 1915 that immigrants needed to be protected against economic exploitation. This could be done primarily by supporting the labor movement, persuading the immigrants to join unions, and democratizing industry. In a subsequent letter, Walsh charged that by willfully neglecting the trade union as a primary Americanizing influence, the Committee aimed at "docile subserviency," not Americanization.[7] Despite the growing fears of reformers that the

---

5. Lombardi, *Labor's Voice in the Cabinet,* 138–39; Higham, *Strangers in the Land,* 241–43.
6. Mattern, *Pi Chapter of Phi Gamma Delta:* 350; form letter dated May 22, 1915, in Theodore Roosevelt Papers, Library of Congress, reel 200; *Survey* 34 (May 29, 1915), 188, and (June 19, 1915), 261; FCH to Colonel Edward M. House, October 26, 1915, House Papers.
7. George P. West to Frank Walsh, November 27, 1915; Walsh to West, November 19, 1915; Letter Addressed to Americanization Committee, December, 1915; Frances A. Kellor to Frank Walsh, December 22, 1915; press release from Committee on Industrial Relations, January 19, 1916, Frank Walsh papers, New York Public Library.

Americanization movement had come to represent a pressure for conformity and a shield for antilabor activities, Howe remained a member of the National Americanization Committee at least until early 1917 (at any rate, his name continued to appear on its letterhead until then).

One of the early consequences of the war in Europe was increased unemployment in America as the conflict disrupted the normal currents of trade. Despite the detainment of aliens who could not be deported under wartime conditions, the greatly reduced number of immigrants passing through Ellis Island meant that there was empty space at the station. In the winter of 1914–15, Howe opened two buildings to New York City's unemployed and homeless, many of them recent immigrants. Seven hundred and fifty men, who had been reduced to abject misery because they lacked food and shelter, were given at least a roof over their heads at night during the severe cold weather. The government ferry took them back to the city each morning so that they could look for work.

Howe believed that the immigrants responded well to the changes he had instituted at Ellis Island. "I found the immigrant well worth the interest he inspired. He was helpless and confused; he responded to any kindness and was far better material than I had anticipated." He liked the new Irish and Italian arrivals most. They were independent-minded and had a certain dignity. The British gave him the most trouble. As soon as a British subject was detained, he hurried to phone his consul in New York or his ambassador in Washington. "All Englishmen seemed to assume that they had a right to go anywhere they liked, and that any interference with this right was an affront to the whole British Empire."[8]

At first, Fred thought the staff at Ellis Island cooperative and willing to consider changes. He introduced a system of representation so that their proposals and complaints could reach his office. As part of his efforts to change the image of the immigration station as an "island of fear," he posted on the bulletin board a directive that workers should smile. They did, or so he believed. "They found it was a good deal pleasanter to be pleasant than it was to be brusk.... Out of a working force of scrub women, matrons, laborers about the place came a joyousness in their work, simply because they felt they were doing something that was helpful and useful rather than something that was not useful."

As Fred became more experienced in his job, he became more realistic and more critical of his staff. He noted in his autobiography that had he known "the psychology of the permanent employee and his power, I should have hesitated before initiating the changes I had in mind to humanize the island." He learned

---

8. W. B. Wilson to FCH, February 19, 1915, General Records of the Department of Labor, 1907–1942 (Chief Clerk's Files), File 19/31, National Archives.

that "we were governed by petty clerks, mostly Republicans. The government was their government." Presidents came and went, but the permanent official, protected by the Civil Service regulations, was there for life. The Civil Service reform movement in America had created an "administrative state... an official bureaucracy moved largely by fear, hating initiative, and organized as a solid block to protect itself and its petty unimaginative, salary-hunting instincts."[9]

As commissioner, Howe was at least nominally responsible for a host of administrative duties at Ellis Island. Since he knew little about the bureaucratic routines there, he relied much upon the assistant commissioner, Byron Uhl. Uhl was a career civil servant who was to rack up some forty years in the immigration service. Howe could delegate many of his responsibilities to Uhl and, when absent on speaking engagements or vacations, could rely on him to run the station. Among Howe's administrative tasks were the transfer of employees to other immigration offices or stations; recommendations for promotions and salary increases; general supervision and maintenance of discipline among the staff; and the solution of problems of many kinds.[10] For those on the payroll at the station, Howe fought for salary increases, especially for the lowest-paid workers. He believed that government should be a model employer and should not "sweat" its employees.

Howe was able to use his position to do a few favors for friends and to seek action within government on matters that interested him. Escaping the war in Europe, pupils in Isadora Duncan's dance school, some of whom were German, arrived at Ellis Island in 1914 and were detained because their sponsors lacked guardianship papers. Howe cut through the red tape and secured the children's release on five hundred dollars per capita bonds. He wrote letters of introduction for friends traveling abroad. He tried unsuccessfully to get Secretary Wilson to order an official investigation of the case of Patrick Quinlan, convicted for actions in the Paterson silk mills strike. He promised Mabel Dodge to take up with the secretary of the Interior her complaint about the incompetence of a doctor working for the Bureau of Indian Affairs.[11]

It seems clear that Howe's first months as immigration commissioner were satisfying and productive ones. There were troubles looming, however. The outbreak of the European war in August 1914 had curtailed immigration and eased

9. *Confessions*, 253–56.
10. FCH to Commissioner General of Immigration, June 17, 1916, Immigration and Naturalization Service Central Office, Subject Correspondence, 1906–1932, File 539358B and File 53854/58, National Archives.
11. Blair, *Isadora*, 237–38; Kurth, *Isadora*, 324; FCH to "To Whom It May Concern," May 22, 1915, Inez Milholland Papers, Schlesinger Library, Radcliffe; FCH to W. B. Wilson, November 9, 1915; Wilson to FCH, November 22, 1915, General Records of the Department of Labor, 1907–1942 (Chief Clerk's Files), File 16/327; Rudnick, *Mabel Dodge Luhan*, 176.

the burden on Ellis Island. But wartime conditions also limited deportations. After the sinking of the *Lusitania* in May 1915, the president ordered a halt to them. The number of reluctant or unwilling guests on the island gradually increased, and their presence presented custodial problems in a time of budget cuts for the immigration service. In October the commissioner general issued a general directive to all the immigration commissioners, ordering them to take "very strict methods of retrenchment."[12]

Retrenchment meant that Howe had to battle hard with Washington over the next few years as he tried to retain as many of his 650-person staff as possible and to get the best arrangements possible for those who had to be laid off. Finding that reductions in force were inevitable, Howe tried to ease the pain. He persuaded Secretary Wilson to agree to furloughs for all employees in rotation for short periods, rather than layoffs for indefinite periods. By April 1915 the number of employees at Ellis Island was sixty-four less than in July 1914, and Howe wrote Caminetti plaintively: "I want to call your attention to the fact that we must have some active men left at this station."[13]

The furlough system lasted throughout 1915 and into 1916. Howe continued his complaints about both the hardship for individuals and the difficulty of doing the station's work with a depleted force. By the spring of 1916, however, he could turn from fighting to hold on to his staff to urging increases in it. After America entered the war and the government began to detain German and other enemy aliens, Howe increased his demands for additional guard and inspectors and generally was successful in his efforts.[14]

After the European war began, pressures to impose new controls on immigration—never absent from American discussion—once again increased. Howe did not share the apprehensions of the restrictionists. He took issue with his old friend Edward A. Ross, who feared "race suicide" as "new immigrants" from Eastern Europe outbred the "Anglo-Saxon" stock. The commissioner told an interviewer that he anticipated no such danger. "'The races now coming to our shores have solved many problems more intelligently than the countries of northern Europe, and as they are assimilated in America, I think we will gain rather than lose in the process.'"[15]

The Ellis Island commissioner had no quarrel with the policy on exclusions contained in existing immigration laws. "I do not mean to suggest that our

12. FCH to Commissioner General of Immigration, September 12, 1914, ibid., File 53935/8; F. H. Larned (acting commissioner general) to FCH, October 22, 1914, ibid.; Message to all Commissioners from Commissioner General of Immigration, October 8, 1914, ibid., File 53854/39D.

13. FCH to Commissioner General of Immigration, December 1, 1914, November 16, 1914, and May 22, 1915, ibid.

14. FCH to Commissioner General of Immigration, May 23, 1916, and July 11, 1917; Commissioner General to FCH, July 14, 1917, File 539358B and File53935/8D, ibid.

15. Interview in *New York Sun,* October 25, 1914, in File 53854/39D.

inspection should be weakened or that we should admit those in excludable classes," he told a conference of immigration officers. "We know the effect of the imbecile who drifts in like the Jukes case. . . . There are none who would open our doors to those who are likely to become a public charge or those who will add a strain of feeble-mindedness, imbecility, or insanity to our population."[16]

Among the excludable classes were prostitutes. The first decades of the century had seen a crusade against the "white slave traffic" that had led to a tightening of the laws against the "social evil." An 1875 statute had forbidden the entry of prostitutes into the United States. A 1907 law increased the penalties for importing women for prostitution and made alien women who practiced the trade within three years of their arrival subject to deportation. A 1910 amendment eliminated the time limit, and in the same year Congress passed the White Slave Traffic Act (the Mann Act), banning the transportation of women for immoral purposes both in interstate and foreign commerce. Enforcing these laws, local authorities and immigration inspectors rounded up alien women alleged to be prostitutes, incarcerated them in local jails, and then sent them on to be deported, principally through Ellis Island. The war brought an end to most deportations but not to the arrest of aliens throughout the country, including women charged with immorality. Most of them could not be returned to their homelands and remained in custody.

After 1914, Howe found that he had become "a jailer instead of a commissioner of immigration; a jailer not of convicted offenders but of suspected persons who had been arrested and railroaded to Ellis Island as the most available dumping-ground under the successive waves of hysteria which swept the country." Legally, his role was only that of administrator of the laws and custodian of the detained aliens. His sense of justice rebelled, however, at the "flimsy," "emotional," and "unlegal" testimony on which detention and deportation seemed so often based. He could not be simply a silent administrator of the laws and regulations. "I quarreled with the Commissioner-General of Immigration, who was working hand in glove with the Department of Justice; I harassed the Secretary of Labor with protests against the injustice that was being done. I refused to believe that civil liberties should be thrown to the winds. . . . But in this struggle there was no one to lean on; there was no support from Washington, no interest on the part of the press."[17]

---

16. Immigration and Naturalization Service Central Office, Subject Correspondence, 1906–1932, File 53854/39D, National Archives, 246–50, 265–67; FCH, "Immigration After the War," 639.

17. Reviewing the crusade against immoral aliens a decade later, Howe wrote: "For over a year America seemed convinced that our social and political life was honeycombed with a vice traffic that was threatening the foundations of the nation. I do not know whether there was any more

The increasing number of allegedly immoral aliens detained at Ellis Island presented Howe with a dilemma. The island was not a suitable place for long-term incarceration. Discovering that the women would not speak freely to him, he asked a number of prominent New York City women—Marie Howe, Mary Simkhovitch, Lillian Wald, and others—to come to the island and listen to the stories of the arrested women. They looked at individual cases not in terms of legal guilt or innocence but in an effort to understand the circumstances and to consider whether temporary work could be found for the women. They found that "the great majority of the women were casual offenders who would not have been arrested under ordinary circumstances. In many instances their misfortunes were the result of ignorance, almost always of poverty."[18]

Armed with their report, Howe proposed to Secretary Wilson that casual offenders be paroled until the war's end made deportation possible. During their parole, they would be supervised by responsible persons or organizations, and they would report regularly to immigration officers. The plan was approved, and the commissioner reported that few violated the terms of their release. Nevertheless, the program made him enemies who could charge him with overly gentle treatment of immoral women.

Howe found himself in even more serious trouble when he tangled with powerful outside interests, the railroad and steamship companies and other concessionaires who were profiting substantially, and, it seemed to him, unfairly in their services to the immigrant. Transatlantic steerage passengers were unloaded at landing piers and transferred to Ellis Island by smaller vessels, operated by a contractor for the steamer line. These barges also took the aliens after their processing from the island to the railroad docks in New Jersey. This service was performed under contract with the railroad companies. The boats were old, slow, often overcrowded, and lacking in sanitary facilities. After reaching the island, immigrants sometimes had to remain on them for hours before they could disembark and be examined. Collusion through a pool arrangement involving a dozen railway companies and three steamship lines divided up the movement of the immigrants from Ellis Island. The process seldom considered the wishes of or the consequences for the immigrant, who might find himself routed under poor conditions and in roundabout ways at a cost in both time and money. Howe's predecessors had tried to improve conditions but with little

---

organized vice in the country in 1916 than there is to-day. . . . Certainly there was little official evidence to substantiate the assumption that our morality was being undermined by commercialized vice organized into an international system by the most depraved of alien promoters." *Confessions of a Reformer*, 268–69. All the quotations from Howe dealing with the detentions of the alleged prostitutes are taken from ibid., 266–72. On Progressivism and prostitution generally., see Feldman, "Prostitution"; Connelly, *Response to Prostitution*.

18. For summaries of some of the stories they heard, see *Confessions of a Reformer*, 270–71.

success. "Guerilla warfare constituted the normal relations between the commissioner of immigration and the steamship companies," and, it may be added, with the railroad lines as well.[19]

Adding to the "warfare" was controversy over the differential treatment of steerage and second-cabin passengers. The immigration laws and immigrant inspection for years had been most strictly enforced against steerage passengers. The steamship companies protested any attempt to apply the same rules to cabin passengers, and the immigration authorities tended to yield and to conduct only a superficial examination of cabin passengers. Knowing this, aliens who could afford it paid a little extra to travel cabin class rather than steerage. They were inspected aboard ship and did not have to go to Ellis Island. Once ashore, they were often cheated by hotels and baggagemen and lured into saloons and houses of prostitution. In the end, many of them found that they still had to go to the island to arrange their railroad transportation.

The remedy seemed simple; Howe convinced his superiors to order that all second-cabin passengers be examined at Ellis Island. After loud protests from the steamship companies, the order was suspended, and Commissioner General Caminetti ordered a hearing at which all those who were making money from the immigrant put in an angry appearance. "They looked upon the money which they took from the alien as a vested interest. It was sacred." The steamship companies promised improvements so that shipboard inspections could be more easily accomplished, but, Howe noted sadly, "the order for change was never made."

Nor was he able to accomplish changes to prevent abuses by the railroads or to curb "fly-by-night bankers" who cheated immigrants in money exchanges. He succeeded in getting the steamship companies to pay a fair amount for the medical care of aliens whom they had brought to the United States but whose return had been ordered. Howe ordered accountants to work out the actual costs and secured an order to make companies pay on that basis. "It increased the revenues of the bureau [of immigration] by hundreds of thousands of dollars. But it organized the hostility of the steamship companies."[20]

The major controversy of 1916 involved another concession at Ellis Island. Howe wrote later: "Unconscious of the interrelation of all these interests with one another, with New York congressmen, with bureaucratic officials, I had built a fire which needed only a spark to start a blaze. The attempt to deprive the food contractor of his concession started the conflagration."[21] He found

19. Pitkin, *Keepers of the Gate*, 91.
20. Unless otherwise indicated, quotations from Howe dealing with the steamship and railroad problems are drawn from *Confessions of a Reformer*, 260–63.
21. Quotations from Howe on the controversy with Representative Bennet are from ibid., 258–64, unless otherwise noted.

himself embroiled in a new kind of battle. "In Cleveland I had been shielded by Tom Johnson's commanding personality. He took the blows; I was one of his seconds, on the edge of the ring. And the fighting had been for the most part fair. Now I was to enter the ring myself. It was a new experience to me to be a principal in the fight."

The conflagration began with a dispute over the very profitable contract to feed the detained aliens and the employees on the island. In 1916 the old contract, held by the firm of Hudgins and Dumas, expired. Howe had come to believe that it was wrong for private contractors to enjoy concessions on government property, and he thought the government could do a better job than a private firm. He had been warned that the concessionaires had power and influence with Congress, but he pooh-poohed the warning. "Everybody, I assumed, wanted the alien protected; everybody wanted the administration to be as kindly as possible." After obtaining favorable opinions on the plan's legality from the attorney general and the comptroller of the Treasury, Howe recommended it to Secretary Wilson, who approved, and an authorizing amendment was added to an appropriations bill pending in the House of Representatives.

Howe and his superiors were caught napping, however, by the quick action of Congressman William S. Bennet, a Republican from New York City who had been active on immigration issues and who at one time had been the attorney for Hudgins and Dumas. Bennet introduced and secured passage of an amendment that effectively forbade the federal government to use any money for the food service at Ellis Island and other immigration stations. He had not informed the secretary of labor or the immigration authorities of his intention, and the bill had passed the Senate before any protest could be made.[22]

After Howe criticized the congressional action, Congressman Bennet took the floor in the House on July 18, 1916, for a full-scale assault on the Ellis Island commissioner. Who is this Frederic Howe? he asked his colleagues rhetorically. He is a man "more radical in his views in regard to governmental affairs than any Member of this House, and that gives somewhat of an idea of him as an extremist.... Mr. Howe does not believe that anything ought to be done by private contract which by any possibility the Government can do." The controversy over the food contract had brought Howe's activities at Ellis Island to Bennet's attention. He said that he had looked into the situation at Ellis Island and found that "this commissioner of immigration is the most negligent commissioner of immigration that we have ever had, the most frequently absent, and that he pays the least attention to his duty of any commissioner in my time."

22. *New York Times*, July 1, 1916, 20. Bennet had served on President Taft's Commission on Immigration.

Specifically, the congressman charged that Howe had admitted prostitutes to the United States in violation of the laws and that his administration had promoted or protected immorality at Ellis Island. He had "permitted the prostitutes, the pimps, the procurers, to mingle at will with the other inmates." He offered the House the example of "Juliette," a prostitute who continued "plying her vocation for money" while interned at the island. Introducing a resolution for an investigation of conditions at the immigration station, Bennet concluded: "It is of tremendous importance that a half-baked radical with free-love ideas who has no proper idea of the effect of the mingling of bad with good, should be spoken of plainly."[23]

Howe replied to the congressman's charges in a lengthy statement. The basis for the charges was the food contract, he said. "I wanted the Government to do it right, and take the element of profit out of it. . . . Mr. Bennet said it was socialistic to feed the immigrants, and prevented its being done." Turning to Bennet's indictment, Howe declared that he had no power to admit aliens to the United States. This was done by the Department of Labor, mostly after personal hearings held by representatives of the department. As to immorality, he had heard of only two complaints during the two years he had served as commissioner, and, after investigation, neither was proved. The facts in the specific case of the alleged prostitute, "Juliette," were other than those cited by Bennet in his speech. "I have done everything in my power to relieve the suffering and misfortunes of the thousands of persons who have been detained at Ellis Island, and have found homes for many of them," Howe stated. "I have, I admit, thought of the poor, ignorant, immoral women detained at the Island as human beings entitled to every help to a fair start in the world. . . . They have not been convicted or found guilty by any court, and they deny their guilt, and we can only guess at guilt in most cases."

The station had not been built to be a prison, Howe pointed out, but had been turned by the war into a detention camp. Given the openness of the island to thousands of visitors, the presence of representatives of seventy religious and philanthropic societies, the availability of the commissioner in his office, and the complaint boxes placed all over the station, "it seems incredible that any such conditions as Congressman Bennet describes could be true and not have been known long before this."[24]

In reporting on the Bennet-Howe controversy, most newspapers and periodicals criticized the congressman. The editorial writer of the *New York Times* had no admiration for Howe's political and economic ideas, calling him "a glib

23. *Congressional Record*, 64th Cong., 1st sess., vol. 53, 11260–62. Bennet dropped the phrase "with free-love ideas" when he revised his remarks for publication in the *Record*.
24. *New York Times*, July 20, 1916, 4.

spokesman of glittering and ignorant theories, a thinker of vealy thoughts, an individual whose public utterances are often of the half-baked kind." The writer came down on Howe's side in the dispute, however. Even a fuzzy thinker like the commissioner might have "a kind heart and a soul that revolts from cruelty and injustice, and these he has." As the "petty Czar" of Ellis Island, Howe had "devoted himself to mitigating the savagery of the hard laws, to making as bearable as possible the frequently intolerable lot of the persons who—through no fault of their own, except in the cases of professional criminals—have fallen under it." The editorial concluded: "Mr. Bennet's resolution should be pigeonholed, he should hear from his constituents their opinion of his conduct as soon as possible, and Mr. Howe should be encouraged to go on with the beneficent work he is doing at Ellis Island—and to stay off the lecture platform and shun Cooper Union."[25]

Other New York newspapers chimed in. Frank Crane, a popular syndicated columnist whose essays appeared daily in many newspapers, praised Howe as "a man of scholarly mood, a student of conditions and not a declaimer of theories, an author of books that are standards in civics, a solid sort of man, not at all the type that gets votes and has pulls, and trades in friendships, and gets on by the usual devious ways of politicians." He pointed out that Bennet's charges were self-serving, and Howe's replies to them careful and factual. "Not one word of recrimination, no heat of denial, no snarling retort, mars the clean page of his apology. He does not strive or cry. He does not answer the charges against his character; he does not see them. When you read this dignified yet satisfactory answer of a public man under fire you realize what a tremendous advantage is possessed by a gentleman." You promote the commissioner to a higher office, "and dub him Frederic C. Howe, Gentleman."[26]

Howe defended his record in testimony under oath to executive sessions of the House Committee on Immigration and Naturalization on July 27 and 28, 1916. He argued that the facts on the specific case cited by Representative Bennet were quite different from the congressman's assertions. Detained at Ellis Island as an alleged prostitute, Giulietta La Marca had been released on the recommendation of the St. Raphael Society for Italian Immigrants. Howe had approved her parole to work as a servant for one of the public health service physicians at Ellis Island. She had not been released by the commissioner to be a servant for one of his friends. To the more serious charge that he had encouraged the admission of large number of warrant cases to the United States, he stressed

---

25. Ibid., July 21, 1916, 8.
26. Clippings from the *World* and the *Tribune* and a copy of Frank Crane's column, "Frederic C. Howe: Gentleman," were enclosed in Howe's letter to President Wilson, August 11, 1916, Woodrow Wilson Papers, Series 4, Case Files 19 and 20.

that he had no power to admit anyone, only to recommend admissions. He had recommended nine cases in two years.

To the charges of negligence in his official duties and of inefficiency in his administration of Ellis Island, Howe emphasized that the immigration law gave the commissioner the duty of protecting immigrants against fraud and loss. He took this obligation seriously, he said, and it occupied much of his time. Bennet's reference to Howe's absence from the island led the committee chairman to raise that question, and the answer gave a good picture of the commissioner's work schedule. He arrived at the Ellis Island station at about 9:30 and left at 4:15, earlier if he had got all his work done. "On many days I leave before that when I clean up all the work and there is nothing more to do. When the work is cleaned up and there is nothing further to be done, I leave." He denied the charge of absenteeism, pointing to the many days he had to spend in Washington on official business and to the numerous speeches on immigration he had made throughout the country. Committee members asked Howe a number of questions about his actions at Ellis Island, and he responded without hesitation or difficulty. He rejected all charges that he had permitted or condoned conditions of immorality.[27]

Several weeks after his appearance before the Committee, Howe sent President Wilson a copy of his statement to the *New York Times* and clippings about the Howe-Bennet controversy from several other newspapers. After indicating Bennet's past connections with the food contractor, he observed: "Possibly Mr. Bennet honestly believed that the poor immigrants who have been herded at Ellis Island since the outbreak of the war ought to be treated like criminals and kept locked up day and night in dark rooms with absolutely nothing to do. That, however, was a policy repugnant to the Department, and to me as well." The president replied with a vote of confidence: "You know how thoroughly I have approved and admired what you have been doing."[28]

Representative Bennet returned to the fray on September 5, taking the floor in the House to repeat his critique of Howe's actions at Ellis Island. The congressman maintained again that Howe was "the most negligent commissioner we have ever had at Ellis Island." In his important position, he received a salary of sixty-five hundred dollars a year, "and he ought to attend to his business." He called himself "a professional writer," and he must have done some of his private work at the station. "Here are 100 or 150 pages of manuscript of one of his books, written on Government paper at Ellis Island by a Government

27. *Congressional Record*, 64th Cong., 1st sess., September 5, 1916, 13890–93.
28. FCH to Woodrow Wilson, August 11, 1916; Wilson to FCH, August 12, 1916, Woodrow Wilson Papers, Series 4, Case Files 19 and 20.

stenographer. That is the way that Mr. Howe has discharged his duties as Commissioner of Immigration at Ellis Island."²⁹ Following its hearings, the Committee on Immigration and Naturalization took no action on Bennet's charges, and Howe considered that he had been vindicated. By then, however, he must have agreed with one of his Ellis Island predecessors, Robert Watchorn, that "a saint from heaven actuated by all his saintliness would fail to give satisfaction at this place."[30]

Howe had rejected Bennet's charges of absenteeism from Ellis Island, but during his tenure as commissioner he certainly had found time for an amazing number of activities unrelated to his immigration duties, including the usual lengthy summer vacations on Nantucket. He continued to send unsolicited advice on policy matters to President Wilson, Secretary McAdoo, and Colonel House. He approached the president both directly and through Tumulty and House. Howe encouraged Wilson to act so that the Democratic Party would inherit "the group of socially minded men and women who have been the heart and brain of the Progressive party." The Democrats should develop "a comprehensive social and industrial programme both national and local, such as Germany and Great Britain have developed in recent years." That might include extension of social insurance for accident, sickness, old age, and unemployment; nationwide employment agencies or labor exchanges; "wandering artisans' homes" or lodging houses, perhaps associated with immigration stations; an insurance and pension scheme for federal employees; land credit banks; and a variety of services to the immigrant. The president should consider appointing a commission to work out the details of the program.[31]

A piece of legislation that won Fred's approval was the Keating-Owen child labor law, passed by Congress in August 1916. He wired the president, suggesting that he issue a statement when he signed the law, "referring to it as the children emancipation proclamation." Wilson replied that he planned to sign the bill "and I shall certainly make a little speech in which I will make special reference

---

29. Bennet's charges are found in *Congressional Record*, 64th Cong., 1st sess., September 5, 1916, 13883-87.

30. Quoted in Pitkin, *Keepers of the Gate*, 65. According to Howe's autobiography, he challenged the congressman to three debates on the charges during his campaign for re-election. The debates, held at street meetings, found the commissioner "thoroughly angry, at home with the subject, and in a mood to fight." When he demanded that Bennet answer a dozen questions, his opponent equivocated despite demands from the crowd for a response. Howe suggests that the debates were a factor in Bennet's loss in November, when his Democratic rival defeated him by nearly three thousand votes. *Confessions of a Reformer*, 264-65. We have only Howe's account of these debates.

31. FCH to Woodrow Wilson, November 21, 1914, in Link, *Papers of Woodrow Wilson*, 31:342-43.

to the Child Labor Bill." A pamphlet used by the Democratic national committee in the 1916 presidential campaign bore the title *Children's Emancipation Day*.[32]

Howe also interested himself in questions of foreign policy, especially with American actions in Mexico and China (leaving aside for now his attitude and activities toward the war in Europe). The Mexican Revolution had become a civil war. In the summer of 1914 the forces of Venustiano Carranza had ousted Victoriano Huerta from power, but fighting continued between Carranza's troops and an army led by Francisco "Pancho" Villa. The Wilson administration at first backed Villa. After Carranza defeated Villa militarily in the early months of 1915, the administration changed to a policy of neutrality, despite increasing pressure from business interests for direct intervention. The situation was complicated since the United States was at the same time embroiled in a crisis with Germany over the use of submarines against merchant ships. Fearing that this dispute might lead to war with Germany, the administration had no desire for a military conflict with Mexico. Hence it worked for a Mexican settlement that would bring into power a new and representative government that would oust Carranza. When the Carranza forces triumphed, however, Secretary of State Lansing successfully pushed for a change in policy, and on October 9, 1915, the United States and six Latin American nations extended de facto recognition to the Carranza government.

Howe offered President Wilson some unsolicited advice on American relations with Mexico. He expressed his belief that the Mexican Revolution was like the French in that it was "primarily agrarian, economic and social . . . moved by the same kind of feudal abuses that prevailed in France under the old regime." Of paramount importance in dealing with Mexico would be the American ambassador. "If he is sympathetic with the Mexican government, if he has a really democratic knowledge of the wrongs from which they have suffered, of the land question, of the methods employed in securing these concessions, and if he is willing to be a little tolerant of delay and of Mexican methods, he may cement the relations of the two countries, and also wipe away the suspicions of the Central and South American states, which have been rather apprehensive of the activities of American promoters." In addition, if the minister had a knowledge of American experiences with privileged interests, and if he knew something about banking, credit, finance, taxation, and labor matters, he could be of great service to the new government. An ambassador who was "a really democratic Democrat" would have in Mexico the same opportunity Franklin and

---

32. FCH to Woodrow Wilson, August 21, 1916; Wilson to FCH, August 22, 1916, in Link, *Papers of Woodrow Wilson*, 32:61, 63; Link, *Woodrow Wilson and the Progressive Era*, 243.

Jefferson had had in France, the chance to write "a new page ... in our history as pleasant to contemplate as that of our relations with France one hundred years ago."

Undoubtedly, given the criteria he had set out for the position, Howe was thinking of himself for the appointment as ambassador, but he gave the president a list of three—Newton Baker, Brand Whitlock, and Lincoln Steffens. To all of this, President Wilson replied that he had already noted "the extraordinary similarity" between the Mexican and French revolutions. It was difficult to choose an ambassador because "we must not only have a man of the right principles but a man thoroughly versed in Latin-American affairs and accustomed to dealing with a sensitive people in a way they wish to be dealt with. Your suggestion of names interests me very much indeed."[33] In the end, Howe's advice was not persuasive with Wilson. When the president recognized the Carranza government in October 1915, he appointed Henry P. Fletcher, then ambassador to Chile, to the post in Mexico.

China was a second area of foreign policy interest for Howe. The United States had been a member of the Six-Power Consortium, formed during the Taft presidency to make China a loan for railroad building. In March 1913 the president announced American withdrawal from the Consortium, explaining the step as necessary to avoid excessive interference in Chinese affairs. A few weeks later the United States unilaterally recognized the Republic of China without seeking prior agreement from other major powers. Early in 1915 Japan took advantage of the war in Europe to issue twenty-one demands on the Republic. The United States objected to the demands, especially to Article V, which would have given Japan control over much of China's administrative, financial, and military affairs. Japan yielded to American pressure and abandoned Article V, while securing Chinese consent to the rest of its demands.

Writing to the president in August 1916 concerning a proposed loan to China by American bankers, Howe suggested a direct loan by the United States government. This would be "a very splendid international act" that might save China from the financial grip of foreign powers. Wilson welcomed the idea and wished "with all my heart" that what Howe suggested could be done. "I am afraid that in the present need for money and the piling on of new taxes the Congress would back off from the thing," he wrote, "but I am going to discuss it at least with some of the men on the Hill to see if it is by any chance feasible."[34]

---

33. FCH to Wilson, October 29, 1915; Wilson to FCH, November 1, 1915, ibid., 35:132–34, 146.
34. FCH to Wilson, August 5, 1916; Wilson to FCH, August 7, 1916, in Link, *Papers of Woodrow Wilson*, 37:534, 537.

Earlier, combining his interest in Mexico and China, Howe had sent Wilson a proposed plank for the 1916 Democratic platform. It called for adherence to "the democratic doctrine that all peoples have a right to establish their own form of government and control their internal affairs." The doctrine that the State Department and the flag should follow the investor was condemned as "undemocratic and dangerous." Imperialism was "one of the gravest dangers to democracy," and the Democratic Party was "irretrievably opposed to dollar diplomacy, the acquisition of new territory, or to any act which threatens the sovereignty or political integrity of any people."

Howe wanted this plank to state clearly the issue between democracy and imperialism and to answer those privileged interests that were "urging what they term 'a strong foreign policy' as an aid to the same kind of financial imperialism that has brought over 100,000,000 people under the dominion of the greater powers of Europe during the last thirty years, and led to countless irritations, conflicts and diplomatic contests, which formed a prelude to the present war." Howe believed "it is eminently good politics to place this issue in the forefront and frankly develop it before the people." The president rejected Howe's plank but thought that "when the platform is finally completed you will find that it breathes throughout just the spirit of what you have embodied in what you have sent me." He was "warmly obliged" for the suggestion, he wrote.[35]

Howe did not limit his role in national affairs to offering advice to the president and other officials. In 1915 he became involved in the work of the Committee on Industrial Relations, the nongovernmental successor to the Commission on Industrial Relations. That Commission had originated in the desire of a group of reformers for a federal investigating committee to discover the facts on labor disputes, strikes, violence, unsafe working conditions, wages, and the place of unions and employer associations. Its progenitors included many of Howe's friends or associates. They persuaded President Taft to recommend to Congress a measure authorizing a commission, prepared a draft bill, lobbied hard for its passage, securing the backing of the American Federation of Labor, the National Civic Federation, and prominent individuals, and hailed its enactment in August 1912. The law provided for a commission made up of three representatives of labor, three of industry, and three of the public, and gave it the task of discovering "the underlying causes of dissatisfaction in the industrial situation." Confirmation of Taft's appointees was held up in the Senate until Wilson took office. The new president nominated his own choices in June 1913. Reformers liked the appointment of John Commons as a public member but

---

35. FCH to Wilson, June 9, 1916; Wilson to FCH, June 15, 1916, ibid., 37:180–81, 230.

were sparing in their praises of the others. Frank Walsh, another public member, was designated chairman.

The Commission on Industrial Relations divided its efforts between public hearings in major American cities and basic research. After several years of hearings, investigations, and public bickering among its members, the Commission finally produced in 1915 three separate sets of recommendations. One report, drafted by Basil Manly and endorsed by Walsh and the three labor representatives, found the question of industrial relations "more fundamental and of greater importance to the welfare of the Nation than any other question except the form of our Government." It declared the only hope for its solution to be "the effective use of our democratic institutions and in the rapid extension of the principles of democracy to industry."[36] A second report came from the three industry members, and a third from Commons and Florence Harriman, with partial endorsement from the industry representatives.

The outcome of the Commission's work pleased hardly anyone. Ralph M. Easley of the National Civic Federation called the Manly report "a 'soap-box socialist' harangue from start to finish.... The report itself would not be worth considering were it not for the unfortunate fact that the labor movement of the country is taking it seriously, on account of its having been signed by the labor men on the Commission." He referred in another letter to the "populistic, socialistic and anarchistic contents" of the report and wrote of the need for action "to neutralize and utterly destroy its evil effects.... The pity of it is that many otherwise sane labor men are going to feel bound to support the labor members of the Commission, however wild and inane their statements."[37] Businessmen and industrialists shared Easley's views.

Following the report of the Commission, Walsh and others sympathetic to the labor movement began to think of creating a nongovernmental Committee on Industrial Relations. One of the persons he turned to was Fred Howe, who quite properly took to the secretary of labor the question of the compatibility between membership and his position as immigration commissioner. Wilson not only saw no problem but expressed his own support. In mid-November it was announced that the Committee had been formed to promote the recommendations of the Manly report of the Commission on Industrial Relations. Its

---

36. U.S. Commission on Industrial Relations, *Final Report and Testimony*, 1:1:17. On the work of the Commission, see Adams, *Age of Industrial Violence*; A. Davis, *Spearheads of Reform*, 208–13, 216–17; Commons, *Myself*, 166–79; Milton Derber, *American Idea of Industrial Democracy*, 118–23; McCartin, *Labor's Great War*, 12–30; Weinstein, *Corporate Ideal in the Liberal State*, chap. 7. One of the public members, Florence Harriman, gave her view of the Commission and its work in *From Pinafores to Politics*, 133–46, 165–75.

37. Ralph M. Easley to Professor E. F. Humphrey, December 13, 1915; Easley to John Hays Hammond, September 8, 1915, National Civic Federation Papers, New York Public Library.

primary object, according to Walsh, would be to support organized labor, chiefly by "removing governmental obstacles to the efforts of the wage-earners to organize, and insisting that wage-earners and their representatives have a fair and free field." Its stand against the forces of privilege echoed Howe's beliefs: "The Committee on Industrial Relations believes the opportunity is great to lessen or shake off the hold of special privilege on our natural resources and our industrial production. It believes the workers and those who think with them as to collective bargaining and the fairer distribution of wealth are the ones to use this opportunity for the best results."[38]

Founding members of the Committee on Industrial Relations were Walsh, seven labor union representatives, Fred Howe, Amos Pinchot, Bishop Charles D. Williams of Michigan (a proponent of the Social Gospel), and Dante Barton. It was quickly noted that many of the members were, like Howe, single taxers. Howe became one of the principal fund raisers for the Committee.

As the presidential and congressional elections of 1916 neared, Howe, Walsh, Pinchot, and other Progressives began to think about the Committee on Industrial Relations as the nucleus of a larger political movement. Fred wrote Amos in January 1916 that he had talked with Gifford Pinchot about getting together "a group of radical minded persons to formulate a programme of state and national legislation, and start a propaganda behind the programme for the purpose of getting it into the consciousness of progressive minded leaders throughout the country." At a meeting of the Committee sometime in March 1916, there was a least a tentative decision "to try to get a labor party of at least fifty members in the next Congress," Barton wrote Walsh. "Fred Howe brought up the subject." In a 1916 article, Howe asserted his hope for "a real labor party in America: a party that thinks in terms of organized labor rather than socialism, and that makes common cause for advanced labor legislation, for government ownership of the natural monopolies, and for a program of social legislation like that of Germany and Great Britain."[39]

The drive toward a new political movement was sidetracked by what Arthur S. Link called "the astonishing metamorphosis in Democratic policies" that took place in the spring and summer of 1916. "Regardless of the motivation behind Wilson's commitment to advanced doctrines, the fact was that the Democratic congressional majority had, by the fall of 1916, enacted almost every important

---

38. Basil Manly to Frank Walsh, October 8, 1915, Walsh Papers, box 34; "A Follow-up Committee on Industrial Relations," *Survey* 35 (November 13, 1915): 155; Letter Addressed to Americanization Committee, December, 1915: Draft of General Letter Asking Financial Support, November, 1915, Walsh Papers. See also McCartin, *Labor's Great War*, 30–37.

39. FCH to Amos Pinchot, January 11, 1916, Amos Pinchot Papers; Dante Barton to Frank P. Walsh, March 25, 1916, March 30, 1916, Walsh Papers; FCH to Pinchot, April 15, 1916; Pinchot to FCH, April 20, 1916; FCH, "Wage-Earner's Innings," 298.

plank in the Progressive platform of 1912." Barton could write Walsh just before the election that its political issues were "clearly identified with the industrial, economic conditions the Committee is interested in. Every member of the Committee, without regard to ordinary partisanship, and without any agreement reached within the Committee, is quite actively for the election of Mr. Wilson."[40]

Wilson's reelection and America's entry into the war soon thereafter halted temporarily the attempt to develop a new political movement. Even in 1916, preparedness was supplanting labor conditions as the focus of the Committee on Industrial Relations. The organization closed its offices in October 1917. An important factor in the decision to end the Committee was probably the untimely death, in August 1917, of Dante Barton, who had been such an active force in all its efforts.

President Wilson's nomination of Louis Brandeis to the Supreme Court in January 1916 also helped rebuild his ties with Progressives. There was an immediate storm of protest from leading lawyers and businessmen, deans of law schools, the president of Harvard, ex-president Taft, and others. Opponents of the nomination called Brandeis antibusiness, a theorist, too radical, lacking in judicial temperament. Covert anti-Semitism was also at work. Springing to Brandeis's defense was a host of Progressives, including Frederic C. Howe. Howe admired Brandeis, had worked with him in the National Progressive Republican League, and had often talked and corresponded with him. In February he joined with a group of assorted reformers in a letter to the chairman of the Senate Judiciary Committee in support of the nomination. After the Senate confirmed Brandeis in June, he wrote the new justice: "I cannot tell you how happy I am over the confirmation of your nomination by the Senate. I know I am voicing the feelings of millions of people in this expression, as well as the gratification of the many friends you have made in your courageous fight for progressive things. Your nomination is one of the big forward steps that constructive politics has taken in recent years, and we are all heartened by reason of it." Brandeis replied with his thanks and his hope that "we may meet soon and talk over the future as well as the past."[41]

40. Link, *Woodrow Wilson and the Progressive Era*, 229; Dante Barton to Frank P. Walsh, November 1, 1916; Walsh to Barton, November 28, 1916; Barton to Walsh, December 3, 1916, Walsh Papers.

41. Mason, *Brandeis*, 489; Letter to Senator William E. Chilton, Chairman, Senate Judiciary Committee, February 23, 1916, Amos Pinchot Papers; FCH to Louis D. Brandeis, June 3, 1916; Brandeis to FCH, June 23, 1916, Louis Dembitz Brandeis Papers, University of Louisville. Other signers of the letter to Senator Chilton included Lillian Wald, Walter Lippmann, Florence Kelley, Rabbi Stephen Wise, Paul U. Kellogg, and Frances Perkins. On the fight over Brandeis's appointment, see Mason, *Brandeis*, 465–508; Strum, *Louis D. Brandeis*, 290–99; La Follette and La Follette, *Robert M. La Follette*, 2:567–69.

Fred and Marie became involved for the first time in matters of race relations in their New York years. Although they arrived in the city after the establishment of the National Association for the Advancement of Colored People in 1909, they quickly lent it their support. Marie was an "Honorary Vice-President" of the NAACP's annual meeting in February 1915, for example. In March 1916 the Howes joined with other liberals to form the Civic Club of New York, whose object, its constitution declared, was to offer "opportunity for social intercourse for people actively interested in civic affairs, to facilitate the consideration of civic problems and to maintain a club house in the city for the use of its members." Fred and Marie were both on its organization committee, and Marie served on its first executive committee. The club was notable in that it admitted men and women on an equal basis and did not use the titles "Mr." and "Mrs." The organizers believed there was no other body in the city which "responds fully to this modern demand."[42]

The Civic Club was also unusual in its treatment of African Americans. James Weldon Johnson, later the executive secretary of the NAACP, wrote that "in the discussions of the plans, the question of Negro membership was brought up. Finally, after considerable debate, it was settled upon that there would be no bar to membership on account of race or color. Dr. Du Bois and I were invited to become charter members, and we did." Johnson reported that Marie chaired one of the first special committees formed by the Club, on "The Negro in New York." "The first case undertaken was that of admittance to internship [sic] at Bellevue Hospital of a young colored woman doctor. Mrs. Howe worked earnestly on the case and it was won, but the young lady did not take the interneship; she got married." Johnson, who served for a number of years on the executive committee and then as president, believed that the Civic Club became "a strong influence on the life of Negro New Yorkers."[43]

New York City's economic and political problems also engaged Howe's attention. As economic distress in the city continued, Mayor Mitchel appointed a blue-ribbon Committee on Unemployment and Relief, headed by Elbert H. Gary, chairman of the board of the United States Steel Corporation. Committee members opposed direct relief efforts but approved municipal workshops to provide temporary employment at low wages. Howe and Agnes Warbasse

---

42. *New York Times,* March 12, 1916, 16. Many of the woman members were also members of Heterodoxy. Others on the organization committee were such reform stalwarts as Crystal and Max Eastman, Inez Haynes Gilmore, Walter Lippmann, Inez Milholland Boissevain, Amos and Gertrude Pinchot, Rose Pastor Stokes, Ida Tarbell, Herbert Croly, Norman Hapgood, Florence Kelley, Benjamin Marsh, and James and Agnes Warbasse.

43. J. Johnson, *Along This Way,* 328–29. Both Johnson and Mary White Ovington give the date of the club's founding as 1917, but the *New York Times* reported its first meeting in March, 1916. Johnson's wife, Grace Nail Johnson, was a member of Heterodoxy.

helped arrange a People's Institute "town meeting" to discuss the unemployment situation and the work of the Gary Committee. As one of the speakers, he challenged the city's policy of "letting the poor bear their poverty alone," and condemned the abandonment to private charity of those who were "maimed and hurt in the industrial battle." "We must shift the burden from the backs of the poor to the backs of all of us," he declared. The meeting unanimously adopted Howe's resolution calling for creation of a city department to provide relief work.[44]

Howe became more deeply involved in the campaign for municipal ownership, a cause he had espoused since the Cleveland battles over franchises and street railways. The immediate controversy in New York City was over ownership of the subway system. A Society to Recapture the Subway, formed in April 1916, gave way a few weeks later to an organization with a broader focus, the League for Municipal Ownership and Operation in New York City. Howe became its first president, and the indefatigable Benjamin Marsh was executive secretary. Besides municipal ownership of the subways, the League's goals included reduction of transit fares, legislation to "terminate present perpetual franchises," and prevention of future partnerships between the City and public utilities corporations. After a long debate in the May 8 meeting, the group agreed that its constitution should retain the goal of "[securing] revenue for financing municipal ownership through the taxation of land values."[45] Fred's name was often in the newspapers as spokesman for the League for Municipal Ownership.

The approach of the 1917 mayoral election turned the thoughts of many in the League to the possibility of a municipal ownership candidate. By 1916 Mayor John Purroy Mitchel had lost the backing of many reformers. His critics believed that he had failed to act to alleviate economic distress and to find work for the jobless. Mitchel also had become a vociferous advocate of preparedness and sometimes questioned the patriotism and loyalty of those who disagreed with him, at a time when a number of Progressives equated preparedness and militarism. Amos Pinchot was completely disillusioned with the mayor. He wrote Rabbi Wise: "Mitchel's administration has been a perfect model of intelligent, enlightened, Christian non-interference with the big grafters, i. e., the real estate ring and the public utilities ring, which form the strength of the by-partisan [sic] machine." Howe later observed: "As mayor Mr. Mitchel drifted away from

---

44. Agnes D. Warbasse to Amos Pinchot, February 26, 1915, Amos Pinchot Papers; *New York Times,* March 13, 1915, 9. See Ritchie, "Gary Committee."

45. *New York Times,* May 9, 1916, 18. Others involved in the League besides Howe, Pinchot, and Marsh included the Reverend J. Howard Melish, Rabbi Stephen Wise, the Reverend John Haynes Holmes, John F. Hylan, and James P. Warbasse.

his early militancy, he lost interest in the things he had stood for, and alienated the great mass of the people who had previously supported him."[46]

Mitchel was silent on his reelection plans throughout 1916 and well into the election year of 1917, leaving the door somewhat open for an independent reform candidate. Pinchot thought that he had a candidate. He wrote Stephen Wise: "I would like to see Fred Howe run for mayor, if he would stand the gaff. Of course, he could not be elected, but we would make the people ask why the city had to pay such heavy tribute to the grafters, and we would link up the connection between the government and the pocketbook of the average citizen." Pinchot and others sounded Howe out on the possibility of running as an independent candidate. He asked his friends to let him postpone a decision until the summer of 1917. As late as February 1917, Pinchot was still hoping that Howe would run as an independent. He met with him, Rabbi Wise, and Bainbridge Colby (a well-known lawyer who had backed Roosevelt in 1912), and found all of them except Colby receptive to the idea. "They think . . . that the only solution is to run an independent municipal ownership and tax reform candidate," Pinchot wrote. "I think this will be done. . . . What the attitude of the federal administration will be towards Mitchel, I have not learned, but I think that if Tammany put up a decent man, they would not support Mitchel, and if we ran an independent candidate like Fred, the administration would swing to us."[47]

At some point Howe declined to run, and one doubts whether he had even considered the idea very seriously. He knew that he would have no chance to win, even though there might be as many as four other candidates in the race: Mitchel on the Fusion and perhaps the Republican ticket, a Tammany Democrat, a regular Republican if one could beat Mitchel in the party primary, and the socialist Morris Hillquit, who would benefit from the antiwar vote. Contrary to Pinchot's prediction, the national administration did not favor an independent Democrat—it was anti-Tammany but did not want to risk an electoral loss in New York City. President Wilson was neutral and advised others in the administration to be the same. It was highly unlikely that Howe would oppose the president's wishes, since that might well lead to the loss of his position as commissioner of immigration and of his chance to influence Wilson and others in the administration. There was a price to be paid for waving the flag of municipal ownership as a gesture in a losing campaign. Howe also might well have

---

46. Amos Pinchot to Rabbi Stephen Wise, November 22, 1916, Amos Pinchot Papers; FCH, *Confessions of a Reformer*, 245. "[Mitchel] saw economy, efficiency, and social reforms as ends in themselves rather than as means leading to the end of human comfort, welfare, and betterment." Lewinson, *John Purroy Mitchel*, 246.

47. Amos Pinchot to Rabbi Stephen Wise, November 22, 1916, Amos Pinchot Papers; Amos Pinchot to A. J. McKelway, December 13, 1916, McKelway Papers, Library of Congress; FCH to Pinchot, December 14, 1916, and December 19, 1916, Amos Pinchot Papers; McKelway to Pinchot, January 29, 1917, Amos Pinchot Papers; Pinchot to McKelway, February 2, 1917, McKelway Papers.

been shrinking from a political battle so soon after his noisy fight with Congressman Bennet and after the ups and downs he had experienced as a candidate for various offices in Ohio. Perhaps this was what Pinchot had in mind when he wondered if Fred could "stand the gaff." In any event, Howe did not become a candidate, and Mitchel lost to Tammany's candidate, John F. Hylan. Hylan was a member of the League for Municipal Ownership, but he failed to pursue its goals during his term and "let his office drift."[48]

In the League and other organizations, Howe was able to continue his advocacy of the single tax. During 1916 and 1917 he was a leader in such organizations as the New York State Single Tax League, the Provisional National Single Tax Commission, the Joseph Fels Fund Commission, and the National Single Tax League. Ratification of the Sixteenth Amendment in February 1913 introduced a new controversy over taxation. The Amendment made an income tax constitutional, and Congress quickly added a mildly graduated tax to the 1913 tariff law. In 1916 Senator La Follette and Representative Claude Kitchin, chairman of the House Ways and Means Committee, led a congressional fight to boost the income tax rate on wealthy individuals. Support for this came from critics of higher military expenditures who argued that big business and the rich should pay a larger share of the cost.

A number of Progressives, joined by labor and farm leaders, thought the proposals placed the burden of taxation disproportionately on the poor and middle classes, to the benefit of the rich. To combat such taxes, Howe, John Dewey, George Record, Pinchot, Benjamin Marsh, and others formed the Association for an Equitable Federal Income Tax and lobbied vigorously for their goals. Responding to such pressures, the Southern and Western members who controlled the House Ways and Means Committee pushed through a bill that went far beyond the administration's proposals and substantially increased the rates of income and inheritance taxes. The Senate went even further in that direction, and the final outcome, the Revenue Act of 1916, was a watershed in federal tax policy. "Heretofore, the advocates of a progressive tax policy—the single taxers, the Socialists, and the labor and agrarian progressives—had been a minority, scourged and ridiculed by conservatives as purveyors of class prejudice and despoilers of the rich. Now for the first time in the saddle, these progressives used the necessity for vastly increased revenues as the occasion for putting their advanced tax theories into effect. The new income and inheritance taxes constituted, for that day, a powerful equalitarian attack on great property, unrivaled even by Lloyd George's 'Tax on Wealth' of 1909."[49] Howe and his fellow Progressives rejoiced in their victory.

48. Sayre and Kaufman, *Governing New York City*, 697. On the 1917 election for mayor, see Lewinson, *John Purroy Mitchel*, 206–45; Finegold, *Experts and Politicians*, 62–64.
49. Link, *Woodrow Wilson and the Progressive Era*, 195–96. See Ratner, *American Taxation*, 345–61; Link, *Wilson: Campaigns*, 60–65.

Besides the income tax, another emerging controversy that was to engage Howe in 1916 and in later years concerned the nation's railroads. In the summer of 1916 the railroad brotherhoods tried to negotiate a contract that would give them a long-sought goal, the eight-hour day. When the owners resisted, the unions scheduled a nationwide strike for August. Faced with the likelihood of a national economic crisis, the president appealed to the parties for a settlement and then, when labor and owners stood firm, proposed legislation to a joint session of Congress. In a hectic atmosphere, the national legislature quickly passed the Adamson Act, imposing the eight-hour day. This action failed to resolve the dispute, since the railroad executives began a publicity campaign that charged the unions with disloyalty, lobbied for binding arbitration of disputes, and appealed to the Supreme Court to find the Adamson Act unconstitutional. The brotherhoods suggested mediation, rather than arbitration, and, grateful to the administration for its actions, threw their political support to Wilson in the presidential election.[50]

Fred Howe's sympathies lay with labor. In November 1917 he discussed with Pinchot, Benjamin Marsh, and others how the public side could best be presented to the Joint Congressional Committee on Railroads, and in December he became acting chair of the preliminary organizing committee (whose members included, besides the three horsemen of good causes, Howe, Pinchot, and Marsh, such other Progressives as Record and Stephen Wise) for a Committee for Federal Ownership of the Railroads. Very shortly these first involvements by Howe with railroad issues were to lead him into the thick of wartime and postwar problems of the industry and its workers.

Congressman Bennet had charged that Howe's fecundity in publications meant that he was neglecting his duties at Ellis Island. It was certainly true that while he was holding down a presumably full-time job as commissioner of immigration and engaging in a wide range of political activities, he still found time to produce three books and two dozen articles in the years 1914 through 1916. About half of this output dealt with urban issues or immigration. He often returned to familiar themes: municipal ownership and the lessons for America of British and German experience; home rule; city reform; municipal enterprises in Cleveland.[51]

In the winter of 1914, Howe completed *The Modern City and Its Problems*, which Scribner's published in 1915. The message of the book was clear: "The

---

50. For a summary of the dispute, see Link, *Woodrow Wilson and the Progressive Era*, 235–38, 240. The Supreme Court found the Adamson Act constitutional in March, 1917.

51. Howe's publications included "Leisure"; "Joseph Fels"; "German System of Labor Exchanges"; "What to Do with the Motion Picture Show"; "Immigration, Industry, and War"; "Immigration After the War"; "Turned Back in Time of War"; "Municipal Ownership—The Testimony of Foreign Experience"; "Home Rule for American Cities"; "Better Towns"; "Municipal Ownership in Cleveland."

American city lags behind the work it should properly perform." It was negative in its functions, not positive in its activities. It was politically weak, and it failed to protect and serve its citizens. "We have failed to shift to society the burdens of industry which the coming of the city has created. We have permitted the sacrifice of low wages, irregular employment, and disease to be borne by the individuals rather than by the community. Those who suffer from these conditions are in reality a vicarious sacrifice; a sacrifice which society has no right to accept."[52]

Much of the book covered ground that Howe had explored in his earlier works. There was an extensive descriptive survey of the development of the modern city, its achievements and failures in America, its policies and programs, recent changes in city charters, the need for home rule and comprehensive city planning. There was the usual presentation of the Georgist argument for taxation of land values. There was a strong advocacy of municipal ownership. There was the not-unexpected comparison of American cities with those of Germany and England. Once again, Howe found the German city the "freest city" and the "most wonderful city" in the modern world, to be criticized only for its limited democracy and its government by business men. The British city was ahead of most American cities in its administration and services, but it was more hampered than the German because of dependence for its powers on a Parliament dominated by landowning interests. Municipal ownership was a proven success in both Germany and Britain.

Howe concluded with a message of hope and an agenda for action. The public was starting to realize the costs of individualism and to abandon laissez-faire. They were beginning to believe in democracy. They were securing new city charters and experimenting with new governmental arrangements (strong mayor, commission, and city manager forms). The changes were not yet sufficient, and more freedom was needed. "Through freedom to experiment, variety will be substituted for uniformity, while a new sense of affection will lead to an awakening in municipal politics and to constructive policies of city building." Those policies included new municipal services, municipal ownership of public utilities, and reform of the tax system to find new sources of revenue in the increasing urban land values.[53]

Fred Howe's *Modern City and Its Problems* joined the idealism of his *City* to a description of the achievements of municipal reform in such cities as Cleveland and Chicago and a statement of the steps that he believed still had to be taken. His writing was clear and his arguments cogent. All in all, *The Modern*

---

52. FCH, *Modern City and Its Problems*, v.
53. Ibid., 371, 376.

City was a livelier book than several of his volumes that had preceded it. It confirmed his position as a leading analyst of municipal problems and exponent of urban reforms. Ironically, it did so at a time when he was abandoning that field. It was to be his last book on the city.

Many of the reviews of *The Modern City and Its Problems* found it Howe's best work on urban problems since *The City*. The *Independent* thought, for example, that he had "combined much of the material of his earlier books and to very great advantage" and that he had presented his ideas "clearly and forcefully."[54] Some other reviewers were more critical. They took issue with Howe's theories and generalizations, though agreeing that the work was still worth reading.[55]

54. *Independent* 81 (March 1, 1915): 332–33. The *Bookman*'s reviewer declared it "a clear-cut easily comprehended treatment of a subject which is of great timely interest of many." The author's "mental attitude toward his subject, pleasingly evident in this latest volume, as in all the others, is that of one not content merely to understand and describe things as they are, but who illuminates existing conditions by the white light of a vision that might and can become actuality. . . . We feel that Frederic Howe loves the city because after all it is but a huge aggregation of humanity and he loves humanity with an abiding affection." *Bookman* 41 (March 1915): 96–97. The *Annals* observed that Howe's contributions to the study of municipal problems "occupy a unique position in the literature on the subject. No writer has contributed so much toward the development of a fruitful social point of view." Although there were many books on urban topics, "it would be difficult to find any work in which a clearer and more inspiring picture of the possibilities of municipal action is presented. . . . It combines the merit of accurate presentation of fact with an inspiring picture of the possibilities of social betterment." *Annals of the American Academy of Political and Social Science* 62 (November 1915): 294–95. The reviewer for the *American Journal of Sociology* concluded: "Would that all persons dealing with the social sciences had the knowledge of Dr. Howe and could act on his convictions in these respects. This is not Dr. Howe's most original, but it is his most profound, book about the city." *American Journal of Sociology* 21 (July 1915): 105–6. The *Dial* observed that "whatever [Howe] writes bears the stamp of experience and of conviction, and is, in addition, eminently readable." Some "errors of generalization" there might be, but "the fault is one which can be overlooked by any one who cares for fresh, vigorous, and stimulating writing on a subject of vital present-day importance." *Dial* 58 (April 1, 1915): 266–67. The *American Review of Reviews* praised the author's "constructive criticism." *American Review of Reviews* 51 (March 1915): 376.

55. Writing in the *American Political Science Review,* William Bennett Munro described *The Modern City* as a restatement of "facts, opinions, and prophecies" from Howe's earlier books. The author wrote cogently and presented his "clean-cut opinions" in "forceful English." These were qualities that would give real value to any book. "On the other hand the serious student of municipal affairs has nowadays come to expect something more than rapid generalizations which dissolve the most complex problems into naked simplicity and solve them in the twinkling of an eye. If all our municipal quagmires are so easily sidestepped as this book implies, what a marvel that both the saints and sinners of American public life keep stumbling into them with such blind perversity!" It was, nevertheless, a book worth reading, whether or not one agreed with Howe's civic philosophy. *American Political Science Review* 9 (May 1915): 411–12. The *Nation*'s reviewer praised Howe's discussion of facts but disliked his theories. He thought the author failed to realize that "our cities are assuming positive social tasks without revolutionary changes in political theory." *Nation* 100 (March 18, 1915): 310. The most hostile review came from the *New York Times:* "The book is not unlike the picture of such a sunset as nature ought to have produced, but such as man never saw, or at least hardly ever on this side the ocean. This country has not yet produced a city fit to be intrusted with unlimited powers." *The Modern City and Its Problems* was "a counsel of perfection, and it has the

A 1915 referendum on revising the New York state constitution gave Howe an opportunity to summarize some of his basic ideas about government. In "The Constitution and Public Opinion," he argued that American political institutions had been designed on the principle of distrust. "*Fear* of the people, *fear* of the legislature, *fear* of the executive, has inspired constitution makers and law makers from the very beginning. *Fear* has shaped our political machinery in city, state and nation." Fear had led to restraints on freedom and to obstacles to government action like the separation of powers, judicial review, and restrictions on the powers of states and cities. The cards were stacked against reformers. "Inaction has to win but one skirmish, while action has to win a series; reaction need control but one agency of the government, while progress has to control them all. Before public opinion becomes the final law of the land it has to struggle to the point of exhaustion to bring about the change desired, while democracy has frequently to survive many elections to achieve its end. . . . We have organized our politics in fear of the bad man, and by so doing have left little opportunity for the capable one." The failures of American government were due not to the American people but to the structures they had inherited.

Constitutional revision should follow four axioms: (1) Simple and easily understood politics—"a direct line of vision between the voter and the end desired and a means for the immediate execution of the common will, once it is declared at the polls." (2) A direct relation between voter and government. "There should be the fewest possible intermediaries, such as electoral colleges, delegates, conventions, and caucuses between the citizen and his servant." (3) Responsive government, responsible "not to the past, not to political parties, not to interests, but to people." (4) Machinery of legislation and administration that was "simple, direct, and final. . . . Once the public will express itself, it should be registered into law."

If one followed these axioms, the New York constitution should be brief and flexible so as to respond to social change. Important questions—woman suffrage and prohibition, as examples—should be submitted to voters as separate constitutional proposals, rather than incorporated into the body of a proposed new constitution. The legislature should be small and unicameral. The governor and his appointed cabinet members should have seats in the legislature, with the right to discuss but not to vote. The ballot should be short, and terms of

---

fault of the merit that it is so enticingly prepared, with a look ahead so fixed that there is no opportunity for hindsight. If only [Howe] would file a bond to produce his results he might be given a license to proceed. Until then bitter experience has taught Americans to be wary of those who promise faster than they can perform, and obscure their failures with fresh proposals." But even the *Times* praised Howe as a man who had "traveled and seen and written much, but never better than this." *New York Times*, March 14, 1915, 91.

office should be lengthened to four years. Judicial review should be limited. Municipalities should have complete home rule. Voters should have the opportunity to legislate directly through the initiative and the referendum. "The underlying motive of the foregoing philosophy is fluidity, responsiveness, freedom; freedom of society, in its collective capacity, to develop its own political life; freedom to evolve, to grow by change, just as does the individual, just as does the whole animal and even the vegetable kingdom. And I have no more fear of mankind in its collective capacity than I have of mankind in its individual capacity." Howe reiterated these views in speeches during 1915 as a constitutional convention drew up revisions to submit to the voters in the fall. The delegates failed to heed his advice, however, and produced a constitution that, in Al Smith's words, "assumed the proportions of the New York telephone directory."[56] The voters turned it down.

After the advent of the European war, Howe began to abandon his staple topics on municipal government and politics. Between 1914 and the end of 1916, he published two books and a dozen articles on war and international relations. All in all, the total number of his publications on both domestic and foreign subjects during this period was impressive. It must be kept in mind, however, that those on the city and its problems broke no new ground. Those dealing with immigration grew out of the responsibilities of his job, were to some extent speculative, and needed little if any research. Though Congressman Bennet may have exaggerated the leisure Howe had at Ellis Island, the position of immigration commissioner apparently gave him plenty of time for his writings. It is arguable whether this freedom resulted from his ability or willingness to delegate tasks to experienced subordinates like Byron Uhl or simply from the fact that the commissioner's duties were not especially onerous and could be treated as essentially part-time.

Both Fred and Marie Howe had become public figures. Fred was nationally known as a reformer, a writer, and a political activist. Marie was certainly well known in women's circles, especially in New York and the Northeast. Unfortunately, we have only a few glimpses of their private lives during this busy New York City period. They had a circle of close friends—Newton Baker, Lincoln Steffens, Fola La Follette, Inez Milholland Boissevain, the Garfields (though seen less frequently than in the Cleveland days). Others were friends but not as close—Walter Lippmann, the Amos Pinchots, Jane Addams, to mention a few.

Fred seemed to liven up the circles to which he belonged. Dante Barton said he supplied "ginger" to such groups, and George Creel complained once that,

---

56. "Constitution and Public Opinion," 7, 10, 11, 13, 18–19; Al Smith, quoted in E. Warner, *Happy Warrior*, 74.

with Steffens and Howe away, "there isn't a damned soul here I can talk to." He liked to be surrounded by remembrances of his heroes. He inherited Tom Johnson's "big chair" and hung pictures of Johnson and Robert La Follette in his office. He was honored by his alma mater when Allegheny College awarded him the degree of Doctor of Laws on June 23, 1915, and when the college's newly organized chapter of Phi Beta Kappa elected him to membership. He was no doubt also pleased when in May 1915 he was elected a member of the prestigious Cosmos Club in Washington, D.C. He kept up an interest in his very first organization, the Phi Gamma Delta fraternity, serving as third vice chairman and a member of the Permanent Organization and Constitutional Amendments committees at its national meeting in Atlantic City in 1913 and as a member of its committee on the Cheney and Baker Cups in the New York City convention of 1917.[57]

Although Howe sometimes listed Unitarian as his religious affiliation, he was not a churchgoer. Any quasi-religious activity he engaged in was nonsectarian and centered around the Ethical Culture Society and the Humanitarian Cult. He was one of the "men eminent in various walks of life" whom Felix Adler invited to speak at the dedication of the Ethical Culture Society's new meeting house in New York City in October 1910. His theme then was that "our ethical conceptions, the relations of men, virtue and vice, are largely,—almost exclusively,—the product of social conditions." Guilts were not personal but "the products of the complex civilization which the industrial revolution has ushered in. We, ourselves, produce the wreckage of the modern system. We produce it by the sanction which we give to the private ownership of the earth, to the private ownership of the highways, to the class control of the departments of government." The goals of the Humanitarian Cult, founded in 1907 by Misha Appelbaum, were similar to those of Ethical Culture. Howe became a member of the Cult, spoke to its meetings, wrote occasionally for its magazine, the

---

57. Dante Barton to Frank Walsh, November 17, 1915; George Creel to Walsh, August 23, 1915, Walsh Papers; Newton Baker to FCH, April 19, 1911, Baker Papers; FCH to Robert M. La Follette, March 16, 1914, La Follette Papers; letter from Margaret C. Clark, administrative assistant, the Cosmos Club, December 3, 1985. Howe was nominated for membership in the Cosmos Club by Louis Post and Royal Meeker. Meeker was an economist and statistician who established the federal Bureau of Labor Statistics and served as its commissioner from 1913 to 1920.

Howe received his honorary degree at Allegheny College's centennial celebration and he joined in the academic procession from the campus down Main Street to the Stone Church. Fifteen others also received honorary degrees, including Andrew Carnegie, Alexander Meiklejohn (then president of Amherst College), and Ida M. Tarbell. Fred's election to Phi Beta Kappa was probably a recognition of the achievements of his post-Allegheny career rather than of his grades as an undergraduate. Letter from Glenn Holland, secretary, Phi Beta Kappa, Allegheny College, June 20, 1991.

Humanitarian, and was especially interested in its Anti–Capital Punishment Branch.[58]

Besides the friends that she shared with Fred, Marie had her own separate circle, centering upon Heterodoxy, the Town Hall Club, and the Women's City Club. She was also close to Lincoln Steffens, who wrote her frequent gossipy letters. He sought to draw her out, urging her to "tell me something from out of the privacy of that secret cave of yours." In another letter he invited her to "give my love to Fred and all our friends. You didn't before. You seem to think that love is like money: gone when spent. It isn't, you know. It's more like strength, increased by use."[59]

After six years of residence in the Village, the Howes moved northward in 1916 to the small town of Croton-on-Hudson, New York, within easy commuting distance by rail to the city. In 1903 Clifford B. Harmon had purchased land from the Van Cortlandts and planned a development as a colony for writers and performing artists, "a complete community of rural charm." The actors, playwrights, and musicians who found homes in Harmon were soon joined by a migration of artists and writers from Greenwich Village, who built small houses and stone cottages at Mt. Airy in the hills above Croton. For many years, Mt. Airy Road was known as "Red Hill." "The colony caused considerable excitement among the natives; it was reported that the women wore shorts, smoked cigarettes, and took sun baths, and that the men indulged in similarly shocking activities."[60] Living on Mt. Airy or in Harmon, at one time or another, were such rebels and reformers as Max and Crystal Eastman, Mabel Dodge, Doris Stevens, Floyd Dell, Dudley Field Malone, John Reed, Louise Bryant, and Edna St. Vincent Millay. Isadora Duncan's sister, Elizabeth, reestablished their School of the Dance, first in Harmon and then on Mt. Airy.

The Howes apparently moved first to a house named "Wayside" in Croton-on-Hudson, probably in the summer of 1916. They resided there until the spring of 1919 when they moved to an attractive two-story house, high above the Croton River on Observatory Drive in Harmon. There, in the home they called Shadow Edge (the name perhaps modeled on Woodrow Wilson's summer home, Shadow Lawn, at the New Jersey shore), they were to live until the early

---

58. *Dedication of the New Meeting House,* 73; *History, Object and Aims of the Humanitarian Cult,* 1, 3. Other members or associates of the Humanitarian Cult included David W. Griffith, Reverend John Haynes Holmes, Edwin Markham, Lillian Wald, and Rabbi Stephen Wise.

59. Lincoln Steffens to MJH, April 4, 1913, May 3, 1913, in Winter and Hicks, *Letters of Lincoln Steffens,* 1:321, 322.

60. Northshield, *History of Croton-on-Hudson,* 156; *New York,* 580; Max Eastman to Amos Pinchot, September 15, 1916, Amos Pinchot Papers.

1930s.[61] Their departure from the Village brought them fresh air, more space, and a small-town environment, while at the same time offering a stimulating intellectual and artistic community that was an easy commute from the metropolis. The move from New York City to the suburbs seems almost symbolic of Fred's shift of interest at the same time from urban problems to other issues. The Howes did maintain a pied-a-terre on East Thirty-third Street in Manhattan for a while.

There were always the summers on Nantucket for refreshment and relaxation. Fred's view of their haven at Sconset is well conveyed in a letter of July 29, 1914, inviting Senator La Follette to come for a visit.

> It will do you a world of good and Marie and me an equal amount of good. We are pretty comfortable in our arrangements here; we are fifteen miles out to sea; the wind sweeps over the end of the island where we live and you can be just as much alone as you want to. Do come. We'll make you all over in a few days.... Your indigestion will pass away under the invigoration of the sea air.... You can sleep all the time if you want to and you probably will want to. We'll only wake you up to give you food. Bob [La Follette's son] won't want to sleep. There are too many pretty girls here and too good swimming, tennis and golfing.[62]

Fred and Marie remained a two-person household. If they had ever wanted children, time had passed them by. That Fred, at least, felt a lack was indicated in his testimony to the House Committee on Immigration and Naturalization in the summer of 1916. He spoke feelingly of an Irishwoman detained at Ellis Island as a person likely to become a public charge. Her husband had been killed in Flanders, leaving her with "three beautiful children," one seven years old, one nine, and one thirteen. Fred urged his superiors to admit her and added in his letter that "the children had won me so much and I liked them so much that, if nothing else could be done with them, I would adopt them." The department paroled the woman and her children in his custody, and, he testified,

> I carried them up to my own home and wanted to adopt two of the children. I got a cottage for them and I expected to get a job for the woman as a nurse. They were on my hands for five months and cost me $200 before I could find employment for them. I finally sent them down

---

61. I am greatly indebted to Jane Northshield, Croton-on-Hudson's local historian, both for information and for her willingness to serve as a guide to the area and to the Howes' house. I am also grateful to Mrs. Sandra Williams, who let us visit the house on Observatory Drive.

62. FCH to Robert M. La Follette, July 29, 1914, La Follette Papers, Library of Congress.

to a farm in West Virginia, where they obtained work. . . . They were the most beautiful children you ever saw. They were round, rosy, laughing children, climbing all over you in a minute. It almost broke my heart to send them away. I would adopt them in a minute if I had some place to send them.[63]

How Marie felt about a possible adoption is unrecorded.

63. *Congressional Record,* 64th Cong., 1st sess., September 5, 1916, 13891.

12

LIBERALS AND THE GREAT WAR

Almost as soon as the European war began in August 1914, Americans found themselves divided on issues of preparedness and peace. The first organized manifestation of antiwar sentiment was the women's peace parade in New York City, shortly after the outbreak of hostilities. Organizers enthusiastically canvassed women's groups, raised money, and distributed posters throughout the city. They turned down offers by men to help—this was to be a women's achievement, "a woman's protest against all warfare amongst civilized nations."[1] President Wilson endorsed their plans, requesting only that the marchers strictly observe the neutrality he had called for in his public statements on the war.

Preceded by a large white flag with a dove carrying an olive branch in its center, fifteen hundred black-clad women marched down Fifth Avenue to muffled drums on August 29. Even the *New York Times,* which earlier had poked fun at the idea of women parading, was impressed. The parade was evidence, said the *Times,* of a "definite determination on the part of a considerable number of women to exert a practical influence on a field of public action from which in the past they have been almost wholly withdrawn."[2] The parade was a dramatic protest against war, as well as a reminder of the strength of a united womanhood, but it had no lasting effect. The marchers had not agreed on any program or set of principles, and the broad coalition of groups could not be maintained.

The Woman's Parade Committee, whose formation had occurred almost spontaneously, was soon replaced by a more focused group, the Woman's Peace Party (WPP). A conference in Washington in January 1915 adopted a comprehensive platform for world peace that included an immediate convention of

---

1. Press release, n.d., quoted in Steinson, *American Women's Activism,* 11.
2. *New York Times,* August 30, 1914, 11.

neutral nations, limitation of armaments and nationalization of their manufacture, democratic control of foreign policies, an international police force, removal of the economic causes of war, organized opposition to militarism in the United States, the further humanizing of governments by extension of the franchise to women, and gradual organization of the world to substitute law for war. Though overwhelmingly approved by the delegates, the woman suffrage plank was to prove somewhat divisive and to lead to debate at subsequent WPP conferences.[3]

New York City soon had one of the largest and most active branches of the WPP, one that became increasingly more radical under the leadership of Crystal Eastman. Attracting many young feminists, it organized protest meetings, sponsored forums that offered speakers with varying viewpoints, worked against military training in the schools and lobbied in Albany against bills providing it, and generally took a strong antipreparedness stand. For Marie Howe, who was an honorary vice president of the New York City branch (along with Catt, Gilman, Lillian Wald, and others), a meeting of the branch's officers must often have resembled a committee of Heterodoxy.

Marie seems not to have taken much part in the WPP's activities, probably because she was still deeply involved in the suffrage battle in New York State. Lending his help, Fred spoke at a WPP antipreparedness meeting at Cooper Union on June 15, 1915. He suggested that the people should have a chance to vote on a declaration of war, with the understanding that those who favored it would be the first sent to the front. To his surprise, this proposal drew warm applause, and he remarked, "I thought you would consider that the silliest thing I would say." The *New York Times* agreed the next day that his statement was silly: "It must have dawned on [Howe] that by some accident there had been brought together under one roof an audience capable of swallowing anything and incapable of seeing anything foolish in the most preposterous arguments or anything pathetic in the most darkened mind."[4]

Men—Teddy Roosevelt, Elihu Root, Bernard Baruch, General Leonard Wood, Senator Henry Cabot Lodge—dominated the preparedness movement. As individuals and through such organizations as the National Security League (NSL), they called for compulsory military training for young men and for a larger army and navy. Patriotism and Americanism became the themes of the movement's propaganda. It was easy for the Americanism theme to slide over into opposition to potentially disloyal "hyphenated" Americans as the United

---

3. On the formation of the Woman's Peace Party, see Steinson, *American Women's Activism*, 16–47; Marchand, *American Peace Movement and Social Reform*, 194–208; O'Neill, *Everyone Was Brave*, 169–78; Degen, *History of the Woman's Peace Party*.

4. *New York Times*, June 16, 1915, 4; June 17, 1915, 10.

States edged closer to war. Antiwar Progressives, on the other hand, equated preparedness with militarism and the suppression of dissent. They also feared that the financial backing of the NSL by wealthy men heralded an attack on political and economic reform at home.[5]

One of the organizations trying to counter the activities and propaganda of the preparedness movement had begun with a group of social workers. In September 1914 Jane Addams of Chicago's Hull House, Lillian Wald of New York's Henry Street Settlement, and Paul Kellogg, editor of the *Survey*, the principal journal of the social workers, invited some three dozen individuals to come to Henry Street for luncheon, dinner, and "a round table conference on the war." The roundtable would provide "a means by which in humbleness and quiet some of us who deal with the social fabric may come together to clarify our minds and, if it seems wise, to act in concert." One of those receiving and accepting the invitation was Fred Howe, who found himself in the company of many friends. Nearly all those in attendance had had some association with settlement houses.[6]

Nothing much came of the first meeting of the "Henry Street group." Discussion was rambling as participants agreed on the evils of war and militarism but reached no consensus on courses of action against them. Fred told the group that President Wilson's mind was "in bits" and that somebody had to "think hard." "Groups of social workers have thought hard in the past and put over the Children's Bureau, Industrial Relations Commission, etc." He moved that the chair appoint a committee to draft a statement which would voice the feeling of social workers in America. The motion carried but offered no specific guidance or program. The group met again on January 23, 1915, and this time Howe got it on record on a specific point with a successful motion that "we endorse legislation and any movements for the nationalization of production of armaments for use by the governments."[7]

Leaders of peace groups, hoping, even believing, that President Wilson was sympathetic to their position, met with him on various occasions to urge him to support their efforts. After the *Lusitania* sinking in May 1915 the president moved slowly toward a strengthening of national defense. On November 4 he announced a program of "reasonable" preparedness, comprising expansion of the army and a stepped-up naval building program. In a message to Congress in December, he not only recommended passage of this program but also spoke

---

5. See Mooney and Lyman, "Some Phases."
6. Form letter signed by Lillian Wald, Jane Addams Papers, Swarthmore Peace Collection.
7. Minutes of the Henry Street Peace Committee, September 29, 1914, January 23, 1915, Jane Addams Papers, Swarthmore Peace Collection.

out in criticism of those immigrants "who have poured the poison of disloyalty into the very arteries of our national life."⁸

After Wilson's approval of a preparedness policy, members of the Henry Street group decided that the time had come to move from discussion to action. An Anti-Preparedness Committee adopted the proposals embodied in a "platform of real preparedness" that Crystal Eastman had published—an investigation of the state of America's defenses, nationalization of armaments manufacture, independence for the Philippines, student exchange programs between the United States and Japan, a union of American nations to replace the Monroe Doctrine, and eventually a workable world federation.⁹ In April 1916 the Committee changed its name to the American Union Against Militarism (AUAM).

The list of original members of the Committee included most of the Henry Street group, but Fred Howe's name was absent. He had been suggested for membership on a steering committee but apparently had declined. In fact, Howe's name virtually disappears from the records of the Committee and the AUAM after 1915. The reason is obvious. The president had declared his policy, and the immigration commissioner for the Port of New York, as a federal officeholder and presidential appointee, could not overtly and directly oppose the chief executive's position. AUAM members outside the government faced no such limitation. They testified in Congress against the president's national defense bill and held a series of mass meetings to make their case with the American public. Howe could hardly participate in such activities, given his official position. His official position may have limited Marie's pacifist activities as well, but it is likely that the rigors of the suffrage campaign were more important in this respect.¹⁰

Indicative of the pressures for conformity to administration policies was the controversy over Henry Ford's "peace ship." Ford, who had been supporting the antipreparedness movement and attacking war, announced that he would charter a ship to take the peace advocates to Europe, expressing his intent to "get the boys out of the trenches by Christmas." President Wilson refused to endorse the plan or to appoint an official delegation to attend.

Invitations went from Ford to a host of distinguished Americans. When both Fred's and Marie's names appeared on the list of invitees, his friends began to ask him about his intentions, and those in the Wilson administration grew

8. Quoted in Higham, *Strangers in the Land*, 200.
9. Benedict, "Platform of Real Preparedness."
10. Minutes, Anti-Preparedness Committee, November 24, 1915, Jane Addams Papers, Swarthmore Peace Collection. See "Swinging Around the Circle Against Militarism," *Survey* 36 (April 22, 1916): 95–96, and Hallinan, "Putting Pins in Preparedness."

concerned that he would go. Colonel House noted in his diary on November 30 that he had asked Dudley Malone to tell Howe not to go but not to hint that the directive came from the president.[11] Fred told Malone that he had no intention of joining the expedition, and he so wired Louis Lochner, Ford's "peace secretary": "All kinds of obsctacles [sic] prevent my going to Europe. Am sorry." Marie also declined Ford's invitation. In fact, nearly all the prominent people on Ford's list turned him down, including all the socialists and the whole WPP executive committee. No federal officeholder seems to have accepted Ford's invitation. Newsmen aboard the *Oscar II* had a field day ridiculing the enterprise and its participants, and cartoonists found the trip a rich source of fun. Ford abandoned the enterprise in mid-Atlantic, though he continued to pay the bills.[12]

Despite his denial, it is clear that there had been pressure on Howe to decline the Ford invitation. The episode indicated the tightrope he had to walk between administration policy and the freedom to speak his mind on issues of preparedness and war. He shared the views of the AUAM and other peace groups, however, and he could express his views independently and associate with organizations that were not overtly antiadministration.

Probably the AUAM's most successful achievement was its help in averting war with Mexico in 1916. War had seemed a real possibility, especially after some newspapers blamed the Mexicans for a clash with American troops at Carrizal in June 1916. The AUAM purchased space in leading newspapers and published a firsthand account by an American officer that showed the Americans to be the aggressors. Its appeal stimulated an outpouring of letters and telegrams to the president, who then began to urge a peaceful settlement. Later in the summer the two governments agreed to appoint a Joint High Commission to investigate problems and recommend solutions. Lincoln Steffens and others made efforts to get Fred Howe appointed to the commission. President Wilson at first seemed receptive to the suggestion. He told Secretary of State Robert Lansing that he thought it a good idea to appoint an adviser to the American commissioners but did not know whom to select. "The closest and most comprehending student of such questions as those which undoubtedly lie at the bottom of the whole Mexican domestic settlement (so far as my acquaintance goes) is Frederic C. Howe, the Commissioner of Immigration at New York. It was for that reason, chiefly,

11. Gilbert E. Roe to FCH, November 27, 1915, and telegram, Ben Lindsey to FCH, November 27–28, 1915, Ford Peace Plan Papers, Library of Congress; E. M. House to Woodrow Wilson, December 1, 1915, in Link, *The Papers of Woodrow Wilson*, 35:279.

12. Telegram, FCH to Louis P. Lochner, November 27, 1915, Ford Peace Plan Papers, Container 1; *New York Times*, November 30, 1915, 6.24. On the Ford peace ship, see Steinson, *American Women's Activism*, 76–95; Larsen, *Good Fight*, 128–39; Merz, *And Then Came Ford*, 149–60; Hershey, *Odyssey of Henry Ford*.

that I thought of him as a member of the Commission itself."[13] In the end, the president chose Howe neither as commissioner nor as economic adviser.

Perhaps Howe was already deemed too controversial for such an appointment. By the summer of 1916 he was embroiled in the controversy with Congressman Bennet. The *New York Times* had attacked his antipreparedness views on several occasions, in one editorial calling his position on the war a "pestiferous preachment," which, "coming from a man holding a high office under the Federal Government, may easily influence the minds of thousands of persons unable to see wherein Mr. Howe's talk differs from right reason and common sense." The president received at least one anonymous letter attacking Howe and asking how Wilson could tolerate direct opposition from one of his appointees. "Mr. Howe is a single-taxer, a pronounced socialist and in politics a died-in-the-wool [*sic*] republican. He has always been a republican even while serving under democratic appointments." Wilson forwarded the letter to Secretary of Labor Wilson, who appended only the laconic comment, "Noted." There is no indication that the president gave any credence to the charges of an anonymous letter-writer, but they foreshadowed later attacks on Howe.[14]

Howe had done little systematic thinking on international relations prior to the outbreak of the European hostilities. His writings on the tariff had centered on domestic issues rather than its international impact. His frequent trips to Europe had been mainly to study urban conditions, though he had also garnered information about politics and policies in many countries. He had given particular attention to Britain and Germany and had accorded high praise to their municipal achievements while criticizing other aspects of their governments and politics. He had acquired some knowledge about international business through his European sales trips for the Long Arm System Company. In his study of cities, he had found a system of economic privilege at the root of urban problems, and he was predisposed to accept an economic theory of imperialism and war. Indeed, his 1910 book *Privilege and Democracy* was a major step toward that interpretation. As director of the People's Institute, he began to introduce more international topics into its forums and lectures as the world crisis deepened.

13. Link, *Woodrow Wilson and the Progressive Era*, 141–44; Lincoln Steffens to Lou and Allen Suggett, July 16, 1916, in Winter and Hicks, *Letters of Lincoln Steffens*, 1:377; Robert Lansing to Woodrow Wilson, August 24, 1916; Wilson to Lansing, August 26, 1916, in Link, *Papers of Woodrow Wilson*, 38:83, 84. On June 27, 1916, a mass meeting sponsored by the Civic Club had adopted a resolution asking the president to submit the Mexican troubles to a board of arbitration. Steffens and Pinchot spoke at the meeting; Howe was present but was not listed as a speaker. *New York Times*, June 28, 1916, 4.

14. *New York Times*, June 8, 1916, 8; anonymous letter to President Woodrow Wilson, January 21, 1916, General Records of the Department of Labor, 1907–1942 (Chief Clerk's Files), File 2/288.

After the war's outbreak, Howe's membership in the Henry Street group and other peace organizations began to put him on record on many of the issues in America's foreign policy and national defense. In November 1915, at a dinner honoring Frank Walsh for his work as chairman of the Commission on Industrial Relations, he observed that he had heard a great deal of talk about preparedness but had "never heard the question asked whether the cost of it was to be borne by the bended backs of labor." He had also heard a great deal of talk about "hyphenated Americans," he said, "but the only class of this kind whom I consider to be dangerous is the hyphenated patriots in whose case patriotism is united in unholy wedlock with profit." To the applause of his listeners, he urged that the government enter the business of munitions making and limit private manufacturers of arms and ammunition to a profit of no more than 5 or 6 percent. Howe became, in Dante Barton's words, "a bug on the preparedness proposition."[15]

Howe clearly saw increased military expenditures as a threat to social reform. Preparedness proposals made him "mentally sick," he wrote Oswald Garrison Villard. "War preparation and emphasis upon militarism is national suicide to all the things I am interested in. I could stand the financial cost if it were equitable [sic] distributed, but I can't stand the social cost. It is, as you suggest, taking poison into the system." He seemed gradually to become reconciled toward some measure of preparedness, however, provided that the burden did not fall on the wage earners. In January 1916 he told an interviewer that although he was an antimilitarist, he did not care how large the American army became as long as its organization provided industrial training for every soldier. America's need for skilled workers could be met through "a great industrial army, mobilized about Government workshops, which should be, in effect, vocational training schools. Scatter them all over the country in the localities of the special industries taught in the several schools." Such an industrial army would enhance both America's defenses and its economic strength.[16]

"Everyone is agreed that the new preparedness is in the nature of insurance or precaution against war, or a means of defense in case of war," Howe wrote in a *New Republic* article a month later. "We are preparing to protect democracy, the traditions, honor and dignity of the nation." Preparedness should be a complete program, however. "We should know not only the military and naval

---

15. *New York Times*, November 7, 1915, 19; Dante Barton to Frank P. Walsh, December 14, 1915, Walsh Papers, New York Public Library; "A Follow-Up Committee on Industrial Relations," *Survey* 35 (November 13, 1915): 156.

16. FCH to Oswald G. Villard, October 1, 1915, Villard Papers, Call Number 1323 (1790), by permission of the Houghton Library, Harvard University; "Would Teach Every American Soldier a Trade," *New York Times Magazine*, January 23, 1916, sec. IV, 5.

program and how much it is to cost, but who is to pay the bills, and what precautions are to be taken to avoid the known dangers of war and preparations for war." Equality of sacrifice, especially financial sacrifice, should be an axiomatic principle. The costs of preparedness should be covered by taxes on incomes and inheritances, rather than by indirect taxes on consumption, paid mainly by the poor. No one should profit from war or preparation for war. Concluded Howe: "Democracy has a right to insist that preparedness does not mean the creation of new privileges and an end of its traditions and aspirations."[17]

The coming of the European war had afforded Howe an opportunity to present his views on the power of modern Germany and the lessons that the United States should derive from the German experience. By the fall of 1915, when his book *Socialized Germany* appeared, the early victories of the Kaiser's armies made it an appropriate time to analyze the nonmilitary foundations of Germany's strength and to examine that nation's democratic weaknesses more critically than in his previous books.

Howe began *Socialized Germany* with a disclaimer: he was neither defending militarism and the Prussian idea of the state nor making a plea for socialism. He himself was no socialist, he avowed. He still believed that "with special privileges abolished and industrial freedom assured, society would realize an approach to economic justice that would exclude the necessity of socialism. And I believe in democracy, and all that democracy implies." He was attacking not the socialism of the German Social Democrats but the "socialism" of the Junkers, "the socialism of the ruling caste, the great estate owners and the capitalists." Germany presented a riddle, a paradox. He admired the German people, their orderly and efficient cities, their generous provision for the cultural things of life, their wonderful educational system, their far-seeing social legislation. How were these achievements compatible with German militarism and paternalism?[18]

Germany had replaced English and American individualism with "the coordination of the individual into a machine of national rather than purely personal dimensions. All Germany, in fact, acts as a unit." As a result, it had developed "a wonderful efficiency" in the production and distribution of wealth. In chapters replete with facts and figures, Howe surveyed German achievements in public ownership, social legislation, labor relations, education, health and

---

17. FCH, "Incomplete Preparedness." For an exchange of views on the article, see Lippmann, "Trade and the Flag"; Lippmann to FCH, February 18, 1916; FCH to Lippmann, March 1, 1916; Lippmann to FCH, March 2, 1916; FCH to Lippmann, March 7, 1916, Lippmann Papers, Yale. Howe's article, "The Flag and the Investor," appeared in the *New Republic* on June 17, 1916.

18. FCH, *Socialized Germany*, 1, 2. The principal arguments of the book are summarized in Howe's article "The Background of Modern Germany."

sanitation, cities, housing, and land use. Germany had tackled the problems of modern industrial society in a thoroughgoing and efficient way, giving "a new conception of the state to the world."[19]

Germany's defects were not economic but political, Howe argued. The old feudal class remained the ruling class. It filled all important posts in government, it controlled the armed forces, it directed society. There were, in effect, "two Germanys: the Germany of politics, militarism, and aggression, and the Germany of culture, sweetness, efficiency, and life." Official, feudal Germany was separate from the real Germany of workers, peasants, merchants, and most of the property-owning classes. "The voice of the class which rules is not the voice of the people."[20]

The great estate owner, the Junker, ruled Germany and was "ultimately responsible for the militarism and jingoism which seem to characterize the whole nation." The caste system he represented was the bane of Germany. Nowhere in German statecraft was there any belief in democracy, representative institutions, or manhood suffrage. Instead of freedom, "there was endless supervision of the individual. *Verboten* is the law of the land. The daily life of the German is supervised by countless officials under the police power of the state; he is subject to regulations without number upon his daily personal acts."[21]

Both the United States and Germany had their defects, Howe concluded. "We have so weakened the state that great aggregations of wealth have become more powerful than the community, while Germany has so strengthened the state as to devitalize the individual." Even with its controls on political rights, Germany in some respects provided more freedom for its people than did either America or England. "Germany protects industrial and social equality, while America protects political and personal equality. Her freedom is in the economic, ours in the political field." State socialism had "largely made Germany what she is, a menace and a model, a problem to statesmen of other countries, and a pathfinder in social reform."[22]

Howe realized that he was open to criticism for his attempt at a balanced assessment of the German model, and many of the reviewers took issue with his treatment of it.[23] Despite the criticisms, Howe stuck by his guns. "There is a

19. *Socialized Germany*, 5, 6.
20. Ibid., 11, 12.
21. Ibid., 32, 332, 334.
22. Ibid., 81, 85, 327, 335.
23. For reviews, see *Dial* 59 (December 9, 1915): 567; *American Economic Review* 6 (June 1916): 357, 358; *Nation* 102 (January 13, 1916): 52; *New Republic* 4 (October 30, 1915): 343; *North American Review* 202 (November 15, 1915): 782; *Survey* 35 (February 26, 1916): 644; *New York Times*, September 12, 1915, 16–17, and October 24, 1915, 404; *Journal of Political Economy* 24 (January 1916): 91; *Publishers' Weekly* 88 (October 16, 1915): 1240–41; *Annals of the American Academy of Political and Social Science* 64 (March 1916): 256.

kind of economic democracy in Germany that to my mind is very much more wide spread than in England or America," he wrote Bolton Hall in May 1916. "This, of course, is a very different thing from political equality or political democracy."[24]

Howe pulled together his thinking on war in general, and the European war in particular, in a book *Why War,* published in the spring of 1916. He argued that wars were "born of privilege in politics, privilege in finance, privilege in trade." Primarily, they resulted from "powerful economic interests radiating out from the capitals of Europe, which, with the foreign office behind them, have laid the whole world with explosives which only needed a spark to set all Europe aflame." With few exceptions, the European state in its foreign relations was "little more than the political and financial will of the ruling classes."[25]

According to Howe, "the ruling class is the owning class, much as it was in the eighteenth century. The old aristocracy continues to rule because it owns the land that gave it power from the tenth to the eighteenth century.... Political power is a reflection of economic power, just as it was under the old regime." The aristocracy used its political power to fasten its privileges on the people, and then it used its privileges to maintain its political power. Through indirect taxation, it shifted the burden to the poor, and everywhere it prevented the taxation of land. "All of the machinery of organized society is really arrayed on the side of militarism."[26]

The new imperialism originated in the rapid increase in the landed aristocracy's rents and royalties, stemming from the growth of industry and the urban population; the development of combinations and monopolies in nearly every industry (resulting in larger profits and an increase in the surplus capital seeking investment); and the concentration of the world's investing capital in London, New York, Paris, Berlin, and a few other cities, under the control of powerful financial groups in these centers. A new ruling class has been created through the merger of the old landed aristocracy with the new financial aristocracy. Its diplomatic policy was "protection to foreign investments, the doctrine that the flag follows the investors and backs up his private contracts." Allied with the investor was the trader in munitions, whose nefarious commerce brought him huge profits. "The public mind is infected by an appeal to the necessity for preparedness. Peaceful nations are subjected to war scares promoted by the

---

24. FCH to Bolton Hall, May 22, 1916; FCH to Hall, July 15, 1916, Bolton Hall Papers.
25. FCH, *Why War,* viii, ix–xi, 300. Quotations are from the 1970 edition. The themes of the book appear in Howe's article "Reservoirs of Strife," part of a symposium under the general title "War and Reconstruction."
26. *Why War,* 154, 31, 301, 59.

press influenced by the munition dealers." Public ownership of the munitions industry must be adopted to remedy these evils.[27]

Howe intended *Why War* as a cautionary tale for the United States and for President Woodrow Wilson, to whom the book is dedicated. He noted that since the Spanish-American War, a growing militarism had threatened to cause the United States to follow the European path. "Ambitions and fears have been aroused that have united the privileged classes in a movement for financial imperialism, for a great naval programme, for colossal expenditures for preparedness, and unless some hand interpose to prevent it the ideals of America and the democratic traditions of a century will be submerged in the new imperialistic programme that has no place in our life."[28]

The forces of militarism and imperialism were part of the same "invisible government" that had been battling democracy in the United States for the past twenty years, Howe argued. "War and preparations for war are the international expression of the same struggle that has convulsed San Francisco, Cleveland, Chicago, Denver, or Toledo in the conflict of franchise corporations to protect their grants from the city.... Privilege is no more ruthless in its international dealings than it is in its domestic activities." The same business classes united "the press, the investing and ruling classes in the jingoistic appeals for armaments, for navalism, for a strong foreign policy, and for all of the aggressions and activities that lead to war."[29]

Was world peace possible? Howe asked in conclusion. Only if there were "a common factor of interest in peace," he answered. The solution lay in the triumph of democracy and the application of the principle of freedom—"freedom of each nation to expand without let or hindrance from any other nation; equal freedom in colonial markets and freedom of the seas." No permanent peace would be possible so long as the privileged classes ruled. Even democratic nations had to adopt "measures of precaution" to ensure against forces making for war.[30]

In *Why War* Howe sought to do more than explain the causes of the First World War. He offered a general explanation of the causes of modern war. In this, he agreed with two British writers, J. A. Hobson and H. N. Brailsford, whose arguments he cited to support his own.[31] Though he made no detailed examination of American foreign policy in the late nineteenth and early twentieth centuries, he recognized the dangers of American economic imperialism and

27. Ibid., 62–63, 107, 303–4. See also FCH, "Flag and the Investor"; "Democracy or Imperialism."
28. *Why War*, 145, 322.
29. Ibid., xi–xii, 317, 307–9, 314–15.
30. Ibid., 332, 337–38.
31. See Hobson, *Imperialism*, and Brailsford, *War of Steel and Gold*.

praised the Wilson administration's retreat from dollar diplomacy. The United States might still follow the European road, but there was hope of averting this calamity.

The relation of Howe's views on war to his ideas and experiences in domestic policy is clear. Both at home and abroad, the dangers came from the ruling classes. They, not the people, were responsible for the ills of society. The ruling class was the owning class and the war-making class. "Surplus wealth seeking privileges in foreign lands is the proximate cause of war just as wealth seeking monopoly profits is the cause of the civil conflicts that have involved our cities and States." Both at home and abroad, the remedy was democracy. Once the people knew the facts, they would act rightly. They would recognize that a key to democracy and peace was a more equitable distribution of wealth.[32]

Reviews of *Why War* were mixed but generally favorable.[33] Hoping to influence American policy, Howe sent copies of the book to President Wilson and Colonel House. He also sent a copy to the La Follettes, suggesting that the senator might want to read parts of it into the *Congressional Record*. In the Senate on July 20, 1916, Senator La Follette did just that. He praised *Why War* and added: "Dr. Howe is one of the Nation's ablest writers, thinkers, and publicists. He is a practical statesman." The senator was so impressed with Howe's volume that in 1918 he recommended it to his son as must reading in preparation for the battle between Progressivism and reaction. "We must be ready. Begin storing your mind with the vital things that will constitute a real *preparedness* for

---

32. *Why War*, viii, 301.
33. The *Annals* found it a sane analysis of the causes of the European conflict, one "entirely free from prejudice, special pleading and hypocrisy." The *Literary Digest*'s review provided mainly a summary and praised the writer's approach: "Of highest interest and in strong contrast to certain recent amateur efforts, is this author's masterly survey of the psychological *terrain* of the war, wherein he lets in light upon certain phases of the conflict purposely kept in darkness by a too one-sided press." The *Bookman*'s reviewer thought that Howe had brought together an immense amount of material on the development of politico-economic power during the last twenty years and had handled it in "a calm, judicial manner. His book is one of the most interesting of the investigations and arguments that have been produced by the war." Edward Raymond Turner, writing in the *American Political Science Review*, was critical, finding the author's ideas "larger than his knowledge or his comprehension of historical relations and development. His penetration is less profound than his manner, his condemnation is too ready, his suspicions too certain, his solutions too easy and thorough." Nevertheless, the writing was "for the most part . . . so clear and forceful that the reader will not wish to lay the book aside. It is not free from errors, but it also contains large ideas and vigorous thinking, which, in so far as they are correct, are valuable and striking." The *Nation* was less kind. Howe's theory of wars presented "an incomplete, and in some respects a much exaggerated picture." Foreign investments were strong incentives to peace as well as to war; "and certainly no treatment of the subject is complete which does not attempt to estimate the good as well as the evil consequences of a complex phenomenon." *Annals of the American Academy of Political and Social Science* 69 (January 1917): 288; *Literary Digest* 53 (July 8, 1916): 82; *Bookman* 43 (August 1916): 629; *Literary Digest* 53 (July 8, 1916): 82; *American Political Science Review* 10 (August 1916): 607; *Nation* 103 (October 5, 1916): 327.

this coming contest. Read Fred Howe's book WHY WAR. Read it again and again until the facts *stick*."³⁴

Many Progressives were unhappy with President Wilson's preparedness program, but when the chips were down, most of them backed his reelection in 1916. Leading reformers who had followed Teddy Roosevelt's banner in 1912 were in Wilson's camp four years later; Amos Pinchot no doubt expressed the view of the others when he wrote, "Colonel Roosevelt steered the Progressive ship as long as the sailing was good. But when it got into rough water he promptly changed back to the Republican craft. And, incidentally, he did not take much with him. Unlike the boy who stood on the burning deck 'whence all but him had fled,' he took a quick leap and left behind his progressive principles and most of the real men of the party."³⁵ It was crucial for Wilson to have the support of a substantial number of those who had voted for Roosevelt in 1912 if he was to win in a normally Republican national electorate.

For Fred Howe, endorsement of the president for a second term presented no problem at all. Besides being an officeholder in the Wilson administration, he had ties of respect and friendship with his former professor going back to Johns Hopkins days. He was pleased with Wilson's domestic policy—the Federal Trade Commission, the child labor law, the Brandeis appointment, the Adamson Act for the eight-hour day for railroad workers. He considered "the humanizing of the immigration service and the development of a constructive immigration policy" one of the administration's major achievements. In foreign affairs he seemed ready to follow the president's lead, though he advocated a different kind of preparedness. Howe favored neutrality, indicating his belief in "a continuance of the policy of isolation and detachment that has served us so well for a century." He praised Wilson's opposition to financial imperialism in America's dealings with Mexico and China—in fact, he referred to dollar diplomacy as the "paramount issue" in the 1916 campaign.³⁶

Going beyond mere endorsement of the president, Howe played an active role in the campaign. In June he sent the president a plank he had drafted for the Democratic platform, putting the party against financial imperialism. Showing an awareness of the increasing need for systematic publicity in election campaigns, he proposed to William Gibbs McAdoo that the Democratic campaign

---

34. FCH to E. M. House, April 12, 1916, House Papers; Woodrow Wilson to FCH, April 18, 1916, Wilson Papers; FCH to Belle Case La Follette, April 7, 1916, Belle Case La Follette Papers, La Follette Family Collection; *Congressional Record*, 64th Cong., 1st sess., July 20, 1916, vol. 53, 11341–44; Robert M. La Follette to Robert M. La Follette Jr., November 26, 1918, quoted in ibid., vol. 2, 913. See also La Follette and La Follette, *Robert M. La Follette*, 1:575–78.

35. Amos Pinchot to Judge Seabury, press release dated September 17, 1916, Amos Pinchot Papers.

36. FCH to *New York Times*, August 10, 1916, 8; "Democracy or Imperialism," 250; "Dollar Diplomacy and Financial Imperialism," 312.

enlist "a group of vital, young, democratic-minded writers and speakers." "Modern publicity is an advertising art," he wrote. "The average man wants material served up to him in a direct way. He has been trained to expect this by the magazines and the press. He expects directness, the dramatic. He is trained to short sentences and is familiar with certain names." No administration in the past fifty years had made good use of the material available. "It ought to be lifted out of the cold storage of Government reports and the Congressional Record and popularized." The country was eager to hear the story of the Wilson administration's achievements.

Howe was thinking both of the need to win over the Roosevelt voters of 1912 and of the future of the Democratic party. "I think the cleaveage [sic] of privilege and democracy between the Republican and Democratic party ought to be emphasized, and that democracy identify itself with all those classes that desire merely a square deal, whether they be business men, farmers or working men." The Democratic party was traditionally the party opposed to privilege. "We receive little or no support from the privileged interests. And without raising any class divisions we should, I think, interpret what has been achieved during the past four years to the great mass of the American people, and lay the issue of privilege or democracy frankly before them." As for himself, he was ready "to enlist in any capacity that is open to me."[37]

McAdoo replied that he was sending Howe's letter to the new Democratic national chairman, Vance McCormick, a young newspaper publisher in Harrisburg and a leader of Progressive Democrats in Pennsylvania. Other Democrats had made similar suggestions, and McCormick needed little urging to respond to them. He put the party's publicity bureau under the innovative direction of Robert W. Woolley, the director of the United States Mint and a former newspaperman. Woolley was ably assisted by George Creel and a large staff of writers. The Republicans used similar techniques but seemed slow and uninspired in their publicity efforts. "For the first time, advertising completely overshadowed the oratory and didactic pamphlets of education. Run like modern ad agencies, the national committees shaped the public perception of their candidate-clients through press releases and paid advertisements."[38]

Fred Howe's most direct role in the 1916 campaign came in the Wilson Volunteers, a small group of progressive-minded Democrats, Republicans, and independents. He joined with Pinchot and Wise to invite a dozen other men to a luncheon at the Yale Club in New York City on October 5, 1916. The purpose of the conclave was "to evolve plans looking to vital and effective participation

---

37. FCH to William Gibbs McAdoo, June 13, 1916, McAdoo Papers.
38. McAdoo to FCH, June 16, 1916; McGerr, *Decline of Popular Politics*, 162–63.

in the Wilson campaign." The group would be a "voluntary and independent . . . organization, the purpose of which is to enlist independent voters of all parties in the fight for President Wilson's re-election." Out of the Yale Club meeting came the Wilson Volunteers, whose ranks included (besides Howe, Wise, and Pinchot) such Progressives as A. J. McKelway, Ray Stannard Baker, Walter Lippmann, Norman Hapgood, Dante Barton, Frank Walsh, Walter Weyl, Will Durant, and John Dewey. Summing up their view of the import of the presidential election, Pinchot used the language of Fred Howe. Independent voters had to be made to realize "that the great issue of this campaign is that of Privilege against democracy."[39]

The Wilson Volunteers laid plans for a speaking tour by automobile through New York State, "from the Battery to Buffalo and back," as they enjoyed describing it. The operation was launched after a meeting with the president at Shadow Lawn, his summer residence at Long Branch on the New Jersey shore, on October 16. The format of the gathering, which Wilson treated as an important campaign event, was simple. Speaking through Howe, Pinchot, and Wise, the Volunteers asked the president for "a personal message giving your conception of the issues of the campaign." Stressing that they were a group of political independents, they presented a series of resolutions that praised Wilson and the policies of his administration. Added Howe: "We want to see continued another four years of the progressive legislation started by President Wilson, who has done more for the plain, common, unprivileged people of the United States than all the administrations combined since the Civil War."[40]

In reply, Wilson stressed the importance of his party as "a genuine progressive force." In the fight against the reactionary elements in the Republican Party, he was appealing, he said, to the millions of voters who had backed the Progressive candidate in 1912. "The Democratic Party may have been inefficient upon occasion, it may have been misled upon occasion, but it has always had a soul under its jacket. It has always had its sympathies in touch with the great body of the struggling mass of the people."[41]

For Fred Howe, the automobile tour that began the next day must have reminded him of politicking through Ohio with Tom Johnson in his "big red car." After a 5:30 breakfast at the Yale Club, a party of six headed out from New York City. They stopped first to speak to workers at the Isaac G. Johnson

39. FCH, Stephen S. Wise, and Amos Pinchot to Ray Stannard Baker, October 1916, Ray Stannard Baker Papers, Library of Congress; form letter by Amos Pinchot, October 6, 1916, Pinchot Papers. Other Wilson Volunteers included Timothy Healy, Isidor Jacobs, John Martin, Charles Zeublin, Herbert J. Browne, and Sumner Gerard.
40. *New York Times,* October 17, 1916, 1, 3; Barton, "Wilson Volunteers," 2–3.
41. *New York Times,* October 17, 1916, 3.

Foundry in Spuyten Duyvil and then drove on to an open-air meeting at Getty Square in Yonkers. From there, "the run across New York State was along the Knickerbocker country up the Hudson to Troy, then up the Mohawk Valley, and beyond to Buffalo, then almost due south to Jamestown in the Chautauqua center, and then east through and over the Allegheny spurs to the great city." The Volunteers were preceded by an advance man who worked with local Democratic politicians to prepare the way for meetings. Within the group, Howe, Pinchot, and McKelway became known as "the Three Musketeers" of the Volunteer Expedition—they were the only ones to make the entire journey. Their themes were democracy over privilege, prosperity, and peace.

McKelway later wrote Howe: "The Wilson Volunteers tour will always be a delightful memory to me, mainly on account of my association with you and Amos Pinchot." The Volunteers were generally pleased at their reception, though not every meeting could be considered a success. "We had a few very good meetings and some punk ones," Barton observed. By election day, the Wilson Volunteers had covered 1,400 miles and spoken in 108 cities, towns, and villages. It was "possibly the greatest whirlwind tour that has ever been made in New York State," wrote the *Olean Evening Herald*.[42]

Despite the efforts of the Volunteers and other Democratic campaigners, Wilson failed to carry New York. He had won the state's forty-five electoral votes in 1912 by a minority vote in a three-way race in which the Republican and Progressive candidates had outpolled him by nearly two hundred thousand ballots. Now, in a two-way contest, he improved his total by one hundred thousand votes but still lost to Hughes by one hundred thousand. The Democrats did better in upstate cities than they had in 1912, but it is impossible to relate those gains to the activities of the Volunteers. After the election, McKelway wrote to Vance McCormick, the Democratic national chairman, that "the automobile tour of the State . . . seems to have been useless," but he perhaps meant that Wilson had lost rather than that the Volunteers' participation had been futile. For many of those who had been Wilson Volunteers, their campaigning seemed to have forged a political unity that might in time become the nucleus of an independent liberal party. As Rabbi Wise put it in a letter to Amos Pinchot: "We have formed a little fighting group interested not in the fortunes of any one man but in the cause of democracy. Ought we not stay together?"[43]

---

42. Ibid., October 19, 1916, 3; Barton, "Wilson Volunteers," 3, 4; Dante Barton to Frank Walsh, October 30, 1916, Walsh Papers; A. J. McKelway to Vance McCormick, December 15, 1916; McKelway to FCH, November 3, 1916, McKelway Papers; *Olean Evening Herald*, October 24, 1916, quoted in Pinchot, *History of the Progressive Party*, 68–69.

43. A. J. McKelway to Vance McCormick, December 15, 1916, McKelway Papers; Stephen Wise to Amos Pinchot, November 15, 1916, Amos Pinchot Papers.

"He kept us out of war" may have been the slogan that won the presidential election, but less than six months later, after Germany's resumption of unrestricted submarine warfare and after the revelation of the Zimmermann telegram, Wilson asked Congress to declare war. The Senate passed the war resolution on April 4, 1917, and the House followed suit on April 6. We have no information about any changes in Fred Howe's attitudes on the conflict during the spring months while the president was reaching his decision. It is likely that he continued to favor American neutrality. In January 1917, upon being invited to become a director of the New York Peace Society, he had written of his strong belief in peace: "I hate war in all its forms. It is difficult for me to conceive of a condition which would justify war except for absolute defense. I am almost one of those despised pacifists, for I think that wars are almost always the result of the activities of enemies within the country rather than of enemies without." But Howe continued to have confidence in the president and was willing to follow his lead.[44]

At the time America entered the war, his job at Ellis Island was in some respects lighter than in previous years because of the sharp drop in immigration from Europe. After the declaration of war against Germany, Howe became responsible for some 1,150 sailors from German ships seized in the harbors of New York and New London. According to the *New York Times,* the chief complaint of the Germans was the unavailability of beer on the island. Howe was reported as replying that "the fresh sea breezes which blow over Ellis Island are very invigorating, and the water is cold, clear and abundant." He denied that the sailors were harshly treated. "Calisthenic classes have been organized by the officers and men for morning and afternoon, while papers, books, games, and other means for whiling away the time have been provided. The food supply is good and adequate and is cooked under proper inspection. . . . The hours for retiring and rising have been arranged to the satisfaction of the men."[45]

As time went by, the interned Germans were joined by other enemy aliens who had been arrested throughout the country and sent for custody at Ellis Island. The sharp drop in normal immigration had brought reductions in staff, and Howe was kept busy arguing with his superiors for more help. He needed additional watchmen because of the internments, and more inspectors and other personnel because the new immigration law of 1917 required stricter examination of incoming aliens (including all those who were crew members on merchant ships). Apparently the commissioner general appreciated Ellis Island's

---

44. Rebecca Shelly to Henry Wadsworth Longfellow Dana, December 13, 1916, Dana Papers, Swarthmore College Peace Collection; FCH to A. M. Molter, January 8, 1917, Records of New York Peace Society, Swarthmore College Peace Collection.

45. *New York Times,* April 8, 1917, 6; April 15, 1917, 12.

needs, for he met Howe's requests fairly promptly. Eventually the Germans and many of the other interned aliens were moved to other custody centers. During the course of the war, the army and navy took over much of the space at Ellis Island and used its hospitals and other buildings until 1919.

Howe's administrative duties did not prevent him from taking a leave of absence for February and March 1917 for a lecture tour on "questions for the most part suppressed by the press and the magazines." He had a long list of topics on which he was prepared to speak: "After the War—What?" "Some New American Problems," "The City of Tomorrow," "Municipal Ownership in America and Europe," "Town Planning and City Building," "Why War?" "Standing at the Gates of Ellis Island: The Incoming Immigrant," "Confessions of a Reformer." His fee was one hundred dollars a lecture (or the same amount for two lectures on the same day in the same city) plus travel expenses. His friend Daniel Kiefer used the single-tax network to secure bookings for the tour and urged Georgists to bring the availability of this "author of international reputation" to the attention of those responsible for arranging lectures in their cities. Howe spoke in the Middle West and Texas and on the West Coast. During his absence, Byron Uhl served as acting commissioner at Ellis Island.

For Progressives, the battle for reform did not end when America declared war. Indeed, many of them hoped that the stringencies of war would help bring about a reorganized economic system, a better deal for labor, and a more cooperative society generally. Walter Lippmann spoke for many of his fellow reformers when he predicted in May 1917 that "we stand at the threshold of a collectivism which is greater than any as yet planned by a socialist party." Fred Howe agreed, writing in 1917: "The old order has gone, never to return. The war has discarded the economic and political ideas which have dominated our life for three centuries. The *laissez-faire* philosophy that the government should do as little as possible is a thing of the past."[46] He, too, was eager to see a more democratic and humane social order emerge from the world conflagration. He did more than write about the changes needed—he threw himself into the battle to secure them. During the 1917–19 period, he fought for a fair tax system, remedies for the high cost of living, a publicly owned railroad system, reform of land policy, a planned demobilization and postwar reconstruction, and a just peace settlement. Inevitably, as these efforts fell short of accomplishing their goals, he began to lend his support to the formation of a new political party.

Howe had made his position clear on wartime taxes well before America entered the conflict: wars should be paid for by those who made them—the

---

46. Walter Lippmann to J. G. Phelps Stokes, May 1, 1917, quoted in J. A. Thompson, *Reformers and War*, 212; FCH, *High Cost of Living*, 259.

rulers and privileged classes. War taxes should be levied on "incomes, inheritances, land values, and from monopoly, and not shift the cost of war onto the backs of the poor, where our Federal taxes now fall."[47] After war came, Amos Pinchot organized and largely paid for the American Committee on War Finance, whose members advocated increased direct taxation that would fall most heavily on the wealthy, pay-as-you-go financing for military expenditures, and legislation to prevent excessive wartime profits from the sale of the necessities of life. Howe was one of those who signed the Committee's declaration.[48]

Congressional proponents of heavy progressive taxation of large incomes (especially La Follette and Congressman Claude Kitchin) succeeded in increasing the rates on high incomes in the Revenue Acts of 1917 and 1918. For the first time in American history, the earnings of individuals and businesses were taxed at substantial rates, and the income tax, rather than tariffs and excises, became the main source of federal revenue. Although the 1917 Act failed to go nearly as far as members of the Committee on War Finance wanted, they found it an acceptable compromise and ended their Committee's existence in the summer of 1917.

The Wilson administration had hoped to finance half the cost of the war through taxation, but huge military expenditures led to abandonment of that goal and to reliance on loans, especially Liberty bonds. Exhorted to do their patriotic duty, people borrowed money to buy bonds, and with the increase in the money supply, inflation brought rising prices for the necessities of life, a serious problem summed up as "the high cost of living" (soon abbreviated to HCL).[49] For Howe, the problem of the high cost of living brought together a number of interrelated issues: elimination of monopoly, changes in land policy and land taxation, reorganization of the railroad system.

In 1917 he expanded a series of articles bearing on HCL and land policy into a book, *The High Cost of Living*, published by Scribner's in October 1917.[50] Howe

---

47. FCH to editor, *New York Times*, June 11, 1915, 14.
48. American Committee on War Finance, "To All Loyal Americans," April 1917, Amos Pinchot Papers; FCH to Robert M. La Follette, May 1, 1917, La Follette Family Collection.
49. Howe's own income was affected adversely by the economic dislocations of the war. As commissioner of immigration he had a decent salary—$6,500 a year—but his investments did not fare well. He wrote Louis Post on November 14, 1918: "My old Cleveland affairs have gotten in a bad way because of war conditions. All told the adverse business slump nearly cleaned me out. And I had to spend a couple of days straightening matters out making loans and satisfying people." FCH to Louis F. Post, November 14, 1918, General Records of the Department of Labor 1907–1942 (Chief Clerk's Files), File No. 20/740, National Archives.
50. Howe's contract with Scribner's for the book is dated October 17, 1917. The manuscript must have already been completed, for the book was published the same month, even though it is dated 1918. *The High Cost of Living*, the articles, and a pamphlet covered essentially the same ground: "Why Men Do Not Go to the Farm"; "Problem of the American Farmer"; "Decay of Agriculture"; *People, the Land*.

argued that HCL resulted not from the war but from monopolies and the exclusion of people from the land. It was monopoly that "controls the natural resources, the agencies of transportation, distribution, and marketing. It has increased prices. It has discouraged agriculture. Tribute is exacted from the consumer at one end of the line and the producer at the other. It reduces the output of wealth of all kinds. It limits the opportunities for labor and keeps down wages and salaries." Monopoly in the land, monopoly in transportation, monopolies of the middlemen brought the decay of agriculture and, if unchecked, a national disaster. "They mean a continuing increase in the cost of living, a lower standard of living, a decadence of the state, and ultimately a nation of city dwellers on the one hand and a farming peasantry on the other."[51]

For Howe, the remedies were clear. The United States needed a constructive agricultural program that was more than exhortation, education, or regulation. An example of such a program could be found in Denmark, "an experiment station whose achievements must be copied, in part at least, if the United States is to save agriculture from decay and keep her people on the soil." Through both government action and the development of cooperatives, that nation had adopted sound farm policies on the basis of democracy and equality. The Danes had eliminated special privileges and had "no parasitical class." The government was run by the producers.[52] Australia and New Zealand were also exemplars of successful government action.

A constructive American farm policy would encompass government ownership and operation of the distributing agents through publicly owned terminal and storage warehouses, an organized system of municipal markets, the use of the parcel post as a marketing agency, and public ownership of abattoirs and stockyards. Tenancy would be abolished by breaking up the large feudal estates of the West and opening the land for settlement. The transportation system, and especially the railroads, should be publicly owned.

The land monopoly should be ended by taxation of land values—the old single-tax remedy. An additional remedy was farm colonies, planned and protected by the state. "The farm colony involves the sale of ready-made farms to would-be farmers, to be paid for by them on easy terms. It involves state credit to the would-be farmer, and the organization of marketing and purchasing. It involves also a new kind of education. But most of all it means the organization of agriculture along modern industrial lines."[53]

The goals should be both the salvation of agriculture and, in a broader sense, the extension of freedom, Howe concluded. The program was not socialism

51. *High Cost of Living*, v–vi, 18.
52. Ibid., 104, 115.
53. Ibid., 174, 228–29, 231; "Decay of Agriculture," 1036.

because government ownership would be limited and competition would prevail throughout the rest of the economy. "The motives of such a programme are not paternalism but freedom."[54]

The High Cost of Living was a somewhat unusual book for Howe. Though it continued old themes—the battle of democracy against privilege, opposition to monopoly, the virtues of the single tax—it brought in a different, quasi-Marxist terminology as he spoke of a "peasant proletariat," of "feudal estates" in the American West, and of "the organization of agriculture along modern industrial lines." Yet he also took a Jeffersonian approach, praising life on the land and hailing the country as "the great vitalizing force" while the city "uses up people." He saw no need for public ownership of the land, but called for government intervention in the farm economy to ensure freedom and competition. How much Howe really knew about the specific problems of American agriculture is questionable. The establishment of farm colonies—one of his pet ideas—hardly seemed likely to prevent "the permanent reduction in food supply" and the general decay of agriculture that he feared. Regulation of the monopolies that harmed both producers and consumers was a more fruitful approach, one that he was to return to in the 1920s and 1930s.

The book had a favorable reception in the usual quarters but was also subjected to several highly critical reviews. In a brief note, the *Independent* found Howe's arguments based on "solid facts" and his solutions "the logical result of thoro [sic] study into the economic and social causes of the situation." Calling the volume a "most valuable and timely work," the *Bookman*'s reviewer agreed wholeheartedly with Howe's analysis of the state of American agriculture. The author had "driven home with relentless logic . . . the imperative necessity for the socialisation of man's first industry, which precedes all others in immediate, material importance, the industry of keeping himself alive." The *Survey* took issue with Howe's condemnation of farm tenancy but thought that he presented the main facts on the farm problem.[55]

Two other reviews were scathing in their criticisms of Howe's analysis and solutions. In the *American Economic Review*, B. H. Hibbard found little good in the book except for the chapters describing cooperation in Europe. The rest offered a very unfavorable picture of farming, presented "apparently for the ultimate purpose of introducing the remedy, which is a specific, the single tax. . . . It is all well and good for a single-taxer to believe in his vision, but in trying to realize it, it would seem to a skeptic to be better to face the issue squarely, to confine oneself to the facts as they are, rather than to undertake to

---

54. *High Cost of Living*, 270–71.
55. *Independent* 92 (November 17, 1917): 344–45; Archibald Henderson, "H.C.L.," *Bookman* 46 (December 1917): 469; *Survey* 39 (December 8, 1917): 297.

prove by statements, no matter how honest, that reform is demanded by deplorable conditions, conditions which to most people are not apparent." The *New York Times* also disagreed with both Howe's analysis and his remedies. His book might have a wide appeal because "it contains promises of relief that all long for, and presents them seductively. It is a cause of regret to contrast his diagnosis of our trouble with the facts, and to doubt that his promise of a remedy of economic troubles by law is capable of fulfillment. Of what use are memory and experience if their teachings are to be abandoned whenever fancy paints rainbows?"[56] Despite these mixed reviews, *The High Cost of Living* sold fairly well.

Howe had long considered America's railroads as natural monopolies that should be publicly owned. In his first major book, *The City*, he had placed the railway companies among those powerful privileged interests who had "subverted local and state institutions to their ends."[57] As a state senator in Ohio, he had witnessed firsthand the power of their lobbyists, and as immigration commissioner, he had seen their exploitation of immigrants at Ellis Island. He had found their monopoly position to bear a large share of responsibility for the high cost of living. He well understood that they were a major force in American life, indispensable to American economy.

Soon after the United States entered the war, the railroads were in crisis. The government had to move vast quantities of men and materiel over their tracks to the Atlantic ports for shipment on to the battlefields of France. At the same time, the railways were expected to handle the normal loads of raw materials, food, and manufactured products for the domestic market. The result was near-chaos. The rail lines' attempts to cope were plagued by lack of coordination, an old and poorly maintained infrastructure, and a shortage of freight cars that not only hampered the movement of troops and munitions but threatened to close down steel mills, coal producers, and other shippers.

The railroad operators saw the remedy for their problems in higher rates, less regulation by the Interstate Commerce Commission, and suspension of the antitrust laws. Shippers opposed these remedies. For once, railway labor found a common interest with management because higher rates would make possible higher wages. When, in December 1917, the ICC turned down the owners' request for increased rates, the railroad brotherhoods threatened a nationwide strike. Reformers, who had been seeking more government control over the railroads since the days of the Grangers and the Populists, saw in the crisis an opportunity to achieve public ownership.

56. *American Economic Review* 8 (September 1918): 601, 607–8; *New York Times*, February 17, 1918, sec. 6, 64.
57. *City*, 108.

In dealing with the railroad crisis, Howe applied his usual methods for working on public issues. He tried to sell his policy proposals through his contacts with friends in government, through his writings, and by joining organizations that would work for his aims. Generally he combined the three methods. He would send a letter or a memo to the president or Newton Baker or Senator La Follette or William Gibbs McAdoo or Colonel House. He would publish an explication or expansion of the memo's ideas in one or more articles or perhaps in a pamphlet or a book. He would work with an organization to present the ideas to the general public, to take them into the political arena, or to lobby for their adoption.

Thus he began his wartime concern with the railroads on May 19, 1917, by sending President Wilson a pamphlet he had written on the mobilization of transportation. Stopping short of a plea for complete public ownership of the railroads, he proposed that the government immediately take over the two hundred and twenty-five thousand privately owned freight cars and operate them from a central office as a "flying squadron" to relieve freight congestion in critical areas. Wilson thanked him for the pamphlet and observed: "I shall expect to get some very serviceable ideas out of it." Howe followed up with an article in the *Public*, repeating the gist of his earlier pieces.[58]

His arguments for a first installment could easily be expanded to justify complete public ownership as the rail crisis deepened. He took that step a month later and set forth in a number of writings the case for nationalization. Not only were the railroads in a monopolistic position in transportation, but they were "interlocked with so many other agencies and so many other monopolies that their operation by the government would automatically break the power of the warehousemen, packers, exchanges, and other parasites that live off the industry of the country and contribute little or nothing to it." The railroads' wastefulness and inefficiency were drags on the economy. Their need for capital could only be met from the public treasury. The railroad owners gave no thought to the interests of the nation as a whole. "They are interested not in the welfare of industry or agriculture, but in the flotation of watered securities, in stock gambling and speculation. . . . Railroads should be run for the producers and the consumers." Regulation had been a failure and had helped the owners. Railroad earnings had gone steadily upward; the trusts had grown more powerful; the conditions of life for the producing and consuming classes had become harder.

---

58. FCH to Woodrow Wilson, May 9, 1917; FCH, *Mobilization of Transportation;* Wilson to FCH, May 14, 1917; *New York Times,* May 28, 1917, 17; FCH, "Shall the Government Mobilize Transportation?"

"Regulation has not only failed; it has become the bulwark of monopoly." The only remedy was immediate nationalization.[59]

Howe drafted a bill providing for government takeover of the railroads, and the Fels Commission organized support for it throughout the country. Under its terms, a government corporation would operate all the lines, paying railroad stockholders the average rate of interest and dividends received over the past decade and placing any surplus revenues into a sinking fund for the purchase of the railroads. Howe sent the bill and a memo explaining it to all the members of Congress.[60]

He also drew up a proposal to put the railroads in trust and sent it first to Baker and Creel and then to the president, who transmitted it to Secretary of the Treasury McAdoo. Howe suggested creation of "an operating trust or operating committee, appointed by the President, or an operating corporation like the Shipping Board, to operate the railroads either temporarily or permanently as a unit, and in trust for owners and the nation." The trust should include representation from industry, agriculture, and transportation. He pointed out the great advantages that would ensue: an end to the immediate emergency through consolidation of operations, simplification of freight rates, an end to rebates and other discriminations and to the political activities of the railways, and public acquisition of forest, oil, and mineral lands owned by the railroads. In a letter to the president on December 15, 1917, he reiterated the points of the memo, adding that his studies of railways in Germany, Switzerland, Belgium, and Denmark had showed clearly the gains that came when the rail lines were operated for service and not for profit.[61]

The president had been receiving much advice from many quarters on the rail emergency, and Howe's suggestions were only a small part of those coming to him. Secretary of the Navy Josephus Daniels was one of the first cabinet members to advise federal control, and McAdoo, the president's son-in-law, had asked Wilson to act "promptly and decisively" for a government takeover. With few exceptions, spokesmen for the major shippers agreed, as did the railroad brotherhoods. The rail executives called publicly for rate increases and federal aid but privately seemed ready to accept government supervision of their operations. By mid-December the president reached his decision, and on December

---

59. *High Cost of Living,* 81, 82, 174; "Railroads, the Mine Owners and the Government," 646; *People, the Land,* 11, 12–13, 14–15, 81, 82; *High Cost of Living,* 174; "The Railroads, the Mine Owners," 646.

60. *New York Times,* July 23, 1917, 13.

61. FCH to Newton D. Baker, December 6, 1917, Baker Papers; Woodrow Wilson to William Gibbs McAdoo, December 13, 1917, enclosing Howe's "Memorandum for Placing the Transportation Agencies of the Nation in Trust for the Nation and the Security Holders," in Link, *Papers of Woodrow Wilson,* 45:283–85 (Howe's italics); FCH to Woodrow Wilson, December 15, 1917, ibid., 309–10.

28, 1917, he issued a proclamation calling for federal control. He appointed McAdoo as director general of the Railroad Administration.[62]

Howe praised Wilson's decision as "*the greatest peace* measure ever taken in America. For there is war within America, just as there is war without. . . . It is a war that divides America into two camps; a war that aligns the financiers, monopolists, public utility corporations, lawyers, the press and privileged interests in one camp and the manufacturers, producers, farmers, consumers and labor in another camp." Government ownership would end this conflict.[63] The president's action left open the question of the railroads' fate after the war ended, and Howe continued to press the case for public ownership in his writings, as well as in his political activities. He helped organize the Committee for Federal Ownership of the Railroads, and he was soon to plunge into battle for the Plumb Plan.

The future of the railroads was part of a much broader concern of Howe and other reformers, who hoped that wartime necessities would push forward some of the societal changes that they desired. In 1917 and 1918 one began to hear more and more frequently about "reconstruction." The word had different meanings for various groups, but to Progressives it conveyed the idea of a restructuring of both the national and the international order.[64] To some of them, reconstruction meant continuing wartime programs and agencies—the minimum labor standards established by the War Labor Board, government control of the railroads, extension of social insurance to others besides returning veterans. It meant a planned transition from a wartime to a peacetime economy. Severe problems of readjustment—especially unemployment and inflation—loomed ahead, and only government could meet them by policies such as employment services, public works, and continued price controls. Advanced Progressives moved beyond demands for these programs to call for industrial democracy and a more equitable distribution of wealth. Despite disagreements on specific policies, Progressives appeared confident and optimistic. They were united in a recognition that reconstruction was necessary and desirable and in an optimistic belief that it was possible. They could work together on many issues.

Fred Howe was to be found among those who did not fear the power of the state. Even before the declaration of war, he had written Joseph Tumulty of his apprehension that "we are going to be confronted with a terrible condition after

62. Woodrow Wilson to FCH, December 20, 1917, ibid., 334. See Kerr, *American Railroad Politics*, 39–71, on the transportation crisis of 1917 and the government takeover of the railroads.

63. FCH, "Railroads and the New Democracy," 14. See also "Necessity for Public Ownership of the Railways."

64. See Kennedy, *Over Here*, 245–47; Chambers, *Paul U. Kellogg and the Survey*, 68–71.

the war. Hundreds of thousands of men are going to be dislocated. War orders will be cut off. Factories will have to be shaped to new undertakings. Credit may be temporarily paralyzed. There may be a great influx of immigration. Whatever happens we are going to have a temporary labor slump that may reach immense proportions." He urged the White House to back a bill, pending in the House of Representatives, that would set up a Bureau of Employment in the Labor Department and "create a great national clearing house or labor exchange with agencies scattered all over the country for the distribution of men to their proper employment, and of immigrants as well."[65]

Howe quickly directed his own efforts within the Labor Department toward the broad problems of demobilization and reconstruction, incorporating into his proposals such policies as public ownership of the railroads, farm colonies, and taxation of land values. As the fighting in France neared its end, he began working to make the department a center for postwar change. He proposed to Secretary Wilson and Assistant Secretary Post a publicity campaign for industrial and social reconstruction, in which special attention should be paid to "such big questions as the land, different kinds of farming communities and forest settlements, provisions for emergency work by Federal, State, and Municipal agencies, mobilizing education along democratic lines, and the problems of actual military and industrial demobilization." The department should supply feature stories to the editors of weekly magazines that shaped public opinion (*New Republic, Dial, Nation, Public, McClure's*), the labor press, and the Scripps newspapers. "It seems to me that a drive such as this should be an influence in forming opinion around a generous and democratic program of reconstruction," he wrote Post. The department should also try to influence legislation and to work with governors and legislatures to promote such activities as housing, town planning, road building, education, and forestry. The stakes were high, Howe argued. "They involve the question of who will pay the taxes; what will be done as to banking and credit; the disposition of the railroads and transportation agencies, and along with that, the whole status and position of labor. . . . A period of industrial depression may lead to acute disorders and political changes. It is quite conceivable that the future political evolution of America will be influenced by and possibly dependent upon the way these questions are met and the generosity with which they are handled."[66] Post and Wilson quickly approved the plan, and the secretary designated its author to direct it.

---

65. FCH to Joseph Tumulty, January 3, 1917, Woodrow Wilson Papers.
66. FCH to Louis F. Post, November 1, 1918, General Records of the Department of Labor 1907–1942 (Chief Clerk's Files), File No. 20/740, National Archives.

Howe's thinking about postwar readjustments went beyond a mere publicity campaign. He suggested that the efforts might "grow into an institution," in which the labor movement would be central. He submitted to Post a revised program for "Labor Readjustment," in which he suggested the use of conferences to create public opinion and influence legislation. "The activities of the Department would not be in the open."67

Howe went public with the general outlines of his program in an article in the *Annals* in November 1918. It included government aid to unemployed workers; programs for returning soldiers in colleges and secondary schools to equip them to meet the industrial and social needs of the country; vast public works projects for afforestation, reclamation, road and highway building, and other construction; a large transportation program, aimed at developing a unified rail, water, and terminal system; "a great hydro-electric power system, with central stations in different parts of the country"; government-sponsored farm colonies throughout the nation, "with educational, recreational and cooperative agencies for marketing and buying," and with common ownership of tractors and farm machinery. Only government could develop an adequate program for reconstruction, he argued. "It cannot be left to chance, to chaos, to private initiative. The consequences would be too terrible. . . . Only the government can take up the slack, for only the government has the resources to do so."68 It sounded like a blueprint for the early New Deal, fifteen years in advance.

Post and Wilson apparently went along with Howe's ideas on publicity but balked at the department becoming a political force to advance a program like British Labour's. When Howe went off to Europe for the peace conference, Post found that three sets of officials—Howe, the Information and Education Service, and the War Labor Policies Board—seemed to be doing similar work on labor readjustment and recommended that the activities be concentrated in a bureau within the Information and Education division. Howe's sweeping plans were shunted aside.69

In December 1918 Fred wrote to W. C. Brownell, his editor at Scribner's, that Marie was bringing him "the manuscript of a little book which seems to me to have some value for immediate publication if that can be arranged." He observed that "Mrs. Howe is rather keen at reading proof and if you would feel

67. FCH to Louis F. Post, November 6, 1918; FCH to Post, November 15, 1918, ibid.
68. FCH, "Constructive Program for the Rehabilitation of the Returning Soldiers." Within Wilson's cabinet, Secretary of the Interior Franklin K. Lane was a strong proponent of providing government land to returning soldiers. See his letter to Wilson, May 31, 1918, in F. Lane, *Letters of Franklin K. Lane*, 284–90. Lane sought the necessary legislation, but the Republican-controlled Congress failed to pass it.
69. Louis F. Post to Secretary of Labor, January 9, 1919, General Records of the Department of Labor 1907–1942 (Chief Clerk's Files), File No. 129/10-B, National Archives.

more comfortable to have it pass through my hands vicariously she will read the proofs." (Fred was in Europe by this time.) The reason for haste was that a farm colonies bill would soon be introduced in Congress. "The subject is bound to be considered widely and members of Congress, of the state legislatures, governors, Chambers of Commerce etc. should be circularized." The contract with Scribner's for *The Land and the Soldier* was not signed until March 1919, but in the meantime Marie read the proofs and made something of a hit with Brownell, who wrote Fred that he was "extremely pleased to have made the acquaintance of Mrs. Howe, from whom I have received two or three pleasant visits and who has more than justified your recommendations as a proof-reader, and I feel sure that your literary interests have been looked after with more scrupulousness and probable success than ever heretofore."[70]

Although Howe reiterated his general remedies for America's agricultural problems, he was most concerned in *The Land and the Soldier* with one part of the solution, the farm colony. The book was full of optimism. American achievements in waging war had shown what could be accomplished in peace. "We should justify ourselves in the war for democracy by providing for the soldier a home-coming that will not be a 'hand-out' from a job-giver but a free life in a free state."[71]

For Howe, the homecoming for the restless returning soldier should include the option of a fresh start in a farm colony of fifteen hundred to two thousand people. "The farm village is the rural expression of the garden suburb. It is a community organized for production as well as life. . . . It includes the addition of a farm for the man to work upon and make a living from. The government advances the money. The architect plans the community. The farm expert lays out the land and aids the individual farmer."[72] As in his previous writings, he pointed out and praised the steps in this direction that other nations—Denmark, Australia, Canada, Ireland, Britain—were already successfully undertaking.

His was a proposal to "socialize agriculture," Fred wrote. A farmer would own his house and barn and "a piece of land large enough for an unaided man to cultivate" (about thirty acres). He would live in a community that would provide the comforts and amenities of life—education, recreation, water, electric light and power, good roads. "Co-operation should be the key-note of the farm village, co-operation in production, in buying and selling; in the ownership of machinery and of much of the work as well." Community ownership of

---

70. FCH to W. C. Brownell, December 7, 1918; Brownell to MJH, January 23, 1919; MJH to Brownell, January 27, 1919; Brownell to FCH, February 24, 1919, Scribner Archives.
71. FCH, *Land and the Soldier*, 3–4, 5, 7.
72. Ibid., 12–13.

warehouses, cold-storage plants, dairies, and slaughterhouses would enable the farmer to sell his produce directly, thus eliminating the middleman. Local, state, and federal governments should help develop the colonies, but administration should be decentralized. Experts would plan the village. "They would select the most attractive site, with water, trees, and a pleasing outlook on the surrounding country. There would be generous allotments of land for schools, playgrounds, and public buildings. Possibly a substantial acreage would be set aside for common forests and pastures."[73]

The most difficult problem would be ownership of the land. Howe preferred a system in which the government retained title to the land, capitalized its investment at cost, and leased it to the farmers at an annual ground-rental sufficient to cover interest charges on the investment. "From time to time the ground-rental would be revalued as land values changed, and any rental collected in excess of the original interest charges could be dedicated to community use.... By this means the individual who happened to get a favored site would be on a plane of equality with the individual who was less fortunate. He would not be enriched by the growth of the community." The farmer would pay for and own improvements on the land. "His only obligation would be the natural obligation that he should not make use of the generosity of the state as a means of speculation or to the disparagement of the community enterprise."[74]

The farm colony that Howe envisaged would be an alternative to the city. These idyllic, semisocialist, democratic rural colonies would attract handicraft industries, and "many persons of small means, teachers, professional persons and artists . . . would find such a colony an attractive place of residence." Using its constructive imagination, America should develop the farm colony, "not alone as a means of producing food or of keeping men on the land, but as a means of creating an opportunity for a free, comfortable, and alluring life, not for the returning soldier alone, but for other land-hungry peoples as well."[75]

---

73. Ibid., 24, 25, 30, 54–55, 78.
74. Ibid., 88–90, 92–94.
75. Ibid., 73, 38, 140. Howe supplemented *The Land and the Soldier* with several articles on land policy, farm colonies, and the plight of the returning soldier ("Soldier and the Land"; "Land Settlements and the Soldier"), and he had covered some of the same ground in his *High Cost of Living*.

Reviews of *The Land and the Soldier* were satisfactory, though hardly numerous. The *Dial* reported that "within its limits (and the field is no small one) there is a touch of freshness in the survey of the land problem." *Dial* 67 (July 12, 1919): 34. The *American Journal of Sociology* found the book "rationally practical, presenting an understanding of the present and plotting the development of the future, socially and agriculturally." *American Journal of Sociology* 25 (September 1919): 242. The *Nation* thought this "admirable" book had "great value as an outline of what a conscientious people might do through its government towards the opening up of opportunities for its fighters in the recent war." *Nation* 109 (October 18, 1919): 522–23. *Survey* was a little critical: "Aside from the obvious haste with which the book has been put together, one regrets that Dr. Howe has relied so fully upon reports and documents rather than on his own much-traveled experience." *Survey* 42 (July 5, 1919): 551.

Once again, as in his book on the high cost of living, Howe's pragmatic radicalism was tempered by utopian praise for the virtues of the small democratic community. He presented a scheme for a socialized agriculture, but one in which the single tax would reconcile the collective and the individual. The farm colony, not the city, became the hope of democracy. Liberty and equality remained the goals, but they were to be achieved through large doses of government intervention and planning in a kind of Jeffersonian collectivism.

After the armistice, the hopes of Howe and other Progressives for a planned and reformist demobilization, and for new projects like farm colonies, were quickly dashed. President Wilson was lukewarm at best, and his attention was almost at once diverted to the intricacies of peacemaking. Wartime agencies like the War Industries Board and the Fuel Administration went quickly out of existence, and most government controls were dropped as the nation turned back to business as usual. Only the fate of the railroads seemed to present an issue on which reformers could stir up much of a fight. And that would be a battle in which Fred Howe would be heavily engaged.

13

PEACEMAKING AND RED BAITING

The period from 1917 through 1919 was one of the busiest and most demanding of Frederic Howe's career. He had his routine duties at Ellis Island and his involvement in domestic policy matters, but he devoted the major portion of his time to questions of war and peace. In his writings and correspondence, he continued to find financial imperialism or "dollar diplomacy" the root cause of war. Britain, France, Germany, Russia, and the United States had all engaged in it. The remedy, he suggested, was to allow capital to enter foreign fields only at its own risk, with no government backing.

Although he saw all the European powers as imperialist, Howe was most critical of Great Britain and Germany. The ambitious British ruling classes were more concerned with control of Mesopotamia, the Baghdad Railway and the Mediterranean Sea, and Egypt than about any other single issue of the war. He did not mean to minimize the German menace. "I feel that it would be a calamity to the world for Germany to secure anything approaching political or military supremacy in this territory." But, Howe warned, "we are getting a very British slant on the war."[1]

The changes in Russia after the overthrow of the czar in March 1917 drew his attention to American policy there. Learning that the president was planning to send a commission to Russia, he advised Colonel House to send representatives who were "thoroughly sympathetic with fundamental democracy and also intelligently understanding of the psychology of the Russian and what the Russian democrats really want to do." The major question in Russia was land distribution. A satisfactory system of land tenure would make democracy permanent in Russia and would probably end its imperialistic ambitions. Howe worried that

---

1. FCH to Edward M. House, September 18, 1917, House Papers.

the United States might send a group who did not understand the fundamental hunger of the people for land and who might support a "plutocratic middle-class government."[2]

Fred may well have been angling for his own appointment to the commission. Perhaps at his behest, Carrie Chapman Catt, in her capacity as president of the International Woman Suffrage Alliance, suggested to Wilson that he add to his Russian Commission "a man whose interest in real democracy is in full harmony with your own, Frederic C. Howe. . . . He is sincerely interested in the extension of self-government to women as well as to men, and would do all that he could to carry to both men and women in Russia your message of democracy founded upon the consent of all of the governed."[3]

Wilson's reply to Catt expressed sympathy for the rights of Russian women but pointed out that the Russian government would resent any attempts at political guidance by Americans. He made no mention of, or commitment to, Fred Howe as a commission member, and there is no evidence that he considered him. The commission that the president ultimately chose was headed by the conservative Elihu Root and included only two men who could be considered Progressives: Charles Crane, the publisher, and Charles Edward Russell, a prowar socialist.[4]

Howe continued to believe that settlement of the land issue was crucial, writing in the *New Republic* that "our only hope in Russia lies with the revolutionary groups. Not necessarily with the Bolsheviki, but with whatever government the peasants and the artisans may see fit to erect. And these are our natural allies."[5] Howe kept up with the news from Russia through friends like Lincoln Steffens who had journeyed there to see for themselves.

After American entry into the war in April 1917, a principal topic of discussion among Progressives had become the question of war aims and peace terms. In November, publication by the Bolsheviks of the secret treaties by which the Allies divided up the spoils of victory invigorated the debate. Were we fighting for freedom and democracy, or was it for annexation of territory, the restoration of the czar, and a return to the international status quo once the Central powers had been punished? Lincoln Steffens worried that it was only in the United States that no clear public opinion was forming on peace terms. But, he noted approvingly in a letter to a friend, "Fred Howe is on the job."[6] There were

    2. FCH to House, April 25, 1917.
    3. Carrie Chapman Catt to Woodrow Wilson, May 4, 1917, in Link, *Papers of Woodrow Wilson*, 42:215.
    4. Wilson to Catt, May 8, 1917, in Link, *Papers of Woodrow Wilson*, 42:241.
    5. FCH to W. C. Brownell, March 18, 1918, Scribner Archives, Princeton University; FCH, "Realpolitik in Russia," 203.
    6. Lincoln Steffens to Allen H. Suggett, February 8, 1918, in Winter and Hicks, *Letters of Lincoln Steffens*, 1:420.

increasing appeals to President Wilson for a clear statement of America's war aims.

The president had already given indications of the direction of his own thinking, most notably in his reply to Pope Benedict XV's appeal for peace in August 1917. Feeling the need to have something ready for a peace conference, he asked Colonel House to form a group to consider war aims and plan for a future peace conference. House at once drafted Walter Lippmann to set the wheels in motion, and by October the operation known simply as "the Inquiry" was underway.

Fred Howe was engaged in conducting his own "Inquiry" during 1917 and 1918. In a series of memoranda to the president and Colonel House and in several articles and a book, he developed his ideas for the peace settlement. A memo to House in October 1917 was typical. In it, he asked the colonel what would happen "if the President were now to publicly, or through diplomatic channels, lay before the warring powers a simple, direct proposal, amplifying his fundamentals of peace, for a termination of hostilities" on the following principles:

(a) Disarmament.
(b) An open door policy for trade.
(c) Neutralization or internationalization of all waterways, including the Mediterranean, the Suez Canal, and the Panama Canal.
(d) Equality of economic exploitation, such as the lending of money, the building of railroads, the development of mines, etc.
(e) Revision of the idea of sovereignty so as to cover the right of all the powers to the necessary elements of economic independence—iron, coal, cotton, etc.
(f) The freedom of the sea.
(g) Neutralization of the eastern Mediterranean territories, including the Balkans, Turkey, Asia Minor, Armenia, and Mesopotamia.
(h) Guarantees of the principles of peace through international tribunals or international military and naval force.

A presidential declaration along these lines would mean "tremendous gains to democracy in all of the countries, and a possible avenue of approach to a settlement which saves the amour propre of all the powers if territorial aggrandizements are swept away and the idea of peace based upon freedom, liberty and equality of opportunity is substituted in its stead."[7]

---

7. FCH to Edward M. House, October 9, 1917. Harry Garfield transmitted a similar memo from Howe to President Wilson on October 30, 1917. Harry A. Garfield to Woodrow Wilson, October 30, 1917, in Link, *Papers of Woodrow Wilson*, 44:474. At the same time that Howe was trying to

The president had already decided by December 18 that an address on war aims might become the moral turning point of the conflict. At his behest, Colonel House set the Inquiry team to work on a draft, and after three weeks of virtually round-the-clock labor Lippmann could give the colonel a paper entitled "The War Aims and Peace Terms It Suggests." With modifications by the Inquiry and revisions by Wilson, the memo became the basis for the president's Fourteen Points address to Congress on January 8, 1918.

Although Wilson's Fourteen Points were in harmony with the points of Howe's October memorandum, it is unlikely that Howe's suggestions had had much influence on the president's ideas, except perhaps to reinforce views already held. Certainly the basis for the Fourteen Points was the Inquiry's draft. Both Wilson in his address and Howe in his memos took similar positions on freedom of the seas, lower tariffs, disarmament, the rights of colonial peoples, open covenants. Both called for a league of nations, though Howe saw the organization operating primarily to prevent economic exploitation by great powers. Doubtless Howe was sorry that the president had not dealt more thoroughly with such issues. Wilson was much more specific on self-determination and territorial adjustments than Howe had been in his memos, though he was vaguer on arrangements in the eastern Mediterranean.

It was surprising that Fred had not had more to say about national self-determination in his memos to Wilson and House, for that was a subject in which he had grown increasingly interested. In 1917 he had become president of a new League for Small and Subject Nationalities, an organization that hoped to ensure the right of each nationality to direct representation at the peace conference and to presentation of its case to the world. The League's effectiveness as a voice was marred by the fractiousness and suspicions of its members, who claimed to speak for a host of territories throughout the world. Some spoke as representatives of areas longing for incorporation or reunion with another state, such as Alsace-Lorraine. Some sought independence, such as Scotland and Armenia. Some were from small independent states, such as Belgium and Serbia. A few represented bits of ancient history, such as Assyria (the League's secretary was uncertain what territory was included in Assyria but thought it the same as in the time of Sennacherib). The spokesmen for this assortment of states or would-be states came from a variety of nationalist organizations or were self-appointed. As president, Howe had to walk a fine line between upholding each group's freedom of expression and yet maintaining some semblance of a united organization. He and the League looked to Wilson as the hope for the various independences desired, and in December 1918 he sent the president a telegram

---

influence House and, through him, Wilson, the colonel was seeking to steer Howe and other friends in the right direction in their thinking about war and peace. See Lasch, *New Radicalism in America*, 234–36.

calling his attention to the League's "unanimous endorsement of self determination for all nations," considering it the "indispensable basis of a league of nations which could claim universal support [from] league of small and subject nationalities."[8]

Howe elaborated on his various memoranda in a book, *The Only Possible Peace*, published by Scribner's in January 1919. The new book presented to the public, in a more developed form, the ideas he had been sending Wilson and House. There was little in it that he had not covered in his memos or articles. Much of it was a historical survey of the foreign adventures of the great powers, especially of German efforts to penetrate the territories of the eastern Mediterranean. That area should be administered in the interest of the world. Instead of private control of the Mediterranean, there should be international control; instead of exclusive possession of waterways and harbors, there should be international waterways and harbors; instead of private concessions and the closed door, there should be international concessions and the open door; instead of exclusive exploitation, there should be international financing and an end of exploitation. All the dependent territories of the Mediterranean—the Balkan states, Turkey, Armenia, Persia, Mesopotamia, Syria, Palestine, Egypt, Tripoli, Tunis, Algeria, Morocco—should be demilitarized and freed from political or economic control by any of the powers. An international organization, possessing a parliament, a judiciary, and a military force, should settle disputes and protect the peace.[9]

"We are fighting that the world may be free from wars, free from the things that make for war," Howe declared. "We desire that the world may be a safe place for all people to live in; to develop their own cultures and civilizations unmolested by any other Power." The peace conference should apply the principle of self-determination that Wilson had set forth. Those drawing up the peace treaties would have to abandon secret diplomacy and give up any idea of parceling out the world to the victors. America must take the lead in establishing a durable peace, resting on foundations of freedom and equality of opportunity. "Freedom to the subject world should be America's contribution to the peace conference."[10]

---

8. "Small Nations Leagued Together," *Survey* 38 (May 5, 1917): 212; *New York Times*, October 29, 1917, 9; October 31, 1917, 13; November 1, 1917, 5; telegram, FCH to Woodrow Wilson, December 16, 1918, Wilson Papers. Howe also joined the League of Oppressed Peoples, whose chairman was Dudley Field Malone.

9. See FCH, "Heart of the War"; "New Ideals for Peace"; "Economic Foundations of the League of Nations"; *Only Possible Peace*, 229, 189–90, 191–92, 193.

10. *Only Possible Peace*, 200–201, 218–19, 222–23, 265, 228. The reviews of the book were generally favorable. The *New York Times* reviewer praised it: "Who ever reads this volume will lay it down with a broader conception of what the problems of the war have been, and how much of the happiness of the world depends upon the work at the Peace Conference now in session in France.

In his writings on foreign policy, war, and peace, Howe had centered much of his attention on the eastern Mediterranean. He was sure that the origin of the war had been the clash of imperialisms there. "I pictured renaissance in industry, in culture, and in art that would make it again the centre of a civilization of its own."[11] Fred kept his friends in government aware of his views on the Mediterranean and the Near East and sought to stake a claim to the status of expert on the politics of the region. He wrote his old comrade, the secretary of war: "I think I know more about the conflict that has been going on in Europe for the last thirty years over what is commonly known as the 'Drang nach Osten' than anybody in this country with one or two exceptions." He had gained his knowledge through direct experience, he pointed out. He had negotiated for the Long Arm System with munitions makers and diplomats from England, Germany, and France, and he had learned about the German ambitions in Asia Minor from German businessmen and friends. "I have read most of the literature—French, English and German—on this vision of empire with which almost every German is familiar, but which across the Channel in England is only known within diplomatic circles." He predicted to Newton Baker: "Sooner or later the allies are bound to be confronted by this Near Eastern question; and it may be that it will be put up to us for settlement."[12]

In letters and memoranda to House and Wilson, Howe sought to emphasize his knowledge and expertise on Middle Eastern questions. It seems clear that he was seeking some kind of post with the American peace delegation and an opportunity to have his views enter into the postwar settlement. As he later wrote, "I was captivated by the President's eloquence and thoroughly believed in his programme. And I wanted to have a part in it; a share in the settlement of the Near Eastern problems. I wanted to be around when the hand of the Western world should be lifted from the peoples of the Near East, the glories of whose ancient civilization I dreamed of seeing restored."[13]

To get a post, Fred worked directly through a fellow Progressive who had access to the president, George Creel, the head of the government's Committee

---

With a fluent pen that is the direct expression of a logical mind and large vision, Dr. Howe has made a highly valuable contribution to the education in democracy that is the chief compensation to be derived from the hideous outbreak which has brought so much sorrow to the universe." *New York Times*, February 19, 1919, 77. The *New Republic* thought that despite Howe's "inherently laissez-faire position" on international trade, he had provided a valuable analysis of the dangers of America's creditor position in the world. Whether or not one accepted his remedies, "one cannot but be impressed with the candor and earnestness of Mr. Howe's exposition." *New Republic* 20 (August 13, 1919): 65. The *Survey*'s reviewer was more critical: "This study is rapid, spirited, interesting, but not convincing. It is the chief part of the truth but not the whole truth." *Survey* 42 (May 10, 1919): 257.

11. *Confessions of a Reformer*, 284–85, 287.
12. FCH to Newton D. Baker, June 26, 1917, Newton D. Baker Papers.
13. *Confessions of a Reformer*, 288.

on Public Information. Creel urged Wilson to give Howe an unofficial appointment to the American mission, and several weeks before the Armistice he was able to tell him, "'The President wants you to go to Paris.' . . . It was not very clear, but it meant definitely to me an opportunity to press my ideas about the Mediterranean. That was what I wanted." Lincoln Steffens also wangled an appointment, working through Colonel House.[14]

In a Paris crowded with newsmen, diplomats and their staffs, and numerous observers and hangers-on, Howe and Steffens managed to find rooms in the Hotel Chatham near the Place de l'Opéra. Many of their friends were there— Creel, Ida Tarbell, William Allen White, Ray Stannard Baker. Together and separately, they moved through hotel lobbies, press rooms, and the antechambers of the Hotel Crillon, where the American delegation's staff was quartered. "Paris was a chaos of gossip masquerading as history." Fred picked up gossip or information at informal dinner meetings with such men as C. J. Doherty, the Canadian minister of justice, James T. Shotwell, one of the Inquiry's leading figures, and members of Lloyd George's entourage. He sometimes managed to get into official sessions by masquerading as a journalist for a mythical magazine. He and Steffens conversed with Prince Emir Feisal and Lawrence of Arabia, whom Howe could not figure out. "Was Lawrence guarding Arabia for the British? Was he one of the thousands of young men in the British foreign office who forget themselves to forward Britain's empire and protect her outposts from German or Russian penetration? Lawrence gave no hint."[15]

Howe grew discouraged as he waited around for something constructive to do. At the end of 1918, he advised Jane Addams not to come to Paris. He felt stymied, he told her. "Up to date there is no hook that I can find on which to hang a plea, a memorial or even a presentation of a claim. . . . I had some pretty well worked out ideas that I hoped to present but for the life of me I don't know where to present them or to who to go who has any authority to receive them." Nevertheless he remained confident in Woodrow Wilson, picturing him as the Moses of the peace conference. He wrote House:

> It looks as though we were going to be permitted to look over into the promised land. Possibly we may be permitted to enter it as well. I've forgotten who it was had the grouch on all the time because the roads were

---

14. Ibid., 290; Lincoln Steffens to Laura Suggett, November 1, 1918; Steffens to Allen H. Suggett, November 5, 1918, Winter and Hicks, *Letters of Lincoln Steffens*, 1:438, 439; Kaplan, *Lincoln Steffens*, 229–31; Steffens, *Autobiography*, 778, 783.

15. Kaplan, *Lincoln Steffens*, 233; Shotwell, *At the Paris Peace Conference*, 136, 165, 184; *Confessions of a Reformer*, 293–94; Steffens, *Lincoln Steffens Speaking*, 228–29. "Prince Emir Feisal" was Faisal, later the king of Iraq.

so bad. I think it was Aaron. And I don't remember how God disposed of him. Did he let him in too? Well there is more elbow room now even if there are more Aarons. And this time I believe Moses will be permitted to go in too. That ought to go a long way toward squaring what always seemed to be the great injustice of all history.[16]

Howe's opportunity came in late January 1919, when House informed him, through William Bullitt, that the president planned to send a mission to Syria to find out the wishes of the Syrians regarding a "mandatory." He asked Fred to familiarize himself with the secret treaties and other documents pertaining to Allied aims and commitments in the Near East, and to be ready to leave at a moment's notice. His companion on the mission would be Dr. James L. Barton, secretary of the American Board of Commissioners for Foreign Missions, who had been a missionary in Turkey. Howe got the impression that the British approved of the expedition, but that the French did not.

He immediately plunged into a close reading of the materials. He found the secret treaties full of "astounding revelations," in which betrayal was heaped upon betrayal. Britain and France had agreed with Arab leaders that Arab forces would join them and that together they would drive the Turks from Arabia. In return, the Arabs would get their freedom, the British would leave Mesopotamia, and France would give up Syria. Scarcely was the ink dry on this agreement than the French and British negotiated another secret treaty with each other, under which Britain was to keep Mesopotamia, France was to retain Syria, and Russia was to gain Armenia. When the Jews asked for Palestine, Lord Balfour, the British foreign secretary, agreed that they should have it, even though it had already been promised both to the Arabs and to the French. Howe wrote later: "My vision of a free world was clouding. Self-determination for peoples began to ring like an empty phrase. Still I believed that President Wilson had guaranties that would permit him to turn a trick at the proper time and restore the situation. I would not believe that we were going back to the old order; would not credit what I saw about me."[17]

The mission was given official sanction on February 1 in a letter from Secretary of State Robert Lansing that the president had approved. It described the purpose of the two-man commission in the vaguest of terms. Howe and Barton were to visit Syria and Asia Minor and report their findings to the American Commission to Negotiate Peace. A week later, Howe was ready to depart. He wrote House that he planned to leave that night for Rome and then to meet Dr.

16. FCH to Jane Addams, December 27, 1918, Jane Addams Papers, Swarthmore; FCH to Edward M. House, January 24, 1919.
17. *Confessions of a Reformer*, 294–95.

Barton in Constantinople. "From there we will proceed to Beirut to make the enquiries as to the desires of the Syrians." He had credentials and letters of introduction, five thousand dollars for the expenses of the mission, a promise of transport from the U.S. Navy if needed, and a promise of assistance from General Allenby. "I need not tell you how honored I feel that you should have selected me to go or how appreciative I am of your confidence."[18]

Howe's mission proved a fiasco. He expected to meet Dr. Barton in Rome (despite the statement in his letter to House that he would join his fellow emissary in Constantinople). The express train to Rome was cold and packed with people, many of whom had to stand in the unheated corridors for thirty-six hours. Not finding Barton in Rome, he pushed on to Brindisi, planning to take a destroyer from there to Constantinople. Conditions in Brindisi were miserable, and Dr. Barton was nowhere to be found. Howe's discomfort was still vivid in his mind when he later penned his autobiography. He recalled that the hotels were crowded to the last bed. It was bitter cold and raining. The streets were filled with troops of every nationality and every color, drunk and sober. An Italian cab driver helped him and finally took him into a wine room filled with drunken sailors. "The driver explained that I wanted a room, and the host took my bags and started up a series of dirty stairs to the top of the tenement. He threw open a door and motioned to a double bed, already occupied by a rough-looking customer, who might have been of any color or nationality. There were a dozen men in the room and more to come."

Howe quickly fled. "It was night-fall before I found a bed. Wet and cold I crawled into it." That night, his dreams of a free Mediterranean were "confused with drunken sailors, with dark-skinned murderers, with filthy wine-rooms and bitter, inhospitable weather. Alternating with chills and fever, the Arabs, French, or English could have Syria and the Syrians for all of me. If the Lord's chosen people wanted Palestine, they could take it for themselves."[19]

For Howe, the mission was over. He could not find his traveling companion (and probably did not really look for him), and he convinced himself that nothing could be accomplished by going on alone. The French who controlled Syria were hostile. America's allies wanted the United States in the Near East only "to pull the chestnuts out of the fire for England and assume responsibilities that would embroil us forever in European affairs." He decided to return to Paris and lay the situation before Colonel House. "A one-man effort under any circumstances would be of little value; if moral effect were desired it should be on a more imposing scale. If such a mission were sent, it should have power to get

18. Minutes of the Daily Meetings of the Commissioners Plenipotentiary, February 1, 1919, in *Paris Peace Conference, 1919*, 11:8; FCH to Edward M. House, January 31, 1919, and February 8, 1919.

19. *Confessions of a Reformer*, 300–301.

the information desired from the people themselves." He explained to James Shotwell that at Brindisi he had decided that "he might easily be made the tool of a certain interested government and came back in disobedience of orders."[20]

Howe's superiors were surprised and taken aback by his quick return. "Mr. [Henry] White said that Mr. Howe apparently felt that under present conditions of British and French occupation he would be unable to do any useful work. Some doubt was expressed as to whether Mr. Howe's expenses should be paid for this useless journey."[21] On February 22 they received Howe's request to be relieved of his assignment. Lansing and House discussed "the strange manner in which Mr. Howe had acted by returning from Brindisi, half way on his trip to the Near-East. They felt that in view of his actions it would be better to drop him all together, but at the same time to ask Mr. Barton to go on alone." The secretary of state noted that he was skeptical of the wisdom of sending anyone to Syria at this time. In March, however, the commissioners decided to proceed with another mission, headed by two men whom the president felt "particularly qualified to go to Syria because they knew nothing about it."[22]

All of Howe's efforts to assume the role of a Middle Eastern expert and to play an active part in the peacemaking effort had now ended in ignominious failure. It was true that the conditions for his mission were highly unfavorable. Its goal was nebulous, and the expedition had been poorly planned. There is no indication that much thought had been given to which persons Howe and Barton were to meet or how the views of the Syrians were to be ascertained. Since his only knowledge of the area was from books and not from direct experience, Howe would have had to rely heavily on local authorities. If France was hostile to the mission, its representatives in Syria would likely extend only grudging cooperation at best. But granted all these difficulties, Howe's decision to abandon his assignment even before he had arrived on the scene and made some attempt to carry it out can only be described as a failure of nerve. If the disorders and discomforts of Brindisi were more than he could cope with, how much more miserable and unpleasant were conditions likely to be in the *terra incognita* of Syria? Unable or unwilling to face the unknown, he fled back to Paris.

Fred put the best face possible on his inglorious failure and used it later as an example of the problems of the peacemaking process. He left Paris within a week of his return from Brindisi, but before his departure he sent House another

20. Ibid., 301; Shotwell, *At the Paris Peace Conference,* 184. Shotwell's diary entry is dated February 18, 1919.
21. Minutes of the Daily Meetings of the Commissioners Plenipotentiary, February 20, 1919, in *Paris Peace Conference, 1919,* 11:61. Together with President Wilson, Lansing, White, Bliss, and House made up the American Commission to Negotiate Peace.
22. Ibid., February 22, 1919; February 24, 1919; March 27, 1919, 11:66, 72, 133. The leaders of the larger and better-financed mission to Syria were Charles Crane and Henry Churchill King.

memorandum on the Near East, as well as a proposal for a study of "economic internationalism and what may be called financial imperialism for use in connection with the drafting of the terms of mandatories so as to protect not only the dependent peoples but to prevent friction as well." It sounded as if he was hoping to be asked to undertake the project. There is no record of a reply from House (who at this point must have been amazed at Howe's effrontery), or indeed of any subsequent correspondence between them. Fred sailed for New York on the *Mauretania* on February 27, his adventure in peacemaking over.[23]

Howe had gone to Europe with faith and hope in Woodrow Wilson as a peacemaker, but also with misgivings. As he saw it, he had tried to educate his former teacher on imperialism and war, but he could never get as close to the president as he wanted. Letters and memos were fine, but face-to-face appointments were hard to get and unsatisfactory when obtained. Wilson always received him attentively and seemed interested in Howe's views. "He was scrupulously attired, trim and erect, even debonair—every inch the gentlemanly President. And master of every subject. He would listen for a moment, then take up the matter, state it in a few phrases better than I had done—and treat the interview as ended. By taking the initiative he protected himself from divergent views, from discussion of questions that he had settled. . . . I would go away with a feeling that there was nothing more to be said; the subject was closed, it could not be debated." After such conversations, Fred was confused and unconvinced, feeling that he had run into a stone wall. Then he would get a letter from Wilson, "breathing his old belief in freedom. That was the Woodrow Wilson that I knew, my model of the university statesman; the new intolerant one was a product of the war."[24]

Nevertheless, when the armistice was signed, Howe wrote, "I felt that the international millennium was at hand. The President's idealism had carried the world; his Fourteen Points had been accepted; armies were to be disbanded, armaments scrapped, imperialism ended. Self-determination was to be extended to all peoples, hates were to be assuaged, and peace to reign."[25]

Howe's experiences and observations in Europe quickly disillusioned him. The principle of self-determination was soon abandoned in the Middle East as France and Britain betrayed their Arab allies and divided up Syria and Mesopotamia. The opportunity for a rapprochement with the new regime in Russia was lost. The foundations of the League of Nations were undermined when Wilson

---

23. FCH to Edward M. House, February 25, 1919, House Papers, Yale University Library. There are two letters of this date.
24. *Confessions of a Reformer*, 283–84.
25. Ibid., 287–88.

made concession after concession to Lloyd George and Clemenceau. The president had no interest in the economic issues that underlay the war, even though "economic forces moved the conference, like players about a chess-board.... The imperialist interests that had kept the world on edge for thirty years before the war were making a killing; they would end the old controversies; would sanction their loot by treaty agreements; perhaps rivet them by the League of Nations." As he became increasingly fearful of disorder and revolution, the president yielded to the strong-minded leaders of Britain and France, who knew exactly what they wanted.[26]

Looking back from the mid-1920s, Howe concluded that Wilson had failed partly because of his lack of preparation for the peace conference and partly because of basic flaws in his character. By his own choice, the president stood alone. He could not delegate responsibilities, and he resented any appearance of independent action by his aides, even by Colonel House. Even more fundamental to his failure at peacemaking was a kind of schizophrenia, although Howe did not use that term. There were two Woodrow Wilsons, he thought. One was Wilson the idealist, the statesman-philosopher, the evangelist. The other was Wilson the intolerant hater of those who disagreed with him, the vindictive man who turned on old friends, sanctioned hate propaganda, and seemed determined that no one should question his will. Had the president remained a messiah, he might have won.[27]

Woodrow Wilson was a "powerful, baffled, lonely personality," Howe concluded. As an evangelist, he ranked among the great men of history, but he was made vulnerable by his sense of insecurity. His life ended in tragedy. "He saw life in great principles; he knew what the distracted world needed. His phrases won permanent victories; they inspired peoples; possibly they won the war. He left humanity better for what he said; he enriched it by the unsullied idealism of his messages. He missed being one of the world's great heroes by choosing to be something other than what he was. He would not remain what his instinctive self would have chosen to remain, a maker of ideals by which other peoples should chart their course."[28]

Fred Howe returned from France to an America in which dissent had become increasingly branded as disloyalty. Shortly after the declaration of war, President Wilson had set up the Committee on Public Information and appointed George Creel as its director. Creel, a crusading journalist from Denver and a Progressive, was a longtime friend of Howe. His goal was publicity, not censorship, and he recruited writers, artists, movie directors, and speakers to publicize the war

26. Ibid., 313–14, 304, 310.
27. Ibid., 313, 305.
28. Ibid., 314, 316.

effort and obtain support for it. Inevitably, however, the Committee became concerned with creating the "correct" public opinion about the war.[29] Throughout the land, government officials, representatives of private organizations, and local vigilantes joined in word and deed to encourage conformity and 100 percent Americanism and to root out the disloyal and the "pro-Germans." New legislation gave the federal government sweeping powers over dissent. Under the Espionage Act of 1917, the postmaster general could ban from the mails any materials that advocated treason, insurrection, or resistance to law. The Trading with the Enemy Act extended these powers. In May 1918 Congress adopted amendments to the Espionage Act. The Sedition Act, as it was called, prohibited "any disloyal, profane, scurrilous, or abusive language about the form of government of the United States, or the Constitution of the United States, or the flag of the United States, or the uniform of the Army or Navy," or any language that might bring such institutions into "contempt, scorn, contumely, or disrepute." Interpreting these laws broadly, the postmaster general and the solicitor general, acting for the Justice Department, began to move vigorously against critics of the war and other dissenters and radicals.

Fred was soon included among those liberals increasingly named as pro-German or wild-eyed radicals. Sometimes the charges were leveled anonymously. Sometimes he did not even know he was under attack. Unknown to Howe was an attack by Richard Ely, his old mentor. Fearing that a German victory would threaten America, Ely had taken a pro-British stance on the war and joined those who called for a strong program of preparedness. Once the United States had entered the war, he became utterly intolerant of anyone who criticized entry or seemed sympathetic to Germany. He considered Senator La Follette a traitor, urged his ouster from the Senate, and encouraged his fellow faculty members at the University of Wisconsin to adopt a similar position. Though a member of the academic freedom committee of the American Association of University Professors, he believed that any professor who expressed opinions that "hinder us in this awful struggle" should be "fired," if not "shot." He organized and became president of the Madison, Wisconsin, chapter of the Wisconsin Loyalty League, whose members promised to "stamp out disloyalty, and to stimulate those whose loyalty is weak and thin into a militant love for our country and the principles for which it stands," to support the Espionage Act without reservation, and to "work against La Folletteism in all its anti-war forms, realizing that any encouragement to the supporters of La Follette is in fact support of La Follette himself."[30]

29. On Creel and the CPI, see ibid., 59–66; Creel, *Rebel at Large*; Schaffer, *America in the Great War*, 4–12; Mock and Larson, *Words That Won the War*; Vaughn, *Holding Fast the Inner Lines*.

30. Quotations are from Rader, *Academic Mind and Reform*, 183, 185. Ely later regretted his campaign against Senator La Follette.

Anything that smacked of pro-Germanism was anathema to Ely, and he would not spare even a former student and friend who continued to find some good things in the enemy nation. Unknown to Howe, he undertook a campaign of correction. He sent Carl Vrooman, the assistant secretary of agriculture, several extracts from Howe's *New York Times* article on postwar immigration and took serious issue with favorable comments about land reform in Germany. He apparently wanted Vrooman to bring these allegedly pro-German statements to the attention of the proper governmental authorities. When he received no immediate reply, he wrote again, asking what Vrooman had done with the information. "I take it for granted, of course, that you did not and will not make any mention of my name in this connection. Dr. Howe is one of my former students and in many ways is an excellent man who has, in some respects, gone wrong. Perhaps a course of vigorous criticism will bring him around to sounder views regarding the land. He is too good a man to be blinded by fanatical adherence to any theory, i.e. he is blinded, but should not be." Noting that Fred had made "perfectly absurd statements" in his *High Cost of Living,* he concluded: "Sometimes I have thought of having a frank talk with Howe, but I am sure he has too long adhered to certain economic doctrines as a religion readily to come around to see facts as they are." Vrooman tried unsuccessfully to see George Creel about publicizing Ely's information. He advised Ely: "It could do no harm for you to have a heart-to-heart talk with Fred Howe. You could go at him from the point of view of making his work more effective, rather than from the point of view of criticism. It certainly would make his work much more effective if he would be sure of his facts before he writes them. One sloppy statement, such as he makes only too frequently, destroys the influence of a large mass of other perfectly sound work that may accompany it."[31]

It is ironic to note that at the very same time that Ely sought action against Howe, he was also seeking his support. Perhaps "duplicity" is a more appropriate word than "irony." On March 7, 1918, Ely asked Howe to join the new American Association for Agricultural Legislation, which the professor had helped organize. "I should be very glad to have you join," he wrote. "I think we are going to develop a really constructive program and do many things well worth while." Howe responded that he was "very much interested" and that Ely was at liberty to use his name in any way he saw fit. Ely's letter of thanks touched briefly upon his disagreement with Howe: "However much we may differ as to

---

31. Richard Ely to Carl S. Vrooman, January 18, 1918, Ely Papers; Ely to Vrooman, March 13, 1918; Vrooman to Ely, March 21, 1918. The article was an interview with Howe entitled "Immigration Tide May Turn from West to East" in the *New York Times Magazine,* October 14, 1917. See Paulson, *Radicalism and Reform,* 233.

some ultimate theories, there are certain things which must be done now or in the near future and upon which we can all agree. Perhaps when we get to working on definite concrete problems in a constructive way, we will forget all about our formulas and panaceas."[32] This was a gentle admonition that gave Fred no indication of the more specific criticisms that Ely had sent to Vrooman. Although Ely contributed to the postwar "Red Scare" through his attacks on Bolshevism, he did not again single out Howe, and the two men remained on friendly terms throughout their lifetimes. There is no indication that Howe ever learned of his mentor's dealings with Vrooman.

Before leaving for Paris in November 1918, Fred found himself attacked publicly by Senator Lawrence Sherman, Republican of Illinois, who charged that a number of Wilson supporters were "Socialists and economic freaks . . . half-pacifists, firebrands, and fiends of sedition." Included in the senator's indictment along with Howe were Secretary of War Baker, Postmaster General Burleson, Secretary of Labor Wilson, Creel, and Post. Sherman called Howe a "trusted friend and adviser of the Administration," and reported that he "once heard a long-haired, ill-clad, oppressed and unbathed victim of society, speaking in a back hall in Chicago, say that Mr. Howe's book, Socialized Germany, was the greatest thing since Carl [sic] Marx, and that even August Bebel used it." As a single taxer, Fred was included in Sherman's complaints about that ilk: "Even a single taxer can stifle his lifetime convictions of yesterday to get on the Government pay roll. He can then draw a salary from unprincipled Democrats and rascally Republicans who hold real estate. He can console himself by meditating on the iniquity of consuming the unearned increment of Democratic politics." Sherman had singled out *Socialized Germany* for criticism, but this was not the only one of Howe's books to be branded as subversive or pro-German. *Why War* was included on a list of nearly a hundred objectionable books that were banned from American military establishments.[33]

Attacks on Howe and other liberals and radicals continued while he was in France. In January 1919 Archibald E. Stevenson, a New York lawyer identified as a member of the Military Intelligence Service, gave a Senate committee investigating German propaganda a list of sixty-two men and women, purported to be leaders of pacifist and radical movements, who might have been "actively engaged in opposing the military of the country." Fred found his name in what must have seemed to him good company: Jane Addams, Charles Beard, the

---

32. Richard F. Ely to FCH, March 7, 1918; FCH to Ely, April 25, 1918; Ely to FCH, April 29, 1918.
33. *New York Times,* April 24, 1918, 13; *Congressional Record,* 65th Cong., 2nd sess., April 25, 1918, vol. 56, 5599; Mock, *Censorship, 1917,* 168–70; Mock and Larson, *Words That Won the War,* 178; Carl Sandburg to Sam T. Hughes, September 12, 1918, in Mitgang, *Letters of Carl Sandburg,* 134–35.

Reverend John Haynes Holmes, Amos Pinchot, Norman Thomas, Oswald Garrison Villard, Lillian Wald, Eugene Debs. Stevenson helpfully provided the committee with a thumbnail sketch of each person's subversive associations. For Howe the damning information was: "Studied in Germany; gen. comm. Amer. Neutral Conference Comm.; pres. League of Small and Subject Nationalities; Member of League of Free Nations Ass'n; advisory board Brown Open Forum."[34]

Jane Addams and others on the list organized a letter-writing campaign of protests to Newton Baker, who responded with a denial that Stevenson had ever been an officer or employee of his department's Military Intelligence Division. The War Department did not try to censor the people of the United States, he pointed out, nor had it any authority to classify their opinions. "In the particular list accredited to Mr. Stevenson there are names of people of great distinction, exalted purity of purpose, and life-long devotion to the highest interests of America and of mankind. Miss Jane Addams, for instance, lends dignity and greatness to any list in which her name appears." Senator Lee S. Overman, chair of the investigating committee, stood by his witness, quoting a memo from a captain that indicated Stevenson, a member of "the propaganda section," had been studying German propaganda in the United States for more than a year.[35] Earlier, Stevenson had been a leader in a raid by FBI agents and volunteers from the Union League Club on the office of the National Civil Liberties Bureau, the precursor to the American Civil Liberties Union. Roger Baldwin described the federal agent in charge as a "seventy-five per cent good guy" but called Stevenson, whom he knew, a "son of a bitch."[36]

When Howe returned to his desk at Ellis Island in March 1919, he found that his immigration station had become "the most available dumping ground under the successive waves of hysteria which swept the country." He described his life in the time between American entry into the war and the Armistice as a "nightmare." "On the island I had to stand between the official insistence that the German should be treated as a criminal and the admitted fact that the great majority of them had been arrested by persons with little concern about their innocence or guilt and with but little if any evidence to support the detention." Then, for his attempts at fairness, he had been branded a pro-German. Now,

---

34. *New York Times*, January 25, 1919, 1, 4.
35. Statement of Newton D. Baker, January 27, 1918, Wilson Papers, 54:398; *Congressional Record*, 65th Cong., 3rd sess., January 28, 1919, vol. 57, pt. 3, 2187.
36. Lamson, *Roger Baldwin*, 83–85. According to Baldwin, "my inquiries as to the Union League Club revealed the fact that some wealthy young men of that aristocratic organization were serving as dollar-a-year agents of the Department of Justice. Their patriotic duties, I learned, exempted them from the draft." R. Baldwin, "Reminiscences," pt. 1, vol. 1, 67, in the Columbia University Oral History Research Office Collection.

from the winter of 1918 through 1919, he was to be attacked as a dangerous radical, a friend and ally of anarchists and revolutionists.[37]

The immigration law of October 1918, by introducing the principle of guilt by association into the deportation process, had made it much easier for the government to deport alien radicals. An alien could be deported merely for being a member of a group that advocated sabotage, anarchism, or violent revolution. Even before the act's passage, Anthony Caminetti, the commissioner general of immigration, and A. Warner Parker, the Bureau of Immigration's chief law officer, had begun to reinterpret existing legislation and to change the standard for deportation so that members of the Industrial Workers of the World (IWW) and other radicals could be detained and then quickly deported.

Awaiting Fred Howe on Ellis Island in March 1919 were some thirty-eight "Wobblies"—IWW members—who had been shipped there from Seattle in February 1919 on a train dubbed the "Red Special." Newspaper editorials throughout the country hailed the detentions and called for immediate deportation of "this motley crew of IWW troublemakers, bearded labor fanatics, and red flag supporters," as the *New York Times* described them, and Caminetti and Parker were quite willing to cooperate. Byron Uhl, the acting commissioner at Ellis Island in Howe's absence, had tried to hold the detainees incommunicado and had denied access to their lawyers until thwarted by the Labor Department and the courts. Howe decided that there was no need to rush to deport and that the prisoners were entitled to full hearings. He took that stand even though he had been "advised by the Commissioner-General to mind my own business and carry out orders, no matter what they might be." He won the support of Secretary of Labor Wilson, who instructed Caminetti that each alien was entitled to have his case considered on its own merits. Neither Wilson nor Howe was disposed to accept mere membership in an organization—even a revolutionary one—as sufficient grounds for deportation. As a result of hearings and court actions, only a handful of the detained Wobblies were deported, and the *New York Times* groused: "At the water's edge an indulgent Government hesitates. By official magic some of the goats are transformed into probationary sheep."[38]

Coinciding with Howe's resumption of his immigration duties was a raid by the New York City police bomb squad on the office of the Union of Russian Peasant Workers of America and the arrest of two hundred persons. Most were released fairly quickly, but the assistant district attorney sent a few to Ellis Island and asked the commissioner's help in their deportation. According to the DA, Howe told him that he was "too busy with other matters just then and let the

---

37. *Confessions of a Reformer*, 267, 273.
38. Ibid., 274; *New York Times*, February 10, 1919, 1; March 29, 1919, 12.

men go on surety of $1,000 each, furnished by their attorney." The commissioner defended his action by pointing out that Washington had authorized the bail after extensive hearings had been held on the island.[39]

In his autobiography, Howe describes his activities and thoughts during these difficult days.

> I quarrelled with the Commissioner-General of Immigration, who was working hand in glove with the Department of Justice; I harassed the Secretary of Labor with protests against the injustice that was being done. I refused to believe that we were a hysterical people; that civil liberties should be thrown to the winds. But in this struggle there was no one to lean on; there was no support from Washington, no interest on the part of the press. . . . I took the position from which I would not be driven, that the alien should not be held incommunicado, and should enjoy the right of a writ of habeas corpus in the United States courts, which was the only semblance of legal proceedings open to him under the law.[40]

The more firmly Howe stuck to this position, the louder became the demands that this Red sympathizer be removed from his post.

Some of the fears about radical bombers appeared to become realities just prior to May Day in 1919. On April 28 Seattle's Mayor Ole Hansen, who was embroiled with IWW strikers, received a bomb in the mail. On April 29 a package sent through the mails to former senator Thomas Hardwick's Atlanta address exploded, blowing off the hands of his maid and also injuring his wife. On April 30 an alert clerk in the New York City post office noticed sixteen packages that had been put aside because of insufficient postage, recognized that their appearance coincided with newspaper descriptions of the bombs, and reported them to postal inspectors, who called in the police. The packages, which proved indeed to be bombs, were addressed to a roster of prominent public officials and business men. Among the intended recipients were Fred Howe, Secretary of Labor Wilson, and Commissioner-General Caminetti. It was thought that the three immigration officials were included because they were involved in the deportation of the IWW members from Seattle. Intensive investigation by local and federal authorities produced no result.[41]

Fred's inclusion on the list of potential bomb victims did nothing to mitigate the condemnations he was receiving for his actions as immigration commissioner. When the House was considering appropriations for the immigration

---

39. Pitkin, *Keepers of the Gate*, 122–23.
40. *Confessions of a Reformer*, 267, 275.
41. *New York Times*, May 1, 1919, 1, 3; June 5, 1919, 1, 2; Murray, *Red Scare*, 68–73.

service in June 1919, Representative Fiorello La Guardia of New York City moved for a reduction in Howe's salary from sixty-five hundred dollars to twenty-five hundred. The congressman, who was familiar with Ellis Island from his work there as an interpreter from 1907 to 1910 and who was sympathetic to the plight of immigrants, had fallen under the sway of anti-Red emotions. Charging Howe with absenteeism, he declared that the commissioner was "very rarely at the station, unless he goes there for the purpose of defending a detained anarchist." When he was present for duty, his actions ran contrary to the law. "We are able to take care of the anarchists in New York City by our municipal police, but after we get these anarchists and turn them over to the immigration office at Ellis Island we find that the immigration commissioner, instead of deporting them according to the law, acts as their counsel."

Continuing his indictment, La Guardia charged that the commissioner had personally delivered subversive literature to the detainees at Ellis Island, including such publications as the *Rebel Worker*, the *Red Dawn*, the *Truth About the I.W.W.*, the *New Solidarity*, *I.W.W. Songs*, and the *Seattle Union Record*. The only way to rebuke this official and to show congressional displeasure was by cutting his salary. On the urging of another congressman, La Guardia amended his motion to provide that no part of the immigration appropriation should be used to pay the salary of Frederic C. Howe.

No one spoke in Howe's defense, but Congressman Joseph M. Byrns of Tennessee pointed out that this was hardly the right way to remove the immigration commissioner from office. He advised the House to vote down the amendment and allow charges to be brought against Howe and his removal to be sought in a legal way. The amendment was then defeated by a forty-four to eight vote.[42] Neither Howe nor La Guardia mentioned this episode in their autobiographies. The ill feeling that it must necessarily have aroused had certainly disappeared in the 1920s. Howe joined other leading Democrats (including senators La Follette and George Norris) in endorsing La Guardia for reelection to the House in 1932, and as the AAA's consumers counsel, he worked with the by then mayor of New York in the 1930s.[43]

Federal agents kept their eyes on alleged radicals and other subversives. Senator La Follette reported indignantly to his family a "very ugly story" he had heard about the mistreatment of Marie Howe. "Secret service hounds" had seized her in front of her apartment and held her for a while, not permitting any communication with Fred or a lawyer. Fred was under surveillance by the Military Intelligence Division, one of whose agents, Inspector Purdie of the New

---

42. *Congressional Record*, House of Representatives, 66th Cong., 1st sess., June 12, 1919, 1522–24. See also Mann, *La Guardia*, 101.

43. Mann, *La Guardia*, 316; Zinn, *La Guardia in Congress*, 246–49.

York City office, reported on a debate that Howe moderated in April 1919. The debate, sponsored by the Rand School, had Professor Bushnell Hart and Scott Nearing arguing the topic "Will the League of Nations Benefit Labor?" before an audience of three thousand, "composed almost entirely of Russian Jews." Hart supported the League, but Nearing saw it as a capitalist plot and called for revolution, according to the inspector, who put Howe in Nearing's camp. Reported Purdie: "The Chairman of the meeting . . . was Dr. Frederick [sic] Howe . . . I saw no indication on his part to resent any of Scott Nearing's remarks. He did not even exercise the authority of a chairman to suppress the applause which constantly interrupted Nearing, even though Nearing himself repeatedly asked the audience to refrain." In a memo forwarding the agent's report to the Director of Military Intelligence in Washington, Captain John B. Trevor devoted his comments almost entirely to Howe: "A particularly noteworthy feature of this meeting is that fact that Frederic C. Howe . . . acted as the presiding officer and allowed in his presence a program for the overturn of our government and remarks tending to incite sedition and revolution to pass without any protest whatsoever. Aside from this fact, it is a question of propriety whether an important official of the United States should preside at meetings in which the representatives of powers, and, indeed, the powers themselves collectively are characterized in a manner to which Prof. Scott Nearing is prone to adopt."[44]

Fred felt the heat directly after he chaired a "Justice to Russia" meeting at Madison Square Garden on May 25, 1919. Held to protest the intervention of Allied troops into Russia and a blockade against food shipments to that country, the rally heard from such men as Amos Pinchot, the Reverend John Haynes Holmes, Lincoln Colcord (writer and sometime Washington correspondent for the *Philadelphia Ledger*), and Rabbi Judah L. Magnes. In his brief opening remarks, Howe urged help to the sick and starving Russians and called upon the allied powers to recognize their right to work out their own destiny free from outside intervention. He concluded that Russia was "seething with something new that can not be quenched by arms. It can only be overthrown by ideas. To attempt to police Russia in the interest of reaction means a continuation of wars and possibly the complete destruction of the European world—it may be by disease and pestilence bred of hunger, and the emancipation of the people." The *New York Times* reported that the meeting was orderly and that the speakers were interrupted only by applause, except for some booing when

---

44. La Follette and La Follette, *Robert La Follette*, 2:938; memo from John G. Purdie to Lt. W. L. Moffat Jr., April 28, 1919; memo from Office of Military Intelligence Division (signed by John B. Trevor, Captain) to Director of Military Intelligence, April 29, 1919, in *United States Military Intelligence Reports*.

Magnes mentioned President Wilson. The *Times* story did not refer to any of Howe's remarks. The meeting ended with the adoption of resolutions calling for an end to the blockade, for freedom of Russia to determine its own institutions and fate, for the recall of all American troops, and against recognition by the American government of any counterrevolution or any regime representing the old monarchy.[45]

A *Times* editorial uttered a general condemnation of the meeting but made no mention of Howe. It said that "the sincere milk of Leninism flowed freely" at the rally and referred to participants as "our amateur New York Bolsheviki." In subsequent days, several letters to the editor targeted Howe for specific criticism. How could he continue to draw a government salary while "the Bolsheviki over whose meetings he presides" desire to overthrow the government, one writer asked. How could he preside over a meeting at which the president who appointed him was "vigorously hissed," asked another. "It would be interesting to know just what proportion of his time Mr. Howe devoted to the office for which he is receiving a salary of $6,500 from the people."[46]

Howe issued a statement in his own defense on June 4. The meeting was not pro-Bolshevik, he declared. Its limited purpose was to urge that Russia be allowed to buy food (Howe cited Herbert Hoover's support for this) and that the United States should not recognize the czar or the old monarchist regime. "I believe both these demands are just; that they are in keeping with American traditions," he maintained.[47]

The *Times* then took up the cudgels. It now found Howe's action in presiding over the "Justice to Russia" meeting "obviously improper" and "intolerable." "How can such a Commissioner be trusted to shut the gates on those alien enemies of free and ordered government, of equal political privilege, those desperate plotters of class war of whom there are too many already in the United States?" He should have restrained the speakers or protested against the audience's insult to the president, or left the meeting. The *Times* thought the senators' criticism was just and agreed with them on the "impropriety" of Howe's role. The paper concluded: "So fond a friend of the I.W.W., a so sympathetic President of a Bolshevist meeting, so liberal a thinker, so singular a Commissioner of Immigration!"[48]

By the summer of 1919, Howe felt himself under attack from all sides—from the press, from members of Congress, from critics on both the Left and the

---

45. "Justice to Russia," *Bulletin of the People's Council of America* (June 1919): 1–2; Amos Pinchot Papers; *New York Times*, May 26, 1919, 17; Grubbs, *Struggle for Labor Loyalty*, 142.
46. *New York Times*, May 27, 1919, 14; Edward G. Riggs to editor, *New York Times*, May 27, 1919, 14; E. N. Vernon to editor, *New York Times*, June 2, 1919, 14.
47. Ibid., June 4, 1919, 14.
48. Ibid., June 5, 1919, 12.

Right. Within the immigration service, he was constantly battling with his superior, Commissioner General Caminetti, who was cooperating with the Department of Justice for the speedy deportation of alien radicals. Howe found that promises of hearings before aliens were deported were being broken and that orders of the secretary of labor were being ignored by bureau officials. He hurried to Washington to protest to the secretary of labor and succeeded in getting deportation orders put aside in several of the cases he was concerned with.

> But I was through. The Red hysteria was at its height. The Commissioner-General and Attorney-General were directing it. I might be asked to carry out any order and be compromised in any promise which I made. There was talk of chartering a vessel and sending a boat-load of deportees back to Russia. Many of them I had personally examined and found held on the most trivial charges. Driven by business organizations back home, congressmen were demanding action, no matter how innocent the victims might be. I had exhausted my power. Even the secretary was being carried along by the hysteria. . . . There were some orders which I would not carry out. And I wanted to be rid of political office that compelled compromise.

The next day, Fred collected all his personal correspondence and records, which he had been planning to use in a book. Together with a porter, "we carried them to the engine-room, where I consigned them to the flames."

Then, thinking "I will end that chapter forever," he sat down and wrote his resignation to the president. It was brief and made no mention of his tribulations: "I beg to tender my resignation as Commissioner of Immigration at the Port of New York. There is very little immigration and no signs of an early increase. Moreover I very much desire to return to the practice of law and for the immediate present devote myself to the work of the committee that was recently organized in Washington in connection with the Plumb Plan for the settlement of the railroad question." "I left with a feeling of exhilaration," he later wrote. "I had entered whole-heartedly into my principality of Ellis Island, hoping to make it a playhouse for immigrants. I left a prison. I recalled what Wendell Phillips said about negro slavery, that 'it made a slave of the master no less than the slave.' "[49]

Fred's resignation failed to remove him from the line of fire, however. In November 1919 members of the House Committee on Immigration and Naturalization arrived in New York City to investigate conditions at Ellis Island.

---

49. *Confessions of a Reformer*, 326–28; FCH to Woodrow Wilson, September 6, 1919, Wilson Papers.

According to its chair, Representative Albert Johnson, the Committee's visit was part of a detailed study of immigration laws, not as an investigation of Howe (though Johnson did mention charges of absenteeism and sympathetic indulgence of radicals that would doubtless be looked into).[50]

In the course of its hearings, however, the Committee did focus on the former commissioner of immigration. Much of the testimony came from Byron Uhl, Howe's second-in-command and now acting commissioner at the island. Uhl seemed quite happy to respond to the congressmen's leading questions. When Johnson suggested that Howe had intended to make the station "a place of individual government, letting everyone do as he pleased," Uhl agreed: "That was the impression created on me, sir." He agreed that prostitutes and loose women had been given privileges under Howe's administration that they had not received before.[51] To the suggestion that each individual could do as he pleased, Uhl replied, "Pretty nearly; yes, sir." He testified that the staff at Ellis Island disapproved of Howe's policies and that the commissioner had frequently bypassed Caminetti to deal directly with Post and Wilson. Uhl also testified that Howe had been absent from the station from February 1 to April 7 or 8 in 1917 and from September 1918 to mid-February 1919. (In both periods, Howe had been on approved leave, during the first for a lecture tour and during the second on his assignment to the Paris peace conference.)

A great many of the committee members' questions and comments focused on Howe's alleged friendliness to radicals. They implied that he coddled them, pointing to one of his orders that said, "Please supply men detained as political deportees with medicine balls and other means of amusement." They charged that Howe had allowed radical literature to circulate among the detainees and got Uhl to agree that although the commissioner had signed an order to the inspectors to control such dissemination, he had delayed nearly two months before giving it to them. When Howe interrupted the testimony to deny this, Representative J. E. Raker quickly put him in his place and shut him up. The Committee members made much of their discovery in the files of friendly letters to Howe from two "notorious agitators," Emma Goldman and Elizabeth Gurley Flynn, as well as other correspondence on the stationery of *Mother Earth*, the anarchist magazine. They charged that Howe had intervened to delay the deportation of alien radicals or had secured their release on parole or bond. Of more than six hundred aliens sent to Ellis Island for deportation, only sixty had actually been deported.

Howe tried to defend himself. In an interview with the *New York Times*, he pointed out that the charges of immorality and gambling went back to his 1916

---

50. *New York Times*, November 24, 1919, 1.
51. Unless otherwise indicated, quotations are from *Conditions at Ellis Island*.

fight with Congressman Bennet over the food contract and had been refuted at that time. "If it has been charged that I have released radicals or any one else held for deportation, the charges are entirely false. I had no power to release anybody. All releases were made at Washington." It was true that he had allowed men held for deportation to have lawyers. As to circulation of radical literature on the island, detainees received publications by mail, but a Justice Department representative examined their reading matter before giving it to them. He did not recall the letter from Goldman and had only very vague recollections of the one from Flynn. Asked if he was a friend of Goldman, he replied: "I have seen her only three or four times in my life. I don't remember seeing her at all, except at meetings at the People's Institute." Howe gave a similar interview to the *New York World*.[52]

Howe's attempt to speak directly to the Committee was rebuffed. He asked leave to make a statement, but Congressman Raker objected to "any statement being made by any witness before this committee unless he is under oath. We are not ready to hear anyone unless we ourselves call him." The chair ruled that Howe could not be heard but that he could submit a letter for the record. After the session, when reporters asked him if he belonged to the Communist Party, he said that he did not. "I am a democrat with a small 'd.' I am not attached to any party, and I never tied to any party."

On November 30 the Committee returned to Washington, determined to do all it could to speed up deportation of the Reds held at Ellis Island. It indicated it would send evidence on Howe to the Justice Department for action, and it planned to cross-examine his superiors in the Labor Department, Wilson and Post. The committee demanded that Wilson release a report prepared by A. W. Parker, the Immigration Bureau's law officer, on Howe's administration at the island, but the secretary refused, citing its confidential nature. The *New York Times* saw this as an attempt to protect Howe.[53]

Led by Attorney General A. Mitchell Palmer, the Justice Department began mass arrests of alien "Reds" in November 1919, and soon Acting Commissioner Uhl had a full Ellis Island. Caminetti was cooperating completely with his friends in Justice to speed up deportations. Secretary Wilson continued to insist that prisoners had a right to counsel and, in many cases, to freedom on bail. Louis Post, serving as acting secretary during Wilson's illness, undertook to review the case of each Communist Labor Party member and ordered some seven hundred deported, canceling another twenty-seven hundred warrants. He also undertook to limit Caminetti's actions. Post's efforts brought a critical

---

52. *New York Times*, November 27, 1919, 3; Pitkin, *Keepers of the Gate*, 125.
53. *New York Times*, December 12, 1919, 16.

report from the House Immigration Committee and introduction of an impeachment resolution. Post defended himself ably before the House Rules Committee, and the effort to impeach him collapsed.[54]

Looking back on the period of the Red Scare, Howe saw it as the betrayal of the American principle of freedom. "The Department of Justice, the Department of Labor, and Congress not only failed to protest against hysteria, they encouraged these excesses; the state not only abandoned the liberty which it should have protected, it lent itself to the stamping out of individualism and freedom." He had believed that Americans held human rights sacred and would protect them at all costs. He had found instead that his fellow countrymen were "lawless, emotional, given to mob action. We cared little for freedom of conscience, for the rights of men to their opinions." The subversion of civil liberties "was an incident in the ascendancy of business privileges and profits acquired during the war—an ascendancy that could not bear scrutiny or brook the free discussion which is the only safe basis of orderly popular government."

While he was a government official, people all over the country had turned to him for help. "Many of them were young people, many were college men and women." All sought protection and saw him as someone who could take their cases to the president. "I was part of this liberal movement. To me it was a renaissance of America rising from the orgy of commercialism. And I could not reconcile myself to its destruction, to its voice being stilled, its integrity assailed, its patriotism questioned, especially by a war that promised to give these democratic ideals to the world." The crushing of this movement made Howe hate in a way he had never hated before.

> I hated the new state that had arisen, hated its brutalities, its ignorance, its unpatriotic patriotism, that made profit from our sacrifices and used its power to suppress criticism of its acts. I hated the suggestion of disloyalty of myself and my friends; suggestions that were directed against liberals, never against profiteers. . . . I hated the new manifestation of power far more than I had hated the spoilsmen, the ward heeler, the politicians, or even the corruptionists who had destroyed my hope of democracy in Cleveland. I had cherished a free city, but I cherished a free people more.

His role as an agent of that system weighed heavily on his mind. He found himself fighting "a moral battle that went to the bottom of things. . . . For months I lived in a state of fear. I feared something impending, something

---

54. See Post, *The Deportations Delirium;* Lombardi, *Labor's Voice in the Cabinet,* 343–49; Easterly, *Louis F. Post,* 229–37, 234; Preston, *Aliens and Dissenters,* 223–26; Murray, *Red Scare,* 247–49; Coben, *A. Mitchell Palmer,* 230–41; Ackerman, *Young J. Edgar,* 135–214.

mysterious that hung over men." A psychiatrist friend told him he was sick and that the only way to straighten himself out was to "blurt out what you have in your mind. Say what you think about the things that bother you. You have been living through a conflict that can only be gotten rid of through the confessional. Make an opportunity to get it all out of your system." Howe tried it, and it worked. "Confession had been good for me. My fears began to disappear. I recovered health when I recovered honesty—not entirely, for I could not erase from my mind the things I had done; the fine edge of courage was dulled. Accusations of self against self had sunk deep during those years and created a sense of shame. The fears that had possessed me would not be wholly exorcised."[55]

Despite his fears and his feelings of failure, Fred Howe did not stand alone. Surely he would have been heartened if he had read a letter Lincoln Steffens sent from Paris to Allen Suggett:

> All my friends seem to be under suspicion or investigation, on trial or in jail; and my name is mentioned repeatedly. "My country" . . . has gone mad. Safe over here, I might laugh; and I do most of the time. It is so ridiculous. But it cannot be funny to the fellows who are in trouble. Think of Fred Howe under charges! So far as I can gather, he is accused only of humanity, sanity and mercy, but those are great crimes nowadays; and Fred is sure to have been guilty of them. He would not hurt even an investigator; no, not even a Lusker, if he had one in his power. Fred was kind to the Germans in his custody on the Island.[56]

Accusations of subversive radicalism were still to plague Howe from time to time in the 1920s, but they proved no deterrent to his political activity. Freed now of any governmental responsibilities, he could plunge into new efforts to reshape the American polity in the postwar world.

---

55. *Confessions of a Reformer*, 276–82.
56. Lincoln Steffens to Allen Suggett, December 23, 1919, in Winter and Hicks, *Letters of Lincoln Steffens*, 1:513. By "Lusker," Steffens meant a member or supporter of the Lusk Committee, set up by the New York Legislature to investigate "seditious" activity.

14

SEARCHING FOR A NEW PARTY

"The people demanded a leaderless nation. For the first time in twenty years, we were tired of men with burning convictions, curative or palliative panaceas or reforms; ideas that might develop into causes. We were sated with all kinds of spiritual fidgets. The land was more or less afflicted with moral shell-shock." So wrote William Allen White on the advent of Warren G. Harding and the conservatism of the 1920s. "But as for the men themselves who held these high plans for humanity, their day in Washington was done," continued the Sage of Emporia. "The scribbler went back to his attic, the dreamer to his study, the ascetic to his cloister." Though not all reformers were in the full retreat that White described, many did appear to have abandoned the battlefield. Lincoln Steffens stayed on in Europe, observing world events from his Italian villa and writing his autobiography. Walter Lippmann left the *New Republic* to devote his time to other journalistic and literary pursuits. Brand Whitlock remained as ambassador to Belgium till 1921 and then went into semiretirement. Newton Baker returned to civic endeavors in Cleveland. As for Fred Howe, several historians have portrayed him as a fugitive who "retired to a remote hideaway," "sequestered himself on Nantucket," "renounced public life, dividing his years between Nantucket and Europe," and "lapsed into political torpor." Another included him among those reformers who "laid down their burdens of duty and conscience and sought entirely private ends in the years that remained to them."¹

Progressivism in the twenties may have appeared to be as Eric Goldman described it: "a beaten army, muscles aching, its ranks seriously depleted." Many liberals (a term that was supplanting "Progressives") considered their defeat

---

1. White, *Masks in a Pageant,* 410, 418; Rochester, *American Liberal Disillusionment,* 118, 119; Kennedy, *Over Here,* 292; O. Graham, *Great Campaigns,* 120; Kaplan, *Lincoln Steffens,* 291.

temporary, however. They were no longer at or near the levers of power in the White House, but they could point to reform activities in the states and to some triumphs in Congress. Farmers and elements of organized labor, especially the railroad brotherhoods, remained politically active, as did advocates of public control of the electric power industry. It is true that Progressivism no longer dominated national policy—if it ever had—but it seemed far from dead even in the age of Wall Street riches, flappers, and bathtub gin.[2] Though their muscles may have been "aching," a good share of the independent liberals and radicals who had backed reform causes before and during the war were still fighting for them in the 1920s. The list included such stalwarts as Amos Pinchot, senators Norris and La Follette, Jane Addams, John Dewey, Charles Edward Russell, Upton Sinclair, Rabbi Stephen Wise, William Allen White, Lillian Wald, Florence Kelley, and Benjamin Marsh.

As for Fred Howe, although he was not as active in the twenties as he had been in the two previous decades, he could hardly have been described as a man who fled from politics to settle down as a torpid hermit in Sconset. During the "prosperity decade," he campaigned in two presidential elections; worked for the Plumb Plan for public ownership of the railroads; joined in efforts to form a new political party; attempted to help bring about a settlement of the Irish question; wrote three books and a clutch of articles; started and ran a summer school on Nantucket; traveled in Europe and observed closely political developments there; and continued his involvement in the single-tax movement and in such organizations as the American Civil Liberties Union, the Public Ownership League of America, the League for Industrial Democracy, and the American Committee for the Relief of Russian Children. This is hardly the picture of a man who had abandoned the battlefield and entered into an early retirement from politics and public life.

By the early months of 1920, the national antiradical hysteria of the Red Scare seemed to be fading away, although the hunt for Bolsheviks and other "subversives" continued with vigor in some states. In March 1919 New York's legislature had authorized formation of a committee to investigate "seditious activities." Senator Clayton Lusk chaired the inquiry, and Archibald Stevenson was its assistant counsel—indeed, it was Stevenson's testimony before the Overman Committee that, with the backing of the Union League Club and other groups, had helped bring the Lusk Committee into being. The new Committee not only investigated but also raided organizations that it suspected of radical or revolutionary activities or tendencies. It seized their literature, and it began

---

2. Goldman, *Rendezvous with Destiny*, 223. See Link, "What Happened"; O. Graham, *Great Campaigns*, 114–19; A. Davis, "Welfare, Reform, and World War I."

to compile a list of "all parlor bolsheviki, IWW, and socialists" (Lusk's terminology). The chairman claimed to have evidence that radicals controlled at least a hundred labor unions and that such organizations as the socialists' Rand School were working with Soviet agents to "bolshevize" American workers. The Committee presented the legislature with five bills, which, among other things, outlawed the Socialist Party, required loyalty oaths from teachers, and set up a State Bureau of Investigation to continue weeding out sedition, disloyalty, and criminal anarchism. The legislature passed the bills in April 1920, but Governor Al Smith vetoed them. In 1921 the lawmakers again passed the bills, and Smith's successor signed them.

Fred Howe came out of the fire of the wartime Red Scare with a stronger appreciation for the worth of individual liberties and with a diminished regard for the state and its agencies. Like other liberals, he realized the value of a new organization, the American Civil Liberties Union (ACLU). The ACLU was a descendant of an earlier organization that Howe had helped form, the American Union Against Militarism (AUAM). After the United States entered the war, the AUAM set up a Bureau of Conscientious Objectors, soon renamed the Civil Liberties Bureau. Roger Baldwin became its director. AUAM members disagreed over the new unit's relationship to its parent, and in October 1917 it became independent as the National Civil Liberties Bureau (NCLB). Its name was changed to the American Civil Liberties Union in January 1920.[3]

Fred's government post precluded active participation in the AUAM after its early days, but he gave his support to its new civil liberties offshoots. He joined with NCLB members in their July 1917 protest to President Wilson against the banning of socialist and pacifist periodicals from the mails. At Baldwin's request, he wrote a letter stating his opposition to a peacetime sedition law. Once the ACLU came into existence, Baldwin urged him to accept membership on its first national committee, and Fred quickly agreed. On the Committee he found himself among friends—Addams, Crystal Eastman, Elizabeth Gurley Flynn, Felix Frankfurter, Morris Hillquit, Helen Keller, William U'Ren, Oswald Garrison Villard. He remained on the ACLU's National Committee throughout the 1920s. Membership did not entail heavy responsibilities. Baldwin considered Committee members as "good for letterheads as public relations. They were, further, personalities on whom we could count for judgment in controversy—for the mail vote of the National Committee on referenda guided policy." He

---

3. See Walker, *In Defense of American Liberties*, 16–47; D. Johnson, *Challenge to American Freedoms*, 14–25, 145–48; Lamson, *Roger Baldwin*, 70–75, 123–27.

was delighted to have Howe's support, calling him "a very good man to have on our side."⁴

The Lusk Committee had concluded that the ACLU was one of "a large number of groups in this country engaged in an effort to undermine our institutions, to weaken property rights and to set up in place of government by the majority, a government controlled by a militant minority of the workers." The Committee listed Fred Howe as a member of the ACLU's National Committee, mentioned him as a speaker at the Justice to Russia meeting in 1919, and named him as a staff correspondent/writer for the Federated Press, a national news agency that supplied mainly labor papers with news of interest to the trade union movement. Marie Howe's name also made the report as a leader in the Woman's Peace Party.⁵

For many years, government agencies and "professional patriots" in private organizations used information and allegations from the Lusk Committee's four-volume report as a source for their own lists of radicals and revolutionaries. Thus the Industrial Defense Association—"Organized to inculcate the principles of Americanism in Industrial, Religious, Fraternal and Educational circles," according to its official publication—condemned the ACLU in 1926 as "the most influential and dangerous among the organizations devoted to destruction" and described the Federated Press as "an international communistic news-gathering organization." Behind both of them squatted "the sinister figure of Russia, pulling the wires and pouring in the money." It cited as evidence the findings of the Lusk Committee and quoted extensively from its report. Naming names, it found Howe guilty of being both an ACLU member and a "Red" exposed by the Overman Committee. Among government agencies, the Radical Division of the federal Department of Justice, directed by the young J. Edgar Hoover, kept its eye on the ACLU and its National Committee members.⁶

4. FCH to L. Hollingsworth Wood, January 10, 1920; Roger Baldwin to FCH, January 13, 1920; FCH to Wood, January 28, 1920, ACLU Papers, Reel 14, Princeton University; 10; R. Baldwin, "Reminiscences," pt. 1, vol. 1, 124, in the Columbia University Oral History Research Office Collection; Lamson, *Roger Baldwin*, 135. With Addams and a number of other "leading men and women of the country who are of the Christian faith," Howe joined in a statement against anti-Semitism and in a request to President Wilson to approve their "condemnation of anti-Semitism as subversive of our American traditions, ideals and institutions." John Spargo to Woodrow Wilson, December 22, 1920, in Link, *Papers of Woodrow Wilson*, 6:540–42.

5. Joint Legislative Committee Investigating Seditious Activities, *Revolutionary Radicalism*, 1:1000, 1076, 1102, 2:1979, 1982, 1989, 1997. On the Lusk Committee, see L. Chamberlain, *Loyalty and Legislative Action*, 9–52. Others listed as correspondents or writers for the Federated Press were Scott Nearing, Anna Louise Strong, Carl Sandburg, and, from the British Labor Party, George Lansbury and E. D. Morel.

6. "American Government and Institutions Are in Danger from Radical Propaganda," *What's What* 1 (September 1926): 1–4. See, for examples of the Radical Division's surveillance, its Bulletin Number 21 for the week ending June 19, 1920. *United States Military Intelligence Reports*, reel 14.

Howe expressed his concern over one aspect of civil liberties in a 1920 *Nation* article entitled "Lynch Law and the Immigrant Alien." He started from the premise that "the test of America's love of liberty is our willingness to insure it to others. Our reverence for Anglo-Saxon justice is to be measured by the way we apply it to those who have never known justice; to those who have no means of protest, no power to which they can appeal for protection." That test failed when applied to the unnaturalized alien, who was "outside the protection of the commonest safeguards which we throw about a criminal. He has no claims on the Bill of Rights; he is not protected by the Constitution." If the economy broke down, he could be deported because he had become a public charge. He could be deported for his political opinions. "A Tolstoy would have to be deported. So would Bernard Shaw. There is scarcely a critical political philosopher in Europe today who would not be deportable under our laws." In the cruel deportation process, the alien had no day in court in which he could tell his story. He had none of the protections of American law—no impartial judge or jury, no indictment by grand jury, no proceedings in open court, no protection against prosecutorial abuses. The immigration inspector, who might be arresting officer, prosecutor, judge, and jury in his case, could be honest and sincere, but he and his fellows were subject to almost irresistible pressure. "They, too, were indicted as 'reds' and revolutionists if they resisted the hysterical clamor of their locality, a clamor supported by the police, by chambers of commerce, and by the press. For we have been trying the alien by hue and cry, by the methods practiced in the South against the Negro. And the immigrant inspector is but human. He wants to live at peace with his community." If the nation was in peril, government action without legal restraints was perhaps justifiable, but there was no evidence of such an emergency. A pattern of wholesale arrests and deportations worked against Americanization "by poisoning the minds of those whom with one voice we profess to desire to free, while with another we deny them the only thing save a job that America means to them."

As he often did, Fred recycled this article, using it in a talk to the Civic Club on April 12, 1920. The indefatigable J. Edgar Hoover's Radical Division took note of the speech, summarized it briefly in its bulletin, and concluded: "As applied to the hearings of aliens at Ellis Island, the statement made by Mr. Howe has, of course, no basis in fact as the hearings are administrative and not judicial."[7]

---

7. FCH, "Lynch Law and the Immigrant Alien"; Bulletin Number 13 for the week ending April 17, 1920, *United States Military Intelligence Reports*, reel 14.

Howe's interest in immigration continued for a time after his departure from his post at Ellis Island. He became a member of the Committee of One Thousand of the National Committee for Constructive Immigration Legislation, an organization founded in 1918 to promote an alternative to

During his last months at Ellis Island, Howe had thought that he would soon be through with politics. Of his ideas at the time, he wrote: "I had seen the government at close range, with its mask off: it existed for itself and for hidden men behind it. . . . It was as dangerous to the innocent as to the guilty. It was frankly doing the bidding of business." The Department of Justice had become "an agency to protect profiteers, high officials, and business men who looked upon the government as their own; it meant crushing liberalism by deportations, arrests, a terrorism of fear. This was the democracy that the boys were to come back to from the trenches. There was no place for the liberal in it." Shortly after his resignation, he told his friend William Kent that "there must be something the matter with politics. I am quite clear that there is, but I don't know what to substitute for it."[8]

Yet he found that he could not abandon his desire for society's improvement, and he continued to dream of the changes he wanted.

> I had a passionate desire for a society of economic freedom, in which every power and talent of man could function freely. I saw the abundant wealth that could be produced with the land opened up by taxation; saw this wealth running freely from one end of the country to the other, with publicly owned railroads operated for service; saw the wealth of all the world enriching the culture of America through free trade. I had a mental passion for a free society, with the state owning a few industries strategic to its life and functioning more as an administrative than a political thing. I hated anything that blocked effort, that levied unnecessary tribute, and interfered with freedom. My passion for these ideas made inactivity impossible to me. I could not be through with politics.

So, at the same time that he resigned as immigration commissioner, he announced that he was going to work for the Plumb Plan.[9]

---

the very restrictive proposals being pushed in Congress. Members along with Howe included such friends as Norman Hapgood, Ida Tarbell, Lillian Wald, William Allen White, Oswald Garrison Villard, and Louis Post. John Higham notes that "even this modest dissent from prevailing views lost force after 1920, and the committee disappeared from sight." Fred wrote articles on the future of immigration in 1922 and 1923, but then the subject dropped from his agenda as well. Higham, *Strangers in the Land,* 303; FCH, "Has the Westward Tide of Peoples Come to an End?"; "Alien." The *Congressional Digest* published an extract from the *Scribner's* article under the title "The Westward Trend of Immigration."

8. *Confessions of a Reformer,* 328; FCH to William Kent, November 19, 1919, William Kent Papers, Yale University Library.

9. *Confessions of a Reformer,* 328–29. In his autobiography, Howe says that he resigned, planned to leave politics, and then began thinking about going to work for the Plumb Plan. However, the evidence clearly shows that he had made that decision before tendering his resignation.

The government takeover of the railroads in December 1917 had left open the question of their postwar fate. Desirous of maintaining wartime gains in wages, members, and bargaining power, railway labor looked with favor on public ownership. For their proposal, the brotherhoods turned to their attorney, Glenn E. Plumb. Like Fred Howe, he was a veteran of the city traction wars. Before going to work for the unions, he had been the counsel for the City of Chicago in its battles with street railway interests.

The Plumb Plan called for the federal government to sell bonds and use the proceeds to purchase the railroads. Reorganized into a unified national system, the lines would be operated by a public corporation whose board of directors would give equal representation to railroad management, the unions, and the general public. The Interstate Commerce Commission would continue to regulate rates. At the end of each year, surplus revenues would be divided equally, one half going to the government for a sinking fund to retire the bonds and the other half going to railroad employees. Plumb saw his plan as a form of industrial democracy that would "supplant the old system of competition under which the profits of the laborer's industry went to another, and in which he could never hope to share, by a new system where the profit of his industry accrued to himself alone, where all employees were united by a common purpose, all working toward a common end, inspired by the same motives, by the same incentives, and with no opportunity for a division of interest and no apprehension that another would reap what he had sown." The four railroad brotherhoods endorsed the plan; set up a Plumb Plan League to drum up grassroots support; published a weekly newspaper, Labor, to make the case for it; lobbied Congress for its passage; and attempted to find allies in other labor and farmer groups.[10]

As a longtime advocate of public ownership, Howe needed little persuasion to give the Plumb Plan his adherence. He was impressed with the caliber of the railroad union leaders, who were "men of bigger personality than many of the men I had known professionally or in business.... They were far more scrupulous; they fought fair; they took pride in keeping their contracts; they had the old-fashioned moralities of my boyhood. They were often trapped through their respect for the law, their reliance on old ethical standards." When he turned in his resignation as immigration commissioner, he could announce that he was

---

10. Plumb, *Labor's Plan*, 9. The pamphlet was based on Plumb's testimony before the Senate Interstate Commerce Committee. See also his "Labor's Solution of the Railroad Problem." On the Plumb Plan generally, see Kerr, *American Railroad Politics*, 160–78; Derber, *American Dream of Industrial Democracy*, 148–51. Former Congressman Edward Keating, who was editor of *Labor* from 1919 to 1953, gives a rather fragmented account of the paper's history in his *Story of "Labor."* On the railroad unions' turn to politics, see Olssen, "Making of a Political Machine."

taking up the post of executive director of the Conference on Democratic Control of the Railroads, an organization set up by the brotherhoods. In a statement released by the Plumb Plan press bureau, he declared: "Steps will be taken to organize about this committee the liberal thought of America on a program of railroad control that will be industrially democratic and that will protect the interest of the public." Only through democratic control of the transportation agencies would industry, farmers, and workers be released from "the endless cycle of higher costs and then higher wages, which will go on indefinitely under the private monopoly control of transportation by persons interested only in profits. Transportation must be an agency of service, and of service alone." Howe was optimistic about the chances of success. He wrote Walter Clark, the chief justice of the North Carolina Supreme Court and the chairman of his executive committee: "The labor forces of the country are mobilizing around democracy and industry very rapidly and irrespective of immediate legislation. The mind of the country is undergoing a substantial change in the right direction."[11]

The Plumb Plan appealed to many independent liberals because of its support for economic democracy, its call for social harmony, and its emphasis on efficiency and administration by experts. Fred became a bridge between those reformers and labor. He asked a number of his friends to join the conference's advisory committee. Perhaps to broaden the appeal of the organization, he noted that the conference would not be committed to any particular plan but would determine its stand after considering a number of proposals.[12]

Some of his friends, like Walter Lippmann and William Kent, responded enthusiastically to his invitation. Others declined to serve on the advisory committee. William Allen White was unwilling to join, writing Fred that he was "as anxious as you to take the control of industry out of the hands of the bankers, but I feel that the community should be primarily interested in the transfer of power rather than anyone else, even the workers." Calling White's reply "a bully letter," Howe sought to answer his objections. The profit motive was not to disappear, as the Emporia editor believed. Profit was to be "re-distributed . . . shared by the officials and men and by the public as well." He opposed the idea that railroad workers should become government employees and pointed to "the deadening effect of public office on the minds of men." It was far better to

---

11. *Confessions of a Reformer*, 329–30; *New York Times*, September 7, 1919, 1; FCH to Walter Clark, September 20, 1919, in Brooks and Lefler, *Papers of Walter Clark*, 2:406. Members of the Conference's executive committee, along with Howe and Clark, were Governor Henry Allen of Kansas, former governors E. F. Dunne of Illinois and Joseph W. Folk of Missouri, Professor E. W. Memis, and Morris L. Cooke.

12. FCH to Felix Frankfurter, September 15, 1919. This was a form letter sent by Howe to a number of people.

leave operations in the hands of the workers. "I personally do not believe in limiting the right of men to strike, for just as soon as you take that right away you make it impossible for them to do anything to better their conditions. . . . We may try to blink it, but class interests are very ascendant, as you know, not only in our politics, but in our thought as well. That is why I am perfectly willing to see teachers, Federal employees and everybody else get into the labor movement as quickly as possible." He had more faith than White in the joys of serving the community: "I have lived in it in Cleveland; I have seen it at Ellis Island. It was in evidence in Washington during the war. All it needs is to be awakened by some motive which I think the Plumb Plan supplies. Everybody has tucked away within himself an unrecognized desire to be of service to the community, and whenever that motive is attacked it comes out very strong."[13] Despite these arguments, White remained outside the fold.

Howe worked hard for the Plumb Plan League and its affiliate, the Conference on Democratic Control of the Railroads. He traveled around the country, arguing for the plan before varied groups. He was disappointed in the response of trade unionists. "I have had some good meetings," he wrote Pinchot, "but the labor meetings, as you probably know, are not nearly as keen as the audiences you get in New York." Howe's speeches often reappeared in the pages of *Labor*. Thus an address to the Academy of Political Science in New York City on November 22, 1919, became an article, "The Railroads, the Public and Labor under the Plumb Plan," in *Labor* on December 6, 1919. A dozen of his articles explaining and advocating cooperatives appeared in *Labor* from January to April 1920. He wrote on the plan for other publications as well, arguing the need for a national transportation policy in the *Nation*, for example. Howe was also a vice president of the Public Ownership League of America, which backed public ownership of the railroads, though it was willing to accept a five-year test period of government operation before a final decision was made.[14]

Despite their best efforts at organizing and politicking, the railroad unions saw the Plumb Plan go down to defeat, without even a vote in Congress on it. They were never able to develop the coalition with major farm organizations

---

13. Walter Lippmann to FCH, September 9, 1919; FCH to Lippmann, September 10, 1919; Lippmann to FCH, September 14, 1919, Lippmann Papers, Yale University Library; William Kent to FCH, December 3, 1919, Kent Papers, Yale University Library; William Allen White to FCH, October 2, 1919; FCH to White, September 29, 1919, White Papers, Library of Congress. Apparently White had stated his objections in a letter prior to October 2, but that has not been found.

14. *New York Times*, October 4, 1919, 2, and November 23, 1919, 16; FCH to Amos Pinchot, October 27, 1919, Amos Pinchot Papers, Box 39; "The Railroads, the Public and Labor"; "Wanted"; form letter to "The Friends of Democracy" from Albert M. Todd, president, the Public Ownership League of America, June 1919, Henry Wadsworth Longfellow Dana Papers, Swarthmore College Peace Collection.

that they had hoped for. Those who relied on the railways for shipping their products feared that the plan meant higher wages and hence higher freight rates, as well as excessive power for labor. The only organized support from agriculture came from the relatively small Farmers National Council, representing mainly a scattering of western farm organizations. Labor's fight was weakened by disunity within its own ranks. The Brotherhood of Railroad Trainmen pulled back its financial support in mid-1919. Although several annual conventions of the American Federation of Labor endorsed the Plumb Plan, Samuel Gompers and his executive council opposed it. The AFL chieftain observed in his autobiography: "The 'intellectuals' filled the highbrow organs with praise, 'Labor to operate the railroads!' The hard-headed and practical saw the old frame of government ownership in a new dress. Again it was my unpleasant task to point out the pitfalls lurking under appealing phrases." Conservative critics branded the plan socialistic. Most newspapers were hostile. The Boston *Evening Transcript*, for example, called it "'Plumb' Bolshevistic."[15] Even some friends of labor rejected the idea of public ownership. John Commons wrote later that he had considered the Plumb Plan and the entry by railroad labor into banking and other business enterprises "destructive of unionism, because they dissipated the strike funds and took labor over to the side of capitalists with a minority vote, leading them, by way of politics, into socialism or communism. At any rate I knew that labor unions had always been unsuccessful when they ventured into business or politics."[16] Though the brotherhoods disavowed socialism, *Labor* printed favorable articles on guild socialism by two of its leading British exponents, G. D. H. Cole and S. G. Hobson.

In any event, a direct threat to the general interests of labor led the brotherhoods to shunt the Plumb Plan to a siding and to close ranks with the AFL. As Congress considered the future of the railroads, it became apparent that the votes were not there for the Plumb Plan. The Senate's Interstate Commerce Committee reported a bill that returned the lines to private ownership. Senator La Follette was the only committee member to sign a minority report. The bill that Congress later considered—known as the Cummins-Esch bill—contained an antistrike provision that was anathema to labor, and in order to fight it, the brotherhoods and the AFL put aside their differences over the Plumb Plan. Their lobbying campaign was successful in getting the antistrike clause dropped from the bill, but the cost was the loss of the Plumb Plan. La Follette's amendment for a two-year extension of federal control received only eleven votes in

15. Gompers, *Seventy Years of Life and Labour*, 148; *Boston Evening Transcript*, February 25, 1919, 10, quoted in Murray, *Red Scare*, 118. A survey of newspaper opposition to the plan can be found in "The Line-Up on the Plumb Plan," *Literary Digest* 62 (August 23, 1919): 12–13.

16. Commons, *Myself*, 168.

the Senate. Congress passed the Cummins-Esch bill in February 1920, and on March 1 the railroads reverted to private ownership.[17]

The Plumb Plan failure must have seemed to Fred Howe another of the many lost causes that he had joined in. Nevertheless, he had found the work quite satisfying. He had come to know the railroad workers as "intelligent, ... courageous, and independent," and he believed that, if their power could be mobilized, they could both improve their standard of living and exert great influence in their communities. "I was particularly interested in co-operation, labor banking, and direct political action," he wrote. Engagement in the battle for the Plumb Plan, and beyond that for a broader scheme of economic democracy, seemed to Fred to bring him a wholeness that his life had lacked.

> For once I was no longer attempting to be in two camps. My convictions and my class were one. As an editorial writer I appealed to men to follow their own interests, to use their collective power for their own well-being. I was no longer appealing to men of my own class to stop exploiting somebody else. I was urging men to free themselves, not persuading some one to give freedom to others. These men had the power if they would use it. They had billions on deposit in the banks. They had great purchasing power and could organize stores, even factories, for themselves. They could join hands with the farmers, and develop direct bargaining.

He felt the same enthusiasm for the vision of a cooperative commonwealth that he had earlier felt for the city. "I saw a state within a state, creating its own economic life, massing its own power, using it to build up a co-operative society inside the political state. I had the same kind of dream of order that I had had in the city, only it was the order of a class rather than a locality. I was working with a group whose ideals and interests were alike instead of with men whose ideals and interests were diverse."[18]

Howe's interest in cooperatives had grown from his prewar observations of them in Europe (especially in Denmark), as well as from his belief that freedom required both economic and political democracy. "Cooperation gripped me as Socialism had not. It was voluntary, open to individual initiative; it trained leaders and minimized the state. Apparently it achieved all the ends that Socialism promised and left the individual free from bureaucratic control. I saw labor and the farmer rising to political power through the training which co-operation gave."[19]

---

17. On the fight over railroad legislation in 1919–20, see Kerr, *American Railroad Politics*, 204–27; Kennedy, *Over Here*, 256–58; La Follette and La Follette, *Robert M. La Follette*, 2:985–99.
18. *Confessions of a Reformer*, 330–31.
19. Ibid., 332.

Howe was fortunate that the ideas of Warren Stone, the leader of the Brotherhood of Locomotive Engineers, tended in the same direction. The grand chief had been one of the organizers of a farmer-labor conference that met in Chicago in November 1919. From that conclave came the All-American Farmer-Labor Co-Operative Commission, formed in January 1920. Stone was treasurer; the other officers were drawn from the brotherhoods and those farm organizations that had supported the Plumb Plan. Union leaders saw the organization as one that would attack the high cost of living by promoting cooperative buying, production, and distribution. It aimed at conducting "a vigorous campaign for direct dealing between farm producers and city consumers and, as soon as feasible, between city producers and farm consumers."[20] Howe became executive secretary of the Commission's Committee on Banking and Credit, which Stone chaired.

For some time, the Engineers union had had plans to establish a cooperative bank; but action had been postponed because of the war. In late 1919 or early 1920, Stone employed Howe to lay the groundwork for the bank. As he recounted:

> I spent six months in this study. I saw the power of credit in private hands, saw its possibilities when dedicated exclusively to productive uses. Credit was power in the modern world; through the mobilization of the credit power of labor co-operative enterprises could be started, homes built, talent encouraged, and men equipped with tools, machines, and capital. And labor had colossal deposits at its disposal, which only needed to be mobilized and dedicated to new ends. I suggested a co-operative bank with dividends limited to ten per cent; a bank that would distribute some of its earnings back to depositors and that would utilize its resources exclusively for productive uses.

The Brotherhood's executive board approved the proposal, and together Howe and Stone drew up the necessary papers. In June 1920 the Engineers could announce the federal Treasury Department's approval of an application for a charter for "The Brotherhood of Locomotive Engineers Co-operative National Bank of Cleveland, Ohio," capitalized at one million dollars.[21] The bank was an immediate success, and other banks were purchased or organized in New York, Minneapolis, and Hammond, Indiana. The union went on to develop a coal mine and other enterprises.

---

20. Bert M. Jewell, an officer of the Commission, quoted in *New York Times*, January 8, 1920, 1.
21. *Confessions of a Reformer*, 333; *New York Times*, June 29, 1920, 17.

Howe worked at promoting these ventures and presenting the merits of cooperatives to labor and farm groups. For the Engineers he wrote a pamphlet, *Banking for Service: The Need of Banks for Workers and Farmers and the Service They Can Render,* in which he explained in simple terms the nature of banking and pointed to the merits of cooperative banks. Banks operating for the nation's good would spend their money in their localities. The money would be loaned to the people of the community—farmers, merchants, workers—instead of being used for speculation. "It would build homes, it would go out to the man of no capital, if he could furnish good security. . . . We will never have a proper banking system until the control of credit is invested with a public trust and is so controlled that it will be used to aid people rather than exploit them." Credit was the life of society. Our economic life depended on it. "That is why banking must be under some kind of public control."[22]

Pushing for changes in state laws to allow the formation of cooperative banks, he argued that no banking reform could be expected from Congress. "There are too many bankers in Congress. They seem to be everywhere. If a man is not a director he is a stockholder. And if he is not a stockholder, he is very profoundly responsive to the bankers of his locality, who use their power to keep him in a state of fear."[23] By the mid-1920s, Howe believed cooperative banks to be a success. The example of the Engineers had been followed by the Amalgamated Clothing Workers, the Railway Clerks and Telegraphers, and other labor groups. "Soon there were nearly thirty labor banks throughout the country, with resources of close to a hundred million dollars."[24]

22. FCH, *Banking for Service,* 13.
23. FCH to Charles McCarthy, October 21, 1920, Ely Papers. Howe's views on banking were attacked by George E. Roberts, vice president of the National City Bank of New York, in an article in *Nation's Business,* later republished as a pamphlet. Howe's writings on banks "reveal the kind of thinking that a restless, speculative type of mind may do if isolated from practical affairs," he wrote. "The constant outpouring of such misrepresentations has harmful effects. It is the kind of writing which sets the world awry." Roberts, "Banking Fancies—and the Facts," 34, 36, 38.
24. *Confessions of a Reformer,* 333. Milton Derber calls the Engineers' banks "disastrous failures," but the Amalgamated Clothing Workers' banks did well. *American Idea of Industrial Democracy,* 245. Selig Perlman and Philip Taft report the fate of the Engineers' banking ventures: "By 1925 the parent bank in Cleveland realized that its portfolio left much to be desired. To put itself on a sounder basis it was decided to invest heavily in Florida land. The membership, too, would be given the opportunity to grow rich from Florida investments. A town poetically called Venice was built and widely advertised as a 'New Eden' in the *Locomotive Engineers' Journal.* Unfortunately the New Eden was completed at a heavy cost just on the eve of the expulsion of the unsuspecting Adams and Eves. Rumblings of the collapse of the whole huge edifice had been heard as early as 1926, but the extent of the *débâcle* was not known until after the convention of 1927 set up a Committee of Ten to disclose the unvarnished truth. . . . The disclosures revealed a story of incompetence and unfathomable recklessness of those who had come to imagine themselves as Napoleons of finance. . . . Thus ended the dream of beating capitalism at its own game. In March, 1930, the parent institution, the Engineers' National Bank of Cleveland, merged with a non-labor bank." *Labor Unions,* 576–77. Benjamin Marsh noted that Warren Stone, who died in 1925, was "vigorously opposed to having

Howe undertook to show the feasibility of cooperatives as a solution to economic and social problems in his *Denmark: A Cooperative Commonwealth*, published in January 1921. "Denmark seems to me to be quite the most valuable political exhibit in the modern world. It should be studied by statesmen," he wrote. "Denmark is one of the few countries in the world that is using its political agencies in an intelligent conscious way for the promotion of the economic well being, the comfort and the culture of the people." He described the role of Danish cooperatives, piling fact upon fact (the number of fowl in the country, the total amount paid for pigs by the cooperative slaughterhouses, etc.). Admitting that Denmark was not a paradise and that some poverty remained, he argued that Danes had the opportunity to rise from humble beginnings. So too could Americans if they turned toward cooperatives and some necessary state intervention. Of course, they could not simply adopt the Danish experiments in their entirety—American conditions were different. "The struggle in this country will be far more bitter than it was in Denmark, for the exploiting agencies with us are far more powerfully organized, they have a stronger strangle-hold on politics, the press and on our industrial life than they did in little Denmark a generation ago."

The American farmer had to enter politics as his Danish counterpart had done. He had to look after his own interests, for no one else would look after them for him. Reliance on existing parties had left him the prey to privileged groups and interests. "Having no political power he has lost his economic power. He has been exploited by one group after another until he is shorn of the dignity and standing that he had for many generations." Denmark was an experiment station in freedom, Howe concluded, "a demonstration that the political state can be used by democracy for its own ends. It can be used as an agency for culture and education, as an agency for developing home ownership and farm ownership, as an agency of justice in all of the relations of life." Denmark had abolished privilege and ended many of the economic injustices resulting from privilege. "With privilege abolished democracy has taken its rightful place. And democracy has ushered in a larger degree of economic justice than in any other country in the world."[25]

---

the Engineers Bank make its disastrous plunge in real-estate in Sarasota, Florida." *Lobbyist for the People*, 86. See also R. Richardson, *Locomotive Engineer*, 376–83.

25. *Denmark: A Cooperative Commonwealth*, iii–iv, 183, 196, 198–99.

Reviewers did not find *Denmark* as valuable as Howe's other books, though they tended to recognize its usefulness as a compendium of facts. The *Outlook*'s review thought that Denmark's remarkable progress offered "a lesson, well presented in this book, which American publicists, statesmen, industrialists, and citizens generally should learn and take to heart." *Outlook* 128 (May 11, 1921): 72. According to the *Freeman*, "what distinguishes Dr. Howe's book from others on the same subject is the fact that he never loses sight of fundamental principles. Co-operation in Denmark he shows, has succeeded because it is based on democracy." *Freeman* 4 (January 11, 1922): 428.

As his postwar enthusiasm for labor grew, Howe became convinced that the unions had to resort to independent political action if their economic and social goals were to be attained. He had been thinking about a new party based on labor for some time. He had followed closely the origin and growth of the British Labour Party and, like many Progressives, welcomed its program for postwar reconstruction, "Labour and the New Social Order." In the spring of 1916, he had suggested that the Committee on Industrial Relations become the nucleus for an alliance of single taxers and trade unionists. The goal of the new organization would be the election to Congress of prolabor members. The plan was discussed in a circle that included Howe, Frank Walsh, Dante Barton, George Record, and John White, president of the miners' union, but it was shelved by the need to mobilize progressive forces for the reelection of Woodrow Wilson. Fred did not drop the idea completely, however. In the summer of 1916, in an article about the gains being made by American labor, he wrote of "a quiet movement" underway to increase the size of the labor group in Congress, "with the aim of holding the balance of power on economic and industrial questions." It would be a class-conscious, but not a socialist, delegation. "Should the next House of Representatives be evenly divided between the two old parties, such a group might lay the foundations for a real labor party in America; a party that thinks in terms of organized labor rather than socialism, and that makes common cause for advanced labor legislation, for government ownership of the natural monopolies, and for a program of social legislation like that of Germany and Great Britain."[26]

After Wilson's victory, Howe resumed his quest for a new party. To John Spargo, who had left the Socialist Party because of its stand on the war and who was now trying to form a new party, he sent suggestions for its platform. He

---

The *Literary Review* observed: "They do many things surprisingly well in Denmark, and anyone wishing to become familiar with their ways can do so by reading this volume. It is as full of facts as a 'World almanac' and in moralizing is the equal of John Bunyan." *Literary Review* (April 30, 1921): 11. The *Survey* praised "Mr. Howe's usual lucid style," but concluded that the book's chapter on Denmark's lessons for the United States was unsatisfactory. "It does not with sufficient directness point out exactly how the measures that have succeeded to overcome [problems] in Denmark may best be applied here." The volume had "a high educational value and is to be recommended especially for use in agricultural colleges and normal schools." *Survey* 46 (September 24, 1921): 718. The *New York Times* gave *Denmark* a five-column review that was almost entirely summary. *New York Times*, May 29, 1921, sec. 3, 8. Finding the book "not statistically exact nor scientifically accurate" and "superficial" in its application to the United States, the *American Economic Review* concluded that the material on Denmark was nevertheless "very well compiled and presented and merits wide popular reading." *American Economic Review* 11 (September 1921): 504. Reviewing *Denmark* and *Revolution and Democracy* together, the *American Political Science Review* commented: "After reading Mr. Howe's books one is inclined to believe that Shakespeare was wrong and Barnum was right. There is nothing rotten in the state of Denmark, and the great American public likes to be humbugged." *American Political Science Review* 15 (August 1921): 453.

26. FCH, "Wage-Earner's Innings," 298.

probably had little more to do with Spargo's enterprise, judging from a letter of Albert Jay Nock to Pinchot. Nock wrote that the Chicago convention of the new party looked "pretty negative, both as furnishing the rousing note of protest and also of squarely facing issues that I cant [sic] somehow feel that our Adullamites are really much in earnest about. So I reckon you and Fred are pretty right in being lukewarm; I am lukewarm too, to tell the truth. . . . The ship rolls dreadfully, and my innards with it."[27] Fred also submitted detailed suggestions for its legislative program to the Non-Partisan League, which had become a neo-Populist political force in North Dakota and Minnesota. In a letter to Arthur Le Sueur, the League's executive secretary, he expressed his belief that the producers must gain political control, with a program worked out on "quasi-cooperative" rather than "state socialistic" lines. "I should not be so fearful of state socialism if the political machinery were better adjusted to our purposes or if the producing classes had more cohesive training, as they have in some European countries. In addition, there are substantial ethical reasons for emphasizing the cooperative as opposed to the state-socialistic motive."[28]

By 1919, according to his autobiography, Fred had come to support fully the movement for a new party. In his case, this meant a labor party, "a party of primary producers, of workers and farmers, of men whose economic interests would exile war from the earth, at home as well as abroad." His desire for such a party strengthened as he worked with trade union leaders for the Plumb Plan and for cooperative banks. His mind exercised "its old affinity for fortifying facts and ideas," he wrote. A party of primary producers was the last step in political evolution, justified historically and scientifically. Kings had given way to landed aristocracies, which had been supplanted in their turn by the commercial classes. Farmers and workers constituted a natural economic class that should form its own party and send its own members to Congress to serve the great majority of the people. "Individuals of the new group might be selfish like other men—dishonest; but collectively they had to follow the economic needs

27. Draft form letter to "Dear Friend" from John Spargo, September 14, 1917, Pinchot Papers; Albert Jay Nock to Amos Pinchot, September 21, 1917. J. A. Hopkins urged Fred to go to the Chicago meeting but there is no indication that Fred attended. J. A. Hopkins to Amos Pinchot, enclosing letter to FCH, September 21, 1917, Pinchot Papers.

28. FCH to Arthur Le Sueur, April 22, 1918, courtesy Arthur Le Sueur Papers, Minnesota Historical Society. Le Sueur wanted very badly for Howe to come to Minnesota and work on developing the program, writing that "he is one man in the United States who can and ought to be of tremendous service in carrying out the practical program that we are driving at, and that if it is possible for him to give us a month or two now it would be of tremendous value and we are ready to tread and have you get busy with us if you can. . . . Now dod gast it, let there be no ifs nor ands nor buts." Le Sueur to FCH, July 23, 1918. There is no evidence that Howe answered this plea, even though the League was willing to pay him for his time. Of course, he was still employed as immigration commissioner in July 1918, and planning to go to Europe in the fall. See also Le Sueur to FCH, July 8, 1918, and FCH to Le Sueur, July 12, 1918.

of their class. They represented the many, not the few. They would have to oppose exploiting agencies and the private monopoly of natural resources." The interests and instincts of a labor party would be "to produce as much wealth as possible, to distribute it as equitably as possible; to insure a free field and no favors to themselves and their children. It was my old dream of equal opportunity."[29]

In his quest for a new political alignment, Fred found himself with a foot in each of two camps of advocates for a third party. One camp was made up of the people with whom he had worked in reform causes since 1912 or before, people like Amos Pinchot, George Record, and the single taxers. Many of these were now members of a new political organization, the Committee of Forty-Eight. The other camp was made up of socialists and former socialists, leaders of such farm organizations as the Non-Partisan League, and labor leaders activized politically by their wartime experiences. The two groups agreed on specific reforms, but their accord on many issues obscured some basic ideological conflicts. The "independent Progressives," to use Eugene M. Tobin's nomenclature, thought in terms of general social harmony, and their leaders were chary of politics based on the interests of a particular class. Hence they were inhospitable to the idea of a labor party. On the other hand, farmer and labor leaders who were looking for new political avenues supported formation of a party that based itself firmly on the interests of those whom Howe called the producing classes. Many liberals found themselves somewhere in between the two groups, and the disagreements were often greater between the leaders than among the rank-and-file.

Taking the initiative in founding the Committee of Forty-Eight was J. A. H. Hopkins, who had been national treasurer of Teddy Roosevelt's executive committee in the 1912 Bull Moose campaign and who, after the Progressives' ill-fated electoral ventures in 1916 and 1918, had become custodian of the party's name and assets. Authorized to turn them over to "the first political re-organization conforming to our principles," he had decided that the opportunity for a new party had come in January 1919. Then, "a number of people, feeling that the Democratic Administration had been a failure as far as meeting present industrial and economic problems were concerned, and having no faith whatsoever

---

29. *Confessions of a Reformer*, 329, 333–35. Although he advocated a new party, Howe was not opposed to other efforts to unite Progressives before a political realignment came about. Thus he wrote to Senator La Follette in the fall of 1920 suggesting "a meeting in the middle west ... to frame up a programme of state legislation of the half dozen states that seem to promise results. The conference should include not only the Non Partisan league, your friends and associates, but representatives of the strong farmers organizations and labor. There are a half dozen things I am sure we could agree on and if we can get a belt of states across the country committed to a like programme we will have begun to eat into the system." FCH to Robert M. La Follette, October 31, 1920, La Follette Papers.

in the elasticity of the Republican Party, gathered to discuss ways and means of political action that would answer the needs of the day. The Committee of Forty-Eight was the result."[30] Hopkins brought together at dinner meetings a number of veterans of liberal causes, including in the early ones Pinchot, Record, Will Durant, Dudley Field Malone, John Haynes Holmes, Allen McCurdy, and Arthur Garfield Hays. With Hopkins providing most of the money for it, the Committee soon had a headquarters at 15 East Fortieth Street in New York City. During the spring and summer of 1919, it published announcements in liberal journals and sent out letters to people it thought might be interested. Organization meetings recruited new members who were asked to suggest others who might join. Hopkins, Pinchot, Record, and McCurdy formed the nucleus of the group, though it soon included within its ranks a varied lot of other reformers. If Fred Howe had not been spending most of his time in Washington on Plumb Plan affairs, he would likely have been a part of the Committee's inner circle. As it was, he became a member of its national committee and lent his name to the organization's activities.

In March 1919 the Committee of Forty-Eight called for a gathering of leaders of American "liberal thought" to devise a program. After distributing ten thousand copies of a questionnaire on political issues, it announced that a national conference would meet in St. Louis in December. Overcoming threats to the assembly by American Legion members, the delegates, led by Pinchot and Record, proceeded to draft a platform. Arthur Garfield Hays described the hearings that preceded its completion:

> We sat up long hours listening to every variety of crank suggestion presented as the only road to salvation. We heard from single-taxers and birth-controllers, from health enthusiasts, gymnosophists, nudists, fundamentalists and scientists, from back-to-nature and forward-to-technology orators, from silver, gold, and fiat-money adherents. One delegate proposed the building of an Arcadian highway around the world with little

---

30. J. A. H. Hopkins to Kenneth Campbell MacKay, June 12, 1923, in MacKay, *Progressive Movement of 1924*, 57; interview with Hopkins, *New York Times*, July 4, 1920, sec. VII, 2; See also Durant, *Transition*, 296–306.

Arthur Garfield Hays recounted the origin of the group's name: "We talked Progressive politics until well into the night, but none of our discussions of policies and programs equaled in length or intensity the matter of selecting a name. 'The Committee of Forty-Eight' was finally picked on as a compromise, indicating that we had representation in the forty-eight states of the Union, an optimistic bit of wishful naming. The public, to be sure, generally thought that the name meant that we had but forty-eight members. The size of the organization always was the butt of jokes. I once appeared at a Socialist summer camp together with Hopkins. As we walked up the path to the meeting hall, Morris Hillquit, the shrewd and skeptical Socialist chief, announced: 'Here comes the leader—and the membership—of the Committee of Forty-Eight.'" Hays, *City Lawyer*, 251.

houses, each with its own garden, dotting the road, as a path to international understanding and a method to end war. The suggestion was made that we should set up as our standard a sign from a near-by candy store: "If there's a nut, we have it."[31]

Eschewing all such fads, the platform's introductory section announced the conference's purpose "to formulate and present to the American people a program of political action that is honest, workable and fundamental. Such a program must be economic in nature, since the ills from which the country suffers are largely economic. Reforms in the political machinery itself will not meet the need." Measures to reduce the high cost of living and to control the trusts would not come from the two old parties, since an "invisible government" of the same economic forces controlled both of them. The conference adopted a platform with three planks: (1) public ownership of transportation, other public utilities, and the principal natural resources; (2) taxes to force idle land into use—"no land (including natural resources) and no patents to be held out of use for speculation or to aid monopoly"; (3) "equal economic, political and legal rights for all, irrespective of sex or color," immediate restoration of free speech, press, assembly, and other civil rights; abolition of injunctions in labor cases; and endorsement of "the effort of labor to share in the management of industry and labor's right to organize and bargain collectively through representatives of its own choosing."[32] After unanimously adopting this platform, the delegates adjourned to turn their efforts to creating a coalition of liberals, labor, and single taxers.

Agents from Military Intelligence and the Justice Department kept a watchful eye on the activities of the Committee of Forty-Eight. In April 1919 one of them posed as a freelance reporter, visited the group's headquarters, and talked with Allen McCurdy about the organization. Another reported on the Committee's dinner meeting of May 3. Surveillance continued throughout 1919 and 1920, and several of the reports referred to Committee members as "parlor Bolshevik" types. Among individuals, Fred Howe came in for his share of attention. J. Edgar Hoover's agents referred to him as the "Plumb Plan agitator" and monitored his speeches and writings.[33]

31. Ibid., 256.
32. "Platform and Statement of Aims, Adopted by the National Conference of the Committee of Forty-Eight at St. Louis, December 11, 1919," Mercer Johnston Papers, Library of Congress.
33. See United States Military Intelligence Reports, reel 12 (memo of April 23, 1919; report of May 3, 1919), reel 14 (surveillance of Committee of Forty-Eight convention, Chicago, July 13, 1920), reel 16 (Bulletin No. 8 on Radical Activities, period from March 1 to March 13, 1920; Bulletin No. 14, for week ending May 1, 1920; Bulletin No. 21, for week ending June 19, 1920. See also Belknap, "Mechanics of Repression"; Williams, "Bureau of Investigation and Its Critics"; Gentry, *J. Edgar Hoover,* 70–105; Powers, *Secrecy and Power,* 44–92.

Besides canvassing its members for their opinions on such issues as American entry into the League of Nations, the release of political prisoners, universal military training, and universal disarmament, the Committee early in 1920 took a poll on their choices for presidential and vice-presidential candidates. Tabulated in June, the returns from 1,500 questionnaires showed Senator La Follette as the favorite (259 first choices and 51 second choices, for a total of 310), followed by Herbert Hoover (177 total), Senator Hiram Johnson (155), and Eugene Debs (151). Fred Howe was eighth on the list (28 total—22 first choices and 6 second choices). Though far behind the top four, he was perhaps pleased that he had outpaced such other reform stalwarts or national figures as Amos Pinchot, McAdoo, Post, Record, Brandeis, Whitlock, and senators Borah and Capper. He was ninth among vice-presidential choices, receiving 23 votes (the front-runner, former governor Lynn Frazier of North Dakota, had 62).[34]

Negotiations to bring together into a new party the Committee of Forty-Eight, the Non-Partisan League, and the National Labor Party fell apart in Chicago in July 1920. The Forty-Eighters split over joining the Labor group, as Pinchot, Record, and others rejected the idea of a "class" party. On his return from Chicago, Pinchot told reporters that the Committee of Forty-Eight had been "infiltrated by a lot of honest, well meaning mushheads." To all intents and purposes, the Chicago debacle ended the Committee of Forty-Eight, although it lingered on for a few years. Fed up, Pinchot resigned in November 1920, writing a friend: "I do not want again to be off shore in a boat without a compass, and with the quartermaster steering consistently for the breakers. I am willing to pull oar, but not in that direction."[35]

Though much interested in the third-party movement, Fred Howe was only peripherally concerned in its activities in 1919 and 1920. Besides his work for the Plumb Plan and cooperative banking, he had taken on another responsibility as he involved himself in the campaign for the independence of Ireland. As soon as President Wilson embraced the principle of national self-determination, Irish Americans began to demand its application to their homeland. They organized mass meetings and applied pressure to both the president and Congress. They became increasingly bitter when the Versailles Treaty failed to recognize their demand. In Ireland itself, nationalists had set up a republic under Eamon de Valera. The British government refused to recognize it, and violence escalated

---

34. Results of the poll can be found in the Mercer Johnston Papers.
35. Amos Pinchot, statement to press, July 16, 1920, La Follette Family Papers; Hays, *City Lawyer*, 263; Amos Pinchot to Frank Stephens, December 3, 1920, Pinchot Papers. After Pinchot's departure from Chicago, the convention agreed to call its new entity the Farmer-Labor party and, when Senator La Follette declined its nomination, named Parley Christensen its presidential candidate. The national ticket received only about 265,000 votes in the 1920 election.

in the so-called Anglo-Irish War of 1919–21, in which Irish Americans strongly backed the republican forces.

The editor of the *Nation*, Oswald Garrison Villard, was a fervent apostle of self-determination. Shocked by the brutal methods of British mercenaries, the Black and Tans, he called in his journal in the fall of 1919 for creation of a hundred-member committee to study conditions in Ireland. He expressed fear that the Irish issue might ultimately lead to war between the United States and Britain.[36] Once set up and with its numbers enlarged to nearly 150 members of Congress, governors, mayors, clergymen, lawyers, businessmen, labor leaders, professors, and writers, that organization selected a smaller group of five persons (later increased to eight) to conduct the inquiry. The American Commission on Conditions in Ireland's members were Jane Addams, senators David G. Walsh and George W. Norris, L. Hollingsworth Wood (chairman of the Commission, a lawyer who was a founding member of the ACLU, the American Friends Service Committee, and the Urban League), James H. Maurer (president of the Pennsylvania State Federation of Labor), Norman Thomas, Major Oliver P. Newman (former president of the Board of Commissioners of the District of Columbia), and, as vice chairman, Frederic C. Howe.

Fred probably had no reluctance to serve on the Commission. He had long been a friend to the Irish, from his boyhood days when he envied the freedom of the "wild, delightful Irish boys," to his friendship with Jerry, the Irish bartender in New York City, and his observations of the Irish political role there, to his good times with Patsy Sheehan when reading law in Meadville, to his respect for Irish immigrants at Ellis Island. Entitling a chapter in his 1925 autobiography "My Friends the Irish," he wrote that "in the decades that have passed since that illuminating winter [of 1892 in New York City] I have never ceased to like the Irish. I should not like to think of America with them left out."[37]

Howe presided over a number of the Commission's sessions, held in Washington in November and December 1920 and January 1921. At the first hearing on November 18, he announced the group's purpose and plans: "Conditions in Ireland have profoundly stirred millions of American citizens of Irish descent. They have created and are creating a widening rift in the friendly relations of English speaking peoples, not only in America but all over the world. . . . The Commission has set itself to the task of ascertaining the facts. It plans to learn as nearly as possible just what the conditions in Ireland are and what has brought them about."[38]

36. *Nation* 111 (September 25, 1920): 340. Nearly every subsequent issue has a story about the Commission's activity.
37. *Confessions of a Reformer*, 60.
38. *Nation* 111 (December 15, 1920): 703–4.

The British government refused to recognize the Commission or to cooperate in its investigations, and it would not allow a subcommittee to visit Ireland. As a consequence, nearly all those who testified were sympathetic to Irish independence, and soon the record was filled with accounts of victimizations and malevolent actions by British troops and their cohorts. Irish Americans supported the Commission, but others found little to approve in the group's work. Critics charged it not only with meddling in matters that were not its concern but also with taking the side of Sinn Fein and the Irish republicans against the British and with encouraging and increasing anti-British sentiments in the United States. Howe found himself heckled when he spoke on the Irish question at a Community Church forum. He responded: "Ireland is a nation—economically, politically, judicially and essentially a nation. . . . She is developing a new culture, which under oppression is becoming something very fine." The Irish issue had been "manufactured by the interests," he charged. The republicans' de facto government was functioning, and sooner or later Ireland would win its freedom. Though these remarks by one of its members may have appeared one-sided, the Commission maintained that it was performing its task in a nonpolitical and even-handed way. In a letter to Wood, Howe indicated that he had something more in mind than just collecting the facts: "We can go a long way toward molding and shaping American opinion on the Irish question, and in giving character and standing to the Irish movement, by placing this report in the hands of thousands of persons who will be influenced by it."[39]

The Commission's report, published in March 1921, concluded that "the Irish people are deprived of the protection of British law, to which they would be entitled as subjects of the British King. They are likewise deprived of the moral protection granted by international law to which they would be entitled as belligerents. They are at the mercy of the imperial British forces, which, acting contrary both to all law and to all standards of human conduct, have instituted in Ireland a 'terror.'" The report called for an end to violence, withdrawal of troops, release of political prisoners, and transfer of responsibility for law and order to "Irish local elected bodies, thus creating conditions under which the Irish people may determine their own form of government."[40] The Commission noted that its work had been impeded by inability to secure pro-British witnesses and by the British government's failure to participate and its ban on travel to Ireland by the Commission.

39. Villard, *Fighting Years,* 487; *New York Times,* January 24, 1921, 3; FCH to L. Hollingsworth Wood, February 2, 1921, Wood Papers, Haverford College Library. See also Humes, *Oswald Garrison Villard,* 233–41.
40. American Commission on Conditions in Ireland, *Evidence on Conditions in Ireland,* 625. Records of the Commission's activities can be found in the L. Hollingsworth Wood Papers, Haverford College Library.

A statement from the British Embassy held that the report was "entitled to exactly the amount of weight which should be given to any judgment based entirely upon the evidence of ex parte statements put forward for the most part by persons admittedly holding extreme views. It is biased and wholly misleading, both in its general conclusions and in the statements it contains in matters of detail." In London, the Chief Secretary for Ireland repeated the gist of the Embassy comment, adding: "I need hardly say the commission has no official character and therefore affords no occasion for representations from his Majesty's Government."[41] Villard believed that the Commission's work had been constructive and was much pleased by the judgment Albert Shaw delivered some years later. "This was a difficult undertaking and, in the end, it was proved to be a remarkable achievement," Shaw wrote. "This commission, composed of men and women of great influence, assembled a mass of testimony that could not be refuted. Mr. Lloyd George realized that the time had come for a truce to be followed by an arrangement far more favorable to Ireland than had been proposed in the Home Rule programs of Parnell and Gladstone."[42]

As his work for the Plumb Plan and the Ireland commission wound down, Howe could once again involve himself in the movement for a third party. This time the impetus for that endeavor came from men with whom he was closely associated, the leaders of the railroad brotherhoods. Early in 1922 a committee representing the fifteen unions issued an invitation to a "conference of Progressives" to meet in Chicago in February. The conference's goal was "to discuss and adopt a fundamental economic program designed to restore to the people the sovereignty that is rightly theirs, to make effective the purpose for which our Government is established, to secure to all men the enjoyment of the gain which their industry produces." Using cautious language, the brotherhood leaders declared: "This is not an attempt to form a new political party. It is an effort to make use of those constructive forces already in existence and by cooperation bring about political unity."

The broadly worded invitation aimed at attracting as many as possible of the varied body of liberals and reformers without raising divisive issues of program or tactics. The three hundred delegates to the Conference for Progressive Political Action (CPPA) came from labor unions, farm organizations, the Non-Partisan League, the Committee of Forty-Eight, the Socialist Party (after some debate about participation), the Methodist Federation of Social Service, the National Catholic Welfare Council, the Farmer-Labor Party, the Church League for Industrial Democracy, the single taxers. On its first day, the conclave appointed

---

41. *New York Times*, April 2, 1921, 3; April 9, 1921, 2.
42. Albert Shaw to Oswald Garrison Villard, October 17, 1938, in *Fighting Years*, 490–91.

a Committee on Organization, chaired by Fred Howe. Next day, that Committee recommended appointment of a Committee of Fifteen to give national leadership and to work with local organizations. It also called for a second national conference of the CPPA, to meet in December 1922. It suggested that those invited to attend should represent a broad collection of progressive organizations. The delegates adopted the report and elected the Committee of Fifteen. William H. Johnston of the Machinists union became its chairman, Warren Stone of the Locomotive Engineers its treasurer, and Howe its secretary. The labor unions had seven representatives on the committee (four from the railroad brotherhoods, plus Sidney Hillman of the clothing workers, William Green of the mine workers, and Agnes Nestor of the Women's Trade Union League). One member each came from the Farmer Labor Party, the Socialist Party, and the Non-Partisan League. Four "independents"—Howe, Benjamin Marsh, Basil M. Manly, and Edward Keating—were men with considerable experience in organization for reform battles, as well as close ties to labor.[43]

The CPPA's first conference also adopted a brief platform that reiterated the principles of the Declaration of Independence and applied them to contemporary America. After a litany of charges against the ruling oligarchy, it concluded that "our government of right ought to be administered for the common good and for the protection, prosperity, and happiness of the people; that its present usurpation by the invisible government of plutocracy and privilege must be broken; that this can be best accomplished by united political action suited to the peculiar conditions and needs of each section and state." To that end, the delegates pledged themselves "to organize for the coming campaign in every state and congressional district, so that this may become once more in very truth a government of the people, for the people, and by the people."[44] The meetings were harmonious as the delegates sought common ground. No one pushed very hard for any issue that was likely to be divisive or to arouse ideological debate. The question of a third party was deferred, even though most delegates seemed to assume it as the ultimate aim. It was agreed that the conference in December, meeting after the congressional elections, would have a better idea of exactly how to proceed. In the meantime, the CPPA would endorse and work for Progressive candidates for Congress throughout the country.

As CPPA secretary, Fred Howe threw himself into the work of organizing. He had his own view of how the seeds of a third party should be planted and nourished. He thought that "labor should begin at the bottom, in city and State

---

43. The name of the Committee's fifteenth member, Mrs. Mabel (Edward P.) Costigan, soon disappeared from the list, although she remained active in the CPPA.

44. "Declaration of Principles Adopted by the Conference for Progressive Political Action, Chicago, February 20–21, 1922," in MacKay, *Progressive Movement of 1924*, app. 2, 269.

elections; that in national affairs it should concentrate its power on congressmen and build up a labor-farmer bloc in Congress." He urged the nomination of "dirt farmers, actual workers rather than liberals outside of the ranks." The necessary preliminary training for members of the party would be gained in city, state, and congressional elections. "Gains of this kind would not be lost. In time we would have the group system in Congress; ultimately workers and farmers, being in the majority, would control it. Then a third party would come. It could probably come, I thought, in no other way."[45] The CPPA's instructions to its supporters to back Progressive candidates in the 1922 elections did not explicitly commit the group to forming a third party, but they certainly tended in that direction and fitted in with Howe's goal.

It was no small measure of the respect other Progressives had for Fred Howe that within the national committee a large share of responsibility for organizing fell upon him. He was well prepared for it through his past experience in state and local politics, the National Progressive Republican League, and the Plumb Plan, as well as through his wide circle of acquaintances in political life throughout the nation. His tasks included developing propaganda that could be used by the disparate elements in the nascent third-party movement, building up and encouraging local organizations (which often meant mediating between discordant factions and securing their cooperation toward the common goal), and providing aid for Progressive candidates insofar as this could be done by a national headquarters with very limited resources.

Howe was optimistic but realistic about the organizing activities. To Morris Hillquit (the Socialist Party's representative on the CPPA national committee), he observed that he felt "very well satisfied with the way things are going. The results are spotty. Some places there is every evidence of movement being permanently grounded on the right foundations; in other places they are ephemeral. Wherever the movement is a group movement, and wherever the Nonpartisan League and the Socialists have done a lot of preliminary work, things are going amazingly well." This he thought was true in Texas, Oklahoma, Wyoming, and the Dakotas. Things were also going well in Iowa, Minnesota, and Pennsylvania. "In a lot of other states, preliminary work is being done. It may or may not yield results. Incidentally a lot of municipal movements have gotten started and in a number of towns the entire labor ticket has been nominated. A great many labor men have been nominated for Assembly, and quite a number for Congress. Speaking generally I should say that things are proceeding quite naturally and that we are planting seed rather than getting ready for the harvest." There were financial problems, however. "We have generous promises

---

45. *Confessions of a Reformer*, 335.

of support, but very little money has, as yet, come through. However, we are proceeding as though we would be adequately financed for a twelve-month's campaign."[46]

The organizing efforts of Howe and others and the vigorous campaigning by labor unions, socialists, and many state and local groups paid off for the CPPA in the fall 1922 elections. Of the 27 candidates for the United States Senate whom it had endorsed, 23 were elected. Some 170 of its favored candidates won for the House of Representatives. Twelve of 16 CPPA-backed gubernatorial candidates won, including Gifford Pinchot as a Republican in Pennsylvania and Al Smith for the Democrats in New York. A number of conservative or antilabor incumbents were defeated. *Labor,* the journal of the railroad brotherhoods, called the results "a Progressive triumph, such a victory as the Progressives have not won in this country in many a day. It was gloriously nonpartisan. Party lines were smashed and labor displayed its strength in a manner unparalleled in the history of the country." Howe thought that the 1922 outcome "showed that labor could mobilize its power. It showed the possibility of union with the farmers; time alone was needed for the inevitable steps that should bring them into united political action." There is no way of determining how much credit for the victories should go to the CPPA, but certainly its existence helped to focus and channel the postwar economic discontent of many farmers and workers.[47]

---

46. FCH, form letter, April 19, 1922, Johnston Papers. Other quotations in this paragraph are drawn from correspondence in the Hillquit Papers: William H. Johnston, form letter, March 15, 1922; Morris Hillquit to FCH, April 6, 1922; FCH to Hillquit, April 17, 1922; Hillquit to FCH, April 21, 1922; FCH to Hillquit, May 25, 1922; Hillquit to FCH, June 26, 1922; CPPA to Organizations of Labor, Farmers and Teachers in Maryland, August 3, 1922; William F. Kehoe to Edward F. Cassidy, June 18, 1922.

Illustrative of the range of Howe's activities was his correspondence with Morris Hillquit, the Socialist Party's representative on the CPPA national committee. Fred produced (probably wrote) a pamphlet entitled *Producers of Wealth Unite: Use Your Ballot for a Better America* that won the socialist's praise: "The systematic education carried on by literature of that character will undoubtedly show results." In a form letter sent out about the same time, Howe made a similar argument, stressing the difference between "the class that produces and the class that lives off those that produce. The producers should vote together, and leave the exploiters to vote together." At his request, Hillquit provided a list of all the branches of the Workmen's Sick and Death Benefit Fund and the names and addresses of the branch secretaries of the Workmen's Circle, and, again at Howe's request, sent letters to all of them, emphasizing particularly "the phase of our activity which, I believe, will appeal to them most strongly, i.e., the effort to organize the forces of labor and farmers for united political action on a permanent basis." Hillquit kept Howe informed of state and local organizations' disputes over candidates and political tactics, especially in Oklahoma and New York. Presumably the CPPA secretary brought these to the attention of national committee members for mediation efforts. The national committee had no power of sanction over local organizations and could not order them to take particular actions. It could only seek to persuade and to educate them by timely reminders.

47. *Labor,* November 11, 1922, quoted in Hicks, *Republican Ascendancy,* 89; *Confessions of a Reformer,* 337. The historian David Burner found three trends in the 1922 elections for the House: "First, states of the character of Missouri and Indiana showed merely a resurgence of traditional

The 1922 successes spurred on the proponents of a third party, but although some pushed for immediate action, for most of them the steps toward that goal remained slow and cautious. In December Senator La Follette, who had had a notable reelection victory, called a meeting of Progressive members of Congress and several hundred nonlegislators, many of whom were CPPA activists. Fred Howe was in attendance, along with such notables as Samuel Gompers, Warren Stone, William H. Johnston, Roger Baldwin, and Herbert Croly. A handwritten note by La Follette listing members for the meeting's committee on resolutions had Fred's as the first name, and he became chairman of the committee. The gathering adopted resolutions urging unity of Progressives "to aid in the advancement of liberal laws and general reconstruction" and calling for a model primary law for each state to adopt and for direct nomination of presidential and vice-presidential candidates. The meeting also set up an advisory committee, and here again La Follette suggested Fred as one of its members.[48]

No specific steps toward a third party came out of the La Follette meeting or from the CPPA's second conference, held in Cleveland later in December. After excluding a Communist delegation led by William Z. Foster, the delegates had a lively debate over a motion to set up a new party and then defeated it by a vote of sixty-four to fifty-two. Generally speaking, the Socialists and many of the unattached intellectuals liked the idea of an independent party; the railroad brotherhoods adopted a wait-and-see position (some of their leaders hoped that McAdoo would win the Democratic presidential nomination in 1924, in which case they would back him); and the farmers continued to think about capturing the primaries of the old parties. Once again the CPPA deferred action, deciding to see what would happen in 1923. It adopted a brief six-point platform of reforms and called for continuing efforts at organizing. Fred Howe was again elected to the national committee.[49]

At the CPPA's third conference in February 1924, Chairman Johnston could report the existence of some thirty state organizations. Enthusiasm for third-party action had been growing during 1923, and the conference issued a call for

---

Democratic strength. Second in certain districts of the West, discontent reminiscent of populism, though now more narrowly centered on agricultural problems, may have sent some radical Democrats to Congress. Third and most important, the big cities—chiefly but not solely in the East where over forty per cent of the shifts occurred—moved strongly toward the Democratic party." Burner, *Politics of Provincialism*, 104, 106.

48. Robert M. La Follette, note dated 1922, La Follette Family Papers; La Follette and La Follette, *La Follette*, 2:1066–68; *New York Times*, November 19, 1922, 1, 17; December 3, 1922, 1. Kenneth MacKay has observed that the La Follette gathering in Washington got more publicity than either of the CPPA's two conferences in 1922. "Without any formal or official connection with the CPPA, the progressive meeting at the City Club undoubtedly served to stimulate the interest of farm and labor groups in the formation of an independent political organization." MacKay, *Progressive Movement of 1924*, 66–67.

49. *New York Times*, December 13, 1922, 4; MacKay, *Progressive Movement of 1924*, 67–72; Tobin, *Organize or Perish*, 142–43.

a presidential nominating convention in July and set up the machinery for the assemblage. There seemed little doubt that the delegates then would select "Fighting Bob" La Follette as their candidate. The senator had professed a willingness to run if both the Republicans and the Democrats nominated reactionary candidates. La Follette for President clubs began to appear, and the senator's friends began to talk with key men in various states. On July 3, 1924, the chairman of the national La Follette for President Committee, W. T. Rawleigh, accompanied by Zona Gale, Gilbert Roe, and several others, brought to La Follette at his home a box of petitions with more than two hundred thousand signatures, all asking him to run for the presidency. The senator promised a definite answer the next day. That night he received a telegram from William H. Johnston conveying the unanimous request of the CPPA's national committee that he, as "the outstanding leader of the progressive forces in the United States, become a candidate for President of the United States."[50] The nomination was assured even before the CPPA's convention met on July 4.

La Follette sent his son, Bob Jr., to the convention with a letter to be read to the delegates. In it he announced his willingness to run as an independent candidate for the White House on a platform that he outlined. By acclamation the delegates nominated him and adopted a platform that embodied his recommendations. There was less enthusiasm for his desire to run as an independent, as socialists and others urged that the convention create a new party and put up candidates for lesser offices as well as for the presidency. La Follette insisted that a third-party ticket would doom to defeat many Progressive Democratic and Republican governors and members of Congress and that steps toward a third party should wait till after November. The delegates acquiesced in La Follette's view, adopted the name of Progressive Party, and authorized the national committee to select a vice-presidential candidate. Two weeks later, the committee picked Senator Burton K. Wheeler of Montana, a Progressive Democrat, as La Follette's running mate.[51]

Pledges of support for the Progressive candidate rolled in from throughout the nation. The Socialist Party, the railroad brotherhoods and other unions, even the American Federation of Labor, gave their endorsement, as did groups of clergy and educators. Oswald Garrison Villard headed a Committee of One Hundred that declared in a telegram to the candidate: "Without this action of yours millions of your fellow citizens would have been compelled to abstain

---

50. La Follette and La Follette, *La Follette*, 2:1110. The text of the telegram is in MacKay, *Progressive Movement*, 118–19.

51. On the convention and the campaign, see La Follette and La Follette, *La Follette*, 2:1107–47; MacKay, *Progressive Movement of 1924*; Waterhouse, *Progressive Movement of 1924*; Hays, *City Lawyer*, 264–75.

from the polls or to choose once more between two corrupt and decadent political parties now separated by no distinction of principle whatsoever. . . . We believe that the time has come for a new deal . . . to put an end to the period of black reaction, of wholesale corruption leading into the cabinet room itself, of the sale of governmental favors, and of administration in the interests of the privileged classes." Fred Howe's name was to be found among the telegram's signatories, who included nearly every prominent reformer in the New York City area.[52]

Earlier in the year, Howe had hoped that William Gibbs McAdoo might be the Democratic nominee. "The men I meet in New York don't like him, but they don't like him for the very reason that I like him," he wrote Gutzon Borglum. "And he did do such a brilliant job in the Treasury and with the railroads. He does the thing he does so easily too." By summer, however, there was no question about Howe's choice for the presidency, given his political affinity with La Follette and his friendship with the senator and his family. Just before the campaign was officially launched with a Labor Day address by the candidate, Fred mused on political developments as he saw them from the shores of Nantucket:

> My feeling is that the present campaign is going to break up the old parties or at least cause such a disintegration that some new formation will follow. That the West is bound to be politically coherent, and that from now on we may have permanent groups in politics, possibly the South, the West, and the East. And I rather like this, for it brings the whole situation out into the open so that we can see it and face it and work it out. And personally I am glad to see the farmer taking things into his own hands, for he is in a very bad way and if something very fundamental is not done for him and by him agriculture in this country will be destroyed. I think we have to face the fact that every economic class or group has to look out for itself. We cannot project our minds very much beyond our personal interests. All of this may sound very materialistic but I have great faith in realism, even though realism challenges old political conceptions and old political moralities.[53]

Howe joined La Follette's staff, helping to draft speeches and accompanying the candidate on his major campaign swings through the East and the Middle West. One can see Fred's hand in the senator's speeches on monopoly—which he

---

52. La Follette and La Follette, *La Follette*, 2:1116, 1224–25.
53. FCH to Maxwell E. Perkins, August 29, 1924, Scribner Archives, Princeton University.

made the main issue in the campaign—and on imperialism and international finance. Musing later on the campaign, Howe wrote: "If a political movement could be gauged by enthusiasm, it seemed from the outpouring of people that [La Follette] was going to receive a tremendous vote. Both the farmers and the workers seemed to be supporting him. Corruption in Washington, the high tariff, high railway rates, the oil scandal, the wide-spread agrarian discontent augured victory for his unquestioned integrity."[54]

The enthusiasm of the crowds could not counteract the weaknesses of the campaign, however. Kenneth MacKay summed these up as "faulty organization, the difficulty of complying with state election laws, insufficient funds, and inadequate supporting tickets." Howe added "fear" to the list: "Fear is one of the assets of the prevailing system. People do not always vote as they shout; they do not even vote as they want to vote."[55] When the ballots were counted on November 4, La Follette had carried only his home state of Wisconsin. Calvin Coolidge had received more than 15 million votes; John Davis, the Democratic candidate, had nearly 8.4 million; and La Follette, 4.8 million (about 16.5 percent of the popular vote). It was not a bad showing for an independent candidate; the Progressive ticket ran second in eleven states (California, Nevada, Oregon, Washington, Idaho, Montana, Wyoming, North Dakota, South Dakota, Minnesota, and Iowa). But it was a defeat nonetheless, and La Follette's insistence that he run as an independent left no adequate third-party machinery and no Progressive officeholders at the grass roots to provide an electoral foundation for later years.

The defeated candidate took his loss in good heart, saying in his concession statement: "The Progressives will not be dismayed by this result. We have just begun to fight. There is no compromise on the fundamental issues for which we stand. The loss of this one battle in the age-long struggle of the masses against the privileged few is but an incident." Pondering on the election, Howe tended to agree:

> The movement has started. It has a following of nearly five millions; it will require time to overcome inertia. No man can call into being a new party; it will come from economic and biological forces. The people will have to learn to use the ballot as they use their hands and their brains to satisfy their wants. Morality does not change men's politics; my class cannot be brought to do justice; justice will come through the efforts of those to whom it is now denied. Justice has never been given to people; they

---

54. *Confessions of a Reformer*, 337–38. For summaries of La Follette's speeches, see Maxwell, *La Follette*, 72–87.
55. MacKay, *Progressive Movement of 1924*, 175; *Confessions of a Reformer*, 338.

have had to take it for themselves. From the beginning men have had to fight for equality of opportunity; they will have to fight for it, I believe, in the end.

Lincoln Steffens thought that his friends were too sanguine. He wrote Marie that she (and by implication Fred) needed a long talk with him to get a true understanding of the modern world. "But for the present I will answer your question: whether I am not interested in the election and Bob's gallant fight, by saying that I am, but in much the same way that I am interested in the ants, bees and spiders in our garden."[56]

Any hope that out of the 1924 defeat would come a new party in 1928 died with Robert La Follette on June 18, 1925. It was unlikely that he would again have been a candidate, but he might well have been a rallying point for the activists of 1924. Fred wired his sympathies to the senator's wife, Belle: "Am heartbroken by the news. You know how much I loved him and the things he was and did. We are all so much poorer than we were and I feel so much lonelier." Marie sent her sympathies to Fola, the senator's daughter. "I keep thinking of you all. I know what it is, the shock, the grief, the sense of utter loss—and then a loneliness, an emptiness that stays and never grows less," she wrote. "And meanwhile the world goes on as though nothing had happened. You wonder how they can, and then after a while you try to go on with them, and finally you *do* go on, but with a sense that things will never be the same again." Nine months later, Fred reported to Robert La Follette Jr., who had been elected to fill his father's unexpired term in the Senate, that he and Marie had visited the Paris studio of the sculptor Jo Davidson to see a model of the senior La Follette's statue.

> My first impression was that it is just what I would want if it were my father and that was my final feeling after being with it rather critically for an hour. Jo has gotten, I think quite perfectly, that mood of your father that I loved the best; it is the mood when he is listening with absorbtion [*sic*] and with sympathy, with lips that are smiling and eyes and brow that are thinking. It is the mood when friends are coming to him with problems, when he and his friends are thinking through some question, when he is weighing all that is said and he is getting ready to make *his own*

---

56. La Follette and La Follette, *La Follette,* 2:1148; *Confessions of a Reformer,* 338; Lincoln Steffens to Marie Howe, November 15, 1924, in Winter and Hicks, *Letters of Lincoln Steffens,* 2:667–68.

decision. . . . It suggests first a listening attitude, a conference, then the possibility of a call to the Senate floor for action.[57]

Davidson's completed marble statue was unveiled in Statuary Hall at the Capitol in Washington on April 25, 1929.

The groups that had supported La Follette in 1924 quickly fell apart after the election. The railroad brotherhoods and the AFL went back to their old politics. The Socialist Party went its separate and electorally futile way. The CPPA did not survive its convention in November 1924, and though a handful of the faithful tried to keep alive the flame of an independent party, their efforts were in vain. Bob La Follette Jr. wrote Howe rather mournfully: "The continued comparative prosperity in industrial centers appears to have completely anesthetized the rank and file [of the people]. No man can say how long the present wave of reaction will continue and yet I have not become discouraged. The only unfortunate result as far as the progressives are concerned, in my view, is that they have permitted this reaction to dampen their ardor. I do not mean that they have compromised in any way in so far as the record is concerned, but there has been a lack of punch in their fighting."[58] For Howe himself, the 1924 defeat brought an end to his attempts to help form a new party. Henceforth, his political activities would be within the Democratic Party.

---

57. Telegram, FCH to Belle La Follette, June 18, 1925, Belle Case La Follette Papers, La Follette Family Collection; Marie Howe to Fola La Follette, June 20, 1925, Fola La Follette Papers, La Follette Family Collection, Library of Congress; FCH to Robert M. La Follette Jr., February 22, 1926, Robert M. La Follette Papers.

Marie Howe was more impressed with some of Davidson's other work: "Genius is an overworked word but one feels he [Davidson] is one. I am thrilled by his Walt Whitman. I would rather have a copy to live with, than any statue I have ever seen. Just to wake up in the morning and see that gallant nonchalant figure swinging down the road. You can see the wind in his beard. Fred has promised when there are copies to be had, to get me one. What a joy. Charlie Chaplin's head is a perfect likeness. La Follette's statue seems the same. But I was so stirred by old Walt I didn't want to look at anything else. I have seen La Follette for years and years so I couldn't be a judge." Marie Howe to Lincoln Steffens, February 25, 1926, Steffens Papers, Columbia University.

58. Robert M. La Follette Jr. to FCH, April 9, 1926, Robert M. La Follette Papers.

15

SEARCHING FOR WISDOM

At the same time that Fred Howe was working with others to create a new party and to send La Follette to the White House, he was also developing a project of his own. Ever since 1900, when as a bachelor he had vacationed at Siasconset (Sconset) and had enjoyed golf and bicycling there, Nantucket had been the place to which he returned nearly every summer. After their marriage in 1904, he and Marie were there in July and August and into September almost every year, and sometimes the sojourn included part of June as well. Marie found the sea breezes conducive to her health. For Fred, Sconset increasingly offered a respite and a refuge from the vicissitudes of politics.

While in Washington working for the Plumb Plan, Fred talked again with his psychiatrist friend from Johns Hopkins who had helped him "get rid of conflicts, poisons, and fears" when he was at Ellis Island. The doctor suggested that the mind had a way of giving daydreams of what one liked and what one wanted to do and be. Howe knew very well what his reveries were about. "They rested me when I was tired. They gave me peace when I was harassed. They were always of an old fishing village on the far end of Nantucket Island, where I had spent many summers; of simple fisherfolk with whom I felt at ease; of a rambling cottage on the edge of the moors into which the sun, rising from the sea, pushed its way in the morning, brighter and gayer and sweeter than sunlight anywhere else in the world." Though satisfied with his work, he felt there was something that he wanted more ardently, even though it might appear selfish. "I wanted to live on the Nantucket moors, to be quit of conflict; to live content with simple, friendly contacts, with horses and dogs, with a fire on the hearth. I wanted to build something with my hands; to plant things and see them grow. These reveries were warmer than any other desire. They had something to do with my deeper self." Every year he waited impatiently for the summer to come; and every fall he left his moorland cottage with greater reluctance.[1]

When Fred first saw Sconset in September 1900, it was a village of around a hundred homes and two hotels and had a summer population of about two thousand. Located at the southeastern edge of Nantucket Island, it had originated as a collection of huts where fishermen lived during the fishing season. Over the years, these were added to and rebuilt as year-round residences, and summer homes, both large and modest, began also to be constructed. Soon Sconset became the favorite summer retreat for Nantucketers. Beginning about 1895 and continuing until around the time of the First World War, the village had a summer actors' colony as word of its attractions spread around the Lambs Club and other New York City spots. Luminaries of the Broadway stage became summer residents. After its opening in July 1900, the Casino, Sconset's social center, entertained its members (a season ticket cost three dollars) with dances, vaudeville and other dramatic offerings, concerts, and tennis, and offered facilities for frequent games of whist, dominoes, euchre, and bridge. In 1912 it instituted a well-attended lecture series that frequently included talks by Fred Howe.

In 1912 he had bought what the local newspaper, the *Inquirer and Mirror*, called an "attractive little cottage near Bunker Hill" (he called it a "farm house"). The Howes named it Edgemoor, and there during the summer months they entertained their friends. In the next five years, Fred purchased more land and had a number of cottages built. By 1919 his name began to appear in the local newspaper's annual list of Nantucket's heavy taxpayers. The expansion of his property holdings can be seen in the increase in his taxes from $89.70 in 1919 to $654.50 in 1925.[2] Although only a summer resident, Fred became a leading member of the Siasconset Improvement Association, an organization of local

---

[1]. *Confessions of a Reformer*, 339–40. Howe wrote Newton Baker that his friends might think him a "lazy quitter" but that a retreat from politics was really salutary. "I am getting quite intelligent I think these last few years. I feel quite wise at times. The two things that interest me and satisfy me completely are friends and nature. I think they will continue very real to me from now on. I messed life up pretty badly by thinking other things more important. But I keep away from the City pretty completely and try and ward off fears of various kinds, and fear is my chiefest curse, and do pretty well considering my evangelical subself which contains a good deal of Calvinism, I regret to say. You see I am a small town or rural-minded person. And I bucked up against too big things a great part of my life. That made me go wrong in so many things. But as I said before I am growing wise as I get over the divide. I think wise thoughts most of the time and my reveries are quite wholesome. . . . The thing that thinks inside of me still says the same things it did years ago but some thing else than the thing that thinks controls the throttle. . . . I try to keep happy and understand a bit. And nature is so wonderful and caressing to me." FCH to Baker, December 27, 1922, Newton D. Baker Papers.

[2]. *Inquirer and Mirror*, September 20, 1919, 3; September 19, 1925. The paper defined heavy taxpayers as "those who will pay more than fifty dollars into the town treasury this year."

citizens concerned with "fairness and justice" in the town's dealings with Sconset and with avoiding the "grievous burden" of taxes.

Some time during 1920, Fred began making plans for a meeting place at Sconset for liberals like himself. He wanted to build a community and make it "a free and happy place for myself and my friends. I would have a herd of my own—for along with my desire for personal freedom was a need for people—people who also wanted to escape other herds and be themselves." He converted the old barn on the farmland he had purchased into a meeting hall and named it the "Tavern on the Moors." "There I planned that we would dine, talk, and have music and dances, intimately, informally, as if we were around a fireside. We would have a little world of our own, bounded on four sides by the sea, unconditioned by any other herd than our own; and we would invite people to share it with us who had something to say about the things we were interested in." His plans began to come to fruition in the summer of 1921 as the Tavern became the center for a variety of presentations by local talent and outside speakers.[3] He was "experimenting in town planning on a small scale," he wrote L. Hollingsworth Wood. "I am very happy, more happy in this work, living quite out of doors, dressed like a farmer and free from care as a man could possibly be than I have ever been before. I greatly fear I have gotten my vocation badly mixed. But I am trying to make up for it."[4]

The events at the Tavern in 1921 laid the groundwork for the more elaborate plans that Fred was developing for 1922. It is hardly surprising that his thoughts should turn toward an intellectual or educational enterprise. His own intellectual development had been stimulated by the people he had heard at Chautauqua in the summers of his youth and by the free pursuit of ideas that he had discovered in graduate study at Johns Hopkins. He had found career models in his Hopkins teachers and had considered devoting himself to the academic profession. As director of the People's Institute, he had had firsthand experience in planning and arranging lectures and discussions so that audiences might be challenged and educated by hearing a variety of viewpoints. Like other Progressives, he had had faith in the power of ideas, and his books, articles, and speeches reflected the belief that the public might be enlightened and brought to support reform by the power of the word.

And, of course, for Howe the interplay of ideas—the challenges and responses of engaged minds—was enjoyable—it was fun! If it could take place in the pleasant surroundings of sun, sea, and moor, so much the better. His friend Lincoln Steffens gave his own slant to Howe's intentions: "You are a

---

3. *Confessions of a Reformer*, 340–41; *Inquirer and Mirror*, July 23, 1921, 2.
4. FCH to L. Hollingsworth Wood, September 28, 1921, L. Hollingsworth Wood Papers.

founder, Freddie. I think you don't care much what you found; a home or a farm, a colony or an Athenian summer school; and, if I am right, you are perfectly unscrupulous where you found your foundations. 'Sconset or Sicily are all the same to you, since it is an instinct, not a conscious, intelligent matter with you."[5]

In his autobiography, Howe wrote that "someone" named his enterprise the "School of Opinion." Probably that someone was Howe himself since he used that title in his first communications about his plans. If he had been surer of his own knowledge, he might have preferred to call it a "School of Wisdom," he wrote. "School of Opinion" was as good a name as any other, he concluded. "The School of Opinion should provide an atmosphere of simplicity and intimacy, in which varying opinions, freely expressed, might give hints of wisdom."[6]

By the early months of 1922, Fred's plans for the school were far enough advanced that he could send them for comment to a number of well-known intellectuals. The proposal pointed to the attractions of Sconset, described Howe's properties at the Sconset Moors, and set forth the concept of the project as "an informal gathering of those who teach and those who listen." Two or three formal lectures each day would be followed by free time for beach, golf, tennis, or "tramps." In the evening there would be dances at the casino and the Tavern. "The object is to reach inquiring, ambitious university students and give them suggestions of what occurs in politics, economics, literature, and the professional world." Speakers would receive little or no remuneration, but Howe would pay their travel and living expenses—he estimated the amount for each one at about one thousand dollars. Costs for students would be kept low, probably set at no more than ten or fifteen dollars for the three weeks in September.[7] It would be "a symposium rather than a classroom; a seminar rather than a forum." Its first week would be devoted to "The American Mind," discussed by such persons as Heywood Broun and Roscoe Pound. Consideration of "The Political and Economic State" would occupy the second week. Oswald Garrison Villard, Frank Walsh, Norman Thomas, and Howe himself were prospective speakers. The concern of the final week would be "International Relations," discussed by people like Amos Pinchot and Walter Lippmann. Obviously Howe did not expect all these people to come to the school, but the list indicates

---

5. Lincoln Steffens to FCH, November 24, 1924, Winter and Hicks, *Letters of Lincoln Steffens*, 2:673.
6. *Confessions of a Reformer*, 341–42.
7. Howe explained to Amos Pinchot that "the cost to the students will be but little more than the cost of table board, for I plan to turn over the property, including a hotel property, without charge." FCH to Amos Pinchot, April 18, 1922, Amos Pinchot Papers. Later the charges became somewhat higher. The preliminary document on the School of Opinion can be found with Howe's letter to Walter Lippmann, March 30, 1922, Lippmann Papers.

the type of speakers he hoped to attract. Most were liberals; nearly all were men (only three women were included in his list of forty-six prospective speakers); a good number were friends or fairly close acquaintances of Howe.[8]

Throughout the summer, Fred publicized the School of Opinion through statements and letters to newspapers and in advertisements in liberal journals like the *New Republic*. Taking due notice of the plans for the school in a tongue-in-cheek editorial, the *New York Times* paid its respects to the charm and simplicity of Sconset and observed that great days were coming to the village. "The 'Sconset air inclines common folks to close the eyes and slumber, but under the guidance of illustrious teachers the pupils of the school will be kept wide awake, and in three weeks such easy subjects as art, science, history, economics and so on should be easily mastered even on 'Sconset moors."[9]

The September sessions of the School of Opinion went well. In the first week Professor E. G. Conklin of Princeton gave three lectures and led a roundtable discussion on "the exact sciences, and especially biology in its relation to the progress of man and the advancement of civilization." Professor Harry Overstreet of the City College of New York spoke on psychology and education. Harry W. Dana presented three lectures on contemporary drama, speaking on "Bernard Shaw and *Back to Methuselah*," "Galsworthy and *Strife*," and "Eugene O'Neill and *The Hairy Ape*." Louise Fargo Brown talked about new viewpoints in history. "On Wednesday afternoon the entire school motored to Wauwinet for an evening picnic, which was followed by a round-table conference in the Tavern. On Thursday evening the Arden Players of Arden, Delaware, gave three Irish plays by Lady Gregory picturing contemporary Irish life," the local newspaper reported.[10] The second and third weeks of the school were just as busy.

One report said that more than 125 persons were in attendance—another said more than 200. A participant described for the *Survey* his impressions of the school and its "more or less gentle rain of opinions." The lecture hall was crowded to capacity for nearly all lectures and discussions. Discussions were so vigorous that they encroached on the time of the lecturers. Students refused to be passive listeners and insisted on playing a part in the making of opinions. "All in all, it was an intensely healthful experience for both students and lecturers. Hence, contrary of most expectations, the school did not degenerate into an orgy of opinions." Fred Howe was pleased. "The lecturing was brilliant beyond my expectations," he declared. Announcing that the school would be held again the next year, he observed: "Whatever we attempt to do here, we

    8. Letter from FCH to "Speakers and leaders of discussion of the Summer School of Opinion at Siasconset, Mass.," July 7, 1922, Lippmann Papers.
    9. *New York Times*, August 20, 1922, 4E.
    10. *Inquirer and Mirror*, September 9, 1922, 5.

must constantly respect the intellectual integrity of those who come. Let us make of this a school of mental integrity."[11]

Given the emotions of the postwar Red Scare, as well as the charges made against Howe during his tenure as immigration commissioner, it is hardly surprising that he and his School of Opinion were under fire for radicalism almost from the start. There were reports that an undercover agent from the Department of Justice had been present during the first session. As the school began its first week, a letter to the editor appeared in the *Inquirer and Mirror*, written by a Nantucket resident, Anne Paddock Ford. She announced firmly that she would not attend the school but suggested that those who planned to do so should find out just who was trying to impose his ideas and what his "acts and utterances" had been during the war. "I would make sure the moving spirit in the School was in no way a part of the perfectly well recognized conspiracy to convert the government in America into an experiment in Socialism; a conspiracy in which radicals of every degree of destructiveness are more or less consciously allied."

A week later, responding, as she said, to numerous inquiries, Ford wrote the paper again and advised those who wanted to find out more about disloyal groups to write to the National Civic Federation's committee on revolutionary movements. The committee had discovered an organization of 150 secretaries to United States Senators and Representatives that was "completely in the hands of the 'Reds,'" she said. "Where do we not find the slimy trail of socialism? Do we realize there are more children learning to war against God and government in the socialist Sunday Schools of New York, than in all of the Christian Sunday Schools of that city!"[12]

Ford's letters brought a reply from two women (who identified themselves as graduates of Columbia University) who had been attending the School of Opinion. Referring to her letters and to a talk in which she had called the school "a hot-bed of revolutionary propaganda," they declared that "all those who have attended the sessions . . . know how utterly unwarranted such assertions are." There had been no propaganda lectures, and the speakers had emphasized the need for patient and scientific study of the complex problems of the day.[13]

An even stronger defense of the school came from a weightier source, William F. Macy, a member of one of Nantucket's oldest families. In a long letter to the *Inquirer and Mirror,* he upheld freedom of speech and assembly against those whose weapons seemed to be "misrepresentation, slander, vituperation,

---

11. J.K.H., "When Opinions Get Together," *Survey* (October 15, 1922): 113–14.
12. Letters to editor, *Inquirer and Mirror,* September 9, 1922, 3, and September 16, 1922, 4.
13. Amy S. Jennings and Marion Fairs to editor, *Inquirer and Mirror,* September 23, 1922, 3.

vilification, and abuse of everyone who begs to differ with them." A few negligible exceptions apart, "those who attended the 'Sconset School . . . report that there was no dangerous radicalism, bolshevism, violent or incendiary doctrine taught or suggested; that, on the contrary, the whole atmosphere of the meetings was one of moderation, thoughtful consideration of the problems under discussion, and general 'sweet reasonableness.'" There was the fullest opportunity to question any of the opinions or conclusions expressed, to disagree if need be, and to present opposing views. Opponents who had attended had pulled a few remarks out of context or had misrepresented them, Macy charged.[14]

Critics of Fred Howe and the school struck back in "a big patriotic meeting" at the Unitarian Church, at which Mrs. Ford again attacked the "Socialist Chautauqua" that Howe was trying to form. She endorsed a newly formed patriotic organization, the Sentinels of the Republic. Also present at the gathering was an outside "expert" on radicalism, Fred G. R. Gordon. A former socialist who had left that faith to become secretary of the American Anti-Socialist League in 1913, he had battled against municipal ownership of utilities as a staff member of the National Electric Light Association. Exactly what he said to the meeting was not recorded, but its tenor is clear from his letter to the *Inquirer and Mirror* in response to Macy's letter. He called the leaders of the School of Opinion "pink socialists" who believed in state paternalism, socialization of private property, and regulation of most human activities. Macy was not courageous enough to join the pure socialists even though he sympathized with them, Gordon suggested. Instead, he had become one of the "mild pink, or parlor socialists, . . . critical of everything and everybody who fails to agree with them, always seeking a change; wishing to jump from the frying pan into the fire and 'sore' because all the rest of us refuse to follow these 'medicine men' into the flames."[15]

Macy's reply to Gordon was succinct:

> Let's wait a few years, friends, and see who the real patriots are. And meantime let us have a little more of Lincoln's faith in democracy—and in the ability of the plain people to think things out and to decide right in the long run. Let's hear any remedy that any one has to offer if he is sincere, and let's not be afraid of the truth wherever we find it, even if we don't like it at first. Let's "know all things, prove all things, and hold fast to that which is good." Let's keep an open mind. . . . Meantime, read "Babbitt."[16]

---

14. William F. Macy, *Inquirer and Mirror*, October 7, 1922, 4.
15. F. G. R. Gordon, *Inquirer and Mirror*, October 28, 1922, 4. On the Sentinels of the Republic (later the Sentinels of America), see N. Hapgood, *Professional Patriots*, 170–72.
16. William F. Macy to editor, *Inquirer and Mirror*, November 11, 1922, 4.

Nantucketers appeared little ruffled by the controversy over the School. Probably most paid little or no heed to it. Some of the islanders came to the lectures, perhaps to see how dangerous they were, and some stayed to enjoy them. Philip Morris, the Sconset postmaster for nearly thirty-five years, said that he "never heard anything derogatory about [Howe] and as far as I know the local citizens regarded him as a very learned man."[17] On the other hand, Edouard Stackpole, who covered the School's activities as a young newspaperman in the 1920s, thought that some Nantucketers—a practical, hard-bitten lot, in his description—considered Howe a "pink." He recalled a former classmate who lived in Sconset calling Fred

> the "liberal front" (not frontier, but a storm coming in), and he said that some of his speakers should be banned and remarks that indicated he didn't have much interest in the matter anyway. . . . Here was a man [Howe] bringing things into the Sconset world that never were there before, and they were suspect. I think many of the villagers took sides, and it was no in-between area. You were either for or "agin." . . . Some of them were very kind in their comments . . . but others were inclined to be a little bit unpleasant in their comments.[18]

No more stories or letters in criticism of Howe or the school appeared in the island newspaper after 1922, however, and the school continued on its course unimpeded. The two natives of Nantucket—Morris and Stackpole—agreed in their praise of Howe. Morris found him "a quiet and affable Gentleman, not inclined to talk too much—but to the point." Stackpole called him "an exuberant person. . . . He sort of drank everything in, and plus he had the kind of mind that could jump from one thing to the other, with ability not just because he enjoyed it but because he had a good deal to contribute." He did not think of him as stuffy or an ivory-tower type and praised his "delightful sense of humor."

In subsequent years, the School of Opinion followed pretty much the format of 1922, though there were variations. Sometimes the sessions were held only during the first three weeks of September, but other times they extended over July and August as well. Fred tried to keep his cottages at Sconset Moors filled during the summer and early fall, both through the school and by treating his

17. J.K.H., "When Opinions Get Together," 114; letter from Philip Morris to author, November 8, 1982.
18. Interview with author, September 17, 1982. Edouard Stackpole had been Curator of the Marine Historical Association at Mystic, Connecticut, and editor of Nantucket's *Inquirer and Mirror*, and was, at the time of the interview, president of the Nantucket Historical Association and director of the Association's Peter Foulger Museum.

holdings as a kind of private club to which persons could come for recreation and intellectual stimulation. From the evidence available, it appears that Howe wanted it both ways, Sconset Moors as a club for people "like ourselves" and as a school for a broader clientele. In his correspondence, he often stressed the former, in his ads and other publicity the latter.

No signs of the "Red" charges of 1922 appeared again in the press, but there was one disturbing incident that seems to have been handled privately rather than publicly. In 1928 Arthur Kellogg, the managing editor of the *Survey*, sent Howe a copy of "a very courteous letter received from one of our many Jewish subscribers and a copy also of the notice received by the subscriber on the letterhead of the Tavern-on-the-Moors. I am very much puzzled as to how to reply." Apparently there was some charge of anti-Semitism, though it is not clear from Kellogg's letter exactly what the situation was. Howe's reply of September 1, 1928, is missing. Kellogg acknowledged the letter and advised: "I venture to suggest that whoever wrote the notice, 'For Prospective Guests to Whom We Have Had No Introduction,' did not make the situation clear enough. That is, did not state flatly that the Tavern on the Moors makes no discriminations in regard to race, religion, and so forth, but that the social clubs on the island to which guests must look for much of their entertainment, etc., do."[19] No further information is available on this episode, and no copy of the notice complained of has been found. There is nothing in the correspondence or publicity materials for the Tavern or the School that suggests any policy or practice of discrimination.

Whether one thought of club or school, the central core of Fred's venture remained the varied lot of speakers and discussants. He could not always secure for the School of Opinion all the "names" he listed in his advertisements and publicity, but he was sure of having a group of well-known teachers, editors, writers, and social scientists in attendance every year. The chance to speak freely on any subject that interested them, and in the pleasant setting of Sconset, proved attractive. The sculptor Gutzon Borglum, who lectured several summers at the School, on one occasion wrote Howe that he had suggested to a university president that "our universities needed a chair for enthusiasm." Fred replied that Borglum had "struck the key of what we are planning to do. The School is a school for enthusiasms, not only the enthusiasm of the speaker but of the auditors as well. I think we have quite a group, just such as you suggest."[20]

Music and dance soon became part of the school's program. The session of 1925 featured Mlle. Roysi Varady of Budapest, a noted cellist, and Mrs. Mildred

19. Arthur Kellogg to FCH, August 16, 1928, and August 21, 1928, "Forget-Me-Not" Files.
20. Gutzon Borglum to FCH, January 30, 1924; FCH to Borglum, February 4, 1924, Borglum Papers, Library of Congress.

Couper of Quidnet, a pianist and composer. In 1926 the Isadora Duncan School of Dancing and Body Development became associated with the School, holding classes for children and adults three mornings a week at the Tavern. The teacher was Anita Zahn, who had been trained by Maria-Theresa Duncan, one of Isadora's three adopted daughters (known as the Isadorables).[21]

The opportunities for fun and recreation at Sconset were not ignored by Howe in his advertising or his letters, and often they received at least equal billing with the lectures and discussions. "The weather in September is usually beautiful.... There are plenty of outdoor sports," he wrote Amos Pinchot in April 1922, "and the tax upon the speakers will not be very heavy." And to the same correspondent later in the year: "There will be a lot of play—golf, tennis and swimming. In other words, we are going to gather together for as playful a time as we can have with our minds and treat the World in Which We Live as playfully or seriously as we see fit."[22]

The Tavern on the Moors—the converted barn—was the center of activities, providing dining room, lecture hall, and meeting rooms. The lecture hall was the old hayloft, on the second floor of the rambling wooden structure. Edouard Stackpole said that Howe "had it all fenced in, of course. There was no danger of anyone falling down the stairs or over the edge or anything like that. He had it well-constructed as a lecture hall." A brochure from about 1926 described the Tavern as "a two-story building, with inviting porches above and below, commanding the sea and the moors. People dine on the upper porches and in the big raftered living room. Here lectures, concerts, dances are given. Below is the office and children's dining room. On the lawn are croquet and clock golf. The cuisine is excellent, southern style. Fish come fresh from the sea; milk and vegetables from neighboring farms."[23] Despite its name, the hostelry was never used as a tavern. After the lectures, those in quest of libations wended their way to the nearby Moby Dick, not a part of the Sconset Moors.

We are fortunate to have a firsthand account of activities at the School of Opinion by Edouard Stackpole.[24] In 1925, four years after graduating from the

---

21. *Inquirer and Mirror*, July 11, 1925; July 24, 1926.

22. FCH to Amos Pinchot, April 18, 1922; August 7, 1922. See ads in *New Republic,* issues of June 30, 1926; June 11, 1927; July 18, 1928. Marie Howe indicated in a letter to Anna Strunsky Walling that participants in the School of Opinion were not all high-minded, at least not all the time: "We have heard nothing but socialism talked this week and I think it has been a good thing for summer visitors to stir them up a bit. I am told that some of the men, wishing to enter their protest against socialism, made loud objections last Saturday night, and arranged a poker party at which they all drank too much by far—an honorable and manly protest against socialism! Truly we may be proud of the enemies we make." MJH to Anna Strunsky Walling, undated, Anna Strunsky Walling Papers, courtesy of the Department of Manuscripts, the Huntington Library, San Marino, Calif.

23. Edouard Stackpole, interview with author, September 17, 1982; "Sconset Notes," *Inquirer and Mirror*, July 31, 1926.

24. Quotations are from the author's interview with Edouard Stackpole, September 17, 1982.

local high school, he had gone to work for the Nantucket *Inquirer and Mirror* as an apprentice printer. In the summer of 1926 one of the paper's reporters fell ill, and the editor asked Stackpole if he wanted to go out to Sconset and cover a lecture. He jumped at the chance and at the School of Opinion heard Alexander Meiklejohn, former president of Amherst, who was about to become head of an experimental college at the University of Wisconsin.

> And he had been accused . . . of being a "pink"—they didn't say "reds," they said "pink." And I didn't find him anywhere near the kind of a rabble-rouser he was supposed to be. He spoke mostly about education, in the field of universities. . . . So, as an embryo reporter, I got nothing sensational. Fortunately I didn't want it anyway; but I was then told that he was a very liberal-minded man, and he *was* a liberal-minded man, nothing of the sort that they made it out to be. And then I suddenly realized that newspapers have a habit of exposing and dwelling on the sensational. In those days, of course, it was even more common than now. But I enjoyed him, I thought he was an able man; and one of the nice things that I remember from that particular night, because it was my first night as a reporter, was that he said that education is a matter of self-adjustment, or words to that effect, and that you learn more by studying on your own steam than with the guidance or propulsion on the part of the teacher, which, while it wasn't a new idea, but it was the way that he said it probably, the way he introduced it into his talk.

So Stackpole was very impressed by his first exposure to the School of Opinion. The next week he asked the editor if his report had been satisfactory. The editor allowed that it had been and asked him if he wanted to go again. "I said, by all means." Fifty-six years later, his memories of the School were still vivid.

> I can see Fred Howe now. He used to come in with a very off-hand manner—you'd never know he was the proprietor of the place—and he'd always introduce his speaker with a few well-chosen expressions, well-chosen words, and would give a sort of a capsule description of his career, either as a writer or an artist or whatever it was; and very much impressed, I think people were, not by the off-hand manner but the very quiet dignified manner in which he would introduce his speakers. And without question I think that in most cases the Sconseters got to respect him from the fact that he could be associated with all these well-known people.

Several of the speakers greatly impressed him: Meiklejohn, of course; Herman Hagedorn, biographer of Teddy Roosevelt; Everett Dean Martin; Dorothy

Thompson ("She was very, very, very good").[25] Others, including Thompson's husband, he found not so good. "Sinclair Lewis I didn't care much for at all—lots of people didn't. . . . I think that the one thing that bothered me about him was the fact that he was so dogmatic. He had not a very good speaking voice either. I will admit though, he had his own brand of humor, which would sparkle on occasion. But maybe he was tired. Maybe he had come to Sconset for a bit of relaxation. It would be unfair to say he was not a good speaker because it just might have been an off night." Stackpole found that not all speakers lived up to their reputations. "I was a little disappointed in some. I think maybe I wasn't quite accustomed, probably, to their delivery; and I never could quite understand why it was necessary to pound the table. That just hit me a little but startled [me]. And I guess two or three of them . . . were products of the elocution age because one fellow had a voice you could hear from one end of the village to the other; and that chap was well endowed with powerful lungs all right. I don't recall that what he said was as powerful as his lungs."

Stackpole was quite taken with the dancer Anita Zahn.

> She used to conduct classes on the lawn of the School, and then the rainy days they would go up in the loft. . . . Anita Zahn one time gave a recital—very short, very dramatic recital—during which she got a splinter in her toe; and I remember one of the Sconseters saying, "What the hell did she expect, dancing in a hay-loft?" But she was a very talented girl, woman, very talented. And she did have some very inspired pupils. I can see them now in their little white gowns, . . . going through the recital of the dance—very much enthused with her.

Stackpole concluded that Howe "was never going to have a dull evening. . . . To me it was a very, very wonderful opportunity to hear these outstanding individuals." Fred felt the same way, writing in his autobiography: "The experiment captivated me. Each year my submerged chromozones [*sic*] became more insistent; they asserted themselves in my reveries, in my thoughts of old age. Each year my escape from political activities was of longer duration. Each summer was a new experience of friendship with others and comradeship with myself such as I had never known before."[26] He was to continue to offer the School of Opinion as a site for the search for wisdom into the 1930s.

During the time when Howe was running the school and taking part in the politics of the Plumb Plan and third parties, he continued to promote his ideas

25. Stackpole later added Will Durant to the list of speakers who had particularly impressed him. Letter to author, October 29, 1982.
26. *Confessions of a Reformer*, 342.

through books and articles. In 1921, along with his book on Denmark, he offered the public his views on the postwar world in *Revolution and Democracy*. He returned to familiar themes—monopoly, privilege, class rule—but his tone was more radical, in analysis if not in remedies.[27] Controlled by privilege, the state was the enemy of freedom. It had corrupted the American mind. "From a distrust of government, we now accept the Prussian idea of the state. From a belief in economic equality, we accept the wage relationship as final. From liberty of thought, of the press and of assembly, we have come to approve of a political censorship on freedom. From an acceptance of change as a most desirable thing, we have come to condemn change. Privilege has decreed we shall have a stratified society. It has decreed there shall be no protest. The present order must be protected at all hazards." Our psychology, our opinions, and even our morals were molded by the owning class, which used the government for its own economic advantage.

> Did the changes in Russia mark an alternative to the exploiting states of the West? Howe thought there was a chance that they did. One need not accept the Russian Revolution or communist methods to see that the Soviet organization of government was "the most nearly natural organization of society the world has ever known," coming into being almost spontaneously when the imperial government broke down. "Equality of opportunity has become the rule of life. The taking over of the tools by the workers is a back to nature movement. Men now live without asking permission from some other man to do so. Industrial freedom has taken the place of industrial feudalism."

The changes remained an experiment, however, and communist "sabotage" was threatening freedom.

If this is a permanent policy of communism, Russia too will pay the cost of its suppression of freedom. But if this is merely a transition stage made necessary or deemed necessary by counter-revolutions, by the imperialistic assaults of the greater powers, by the necessity of securing some kind of stability, which is to

---

27. FCH, *Revolution and Democracy*, vii. Why Howe's book was not published by Scribner's, the publisher of ten of his previous books, is not known. B. W. Huebsch was a crusader against militarism and a defender of civil liberties. Both he and Howe were original members of the national committee of the American Civil Liberties Union, and Huebsch was the ACLU treasurer for many years.

Howe had dealings with at least one other publisher. In 1929 he made a rather strange effort to get Horace Liveright to publish a book of reminiscences by the Grand Duke Ludwig of Hesse-Darmstadt, which Howe would perhaps edit. While expressing mild interest in a completed manuscript, the publisher refused to make any commitment on the book. Horace Liveright to FCH, March 27, 1929, Liveright Papers, University of Pennsylvania.

be changed when security is obtained, then we may see in Russia a new kind of a state, a state in which the natural instincts and powers of the people are given an opportunity to play as they have never been permitted to play in the history of the world.

If failure came, it should be ascribed not to the ideals that animated the revolution but to the old regime's abuses and incompetences and to the organized imperialism of the western powers.[28]

Howe believed that hopeful signs for American democracy could be found in the Non-Partisan League and other movements of political insurgency, in the rapidly growing interest in cooperatives, in the developing political consciousness of labor. "The conditions under which we suffer can be changed by the state, once the state becomes an agency of the class that produces rather than the class that exploits." Such a society could avoid both socialism and communistic syndicalism. It could be brought about by a few changes and by a very few laws and would involve no regimentation of society and little interference with personal liberty. "Rather it protests against such interference as it does against the enlargement of governmental powers. It involves no dictatorship by a class and no violent change in the existing machinery of government."[29]

Not surprisingly, the first of the simple changes that Howe recommended was in land policy. The Georgist remedy would end land monopoly and land speculation and open up the resources of the earth. Industrial democracy would follow as a matter of course. After that in Howe's program came socialization of transportation and communication, conversion of the country's banking and credit resources into public or cooperative agencies, political reforms to make government simpler and closer to the people. There need be no "violent overturn of the government," he observed. "End privilege and freedom will usher in a new world in which justice and equality will prevail."[30]

Except for *Survey*, the reviews of *Revolution and Democracy* were rather unfavorable.[31] Nearly all of Howe's other writings during the rest of the decade were

28. *Revolution and Democracy*, xix, 77–78, 116, 192, 194–95.
29. Ibid., 225–26, 227.
30. Ibid., 204, 231–34.
31. Bruno Lasker wrote that it was a "trenchant indictment" of "the ills that eat into the very heart of human and liberty and well-being." Howe's approach showed him to be "a radical rather than a communist, a realist rather than a dreamer. If some of his pictures are, perhaps, painted in too sombre a hue, if some of his proposals require, perhaps, slower mental readjustments than he would allow for, they cannot be set aside as the ravings of a theorist; for, in a dozen previous books and in long periods of responsible administrative work, Mr. Howe has proved himself a reformer who thinks constructively." *Survey* 46 (May 7, 1921): 185. The *Literary Review* was skeptical, finding Howe "a typical American reformer, earnest, moderate, confident, and hurried. A strong emotional current sweeps through the pages, but there is no intellectual compulsion in them. Not that Mr. Howe is all wrong; perhaps he is mostly right. The trouble is that no one really knows, least of all Mr. Howe himself." *Literary Review* (April 16, 1921): 5. The *Outlook*'s reviewer declared the book

somewhat pedestrian. In April 1925 Paul Kellogg asked him to write two articles for the *Survey,* one on European developments in electric power, the other on British politics. Howe accepted the assignment but never got around to writing either of the articles. He wrote Kellogg that he had no adequate apologies for his failure. "I don't feel like a very good reporter any more. I guess it is really the comfort of a warm fire and books and people that keep me in an assured place." "I don't seem to have that aggressive reporter's instinct that I had twenty years ago," he wrote Kellogg a little later. A few articles on familiar subjects appeared in various journals over the next few years: a piece on the dangers of foreign investment in the *Annals* in 1928; a brief summary of a political utopia based on freedom, cooperation, and the single tax in the *Nation* in 1928; and a recommendation of Henry George's program as a way out of the Depression in the *Christian Century* in 1932.[32]

The principal literary achievement of Fred Howe in the 1920s was his autobiography. Scribner's had agreed to publish it, and he began work, probably in 1923. By August 1924 his editor, Maxwell Perkins, was pressing him for the manuscript. Fred replied that he hoped to have it, under the title "The Confusion of a Reformer," by the last week in September. That timetable proved optimistic, however, and in Paris he worked on the autobiography into 1925. In December 1924 Howe changed the title to "The Confessions of a Reformer," and Perkins approved. Although the editor urged Howe to complete the work in time for Scribner's fall list, he indicated that quality should not be sacrificed to speed. "It will be an original and a highly interesting book in our opinion, so that the nearer to perfection you can bring it, the better."[33]

To make the fall list, the publishers had to have the manuscript by mid-April, 1925, and bending every effort, Howe made the deadline. He wrote Perkins on April 7 that he would be sending the manuscript on either the *Olympic* or the *Mauretania* so that Scribner's would have it by the seventeenth. "So consider that I have come across the line on time and preserve my place at the table. I have been working from ten to fifteen hours a day and the stenographer has hardly gotten to bed at all." A few days later, he expressed his feelings to Perkins more fully.

"remarkable for its earnest conviction as well as for its total lack of either tolerance or humor." *Outlook* 128 (August 17, 1921): 622. The *New York Times* damned the volume with faint praise, finding it "a readable book in that snappy, swift-rushing style of [Howe]," but calling him a writer who could "convince Adam that he wasn't the first man." *New York Times,* May 1, 1921, sec. 3, 19.

32. Paul U. Kellogg to FCH, September 18, 1925, "Forget-Me-Not" Files; FCH to Kellogg, December 25, 1925; January 24, 1926; FCH, "People's Versailles"; memo from Paul U. Kellogg to GS, July 4, 1926; FCH, "Some Overlooked Dangers"; "Political Utopia"; "Way Out? Single Tax!"

33. Maxwell E. Perkins to FCH, August 20, 1924, Scribner Archives; FCH to Perkins, August 29, 1924; FCH to Perkins, November 23, 1924; Perkins to FCH, December 10, 1924; Perkins to FCH, January 28, 1925.

How many times do you hear someone saying: "At last, thank God, its [sic] done." That is what I am saying tonight and tomorrow as the manuscript starts on its way to the Mauretania. There will be sounds of revelry in the Latin Quarter. They may continue to the Dome, though if they do it will be because the revelry has passed beyond the bounds set by one at fifty plus. But it has been long delayed; there are no resolutions to be kept in Paris when the spring sun begins to bring with it spring rains and at last both have put in an appearance.

"Every man should write his own autobiography," Howe declared. "It becomes a sparring match between the truth and bunk. I have tried to catch the latter; but it wriggles in and out and will not be completely denied. I have tried to nail him fast in the end but it required much rewriting and a kind of surgical process to get out the facts. I've made a struggle at the truth but fear some of my friends will say: 'What a damn liar Fred Howe is' just the same."

He was still worrying about the title. He decided to add a subtitle, "A Narrative of Unlearning," but then changed his mind. Perkins agreed: "The title says enough and says it more forcefully for standing alone."[34] Fred began reading proofs "with curious interest" at Sconset in June and once again called on Marie, in Paris, to help with them.

Howe's rejected subtitle, "A Narrative of Unlearning," is an apt description of the central theme of his autobiography.[35] What differed in this book from his earlier writings was his disillusion, his loss of confidence in the prospects and handiwork of the reformers. He was not ready to abandon all hope and turn to a cynical pessimism, however. In the course of his self-examination, he made "one reconciling discovery," he wrote. "My dreams—the things I wanted—were still alive under the ruins of most of what I had thought." Howe decided that he had been wrong on the means to achieve these goals. It could not be through his own class; it had to be through the workers, "those who produced wealth by

34. FCH to Perkins, April 7, 1925, April 13, 1925, August 25, 1925, and September 4, 1925; Perkins to FCH, September 8, 1925. Scribner's sent Howe a contract providing a straight 15 percent royalty on the book.

35. Both Howe and Steffens liked "unlearning" as the theme of their autobiographies. Given the close friendship, correspondence, and conversations of the two men over the years, it is impossible to say who first chose the word, but each thought it appropriate for his life. Steffens wrote Howe after the publication of Confessions: "Marie asks about the title for [my autobiography]. I thought you all knew; it was chosen years ago: 'A Life of Unlearning.' But I'll listen to advice on that. If your title helped your book, I might make mine, 'The Confessions of a Muck-Raker,' or, even, 'A Muck-Raker's Plea of Guilty,' 'A Muck-Raker's Apology,' 'My Apologies to the Muck-Rakers,' or 'A Book for Marie and Peter,' 'A Warning to Little Pete,'—anything that will sell the book will do. I'm indifferent just now to anything but the fun of writing this story." Lincoln Steffens to FCH, December 6, 1925, in Winter and Hicks, *Letters of Lincoln Steffens*, 2:722.

hand or brain." The success of the labor movement seemed historically inevitable. "The next step was the last and it could not be stopped. Labor had to make its own fight; it had to use its own power; the place for the liberal was in labor's ranks."[36]

So Fred Howe concluded the analysis of his "unlearning." He believed he had finally lost the illusions he had hoarded for a lifetime. "Much of my intellectual capital had flown. Drafts on my mind came back indorsed: 'No funds.' But I was still not bankrupt. The new truth that a free world would only come through labor was forced on me. I did not seek it; did not welcome it. But it crowded into mind and demanded tenancy as the old occupants gave notice to leave." He could take part in good faith in labor's struggles for political and economic reform. The irony was, of course, that just as he was pledging allegiance to labor, the unions were pulling back from independent politics after the defeat of the Plumb Plan and of La Follette's 1924 presidential candidacy. He could still continue his quest for self-fulfillment, however. "I began life with a sense of responsibility for my own soul. I returned to the same sense of responsibility thirty years later. Then my concern was as to the hereafter; now my concern was pre-eminently with to-day. Then life was conditioned by fear; now it is conditioned by desire. I was concerned with the poverty of others; now I am concerned with the poverty of my own undeveloped experiences."[37]

Now without obligations to movements or reforms, Howe believed that he had found "a kind of verity that I did not know before. I have few mental conflicts and get a warmth and joy out of life that are new to me." He was living as he chose, he wrote, and being himself. He now knew that he could be his own authority. "A lifetime spent in making good in material ways, in political struggles, and moralistic reform, leaves me aware of gaps in personality; of a fashion of perceiving life fragmentarily. I am committed to such beauty as I can find, to harmony within and without, to friends and the things I love. I have more to learn than the time that is left suffices for. Yet I realize that only a beginning is possible to any man."[38]

Fred intended his autobiography primarily as an account of his intellectual journey. It covers the principal events of his life, though there were some inaccuracies and lapses of memory. It omits some events of importance in his public life. He wrote nothing about the National Progressive Republican League and La Follette's quest for the presidential nomination in 1912, about the Stimson campaign, about his role in movie censorship. The book is sparse on personal

36. Ibid., 324.
37. Ibid., 325.
38. Ibid., 325, 342–43.

details and certainly bears no resemblance to the "tell-all" autobiographies that were to appear later in the century.

Reviews of *Confessions of a Reformer* were an interesting mix. Some were relatively straightforward summaries of the book's contents and evaluations of its merit. The *Literary Review* liked its vignettes of the men whom Howe had come in contact with and who had influenced him and found the volume "stimulating even at the points of greatest disagreement, perhaps most so." Fred's old friend and fellow Georgist, Louis Post, featured the single tax prominently in his review for a Pennsylvania newspaper. Howe's *City* was "one of the best pieces of single tax literature outside of Henry George's." Howe had now "retired from public activities of all kinds to a social observatory from which he may calmly inspect the progressions, the retrogressions and the reactions of social reforms." What seemed most important to Post was that his friend continued to believe intensely in the single tax, "the only secure foundation for every other desirable social reform." Olivia Howard Dunbar, writing in the *Yale Review,* suggested that perhaps in Howe's "stark honesty—an honesty quite untinged with self-idealization—he overstresses both his original naiveté and the abruptness of his successive cures. He has in fact told his story so simply that the book reads almost like a primer of disillusionment." She found it "a unique and suggestive book."[39]

Other reviewers devoted much of their attention to the theory and practice of liberalism as each saw it. Robert Morss Lovett in the *New Republic* viewed Howe as a modern Candide who had written a Pilgrim's Progress, "a record of an experience in which all the various ways of salvation which have been current for the past third of a century were brought to the test of practice." Despair was not the final outcome of the *Confessions,* however. "Rather one is left with a feeling of the vitality, the sheer instinct of life, individual and collective, that went into the process, and which remains undiminished in spite of expense and waste, undismayed by error, ready for the next adventure, the next trial." Despite all the defeats, the lesson of Howe's life was not a pessimistic one. "[He] puts his finger on the cause of the failure of intellectualism from the time of the Utilitarians onward. His whole career is discovery of this illusion in all the insidious forms in which it has thrown away the best efforts of America in these last thirty years." As John Dewey had suggested, "life is not mathematical calculation or a laboratory experiment; it is experience. To this experience Mr. Howe

39. C. R. Woodruff, *Literary Review* (January 2, 1926): 4; Louis Post, *Johnstown (Pa.) Daily Democrat,* Post Papers, Library of Congress; Olivia Howard Dunbar, *Yale Review* 16 (April 1927): 607. Another praising Howe's autobiography was Eugene Debs, who called it "a wonderful book presenting truths and facts in connection with the war and its results upon progressive movements of startling significance." Eugene V. Debs to Mrs. Edward H. Weber, February 3, 1926, in Constantine, *Letters of Eugene V. Debs,* 3:543.

has made a notable contribution, not the least valuable part of which is his story of it."⁴⁰

Far from finding the *Confessions* an affirmation of pragmatic liberalism, Simeon Strunsky, the reviewer for the *New York Times,* considered it a revelation of the creed's failures. He praised the book as "an honest autobiography . . . a valuable contribution to the history of liberal thought and action in the United States during the first quarter of the twentieth century." It was most useful as a "route-chart . . . for the progress from reformism to liberalism." He believed, however, that like other liberals Howe showed himself as too much the doctrinaire and too little the realist. For example, he repeated the "wearisome Liberal tradition" in his accounts of Wilson's failures at Versailles and misunderstood the realities of peacemaking. Likewise with the League of Nations—the liberals wanted a perfect world; Wilson wanted to do what was possible in an imperfect world. Just as Tammany could produce municipal progress, so despite the Clemenceaus and Lloyd Georges and the international bankers, the world could still move forward. "Woodrow Wilson's was the flexible mind at Paris. The Liberal mind was the rigid, schoolmaster, just-so mind and has so remained in large measure."⁴¹

Writing in the *Saturday Review of Literature,* Rexford Guy Tugwell also used his review as an opportunity to criticize liberalism, but from a different perspective. Praising the book, he depicted Howe as an old crusader who was now "looking back upon all those years of strenuous effort not in an apologetic way, that would be putting it too strong, but in a mood of uncertainty concerning their results." His story illustrated the fact that all the prodigious efforts at reform were out of all proportion to the results that were gained. Perhaps his memoirs of failure would teach other younger reformers lessons that he had not perceived clearly. "If, by inference, we learn from them that democracy involves a local leadership which must be carefully organized, and that political forms and election machinery are of little importance; and if we learn that what we are clumsily trying to do is to control an industrial system the owners of which will bitterly contest each encroachment of public control, it will be enough. Their experience will serve to pose our contemporary problems in clearer fashion." While praising Howe's book, Tugwell by inference placed its author among "the wraiths of an old righteousness which no longer counts among our programs of melioration."⁴²

Leon Whipple, a professor of journalism at New York University and for many years the *Survey*'s book review editor, was not ready to put Howe and his

---

40. Lovett, "Candide's Progress."
41. Simeon Strunsky, "A Liberal's Pilgrimage," *New York Times,* November 15, 1925, III:4.
42. *Saturday Review of Literature* 2 (December 26, 1925): 447.

generation of reformers on the shelf. "Fred Howe needed no apologia pro sua vita. He has fought the good fight. . . . [He] has given us a guide book to the liberal movement in the United States for the last quarter century and more. . . . [It is] a book on every page of which is wisdom for the social idealist. It is a plain book, clearly written with little adornment, but full of experience and suppressed suffering." Whipple praised Howe for his frank discussion of the money problems a reformer must face. "It was a blessing for his generation that Fred Howe somehow got money enough to be independent and serve without grinding himself to death in the tread-mill of making a living. But it is a dangerous adventure, and the price is often a man's soul. One must live, and live under the present system, but can one uproot the thing he accepts?" The young men of the next generation of reformers could learn from Howe's frankness, but they could also see that the older liberals had a sense of failure, of "spiritual frustration." Here Howe raised a crucial question: what has happened to the prewar radicals? Did they fail and, if so, why? Who were their successors, and what was the new battlefield? "These are the solemn questions that ring in the heart when you have finished this big, courageous, wide-sweeping book. It is a fine tale that is told here, with a wealth of wisdom garnered and laid by for the inspiration and instruction of onrushing youth. Even the story of their mistakes profits much, and the picture of their final acquiescence teaches . . . its own lesson." If reformers failed at all, perhaps it was from "pride of intellect and impatience. . . . But after all how much they won! Life in America is better for what they did and suffered." No man's ideals ever come true. "But if a man fights the good fight for his day what more can we ask?"[43]

"Stand by to comfort Freddie as the reviews come in," Steffens wrote Marie. "His book is a great chance for all the wise guys to write as if they understand all about the world as we muckrakers exposed it before we did our work. They will not lose the opportunity he gives them to look down upon his (and my) innocence, our childlike faith and girlish ignorance." He had harsh words for the "stupid" review in the *Times*.[44]

Steffens wrote Howe that he was not surprised *Confessions* was selling well. "It's an honest man's story, honestly told, and I think that they have had enough of personal (psychological, sex) confessions and are relieved to find an autobiography which reveals the world; not the author, except as a hero. Most of our recent confessions have made the hero a villain. Yours shows a (near) saint up

---

43. L. Whipple, "Pilgrim's Progress in Politics."
44. Lincoln Steffens to MJH, November 29, 1925, in Winter and Hicks, *Letters of Lincoln Steffens*, 2:720–21. The dates of the correspondence between Steffens and the Howes about the *Confessions*, given in the *Letters* and the Steffens papers, do not correspond with the contents of the letters. I have used the sequence that makes sense, while citing the dates given in the *Letters*.

against the wicked world. And, believe me, you do expose the world." He thought he would imitate Fred's approach in his own autobiography and make himself out to be an innocent sufferer. "My danger is overdoing it. You were, apparently, so unconscious of what you were doing that nobody (but me) gets onto you. I, having read your book, and tumbled to its cunning, I'm afraid that I shall seem (as I am) quite conscious. If we both run for the presidency at the same time, you'll beat me. You'll get the popular vote; I'll get Wall Street's, who will think that they can do business with a slick guy like me."[45]

Steffens also wrote Marie so that she would interpret correctly to Fred the comments he was making. "Lest Freddie take too seriously my letter about his book, I wish to prepare you to explain, if necessary, that all I really mean is that, however he may have intended to abuse himself with his confession, he has as a matter of fact revealed to the world a golden heart and a crystal soul; a dear, honest gentleman and a true follower of the truth: His book is a novel with a beautiful hero.... It's a classic, simple, straight and obviously true and vivid." He had one fault to find, he said. "The book does not end. Freddie may think it does, but the truth does not lie in the Locomotive Engineers." Fred had another chapter to write, but he had to live it first. "I have lived it, I am now. Fred's story is my story; they will be both the same story, but mine will go on another chapter, another part. Fred has need of a look in on Russia." But that was not important now. "What we have is good enough: an honest life of a brave, fine man, and the way to travel through the world."[46]

Marie replied that both letters—the one to her and the one to Fred—had been received "with enthusiasm and read with great enjoyment." His letter to Fred was "delicious" and contained "some truth." "In fact we agree with everything you say."[47]

Another of Fred's friends who was impressed by *Confessions* was Paul Kellogg, editor of the *Survey*. In mid-November 1925 he began circulating interoffice memos pushing for a symposium of the frank reactions of "a lot of ex and oncoming liberals to Fred Howe's Autobiography." What has become of the movement that offered so much promise twenty years ago? Howe had asked. Why had most of the prewar radicals laid down their arms? "Was the fight too hard? Did youth burn itself out? Has the movement become a class struggle,

---

45. Lincoln Steffens to FCH, December 6, 1925, in Winter and Hicks, *Letters of Lincoln Steffens*, 2:721.

46. Steffens to MJH, November 22, 1925, Steffens Papers. Howe visited Russia in November 1927, spending some time garnering information from Dorothy Thompson, who was in Moscow covering the tenth anniversary of the Bolshevik Revolution. Sheean, *Dorothy and Red*, 62, 66.

47. MJH to Steffens, November 25, 1925.

finding its leaders among the farmers and workers? May it be—as some of them feel—that there is little for liberals to do?"⁴⁸

In his review in *Survey* on December 1, Leon Whipple had repeated Howe's questions and set the stage for the journal's symposium. Kellogg wrote to some sixty liberals or former liberals, asking for contributions—"lively, brief, informal, but searching, we hope"—on the questions Howe had raised in his autobiography: "What has become of the pre-war radicals?" or "Who succeeds them and where?"⁴⁹

From Paris, unaware of Kellogg's plans, Fred wrote the editor, asking him to thank *Survey*'s reviewer of his book: "He saw the book more intelligently than any one has thus far and I was most happy to read what he had to say." Kellogg replied that he had just finished reading *Confessions*. "I shan't try to tell you some of the deep things it meant to me—pro and con," he wrote. "I think you have helped scores of us to clear our own thinking. But here just let me say that it was as fascinating as a Winston Churchill novel." (He meant the American novelist, not the British politician and wartime leader.) He had sent the question "What has become of the pre-war radicals?" out to "a big bunch of them," and *Survey* had

> a perfectly corking symposium in the mill. . . . The people whose names counted in 1905 and 1910 and right up to 1915 as those of few men in America; people who could write, too—the muckrakers for one group: Hard, Baker, Tarbell, White, Hapgood, Phillips, et al.; and then a bunch of civic and political leaders such as Newton Baker, Berger, Hillquit, Darrow; and newcomers like Senator Wheeler. . . . There is still kick in the old bunch; and a lively enough breaking with you on this and that; a division of sheep and goats; of people who look back and people who look forward; of people who want more political action and people who want less, and so on.

He asked Howe for a rejoinder to be published in a subsequent issue, and Fred immediately cabled his agreement.⁵⁰

The symposium, "Where Are the Pre-War Radicals?" appeared in *Survey*'s issue of February 1, 1926. A majority of the twenty-three contributors agreed in ascribing the demise or the moribund state of American radicalism to backlash

---

48. *Confessions of a Reformer*, 195–96.
49. Paul U. Kellogg to Norman Hapgood, December 9, 1925, "Forget-Me-Not" Files (for a similar letter see Kellogg to Frank Walsh, December 9, 1925).
50. FCH to Kellogg, December 25, 1925; Kellogg to FCH, January 9, 1926; FCH to Kellogg, January 24, 1926.

from the war, the prosperity of the 1920s, and/or the defects of the reformers themselves. A smaller number of the writers—the socialists (Eugene Debs, Morris Hillquit, Norman Thomas), Ray Stannard Baker, Roger Baldwin, Benjamin Marsh, Louis Post—insisted they were as radical as they had ever been. "If I was indeed a radical then [before the war], I am still a radical, and no hopeless radical either, for my belief in certain great fundamentals of human relationship has not changed," Baker declared. "Where I was mistaken as a 'pre-war radical' was in thinking that what I wanted could be had by adopting certain easy devices of social inventions—otherwise, by shortcuts. What I have gained since is the knowledge that though the thing is true the time appointed is long."

Ida Tarbell's critique of the reformers was shared by others in the symposium: "The fact is that the pre-war radical was often not a wise man—an experienced or patient man. He knew little about human beings, and what as individuals and herds they can be counted on to do under certain circumstances, when his denunciation, his righteous indignation at the stupidities, injustices and wrongs that complicate the daily affairs of the nation . . . when all this had given him an advantage, he frequently lost it because he did not know how to take the next step, did not understand the need of practical cooperation with all men." Stuart Chase summed up colorfully the past and the present:

> Them was the days! When the muckrakers were best sellers, when trust busters were swinging their lariats over every state capitol, when "priviledge" shook in its shoes, when God was behind the initiative, the referendum and the recall—and the devil shrieked when he saw the short ballot, when the Masses was at the height of its glory, and Utopia was just around the corner. . . . Now look at the damned thing. You could put the avowed Socialists into a roomy new house, the muckrakers have joined the breadlines, Mr. Coolidge is compared favorably to Lincoln, the short ballot is as defunct as Mah Jong, Mr. Eastman writes triolets in France, Mr. Steffens has bought him a castle in Italy, and Mr. Howe digs turnips in Nantucket.

Should we, therefore, lay a wreath on the Uplift Movement in America? Chase asked. We might as well. "For the Uplift as a crusading spirit, as a dedication, as a religion, is comatose if not completely ossified—strangled both by the war and its own ineptitude."

Many contributors expected a renaissance of radicalism or liberalism when economic conditions worsened or new issues appeared. A few of the contributors, besides offering their observations on the question Howe had raised, paid their respects to Fred himself. Tarbell pointed out that some of the prewar radicals "like Fred Howe, the lovable reformer whose confessions gave the *Survey* the text for its question, are flitting from one exciting outbreak to another, though few have landed as happily as he—the head of a sublimate gab-fest on his ocean front in summer, an intellectual *flaneur* in Paris in winter. Don't tell me the former does not know how to provide oases for himself!" Hillquit suggested that Howe had "put us all under obligation by the delightful account of his tragi-comical odyssey as a pre-war radical." And Post praised Howe's "deeply rooted and steadily growing confidence in the fundamental reform advocated by Henry George."[51]

In his rejoinder to the symposium, Howe expressed the belief that a majority of the contributors were living their lives as they had before the war, following their own enthusiasms, finding their own happiness in their own individualistic ways. We might be better off, he thought, if each person tended his own garden. It had taken him a long time to realize that he had the right to live his own life and do as he chose. Living in Paris and viewing the New World from the Old gave him a different perspective, he believed. Europe took people for granted, accepted their vices and their virtues, eschewed groups that sought personal reform. America, in contrast, was a nation of zealous reformers. "Reform is a universal passion with us. As a people we will not let either people or institutions alone.... Everyone is a reformer in America. Bankers and Bolshevists, preachers and agnostics, conservatives and radicals, wets and drys, anti-feminists and feminists. There are millions of us."

Why this surfeit of reformers in America? Fred thought it came from our evangelical background. "Our generation in its childhood was deeply saturated with the idea of sin; sin in ourselves, sin in the other fellow. We cannot shake off the impressions made on us in the Sunday School, in the prayer-meeting, in the revival by the exhorter.... We want to change people, not institutions." American reformers were "full of facts," but they did not realize that facts were not enough. "I have never known a business man to be converted by facts against his interest to the public ownership of street railways. I would find it difficult to enumerate a half dozen men who were converted to my ideas against their own economic interest as a result of a score of books, hundreds of speeches and a mass of printed articles. No, the human does not work when men's economic interests are involved. It stalls."

51. "Where Are the Pre-war Radicals?" Contributing to the symposium were William Allen White, Newton W. Baker, Ray Stannard Baker, Ida M. Tarbell, William Hard, Eugene V. Debs, Norman Hapgood, Louis F. Post, Roger N. Baldwin, Fremont Older, Burton K. Wheeler, George W. Alger, Morris Hillquit, Lawson Purdy, Norman Thomas, Stuart Chase, Charlotte Perkins Gilman, Basil M. Manly, John Haynes Holmes, Sherwood Eddy, Benjamin C. Marsh, Clarence Darrow, and John S. Phillips.

The war had all but destroyed his own picture of America, Howe wrote. The hope for change lay in labor as a class. It was being led slowly toward the idea of richer opportunity for all. "All liberals and radicals should be identified with it." The prosperity that some symposium contributors referred to meant little to Howe. "I have never wanted democracy that was satisfied with crumbs from the table, no matter if those crumbs contained occasional bits of cake. As for myself I prefer the rough open warfare of pre-war days to the contentment, the bread and circuses which we are offered today."

Fred admitted that there was some truth in Stuart Chase's charge that he had retired to Nantucket to "dig turnips." But also he had been trying to think. "Digging turnips is easier digging, I find, than thinking. Wisdom comes hard. Political and economic wisdom comes very hard. Personal wisdom comes hardest of all." His patch grew many weeds and some roses. He admired those who were still close to the firing line, taking punishment in an era when reform was "a rather lonely business." He feared that he himself had no claim to the title of "radical"—"I did not have enough iron in my make-up to get on the cross," as Tom Johnson, La Follette, Debs, Baldwin, and others had.

"Digging turnips" had given Howe tolerance and possibly some wisdom, he believed. "I do not now expect my plans for the world will ever be realized. That is too much to ask. Every other man and woman wants a different world from that which I want. And they have an equal right to have it." The future lay between two different philosophies, he thought, between socialism and the single tax, with the odds favoring socialism. "And the majority will rule somehow in the end. That is inescapable," he concluded. "When the pasture lands were opened to the herd by universal suffrage it became merely a question of time when the herd would find its way in. It required forty years of the wilderness to make the Jews humble. And humility is the hardest lesson of all. We only need to trust our instinctive wants for equal opportunity. That is a matter of courage. And America has plenty of courage even though it is temporarily in eclipse."[52]

Howe and his friends had political choices to make as the decade wore on. For those Progressives who had followed Robert La Follette's banner in 1924, the eclipse seemed to be continuing. In 1928 the approaching presidential election presented them with a dilemma. Their hearts might hold lingering hopes for a new party, but their minds told them that it was impossible in the near future. They had no national political organization, save for the moribund Progressive National Executive Committee, which Mercer Johnston finally put to death in 1927. There seemed to be no Roosevelts, Wilsons, or La Follettes to provide a rallying point of national leadership. The labor unions had abandoned the field of new party politics.

52. FCH, "Where Are the Pre-war Radicals? A Rejoinder," 33–34, 50–53.

The major party nominations in the summer of 1928 focused the attention of the old Progressives on the choice that they had to make. Pledged to continue the Coolidge policies, Herbert Hoover was not an alternative. About the Democratic candidate, Governor Alfred E. Smith, many Progressives were uncertain, despite the reforms associated with his administrations in New York. When Smith appointed as new national chairman John J. Raskob, a wealthy industrialist who had voted for Coolidge in 1924 and who sought to show business that the Democratic Party was no threat to their interests, the doubts of Progressives increased. The Democratic platform hardly differed from the Republican, except for a plank endorsing public ownership of water power resources. The Smith campaign's electoral strategy focused on trying to persuade the business community that the candidate was a man to be trusted, not an exponent of economic change.

Still, there were those New York State reforms, there was Smith's backing for public electrical power and for the McNary-Haugen bill and farm price supports, there was his occasional use of the arguments of Republican Progressives in his attacks on Hoover policies. The nearer the election day approached, the better Al Smith looked to those Progressives not willing to bolt to Norman Thomas and the socialists.

Despite the conservative tenor of their campaign, Democratic leaders knew that four years earlier La Follette had received the votes of nearly five million Americans and that, though he had carried only his home state of Wisconsin, he had been the electors' second choice in eleven other western and midwestern states. If those could be considered Progressive votes, then it was crucial to have endorsement by Progressives of the Democratic ticket. The vehicle for this was the Progressive League for Alfred E. Smith, organized in September 1928 by a number of leading Progressives and financed largely by the Democratic Party. The press reported that Fred Howe and Frank Walsh were taking the lead. As Walsh told Peter Witt, "we are throwing the organization together as quickly as possible because, as you so well know, the golden hours are flying by." He reported that Raskob has asked them "to take charge of the progressive end of the fight. . . . While we are working in close co-operation with the National Democratic Committee, we are given naturally a very free hand." They hoped that they could "enroll all of the progressives, even those who balked at 'regular democracy,' 'wet or dry' and the various other points of difference."[53]

As executive secretary of the League, Howe found himself filling much the same role as he had in other political campaigns from 1912 on. He recruited

---

53. Frank P. Walsh to Peter Witt, September 13, 1928, Peter Witt Papers, Western Reserve Historical Society.

members for the executive committee, arranged for speakers, raised money, and helped write pamphlets and press releases. The League's purpose, Howe declared in a typical recruitment letter, was "to give strength to the views of Governor Smith by the confidence we have in his progressive mindedness and forward looking ideals." Its function would be "distribution of literature and possibly the sending out of a few speakers, but primarily in mobilizing progressive groups thruout the country in the support of Governor Smith's candidacy." A form letter, signed by Walsh, Howe, and David K. Niles, made the case for Smith, enumerating the policies that should lead Progressives to support him: his fight against the power trust, his support for free speech and free press, his battle for the rights of industrial workers and the protection of women and children. "As officers of the La Follette–Wheeler campaign committee of 1924, we are assured that the rank and file of progressives throughout the nation see in Governor Smith the best hope for the progressive cause in this campaign."[54]

Whatever aid the Progressive League gave to Al Smith was obviously far from sufficient as, in an election marked by religious animosity and in a time of national prosperity, the Democratic candidate lost decisively to Hoover. Smith lost not only Wisconsin but also all of the eleven states in which La Follette had finished second in 1924. George Norris doubtless expressed the sentiments of many Progressives when he wrote W. T. Rawleigh: "I think the Progressive cause has received a very severe setback, if indeed it is not absolutely defeated. What good does it do, after all, to pass a progressive measure like Congress did enact with regard to Muscle Shoals at the last session if we insist on putting a President in the chair who will veto any law of a progressive nature that we may succeed in passing." Donald Richberg wrote Amos Pinchot about the

> tragic irony of every progressive movement. The conservatives can unite on sticking to everything that is, even though agreeing that a lot of it is rotten. The revolutionaries can unite on smashing everything that is, even though agreeing that a lot of it is good. But when liberal or progressive groups get together to work out an evolutionary program, the conservatives are so fearful they will go too far and the radicals so fearful that they won't go far enough that the total result is they wobble now forward and now backward and when the conservatives and revolutionaries get really to grips they brush the impotent liberals out of the way and have a pitched

---

54. FCH to Paul M. Kellogg, September 13, 1928; Frank P. Walsh, FCH, David K. Niles to Paul M. Kellogg, September 15, 1928.

battle. . . . The whole purpose of a progressive movement, if it has any purpose, is to avoid a pitched battle.⁵⁵

At inauguration time, Fred Howe's discontent was clear in a letter to his friend Pinchot, who had just returned to New York after a vacation in the South. "I hope you had a good time in Florida. I saw the northern end of it and had to come home with a bad tooth," he wrote. "I hope the Ku Kluxers and the good people are not as much in power in the far south as they are in the northern end of the state. They feel that Hoover's election is their victory and they are making the most out of it for God and Country."⁵⁶

---

55. George Norris to W. T. Rawleigh, November 9, 1928, Norris Papers, Library of Congress; Donald R. Richberg to Amos Pinchot, October 7, 1931. A Progressive stalwart in the 1920s, Rawleigh had made a fortune as a purveyor of spices, health foods, and household products through a network of traveling salesmen.

56. FCH to Amos Pinchot, March 4, 1929. Pinchot had a dim view of Florida: "Florida strikes me as more Babbitt than the middle west. Everything is organized for revenue, and they are remarkably vulgar about it, too." Pinchot to FCH, March 12, 1929.

16

FRED AND MARIE

Lincoln Steffens recalled that after Fred Howe completed the manuscript of *Confessions of a Reformer,* he proudly gave it to Marie to read. When she finished, she looked at him "with the humor that is all hers" and said, "But, Fred, weren't you ever married?" "Oh, yes," he answered. "I forgot that. I'll put it in." Steffens's wife, Ella Winter, added that when Fred once again gave the manuscript to Marie, he had added one more sentence: "For the beautiful Miss Jenney was by now my wife." Marie remarked sadly to Ella, "Imagine a woman writing her life story and paying that much attention to her husband." She wrote Steffens that in *Confessions* Fred "tried so hard to be honest—about the things he didn't mind being honest about. And now he's put me in it. O it's terrible. So much more terrible than being left out."[1]

Actually, Fred wrote more about Marie in his *Confessions* than Winter reported—some fourteen pages along with various incidental mentions. He was not exceptional among reformers in limiting the comments on his marriage and his personal life. Tom Johnson's autobiography polished off his courtship and marriage in a sentence. Brand Whitlock's did not mention his wife. Charlotte Perkins Gilman's scarcely referred to her husband, George Houghton Gilman, who "suffers from the invisibility ordinarily associated with the wives of famous men." Steffens, probably not expecting to be taken seriously, asked Marie if he should include his wives in his memoirs—"they are not essential to the story."[2]

---

1. Steffens, *Autobiography,* 153; Winter, *And Not to Yield,* 113; MJH to Lincoln Steffens, April 29, 1925, Steffens Papers. The Columbia annotation makes this a 1926 letter, but the context indicates it was 1925.

2. Murdock, "Life of Tom L. Johnson," 27; Bremner, "Artist in Politics," 243; A. Lane, *To Herland and Beyond,* 190; Steffens to FCH, December 6, 1925, in Winter and Hicks, *Letters of Lincoln Steffens,* 2:721–22.

Nevertheless, the Steffens anecdote, plus other scattered bits of information, have raised questions about the Howes' marriage. The Iowa sisterhood had opposed it, fearing that Marie's independence and radical feminism would be submerged by the tie to a husband with more conventional views on woman's role. Some of them thought that later events proved their fears to be justified. Mabel Dodge, who repeated the Steffens story in her memoirs and found it indicative of the relationship between Marie and Fred, thought that Marie's "loving wit" helped her to accept "the sterility of her domestic life." Fred was a great humanitarian who tried to make Ellis Island hospitable to the immigrants, she wrote, but in his own home he was "one of those husbands who seem to be perpetually engrossed in thought and never on the spot." Among later writers, Cynthia Tucker has observed that "the marriage did not bring the happiness [Marie] had hoped for." Kate E. Wittenstein wrote of "an unsatisfying marriage that ultimately ended [Marie's] career." Judith Schwarz has suggested that "whatever Marie Jenney was led to expect from her marriage, it seems she was sadly disappointed."3

Most of the attempts to describe the Howes' marriage have relied heavily on Hutchins Hapgood's interpretation of it in his autobiography, *A Victorian in the Modern World.* Hapgood was a reporter and editorial and feature writer for various New York newspapers prior to World War I, the author of several interesting books (*The Spirit of the Ghetto* and *The Autobiography of a Thief*), one of the founders of the Provincetown Players, and a moving spirit in Mabel Dodge's salon. He had a wide circle of friends and acquaintances. He certainly was acquainted with the Howes from their Greenwich Village days, but how well and intimately he knew them in the postwar years is debatable. Hutchins's heyday was the prewar Village. Unlike his brother Norman, he was not much of a political activist. A biographer noted his prolabor and anti-middle-class sentiments and observed: "His aversion to self-righteous reformers, especially those who wished to impose their standards on people he liked, kept Hapgood apart, and his estimation of many reformers as wooden and unimaginative was significant."4

Hapgood gave Fred Howe credit for helping stimulate him to write his own autobiography. He told Ella Winter in 1936 that he was "led to do it by the earnest words of my old friend Fred Howe whom I met again last spring in

---

3. Tucker, *Prophetic Sisterhood,* 77–78; Luhan, *Movers and Shakers,* 143–44; Wittenstein, "Heterodoxy Club and American Feminism," 15; Schwarz, *Radical Feminists of Heterodoxy,* 8.

4. Marcaccio, *Hapgoods,* 153, 155. On Hutchins Hapgood, see also Boyce and Hapgood, *Intimate Warriors;* Humphrey, *Children of Fantasy,* 54–83; Marriner, "Victorian in the Modern World." Max Eastman called Hapgood a "philosophical anarchist with a deep voice and a groping mind, both swayed completely by his emotions." *Enjoyment of Living,* 342.

Washington, after long years.... Howe wrote to Harcourt Brace about it and I received an interested letter from them." His wife, Neith Boyce, had added her encouragement; and the result was the publication of *A Victorian in a Modern World* in 1939.[5]

In this volume Hapgood pictured Marie as the prototype of the feminist movement and recalled her founding of Heterodoxy, many of whose members were "moving toward the unknown hoped-for world of feminine predominance. I knew a great many of these women, but Mrs. Howe seemed to me, perhaps because I knew her better than the others, to be curiously significant of the feminist movement of that time." Marie he described as "a woman of very strong mental and emotional character, and one also endowed to an extraordinary degree with what we call femininity, caring more for love and affection even than most women, yet thoroughly impregnated with the feeling that there was a conspiracy of men against women." This was a "vital lie," he believed, untenable but essential to the feminist movement. He praised Marie as an organizer who carried her religious fervor into her passionate suffrage and feminist activities.[6]

Fred he considered "one of the best men and in some ways one of the most effective men of these decades." In contrast to Marie, he was "dominatingly a mental person. He was heart and soul with the deeper reform movement. He could be counted on always to represent courageously, clearly, and truthfully the advancing good." In some ways, Fred and Marie were alike: in their unusual honesty, their lack of personal ambition, their devotion to the good of society. "But they were singularly different, too, in emotional and instinctive ways. Fred was kindness itself, but his was a kindness that didn't enter deeply into the instincts. He was capable of great affection, but he held himself aloof largely from the passions of human beings. He couldn't understand Marie's deep unconscious needs, and she could not understand how he could be so good and kind and yet so aloof."

Marie had chosen George Sand as the subject of a biography because Sand was "the woman who expressed most successfully the tragic situation that life or history or man has put woman into. She felt that George Sand, misunderstood by her lovers, was superior to them, with a great soul, unhappy in a harsh world." This, wrote Hapgood, was certainly the case with Marie, who also was "unhappy in a harsh world, although I think that she, like so many other women

---

5. Hutchins Hapgood to Ella Winter, October 8, 1936, Steffens Papers, Columbia University; H. Hapgood, *Victorian in a Modern World*, 560–61.

6. H. Hapgood, *Victorian in a Modern World*, 332–33. For Hapgood's views on Heterodoxy, see ibid., 377.

of her time with sensitive natures, was against the facts of life and history in thinking that men were the cause of all their inward woe."⁷

It was clear to Hapgood that Fred loved and admired Marie. "But I, who knew Marie well, do not believe that she recognized Fred's love for her, because of her suffrage and feministic poison, which had gone so deep in her whole personality." Nevertheless, he felt that the inspiring thing about the union of Fred and Marie was that "when the man and woman involved are of a superior character, conflicting temperaments, though they may bring about and do bring about great difficulties and emotional conflicts and frustrations, yet keep the marriage alive."⁸

Questions must remain about how close the friendship was between Hutchins and the Howes and how well he had observed their marriage. Fred fails to mention him in *The Confessions of a Reformer,* nor is he mentioned in the surviving letters of Fred and Marie. Several 1919 letters from Steffens indicate that Marie was interested in what Hapgood was writing, if perhaps not in touch with him.⁹ Certainly Hapgood was not a good witness for the post–World War I period. Dividing his time between Provincetown, Key West, and New Hampshire, he did little to attract attention between 1919 and 1939, the year of his autobiography. That he was not in touch with Fred for some time is indicated in the 1936 letter to Ella Winter, when he relates that he met Fred "after long years." Fred was still alive when Hapgood's autobiography appeared. It would be interesting to know his reaction to the description of his marriage.

In his *Confessions of a Reformer,* Fred admitted that he had entered marriage with conventional views of husband-wife relationships. "I wanted my old-fashioned picture of a wife rather than an equal partner," he wrote. In Cleveland, when Marie wanted to go beyond the traditional role of the college-educated wife, he "found reasons for deciding against each suggested activity in turn." His mind led him to support woman suffrage ("without much wanting it") and freedom for women ("without liking it"), but his instincts remained conservative. Looking back from 1925, Fred realized that "I never honestly faced what I was doing or the rightfulness of my wife's claims." Marie had helped him greatly and had given him "generous freedom" to do as he chose with his life.

> There was every reason why I should have allowed my wife any right which I enjoyed, should have given her every freedom which I took for

---

7. Ibid., 333.
8. Ibid., 333–34.
9. Lincoln Steffens to MJH, November 23, 1919, in Winter and Hicks, *Letters of Lincoln Steffens,* 1:493; December 28, 1919, Steffens Papers, Columbia University.

myself, should have encouraged her to express her talents, which I recognized were of an unusual sort. I was proud of these qualities, and my belief in freedom should have made me the first to insist that she use them as she willed. Instead, I discouraged them, because I preferred my early picture of a wife, a picture that fell in with the current assumption of the period that a woman should quite literally "serve," quite literally "obey," her husband.

It was not until they moved to New York, "where the suffrage movement was claiming women of distinction, where no more notice was taken of a woman in work than a man, that I recast my prejudices." New standards brought a change. "Then I was as eager for her to find her work as I had been loath to have her do in Cleveland.... But I had taken many years out of her life, had denied her the opportunity to pioneer, which she feared rather less than did I, and many of the enthusiasms that had been denied her in Cleveland could not be warmed into life again."[10]

In her definition of "feminism," Marie had emphasized independence, whether a woman was married or unmarried. Upon marrying Fred, she had given up much of her independence. In Cleveland she found herself restricted to those public activities that society deemed proper for married, college-educated women of her class: the suffrage movement (carried on in a genteel way), settlement work, consumer protection. Any urge to do more or to do something different was hampered both by Fred's confessed reluctance and by Marie's ill health. Her illnesses, to which Fred devoted much loving care, were a restriction both on her activities and on her ability to join her husband in his many travels.

Improvement in her health and the decision to move to New York City—a decision in which both she and Fred shared—opened up new opportunities for her, and Fred willingly gave his support to her endeavors. She could now work with the more militant woman suffrage advocates, take a leading role in the Woman's Party, join those who resisted preparedness and opposed America's entry into the war, and participate in the heady discussions of the Greenwich Village salons and of Heterodoxy, the club that she founded. Judging from his comments in *Confessions*, Fred welcomed these new chances and willingly backed her efforts.

Nevertheless, except for the years of excitement in the suffrage period, loneliness remained a theme of the Howes' marriage. Fred's needs as a writer on political and economic topics (and articles and books supplied a part of their

---

10. *Confessions of a Reformer*, 233–34.

livelihood) and his commercial responsibilities with Long Arm and other enterprises required frequent trips to Europe. Marie's health—and perhaps a lack of interest—nearly always prevented her from accompanying him. Fred was lonely without her, and no doubt she was lonely without him. That loneliness, emphasized by Marie in the 1920s, apparently was present even in the early years of their marriage.[11]

They had no children on whom their affections could center. One report says that they lost a baby, an infant son, but there is no confirmation of this anywhere in the written record.[12] Marie may have been thinking of her own lot when she wrote Steffens: "I know lots of women who are sad because they don't have children or can't do what they like or live where they like."[13] During the Ellis Island controversies in 1919, Fred expressed a desire to adopt a child. Whether Marie shared this interest is unknown. Doubtless Heterodoxy helped her fill an emotional void in her life—certainly the comments of its members in their "homage to Marie" scrapbook showed them as a close-knit "family." But in the 1920s Marie ceased going regularly to Heterodoxy, probably because of poor health, and her complaints about loneliness increased. It was not just that Fred was frequently absent but that her friends also seemed to have abandoned her. She wrote Fola La Follette from Paris in 1925: "My Adele has gone away and it makes an awful difference as I have no one to talk to. Maria gets my dinner and I do the rest. Maria is an old dear but we don't talk much. . . . I find it depressing to be alone so much as all my friends have gone."[14] On another occasion, back at Harmon, she wrote Fola: "Fred has cabled me from Paris, so he is that far on his way to Russia. I hated to have him go, and was sick for three days after he left. I went to bed, could not sleep, wept, stared at the ceiling and asked of the hard plaster, Will no one ever stay with me—no-one, no-one? And there wasn't even a raven to croak 'Never more.' No one will ever stay with me. That's settled. And I am just as emotional as when I was thirty, that's evident too." Yet at other times Marie indicated that she did not mind a somewhat solitary, sedentary life. Religion provided no consolation. She observed to Fola: "What troubles me more than anything is that I wish there were a God. I want a Something, a Someone. I can't get over it. That's childishness I suppose, or what is called the religious temperament."[15]

    11. FCH to Robert M. La Follette, June 15, 1911, La Follette Papers.
    12. The report is from Cynthia Tucker in *Prophetic Sisterhood,* 79 and 251n23, who credits the information to Mary Ella Holst, who learned of it from a nephew of Marie. I have found no mention of this in any of the letters and papers relating to Fred and Marie.
    13. MJH to Lincoln Steffens, ca. December 1925, Steffens Papers.
    14. MJH to Fola La Follette, June 20, 1925, La Follette Family Collection. Adele Fuchs, an associate of the Iowa Sisterhood though not a minister, had been a friend of Marie's since the Iowa days. Maria was apparently Marie's housekeeper/cook in Paris.
    15. MJH to Fola La Follette, undated, 1927, and March 22, 1933.

The scanty evidence does not allow confident generalizations, but it tends to support somewhat Hapgood's description of Fred as mind and Marie as heart—or as reason and as emotion. Their differences appeared in their attitudes toward life stories. Fred's autobiography was primarily a description of a world of political ideas, institutions, and public policies. He sought to explain how his insights into that world had changed over his lifetime as he learned to reject authority and to think for himself. Although he included some personal details, his main concern was ideas—how he had come to believe what he did. Marie was more interested in the personal and the emotional. As she advised Lincoln Steffens when he was working on his autobiography, "Be personal. What was going on inside of you? Let it out. It will all be interesting. The events you describe may be dull. They may be familiar. But your reaction to them will be new, interesting, even thrilling. Let it out. Don't be self conscious."[16]

The 1920s saw Marie's withdrawal from public life. She no longer remained active in the National Woman's Party, and organizations like the Women's International League for Peace and Freedom and the League of Women Voters did not arouse her interest. She ceased to chair Heterodoxy and attended fewer and fewer meetings. Partly her retreat resulted from the fact that the great campaigns for woman suffrage and peace were over and from her belief that it was time for the older generation of feminist leaders to give way to new blood. The crusaders were aging, and few of them had the fight "to reform the world anymore," she told her friend Adele Fuchs. Her withdrawal from public affairs was due even more to poor health and fatigue. She suffered from heart problems as well as other illnesses, had an appendectomy, and was hospitalized for a time in Paris in 1926. She wrote Ella Winter from her hospital bed: "Shall be happy if I can feel well again. I want to walk. Haven't had a real walk for five months." Travel did not appeal to Marie—she wrote Fola that she had promised to visit Steffens in Switzerland "but somehow don't feel much like it. Am not very strong, and it seems easier not to move." "When I am sick I have no initiative," she informed Steffens. "I just get passive and drift and don't overcome obstacles. That's one of my worst faults." In 1929 Adele reported that although Marie swore that at fifty-nine she did not feel her age, she was clearly weaker and had to wear reading glasses. It hurt "to see old age set in, often so relentlessly," and those who had been "at the front" now ill and weak and "pushed into the background."[17]

16. MJH to Lincoln Steffens, November 25, 1925.
17. Tucker, *Prophetic Sisterhood,* 222, quoting from Fuchs's diary, 1923–1934, January 6, 1923; MJH to Lincoln Steffens, ca. December 1925; MJH to Fola La Follette, June 20, 1925; MJH to Ella Winter, ca. April 1926, Steffens Papers; MJH to Lincoln Steffens, undated, 1926; Tucker, *Prophetic Sisterhood,* 225, quoting from Fuchs, diary, 1923–1934, February 22, 1926, July 6 and 7, 1929, September 10–23, 1931.

After the war Marie spent much of her time in Paris, living there nearly all of 1924, 1925, and 1926 and parts of other years as well. One of France's attractions was that it was cheaper to live there than in America. Though the Howes were not poor, the lower cost of living was important to them. They supplemented their income from investments and Fred's writings by renting out their Harmon house during their absences.

Interested in French culture and ambitious to write about George Sand, Marie found Paris a congenial place to live. She and Fred resided first on the Left Bank at 20 Rue Jacob, "a quiet residential street lined with plain eighteenth-century facades interspersed with a few bookstores and antique shops, located on the edge of the old Latin Quarter, around the corner from the Church of Saint-Germain-des-Prés." Driven out by construction noise in the Rue Jacob vicinity, Marie later moved to 50 Avenue de la Bourdonnais, to "a commonplace hotel like apartment near Champs de Mars." Fred spent part of his time in Paris with Marie and the rest of it in trips to Vienna, Frankfurt, Russia, and other places and in Sconset during the summer months. Although Marie praised the pleasures of Nantucket to her friends, she was not interested enough in the School of Opinion to leave Paris for it. She wrote Steffens in 1926 that she had been there only once in the school's first four years. After a visit when she found Marie depressed and alone, Adele Fuchs wrote in her diary in 1929: "She does not enthuse over her husband. There has been a let-down there, but who shall criticize a man of F. C. Howe's gifts running a summer hotel and a lecture Chautauqua?"[18]

It has been suggested that a close and intimate relationship with another woman, Rose Young, helped fill an emotional void in Marie's life. About the same age as Marie, Young was an author of several novels, a contributor of stories and feature articles to magazines, a journalist, and an activist in the woman suffrage movement. In 1912 and 1913 she wrote feature stories on the "modern" woman for the *New York Evening Post.* In 1914 the widow of the publisher Frank Leslie bequeathed most of her fortune—more than a million dollars—to Carrie Chapman Catt to use as she saw fit for the cause of woman suffrage. Catt used part of the money to create the Leslie Woman Suffrage Commission, which subsidized suffrage organizations and financed the Leslie Bureau of Suffrage Education as the "news purveyor, publicity expert, and propaganda carrier" for the movement. Young served as director of the Bureau and editor of its political magazine, the *Woman Citizen,* from 1917 to 1922.[19]

---

18. MJH to Fola La Follette, September 7, 1933; MJH to Lincoln Steffens, undated, 1926; Tucker, *Prophetic Sisterhood,* 251n24, quoting from Fuchs, Diary, 1923–1934, September 1929.

19. S. Graham, "Woman Suffrage," 208–13.

Marie came to know Rose through the suffrage campaign and through their membership in Heterodoxy. Both were members of the Woman's Party's Committee of Contributing Editors; both were on the committee to arrange the women's peace parade in 1914; Rose was a speaker at the feminist mass meeting that Marie arranged in 1914. Several writers believe their relationship went beyond friendship. One historian has written that Marie found with Rose "the domestic intimacy and locus for her deepest affections that she had initially hoped to find with Fred. . . . Certainly by the mid-1920s, and possibly earlier, she had replaced Fred as Marie's primary partner." Another writer includes the two women in her list of Heterodoxy members who were "probable lesbians, or at the least, bisexuals," and concluded that Marie's relationship with Young "was at least equal in strength as that with her husband."[20]

Evidence to support these generalizations about Marie and Rose and about the effect of their friendship on the Howes' marriage is scanty, and the statements seem to stretch the available information. It is true that Marie dedicated her biography of George Sand not to Fred but to Rose. It is also true that there are a few references to Rose in Marie's surviving letters; but these are brief, matter-of-fact statements, all from 1933. Rose has finished her biography, a three-year job, and "it's grand"; Rose's sister has rented the Harmon house for two months; Rose is coming to visit for a month. Marie took the lead in finding money to help Rose during the Depression. Friends were concerned with Rose's grief when Marie died, and Rose was "the one consulted about the memorial service and the one who virtually closed the house and sent the news to old acquaintants, sometimes enclosing a scarf of Marie's or some other token as she would have wished."[21] She also supplied the information for Marie's death certificate. All these bits of information may be indicative of a close friendship but not necessarily of a deeper and more intimate relationship. Cynthia Daniels has observed in her biography of Lillian Wald: "It must be remembered that it was common for women reared in the Victorian era and who were kindred spirits to love one another with a feeling of sisterly fellowship and to gain emotional support from one another. The erotic could, but did not have to intrude upon intimate relations."[22]

20. Tucker, *Prophetic Sisterhood*, 79; Schwarz, *Radical Feminists of Heterodoxy*, 69, 72. Schwarz states that her list of Heterodoxy's "probable lesbians or . . . bisexuals" is based on "intuition" and "bits and pieces of scattered information" and needs more verification.

21. MJH to Fola La Follette, January 15, 1933, March 22, 1933, December 13, 1933; Tucker, *Prophetic Sisterhood*, 79. Tucker's source is Fuchs, diary entry, June 18, 1934. I have found no information on the biography Young was writing. Apparently it was never published.

22. Daniels, *Always a Sister*, 73. See also A. Lane, *To Herland and Beyond*, 78, 348–49, and Smith-Rosenberg, "Female World of Love and Ritual." It might be noted that Marie dedicated her second book, *The Intimate Journal of George Sand*, to Fola La Follette, but no one has suggested a homosexual relationship between those two close friends.

There is the barest hint in the extant correspondence that Fred's eye may have wandered on at least one occasion. In 1915 Eugene Boissevain wrote Inez Haynes Irwin that Inez's sister, Vida, had often been in the company of Fred Howe and that Inez's mother was worried that Vida's relationship with him could spoil her marriage prospects. No other reference to such a "relationship" has been found.[23]

Despite differences in personality and outlook and despite the problems that may have existed between them, Fred and Marie remained married for thirty years, their union broken only by Marie's death in 1934. This was at a time when divorce was increasingly a solution for serious marital difficulties—a third of Marie's friends in Heterodoxy had been divorced. After pointing out differences in temperament between Fred and Marie, Hutchins Hapgood had concluded that the couple was an example of how a marriage might live in spite of emotional conflicts. Fred expressed his feelings about Marie in the dedication to *The Confessions of a Reformer*:

TO HER MOST OF MY HAPPINESS IS DUE
FROM HER I HAVE GOT FAR MORE THAN I HAVE TOLD
WITHOUT HER THIS NARRATIVE WOULD NOT HAVE BEEN WRITTEN
PERHAPS THERE WOULD HAVE BEEN NO STORY WORTH TELLING
THEREFORE THIS IS NOT A MERE STORY OF MY LIFE
BUT A GRATEFUL ACKNOWLEDGMENT OF LOVE
AND DEBT TO A COMPANION AND
CO-WORKER THROUGH TWENTY YEARS

Marie was more chary about expressing sentiments in writing. Sometimes she thought of Freddy, as she often called him, as much younger than his years, writing Steffens: "Fred is really more naive than you realize and used to be much much more so than you want to realize. A great part of him has never grown up. It's nice [but] sometimes a bit inconvenient." Sometimes her letters expressed a kind of wry exasperation with her husband, as in one to Steffens about a mix-up in plans to visit: "Fred is so individualistic he doesn't like to do things together. He has to do them alone and I have to let him alone. He can't bear to talk things over and have advice. But he meant to do the right thing in the right way." She could poke fun at his seriousness: "Fred (thank goodness) has finished his book on banking. I have heard nothing but banking for 10 years

---

23. Eugen Boissevain to Inez Haynes Irwin, Inez Milholland Papers, Schlesinger Library, Radcliffe College, Spring 1915, Folder 2; quoted in Adickes, *To Be Young Was Very Heaven*, 157.

and I would like to have a change of subject at the dinner-table. But to my despair he has immediately started another book—on banking. Any other subject would interest me more."[24]

Despite their differences, Fred and Marie had much in common. Both were intelligent and witty and had a sense of humor along with a zeal for reform. Though each had his or her own circle, they had a number of friends in common—Tom Johnson, the Newton Bakers, Steffens and Winter, the La Follettes (especially Fola). Fred remained a public man throughout his lifetime, concerned with good causes and the political action necessary to promote them. Marie turned to private life after the suffrage crusade. Though she may have been lonely, her letters show frequent visits to her in Paris and Harmon by friends and acquaintances. She found close friendships rare, however, writing once that "thousands of people affect me like animals, hundreds that are like poison gas, and here and there the same two-legged animal who is not the same at all because of some quality of spirit or brain."[25]

Marie was cautious about what she revealed in her letters. She came to prefer "heart to heart talk" and wrote Fola: "Somehow one doesn't feel like letting go very fully in writing. And I find as I grow older I grow more careful about other peoples private affairs. I start to talk freely to you and then I remember the awful accidents that have happened to letters and so I keep still."[26] Unfortunately for any effort to discuss Fred's and Marie's lives together, few of their personal letters seem to have survived. The largest number of Marie's letters are to Lincoln Steffens and Ella Winter, and they do not reveal a marriage in trouble. Her letters to Fola La Follette are perhaps franker but are so few in number that it is risky to generalize from them. Fred's surviving correspondence throws little light on their marriage and personal relationships.

Marie's Heterodoxy friends believed she had a talent for writing and urged her to use it. Lincoln Steffens joined in the encouragement, praising one of her letters to him as "the wittiest, wisest and the most satisfying. And it's the best

24. MJH to Lincoln Steffens, November 25, 1925, and undated, 1926; MJH to Fola La Follette, postmarked March 22, 1933. Cynthia Tucker interprets this as showing "a man whose interests and comprehension—as his wife still often complained—ran to banking, not to matters of the heart." *Prophetic Sisterhood*, 79. This suggests frequent complaints by Marie about Fred, which the existing correspondence does not bear out.

25. Lincoln Steffens to MJH, May 3, 1913, and April 4, 1913, in Winter and Hicks, *Letters of Lincoln Steffens*, 1:322, 321; MJH to Ella Winter(?), ca. 1925, fragment, Steffens Papers.

26. MJH to Fola La Follette, September 7, 1933. Tucker ascribes this reticence to Marie's knowledge that on Mary Safford's death, her intimate papers were "literally dumped in her yard and pried into by strangers" and that Mary Collson's papers were similarly despoiled. "If the Safford incident did not prompt [Marie] to destroy her paper trails, and it may have, it at least made her all the more leery of candor in private correspondence and all the less given to writing her life's story for the public's perusal." *Prophetic Sisterhood*, 232.

written. You really should write, Marie; not regularly, not as work, but when and what you 'jolly well please.' "[27] By the 1920s, Marie's published literary output consisted of a handful of articles in the *Meadville Portfolio, Old and New,* the *New Review, La Follette's Weekly Magazine,* and the popular *Anti-Suffrage Monologue.* She turned her hand to movie scripts for a while and learned enough about Hollywood to be able to give Steffens practical advice about selling his autobiography for a film.[28] Her only success in writing for the movies, it appears, was credit with another writer for the screenplay for *The Gray Dawn,* a film produced by Benjamin B. Hampton in 1922. The film was a mishmash of crooked politics, murder, vigilantism, and torture in San Francisco in 1856. Marie would not have been pleased with *Variety*'s review. The movie was "the utmost in melodrama," said the show business bible. "It consists of a series of melodramatic bits linked together by a slight story which at no times reaches importance as far as the screen version is concerned. . . . The picture [is] the proper offering for houses where the patrons are dime novel readers." Apparently script writing had not proven to be Marie's métier.[29]

She was much interested in George Sand and in 1925 began to try to write about her. She was encouraged in this by Lincoln Steffens's resumption of work on his autobiography and by his sending several chapters to her to read and comment upon. In her turn, Marie was quite willing to send him chapters of her own work, and a happy writing relationship ensued. Ella Winter and Marie had plotted to keep Steffens at work on the autobiography. Ella described what they had done: "The next time he despaired, as writers do, I sent some chapters, again secretly, to Marie Howe. Stef valued her judgment, but the first he knew of it was an enthusiastic, delighted letter from Marie, which encouraged him so much that he continued the rest of that winter, with Marie reading each chapter and returning it with hosannas."[30]

During the fall of 1925 and much of 1926, Marie and Steffens lent each other mutual encouragement. While she was writing *George Sand,* he was writing the *Autobiography,* and each sent the other chapters to read and critique. Marie provided Steffens with the praise he seemed to need, and she had specific suggestions on the chapters she read, often in the form of a series of questions.

Marie's book, *George Sand: The Search for Love,* was published in October 1927 and dedicated to Rose Young. It was not "fictionalized biography," she wrote in the preface. "It is history told with as near an approach to story form

27. Lincoln Steffens to MJH, November 23, 1919, in Winter and Hicks, *Letters of Lincoln Steffens,* 1:492.
28. MJH to Steffens, April 21, 1926.
29. Munden, ed., *American Film Institute Catalogue,* 58.
30. Winter, *And Not to Yield,* 213.

as authentic records permit." She had drawn on material from Sand's autobiography, journals, and letters, but had "reassembled" rather than invented. "Imagination has been used, as it must always be used in interpretive biography, to touch up details of a faded background, but not to alter a line of the portrait."[31] Thus the life was told as a story, without any scholarly paraphernalia except a bibliography and with no attempt at deep analysis of Sand's literary works. Interestingly enough, she made no acknowledgment of Steffens's help to her, nor did he acknowledge her aid to his autobiography.

Marie had selected Sand because she was "the greatest feminine genius known to literature. No woman has ever matched her in creative power and none has approached her in productivity."[32] She had tried in the biography "to throw light on George Sand's inner life, to explain the secret of her suffering, the reasons for her loneliness, and the unprecedented situation which has made her the most misunderstood woman in the history of literature." Marie saw Sand's life as "a search for love," a quest fraught with difficulties because of her basic conflict between freedom and detachment. "Poor George! It was the conflict of her life, between theories and emotions, between the desire for freedom and the need of human ties." The fundamental force that welded together her many selves and gave them identity was her need of mystic union with something not herself.[33]

The reviews of *George Sand* tended to agree that the book had its failings as biography but that Marie had presented a very readable story. To a reviewer in the *Boston Transcript*, the volume contained little new or original material, was imprecise in dates and detail, and made it difficult for the reader to separate fact from interpretation. "Taken as a story, the book is thoroughly readable and eminently interesting. The background is feelingly if not exhaustively portrayed and the characters and encounters are happily sketched." A review in the *New York Evening Post* declared that the book would please "amateurs of fiction" and would "interest those who know little about George Sand. The historical facts are followed conscientiously." Marie was too much a partisan, however. "It is obvious that the study of her life has been done with a desire to place George Sand on a pedestal before which pilgrims will worship and admirers pray." The *New York World*'s reviewer observed that "to portray this engrossing character Mrs. Howe has written a biography that reads like a novel. She has selected her data carefully from an overwhelming amount of material, and has

---

31. M. Howe, *George Sand,* x–xi. The book was published in England, by Brentano's, also in 1927. Correspondence between Marie and her publisher about her books on Sand can be found in the archives of John Day Company, Princeton University Library.

32. Ibid., xiii–xiv.

33. MJH to Lincoln Steffens, February 25, 1926.

given us, not a literary biography, but an explanation of George Sand's motives."

For the *New York Times*, Percy Hutchison compared Marie's biography with another that had appeared at the same time, Elizabeth W. Schermerhorn's *The Seven Strings of the Lyre: The Romantic Life of George Sand*. He thought both books were accurate accounts of Sand's life. "Mrs. Howe's book is partisan, Miss Schermerhorn's detached; the first is utterly devoid of humor, the second is brimming over with it." He preferred Schermerhorn's approach, although he thought Marie's volume "a more penetrating and more sustained study." An anonymous reviewer in the *Woman's Journal* thought Marie's role as Sand's "defender" might make some readers skeptical of her judgment. "Yet, because it is written with frank bias and with such warm sympathy, the book becomes a fascinating human story of George Sand's adventures in the pursuit of ideal love and in the achievement of fame. In the present vogue for fictionalized biography none is more successful than Mrs. Howe's volume." Marie had selected the vital elements from the tremendous mass of Sand materials and had presented them logically and dramatically. "Of particular interest to *Journal* readers are the parts of the book which deal with George Sand's struggles as a pioneer among working wives, her advocacy of equal laws for women and a single standard of morality, and her own tilt with the courts over the unfair settlement of her property and children—parts related with special zest by Mrs. Howe, who has herself been a leader in many women's causes."

The review in the *Times Literary Supplement* was scathing. "As a colloquial and superficial record of the outer life of Madame Dudevant—George Sand— divested of all originality of genius, this book may find a public. As a critical contribution to the literature dealing with 'the most misunderstood woman in the history of literature,' . . . it is without appreciable value, and . . . no new light is thrown which conduces in any way to a better understanding of George Sand's achievements, attempts, and failures." Mrs. Howe had left the reader with the impression that Sand's literary life was totally subordinate to her amorous one and chosen to interpret Sand in the light of the author's own preoccupation with "that vexed, if exploded, question," feminism. The result was a distortion of Sand's life, which was not a "search for love" but a search for the ultimate truth in human relations. "The whole book is disappointing and strangely unconvincing."[34] Despite such critical reviews, the book found an

---

34. J.F.S., *Boston Transcript*, December 17, 1927, 2; Joseph Collins, *New York Evening Post*, November 19, 1927, 7; Harry Hansen, *New York World*, November 20, 1927, 10; Percy Hutchison, *New York Times*, December 18, 1927, 5, 12; *Woman's Journal* 13 (April 1928): 30; *Times Literary Supplement* 390, no. 1 (September 20, 1928): 661.

audience; it went through four printings by March 1929 and was translated into Chinese in 1955.

Marie dedicated her second, and last, book to Fola La Follette. This was *The Intimate Journal of George Sand,* published in May 1929. For this volume, she translated and edited three documents hitherto unavailable in English: the journal kept by Sand during her love affair with Alfred de Musset, her imaginary conversations with "the very learned and highly skilled Dr. Piffoël," and a scrapbook of personal impressions, confessions, and letters.[35]

There were few reviews of the *Intimate Journal,* perhaps because it was almost entirely a translation. Herbert Gorman in the *New York Times* noted that it had been "excellently translated and liberally annotated by Mrs. Howe. Mrs. Howe is a little breathless in her admiration of George Sand, so much so, in fact, that she comes perilously near to deifying her subject, but this does not nullify the pertinency of her observations." The *American Mercury* thought the Musset journal "quite tame," the Piffoël part banal, the sketches "mainly rubbish." The translation was "good," but the book added "very little to Mme. Sand's modest stature, either as a person or as an artist."[36] Marie's translation of the *Intimate Journal* remains the standard one cited by later biographers of Sand. It was reprinted in 1975 and 1977.

Marie seemed to have no literary ambitions left after she finished the *Intimate Journal* in 1929. For whatever reason—lack of interest in topics other than Sand, discouragement from some of the critical reviews of her works, fatigue and ill health—she undertook no new writing project and appeared content to read, reflect, and observe the world from the sidelines in her remaining years.

---

35. *Intimate Journal of George Sand,* 13. The *Intimate Journal* was also published in London in 1929 by Williams and Norgate.

36. Herbert Gorman, *New York Times,* May 12, 1929, 19; "Check List of New Books," *American Mercury* 17 (July 1929): n.p.

17

PROTECTING THE CONSUMER

Although they did not suffer as much as many Americans, the onset of the Great Depression hurt the Howes' income. The stock market crash of October 1929 wiped out a significant part of the investment income on which their lifestyle depended. Another source of Fred's income had been articles and books, but it was no longer as easy to sell his writings as it had been, given the depressed state of publishers. Howe seems to have started, or become associated with, a travel agency in 1928, the American-European Travel Bureau. How active a role he took in its operations is not known, but he made its services available to his friends, advised them on itineraries, and informed them of expositions, music festivals, and other special events in Europe.[1] Any income from the travel bureau probably ended about 1930. Rental of the Harmon house in the summer months helped out a little.

Fred felt that he had to soldier on with the School of Opinion, "if only to try to pay his carrying charges," Marie explained. "Very few people go away in summer at present, so we can't expect much," she added. The 1935 session was probably the last for the school. By that time Howe was involved full time in affairs in Washington. He vacationed at Sconset in the summer of 1936, but the Nantucket newspaper made no reference to any activity by the School of Opinion in that year. The same year, he abandoned his Nantucket properties by foreclosure sales of his mortgages.[2]

---

1. FCH to Paul Kellogg, April 25, 1928, "Forget-Me-Not Files; FCH to Lincoln Steffens, February 12, 1930, in Winter and Hicks, *Letters of Lincoln Steffens*, 2:867.
2. MJH to Fola La Follette, March 22, 1933, La Follette Family Papers; Nantucket *Inquirer and Mirror*, July 23, 1932, July 22, 1933, December 19, 1936; Edouard A. Stackpole to author, October 7, 1982, and October 29, 1982; Barbara P. Andrews, Librarian, the Nantucket Atheneum, to author, November 24, 1982; interview, Edouard A. Stackpole, September 17, 1982.

Howe observed to Newton Baker: "Marie and I are quite well and have been. We live in the country and aside from having fired all of our servants and then taken them back again we go on about as usual. However we have pulled in our belts as have all of our neighbors but on the whole we are very lucky." Marie expressed much the same view in a 1934 letter to Steffens. All their friends were hard up, but they were "jogging along as usual. . . . By hook and crook we manage to have food and fuel, so ought to be grateful as that puts us in the capitalist class." Her friend Rose Young was in need, and Marie wrote Fola La Follette that she would send what she could and ask others to help. "But we all have hard times paying our grocery bills, so I suppose we can't send a great deal."[3] Despite their complaints, it was apparent that the Howes were among the fortunate ones in the early years of the Depression. Belt tightening did not materially change their way of life, nor did it prevent the occasional trip to Europe or stay in France.

The School of Opinion had faded in importance for Howe not only because of the difficulty of keeping it running during hard times but also because he was moving onto the national stage and would have little time for Sconset. Shortly after Franklin D. Roosevelt captured the Democratic nomination for president on July 1, 1932, the candidate, in planning his campaign strategy, turned a great deal of attention to dissident Progressive Republicans and independent liberals. Some of the old Progressives had wanted Al Smith to have a second chance; others were inclined toward a new party or to Norman Thomas's socialists. Louis Howe, Roosevelt's devoted adviser, and James Farley, the Democratic national chairman, worked with Frank Walsh and Basil Manly to set up an organization to pursue the Progressive vote. It would present itself as nonpartisan, but the Democratic National Committee would provide its financing.

Manly took the first step in creating the National Progressive League by writing letters on August 26, 1932, to Progressive leaders, including Senator George Norris of Nebraska, Harold Ickes, and Donald Richberg. He suggested the need to organize Progressives in support of Roosevelt and solicited the recipients' opinions. Not surprisingly, Norris, who had already endorsed Roosevelt, replied that there should be some kind of national movement "to bring the Progressive vote of the country to Roosevelt where it naturally and logically belongs. The organization ought to be controlled and handled preferably by Republicans of the Progressive wing." Ickes approved the idea if it was "a semi-independent group." Richberg doubted the value of such separate political organizations.[4]

---

3. FCH to Newton Baker, January 12, 1933, Baker Papers; MJH to Lincoln Steffens, January 12, 1934, Steffens Papers; MJH to Fola La Follette, December 13, 1933.

4. George Norris to Basil Manly, September 1, 1932; Harold Ickes to Manly, August 31, 1932; Donald Richberg to Manly, September 3, 1932, Frank Walsh Papers. The steps taken to organize the League are summarized in a memorandum in the Walsh Papers.

Norris had told Manly and Walsh what they wanted, and doubtless expected, to hear. At a meeting at Walsh's office on September 7, the plans for the League were drawn up, and Roosevelt and Louis Howe were informed about them. The plans provided for three separate offices for the League: one in Washington, D.C., to handle publicity; another, in New York City, to take care of speakers, radio, and finance; and a third, in Chicago, to be concerned with membership and field work. All would be kept separate from the Democratic National Committee. Norris accepted the chairmanship of the Progressive League. Fred Howe was quickly chosen as secretary and worked out of the Washington headquarters. Ickes ran the Chicago office.

Before the official announcement of the League's formation, Manly, Walsh, and Howe proceeded to recruit as many well-known Progressives or liberals as they could to serve on the executive committee or to lend their names to the group's activities. By the time the League's existence was officially announced, its roster included a large number of nationally known Republicans and independent liberals. Keeping its identity separate from Democratic campaign committees, it would concentrate its speeches and publicity on states west of the Alleghenies and north of the Ohio, on the fifteen states with enough electoral votes to elect Roosevelt if he carried the South and the border states.[5]

On September 25, 1932, Fred Howe announced the formation of the National Progressive League in a press release to the nation's newspapers. Besides giving information on the organization's officers, headquarters, and general campaign plans, the statement chronicled the Hoover administration's failings and urged independent voters to ignore party labels and join to support Roosevelt's candidacy and the Progressive principles for which he stood.[6] The slogan of the new organization, suggested by Norris, was "We need a Roosevelt in the White House."

Walsh had consulted again with Louis Howe and Jim Farley and received their assurance of Democratic financial aid for the League's radio addresses and speaking tours. Norris was the principal campaigner, undertaking a coast-to-coast trip in which he gave eleven major speeches. The League sought to make it clear that the Republican Progressives were speaking under its auspices and not under the sponsorship of the Democratic Party. Behind the scenes, of course, the Democrats were footing the bills. A report by a League treasurer of

---

5. "Formation of the National Progressive League, September, 1932," memorandum, unsigned and undated but probably mid-September, 1932, Walsh Papers. Members of the League included Richberg, Henry Wallace, Felix Frankfurter, Ray Stannard Baker, Clarence Darrow, Norman Hapgood, Amos Pinchot (Gifford Pinchot did not join), and Gutzon Borglum.

6. FCH, press release, September 25, 1932, Walsh Papers; *New York Times*, September 26, 1932, 1, 8.

receipts and disbursements from September 5 to November 7 showed that $13,000 of the organization's receipts of $14,815.90 had come as loans or contributions from the Democratic National Campaign Committee. The League spent $13,994.15 ($6,603 for the travel expenses of speakers).[7]

Throughout the campaign, Fred issued news releases, made speeches, and helped arrange and coordinate the League's activities. He engaged in a radio debate with John Dewey, who spoke for those liberals and radicals who rejected both the major parties. Describing himself as a follower of Henry George, Fred emphasized Roosevelt as the only choice for Progressives and pointed to the fact that the governor "has sympathetically sought to understand the needs of labor and has taken counsel from labor itself." Dewey contended that liberal forces should consolidate themselves into a new party "to fight for definite constructive social policies."[8] In addition to these activities, Fred himself ran for office, seeking the post of commissioner of welfare for Westchester County, New York.

As election day neared, the League's officers were pleased with their part in the campaign. Just before Roosevelt's triumph, Manly told Farley: "Practically everything that the National Progressive League set out to accomplish has been achieved.... In addition to lining up the key progressives we were very fortunate in being able to secure the active cooperation of the outstanding leaders of the railroad labor organizations, whose influence reaches into every little railroad town throughout the country."[9] Perhaps Howe's ties with the railroad unions had something to do with their support for the League.

Alas, FDR's coattails were not long enough to carry Howe through to victory in the Republican stronghold of Westchester County. He lost to the incumbent welfare commissioner by more than 39,000 votes, winning only 40 percent of the electors. Hoover carried Westchester by 10,000 votes. The only major Democrat to win the county was Herbert Lehman, the gubernatorial candidate, by a 458-vote margin.[10] This was Fred Howe's last attempt at elective office. Like other Americans, he now had to wait to see exactly what policies the new administration would adopt.

A chance to play a role in that administration came to him during the famous "Hundred Days" that followed Roosevelt's inauguration. One of the major pieces of legislation enacted during that period was the Agricultural Adjustment Act. An omnibus measure full of concessions to the varied agricultural interests, the law's principal purpose was to raise and support farm prices by limiting

---

7. H. F. Quinn to Frank Walsh, November 11, 1932.

8. *New York Times,* September 27, 1932, 14, and October 17, 1932, 3.

9. Basil Manly to James A. Farley, November 4, 1932, Walsh Papers. Henry Wallace was less sanguine about the League's success: "It was like all organizations of that sort—three-fourths letterhead and writing. I think I probably had some stationery out there [in Iowa] and wrote to different folks." Wallace, "Reminiscences," 167.

10. *New York Times,* November 9, 1932, 15.

production. To carry out the new program, the statute set up the Agricultural Adjustment Administration (AAA), and to head the agency the president and his new secretary of agriculture, Henry Wallace, settled on George Peek. The new administrator had no doubt that the AAA had one clear and definite goal: "The job's simple. It's just to put up farm prices."

Within the AAA, two administrative divisions representing producers and processors were quickly set up. A third element—consumers—had no immediate voice, even though success in raising farm prices would certainly hit their pocketbooks. The processing taxes, designed to finance the price support program and pay subsidies to the farmers, would be passed on to consumers through higher prices. The need for a consumer voice in the AAA's structure was quickly perceived by Mordecai Ezekiel, an economist with long service in the Department of Agriculture who became Wallace's chief economist, and Rexford G. Tugwell, one of Roosevelt's close advisers in the brain trust and now assistant secretary of agriculture. Both men had been involved in drafting the new farm legislation.

Ezekiel took the credit for first thinking that there should be a consumers counsel "to serve as a representative for the consumer and to act as a counter force against the pressure groups in the other parts of the organization." He took the concept to Tugwell, who agreed, and the two presented the proposal to Secretary Wallace. The secretary approved it and sent Peek a memo (drafted, according to Ezekiel, by himself and Tugwell) urging prompt action to create the office of consumers counsel. The memo pointed out the need to ensure that the rights of all interests were considered by the AAA. The AAA's administrative divisions dealing with producers and processors were headed by men who had "broad experience and sympathy" with those interests. "If we are to justify our decisions before Congress and other political groups, however, the record must show that we have given equal consideration to labor and consumers' interests. That was why I suggested the creation, within your organization, of a unit specially charged with examining each proposed action from labor and consumers' point of view, and staffed and equipped to carry out the necessary accounting, statistical, and economic investigations as a basis for its reports to you." The memo concluded with Wallace's request that Peek "take prompt action to develop an organization for the investigation of the consumers' interest in the cases now before you, for the preparation of adequate briefs on all the economic aspects of those cases; and for the selection and appointment of the additional persons needed to carry out this work."[11]

11. Mordecai Ezekiel to Rexford Tugwell, October 20, 1939, Tugwell Papers, Franklin D. Roosevelt Library; Secretary of Agriculture to George N. Peek, June 10, 1933, Secretary of Agriculture's Correspondence, 1933, National Archives. The 1939 memo from Ezekiel was a summary of the development of agricultural policy in 1932–33.

Wallace, Ezekiel, and Tugwell pressed the need for appointment of a consumers counsel on Peek. The administrator resisted for a while (according to Tugwell, Peek thought "the consumers could look out for themselves. They were not our responsibility").[12] Eventually Wallace prevailed. No legislation was necessary, and the office came into existence when on June 27, 1933, Peek named Frederic C. Howe as consumers counsel. The administrator later said that the appointment was one of the two big mistakes he had made in setting up the AAA.[13]

Whether Fred had been actively seeking a position as he had in 1914 is unknown, though Jerome Frank later recalled that Howe was "eager to come to Washington. He had talked to me about it."[14] Certainly he could argue that he had earned a place in the administration as a result of his work with the National Progressive League in the presidential campaign. Not having any commitments except to the School of Opinion, which was fading in importance, he was available, and he could see that the next four years would be full of challenges and adventures. His own political weight was not great enough for him to claim a major post like a seat in the cabinet, but a chance to be the tribune of the consumers—and to have a voice in defining that role—must have appealed to him. After all, it would be the first attempt by the national government formally to take account of the consumer interest, save for a few piecemeal interventions like the Food and Drug Act of 1906.

To recruiters for the New Deal, the appointment of Fred Howe must have seemed a most desirable step, one that would bring into the administration a well-known and articulate figure, signal to Progressives that their participation was welcome, and provide a link between present reform and its Wilsonian predecessor. He had friends in Congress, as well as throughout the country in the ranks of liberals. He was no stranger to Roosevelt's inner circle of advisers. Raymond Moley knew him in the context of the Cleveland battles of Tom Johnson, which had sparked his own political enthusiasm. Rex Tugwell thought highly of him, as did Louis Howe. His credentials as a reformer were impeccable. Tugwell wrote that Howe was "venerated by all younger liberals as a warrior in many old battles. . . . Howe was interested in Roosevelt as a progressive; and since he was a surviving embodiment of the movement for reform we had read about as students, what could be more fitting than that he should have a part in our effort? He was still a persuasive liberal. He seemed an ideal person to represent consumer' interests. Above all, as Wallace saw it, his presence among us would be a guarantee that farmers' gains were not to be at consumers'

---

12. P. Campbell, *Consumer Representation*, 202; Tugwell, *Roosevelt's Revolution*, 122.

13. Peek, *Why Quit Our Own*, 107. The other "mistake" Peek cited was the appointment of Jerome Frank as general counsel.

14. Tugwell, *Roosevelt's Revolution*, 122–23.

expense." The political columnist John Franklin Carter, writing under the pseudonym "Unofficial Observer," declared that Howe was "brought into the New Deal picture for sentimental, as well as practical reasons, both as a stimulating survivor of the old pre-war muck-raking and reform days, and as one who has never changed sides or grown weary in the fight for social justice."[15]

Some years afterward, Henry Wallace recalled that he had not known Howe and had chosen him to be consumers counsel on Louis Bean's recommendation. "Here's a fine old liberal of the Tom Johnson school," Bean advised him. Jerome Frank offered a similar account, saying that he brought up Howe's name at a meeting of the top echelon of the AAA. "Fred had been one of the respected men of my college days. He'd written *The City: The Hope of Democracy*, was a great liberal, a friend of Tom Johnson and so on. . . . So I just brought up his name in a very casual fashion." One who did not claim a role in appointing Howe was Ezekiel. He recalled that he had urged appointment of "a well-trained economist, sympathetic with consumer problems." Howe, he thought, was "quite a different person than I had visualized. He made [the consumers counsel] a sort of propaganda, agitating thing, quite different from what I had in mind—he and Tom Blaisdell and Gardner Jackson. It developed into a sort of crusading group, but, in some respects, operating to make sure that the process didn't impinge on consumers too much."[16]

Tugwell indicated that Wallace knew Howe and that he and the secretary together agreed upon Fred for the appointment. Charles J. Brand, Peek's friend and co-administrator of the AAA, was acquainted with Howe and perhaps had some part in the decision. At any rate, although it remains not entirely clear just who recommended Fred—and perhaps there were several recommendations—Wallace suggested his name to Peek, who made the actual appointment.

Fred did not immediately take over the job, and Thomas C. Blaisdell Jr. filled in temporarily as consumers counsel during the summer of 1933. Blaisdell had been brought by Tugwell to Washington from Columbia, where they had been faculty colleagues. Howe was absent on a trip to Germany, where he became very interested in the enthusiasm of the Nazi youth movement. Around this time, Howe became a member of the American Committee Against Fascist Oppression in Germany.[17]

---

15. Frank, "Reminiscences," 78; Unofficial Observer (John Franklin Carter), *New Dealers*, 68. Carter used the pen name Jay Franklin for his columns.

16. Wallace, "Reminiscences," 238; Bean, "Reminiscences," 104–5; Conrad, *Forgotten Farmers*, 38; Tugwell, *Roosevelt's Revolution*, 122–23; P. Campbell, *Consumer Representation*, 204; Frank, "Reminiscences," 78; Ezekiel, "Reminiscences," 62. Ezekiel was assistant chief economist for the Federal Farm Board from 1930 to 1933 and economic advisor to the secretary of agriculture until 1944.

17. Thomas C. Blaisdell Jr. to author, December 12, 1985. The Committee had many of Howe's friends as members. Robert Morss Lovett was chairman, and Ella Winter secretary.

Upon his return from Germany, Fred and Marie began house hunting in Washington but soon gave up the idea of residence there, both because of cost and, even more, because of Marie's distaste for life in the capital. After a disappointing search for an apartment, she wrote Fola La Follette that the cheap apartments were "so cramped that I couldn't bear it. When Fred's at home he always has the radio and his typewriter going together and I have to be a little way off, not right by the noise.... They don't allow a colored maid to sleep in any apartment, so that's not what I want either, as Margaret is a member of the family." So she would stay on at Harmon, and Fred would come home weekends as much as possible. "I am greatly relieved as I don't want to live in Washington anyhow. It's a beautiful town but I should hate to be forced to take any part, however small, in the kind of social life that is there. And Fred would want us to entertain and be entertained which fills me with nervous dread. Our home here at Harmon is surrounded by snow and I don't get out much, but still it is home and I like it best." For a while, Fred shared a house in Washington with Blaisdell, Gardiner Means, and Tugwell, and then he took up residence at the Cosmos Club, where he ran a "rather free wheeling liberal seminar—people from the executive branch and congressmen."[18]

Once he was on board as consumers counsel, Fred's first concern must have been staffing the office. For his top positions he had advice and suggestions from such New Deal recruiters as Tugwell and Frank. Tom Blaisdell had come to Washington at Tugwell's behest and had entered the Department of Agriculture as an economist with an antitrust specialty. After working with the legal division for a short time, he was asked to help the consumers counsel and appointed assistant director. Gardner Jackson described him as "the top intellect in the consumers counsel office."[19] He transferred to the Consumer Advisory Board of the National Recovery Administration (NRA) in July 1934, went on to a distinguished career in government, and then became a professor of political science at the University of California, Berkeley.

Coming to the office in the summer of 1933 was Gardner "Pat" Jackson. He had been a reporter for several newspapers, most recently the Washington correspondent for three Canadian papers. Possessing an independent income, he had frequently abandoned journalism to spend time and money on liberal causes. He joined the fight against the ouster of Alexander Meiklejohn from the Amherst presidency, served for four years as publicist and adviser on strategy for the Sacco-Vanzetti Defense and Memorial Committees, and worked for the release of Tom Mooney from a California penitentiary. He has been described

---

18. MJH to Fola La Follette, December 13, 1933; Arthur Goldschmidt to author, December 17, 1985.
19. Jackson, "Reminiscences," 441.

as "consumed by the flame of social justice"—"the underdog has him on a leash," a friend said.[20]

According to his own account, Jackson's recruitment to the New Deal came directly from Tugwell and Frank, indirectly from Lee Pressman and Nathan Witt, new members of the AAA's legal staff. Frank and Tugwell visited Jackson at his home and told him that Pressman and Witt had talked to them, "saying that I was a guy they ought to get into the show to help remake the world." He would have "an opportunity in cahoots with them down in the Department of Agriculture to fulfill the reforming zeal that somehow had been implanted in me out of my experiences up to that time." They thought that the logical spot for him was with the consumers counsel. They convinced Jackson that it was the right time to enter government service.[21]

Jackson knew something about his new chief. He later observed: "Fred Howe had been in my consciousness quite a lot because of books he had written and because he ran that summer school of discussion on Nantucket at Siasconset, where he had a lot of notables for seminars." He was officially appointed as research assistant on August 21, 1933, but had probably been at work in the counsel's office a few weeks before then. His civil service title soon became senior administrative officer, but he was serving as Howe's deputy and was often referred to as the assistant consumers counsel. "In my work in the department I didn't have a title, by the way," he noted. "One of the hilarities was the civil service trying to figure out how to define my duties." Murray Kempton, a friend of Jackson's, wrote that because of Howe's age, "it was understood that Jackson's youth and energy would make him the [consumers counsel's] division's real force."[22]

Three other new appointees, two with government experience, completed the roster of key people in the consumers counsel office. Donald Montgomery, an economist, came from the Federal Trade Commission. Educated at Mount Holyoke, the University of Wisconsin, and the London School of Economics (where she had done research on the Trades Union Congress), Mary Taylor had been briefly the Madrid correspondent for the *Chicago Tribune* and then an account executive for a New York export-import firm. In 1931 she had joined the Department of Commerce as chief of its Drug and Cosmetic Section. In 1933 she transferred to the counsel office and became editor of its *Consumers Guide*. The fourth member of the group around Fred Howe was Iris Walker, who took over responsibility for working with women's organizations on consumer problems. Years later, Henry Wallace expressed the opinion that Howe—"an old-fashioned liberal of the rather extreme sort"—had recruited "a great assortment

20. Carter, *New Dealers*, 72; Schlesinger, *Coming of the New Deal*, 51.
21. Jackson, "Reminiscences," 422–25.
22. Ibid., 432, 438; Kempton, *Part of Our Times*, 55.

of rather extreme liberals." He mentioned particularly Jackson and Montgomery.[23]

Many of those who found jobs in the AAA and other New Deal agencies were young and inexperienced in government. "Every department was full of bright young people. We were a happy band of brothers, all helping each other," wrote Alger Hiss, who entered the AAA's legal division. "It was an extraordinarily vital time for young people. We acquired a considerable amount of arrogance, because much of what we believed in was opposed by conservative forces." Fred Howe at sixty-six was a graybeard. Among the people with whom he worked, Jerome Frank was forty-four, Rex Tugwell forty-two, Tom Blaisdell thirty-nine, Caroline Ware thirty-five, Mary Taylor thirty-two, Adlai Stevenson thirty-three, Alger Hiss twenty-eight, Lee Pressman twenty-seven, Abe Fortas twenty-three. "Boys with their hair ablaze," George Peek called them (ignoring the women). Some of the young New Dealers had little patience with the oldsters. Thomas H. Eliot (twenty-six years old in 1933), one of the principal draftsmen of the Social Security Act, heard someone call Howe a "retread"—"I guess for the young fellows in the New Deal, the Wilson Administration seemed like very ancient history." Others were much more complimentary, respecting Howe's past activities and welcoming his presence at their side in current battles.[24]

Howe's unit was first called the "trade agreements division," indicating the expectation that its primary concern would be marketing agreements and the various codes transferred by the National Recovery Administration (NRA) to the AAA.[25] By the time the consumers counsel began functioning, the crop-control activities were already underway, and the division began to review them with no questions raised about its right to do so. The announcement of Fred Howe's appointment on June 23 emphasized the consumers counsel's role in reviewing marketing agreements to protect consumers against sharp price increases. He would also look into complaints from consumers and undertake formal investigations when necessary.

23. Wallace, "Reminiscences," 238.
24. Louchheim, *Making of the New Deal*, 238; Eliot, *Recollections of the New Deal*, chap. 1; Conrad, *Forgotten Farmers*, 106, quoting Lord, *Agrarian Revival*, 155; Thomas H. Eliot to author, December 6, 1985. Caroline Ware denied that there was any sharp generational break among the New Dealers. "With a shattered economy, there was a pervasive sense that each one of us had to do what we could, in our various ways, to find a way out. So differences like age were not accentuated." Interview, October 4, 1986.
25. Marketing agreements were agreements entered into by the secretary of agriculture and agricultural producers, providing for either reduction of acreage or reduction of the amount produced for the market, or both. Codes were agreements on fair competition, including provisions on wages and hours, negotiated in each industry with the help of the NRA and submitted to the president for approval.

Given the breadth and vagueness of the delineations of its duties, the consumers counsel division had to develop its own definition of its mission as it went along, subject to any constraints imposed by upper echelons of the AAA or the department. It quickly began to stake out its territory, marking out five activities. (1) It would examine market agreements and codes, watching to see that consumers were protected from unfair price rises. It would participate in working out agreements, taking part in hearings, testifying, asking questions, offering advice, and analyzing alternative programs. (2) It would monitor results of agreements and codes to find their effects on consumer prices and to keep the AAA aware how its actions affected consumers. (3) It would make studies, conduct surveys on food prices, and determine whether processors raised prices more than justified by the processing taxes they paid. (4) It would advise on proposed AAA legislation that might affect consumers. (5) It would educate consumers about wise use of their money and disseminate information through press releases, speeches, radio broadcasts, and publications.

The way was open for a clash of views on how extensive the consumers counsel's scope should be. AAA leaders tended to believe that the consumers counsel should function "largely if not solely as a service agency to the AAA," providing information on the effects that the production and marketing programs were having on consumers' prices, keeping it informed at all times as to the effects which the production and marketing programs were having upon consumers' prices and consumption, and analyzing the likely effects of any contemplated program or agreement.

Many in the consumers counsel unit, including Fred Howe, saw a broader role: the consumers counsel's function must include "representing consumers in the administration of AAA programs, not only fighting for the interests of the consumers within the AAA itself but carrying the issue out into the country. They would even mobilize consumers to help win battles against non-consumer interests." The potential for conflict was apparent, as the consumers counsel and his staff consistently interpreted their public responsibility more broadly than did the higher-ups in the AAA. The consumers counsel found allies in the AAA's legal staff, with whom his office worked closely. Jerome Frank was general counsel and his young attorneys included Thurman Arnold, Abe Fortas, Adlai Stevenson, Alger Hiss, Lee Pressman, John Abt, and Nathan Witt. Gardner Jackson later commented that "in actual practice, from the very start, the consumers' counsel's office and the general counsel's office collaborated with great intimacy and always took the same positions."[26]

26. Nourse, Davis, and Black, *Three Years,* 392, 393; Jackson, "Reminiscences," 436. In performing its functions, the consumers counsel also cooperated with other agencies and organizations, such as the NRA's Consumer Advisory Board (CAB) and the National Emergency Council (NEC).

Within the AAA, because work on the crop-control programs was already underway when Howe became consumers counsel, he had no chance to participate in the discussions that had developed them. Their purpose was to raise farm prices, even if that necessitated exempting marketing agreements from the antitrust laws. Fred's outlook on this trade-off was congruent with his longtime views on the dangers of monopoly. He spelled it out in a series of memos soon after he took up his duties. "The main underlying purpose of trade agreements is to legalize monopoly in industry in return for prospective gains to the farm producer and consumer," he wrote on July 20, 1933. "I think I can speak somewhat as an expert in this field. I know fully the difficulties, personally I should say impossibilities of regulation of monopolies. I have never known it to succeed." His personal experience showed him that monopoly contracts and franchises were always "weasel-worded" and favored the monopoly over the consumer. In his own days as a public utility operator, the thing he had most feared was "a uniform accounting system and publicity of such accounts."[27]

In another early memo, addressed to Louis Bean, Howe argued for a time limit, probably a year, for all marketing agreements. Agreements should require that all records of the contracting parties be filed with the government on standard forms. "These provisions are a kind of Damocles sword hanging over the processor. He will know that complaints against him will be registered; he will not know how closely we follow his accounts; he will be operating with a daily concern for his standing with the third party to the agreement, which is the Government."[28]

Howe soon found that, as a line agency and not just an advisory board, the consumers counsel was in the midst of the policy-making process on marketing agreements. Pat Jackson put their position succinctly: "In essence, our position was that the forces of competition should be encouraged and kept open whenever possible in order to hold distributors' and processors' margins within reason and thus protect the consumer." That goal quickly came into conflict with the priority that George Peek and his aides placed on raising farm prices as rapidly as possible. Tom Blaisdell, a participant on the consumers' side, observed that the consumers counsel became "the focus for internal Agriculture Department conflicts between the traditional conservative elements whose thinking represented the larger, successful farmers and those with a more social outlook who were regarded as liberals or radicals."[29]

27. FCH, "Memorandum as to Approach and Underlying Policies to be Followed in All Trade Agreements," July 20, 1933, Office File of Consumer Counsel 1933–35, Record Group 145, National Archives.
28. Memorandum, FCH to Louis Bean, August 10, 1933, Office File of Consumer Counsel 1933–35, Record Group 145, National Archives.
29. Quoted in P. Campbell, *Consumer Representation*, 212; Angevine, *Consumer Activists*, 181.

On one side were Peek and Charles Brand, the AAA's administrator and coadministrator, as well as most of their division heads. Peek saw the consumers counsel and his group as an obstruction to the effort to raise farm prices. His goal was accepted as one among several for the AAA by the group that Peek called the "reformers," when he was not using stronger language—Tugwell, Frank, Howe, sometimes Wallace, and their supporters in the consumers counsel division and the general counsel's office. The reformers took seriously the responsibility to protect consumers, and they regarded farmers both as producers and as consumers who needed to be protected from excessive price raises if the farm program's goal of parity was to be attained. Howe and his cohorts always interpreted their mandate more broadly than did Peek and the men around him. Working with Tugwell and Frank, the consumers counsel people tried to scrutinize carefully and critically the drafts of marketing agreements that came before them, despite pressure from the administrator and his section heads for rapid action. In the early days of the New Deal, quarrels between the two factions over marketing agreements for tobacco and milk were especially heated.

Along with his work on marketing agreements, Howe had other responsibilities that took up much of his time. Soon after he became consumers counsel, he was asked by Wallace to determine a fair price increase for bread and to publicize his findings. The secretary also asked him to calculate a fair increase in the price of a cotton shirt, taking into account both AAA and NRA programs. Fred quickly broadened his assignment and assumed the role of watchdog for the consumer against excessive price rises generally. His weapons were information, warnings, and publicity. "We are going to do what we can to see that consumers are protected at a time when the administration is trying to pull the farmers and workers out of what President Roosevelt calls the 'economic hell' they have been living in for four years," he told the press.[30]

The first surveys found price increases for bread to have been moderate. Howe was pleased but promised investigations in any city where prices seemed excessive. On a number of occasions he asked the American Bakers Association to look into increases in certain cities. He warned consumers to beware of a possible reduction in quality—"a form of profiteering as injurious to consumers as unreasonable price increases." Overall, Howe's "jawboning" approach on bread prices seemed to work, and increases remained within reasonable limits.[31]

There seemed to be more profiteering in the textile industry, or so both Howe and his AAA superior, George Peek, charged. The consumers counsel

30. *New York Times,* August 4, 1933, 8.
31. *New York Times,* August 22, 1933, 3; U.S. Department of Agriculture, AAA, *Agricultural Adjustment,* 210.

found that some retailers were guilty of "misrepresentation"—they tried to fool the public by asserting that unwarranted increases in textile prices had resulted from the processing tax levied on cotton manufactures. Jay Franklin described how Howe—"an unhesitating and unterrified spokesman" for the consumer—presented the case against such excessive price advances. "From the start, Howe began to get out simple exhibits showing how much of the increased price of a pair of overalls or of a housewife's apron, was due to the processing tax on cotton, how much to higher wages in the cotton mills, how much to better prices for raw cotton, and how much to increased profit." The president borrowed from Howe's information when he took on "chiselers" on the NRA codes in a fireside chat in October 1933. He told his listeners of "the salesman in a store in a large Eastern city who tried to justify the increase in the price of a cotton shirt from one dollar and a half to two dollars and a half by saying that it was due to the cotton processing tax. Actually in that shirt there was about one pound of cotton and the processing tax amounted to four and a quarter cents on that pound of cotton."[32]

Fred was more interested in the informational and public relations aspects of his job than in its administrative nitty-gritty. His colleague, Tom Blaisdell, told Howe's successor as consumers counsel, Calvin B. Hoover, that Howe "devoted most of his attention and the attention of those people who were directly attached to him to various public relations phases of the work of the consumers counsel, holding only an administrative and supervisory check on the economic work having to do with marketing agreements." According to the chronicler of consumer representation in the New Deal, Fred vigorously pursued the consumer interest with great integrity of purpose. "Like Mrs. Rumsey [who chaired the NRA's Consumer Advisory Board], he was promotional rather than administrative in capacity, somewhat given to generalities but with a deep emotional drive toward an abundant life for everyone."[33]

Howe used a variety of means to secure publicity for the consumers counsel's efforts to protect the consumer. He held a weekly press conference, and his office frequently sent out news releases. In cooperation with the General Federation of Women's Clubs, he began a series of weekly radio programs, carried by NBC with 138 stations participating by November 1934. No expert on radio, Howe ran into problems with the preparation of his first talk. He requested thirty minutes of radio time and said he would write and deliver an explanation and justification of AAA price policy that would make the program fifty million

32. Carter, *New Dealers*, 67; quoted in K. Davis, *FDR*, 293.
33. Thomas C. Blaisdell Jr. to Calvin B. Hoover, February 19, 1935, Office File of Calvin Hoover 1934–1935, Records Group 145, National Archives; Blaisdell to author, May 1, 1987; P. Campbell, *Consumer Representation*, 204.

friends in the cities. He kept working on the speech, reciting parts of it to everybody he met at the Cosmos Club. When he thought the moment had come, "he jumped into a taxicab, went alone to his office, turned on the lights, and sat there dictating from nine o'clock in the evening until one o'clock in the morning. . . . He put everything he had into that speech, and in the morning he was worn but radiant. 'Twelve cylinders full!' he said. 'The best I ever did, the very best, I'm certain!' But, unhappily, he had failed in every take to shove down the little lever that makes the needle bite the words into the record; so all he had was blank records."[34]

That experience did not daunt Howe, who believed strongly in the value of radio as a vehicle of information and persuasion. He spoke on the consumers counsel's weekly program (and sometimes also on the Agriculture Department's Farm and Home Hour), occasionally as the only speaker but more often with a representative of the General Federation of Women's Clubs. Topics addressed during the winter of 1933–34 included "Egg Prices," "New Deal in Milk," "What's Happened to Prices?" "The Consumer's Job in 1934," "Surplus Food for Hungry Children," "New Deal for Indians."

Fred wrote some of the talks himself, but the broadcast scripts seem to have been prepared in final form by the publicity unit of his office. Marie Howe believed that his remarks were censored. She wrote Lincoln Steffens: "He tells me beforehand about his good stuff and I listen in, only to hear a lot of garbled material, totally emasculated. . . . Every department has its censors to protect the fine sensitive pride of those who are exploiting us. An excellent way to catch and punish robbers."[35] The AAA found the radio talks valuable and continued them after Fred left the position of consumers counsel.

As part of its informational and public relations effort, the consumers counsel division under Howe's leadership began publication in September 1933 of a semimonthly *Consumers Guide.* Mary Taylor, who had newspaper as well as governmental experience, was its editor for many years. The *Guide* furthered Fred's campaign against unjustifiable price increases and profiteering and presented information on changes in farm prices and their relation to retail prices. It also tried to stimulate consumers' participation in governmental activities affecting their interests, such as public hearings on agricultural programs. Howe's friends in consumer and social service organizations liked the new journal. "My feeling is that you have really started something in this little publication and should push it hard," wrote Paul Kellogg.[36] AAA leaders generally tried

---

34. Lord, *Wallaces of Iowa,* 355–56. Lord gives no reference to the source of this story. A nearly identical account of the incident appeared in the *Salt Lake Tribune* on January 28, 1934, although it had Howe preparing a report for Henry Wallace, rather than a radio address.
35. MJH to Lincoln Steffens, January 12, 1934, Steffens Papers.
36. Paul U. Kellogg to FCH, December 28, 1933, "Forget-Me-Not Files."

to limit *Consumers Guide* to factual and informational presentations and to hold down any effort to take a stand on controversial issues within the AAA.

Although reactions to *Consumers Guide* were largely favorable, there were criticisms in the press and from some Republicans. One attack came from the *Akron Beacon Journal*, which noted the appearance of this "lavishly illustrated, slick paper periodical manufactured by the U.S. Government Printing Office for issuance by the Consumers' Council [sic] of the Agricultural Adjustment Administration in cooperation with the Bureau of Agricultural Economics, Bureau of Home Economics, Bureau of Labor Statistics." The paper observed that the current issue informed its readers of the market song sung by a "Negro vendor" in uptown New York City:

> Ain't nothin' as good as fresh, sweet cawn,
> Or nice young onions wit' ther tops still on.
> But yo' cain't beat carrots fo' keeping strong,
> An' spinach makes yo' inch along!
> Step right chere, folks, an' buy 'em cheap;
> Mah "veg" and prices cain't be beat.

Marveled the newspaper: "And it took only four bureaus to dig that up! Great is the government able to get away with squandering tax money on the distribution of such vital stuff."

Another Akron paper, the *Times-Press,* sprang to the consumers counsel's defense. "The captiousness of critics of the New Deal sometimes carries them to ridiculous extremes. Eager to pounce on anything that might influence people against the present administration, the critics sometimes resort to half truths, or even worse, fractional truths, to get their criticism across." The vendor's song took up about four inches of space in a twenty-four-page issue and was obviously a filler. The *Times-Press* praised the *Guide* as a source of useful information for consumers and observed that it had "already has been of extreme value in several cities in stopping unwarranted rises in the price of food. But this was conveniently ignored." The New Deal was "subject to enough honest criticism without its critics resorting to fractional truths to give it a black eye," the paper concluded.[37]

To the radio addresses and the written word, Fred added speeches to a wide variety of groups throughout the country. He also testified in congressional hearings, such as one on the creation of a federal marketing corporation, and

---

37. *Akron Beacon Journal,* November 17, 1934; *Akron Times-Press,* November 19, 1934; clippings in Office File of Consumers Counsel 1933–35, Record Group 145, National Archives.

he spoke and lobbied hard for passage of a bill creating a federal credit union system. He published an occasional article on the purposes and activities of his office.[38]

In the winter of 1933 the schism in the AAA led to the departure of George Peek. The internecine warfare had found on one side Tugwell, Frank, and most of the lawyers on the general counsel's staff, Fred Howe and Pat Jackson in the consumers counsel office, Paul Appleby, and others, often supported by Wallace; and on the other side, Peek, Charles Brand, the heads of the commodity divisions, and the comptroller's office. The Tugwell-Frank-Howe group saw in the farm crisis an opportunity for social reform as well as for aid to the farmers. David Conrad calls the Peek group "traditional agrarians"—"men who had worked their way up through the ranks of the Department of Agriculture or the farm movements. They came from the triple alliance of Extension Service, Farm Bureau, and land grant colleges. Capable, well trained, and dedicated, they were the ones who made AAA work, and yet they were reconciled to the agricultural status quo and in general sympathetic with the larger and more successful farmers and landlords." They labeled their opponents "liberals," "radicals," "urbanites." Peek considered himself a practical man, standing against theorists, ideologues, and young attorneys who knew little if anything about agriculture. As he later put it, "a plague of young lawyers settled on Washington. They all claimed to be friends of somebody or other and mostly of Felix Frankfurter and Jerome Frank. They floated airily into offices, took desks, asked for papers and found no end of things to be busy about. I never found out why they came, what they did or why they left."

Gardner Jackson bridled at the charge of radicalism and later observed, in language that Fred Howe would have accepted: "We were really not at all radical, ... we were really old-fashioned Jeffersonian guys in our approach to the thing, trying merely to control a segment of the economy that the processing and distributing element had come to dominate pretty completely.... It was simply the old-fashioned effort to get more equity within the system."[39] In those days, "radicals" in the AAA were rarely called "communists." There were communists in the AAA—Lee Pressman, Nathan Witt, Charles Kramer, John Abt, and, according to Whittaker Chambers, Alger Hiss—but their party connections were not generally known at the time. The leaders of the "radicals"—Tugwell, Frank, Howe, Jackson—were not Communist Party members or sympathizers.

38. See FCH to Franklin D. Roosevelt, June 5, 1934; Roosevelt to Marvin H. McIntyre, June 13, 1934; McIntyre to FCH, June 14, 1934; Angevine, *Consumer Activists*, 26–27. The bill on credit unions passed and was signed by the president as the Federal Credit Union Act on June 26, 1934. Howe's articles included "Watchdogs for the Consumer" and "Know Yourself as a Consumer!"

39. Conrad, *Forgotten Farmers*, 105; Peek, *Why Quit Our Own*, 20; Jackson, "Reminiscences," 588.

Given the differences in outlooks and goals, the AAA's internal relationships were tense. Fueling the flames was the personal dislike between Peek and Frank. Brand resigned as coadministrator after only four months. In the fall of 1933, except for his commodity chiefs, Peek seemed to be on the outs with nearly everyone. He was sure that an "inner ring" in the AAA "wanted to purge the AAA of all business men or any others who did not welcome the coming of the new day of revolution." He demanded that Secretary Wallace fire Jerome Frank. After several weeks of public and private bickering between Wallace and Peek over the administrator's ultimatum and other issues, Wallace forced a showdown on December 6 by taking the problem to the president. Roosevelt tried to mediate, but when this did not work, he came down on the side of Wallace, and Peek had to go. Accepting his formal resignation, the president helped him save face by appointing him as his special assistant on foreign trade policy and then, in February 1934, as head of the new Export-Import Bank.[40]

Peek had some advice for his successor, Chester Davis: "Get rid of Jerome Frank and the rest of that crowd as a condition to your acceptance."[41] Peek concluded that his ouster had been engineered by "a curious collection of socialists and internationalists who were neither Republicans nor Democrats. . . . Secretary Wallace, who has an elastic and fantastic mind capable of any stretching, alone managed to be in both groups." The only common characteristic of the groups was "their willingness to make the interests of our country and its people subservient to the practice of their theories and to substitute personal government centralized in Washington for our traditional state and local governments."

Looking back, Peek considered his two greatest errors had been his acceptance of the appointments of Jerome Frank and Fred Howe. Charles Brand, who had recommended Howe's appointment, did not know that "Dr. Howe had been seriously bitten by some kind of pink bug and had accumulated a hazy, half radical, half uplifter set of views and attitudes. It turned out that he was against the profit system and was all for abolishing it—without, however, exactly knowing what he wanted to put in its place." Howe's attitude had spread through the Legal and Consumers' divisions of the AAA "like an epidemic." Liberals and reformers were happy to see Peek go. As one of them outside the AAA put it: "There is certainly a ground swell of interest in the consumer's stake in what is afoot. The AAA split on it; and the elimination of Peek means that the Tugwell-Howe group won out with Wallace."[42]

40. Ibid., 144. Good accounts of the controversies leading to Peek's departure can be found in Perkins, *Crisis in Agriculture*, 179–86; K. Davis, *FDR*, 299–302; Fite, *George Peek*, 260–66; Schlesinger, *Coming of the New Deal*, 56–59. Peek's account is in his *Why Quit Our Own*.

41. Fite, *George Peek*, 266.

42. Peek, *Why Quit Our Own*, 12, 13, 107; Paul U. Kellogg to Arthur Kellogg, December 17, 1933, "Forget-Me-Not" Files.

Meanwhile, during all of Fred's adventures in Washington, Marie continued to live quietly in Harmon. She had been to Washington but didn't like it, she explained to Lincoln Steffens. "A lot of little boys all competing for favors and importance. And they are so afraid of one another, of the President, of Congress, of losing their jobs. Nothing very interesting about all that." Fred came home to Harmon on weekends "and so gets a complete change and rest. He likes to keep his home so I am not abusing him," Marie told Steffens. He was "evidently doing a good job and gets lots of praise. The extent of his acquaintances is amazing and (to me) alarming."[43]

Marie led a peaceful life in Harmon, following the advice she gave Steffens: "Do as you please and get all the comfort and happiness you can in any way you can." She read, mainly French books with occasional exceptions like a biography of Hans Christian Andersen by Signe Toksvig, a member of Heterodoxy. Occasionally she went to a play. After seeing Maxwell Anderson's *Mary of Scotland*, she advised Fola La Follette and her husband that "the play is bad and Helen Hayes is worse. The critics refuse to tell the truth as they have agreed to build up the Theatre Guild."[44]

Marie kept in touch with friends—Heterodites (like Rose Young, Florence Seabury, and Doris Stevens) and others. She continued to correspond with Steffens and to encourage him with his writing. Heterodoxy she attended infrequently, going only for "obituary speeches" for such longtime members as Anne Van Vechten, Rose Pastor Stokes, and Anne Shinn. She saw Mary Heaton Vorse upon her return from a long stay in Russia and observed that "(like the rest of us) she looks 100 years old."[45]

A quiet pleasure came simply from Marie's observation of the little world around her home. "I don't get out much," she told Fola, "but still it is home and I like it best. . . . Living in the country certainly spoils one for noises, for formal society and for good clothes. Here we enjoy feeding nuts to the squirrels and we hang out suet for the birds and have a lot of these small animals to watch from our windows. Then I have books, some bridge, and quite a number of friends so that I am not lonesome."[46] She felt her age, writing Fola in December 1933: "I shall be 63 this month. Have neuritis and rheumatism (especially in right arm,—this is one of my excuses for not writing), a game knee and other

---

43. MJH to Fola La Follette, undated but postmarked March 22, 1933; MJH to Lincoln Steffens, January 12, 1934; MJH to Fola La Follette, December 13, 1933.

44. MJH to Lincoln Steffens, January 12, 1934; MJH to Fola La Follette, January 15, 1933; December 13, 1933.

45. MJH to Lincoln Steffens, January 12, 1934; Lincoln Steffens to MJH, January 17, 1934, in Winter and Hicks, *Letters of Lincoln Steffens*, 2:974; MJH to Fola La Follette, December 13, 1933.

46. Ibid., March 22, 1933; December 13, 1933.

signs of senility. But still enjoy being alive and am ready to go, or glad to stay, as the case may be."⁴⁷

On February 28, 1934, Marie died in her sleep at Shadow Edge, her home in Harmon, from myocarditis. The *New York Times* obituary noted: "Only a few contemporary American women have lived as full or as varied a life as did Mrs. Howe." After listing her activities, the paper continued: "The efforts on the behalf of George Sand rounded out the life of Mrs. Howe, who to her friends was considered among the unusual women of her time."⁴⁸ There was a private funeral from the home, followed by cremation.

On March 25 Marie's friends in Heterodoxy held a memorial service for her at the home of Alice Duer Miller. Inez Haynes Irwin presided over the service, and more than two dozen persons spoke, formally or informally, or sent letters of tribute that were read. Nearly half were Heterodites, among them Zona Gale, Alice Duer Miller, Fannie Hurst, Charlotte Perkins Gilman, Doris Stevens, and Rose Young. There were tributes from other well-known women who were not members of Heterodoxy, including Lillian Wald, Emma Goldman, Mrs. Amos Pinchot, and the woman suffrage pioneers Carrie Chapman Catt and Harriet Stanton Blatch. Eight men were heard from—Newton Baker, Senator Robert La Follette Jr., Lincoln Steffens, Francis Hackett, Floyd Dell, David Seabury, Max Eastman, and James Weldon Johnson. A newspaper reported that the speakers "presented the memory of a person who found through the ministry that churches were not necessarily close to God, and who thereafter embarked on an extensive search, in which her chief solace was in combating injustice and relieving unhappiness, and principally in offering sympathy and understanding to a number of friends."⁴⁹

Marie had been reluctant to have her letters survive her, and, probably in accordance with a request from her, Fred wrote to friends asking for a return of any of her correspondence that they had. It is not known how many were returned, but it appears that Fred destroyed all he received.⁵⁰ Any letters from him that expressed his feelings at Marie's death were probably destroyed at the

47. MJH to Fola La Follette, December 13, 1933.
48. *New York Times*, March 2, 1934, 22.
49. *New York Times*, March 26, 1934, 17. I have found the names of twenty-seven persons who spoke or sent letters to the memorial service. They were Newton Baker, Harriet Stanton Blatch, Carrie Chapman Catt, Floyd Dell, Mary Ware Dennett, Max Eastman, Zona Gale, Charlotte Perkins Gilman, Emma Goldman, Francis Hackett, Ruth Hale, Fannie Hurst, Inez Haynes Irwin, Paula Jakobi, James Weldon Johnson, Fola La Follette, Robert La Follette Jr., Mrs. James Lees Laidlaw, Frances Maule, Alice Duer Miller, Mrs. Amos Pinchot, David Seabury, Lincoln Steffens, Doris Stevens, Lillian Wald, Mrs. Normande R. Whitehouse, and Rose Young.
50. Lincoln Steffens to FCH, in Winter and Hicks, *Letters of Lincoln Steffens*, 2:992. There are a number of letters from Marie in the archives of the John Day Company at the Princeton University Library, but these deal almost entirely with publishing matters and offer no insights into her life.

same time. At any rate, none seem to have survived. Howe disposed of the Harmon and Sconset properties and continued to live at the Cosmos Club for a while. Sometime around January 1936, he bought or rented a "small modernized farmhouse" in Fairfax County, Virginia, and became a commuter. Fred liked to have his friends drop in for long talks. Oswald Garrison Villard was one of his first visitors, and Jerome Frank and Rex Tugwell enjoyed spending time there. Grace Tugwell recalled that "one summer he offered me the use of his little cottage in Virginia . . . while he went to Europe. I stayed in it for several weeks but I have the impression he lived in it alone."[51]

Pat Jackson believed that after Marie's death Fred found companionship with Mary Taylor, who edited *Consumers Guide*. Jackson looked at his co-worker rather critically. He thought she was "a very dominating, but effective, intriguing woman, not attractive in physiognomy, but very attractive in the rest of her body, which she used. One of her first notable achievements was to become, though I can't document this, the inseparable companion of old Fred Howe, the widower." No confirmation of any relationship has been discovered, and indeed there is little to be found about Howe's social life in the 1930s. Grace Tugwell mentioned a solitary life in his Virginia house and observed: "I do not believe that he was socially active."[52]

In his political life, Fred sought to cultivate his ties with the White House and volunteered political advice, if not directly to the president then to people close to him. He kept on good terms with Eleanor Roosevelt and involved her in the work of the consumers counsel as much as possible. When the first lady asked that someone from the AAA's rural planning section speak to "my group at Hyde Park to tell them what has been done in other rural and village communities," Fred volunteered for the job. In later years he was to use Mrs. Roosevelt as a channel to reach her husband. Occasionally he would communicate with the president directly. For example, he wrote him in May 1934, suggesting that the government buy the abandoned C & O Canal in Washington and Maryland for a parkway and waterway for recreation. Roosevelt thought this a good idea and asked the secretary of the Interior to look into it. Thirty-seven years later, thanks in large part to the efforts of Justice William O. Douglas, the C & O became a national historic park.[53]

51. Oswald Garrison Villard to FCH, January 15, 1936, Villard Papers, Library of Congress; Tugwell, *Roosevelt's Revolution*, 151; Grace Tugwell to author, July 21, 1986.
52. Jackson, "Reminiscences," 443; Grace Tugwell to author, July 21, 1986. Mary Taylor's first husband, Rodney Dutcher, died in 1938. She married Donald Montgomery in 1943.
53. See their 1934 correspondence on possible radio talks by the first lady. Eleanor Roosevelt Papers, Franklin D. Roosevelt Library; Eleanor Roosevelt to FCH, January 23, 1935, and February 13, 1935, Eleanor Roosevelt Papers, FDR Library; FCH to Franklin D. Roosevelt, May 1, 1934, President's Personal File, FDR Library; Simon, *Independent Journey*, 328–29.

Fred Howe expressed his views on the administration in which he served and on the liberalism he thought it represented in a talk at the Chautauqua Institution in July 1934.[54] For a year, there had been "sniping attacks" against the administration, charges of "destruction of liberalism," and change of our government to something like Italian fascism or Russian communism, he observed. Coupled with these had been warnings against the "'brain trust,' as though some malignant influence was working in Washington to destroy our political institutions and our liberties. Only occasionally had these criticisms issued from men whose lives have been identified with liberal or humane policies. "Rather, they issue from men who are identified directly or indirectly with the more reactionary and highly concentrated forms of business in the country."

Howe defended the brain trust. He knew the group—indeed, he had about twenty of them on his staff. "Their integrity and devotion to the public is unimpeachable.... There were before them opportunities for advancement; of easy and comfortable relationships; yet, without exception they have chosen the rough, thorny, and unpopular path of disinterested service to the public." They were fighting against monopoly, and it was this fight that had given rise to the hue and cry against them. They were defenders of liberty.

As Howe read history, liberty had broadened from the right to take part in government to industrial rights like the right to work and the right to a decent wage. Agitators like Karl Marx and Henry George "widened the concept of liberty from purely political into economic terms. Today all of us accept some part of this philosophy that a man has a right to work, to a fair share in the wealth that his labor produces."

The rugged individualism that the New Deal's critics sought to preserve "has given us a nation with twenty million people supported by public charity and thirty to forty million more who are on the border line of relief. It dispossessed millions of people of their homes and millions more of their farms. It sunk the most richly endowed continent in the world into an insolvency so deep that nearly a year of effort has made only a beginning of recovery on the collapse." The smokescreen of concern for "endangered liberties" came from the very men who were "responsible for the economic conditions described, for the loss of industrial liberty, if not the loss of real political liberty, which they mourn as passing as a consequence of the administration at Washington."

Sometimes Mrs. Roosevelt also called on Howe for help. At her request, he agreed to serve on the advisory board for the National Home Library Foundation, which was to operate a press in Arthurdale, West Virginia, a model community for homesteaders. Its aim was the publication of good low-priced books. Cook, *Eleanor Roosevelt*, 148–49.

54. A press release with the text of Howe's speech can be found in President's Personal File 3702, FDR Library.

More important than postmortems on the past, Howe thought, was the development of a new liberty—"a liberty which involves first of all, security from fear; second, security from accident and the disabilities of old age; thirdly, security from the uncontrolled power of another human being; and fourthly, and the most important, security from being merely nut 242 in an automobile plant or steel mill." In the new era, "industry will be socially managed, our economic system will be socially managed, agriculture will be socially managed so that our society will not continuously engulf itself in destructive disaster, but will assure all of us the possibilities of a full life, and a fullness made possible by the planning of the inanimate things which man creates, so that they will serve man rather than be man's master."

It was apparent that the Depression and the advent of a new administration had not changed Fred Howe's political views. He was still the reformer, still the independent liberal challenging monopoly and special privilege. He also remained faithful to the single tax, but his advocacy of it was muted since it was not part of the New Deal agenda. Nevertheless, he wrote Georgist articles from time to time, and he continued for a while as a director of the Robert Schalkenbach Foundation to Promote the Economics of Henry George, though his Washington duties prevented more than token service after 1932. He resigned in 1936, probably not because of lack of interest but because he continued to live in Washington while the Foundation's headquarters was in New York.[55]

Fred's political views and his visibility as consumers counsel made him one of the targets of the sniping attacks he referred to in his Chautauqua speech. Tugwell observed that both the AAA's consumers counsel and the NRA's Consumer Advisory Board were "the subject of vitriolic attacks by the business interests, and [the CAB] was treated with contempt by labor. In the consequential bargaining going on among the vast powers of industry, it was a small but irritating matter to have a consumers' counsel speaking up against high prices, poor qualities, and insufficient services. Frederic C. Howe in AAA was soon being pictured as a 'Red.'"[56]

One of those labeling Howe a communist sympathizer was Elizabeth Dilling in her book *The Red Network,* published in 1934. Dedicating the volume to "all those sincere fighters for American liberty and Christian principles who, because of their opposition to Red propaganda and the 'new social order' of Marx and Lenin, are denounced as 'professional patriots,' 'super-patriots,' '100 per centers,' 'patrioteers,' and 'Tories' by their red opponents," she listed and described

---

55. Barker, *Henry George,* 634; FCH, "Way Out? Single Tax!"; "Economic Foundations of Low Cost Housing."
56. Tugwell, *Democratic Roosevelt,* 335.

some 460 organizations and 1,300 individuals whom she considered radical subversives or their dupes. Fred Howe not only made the list but was singled out for additional treatment in her book. Drawing on the Lusk Committee reports and on an article entitled "A Shameless Appointment," she discussed the 1919 congressional investigation of Fred as immigration commissioner and noted his alleged ties to Emma Goldman, Elizabeth Gurley Flynn, and other "Anarchists" and "Communists" and his "aid to their cause."

Howe's entry in Dilling's list merits printing in full:

> HOWE, FREDERIC C.: lawyer; former Professor of Law; national committee American Civil Liberties Union; national council League for Industrial Democracy for New York; Conference for Progressive Political Action; former correspondent Federated Press; People's Legislative Service; Defense Committee I.W.W.; board directors Cooperative League of America; Socialist; communist sympathizer; was Commissioner of Immigration, Port of New York, under President Wilson and resigned following Congressional investigation because of his "unauthorized release of alien radicals held for deportation" (Record 66th Congress pp. 1522–23); Freethinkers Ingersoll Committee; wife in Jane Addams' Women's Peace Party; Congressional Exposure of Radicals; Single Tax League 1896–1925; La Follette supporter; national council Berger National Foundation; Roosevelt appointee as chairman Consumers' Board of AAA.[57]

On Dilling's list of subversive or suspect organizations were many to which Howe belonged or had belonged—the American Association for Labor Legislation, the ACLU, the Conference for Progressive Political Action, the League for Industrial Democracy, the NAACP, the National Popular Government League, the People's Lobby, and such journals as *Survey*, the *Nation*, and the *New Republic*. He probably thought himself in good company on the Dilling list of individuals, which included many of his friends and some of his co-workers in the New Deal (described by Dilling as "the present Socialist administration, labeled as 'Democratic'"). On the roster along with Fred were Newton Baker, Frank Walsh, Rexford Tugwell, Amos Pinchot, Fola La Follette and Robert M. La Follette Jr., Lincoln Steffens and Ella Winter, Henry Wallace, Jane Addams, Benjamin Marsh, Roger Baldwin, Ben Lindsey, George Norris, and Eleanor Roosevelt. The *Red Network* was later to become a handbook for zealous anticommunists,

---

57. Dilling, *Red Network*, 5, 258–59, 83, 291–92. Dilling cites Francis Ralston Walsh as the author of the article she quotes, but the article itself has not been located. I have spelled out Dilling's abbreviations. "Congressional Exposure of Radicals" means that Howe's name was given in Archibald Stevenson's investigations.

but it probably had little effect on Howe's life in the 1930s except as a source of ammunition for some of his critics.

Direct attacks on Howe came from Republican members of Congress, especially in the "Wirt affair." On March 23, 1934, James H. Rand Jr., of Remington Rand and chairman of the Committee for the Nation (an organization formed in 1933 to push for inflationist monetary policies), testified before the House Committee on Interstate and Foreign Commerce against an administration-sponsored bill to regulate the stock exchange. He told members that the proposal was part of a plan designed to take the nation "along the road from Democracy to Communism."[58] To back up his charges, he read into the record a manuscript by Dr. William A. Wirt, longtime superintendent of schools for Gary, Indiana, who wrote pamphlets and gave speeches for the Committee for the Nation. (Twenty years previously, Howe as head of the People's Institute had avidly sought Wirt as a speaker on his educational program in Gary.)

Wirt wrote that Roosevelt's "brain trusters" started with the assumption that the America of Washington, Jefferson, and Lincoln had to be destroyed so that they could reconstruct on its ruins "an America after their own pattern." He recalled a meeting with some of these "brain trusters" in the summer of 1933, during which he asked them about their concrete plans for overthrowing the established social order. "I was told that they believed that by thwarting our then-evident recovery they would be able to prolong the country's destitution until they had demonstrated to the American people that the Government must operate industry and commerce.... They were sure that their propaganda could inflame the masses against the old social order and the honest men as well as the crooks that represent that order."[59]

Representative Alfred L. Bulwinkle, Democrat of North Carolina, immediately introduced a resolution calling for a House select committee to summon Dr. Wirt and to require him to reveal the source of his statements "to the effect that the United States is in the process 'of a deliberately planned revolution,' and to the effect that certain officials or employees of the Government are attempting to thwart the program of national recovery in the United States."[60] Upon the resolution's passage, the speaker appointed Bulwinkle to chair the committee. Its hearings were carried on the radio.

58. Tugwell wrote: "It was the idea of The Committee for the Nation that most of the New Deal was unnecessary for recovery. Its businessman members regarded most of the new measures as 'socialistic' if not something worse. The Committee recommended giving up AAA, NRA, and all the other 'adjustment' measures requiring any social discipline and would have relied altogether on currency manipulation." *Democratic Roosevelt*, 322.
59. Text of statement by Dr. William A. Wirt, *New York Times*, March 24, 1934, 2.
60. This and subsequent quotations are taken from *Hearings Before the Select Committee*.

The first witness was Dr. Wirt, who proceeded to explain how he had learned about the "brain trusters" and their subversive plot. On September 1, 1933, he had attended a dinner party at the Washington home of Alice Barrows, who had been his secretary from 1914 to 1917 and who now worked for the Office of Education in the Department of the Interior. The other guests were Robert Bruere, chairman of the Textile Code Advisory Board; David Cushman Coyle, a member of the Technical Review Board of the Public Works Administration; Hildegard Kneeland of the Home Economics Department of the Department of Agriculture; Mary Taylor, who worked for Fred Howe in the consumers counsel division and who edited *Consumers Guide;* and Laurence Todd, Washington correspondent for Tass, the Soviet news agency. None of the six were prominent New Dealers or close to the president or his brain trust. Wirt admitted that he considered them "satellites" of the brain trusters.

Wirt stated that Kneeland had had the most to say to him, though he indicated at several points in the testimony that he himself had done the largest share of the talking. She had said, "Our group takes the leadership and recognizes the leadership of Dr. Tugwell." According to Wirt, Kneeland and Taylor referred to statements by Tugwell that argued for a planned economy and said that it could not be achieved under present laws and the Constitution.

Wirt also testified to another occasion, in March 1934, when General William I. Westervelt, an AAA division head, visited him in Gary. "He stated that Frederick C. Howe came into his office and was discussing the Federal relief program, that Howe asked him, Westervelt—'Is there any way by which we can stop feeding them? We are going too slowly. If we could stop feeding them, we would make greater headway toward what we are trying to accomplish.'"

Representative Harold McGugin (Republican, Kansas) then moved to call Tugwell, Howe, Wallace, Westervelt, and several others before the committee, though it had earlier agreed to hear only the persons at the Barrows dinner. In advocating his motion, he pointed to Howe's record as a "defender of anarchists" when he was immigration commissioner. The Democratic majority voted down the motion.

Alice Barrows then testified. She said that she considered Dr. Wirt and his wife "among my most devoted, sincere, and loyal friends." She had invited him to dinner to meet a few other friends whom she wanted to hear his educational theories. "At the dinner table he talked about education. After dinner, at about, I think, 8 o'clock, he began talking on the devaluation of the dollar and talked continuously on that subject until, I should say, about 11 o'clock." At no time had Dr. Wirt asked any questions. She declared that Kneeland had made none of the statements the school superintendent attributed to her, except one incidental remark.

The testimony of Kneeland and the other guests agreed with that of Barrows: they had been unable to halt the flow of Wirt's discourse, and they had no recollection of any mention of Tugwell or Wallace or their philosophies. "There was no conversation," said Bruere. "As has been stated there was a monologue unsuccessfully interrupted."

The committee adjourned after taking testimony only from Wirt and the dinner guests. On April 26, 1934, the three Democratic members issued a majority report. They pointed out that although Wirt had mentioned the names of Wallace, Tugwell, Howe, and others, he had testified that he had spoken to none of them. They saw no need to call other witnesses since "the five persons in the employ of the United States Government and the newspaper correspondent, who were present at the dinner in Virginia on September 1, 1933, did not make any such statements as were alleged to have been made by them to Dr. Wirt." In all the evidence presented to the committee, "there was none whatever showing that there was any person or group in the Government service planning to 'overthrow the existing social order' or planning or doing any of the things mentioned in Dr. Wirt's statement."

The two Republican members of the select committee rejected the majority's findings. McGugin charged that the committee had deliberately refrained from securing, or had suppressed, the information it was supposed to find. "Majority members made it inevitable that the proceedings would be a suppression of the truth rather than an uncovering of the truth." This was especially true with reference to Frederic C. Howe. The majority had refused to call witnesses who "could give the true testimony as to whether or not Frederick Howe, a high official in the Government, was doing everything within his power to retard the recovery program." The committee should have heard from General Westervelt and from Howe. The majority were "fearful or believed that the complete truth of this statement would be established, and having been established, every citizen of the land would know that it was the designed purpose of Frederick Howe, Consumers' counsel of the Agricultural Adjustment Administration, to retard recovery for the purpose of bringing about a revolution."

McGugin's Republican colleague, Representative Frederick R. Lehlbach of New Jersey, agreed that the committee had failed to investigate whether the brain trust was trying to establish a socialized America, but he made no attacks on specific individuals.

Fred Howe had been ready to testify before the House committee. To the press he had declared that the quotation imputed to him by Dr. Wirt was "all bunk." He had never said anything to General Westervelt about stopping the feeding of people on relief. "Somebody is evidently misquoting somebody," he added. AAA officials close to the consumers counsel backed him up, saying that it was "unthinkable" that he could have made the statement Wirt quoted. The *New York Times* reported allegations that Westervelt would back up Wirt's assertions, but the general remained publicly silent. Since the committee called neither Howe nor Westervelt, there was no confrontation. Fred's friend Lincoln Steffens had a different slant on the whole affair: "All I wrote you about Tugwell was that I was sorry that he and your brain trust were so innocent of the charges of Mr. Wirt. I wanted them to be guilty. I wanted it to be true that there was conspiracy on to change the very bottom of our system."[61]

The whole episode turned out to be a source of amusement for press and country. The Bulwinkle committee "made [Wirt] to look a fool," said Tugwell, to whom the dinner party had just been a chance for young New Dealers to have "a lot of fun with the scary old gentleman." Another New Dealer, Donald Richberg, offered a bit of doggerel:

> A cuttlefish squirt
> Nobody hurt,
> From beginning to end;
> Dr. Wirt.

Arthur Krock, the *New York Times* pundit, wrote of "the absurdities of the 'brain trust plot' against the President and the American social order" and praised Congressman Bulwinkle's conduct of the hearings. If Westervelt had been called and had confirmed the statement attributed to Howe, then one member of the brain trust might have been "partially hooked. Mr. Howe belongs properly to the group. But he plays in the bush league and a good deal of his time is spent on the bench." The impression "at the end of the Hoosier schoolmaster's testimony was a lot of childish dinner-talk from people with no governing responsibility or position." Under the heading "Pish & Piffle" *Time* magazine reported: "Thus, flatter than a crepe suzette, fell the Red Scare of 1934."[62]

For all the amusement it offered, the Wirt episode had its more serious consequences. As Arthur Schlesinger Jr. observed: "Yet a residue remained. The Wirt affair helped shape a new stereotype—the theory of the New Deal as a subversive conspiracy." Tugwell noted in his diary at the time: "What will come of it no one knows. If there is genuine strength in the present reaction, we may

---

61. *New York Times*, April 11, 1934, 12; Lincoln Steffens to FCH, May 11, 1934, in Winter and Hicks, *Letters of Lincoln Steffens*, 2:985.

62. Tugwell, *Democratic Roosevelt*, 323; Richberg, quoted in Schlesinger, *Coming of the New Deal*, 460; Arthur Krock, "'Brain Trust' Inquiry Proves Triumph for Bulwinkle," *New York Times*, April 11, 1934, 20.

be thrown overboard. . . . The present attack is getting pretty vicious. The Wirt thing has apparently been a complete flop; but it has not ended the attack."[63] As for Fred Howe, he may have emerged unscathed from the controversy, but the publicity and his visibility as a target for enemies of the New Deal and its policies undoubtedly strengthened the hands of those in the AAA who wanted to alter the consumers counsel's role and to get rid of some of the division's people.

---

63. Schlesinger, *Coming of the New Deal*, 460; Namorato, *Diary of Rexford G. Tugwell*, April 8 and 11, 1934, 108, 110. Tugwell later observed: "The publicity this trivial farce commanded can hardly be imagined at a distance in time. What is hard to credit is the prevalence of fear in the minds of most of the nation's pundits and former decision-makers. It was upon this near hysteria that such silly allegations as Wirt's fed. . . . Oppositionist propaganda was put out in great quantities throughout Franklin's first two terms, and every once in a while some one of the inventions would take hold and become, for the time being, a *cause celebre*." *Democratic Roosevelt*, 323.

18

FROM WASHINGTON TO MANILA

George Peek's successor as AAA administrator was Chester Davis, who had been serving as chief of the Production Division. He agreed with Secretary Wallace on emphasizing production control and crop reductions rather than marketing agreements, which he thought useful but supplemental. He was not a rebel and was accustomed to working with the agriculture establishment. No friend of the reform group in the AAA, Davis thought them obstructive and often impractical. "It wasn't necessary that the Triple-A should have all the crackpots in Washington," he observed. "There weren't any in other places to match in number what we had in the Triple-A."[1]

Pat Jackson believed that Davis had determined early on to limit or even to do away with the consumers counsel. The new administrator began meeting with division heads and their assistants in order to reappraise the AAA's activities, and Jackson and Fred Howe came away from their first conference with him saying, "We're in for it. Chester does not approve of our direction in the dairy efforts with the milk industry."[2] Davis's recollections bear out Jackson's suspicions. By the end of the summer of 1934, he found it "evident that the legal division and the consumer counsel, Tugwell, and the Secretary's outer office were certainly not in harmony with what I felt we were set up to do." In his reminiscences he referred to the Tugwell-Frank group as "arrogant," "offensive," "young zealots."[3]

The showdown between the two wings of the AAA came not over milk or meat, however, but over cotton. The dispute centered on the plight of Southern

---

1. C. Davis, "Reminiscences," 319. See also Gilbert, "Eastern Liberals and Midwestern Agrarian Intellectuals."
2. Jackson, "Reminiscences," 585.
3. C. Davis, "Reminiscences," 343, 375, 350–51.

sharecroppers. Cotton contracts mainly benefited the planters, and reductions in cotton acreage forced many croppers and tenants off the land. The 1934–35 cotton contract required a landlord to keep the same number of tenants as in 1933, as far as this was possible. This provision had resulted from several months of interoffice bargaining involving the AAA's Cotton Section, the consumers counsel, and the Legal Division. Owners did not interpret the provision to mean that they had to keep the same individuals as tenants, as long as the number stayed the same.

Among the AAA's "reformers" or "liberals" or "radicals" or "New Dealers," as they were variously called, concern had grown over the treatment of farm labor, especially in the South. Pat Jackson had long been worried about the problem. He was joined in his efforts by other "radicals" in the consumers counsel office, who worked closely with their allies in the Legal Division. One historian sums up the conflict within AAA: "The liberals feared that crop restriction would encourage landlords either to anchor their tenants in place under onerous tenure terms or to drive unneeded tenants from their land. . . . They believed that the AAA represented an opportunity to promote land tenure improvement and to secure some substantial redistribution of income." The conservatives, on the other hand, believed that the AAA's "paramount goal . . . should be crop restriction and price enhancement, not the equalizing of income, the promotion of equality of opportunity for tenants, nor the solving of all the South's ills."[4]

The showdown between the two factions came over a reinterpretation of the cotton contract in the AAA's Legal Division. Several attorneys had a hand in drafting the opinion, which received the approval of Francis Shea, chief of the Opinions Section, and of his superior, Alger Hiss, who was Jerome Frank's assistant on benefits contracts. It took the position that each tenant had a right to continue on the land during the life of the contract. This meant that landlords had to keep the same tenants and not just the same number. Frank, as head of the AAA's Legal Division, approved the new interpretation.

Chester Davis was away from Washington on a field trip in early 1935. In his absence, Frank persuaded the acting administrator, Victor Christgau, to approve the new interpretation as an AAA directive, which was sent out to state administrators in the South. This was done without consulting Davis or other top AAA officials. When the administrator returned to Washington and learned what had been done, he was furious. He immediately revoked the directive and went to

4. S. Baldwin, *Poverty and Politics*, 76–77.

Wallace, demanding the heads of Frank and the others he blamed for the challenge to his authority. On his list besides Frank were Pressman, Shea, Howe, and Jackson.[5]

Wallace was presented with a dilemma. If he failed to uphold Davis, he would lose not only his administrator but also many of Davis's supporters in the Cotton Section and other parts of the AAA. In addition, there would be an outcry from cotton growers and their powerful congressional allies, whose support the administration depended on. If he upheld Davis, he would undermine the role of the Legal Division, bring about the dismissals or resignations of key men like Frank, and incur the wrath of many New Deal liberals. He had been trying to balance the AAA's two factions. His personal sympathies were probably with Frank and the liberals on the immediate issue, but he felt that he must stand with Davis.[6]

As soon as he had Wallace's approval, Davis proceeded to fire Frank, Shea, Pressman, and Jackson. Jackson had not been involved in the reinterpretation of the cotton contract, but Davis considered him, in Jackson's words, "nothing but a goddamn trouble maker." Neither Hiss nor Christgau was fired, but both resigned a short time later. The "purge" included Fred Howe, as Davis took advantage of the firings to square accounts with the consumers counsel division and to remove Howe as its head. He had had no involvement in the cotton contract's reinterpretation, but he was on the liberal side, and Davis had long been critical of his office's role in agricultural policy making. Davis later recorded: "Fred Howe was a man of very high ideals and very little practical sense. He was the 'turn the other cheek' type. He was a well-meaning man who permitted his organization to be loaded down with a group of people who were more concerned with stirring up discontent than they were with achieving the objectives of the act."[7]

Howe was too important and symbolic a figure in American liberalism for Davis summarily to discharge along with Frank and the others. Apparently he called Howe into his office and informed him of the firings and of his removal as consumers counsel. Davis later recalled that he was "awfully sorry" for Howe, who was "very much distressed."

> He came in with tears in his eyes. He said, "I know you've had a lot of trouble, but my God! this is a blow to me!" I told him that I felt his

---

5. On the purge in the AAA, see Benham, "Purge"; Conrad, *Forgotten Farmers*, 136–53; Lash, *Dealers and Dreamers*, 221–30; Lord, *Wallaces of Iowa*, 393–409; Riker, *Firing of Pat Jackson*; Schlesinger, *Coming of the New Deal*, 77–80; Josephson, *Infidel in the Temple*, 280–96; Culver and Hyde, *American Dreamer*, 152–57.

6. Wallace, "Reminiscences," 376.

7. C. Davis, "Reminiscences," 313.

responsibility for consumers counsel had been pretty badly neglected, that he'd let a lot of boys run away with the show and didn't have any control over it at all. I said that he had to go out of consumers counsel but that I would try to find other employment for him so that he would not be affected personally and financially. Fred was broke. We did arrange some continuing employment for Fred, but we got him out where he didn't have a lot of boys clustered under him.

Davis observed that he "never felt personally that Fred did anything more than just permit his office to become a rallying ground for a lot of people who required constant watching.[8]

Howe left Davis's office and called Jackson in to see him. As Jackson recalled the meeting, Howe was "shaking and sweating from nervousness" and appeared to be "a very much beaten Fred Howe. It was noticeable in his manner and his looks." He told Jackson that Davis wanted his resignation. "Fred was in such a state of collapse, nervously and emotionally, that he just left it entirely up to me and said, 'Well, do whatever you want. I'm afraid there's nothing we can do. I'm afraid this is a finished thing.'" Jackson refused to sign the resignation form, and "we went out to lunch to have a council of war. We wanted to figure out some way to fight it."[9]

In a joint press conference on February 6, Wallace and Davis faced sharp questions from a hundred reporters and returned evasive answers. Russell Lord, Wallace's biographer, who was present, has described the scene: "It was an exceedingly trying conference for Wallace. He was gray-faced and haggard. I never saw at any press conference so many plainly hostile representatives of public opinion, with barbed questions prepared, planted. Wallace was sad and uneasy; his guard was down; his questioners were clamorous and loud. It was not a pleasant occasion." Davis, Wallace, and Alfred D. Stedman, the AAA's director of information, had agreed in advance to portray the "purge" as essentially an administrative reorganization, designed to bring greater harmony and efficiency into the AAA's operations. They made no mention of the fight over the cotton contract.[10] All those who worked for the AAA were members of "an exceptionally happy family," Wallace observed. The AAA was "going right ahead.... You see we don't like to have a ship that lists stronger to the left or the right, but one that goes straight ahead."

8. Ibid., 313, 414.
9. Chester C. Davis to Gardner Jackson, February 5, 1935, Jackson Papers, FDR Library; "Statement by Pat Jackson," in Riker, *Firing of Pat Jackson*, 4; Jackson, "Reminiscences," 612–14.
10. Lord, *Wallaces of Iowa*, 406; C. Davis, "Reminiscences," 411, CUOHROC. The transcript of the Wallace-Davis press conference can be found in a number of places. Quotations are from that found in Namorato, *Diary of Rexford G. Tugwell*, 198–217.

Reporters asked a number of questions about Fred Howe. To a query about his new role, Wallace replied: "Dr. Howe will be shifting his activities, but in just what capacity hasn't been determined yet. . . . In the case of Dr. Howe his capacities are not quite the capacities that are necessary for leading up this particular organization."

A few minutes later, Davis tried to explain the alterations being made in the consumers counsel's role that necessitated a change in its leadership. What the director needed was study, analysis, and constructive criticism. "Now, Mr. Howe is in entire agreement with me on this point that he is not the man—he is not interested in that type of activity. He has enormous capacity through his public contact for educational work and promotion, but not this particular type of work which I believe we need." Wallace declared that Howe was not interested in statistics gathering. "His genius runs in other directions, and a very remarkable genius it is." The responses by Wallace and Davis made it clear that the consumers counsel would no longer be involved in policy making and that Fred Howe would no longer be its head. They did not indicate what his new duties would include.

On February 8, Pat Jackson faced the inevitable and turned in his resignation, commenting, "I deeply regret being forced by Mr. Davis to leave the Consumers Counsel Office because the work which has been attempted by Dr. Howe and his staff seems to me to be one of the few efforts of the AAA to protect the consuming public." In the meanwhile, Fred Howe had sent his own farewell message to his colleagues, in a letter addressed to "My dear Pat." He observed: "The political state is a very difficult institution, but not as inefficient, wasteful and dishonest an institution as many people believe. And it heightens greatly my belief and confidence in democracy that I can say at the end of nearly two years working with you and twenty other men and women that there has been a high degree of efficiency and an equally high degree of devotedness and intellectual integrity as to which not even a question has been asked."[11] He left his post and his co-workers with deep regret but also with deep admiration for their efforts and achievements.

In their reminiscences, both Davis and Jackson pictured Fred as a beaten man. Jackson recalled: "He was not in an emotional nervous condition to really put up a battle. He didn't want to battle. He was an old man. His future livelihood was very much at stake. He had virtually nothing on which to live. His book-writing days had passed. So he was very much filled with anxiety about

---

11. Gardner Jackson to FCH, February 6, 1935; Jackson's resignation form, February 8, 1935; FCH to Gardner Jackson, February 7, 1935, Jackson Papers, FDR Library.

his future." Jackson was not sure whether Fred knew at this point that some job would be arranged for him in the Department of Agriculture.[12]

Newspapers and magazines had mixed reactions to the "purge" in the AAA. The *New York Times* in its news columns treated the events as "an enforced separation of 'left-wingers.'" Editorially, it considered the changes as perhaps the beginning of the end for the brain trust. New York's *Journal of Commerce* chortled that the firings were "another victory for the conservative elements within the Administration which have been endeavoring to effect a working concord between Government and business. . . . The activities of AAA are now in the hands of executives in whom industry may safely place its confidence." As for the once-powerful consumers counsel, its left-wing element had been stripped of its power. The *Washington Post* was also pleased with the changes in the consumers counsel office. "Dr. Frederic C. Howe, as consumers' counsel, has been equally energetic [as Jerome Frank] in putting the formulation of policy ahead of its administration. In his case, as in that of Mr. Frank, what has happened was inevitable. The time was bound to come when those saddled with the real responsibility would have to crack down on those whose chief interest lies in the promotion of interesting theories of social evolution." The *Nation*, though expressing both some sympathy with Chester Davis and some criticism of Roosevelt for failing to fight, concluded: "The purge spells the end of an era. It is the defeat of the social outlook in agricultural policy."[13]

David Eugene Conrad, in a solid study of the "purge" at the AAA, concluded that neither Wallace nor Davis could be blamed for their actions. To restore peace in the AAA, they had no other recourse except their own resignations. "In the final analysis, there were no real heroes in the battle. . . . However, it is much easier to excuse the liberals for their brashness, ignorance of agriculture, delay in acting, faulty strategy, and compassion for suffering tenant farmers than it is to forgive the agrarians for their close-mindedness, refusal to tolerate interference with their programs, pro-landlord bias, and hard-heartedness toward tenants."[14]

So ended, in February 1935, Fred Howe's tenure of some twenty months as consumers counsel. It had been a tough job. He had enjoyed being back in action and pioneering as a defender of the consumer, but he had also felt frustrated by the battles within the AAA and by the antagonisms of many inside and outside the agency. Some of the frustrations came from a conflict of purpose written into the AAA statute. The agency's primary purpose was to raise

---

12. Jackson, "Reminiscences," 630, CUOHROC.
13. *New York Times*, February 7, 1935, 2, 18; *Journal of Commerce*, February 8, 1935; *Washington Post*, February 7, 1935; "The Purge at the AAA," *Nation* 140 (February 20, 1935): 216.
14. Conrad, *Forgotten Farmer*, 153.

the prices of farm products while at the same time protecting the consumer against unreasonable price increases and safeguarding against monopolistic practices. Since the consumers counsel section was a line agency and not merely an advisory board, it was necessarily plunged into the agricultural policy-making process, where the outlook and efforts of Howe, Jackson, and their cohorts were often at odds with those in the producers', processors', and distributors' sections. Fred's antimonopoly views and his sympathy for the underdog made him a natural ally of Frank, Jackson, and the other liberals in the AAA.

There is no doubt that the effectiveness of the consumers counsel's office was hampered by the differences in outlook on farm policy and the internecine conflicts and outside pressures that developed. It had other weaknesses as well: a minimal budget, a small staff, a mandate for consumer protection that extended only to agricultural products and not to manufactured goods, lack of an organized grassroots constituency. Despite these problems and weaknesses, Fred and his staff could point to achievements. Van L. Perkins has noted that some have dismissed the consumers counsel division as "an innocuous little office because it was not able to prevent the major burden of the adjustment effort from being placed on the consumer." Such a judgment was essentially unfair. "No one expected the division to achieve such a goal because the act itself made it inevitable that the consumer would bear the burden. Thus the act should bear the criticism, not the division. Within the bounds permitted by the act the division was, in fact, reasonably effective." The office educated the public through the *Consumers' Guide* and Fred's radio talks and press releases. In some cases it was able to limit price increases and to see that marketing agreements protected consumer interests. Tom Blaisdell, who was in on the consumer effort from its beginning and who could look back on it after a long career in government and academe, believed that, in spite of its limitations, "the Consumer Counsel demonstrated what a dedicated staff can do when it knows how to use its inside and outside contacts and effective publicity."[15]

15. Perkins, *Crisis in Agriculture*, 95; Angevine, *Consumer Activists*, 182. The consumers counsel office continued after the "purge." Howe's successor was Dr. Calvin Hoover, an economist on leave from Duke and a member of Wallace's staff. The office's crusading days were over. It became mainly an advisory body, and its publicity efforts were curtailed, though *Consumers Guide* continued to circulate under Mary Taylor's editorship. Chester Davis noted that after the "purge" he did not have to pay so much attention to internal conflicts: "The consumers counsel was fully as effective as it ever had been in representing the consumer's interest. It was less interested in internal politics than it had been before." C. Davis, "Reminiscences," 422. Hoover served till the fall of 1935, when he returned to Duke. His successor was Donald E. Montgomery, who had been a key player in the consumers counsel office from its beginning. A longtime consumers advocate, Benjamin Marsh, observed: "Donald Montgomery, who succeeded Dr. Howe . . . tried valiantly to keep up the pace set when the office [of consumers counsel] was created, but was boxed in, and given practically no funds on which to operate." Marsh, *Lobbyist for the People*, 166. On the changes in the consumers counsel office after the "purge," see P. Campbell, *Consumer Representation*, 243–61.

Throughout his tenure as consumers counsel, Fred Howe's stock with liberals remained high. William Allen White wrote him that although he was leery about the New Deal's farm program, "at any rate, you men are doing a first rate job and should have the cheers of your fellow countrymen." In a book of sketches of contemporary figures, Peggy Bacon paid her respects to him:

> Dr. Fred Howe
> Old New England type, unkempt, unselfconscious, straight, earnest. Seamed and cross-hatched, weathered, worm-eaten, antique, early-American, curly maple. Eyebrows sputtering, hair like hay, forehead evenly seamed in a half-dozen parallels. Eyes deep-set, orbless chinks through which something invisible peeps at you, not slyly but with an observant interest. Nose starts way under brow and develops rapidly to a thick end with scooped nostrils. Upper lip short in meditative pucker. Lower lip perfectly horizontal line, a straight crack across the face. Chin multiplying wrinkles like skin on boiled milk. Expression of relaxed, pondering abstraction. Disinterestedly absorbed in mundane matters. The world his hobby. Potters over it like an old carriage-maker. Think-I-can-fix-it-up look.

Some of his fellow New Dealers later added their recollections of Howe from the AAA years. Grace Tugwell, who was Rex's administrative assistant, recalled Fred as "a mild mannered and kindly man—everyone liked him as far as I know." Alger Hiss, who knew him throughout the AAA battles, observed:

> Fred Howe, as one might expect, was part of the liberal group at AAA. His Progressive credentials were greatly important and he could be counted on to support liberal views. But there was little he could do, I suspect, to aid consumers. Our job was to raise farm prices. As prices were abnormally low during the Depression we didn't think of higher food prices as injurious to consumers, especially as the relief programs soon included some surplus food items. Howe's task must have been an uphill one. . . . Fred Howe had my admiration and respect for his consistent dedication to liberal and progressive principles.

He was "a very nice guy," said Gardiner Means. "Very quiet, firm, not flamboyant, . . . staunch and sturdy like George Norris," added Caroline Ware.

Montgomery did not escape controversy. In December 1939 J. B. Matthews, research director of the House Un-American Activities Committee (the Dies Committee), reported that the Consumers Counsel was aiding communist-dominated organizations. Montgomery denied the charge. *New York Times,* December 11, 1939, 1, 14; December 13, 1939, 19.

Dr. Fred Howe

Old New England type, unkempt, unselfconscious, straight, earnest. Seamed and cross-hatched, weathered, worm-eaten, antique, early-American, curly maple. Eyebrows sputtering, hair like old hay, forehead evenly seamed in a half-dozen parallels. Eyes deepset, orbless chinks through which something invisible peeps at you, not slyly but with observant interest. Nose starts way under brow and develops rapidly to a thick end with scooped nostrils. Upper lip short in meditative pucker. Lower lip perfectly horizontal line, a straight crack across the face. Chin multiplying wrinkles like skin on boiled milk. Expression of relaxed, pondering abstraction. Disinterestedly absorbed in mundane matters. The world his hobby. Potters over it like an old carriage-maker. Think-I-can-fix-it-up look.

Figs. 5/6 Frederic C. Howe, consumers counsel and New Dealer, 1934: sketch and text by Peggy Bacon

"You always knew where he stood, but he wasn't the one that made the noise—Gardner Jackson made more noise, Jerry Frank made more noise, and Don Montgomery made more noise."[16]

Unfortunately, we have no direct testimony about Fred's feelings at the time of the "purge" and his demotion. At the age of sixty-eight, he had reached a

16. William Allen White to FCH, February 21, 1934, White Papers; Bacon, *Off with Their Heads!* n.p.; Grace F. Tugwell to author, July 21, 1986; Alger Hiss to author, December 18, 1985; interview with Gardiner Means and Caroline Ware, October 4, 1986.

time of stocktaking in his life and could look back on a career in which triumphs had often ended in defeats. He mused on this in a letter to Bolton Hall on the occasion of his friend's eightieth birthday: "Many of us have slipped. We have not always clim[b]ed as we should have climbed. You, however, have always kept your eyes upwards and have not made any concession to those who demanded that you be other than what you are or think otherwise than you had to think."[17] Throughout his life, Howe was to have periods of pessimism and depression when he measured his accomplishments against his ambitions. His spirits lightened whenever he had a meaningful task to do.

Such tasks seemed lacking in the first months after Howe's removal as consumers counsel. It appears that the Department of Agriculture did not quite know what to do with him. He was given a new title—special adviser to the Office of the Secretary of Agriculture—but no specific duties. He wrote a number of reports and memoranda—to Tugwell on financial contributions by utility interests to land grant colleges and on housing in Europe, to the president on using executive orders with government contracts so as to maintain fair conditions for labor, on the way to correct adverse rulings on parcel post by the postmaster general that would hurt farmers, and on negotiations with the railroads to reduce passenger fares. Roosevelt sent them all on for consideration to the appropriate officer or agency.[18] Howe could now devote more of his time to writing and to thinking about and offering advice on New Deal politics.

It was not a very productive period for Howe as an author, however. He had completed a book in early 1933—Marie referred to it as a book on banking, but Fred called it a book on the history of gold. Despite the fact that publishing, like other businesses, was suffering from the Depression, he hoped to find a publisher, writing Newton Baker: "I shall be hurt if not for I have done a lot of very hard work on it and there is something like a very personal rebuff in not having one's intellectual child liked by others."[19] Fred had to accept the hurt, for the book was never published.

In March 1934 he wrote a glowing account of Denmark's agricultural achievements for the *Annals,* and his thoughts turned to revision of his 1921 book on that country. He tried to persuade Maxwell Perkins to accept either a book on land and housing in Europe or one on the cooperative movement in Denmark. Perkins replied for Scribner's that "it would be a pleasure to us to be able to publish another book for you," but pointed out the "specialized character of

17. FCH to Bolton Hall, August 1, 1934, Hall Papers.
18. FCH to Rexford Tugwell, June 13, 1935; FCH to Marvin H. McIntyre, June 26, 1935, President's Personal File, FDR Library; FCH to Lincoln Steffens, January 15, 1936, Steffens Papers.
19. MJH to Fola La Follette, March 22, 1933, La Follette Family Papers; FCH to Newton Baker, January 12, 1933, Baker Papers.

the market" for such a book and the difficulty of earning a profit for the publisher, given the current economic situation. As to the Danish book, he wanted to defer a decision and suggested that Howe consider revising his earlier book on Denmark.[20]

Fred liked the idea of a revision, noted the great interest in Marquis Childs's *Cooperative Movement in Sweden,* and reiterated his arguments for a similar book on Denmark. Then Perkins hesitated—certainly the idea had merit, but it was difficult for a publisher to succeed with a book that had already appeared, and the topic of cooperatives in Denmark would have limited appeal. Why not a more complete volume on cooperatives in Denmark, Sweden, the United States, and elsewhere? Howe jumped at the idea, but in the end he could not reach agreement with Scribner's, and when *Denmark: The Cooperative Way* appeared in the fall of 1936, its publisher was Coward-McCann.

Gardner Jackson had observed that Fred's book-writing days had passed, and this, his final volume, justified the remark. It was little more than a revision and expansion of his 1921 work, and like its predecessor, it was chock full of facts and figures on such things as agricultural production, land ownership, producers' and consumers' cooperatives, education, and social legislation. Howe admitted that the fundamental facts about Denmark had not altered since the earlier book. The nation, which had had few flaws in 1921, had even fewer fifteen years later.[21]

It had become a model for the world, a middle way between the excesses of socialism, communism, and fascism, on the one hand, and capitalism, on the other. Its democracy was full—political, economic, social. "All these gains have been achieved in little more than the lifetime of a single generation. They have been achieved without bloodshed or revolution. One abuse after another has been removed by legislation and by cooperative action, while the production of wealth has been increased and retained by the producers, until we have an incontestable exhibit of the fact that poverty, ignorance, insecurity, and fear can be ended in any state which really desires to end them." The cooperative movement "enlists the humblest citizen on a plane of equality with the richest and transfers to those who produce and those who consume many of the activities which in other countries are performed by distant, if not hostile agencies, indifferent to the effect of their acts on the well-being of the people whom they profess to serve. . . . It is the economic equivalent of political democracy."[22]

20. FCH, "Most Complete Agricultural Recovery"; FCH to Maxwell E. Perkins, December 2, 1935; Perkins to FCH, December 5, 1935, Scribner Archives.
21. FCH, *Denmark: The Cooperative Way,* 4.
22. Ibid., 31, viii.

As a successful economic and political democracy, Denmark had lessons for the United States. "As compared with Denmark the American State is a limping, halting thing." Democracy in America was "jug-handled; it is hobbled by our inflexible constitutions, by the limitations on the powers of the nation and the states, and by the all but complete lack of liberty of action on the part of our towns and cities.... As a people we are in a political jungle of legalism, the effect of which is to make government devious, costly, difficult, at times unworkable." Free from these problems, Denmark had a government that was "completely responsible to the will of the people." It was essential that American farmers copy their Danish counterparts. They must organize politically, join with urban labor, and use their power "to realize a life of their own and a complete protection of their industry." They must control their economic destiny through cooperatives and public enterprises and, as in Denmark, work to create a democracy of trust and confidence.[23]

The new book on Denmark was basically an updating of Howe's earlier one. Its style is disjointed, and the text repetitive. There were few reviews. The *New York Times* summarized Danish achievements favorably but doubted that they could be transferred to America. The book had "a faintly nostalgic quality," said the reviewer, since Americans had gone too far into "the barbarism of the machine" to turn back. "Denmark is a solution for Danes, and a good one; it is too small, too homogeneous, too firmly rooted in its soil to be a model for this sprawling nation." *Current History* found the volume "competent and readable ... a clear discussion and explanation," filled with useful information on consumer co-ops. The *Nation* gave it only a brief summary. Howe himself agreed that *Denmark* could have been "a better book if I could have sweated over it some more ... However, it is pretty good for those who understand."[24]

Howe thought about other books he might write. He proposed two books to the John Day Company, but the publishers were not interested in either one. Fola La Follette hoped Fred would write a biography of her father, which he had apparently been thinking of for some time, but he replied regretfully that he doubted he could do anything about it. "I am pretty tired. I have only my evenings and I fear I have lost the willingness to do original research, certainly

---

23. Ibid., xi, 117–228, 271.
24. *New York Times,* January 3, 1937, sec. 7, 5; *Current History* 45 (February 1937): 128; *Nation* 144 (January 23, 1937): 107; FCH to Lincoln Steffens, July 1936 (complete date not given), Steffens Papers. Gardner Jackson had agreed with the *Times*'s comment on "nostalgia." He had written Tom Blaisdell in August 1936 concerning a European trip the latter was planning: "I assume you'll go to Scandinavia since that peninsula of Nordics seems to be becoming the New Deal's ideal of how the U.S. should go—a nice romantic notion, in my opinion, rooted in the worst kind of sentimental wishful thinking. Conditions are so completely different." Gardner Jackson to Thomas C. Blaisdell Jr., August 7, 1936, Gardner Jackson Papers.

of the kind that a biography of your father demands. . . . It is the mental depression I have been in for so many years, and my present inability to freshen up enough to take on a big job." Fola was sorry, too, writing Fred: "I know you could do this in a way that no one else could, and it would have been a unique contribution to the history of this period." Musing to Fola about America as a "wrecked" continent, Howe added: "How is it possible for us to have eroded not only desert lands, but every kind of economic opportunity that nature offered us?" Fola tried to console him. "Your reasons for not doing [the biography], or not having done anything on it, gives me a heart ache, dear Fred," she wrote. "I know the deep satisfactions you always found in your creative work, and that a prolonged depression should be shutting you off from this way of life which was so important to you grieves me."[25]

In the literary field, about as far as Howe could stir himself was a query to Maxwell Perkins about reprinting *Confessions of a Reformer* in an inexpensive edition, but Perkins replied that the plates had been destroyed. Fred's only publication after 1936 was a brief and prosaic article in an educational journal put out by the federal government, describing Wisconsin's folk high school.[26] His days of literary creativity were over.

Despite the personal defeat that Howe had suffered in the "purge" of 1935, he remained a staunch supporter of the New Deal and Franklin Roosevelt. Whatever his feelings may have been about Wallace's actions and the president's failure to intervene, he continued to regard Roosevelt as the essential man, the only one who could save and reform capitalism. The nation might well face chaos if the Supreme Court acted against the New Deal as Howe expected it to. What would the millions of unemployed men and women do if they lost confidence in the government and its leadership? "The president is not only the best, he is almost the only asset the old kind of capitalism has," he wrote Steffens.[27]

As the 1936 election campaign got underway, Howe sent frequent letters and memos to the president, either directly or indirectly through Mrs. Roosevelt, offering advice about tactics and issues. Sometimes the focus was on very specific items. For example, in a letter to Roosevelt in June 1936, he harked back to his experiences with Tom Johnson, Bob La Follette, the CPPA, and the railroad brotherhoods, and recommended that government act to help veterans secure low-cost housing, to restore low parcel post rates for the benefit of farmers and

---

25. Fola La Follette to FCH, May 12, 1936; FCH to La Follette, May 19, 1936; La Follette to FCH, May 21, 1936.

26. FCH to Maxwell Perkins, December 7, 1936; Perkins to FCH, December 9, 1936; FCH, "Wisconsin's Folk High School."

27. FCH to Lincoln Steffens, January 15, 1936, Steffens Papers.

consumers, and to promote credit unions so as to "cut down the interest charges of loan sharks." He called for mobilizing labor as the CPPA had tried to do.[28]

In a broader view of campaign issues, Howe recommended to the president that he point to the menace of fascism. "I think we are quite honestly justified in having someone . . . bring out into the open and keep in the open the suggestion which has been made of the potential Fascist menace involved in Hearstism, the oil interests, the Liberty League. . . . Certainly this is the direction in which these forces are driving, as certainly Hearst has definitely committed himself to that philosophy. This menace has been sensed by labor, by the Socialists, and it is a menace which is potentially here in the Republican set-up."[29]

Perhaps the antifascist theme might best be presented by the National Progressive League for Franklin D. Roosevelt, a supposedly independent organization like that Howe had helped create in 1932. He wrote Senator Robert La Follette Jr., who chaired the new group, about the threat he perceived from the Supreme Court. Whoever was elected president in 1936 would appoint four or more members of the court during his term of office. If the Republicans won, the new justices might "make permanent the whole reactionary philosophy which now permeates the Court for a quarter of a century, just as did the appointments of Wilson and his Republican successors." This possibility was brought vividly to Howe's mind when he overheard a railroad vice president say, "Of course, we are not so much concerned about the Presidency as we are about the Supreme Court. That is what makes this election so vital." The second issue, Howe suggested, was "what seems to me a perfectly possible set-up headed towards Fascism. It is the set-up of Hearst—The Liberty League—the oil interests—and the Old Guard of the Republican Party."[30]

Howe rejoiced in the president's victory in 1936 but warned the first lady: "I fancy this is a bit of gratuitous and needless concern, but just after an election, when passions have been running high and frustrations are widespread, there is more danger from unbalanced persons than at any other time."[31]

Throughout the years Fred kept in touch with his old friends—John Finley, Newton Baker, Amos Pinchot, Fola La Follette, Lincoln Steffens, Harry Garfield,

---

28. FCH to Franklin D. Roosevelt, June 29, 1936, President's Personal File, FDR Library.
29. FCH to Roosevelt, June 30, 1936.
30. FCH to Robert M. La Follette Jr., President's Personal File, FDR Library. Howe sent a copy of his letter to the president, by way of Marvin McIntyre. Roosevelt had spurred the formation of the National Progressive League in a memo to Jim Farley, a copy of which may be found in the Frank P. Walsh Papers, New York Public Library. Many of Howe's friends or acquaintances were members of the League, including Donald Richberg, Judson King, Peter Witt, George Norris, Frank Walsh, as well as La Follette. See Schlesinger, *Politics of Upheaval*, 545–46.
31. FCH to Eleanor Roosevelt, Eleanor Roosevelt Papers, FDR Library, November 4, 1936. Some months later he suggested to the first lady how she might use the radio to build support for what the administration was trying to do. FCH to Eleanor Roosevelt, June 4, 1937.

Paul Kellogg, Oswald Garrison Villard. Finley, by the 1930s an associate editor of the *New York Times* and for a year its editor-in-chief, sent Fred a little poem after he saw a headline "Frederic W. Howe—Dead in 60th Year":

> Dear Frederick C. or "Fred" for short:
> I'm grateful that the middle
> C has saved your life
> Long may it be before you
> Leave this world of strife.[32]

Howe kept up an affectionate correspondence with Fola La Follette and, when she asked for his aid in writing her father's biography, gladly read parts of the manuscript and provided what information he could. "I will be very happy, as you know, to do anything you ask me to do," he responded. She sent him her love and observed: "We have shared so much through the years, and as one grows older such friendships are increasingly precious. We should keep in closer touch." Before he left for the Philippines in 1937, he sent her "some of Marie's things that I had and that mean as much to you as they do to me. . . . You will remember all of them. And I guess they all came from girl friends so you have a further right to them. . . . There isn't anything that you want to happen to you and yours that I don't want also." He reiterated these feelings in a later letter: "You may not know how deep my affection is for you and all of the things that concern you, and how permanent are the attachments made with you all when we were all a bit younger than we are today."[33]

Fred's friendship with Lincoln Steffens remained strong and undiminished, even though the distance between Washington, D.C., and Carmel, California, meant the links were by letter rather than personal visit. They continued to exchange comments on their doings, the books they had read or were working on, political events in America, Europe, and the Soviet Union, and their views of the world, both immediate and long-range. They often reminisced about politics and leaders in the days of Tom Johnson and Bob La Follette. In July 1936 Howe planned a trip to Europe and wrote his friend: "I like the old spots of the world best, as I like many old friends whom I have over there whom I can sit down with and metaphorically hold hands with just as I did twenty or thirty years ago. There is something nice about age as you know and I know. I

---

32. John H. Finley to FCH, August 24, 1934, Finley Papers, New York Public Library. The obituary of Frederic W. Howe, a financier, was in the *New York Times*, August 17, 1934, 15.

33. Fola La Follette to FCH, May 12, 1936; FCH to La Follette, May 19 1936; La Follette to FCH, May 21, 1936; FCH to La Follette, June 30, 1936; FCH to La Follette, June 14, 1937; FCH to La Follette, January 31, 1938.

find that same nice thing in old countries." Steffens died a month later, and Howe wrote Ella Winter: "I do feel increasingly bereft. I was tied very close to Stef and he was about the only link of a confident kind that I had with any friends. As I think of his last years my long admiration of him is greatly increased. At no time in his life was he as outstanding as he had been lately in his courage, in his interest, and his insistence on being a part of his world."[34]

A note of melancholy and depression appeared in many of Fred's letters to his friends in the mid-1930s. He unburdened himself at length to Newton Baker in 1935: "When I think over the years we were together in Cleveland and how nearly cosmic in importance the things we were fighting for seemed to be and how very relatively insignificant they have been in the last quarter of a century, I get a little despairing at times over the inability of society to hold on to its gains or to escape from the purely personal struggle which the competitive system makes so much of." He realized that many of the pioneering ideas of Cleveland had found a place in legislation and were now accepted as commonplace. "So in some lines at least the world does climb up rather than slip down even while human nature remains much the same."[35]

Baker mentioned his friend's melancholy in a letter to Isaiah Bowman, the president of Johns Hopkins, in November 1936. "[He] has a very real mind and a spacious character. For the rest, he is often beguiled by beautiful notions, for which the world should be ready but is not, and he is often rather downcast because his fellowmen just will not do wise and beautiful things!"[36]

Fred's gloom lifted in 1937 when, after several years of drifting at the Department of Agriculture, he suddenly got a job that seemed meaningful to him. On a visit to Washington in April 1937, Manuel Quezon, president of the Philippine Commonwealth, announced that he had appointed Howe as an adviser on rural tenancy problems. Under the Tydings-McDuffie Act of 1934, the Philippines had acquired commonwealth status and a nearly autonomous government. Independence was promised for 1946. Most Filipino peasants were landless, and landlord-tenant relations had been a serious and continuing problem ever since the United States had taken the Philippines from Spain in 1898. Quezon indicated at the time of Howe's appointment that he was interested in land reform policies in Mexico, Ireland, and Denmark that might be applied to his nation and planned to visit the three countries on his trip. (According to Geoffrey

34. Steffens to FCH, January 21, 1936, in Winter and Hicks, *Letters of Lincoln Steffens,* 2:1014; FCH to Steffens, July 1936 (complete date not given), Steffens Papers; FCH to Ella Winter, October 9, 1936, Steffens Papers.
35. FCH to Newton Baker, April 19, 1935.
36. Baker to Isaiah Bowman, November 23, 1936, Special Collections, the Johns Hopkins University Library.

Perret, Quezon's journey was actually "a ten-month round-the world ego trip. He took a huge entourage with him, numbering more than twenty cronies and political friends, all having a lavishly good time at other people's expense.")[37]

It is not known how Quezon learned about or decided to appoint Howe. Perhaps his writings on Danish agriculture had been brought to the president's attention. Perhaps reports that Howe had had a hand in drafting the Farm Tenancy bill then pending in Congress were also important. Perhaps his friends in the administration simply wanted to give him something interesting to do in his waning years. At any rate, he took an indefinite leave of absence from the Department of Agriculture to serve as adviser for what Quezon called a "new attack" on an old problem.[38]

Howe arrived in Manila in the summer of 1937, took up residence in the Manila Hotel, the city's leading hostelry, and remained there during his tour of duty. General Douglas MacArthur and his family lived there, too, in the penthouse apartment, described by Howe as "a palatial suite (and it is palatial)." The hotel was one of the main centers of Manila's social life, and Fred enjoyed its attractions. "Life here is quite perfect, good hotel, lots of fine men and girls, everybody is away from mamma and papa and the day begins about nine at nights for those who want it so," he wrote Paul Appleby after he had been there a few months. "And from now on till February a climate that is more than wonderful in its beauty." It was easy to make friends, he told Fola La Follette, and he enjoyed the climate. "We are pretty far away from books and the theater, but there are good movie houses, and there is very little of that social climbing or other struggle that disturbs life at home. I like it very much."[39]

Almost as soon as he arrived in the Philippines, Howe began sending long letters about his thoughts and experiences to Henry Wallace, Paul Appleby (Wallace's trusted assistant, who passed them on to his boss), and Eleanor Roosevelt, all the correspondence intended to reach the eye of the president. He also wrote at length to Fola La Follette. From these letters it is apparent that Fred fell quickly under the sway of Douglas MacArthur. After a distinguished military career that had culminated in a tour of duty as army chief of staff, MacArthur had been appointed by Quezon as the commonwealth's military adviser. He had arrived in the Philippines in late 1935, accompanied by a small staff that included

---

37. Perret, *Old Soldiers Never Die*, 204.
38. *New York Times*, April 25, 1937, 4. The bill on farm tenancy, which became the Farm Tenancy Act of 1937 (the Bankhead-Jones Act), set up the Farm Security Agency to make loans to farmers to rehabilitate their land and to tenants to buy farms they were renting. President Quezon had already included the purchase of large estates and their resale to their cultivators in his "Social Justice" program.
39. FCH to Paul Appleby, October 31, 1937, and October 29, 1937, President's Personal File, FDR Library; FCH to Fola La Follette, January 31, 1938.

Major Dwight D. Eisenhower as his chief aide. The general's plan for the Philippine military was an army on the Swiss model: a small core of about ten thousand regular soldiers plus a reserve of well-trained conscripts (about forty thousand men to be trained every year) who would be mobilized in event of war. Always optimistic on the development of this army, he constantly reported to Quezon that great progress was being made. Eisenhower thought otherwise and was most unhappy with the conscripts and their training.[40] By 1939 the reserves amounted to only about a quarter of the number that the defense plan called for.

Howe accepted MacArthur's pronouncements at face value and quickly became a booster for the general. A few weeks after his arrival, he observed in letters to Wallace and Mrs. Roosevelt that before coming to the Philippines he had heard a great many bad things about MacArthur, but they were proving untrue. The general "has won my confidence as have few men I have met on the islands," he wrote Eleanor Roosevelt.[41]

Howe's praise for MacArthur continued throughout his stay in the Philippines, and he served as a useful conduit to Washington for the general's views. He spoke less favorably of the incumbent high commissioner from the United States, Paul McNutt. He could not figure McNutt out, he wrote Appleby. "He is very handsome, very circumspect of speech and he has a clever and very ambitious wife." But did he play fair? "Certainly he is ambitious—possibly too ambitious," and he resented MacArthur's residence in a penthouse while he had to live in a rented home.[42]

Manuel Quezon impressed Howe. He told Fola La Follette: "I like him better every time I see him. He is a real statesman. He sees things quickly and thoroughly and he has a real love for a spectacular fight." He had some realization of the Philippine president's limitations, however. He believed that Quezon was "as nearly committed to the interests of his people and to formulas that accord with our own as is possible among peoples who have none of our backgrounds

---

40. "Eisenhower, detailed by MacArthur to create the Filipino force, doubted from the start that an army could be cobbled together, and his frustrations rose as he grappled with the task. . . . As he toured the country, he found training camps to be ramshackle affairs in which the rookies, most of them uneducated farm boys, hated discipline, disobeyed orders and even mutinied. But he was particularly dismayed by the native officers, supposedly the spine of the makeshift army, who impressed him as indolent, corrupt and quarrelsome. He soon came to expect of them, as he confided to his diary, 'a minimum of performance from a maximum of promise.'" Karnow, *In Our Image*, 275.

41. FCH to Henry A. Wallace, August 28, 1937. A copy of this letter may be found in the MacArthur Archives. Howe wrote virtually the same thing to Mrs. Roosevelt. FCH to Eleanor Roosevelt, September 7, 1937, Eleanor Roosevelt Papers, FDR Library.

42. FCH to Paul Appleby, October 31, 1937, President's Personal File, FDR Library.

of political and civil liberty." He considered that among Philippine leaders only Quezon had the "guts" to take on a fight for economic change.[43]

The problems on which Howe was to advise Quezon were both serious and long-standing. In the countryside, where most of the population lived, a "calcified" social structure resembled a feudal system. On the land, most Filipinos were sharecroppers, perpetually in debt to the landowners. According to a census in the 1930s, nearly a fourth of the population—3 1/2 million out of 16 million—were "agricultural day laborers." A description fifty years later could have been made during Howe's tour of duty: "Plantations have belonged to the same dynasties for generations, and tenants can trace their roots on the property back to their grandfathers and great-grandfathers." Those peasants who owned their own land had only small plots and a precarious independence. Short of capital, they lived under the threat of losing what they had and being forced back into tenancy. Desperation led to peasant revolts, the most recent of which, the *Sakdalista* rising, had occurred only about two years before Howe came to the Philippines.[44]

Fred Howe had never set foot in the Far East before. His travels had taken him almost exclusively to Europe, and his investigations and writings on land problems and tax policy had been limited mainly to Denmark, Ireland, and the United States. He had given no indication of any interest in or knowledge of the Philippines until his appointment as Quezon's economic adviser. Except for a brief concern about loans to China in 1916, Asia—and more specifically, the Philippines—had not been on his list of interests.

Nevertheless, after a few months in the country, Fred was sure that he understood the society, politics, and economics of the Philippines. His job put him "on the inside of things governmental and things economic in a very intimate way," he believed. He supplemented the inside information with his own investigations of Philippine life. After ten weeks in the islands, he could tell Paul Appleby that he doubted "if any American has gotten on the inside of economic facts as I have in that time." He had studied the tax system and the national resources "as a kind of national balance sheet, . . . and I had to build everything up from the very bottom."[45]

---

43. FCH to Fola La Follette, January 31, 1938; FCH to Eleanor Roosevelt, September 7, 1937; FCH to Eleanor Roosevelt, October 22, 1937, Eleanor Roosevelt Papers, FDR Library; FCH to Paul Appleby, October 29, 1937, President's Personal File, FDR Library. Historians have not been as sanguine as Howe on Quezon's commitment to democracy and change. "Quezon . . . articulated the language of American democracy, but he was, in practice, an autocrat primarily preoccupied with preserving his power. Recalling his mythical peasant past, he would rattle on about 'social justice' as he wielded nearly absolute authority to control wages, prices and profits as well as to ban strikes and other 'unwholesome agitation.'" Karnow, *In Our Image*, 271.

44. Karnow, *In Our Image*, 22, 272.

45. FCH to Paul Appleby, October 29, 1937, President's Personal File, FDR Library.

Howe concluded that the Philippines presented "a unique blend . . . of East and West." Under American tutelage, many good things had been accomplished—stimulation of "as universal hunger for education as I have ever known . . . a sanitary and health cleansing that is a miracle . . . on the outside at least a tidiness and cleanliness that is remarkable and along with that a refusal of the people to take on Western vices such as drinking or any disorderliness." Little crime existed, and very few people were in the prisons "which are the most advanced I have ever known." As evidence, he cited the example of a self-governing and economically self-sufficient prison colony in Mindanao.[46]

There were serious problems, however. Filipinos lacked the self-reliance that came from experience in doing things for themselves. In part, Howe blamed their Spanish heritage. "The Spaniards have soaked the people with 'duty, obedience and chastity' for so long that the people have no self-confidence." He thought that "the heritage of the Spaniards and the Church hangs on and pretty completely obliterates everything else—certainly civic responsibility, and a relationship to the state. . . . Government is a <u>very personal</u> thing and aside from the President, few other officials will assume any responsibility. Some people are convinced that individual and localized responsibility and initiative never will come." Perhaps "when those generations that knew Spanish and Church rule pass away and when the thousands of young men and women from universities go back to their homes, a new kind of responsibility and initiative will develop." But Howe was not sure that this would be the case.[47]

Americans had to bear their share of blame for Philippine problems, Howe believed. The Filipinos were fine people, "the soul of kindliness and courtesy. But they get damn little if any help from any Americans in connection with their economic wrongs—most Americans out here only know of the New Deal as something awful. It means taxes and disrespect of the courts." He feared that American officials too often were politicians on the make who fell under the sway of the Catholic Church. He thought that Quezon, with MacArthur as his friend, might make a difference, but he had "difficulty in finding any foundations for constructive statesmanship or possible permanency of progress of a social and economic sort, from any other men or any other combination of leaders. All of which I admit . . . may be built on inadequate information or on wrong hunches."[48]

46. FCH to Eleanor Roosevelt, October 22, 1937, Eleanor Roosevelt Papers, FDR Library.
47. FCH to Paul Appleby, October 29, 1937, President's Personal File, FDR Library; FCH to Eleanor Roosevelt, October 22, 1937, Eleanor Roosevelt Papers, FDR Library. The underlinings are Howe's.
48. FCH to Appleby, October 29 and 31, 1937, President's Personal File, FDR Library; FCH to Fola La Follette, January 31, 1938.

Consonant with his general belief in the salience of economic factors, Howe perceived economic change as the crucial need for the Philippines. "The economic power here is in the land," he wrote Fola La Follette, "and it in turn is in the hands of the same people whom we dispossessed of political power forty years ago." The "most important thing of all to do," he told Eleanor Roosevelt, was to end "the terrible system of landlordism and usury that is widespread." Many tenants and sharecroppers never escaped the tentacles of usurers who might charge 150 percent for a six-month loan. People struggled for land, and "as they struggle, the landlord takes more in rent while *iniquilinos* crowd in between the landlord and tenants and push the worker down still further."

Taxes were oppressive. The poor bore the burden, and privileged groups, like the sugar and gold interests, benefited. Howe reported to Quezon that "the people were being skinned clear down to their bones by consumption taxes and charges of all kinds, woven about them by a vast army of officials and collectors, and which differed only in amount from the way it was done a hundred years ago."[49]

Looking for support for economic reform, Howe found little help within the government structure until he turned to General MacArthur and the army. According to Howe, he found in MacArthur a strong ally. There were ways, it seemed, in which the building of the Philippine defense force could also help solve the problems of the land. Along with military training, conscripts received training "in hygiene, in agriculture, in handicraft, in making them ready to take up homesteads and establish them as self respecting citizens. And the one thing the islands need is a body of men who can assume responsibility and accept leadership. Without that I do not see how the Philippines can stand on their feet no matter what assistance is given them." Perhaps the military training camps could be integrated into something like the American CCC camps. Howe concluded that the army and MacArthur were America's best representatives in the Philippines, and about the only disinterested ones. "I go to [MacArthur] a good deal for advice with respect to local men and what can and cannot be done. And he is not only a great executive and probably a great soldier but a great civilian as far as the islands are concerned. . . . Unless I am completely bogged about him he could do more to see these people through their coming independence and possible troubles than any other man I know of, either here or elsewhere."[50]

---

49. Ibid., FCH to Eleanor Roosevelt, October 22, 1937, Eleanor Roosevelt Papers, FDR Library; FCH to Appleby, October 29, 1937, President's Personal File, FDR Library.

50. FCH to Eleanor Roosevelt, September 7, 1937, Eleanor Roosevelt Papers, FDR Library; FCH to Henry A. Wallace, August 28, 1937 (copy of letter in MacArthur Archives); FCH to Appleby, October 29, 1937.

So Howe began to work with MacArthur and members of his staff to develop a land policy. As early as September 27, 1937, he was able to submit two preliminary reports to President Quezon. In them, he argued for establishment of "colony settlements" throughout the islands. "No other problem is as worth while as the problem of the proper relation of the people to the land," Howe argued. "Without its proper solution other problems are difficult, if not impossible." Prime candidates for land ownership in the settlements would be the conscripts of MacArthur's Philippine army, once they completed their required military service. "They are the best of material for the experimental settlements. A homestead and along with the homestead the possibility of administrative positions in connection with the settlements can be held out as prizes. If these men can move directly from the cadres to their homestead the Army would become a civil implement of great value while a homestead as a prize for excellence would increase the popularity of military training." The program Howe proposed, with MacArthur's blessing, thus would have economic, civic, and military value. "Military intelligence might be used in the laying out of roads and enbankments and in setting aside strategic points for purposes of defense."

A second proposal aimed at using taxation to diminish large-scale landholdings and to provide revenues for development projects. Here Howe's continued faith in the single tax was readily apparent. "It is obviously a first obligation on any nation to hand out equal justice to all of its citizens," he declared. "And inequality in assessments and inequality in taxes are as indefensible as any other inequalities of justice on the part of the government." Local authorities should be instructed to correct present inequalities in the assessment of lands for local taxation and to increase assessments to a uniform percentage of the land's selling value or to its real market value. The privileges of major economic interests ought to be curtailed. For Howe, the analysis and the remedy came straight from Henry George. "Much of the value which inheres in land has been created by all of the people and by logic and by justice should be shared in by all of the people. . . . IT IS THEREFORE JUST FOR THE PEOPLE THROUGH THE GOVERNMENT TO SHARE IN THIS WEALTH WHICH THE GOVERNMENT ITSELF HAS CREATED." The right laws would greatly increase local revenues, deflate speculative land values, stimulate the breakup of large estates, compel owners to cultivate idle land and thus increase both the demand for labor and wages, and diminish the need for the national government to subsidize local governments for roads, schools, water, and other improvements.[51] In January 1938 Howe followed up with a longer report on taxation.

---

51. FCH to Douglas MacArthur, September 11 and 27, 1939; FCH to Manuel Quezon, September, 27, 1939, enclosing memoranda "Toward a Better Land Policy" and "Proposal for Land Value Taxation," MacArthur Archives. The capitalization is Howe's.

Howe feared that imperialist interests might subvert the promised independence of the Philippines. In long letters to Wallace, Appleby, and Mrs. Roosevelt, he expressed this concern, hoping they would bring them to President Roosevelt's attention. He reported to Wallace that the Manila Hotel was "a sounding board for interests, especially sugar, gold mining, banking and all the big American interests that want above everything else that the United States stay in the islands and amply protect their interests. They talk it on every occasion and fill every newcomer with an imperialistic patter. I recognize it for my book 'Why War' was about just this sort of opinion building which is the same in every colonial outpost and at home as well." He made the same point to Eleanor Roosevelt. He feared that his friends back home might be being used "as they have been used before, to pull the chestnuts out of the fire for those who want the United States to hold on to the Islands, to scuttle President Quezon and discredit General MacArthur." American investors in gold mines, sugar, and coconuts were doing everything in their power "to involve us so completely in Philippine affairs that we may easily spend hundreds of millions just in armaments and billions in a war, should we ever be led into such a disaster."[52]

The strategy of the imperialists in the Philippines was to discredit the two strong men who were trying to build the new commonwealth. Howe wrote Mrs. Roosevelt that it was the success of President Quezon as an administrator and of General MacArthur in building a defensive citizen army that stood in the way of an imperialistic policy.

> If President Quezon can be discredited and the trainee system like the Swiss army, be halted, almost the only other alternative is American military and naval protection of the islands. And judging by what I hear from home and the attitude of the imperialistic interests in Manila that would seem to be the present insidious line of attack; a line of attack in which pacific minded persons are working hand in glove with the very forces which they most fear. It may easily be that our future policy in the Pacific and in the world at large will be determined by the success or failure of this and similar attempts at disparagement.[53]

---

52. FCH to Henry Wallace, August 28, 1937 (copy in MacArthur Archives); FCH to Eleanor Roosevelt, September 7, 1937, Eleanor Roosevelt Papers, FDR Library. In both letters Howe recited his credentials as a student of imperialism, telling Wallace: "During the Administration of President Wilson I made a study of the Chinese Six Power Loan and activities of American interests in Mexico and Central America under the authority of Secretary McAdoo and in cooperation with Governor Folk. I also worked on the same general subject with Colonel House with respect to the Bagdad Railway and imperialistic activities in Africa and the Near East during the peace conference at Paris."

53. FCH to Eleanor Roosevelt, September 7, 1937, Eleanor Roosevelt Papers, FDR Library.

Howe considered that other imperialist threats existed besides those from American interests. In the Philippines, Spaniards and the church were "sleeping in the same bed with Franco, with Mussolini, and also with Japan, with whom they have much more sympathy and affinity than they have with us." The greatest threat was from the British, however. "I certainly don't want to see America holding the bag for the British who are in a tight spot with the Philippines going it alone," he wrote Paul Appleby. "For about $2,000,000,000 British money is said to be in this part of the world and with India added it must be nearer ten billions. And with us gone Singapore is the only protection of Hong Kong and British power. So look inside of any news stories and you will probably find that marvelous and highly perfected propaganda of Britain at work. It is worth more to her than her navy and it is far more efficient." Little help in countering the British could be expected from American diplomats, and Howe sometimes was angry at "our ladder climbing Harvard boys and their wives who would rather be invited by the British Embassy for dinner than anything else and who come to be ashamed of their own government as well. I could be damn nasty about this if I let myself go."[54] Surprisingly, Howe's surviving correspondence from his Philippine assignment makes virtually no mention of Japan as an imperialist menace (though the War Department's, and hence MacArthur's, defense planning assumed that the Philippines would have to meet a Japanese invasion).

With his reports completed and their fate in the hands of the commonwealth government, Howe left the islands in the late spring or early summer of 1938. The assignment in the Philippines had been invigorating. "You, almost better than anybody else, know how I have been living since our old days in Cleveland and New York, and you know pretty well what my interests are and desires as well," he observed to Fola. "And almost everything I have done or wanted to do, and almost everything I have studied is really a preparation for this job, and strange to say, it is not only being used rather generously but is also appreciated by President Quezon, and . . . by a good many other people as well."[55] Sadly, he returned to a Washington where he no longer had any important place and could no longer hobnob with a president or a field marshal (MacArthur's rank in the Philippine defense force). He escaped the doldrums of Agriculture when the department loaned him to the Temporary National Economic Committee (TNEC) to work as a senior economist.

The TNEC had been established in May 1938 pursuant to a request by President Roosevelt for funds for a study of the concentration of economic power. Chaired by Senator Joseph O'Mahoney, it held public hearings and produced

---

54. FCH to Fola La Follette, January 31, 1938; FCH to Appleby, October 31, 1937, President's Personal File, FDR Library.
55. FCH to Appleby, October 29, 1937; FCH to Fola La Follette, January 31, 1938.

more than forty monographs by government economists in its service. Working for the TNEC, Fred Howe returned to the issues of the dairy industry that had been his concern as consumers counsel. He wrote at least two memos or reports on them, both of which attracted presidential attention and were sent on to cabinet members for further consideration.[56] He also began work on a study of European banking. His attitude toward the European war is unknown, though by 1940 he was ruminating on the peace settlement to come. To Harry Garfield, who had written that the major thing to be kept in mind was "what is good for all the peoples involved," he observed that "a peace in which all the peoples felt that this was the governing motive would be pretty well insulated against another war. And one does not need to be a very wise person to know that another peace based on conquest means simply another war."[57]

By 1940 Fred may have been thinking about retirement. "Just now I am browsing around the coasts of Florida looking for a spot to roost," he wrote Maxwell Perkins from Key West in January. In the summer, on a visit to Roger Baldwin in his summer home in Chilmark on Martha's Vineyard, he became ill, and died on August 3 at Martha's Vineyard Hospital. The death certificate indicated as cause of death "carcinoma of sigmoid," of an estimated six months' duration. Several years before his death, he had given Allegheny College about three hundred of his books. His will provided that most of the rest of his library should go to the college as the nucleus of a library of economic and social problems. The nearly five hundred books were mostly in the social sciences and history but also included works on philosophy and religion, a wide range of literature (including thirteen volumes of Robert Browning's poetry), and several books on contract bridge. Howe was buried in the family plot in Greendale Cemetery in Meadville, Pennsylvania, on August 8, 1940.[58]

Fred Howe's public life had spanned more than forty years. Amidst the multitudinous political and governmental activities that occupied him during those decades, it is difficult to find the private man. There is little direct or specific

---

56. FCH to Eleanor Roosevelt, June 23, 1939, Eleanor Roosevelt Papers, FDR Library; Edwin M. Watson to H. M. Kannee, December 19, 1939; Franklin D. Roosevelt to Henry Wallace, December 19, 1939, and February 6, 1940; Roosevelt to Henry Morgenthau, December 29, 1939; Morgenthau to Roosevelt, January 23, 1940, President's Personal File, FDR Library.

57. FCH to Harry A. Garfield, April 15, 1940, Garfield Papers.

58. FCH to Maxwell Perkins, January 17, 1940, Scribner Archives; certified copy of Certificate of Death for Frederic C. Howe, dated August 6, 1940; Spencer Gordon to Allegheny College, November 23, 1940; Edith Rowley to Gordon, December 12, 1940; Gordon to Rowley, December 17, 1940; Gordon to Ruth Corliss, January 24, 1941, Pelletier Library, Allegheny College; Reis Library, Allegheny College, "The Library of Frederic C. Howe, Class of 1889," Lists 1 and 2, February, 1944, and November, 1945, typescripts; *New York Times*, August 4, 1940, 33, and August 8, 1940, 19.

During World War II, Howe's name was given to a "Liberty ship," the *Frederic C. Howe*, launched in Florida in October 1943. This army tank transport served in the war and continued in use until 1972, when it was scrapped in Kearny, New Jersey.

information about his marriage and other intimate parts of his life. Neither he nor Marie left any collection of letters or other documents. He burned all his correspondence when he left his post as commissioner of immigration, and he collected and destroyed Marie's letters after her death. Presumably he either destroyed the rest of his papers before his own death or left instructions that they be destroyed at that time.

Most of the personal references in his *Confessions of a Reformer* relate to Howe's childhood and youth and occur in the first thirty pages of the book. Except for that with Morris Black, his friendships, though important to him, are only tersely treated. Even friends of long standing are given short shrift. There are, for example, only three brief references to Ida M. Tarbell, whom he knew for more than sixty years. Perhaps reciprocating, she mentions Howe only once in the more than four hundred pages of her autobiography, calling him "my old friend."

Howe's autobiography is limited almost entirely to the man in the public arena. That career is easier to document (since other collections are full of his letters), but a focus on it may make him appear a political technocrat with few human feelings. Through the letters and papers that have survived in those other collections, however, we catch occasional glimpses of his private life.

Fred Howe was a convivial man. He enjoyed the theater and vaudeville, golf, fishing, riding, relaxing in the salt breezes of Nantucket. He liked a drink and a pipe. He had a talent for friendship—among the friends he made and kept, in many cases for nearly fifty years, were James and Harry Garfield, Newton Baker, Lincoln Steffens, Tom Johnson, Amos Pinchot, John Finley, Brand Whitlock, Ida Tarbell, all the La Follettes and especially Fola in later years. He preferred the company of an Irish bartender or politician or a lobbyist to that of a Waspish stuffed shirt or "goo-goo," but he also took pleasure in his membership in clubs like the Century in New York and the Cosmos in Washington.

About one important aspect of his life—his years with Marie—there are tantalizing hints but little real information. There must have been strains between them in the Cleveland years, when Fred retained traditional views of marriage though intellectually accepting the need for equality and women's rights, while Marie felt increasingly stifled by the limitations set by society on her activities. Many of her friends considered her more radical than her husband at that time. To his credit, he came to realize that he was unfair in his expectations, and their decision to abandon Cleveland for New York City—a move desired more by her than by him—liberated Marie and gave her an opportunity to assert her own ideas and interests. Fred paid more than lip service to her causes and supported and worked with her on them, while she carved out her own independent role in the woman suffrage movement and in Heterodoxy. There are hints that Fred, at least, would have liked them to have a child, perhaps to adopt one, but how Marie felt about this is not known.

Their temperaments differed. He was a fact seeker, she more at home in a world of feelings and emotion. He was more serious, once describing himself as "reserved and undemonstrative." She was more playful. She liked to be settled, whether in Paris or Harmon. He liked to—needed to—roam as he handled business affairs abroad for Long Arm or sought information for his writings (an essential source of their income) on numerous European jaunts. They were often apart. Marie seldom joined Fred on his trips, partly because her ill health did not permit it, partly because she preferred a more sedentary life. During the New Deal years, her health and a distaste for the Washington scene kept her in Harmon, while he remained in the capital, returning to Harmon only on weekends. Certainly there must have been problems in their relationship, perhaps major ones, but there is no evidence of any great rift between them. Fred's words in his dedication of *Confessions* to Marie are a token of his love for her, and in her few surviving letters she returns that affection, though not without some exasperation at the serious side of her husband's character.

Throughout his life, Howe was plagued with bouts of melancholy and depression. In part, these stemmed from ambivalence about his career choices. He entered Johns Hopkins, sure that journalism would be the focus of his life, and believing that the day of the college-trained journalist had come. After earning his Ph.D., he met only disappointment—even despair—in his efforts to find a place on a New York newspaper and had to retreat disconsolately to Meadville. A later attempt at journalism also failed with the unhappy attempt to create a regional *Ridgeway's Weekly* in Cleveland.

Faute de mieux, Howe turned to the law. He was a successful lawyer and earned a good living as the firm prospered, but he was never happy about his work. "I never overcame my dislike for the profession, and got little enjoyment out of such success as I achieved," he wrote. Looking back years after he had ceased to practice, he reflected that his dislike was a "deep and fundamental protest" against law as an institution. "I liked change, fluidity, movement. Anything that balked freedom irked me. The law was opposed to change, it thwarted the free movement of life."[59] He left the practice of law without regret.

Unsatisfying as it was, the law helped Howe along other career paths. It was a profession that gave him the chance to spend a good deal of time on things he liked better, especially politics and writing. His principal efforts to win electoral office had little success: a win and a loss for the Cleveland city council, a win and two losses for the Ohio Senate. If he had remained in Cleveland, he

---

59. *Confessions of a Reformer,* 199, 200.

would likely have been returned to the state senate in the 1910 election, which brought the most sweeping Democratic win in twenty years. It is ironic that Howe's abandonment of Ohio politics came just when the Progressives were on the threshold of triumph.[60] He had relinquished his candidacy at just the wrong time. Given a record of success in the legislature, the governorship or perhaps even the U.S. Senate might have been in his political future.

Howe's defeats as a candidate did not mean an exit from politics. He liked the political life, and he was full of ideas on organizing and campaigning, and not at all reluctant to share them with candidates. Arthur S. Link and Richard L. McCormick have suggested that in the first years of the twentieth century "the most important barrier to [political] change was party loyalty."[61] Howe's political career is a case study in the breakdown of that loyalty. He cut free from his Republican moorings to seek a Cleveland council seat as an independent and soon became a Tom Johnson Democrat. Despite his Democratic identification, he was willing and eager to work with Progressives and reformers of all types and parties. He campaigned with Republican Henry Stimson for the governor's office in New York. He helped organize and run the National Progressive Republican League. He backed first the Progressive Republican La Follette and then the Democrat Wilson in the presidential election of 1912, and campaigned for Wilson in 1916. He worked with numerous independent and third-party efforts in the 1920s, returning to the Democratic fold to support Al Smith for the presidency in 1928 and Franklin D. Roosevelt in 1932 and 1936.

Rather than a candidate, Howe became organizer, adviser and idea man, coordinator and campaigner, all very useful roles but far from taking him to the high position he craved. He was ambitious and put himself forward or made himself available for major posts—as Woodrow Wilson's chief of staff, as a cabinet officer, as a regulatory commission member—but none materialized, and he had to settle for midlevel appointments—commissioner of immigration at Ellis Island and consumers counsel in the AAA. These were important jobs in which he could do useful work, but they were hardly the policy positions he had hoped for.

Law, politics, administration—all had their failings, as far as Howe was concerned. The academic life had been another possibility, but he did not pursue academic posts as vigorously as he sought governmental ones and did not seem to be considered a serious candidate for appointments. This left his didactic bent to be satisfied in a less structured way by the People's Institute and the School of Opinion, and by his writings. Law, politics, and even government

60. Griffith, *History of City Government*, 4:27–28; Warner, *Progressivism in Ohio, 1897–1917*, chaps. 10, 11.
61. Link and McCormick, *Progressivism*, 28.

service gave him ample time to write, and he had an urge to present his ideas. "If I have any convictions about life at all, it is that one's first obligation is to express himself," he wrote Lincoln Steffens in 1908.[62] And express himself he did: in the thirty-three years from 1894 to 1926, there were only four years in which no book, pamphlet, or article appeared. His grand total was 17 books, 10 pamphlets, and some 120 articles. Writing was for Howe both a pleasure and a source of income. After the onset of the Great Depression, however, he found publishers reluctant to accept his book proposals and journals not very interested in commissioning articles.

Howe tried many paths to the success he longed for, but each of them had its disappointments and setbacks, which sometimes led to failure of nerve and retreat. Failing to find a job in journalism, he returned disconsolately to Meadville. Buffeted by political defeats, he abandoned Cleveland for a new life in New York City. Faced with criticisms over his activities in the National Progressive Republican League, he gave up his position and went to summer in Nantucket. Assigned a mission to the Middle East during the peace conference after World War I, he got only as far as Italy before being overcome by hardships and scurrying back to Paris. Under fire at Ellis Island, he resigned as commissioner of immigration and took up the Plumb Plan. After the "purge" of rebels in the AAA, he was seen by some of his colleagues as nearly a broken man, worried about his livelihood and willing to accept a nominal post with neither power nor responsibility. Though some of these retreats proved to be only minor setbacks, they added to his feeling that he had failed to measure up to the standard he had set for himself.

Yet the reverses were temporary, and he quickly returned to the political arena. He was a man of courage and a fighter for the causes he believed in. He sprang to the defense of his mentor Richard Ely against charges of "socialism." He defended vigorously his own policies at Ellis Island. He was a stalwart supporter of civil liberties and did not retreat when causes proved unpopular. He stood his ground in the midst of the Red Scare. He was one of the founders of the American Civil Liberties Union. He spoke and acted strongly for the rights of immigrants and aliens, especially for the right of detainees to a fair hearing and the other protections of due process. He became a vigorous advocate for the consumer in his role as consumers counsel in the AAA.

Howe was active in a number of movements for third parties. Unlike many of his reformer friends who worried about "class warfare," he accepted the trade unions as full participants in the political game. A good example of the ambivalence of some Progressives toward labor was Fred's longtime friend Amos Pinchot, who warned his middle-class fellows against "hotheads" who wanted a

62. FCH to Lincoln Steffens, November 15, 1908, Steffens Papers.

class party. "This is where we have trouble with labor, for labor still wants to think as labor and function as labor, though it should be clear enough that there is no place for a class party in a country constituted as ours," he wrote. In contrast, Howe recognized the reality of class conflict and welcomed the growing political role of the unions. "Labor would serve freedom, democracy, equal opportunity for all," he wrote. "The place for the liberal was in labor's ranks."[63] He had no fear of cutting loose from the old parties and seeking new coalitions and new paths for the advancement of reform.

Howe felt that most of his life he was struggling to escape domination by "authority," whether it was the narrow conformity imposed by the American small town or the more benevolent fetters attached by his professors at Johns Hopkins. He perceived his life as one of "unlearning," of releasing his abilities from the bonds of others and pressing on toward self-realization. He was always concerned with whether he had developed true independence of thought or simply had submitted himself to another "herd-mind."

Fred Howe was not a deep or profound thinker, but by the early years of the twentieth century he had developed an outlook on government and politics that guided him for the rest of his life. From his early belief in voluntary action through the settlement house and the Social Gospel, he had moved to acceptance of local government action and municipal ownership, and then to an embrace of social legislation and intervention into the economic order by state and national governments. His experiences during World War I and the Red Scare led him to modify his views on the role of the state and to seek democratic counterbalances to the power of government.

His goal was self-realization, self-fulfillment—the opportunity for each individual to develop freely along the lines of his or her own interests and talents. The enemy of free development of the individual was privilege. He had been aware of the entrenched power of privilege ever since he began to study economics and taxation at Johns Hopkins. In Cleveland he saw it manifested in the monopoly grants to street railway companies, and he found it in his battles with vested interests in the state legislature and the national government. It corrupted politics and subverted democracy. Full freedom for the individual could be achieved only when privilege was destroyed.

How could this come about? First and foremost, by adoption of the single tax on the unearned increment of land. Convinced by Tom Johnson and by his own readings and experiences, Howe adopted the Georgist theory and held to it till the end of his life. The "simple yet sovereign remedy" of the single tax

---

63. Amos Pinchot to James H. Maurer, March 23, 1920, Amos Pinchot Papers; *Confessions of a Reformer*, 325. On attempts to end class conflict in the Progressive Era, see McGerr, *Fierce Discontent*, 48–146.

would end monopoly and speculation in land, free for use the resources of the earth, and bring to the public treasury a colossal revenue that could be used for social purposes. Economic fear would vanish as opportunities abounded in a free and competitive economy. The solution was "so simple, so easily achieved, and so marvelous in its potentialities that it should be the first step in any change."[64]

Howe maintained his faith in the single tax to the end. He wrote in his autobiography that he believed in it "as intensely as I ever did."[65] He knew that there were more problems than could be solved by the Georgist remedy. It might help to create "city republics," but it did not speak directly to the complex problems of an industrial society. Howe did not become a single-issue politician as some in the single-tax movement tended to be. He knew that acceptance of George's ideas might lie far in the future. In the meantime, the reformer could turn his attention to plenty of other problems in society. He saw no contradiction between holding the single tax as an ideal while simultaneously tackling other reforms in cooperation with both single taxers and non–single taxers. He wrote Daniel Kiefer: "I think that the average man is right in thinking that there is no possible single thing that will cure all the troubles in society, and I am for the other forces that make for democracy almost as strongly as I am for the Single Tax." Howe's involvement in so many good causes led his close friend Lincoln Steffens to wonder: "Is Fred a Single Taxer? Hasn't he listened to other thinkers than George? Is he, in a word, strictly orthodox?"[66] For Howe, the proximate goal was a reformed capitalism, a mixed economy with large components of public ownership, cooperatives, and social services.

One of the great appeals of the single tax to Howe was that its adoption would require neither a ponderous bureaucracy nor a powerful political state. Before the First World War, he had tended to see the state as a benevolent institution, once the forces of privilege had been routed. The events of the early twentieth century—the war, the failures at peacemaking, governmental abuses of power and repression of civil liberties, mistreatment of immigrants—brought him to a more pessimistic view. "My attitude toward the state was changed as a result of these experiences. I have never been able to bring it back. I became distrustful of the state. It seemed to want to hurt people; it showed no concern for innocence; it aggrandized itself and protected its power by unscrupulous means. It was not my America, it was something else." His view of the state

---

64. FCH, "Political Utopia," 179.
65. *Confessions of a Reformer*, 342.
66. FCH to Daniel Kiefer, August 5, 1910, Bolton Hall Papers; Lincoln Steffens to Kiefer, February 8, 1920, Steffens Papers.

became "somewhat negative—a state that keeps out of the way of people so that people themselves will be important in themselves and by themselves."[67]

Nonetheless, there were positive functions for the state to perform in the battle against privilege. A free state would involve "a certain amount of socialism": public ownership of the railroads, water power, the telephone and the telegraph, the street railways, gas and electricity. Certain services were so fundamental to the community that they could not be left in private hands.

Howe did not think that accepting a measure of public ownership made him a socialist. He believed there were two solutions for the world's social problems: the industrial socialism of Karl Marx and the industrial freedom of Henry George. In this context, he considered socialism a bureaucratic system that limited freedom. With the adoption of the single tax and the abolition of special privileges, society would achieve an economic justice that would eliminate the need for socialism. His advocacy of public ownership of natural monopolies and a program for social justice did not suffice, in his opinion, to make him a socialist, but clearly he would have been at home in the British Labour Party (whose postwar program he applauded) or in the Social Democratic parties of Scandinavia and Germany.

The gains from collective effort would come not from a socialist bureaucracy but from cooperation, like that which had converted Denmark into "one of the most contented, happy, and on the whole satisfactory commonwealths in the civilized world." Declared Howe: "Co-operation gripped me as Socialism had not. It was voluntary, open to individual initiative; it trained leaders and minimized the state. Apparently it achieved all the ends that Socialism promised and left the individual free from bureaucratic control." Decisions were made by local producers and consumers, and this fostered "the intimacy of people with politics."[68]

How can the cooperative commonwealth be attained? Not by the efforts of his own class (as Howe had believed for much of his lifetime), which could not rise above its own interests, but by those of the producers, "those who produced wealth by hand or brain." Labor could not serve privilege, but it could serve freedom, democracy, and equal opportunity for all. Labor and farmers had to free themselves and take power by democratic means. A political party made up of primary producers would eventually win office and institute the kind of reforms that Howe wanted. "I saw a state within a state, creating its own economic life, massing its own power, using it to build up a co-operative society inside the political state."[69]

67. *Confessions of a Reformer*, 282; "Political Utopia," 178.
68. "Political Utopia," 179; *Confessions of a Reformer*, 332; *Denmark: The Cooperative Way*, 229.
69. *Confessions of a Reformer*, 324, 325, 331. See above, chap. 17, p. [392], for Howe's belief that cooperation meant "the maximum of liberty."

Howe's involvement with civil rights and racial equality was very limited. He welcomed W. E. B. Du Bois as a speaker at the People's Institute, and he and Marie had active roles in promoting color-blind organizations like the City Club, the NAACP, and Heterodoxy. The reforms that he urged and worked for would benefit all Americans, regardless of race. For Howe, as for most Progressives, civil rights and race relations were not his subjects. Probably he assumed that the equality of opportunity that he fervently desired—"freeing the individual so that he could achieve all that was in him"—would conquer the problems of race and ethnicity.[70]

Howe realized that neither of his utopian dreams—the single tax and the cooperative society—was likely to be realized in the near future. He could see only small increments of progress in his lifetime. Indeed, there were steps backward as well as forward. Reviewing an edition of Brand Whitlock's journal and letters in 1937, he mourned the losses in the municipal battle against special privilege. "It was tragic in that the gains in these two outstanding cities [Cleveland and Toledo] seemed quickly lost as soon as the protagonists [Tom Johnson, Sam Jones, Whitlock] were gone. For big business swept quickly over their achievements and left little more than the affection of the masses, their alert public sensibility and public improvements in the form of planning projects, parks, playgrounds, and a beautiful city as a monument."[71]

Howe understood that the conservatives and the special interests had the advantage over the liberals. The deck was stacked against reformers. Back in the beginning of the republic, Alexander Hamilton had given us "the most unworkable of instruments in the constitutions that have been foisted on us, with the two chambers, the courts, the destruction of local rights and liberties. They are all designed to make legislation impossible." If reformers nonetheless managed to succeed in the legislative houses, the judges lay in wait for them, "enveloped in sanctity" designed for "their usefulness to corporate interests, their interference with the legislatures and Congress, their use of the injunction in labor disputes and their concern for property." As a result of limitations on democracy and the entrenchment of the special interests or their agents at the strategic points of policy making, "democratic movements have to survive a series of elections to achieve their ends. . . . The average man is moved by the desire for results. Yet when success is subject to innumerable obstacles, when the end is distant and highly problematical, when the fruits of effort are subject to veto by officials unresponsive to the public will, initiative and effort are discouraged." The road for the reformer, for the democrat, was indeed "rough, thorny and

---

70. Grantham, "Progressive Movement and the Negro," 477; *Confessions of a Reformer*, 253.
71. FCH, "Great American Aristocrat," 292.

unpopular." As Brand Whitlock put it: "It is fatigue that keeps democracy back. It requires so little energy to be a conservative and so much to be a radical."[72]

Nevertheless, despite disappointments and setbacks, Howe continued on the reform road to the end of his life. There were always battles, new and old, to engage in. There were always gains that might be made. Unlike a majority of the "old Progressives," he embraced the New Deal enthusiastically and stayed with it. This meant parting company politically with old friends and allies like Baker, Creel, Ely, Pinchot, and Shaw.[73] Howe was a New Dealer before there was a New Deal. In his 1914 suggestions to President Wilson for a "comprehensive social and industrial programme" for the Democratic Party, and in his proposals for "a generous and democratic program of reconstruction" at the end of World War I, he anticipated a good part of the policies of the New Deal in the 1930s.[74]

The passage of time has not diminished historians' interest in the "age of reform," and there are still disputes over what Progressivism was and what were its driving forces. A new scholarly publication, *Journal of the Gilded Age and Progressive Era*, has continued those controversies since its appearance in 2001. It may be useful to look at Frederic Howe's beliefs and career in the context of several of these recent analyses of Progressivism. Many writers have emphasized class as the principal element to be considered. Historian Robert D. Johnston draws on a detailed analysis of class politics in the Progressive Era's Portland, Oregon (a city which Howe called "the most complete democracy in the world" for its adoption of the instruments of direct democracy), and finds a middle-class populism adhering to the single tax as its political economy. Uncomfortable with the traditional term "middle class," he thinks more analytically useful the concept of an anticapitalist radical coalition of "middling folks" (the petite bourgeoisie) and working people. Single-tax proposals and other land reform issues went down to defeat in Portland in the early decades of the twentieth century, but Johnston still hopes for the success of a lower-middle-class radicalism.[75]

Another historian, Michael McGerr, also relies heavily on a class interpretation of Progressivism in his *A Fierce Discontent*. His approach is more traditional

---

72. FCH to Steffens, February 29, 1908, Steffens Papers; *Confessions of a Reformer*, 202; *Revolution and Democracy*, 109–10; FCH, "New Liberalism or the Old," 3; Brand Whitlock to Newton Baker, July 26, 1916, Newton D. Baker Papers.

73. See O. Graham, *An Encore for Reform*. Political differences did not mean an end to ties of personal friendship between Howe and the "old Progressives."

74. FCH to Woodrow Wilson, November 21, 1914, in Link, *Papers of Woodrow Wilson*, 31:342–43; FCH to Louis F. Post, November 1, 1918; FCH to Post, November 6, 1918; FCH to Post, November 15, 1918, General Records of the Department of Labor 1907–1942 (Chief Clerk's Files), File No. 20/740, National Archives; FCH, "Constructive Program."

75. FCH, "Oregon," 459; Johnston, *Radical Middle Class*, 159.

than Johnston's. He finds four classes in the Progressive years: an upper class of the rich; a middle class, defined mainly by occupation (small proprietors, professionals, clerks, salespeople, managers, bureaucrats); a working class made up mostly of manual laborers; and farmers. Progressivism was "the creed of a crusading middle class." Its adherents were a radical movement, not in the sense that they sought fundamental change in the economic structure, but in "their conviction that other social classes must be transformed and in their boldness in going about the business of transformation." McGerr makes no mention of the single taxers as an important element in the reformers' coalitions. Despite its many achievements, Progressivism had collapsed by 1920, and its failure set limits to later reform efforts. All in all, McGerr offers a cogent narrative of the Progressive Movement, though his attempt to cover all (or nearly all) of its aspects leads to some overbroad generalizations.[76]

Kevin Mattson's *Creating a Democratic Public* maintains that America today is bereft of forums in which citizens talk seriously about public issues and then act on what they have learned from each other in the discussion. These days, political discourse is "shallow, relying less on deliberation than on shoddy slogans and imagery." There are "few ways in which democratic debate and democratic decision making influence politics." We can begin to rescue democracy from the low point it has reached by examining how citizens in the past used community-based forums and meetings to tackle public problems. In the Progressive Era, people discussed seriously alternatives to industrial capitalism and liberal democracy. "The activists and intellectuals studied here believed in creating institutions that would, within the confines of the modern world, sustain a democratic public and public-minded values, not just private, commercial motivation." Mattson then considers the City Beautiful movement and Charles Zeublin, Frederic C. Howe and the forum movement, and the political thought of Mary Parker Follett.[77]

Mattson points to the beginnings of Frederic Howe's interest in creating a democratic public in the tent meetings of Tom Johnson's political campaigns. Howe provided the "intellectual vision" for the mayor's administrations. His major contribution to democratic publics was his leadership as director of the People's Institute in New York City. In its People's Forums, the Institute under Howe continued what Charles Sprague Smith had started. He described the meetings in one of his annual reports as "an open forum, with absolutely free discussion, the audience itself free to act as it sees fit on public questions."

Although Mattson praises Howe, he has some criticisms of his view of democracy. He suggests that Howe saw no conflict between democracy and

---

76. McGerr, *Fierce Discontent*, xiv–xv.
77. Mattson, *Creating a Democratic Public*, 1, 2, 8.

efficiency, "between democratic deliberation and the rule of experts.... Howe's faith in the compatibility of efficiency and democracy weakened his political thought." Mattson says Howe "never concerned himself with the federal bureaucracy," implying that he was thinking of efficient bureaucracy only at the local level. He believes that Howe sometimes fell short as a democrat. "[His] role as a political activist occasionally caused him to envision the forum as a tool for political reform," thus "subordinating the democratic public to his own goals and agenda."[78]

The experiments in creation of a democratic public faded away during and after World War I. Mattson hopes for a revival. "If the activists and intellectuals studied here teach us anything, it is that the 'hope of democracy' will remain a hope until we commit ourselves to building institutions that make it a reality."[79]

Perhaps it is time to give Fred Howe a voice in the discussion. Temporarily somewhat withdrawn from the political fray by the end of World War I, he began trying to make sense out of his own experiences and those of his fellow activists. He did this primarily in his *Confessions of a Reformer* in 1925 and in two articles in *Survey* in 1926, "Where Are the Pre-War Radicals?" and "Where Are the Pre-War Radicals? A Rejoinder."

By that time, Howe had accepted a class analysis of his society. He failed to offer a clear definition of the contours of class, but he seems to have seen the divisions as follows:

- An upper-class elite (big business, monopolists, the wealthy, exploiters generally)
- A divided middle class, composed of honest independent businessmen, merchants, and professionals ("my own class," as he called it) and of a satellite of the upper-class elite, "a small but powerful group that is responsible for most of the publicity, most of the lobbying, and a good part of the corruption" (banks, utilities, industries protected by patents and tariffs, controllers of natural resources)
- Labor, with unions taking the lead
- Farmers

He hoped for a political coalition, headed by the trade unions and bringing together workers, farmers, and members of the "good" middle class, who would defeat the upper class and its satellite. It is clear that in his interpretation of class, Howe mixed together the descriptive, the analytical, and the prescriptive.

78. Ibid., 40, 46.
79. Ibid., 135.

One conjectures that Howe would appreciate the role of the middle class in McGerr's history of the Progressive Movement but would task him for failure to mention the single taxers as an important element in reform efforts and for insufficient attention to the leading role of the working class.

Robert D. Johnston's approach and findings would intrigue Howe. He would be pleased to see the important place given to the single-tax movement. He would be interested in Johnston's treatment of the reform potential of the petite bourgeoisie, a class that Howe made no room for in his analysis. He would likely be puzzled by the historian's analytic tools, but he would approve their use. Howe's own training in political science had been in the historical-constitutional-legal approach of the nineteenth century, but he welcomed the more scientific attitude that was beginning to develop in the twentieth century. He realized that "at bottom I was a moralist, not a realist, not a scientist." He wrote elsewhere: "There were few realists in American reform, few fundamentalists. We were evangelists. I think the failure of pre-war reform is explained by this fact."[80]

Howe would have been stung by Kevin Mattson's criticisms. He would have pointed out that far from lacking experience with the federal bureaucracy, as Mattson alleges, he had tussled with it as commissioner of immigration at Ellis Island and was well aware that efficiency and democracy were not the same thing. He might have recalled how his praise for the prewar German bureaucracy was tempered by his conclusion that Germany had failed in the area of rights and civil liberties. He certainly did not believe that imperial Germany's efficient bureaucracy meant that it was a full-fledged democracy.

Howe surely would have denied that he was manipulative in his role in the People's Institute's forums, and would have cited their openness, vigorous discussion, and adoption of motions on pressing problems to be forwarded to state and municipal decision makers. While admitting his shortcomings, he would likely list among his democratic credentials his vision of the reformed city as "simple democracy, a little republic," his support for the democracy of the cooperatives, his backing for the initiative, referendum, and recall, and his lifelong campaign for equality over privilege. He would not think that he had to prove that he was a democrat.

Frederic Howe was an important part of what Richard Hofstadter called "a sort of informal brain trust to the progressive movement." Through his actions and writings, he helped set the agenda for reform, defining issues and proposing remedies. His *City: The Hope of Democracy* is a classic of American writing on the urban condition, its promise and its problems. The book broke with traditional views of the city as cesspool of sin, depravity, and political corruption

80. *Confessions of a Reformer*, 321; "Where Are the Pre-war Radicals? A Rejoinder," 34.

and stressed its possibilities as a positive force in American life. Through his subsequent books and articles on how European cities and states were tackling and, in Howe's view, solving, their social problems, he suggested to Americans how reforms might be imported to their country. Daniel T. Rodgers called him "the leading interpreter of progressive Europe to American audiences." His writings, though overly enthusiastic about the successes of German and British cities, were a major contribution to the public debate on reform in America. As his friend Paul Kellogg told him: "You stretched men's horizons; you struck a note of faith." He was stalwart, trustworthy, humane, and, in Roger Baldwin's words, "a very good man to have on our side." Fred Howe himself summed it up: "I believe in keeping the mind open to everything that is moving. To me liberalism is open-mindedness."[81]

---

81. Hofstadter, *Age of Reform*, 154; Rodgers, *Atlantic Crossings*, 68; Paul Kellogg to FCH, December 14, 1926, "Forget-Me-Not" Files; *Confessions of a Reformer*, 342.

BIBLIOGRAPHY

Writings by Frederic C. Howe

Books

The British City: The Beginnings of Democracy. New York: Charles Scribner's Sons, 1907.
The City: The Hope of Democracy. New York: Charles Scribner's Sons. Reprinted with an introduction by Otis A. Pease, Seattle: University of Washington Press, 1967.
The Confessions of a Monopolist. Chicago: Public Publishing, 1906. Reprint, Upper Saddle River, N.J.: Gregg Press, 1968.
The Confessions of a Reformer. New York: Charles Scribner's Sons, 1925. Reprinted with an introduction by John Braeman, Chicago: Quadrangle Books, 1967. Reprinted, with an introduction by James F. Richardson, Kent, Ohio: Kent State University Press, 1988.
Denmark: A Cooperative Commonwealth. New York: Harcourt, Brace, 1921.
Denmark: The Cooperative Way. New York: Coward-McCann, 1936.
European Cities at Work. New York: Charles Scribner's Sons, 1913.
The High Cost of Living. New York: Charles Scribner's Sons, 1918.
The Land and the Soldier. New York: Charles Scribner's Sons, 1919.
The Modern City and Its Problems. New York: Charles Scribner's Sons, 1915.
The Only Possible Peace. New York: Charles Scribner's Sons, 1919.
Privilege and Democracy in America. New York: Charles Scribner's Sons, 1910.
Revolution and Democracy. New York: B. W. Huebsch, 1921.
Socialized Germany. New York: Charles Scribner's Sons, 1915.
Taxation and Taxes in the United States Under the Internal Revenue System, 1791–1895: An Historical Sketch of the Organization, Development, and Later Modification of Direct and Excise Taxation Under the Constitution. Library of Economics and Politics 11. New York: Thomas Y. Crowell, 1896.
Why War. New York: Charles Scribner's Sons, 1916. Reprint, Seattle: University of Washington Press, 1970.
Wisconsin: An Experiment in Democracy. New York: Charles Scribner's Sons, 1912.

Pamphlets and Reports

Banking for Service: The Need of Banks for Workers and Farmers and the Service They Can Render. Cleveland: Brotherhood of Locomotive Engineers, 1920?
"The City of Cleveland in Relation to the Street Railway Question." *Bulletin of the Municipal Association of Cleveland* (1897).

The Economic Utilization of the Public School Plant for Educational and Recreational Purposes. In New York City, Board of Estimate and Apportionment, *Report of Committee on School Inquiry.*
Frederic C. Howe on Suffrage. Political Equality Series 4, no. 2. Warren, Ohio: National American Woman Suffrage Association, 1906.
The Mobilization of Transportation for the Relief of Freight Congestion, Car Shortage, Manufacturer, Farmer and Consumer. New York: Joseph Fels International Commission, 1917.
"Municipal Ownership in Great Britain." *Bulletin of Bureau of Labor* 12 (January 1906): 1–123.
[With Frank J. Goodnow.] See Goodnow, Frank J., and Frederic C. Howe. "The Organization, Status and Procedure of the Department of Education, City of New York." In New York City, Board of Estimate and Apportionment, *Report of Committee on School Inquiry,* vol. 3. New York: City of New York, 1913.
The People, the Land, and the High Cost of Living: The Need of a Land and Agricultural Policy. Cincinnati: National Single Tax League, 1917.
What the Ballot Will Do for Women and for Men. New York: National American Woman Suffrage Association, 1912.
Why I Do Not Believe in Censorship of Motion Pictures. New York: National Board, 1923.

Articles

"Address." In *Dedication of the New Meeting House,* 1910.
"The Alien." In *Civilization in the United States: An Inquiry by Thirty Americans,* edited by Harold A. Stearns, 337–50. New York: Harcourt, Brace, 1922.
"The American and the British City—A Comparison." *Scribner's Magazine* 41 (January 1907): 113–21.
"The American City of To-Morrow." *Hampton's Magazine* 26 (May 1911): 573–84.
"Ask Your Congressman." *Everybody's* 23 (August 1910): 158–68.
"The Background of Modern Germany." *Scribner's Magazine* 58 (July 1915): 46–51.
"Baker: Trained Administrator." *Independent* 85 (March 20, 1916): 414–15.
"The Beast and a Boomerang." *Survey* 31 (December 6, 1913): 273.
"'The Best Governed Community in the World.'" *World's Work* 3 (February 1902): 1723–28.
"Better Towns." *Independent* 86 (May 29, 1916): 338–39.
"The Character and Achievements of Chicago." *World's Work* 5 (March 1903): 3240–46.
"Choose Your Congressman." *Everybody's* 23 (November 1910): 593–97.
"Cities That Think." *Outlook* 102 (September 28, 1912): 209–18.
"The City as a Socializing Agency: The Physical Basis of the City: The City Plan." *American Journal of Sociology* 17 (March 1912): 590–601.
"City Building in Germany." *Scribner's Magazine* 47 (May 1910): 601–14.
"A City in the Life-Saving Business: How the City of Cleveland Makes Men of Its Workhouse Prisoners." *Outlook* 88 (January 18, 1908): 123–27.
"City Sense: Introductory." *Outlook* 101 (August 24, 1912): 945–53.
"Cleveland—a City 'Finding Itself.'" *World's Work* 6 (October 1903): 3988–99.
"The Cleveland Group Plan." *Charities and the Commons* 19 (February 1, 1908): 1548.
"Cleveland's Education Through Its Chamber of Commerce." *Outlook* 83 (July 28, 1906): 739–49.
"A Commonwealth Ruled by Farmers." *Outlook* 94 (February 26, 1910): 441–50.

"The Confessions of a Commercial Senator." *World's Work* 9 (April 1905): 6069–79.
"The Confessions of a Commercial Senator II." *World's Work* 10 (May 1905): 6,186–91.
"Conquering a Nation with Bread." *Outlook* 94 (March 26, 1910): 683–89.
"The Constitution and Public Opinion." *Proceedings of the Academy of Political Science* 5 (October 1914): 7–19.
"A Constructive Program for the Rehabilitation of the Returning Soldiers." *Annals of the American Academy of Political and Social Science* 80 (November 1918): 150–52.
"The Decay of Agriculture." *Public* 20 (October 26, 1917): 1035–37.
"Democracy or Imperialism—The Alternative That Confronts Us." *Annals of the American Academy of Political and Social Science* 66 (July 1916): 250–58.
"The Discovery of the Schoolhouse." *Saturday Evening Post* (June 1, 1912): 14–15, 54–56.
"Dollar Diplomacy and Financial Imperialism Under the Wilson Administration." *Annals of the American Academy of Political and Social Science* 68 (November 1916): 312–20.
"Düsseldorf: A City of To-morrow." *Hampton's Magazine* 25 (December 1910): 697–709.
"Economic Foundations of Low Cost Housing." *American City* 49 (March 1934): 60–61.
"Economic Foundations of the League of Nations." *Annals of the American Academy of Political and Social Science* 83 (May 1919): 313–16.
"The End of an Economic Cycle." *Atlantic Monthly* 90 (November 1902): 611–13.
"An Epoch-Making English Budget." *Independent* 66 (June 17, 1909): 1,332–35.
"The Federal Revenues and the Income Tax." *Annals of the American Academy of Political and Social Science* 4, no. 4 (January 1894): 65–89.
"Financial Imperialism." *Atlantic Monthly* 120 (October 1917): 477–84.
"The Flag and the Investor." *New Republic* 7 (June 17, 1916): 170–71.
"The Garden Cities of England." *Scribner's Magazine* 52 (July 1912): 1–19.
"The German and the American City." *Scribner's Magazine* 49 (April 1911): 485–92.
"German City Has Solved Problems Like Our Own." *Cleveland Plain Dealer* magazine, June 13, 1909
"The German System of Labor Exchanges." *American Labor Legislation Review* 4 (May 1914): 300–304.
"Glasgow." *Scribner's Magazine* 40 (July 1906): 97–109.
"A Golden Rule Chief of Police." *Everybody's* 22 (June 1910): 814–23.
"Graft in England." *American Magazine* 63 (February 1907): 398–405.
"A Great American Aristocrat." *Survey Graphic* 26 (May 1937): 291–92. Review of Nevins, *Letters and Journal of Brand Whitlock*.
"The Great Empire by the Lakes." *World's Work* 1 (February 1901): 408–19.
"Has the Westward Tide of Peoples Come to an End?" *Scribner's Magazine* 72 (September 22, 1922): 358–64.
"The Heart of the War." *Harper's Monthly Magazine* 136 (April 1918): 728–34.
"Home Rule for American Cities." *Technical World Magazine* 23 (April 1915): 234–37.
"How Germany Cares for Her Working People." *Outlook* 94 (April 23, 1910): 939–46.
"Immigration After the War." *Scribner's Magazine* 58 (November 1915): 635–39.
"Immigration, Industry, and the War." *Review of Reviews* 52 (November 1915): 598–602.
"Imperial Germany: Emperor William II and German Politics." *American Journal of Politics* 2 (January 1893): 1–8.
"Incomplete Preparedness." *New Republic* 6 (February 26, 1916): 94–96.
"In Defence of the American City." *Scribner's Magazine* 51 (April 1912): 484–90.
"Joseph Fels." *Survey* 31 (March 28, 1914): 812–13.
"Joseph W. Folk." *Cosmopolitan* 35 (September 1903): 554–58.

"Know Yourself as a Consumer!" *Scholastic* 26 (February 9, 1935): 11–12.
"Land Settlements and the Soldier." *Nation* 108 (March 22, 1919): 426–27.
"Land Values and Congestion." *Survey* 25 (March 25, 1911): 1,067–68.
"Leisure." *Survey* 31 (January 3, 1914): 415–16.
"London: A Municipal Democracy." *Scribner's Magazine* 40 (November 1906): 589–96.
"The Lure of the Land." *Scribner's Magazine* 46 (October 1909): 431–36.
"Lynch Law and the Immigrant Alien." *Nation* 110 (February 14, 1920): 194–95.
"Milwaukee, a Socialist City." *Outlook* 95 (June 25, 1910): 411–21.
"The Most Complete Agricultural Recovery in History." *Annals of the American Academy of Political and Social Science* 172 (March 1934): 123–29.
"The Municipal Character and Achievements of Chicago." *World's Work* 5 (March 1903): 3,240–46.
"Municipal Ownership—The Testimony of Foreign Experience." *Annals of the American Academy of Political and Social Science* 57 (January 1915): 194–208.
"Municipal Ownership in Cleveland." *Moody's Magazine* 2 (October 1916): 511–14.
"The Necessity for Public Ownership of the Railways." *Annals of the American Academy of Political and Social Science* 76 (March 1918): 157–66.
"The New Constitution of Ohio." *Survey* 28 (September 21, 1912): 757–59.
"New Ideals for Peace." *Century Magazine* 96 (May 1918): 97–104.
"The New Liberalism or the Old." *Chautauquan* (July 3, 1934): 3, 8.
"Old London." *Scribner's Magazine* 47 (January 1910): 40–52.
"Oregon: The Most Complete Democracy in the World." *Hampton's Magazine* 26 (April 1911): 459–72.
"Our Foreign-Born Citizens." *National Geographic Magazine* 31 (February 1917): 95–130.
"Our Future Immigration Policy." *Scribner's Magazine* 61 (May 1917), 542–46.
"The Peaceful Revolution." *Outlook* 94 (January 15, 1910): 115–19.
"A People's Versailles." *Survey* 57 (January 1, 1927): 456–58.
"Plans for a City Beautiful." *Harper's Weekly* 48 (April 22, 1904): 624–25.
"A Political Utopia." *Nation* 127 (August 22, 1928): 178–79.
"The Problem of the American Farmer." *Century Magazine* 94 (August 1917): 625–32.
"Public Services." *Arena* 35 (May 1906): 512–13.
"The Railroads, the Mine Owners and the Government." *Public* 20 (July 6, 1917): 646.
"The Railroads, the Public and Labor Under the Plumb Plan, *Labor* 1 (December 6, 1919): 4.
"The Railroads and the New Democracy." *Public* 21 (January 4, 1918): 14–17.
"Realpolitik in Russia." *New Republic* 15 (June 15, 1918): 202–3.
"The Remaking of the American City." *Harper's Magazine* 127 (July 1913): 186–97.
"Reservoirs of Strife." *Survey* 33 (March 6, 1915): 614–15.
"The Rule of the Expert." *Outlook* 101 (August 24, 1912): 945–53.
"Shall the Government Mobilize Transportation?" *Public* 20 (June 1, 1917): 526–28.
"Socialized Germany." *Pearson's* 35 (January 1916): 1–9.
"The Soldier and the Land." *Nation* 108 (March 15, 1919): 391–93.
"Some Overlooked Dangers in Foreign Investments." *Annals of the American Academy of Political and Social Science* 138 (July 1928): 19–25.
"Some Possible Reforms in State and Local Taxation." *American Law Review* 33 (September–October 1899): 685–701.
"The Struggle for the Mediterranean." *Scribner's Magazine* 59 (May 1916): 621–24.
"A Suggested Solution of New York's Liquor Problem." *New York Times*, March 2, 1913, 2.

"The Syrian Imbroglio and the Turkish Settlement." *Nation* 111 (July 10, 1920): 37–38.
The Taxation of Land Values. Cincinnati: Joseph Fels Fund of America, 1910.
"Taxation of Quasi-public Corporations in the State of Ohio and the Franchise Tax." *Annals of the American Academy of Political and Social Science* 14, no. 2 (September 1899): 157–80.
"The Taxation of Railroads and Other Public Service Corporations." In *Proceedings of the Providence Conference for Good City Government and the Thirteenth Annual Meeting of the National Municipal League*, 306–16. Philadelphia: National Municipal League, 1907.
"Tom Johnson and the City of Cleveland." *Reader* 10 (October 1907): 502–16.
"Turned Back in Time of War." *Survey* 36 (May 6, 1916): 147–56.
"Two Decades of Penological Progress." *Christian Union* 47 (January 14, 1893): 67–69.
"Unemployment." *Century* 89 (April 1915): 843–48.
"The Vanishing Servant Girl." *Ladies' Home Journal* 35 (May 1918): 48.
"The Wage-Earner's Innings." *Independent* 87 (August 28, 1916): 297–98.
"Wanted—A National Railroad Program." *Nation* 110 (May 29, 1920): 716–17.
"Watchdogs for the Consumer." *Rotarian* 44 (February 1934): 29–31, 53–54.
"The Way Out? Single Tax!" *Christian Century* 49 (November 2, 1932): 1336–38.
"A Way Toward the Model City." *World's Work* 21 (December 1910): 13,794–801.
"The Westward Trend of Immigration." *Congressional Digest* 2, no. 10 (July–August 1923): 293–94.
"What to Do with the Motion-Picture Show: Shall It Be Censored." *Outlook* 107 (June 20, 1914): 412–16.
"Where Are the Pre-war Radicals? A Rejoinder." *Survey* 56 (April 1, 1926): 33–34, 50–53.
"Where the Business Men Rule." *Outlook* 103 (January 25, 1913): 203–9.
"The White Coal of Switzerland." *Outlook* 94 (January 22, 1910): 151–58.
"Why I Want Woman Suffrage." *Collier's* 48 (March 16, 1912): 18, 31. Also in *Public* 15 (March 29, 1912): 302–3.
"Why Men Do Not Go to the Farm." *Public* 20 (August 10, 1917): 765–66.
"Wisconsin's Folk High School." *School Life* (September 1937): 26–27.
"With the Armies of Occupation in Germany." *Scribner's Magazine* 65 (May 1919): 622–29.
"The World's Fair at St. Louis, 1904." *Cosmopolitan* 35 (July 1903): 277–90.

ARTICLE BY FREDERIC C. HOWE AND MARIE JENNEY HOWE

"Pensioning the Widow and the Fatherless." *Good Housekeeping* 57 (September 1913): 282–91.

WRITINGS BY MARIE JENNEY HOWE

Books

George Sand: The Search for Love. New York: John Day, 1927.
[Ed. and trans.] *The Intimate Journal of George Sand.* New York: John Day, 1929.

Pamphlets

An Anti-suffrage Monologue. New York: National American Woman Suffrage Association, 1912.

Articles

"American League for Civic Improvement." *Old and New* 11 (September 1902): 4.
"Feminism." *New Review* 2 (August 1914): 441–42.
"Unselfishness and Resignation: In What Way Are They the Will of God?" *Old and New* 8 (February 1900).
"Women in the Ministry." *Meadville Portfolio* 1 (September 1894): 21–23.
"Women Suffrage in Colorado." *La Follette's Weekly Magazine* (December 18, 1909).
"The Young Women and the Church." *Old and New* 13 (September 1905): 3–5. [Erroneously ascribed to Elizabeth Padgham.]

SECONDARY SOURCES

Books and Articles

Abbott, Virginia Clark. *The History of Woman Suffrage and the League of Women Voters in Cuyahoga County, 1911–1945*. Cleveland: William Feather, 1949.
Ackerman, Kenneth D. *Young J. Edgar: Hoover, the Red Scare, and the Assault on Civil Liberties*. New York: Carroll and Graf, 2007.
Adams, Graham, Jr. *Age of Industrial Violence, 1910–1915: The Activities and Findings of the United States Commission on Industrial Relations*. New York: Columbia University Press, 1966.
Adickes, Sandra. *To Be Young Was Very Heaven: Women in New York Before the First World War*. New York: St. Martin's Press, 1997.
Allen, H. C., and Roger Thompson, eds. *Contrast and Connection: Bicentennial Essays in Anglo-American History*. London: G. Bell and Sons, 1976.
Alpern, Sara. *Freda Kirchwey: A Woman of the Nation*. Cambridge: Harvard University Press, 1987.
American Commission on Conditions in Ireland. *Evidence on Conditions in Ireland, Comprising the Complete Testimony, Affidavits and Exhibits Presented Before the American Commission on Conditions in Ireland*. Transcribed and annotated by Albert Coyle. Washington, D.C.: The Commission, 1921.
Angevine, Emma, ed. *Consumer Activists: They Made a Difference: A History of Consumer Action Related by Leaders in the Consumer Movement*. Mount Vernon, N.Y.: Consumers Union Foundation, 1982.
Bacon, Peggy. *Off with Their Heads!* New York: Robert McBride, 1934.
Baker, Ray Stannard. *Woodrow Wilson: Life and Letters*. 8 vols. Garden City, N.Y.: Doubleday, Page, 1927–39.
Baldwin, R. Leon. *The Purge in the Agricultural Adjustment Administration*. Ann Arbor: University Microfilms International, 1988.
Baldwin, Roger Nash. "The Reminiscences of Roger Nash Baldwin." Columbia University Oral History Research Office Collection.
Baldwin, Sidney. *Poverty and Politics: The Rise and Decline of the Farm Security Administration*. Chapel Hill: University of North Carolina Press, 1968.
Barber, William J., "Political Economy in the Flagship of Postgraduate Studies: The Johns Hopkins University." In *Breaking the Academic Mould: Economists and American Higher Learning in the Nineteenth Century*, edited by William J. Barber, 203–24. Middletown, Conn.: Wesleyan University Press, 1988.
Barker, Charles Albro. *Henry George*. New York: Oxford University Press, 1955.

Barton, Dante. "The Wilson Volunteers in New York State." Typescript, Amos Pinchot Papers, Library of Congress.
Bates, Samuel P. *Our County and Its People: A Historical and Memorial Record of Crawford County, Pennsylvania.* Boston: W. A. Fergusson, 1899.
Bean, Louis. "The Reminiscences of Louis Bean." Columbia University Oral History Research Office Collection, June 1956.
Beede, Benjamin R. "Foreign Influences on American Progressivism." *Historian* 45, no. 4 (August 1983): 529–49.
Belknap, Michael R. "The Mechanics of Repression: J. Edgar Hoover, the Bureau of Investigation and the Radicals, 1917–1925." *Crime and Social Justice* 7 (Spring–Summer 1977): 49–58.
Bemis, Edward A. "The Cleveland Referendum on Street Railways." *Quarterly Journal of Economics* 23 (November 1908): 179–82.
Benedict, Crystal Eastman. "A Platform of Real Preparedness." *Survey* 35 (November 13, 1915): 160–61.
Benham, R. Leon. "The Purge in the Agricultural Adjustment Administration." Ph.D. diss., Emory University, 1987.
Berg, A. Scott. *Max Perkins: Editor of Genius.* New York: E. P. Dutton, 1978.
Bierbaum, Martin A. "'Free Acres'": Bolton Hall's Single-Tax Experimental Community." *New Jersey History* 102 (Spring–Summer 1984): 37–63.
Black, John D. *The Dairy Industry and the AAA.* Washington, D.C.: Brookings Institution, 1935.
Blair, Fredrika. *Isadora: Portrait of the Artist as a Woman.* New York: McGraw-Hill, 1986.
Bourne, Henry E. *The First Four Decades, Goodrich House.* Cleveland: Wm. Feather Co. for Goodrich Social Settlement, 1938.
Boyce, Neith, and Hutchins Hapgood. *Intimate Warriors: Portraits of a Modern Marriage, 1898–1944.* Edited by Ellen Kay Trimberger. New York: Feminist Press at City University of New York, 1991.
Bragdon, Henry Wilkinson. *Woodrow Wilson: The Academic Years.* Cambridge, Mass.: Belknap Press, 1967.
Brailsford, H. N. *The War of Steel and Gold: A Study of the Armed Peace.* London: G. Bell and Sons, 1914.
Bremner, Robert H. "Artist in Politics: Brand Whitlock." *American Journal of Economics and Sociology* 9 (January 1950): 239–54.
———. "The Civic Revival in Ohio." *American Journal of Economics and Sociology* 8, no. 1 (October 1948): 61–68.
———. "Harris R. Cooley and Cooley Farms." *American Journal of Economics and Sociology* 14 (October 1954): 71–75.
———. "The Political Techniques of the Progressives," *American Journal of Economics and Sociology* 12, no. 2 (January 1953): 189–200.
———. "The Single Tax Philosophy in Cleveland and Toledo." *American Journal of Economics and Sociology* 9, no. 3 (April 1950): 369–76.
———. "The Street Railway Controversy in Cleveland." *American Journal of Economics and Sociology* 10, no. 2 (January 1951): 185–206.
———. "Tax Equalization in Cleveland." *American Journal of Economics and Sociology* 10, no. 3 (April 1951): 301–12.
Briggs, Robert L. "The Progressive Era in Cleveland, Ohio: Tom L. Johnson's Administration, 1901–1909." Ph.D. diss., Department of History, University of Chicago, 1962.

Broderick, Francis L. *Progressivism at Risk: Electing a President in 1912.* Westport, Conn.: Greenwood Press, 1989.
Broesamle, John J. *William Gibbs McAdoo: A Passion for Change, 1863–1917.* Port Washington, N.Y.: Kennikat Press, 1973.
Brooks, Aubrey Lee, and Hugh Talmage Lefler, eds. *The Papers of Walter Clark.* 2 vols. Chapel Hill: University of North Carolina Press, 1948–50.
Buhle, Mari Jo. *Women and American Socialism, 1870–1920.* Urbana: University of Illinois Press, 1983.
Burner, David. *The Politics of Provincialism: The Democratic Party in Transition, 1918–1932.* Cambridge: Harvard University Press, 1986.
Camp, Helen C. *Iron in Her Soul: Elizabeth Gurley Flynn and the American Left.* Pullman: Washington State University Press, 1995.
Campbell, Persia. *Consumer Representation in the New Deal.* New York: Columbia University Press, 1940.
Campbell, Thomas F. "Mounting Crisis and Reform: Cleveland's Political Development." In Campbell and Miggins, *Birth of Modern Cleveland,* 298–324.
Campbell, Thomas F., and Edward M. Miggins, eds., *The Birth of Modern Cleveland, 1865–1930.* Cleveland: Western Reserve Historical Society; London: Associated University Presses, 1988.
Candeloro, Dominic. "Louis F. Post and the Single Tax Movement, 1872–98." *American Journal of Economics and Sociology* 35, no. 4 (October 1976): 415–30.
Carter, John Franklin ("Unofficial Observer"). *The New Dealers.* New York: Literary Guild, 1934.
Century Association. *The Century, 1847–1946.* New York: Century Association, 1947.
Cerillo, Augustus, Jr. *Reform in New York City: A Study of Urban Progressivism.* New York: Garland, 1991.
Chamberlain, Lawrence H. *Loyalty and Legislative Action: A Survey of Activity by the New York State Legislature, 1919–1949.* Ithaca: Cornell University Press, 1951.
Chamberlain, Rudolph W. *There Is No Truce: A Life of Thomas Mott Osborne.* New York: Macmillan, 1935.
Chamberlin, William Fosdick. *The History of Phi Gamma Delta.* Washington, D.C.: Phi Gamma Delta, 1926.
Chambers, Clarke A. *Paul U. Kellogg and the Survey: Voices for Social Welfare and Social Justice.* Minneapolis: University of Minnesota Press, 1971.
Chatfield, Charles. *For Peace and Justice: Pacifism in America, 1914–1941.* Knoxville: University of Tennessee Press, 1971.
Christie, Francis A. *The Makers of the Meadville Theological School, 1844–1894.* Boston: Beacon Press, 1927.
Churchill, Allen. *The Improper Bohemians: A Re-creation of Greenwich Village in Its Heyday.* New York: E. P. Dutton, 1959.
Coben, Stanley. *A. Mitchell Palmer: Politician.* New York: Columbia University Press, 1963.
Colburn, David R., and George E. Pozzetta, eds. *Reform and Reformers in the Progressive Era.* Westport, Conn.: Greenwood Press, 1983.
Collier, John. "The People's Institute." *Independent* 72 (May 30, 1912): 1144–48.
Comer, Lucretia Garfield. *Harry Garfield's First Forty Years: Man of Action in a Troubled World.* New York: Vantage Press, 1965.
Commons, John R. *Myself.* New York: Macmillan, 1934.
Conditions at Ellis Island: Hearings Before the Committee on Immigration and Naturalization, House of Representatives, 66th Congress, 1st Session, November 24, 26, 28, 1919. Washington, D.C.: Government Printing Office, 1920.

Condon, George E. *Cleveland: The Best Kept Secret.* Garden City, N.Y.: Doubleday, 1967.
Connelly, Mark Thomas. *The Response to Prostitution in the Progressive Era.* Chapel Hill: University of North Carolina Press, 1980.
Conrad, David Eugene. *The Forgotten Farmers: The Story of Sharecroppers in the New Deal.* Urbana: University of Illinois Press, 1965.
Constantine, J. Robert. *Letters of Eugene V. Debs.* 3 vols. Urbana: University of Illinois Press, 1990.
Constitution of the Bethel Associated Charities for 1893–1894. Cleveland: W. M. Bayne, 1894.
Cook, Blanche Wiesen. *Eleanor Roosevelt.* Vol. 2, 1933–1938. New York: Viking, 1999.
Corsi, Edward. *In the Shadow of Liberty: The Chronicle of Ellis Island.* New York: Macmillan, 1935.
Cott, Nancy F. *The Grounding of Modern Feminism.* New Haven: Yale University Press, 1987.
Cramer, C. H. *Newton D. Baker: A Biography.* Cleveland: World, 1961.
Creel, George. *Rebel at Large: Recollections of Fifty Crowded Years.* New York: G. P. Putnam's Sons, 1947.
Croly, Herbert. *The Promise of American Life.* 1909. Reprint, New York: E. P. Dutton, 1963.
Crunden, Robert M. *A Hero in Spite of Himself: Brand Whitlock in Art, Politics, and War.* New York: Alfred A. Knopf, 1969.
Culver, John C., and John Hyde. *American Dreamer: The Life and Times of Henry A. Wallace.* New York: W. W. Norton, 2000.
Czitrom, Daniel. "The Redemption of Leisure: The National Board of Censorship and the Rise of Motion Pictures in New York City, 1900–1920." *Studies in Visual Communication* 10 (Fall 1984): 2–6.
Dahlberg, Jane S. *The New York Bureau of Municipal Research: Pioneer in Government Administration.* New York: New York University Press, 1966.
Daniels, Doris. *Always a Sister: The Feminism of Lillian D. Wald.* New York: Feminist Press at the City University of New York, 1989.
———. "Building a Winning Coalition: The Suffrage Fight in New York State." *New York History* 60 (January 1979): 58–80.
Davis, Allen F. *American Heroine: The Life and Legend of Jane Addams.* New York: Oxford University Press, 1973.
———. *Spearheads of Reform: The Social Settlements and the Progressive Movement, 1890–1914.* New Brunswick: Rutgers University Press, 1984.
———. "Welfare, Reform, and World War I." *American Quarterly* 19 (Fall 1967): 516–33.
Davis, Chester C. "The Reminiscences of Chester C. Davis." Columbia University Oral History Research Office Collection, November 1954.
Davis, Kenneth S. *FDR, the New Deal Years, 1933–1937: A History.* New York: Random House, 1986.
Dedication of the New Meeting House of the Society for Ethical Culture, Sunday, October 23rd 1910. New York: Society for Ethical Culture, 1910.
Degen, Marie Louise. *The History of the Woman's Peace Party.* Baltimore: Johns Hopkins University Press, 1939. Reprint, New York: Burt Franklin, 1974.
Derber, Milton. *The American Idea of Industrial Democracy, 1865–1965.* Urbana: University of Illinois Press, 1970.
De Witt, Benjamin Parke. *The Progressive Movement: A Non-partisan, Comprehensive Discussion of Current Tendencies in American Politics.* New York: Macmillan, 1915. Reprint, Seattle: University of Washington Press, 1968.

Dilling, Elizabeth. *The Red Network: A "Who's Who" and Handbook of Radicalism for Patriots.* Kenilworth, Ill.: The Author, 1934.
Diner, Steven J. *A Very Different Age: Americans of the Progressive Era.* New York: Hill and Wang, 1998.
Doan, Edward N. *The La Follettes and the Wisconsin Idea.* New York: Rinehart, 1947.
Dorr, Rheta Childe. *A Woman of Fifty.* New York: Funk and Wagnalls, 1924.
Dudden, Arthur Power. *Joseph Fels and the Single-Tax Movement.* Philadelphia: Temple University Press, 1971.
Durant, Will. *Transition: A Sentimental Story of One Mind and One Era.* Garden City, N.Y.: Garden City, 1927.
Easterly, John W., Jr. "Louis F. Post (1849–1928): The 'Henry George Man' as Progressive Reformer." Ph.D. diss., Duke University, 1976.
Eastman, Max. *Enjoyment of Living.* New York: Harper, 1948.
———. *Love and Revolution: My Journey Through an Epoch.* New York: Random House, 1964.
Eliot, Thomas H. *Recollections of the New Deal: When the People Mattered.* Boston: Northeastern University Press, 1992.
Ely, Richard T. *Ground Under Our Feet: An Autobiography.* New York: Macmillan, 1938.
Ezekiel, Mordecai. "The Reminiscences of Mordecai Ezekiel." Columbia University Oral History Research Office Collection, 1972.
Faulkner, Harold U. *Politics, Reform and Expansion, 1890–1900.* New York: Harper Torchbooks, 1963.
Feldman, Egal. "Prostitution, the Alien Woman and the Progressive Imagination, 1910–1915." *American Quarterly* 19 (Summer 1967): 192–206.
Fifty Years of Unity Church, 1885–1935: The Story of the First Unitarian Church of Sioux City, Iowa. Sioux City: n.p., 1935.
Finegold, Kenneth. *Experts and Politicians: Reform Challenges to Machine Politics in New York, Cleveland, and Chicago.* Princeton: Princeton University Press, 1995.
Fisher, Robert Bruce. "Community Organizing and Citizen Participation: The Efforts of the Peoples Institute in New York City." *Social Science Review* 51 (September 1977): 474–90.
———. "Film Censorship and Progressive Reform: The National Board of Censorship and Motion Pictures, 1909–1922." *Journal of Popular Film* 4 (1975): 143–56.
———. "The People's Institute of New York City, 1897–1934: Culture, Progressive Democracy, and the People." Ph.D. diss., New York University, 1974.
Fite, Gilbert C. *George N. Peek and the Fight for Farm Parity.* Norman: University of Oklahoma Press, 1954.
Flower, B. O. "'The British City': A Study of the Beginnings of Democracy." *Arena*, no. 213 (August 1907): 200–208.
Flynn, Elizabeth Gurley. *The Rebel Girl: An Autobiography: My First Life (1906–1926).* New York: International, 1973.
"Forget-Me-Not" Files. Pt. I of Survey Associates Records. Frederick, Md.: UPA microfilm.
Frank, Jerome. "The Reminiscences of Jerome Frank." Columbia University Oral History Research Office Collection, February 1960.
Frederick, Peter J. *Knights of the Golden Rule: The Intellectual as Christian Social Reformer in the 1890s.* Lexington: University Press of Kentucky, 1976.
Freidel, Frank. *Launching the New Deal.* Vol. 4 of *Franklin D. Roosevelt.* Boston: Little, Brown, 1973.

———. *The Triumph.* Vol. 3 of *Franklin D. Roosevelt.* Boston: Little, Brown, 1956.
French, John C. *A History of the University Founded by Johns Hopkins.* Baltimore: Johns Hopkins Press, 1946.
Furnas, J. C. *Great Times: An Informal Social History of the United States, 1914–1929.* New York: G. P. Putnam's Sons, 1974.
Gable, John Allen. "The Bull Moose Years: Theodore Roosevelt and the Progressive Party, 1912–1916." Ph.D. diss., Brown University, 1972.
Garfield, Harry A. "Private Rights in Street Railways." *Outlook* 85 (February 2, 1907): 256–58.
Gelfand, Lawrence E. *The Inquiry: American Preparations for Peace, 1917–1919.* New Haven: Yale University Press, 1963.
Gentry, Curt. *J. Edgar Hoover: The Man and the Secrets.* New York: W. W. Norton, 1991.
Gerber, Larry G. *The Limits of Liberalism: Josephus Daniels, Henry Stimson, Bernard Baruch, Donald Richberg, Felix Frankfurter and the Development of the Modern American Political Economy.* New York: New York University Press, 1984.
Gilbert, Jess. "Eastern Urban Liberals and Midwestern Agrarian Intellectuals: Two Group Portraits of Progressives in the New Deal Department of Agriculture." *Agricultural History* 74, no. 2 (Spring 2000): 162–80.
Gilman, Charlotte Perkins. *The Living of Charlotte Perkins Gilman.* Edited by Zona Gale. New York: Appleton-Century, 1935.
Goldman, Eric F. *Rendezvous with Destiny: A History of Modern American Reform.* Rev. and abridged ed. New York: Vintage Books, 1956.
Gompers, Samuel. *Seventy Years of Life and Labour: An Autobiography.* 1925. New York: August M. Kelley, 1967.
Goodnow, Frank J., and Frederic C. Howe. "The Organization, Status and Procedure of the Department of Education, City of New York." In New York City, Board of Estimate and Apportionment, *Report of Committee on School Inquiry.*
Grabowski, John J. "Social Reform and Philanthropic Order in Cleveland, 1896–1920." In Van Tassel and Grabowski, *Cleveland,* 29–49.
Graham, Otis L., Jr. *An Encore for Reform: The Old Progressives and the New Deal.* New York: Oxford University Press, 1967.
———. *The Great Campaigns: Reform and War in America, 1900–1928.* Englewood Cliffs: Prentice-Hall, 1971.
Graham, Sally Hunter. "Woman Suffrage and the New Democracy." Ph.D. diss., University of Texas, 1988.
Grantham, Dewey W., Jr. "The Progressive Movement and the Negro." *South Atlantic Quarterly* 54 (October 1955): 461–77.
Graybar, Lloyd J. *Albert Shaw of the Review of Reviews: An Intellectual Biography.* Lexington: University Press of Kentucky, 1974.
Griffith, Ernest S. *A History of American City Government.* 4 vols. Washington, D.C.: University Press of America, 1983.
Grubbs, Frank L., Jr. *The Struggle for Labor Loyalty: Gompers, the A. F. of L., and the Pacifists, 1917–1920.* Durham: Duke University Press, 1968.
Hallinan, Charles T. "Putting Pins in Preparedness." *Survey* 35 (February 26, 1916): 632–33.
Hammack, David C. *Power and Society: Greater New York at the Turn of the Century.* New York: Russell Sage Foundation, 1982.
Hapgood, Hutchins. *A Victorian in the Modern World.* New York: Harcourt, Brace, 1939.
Hapgood, Norman, ed. *Professional Patriots.* New York: Albert and Charles Boni, 1928.

Harper, Ida Husted. *History of Woman Suffrage*. 6 vols. New York: Arno, 1969.
Harrison, Dennis Irven. "The Consumers' League of Ohio: Women and Reform, 1909–1937." Ph.D. diss., Case Western Reserve University, 1975.
Hauser, Elizabeth J. "The Woman Suffrage Movement in Ohio." *Ohio Magazine* 4 (February 1908): 83–92.
Hawkins, Hugh. *Pioneer: A History of the Johns Hopkins University, 1874–1889*. Ithaca: Cornell University Press, 1960.
Hays, Arthur Garfield. *City Lawyer: The Autobiography of a Law Practice*. New York: Simon and Schuster, 1942.
Hearings Before the Select Committee to Investigate Charges Made by Dr. William A. Wirt, House of Representatives, Seventy-Third Congress, 2nd Session. Washington: Government Printing Office, 1934.
Hechler, Kenneth W. *Insurgency: Personalities and Politics of the Taft Era*. New York: Russell and Russell, 1964.
Hershey, Burnet. *The Odyssey of Henry Ford and the Great Peace Ship*. New York: Taplinger, 1967.
Heterodoxy to Marie. Album, Inez Haynes Irwin Papers, Schlesinger Library, Harvard University.
Hicks, John D. *Republican Ascendancy, 1921–1933*. New York: Harper, 1960.
Higham, John. *Strangers in the Land: Patterns of American Nativism, 1860–1925*. New York: Atheneum, 1981.
Hines, Thomas S. *Burnham of Chicago: Architect and Planner*. New York: Oxford University Press, 1974.
———. "The Paradox of 'Progressive' Architecture: Urban Planning and Public Building in Tom Johnson's Cleveland." *American Quarterly* 25, no. 4 (October 1973): 427–48.
History, Object and Aims of the Humanitarian Cult. New York: Humanitarian Cult, n.d.
Hitchings, Catherine F. *Universalist and Unitarian Women Ministers*. Journal of the Universalist Historical Society 10. Boston: Universalist Historical Society, 1975.
Hobson, J. A. *Imperialism: A Study*. New York: James Pott, 1902.
Hodgson, Godfrey. *The Colonel: The Life and Wars of Henry Stimson, 1867–1950*. New York: Alfred A. Knopf, 1990.
Hoff-Wilson, Joan, and Marjorie Lightman. *Without Precedent: The Life and Career of Eleanor Roosevelt*. Bloomington: Indiana University Press, 1984.
Hofstadter, Richard. *The Age of Reform: From Bryan to F.D.R.* New York: Alfred A. Knopf, 1955.
Holli, Melvin G. *The American Mayor: The Best and the Worst Big-City Leaders*. University Park: Pennsylvania State University Press, 1999.
Holli, Melvin G., and Peter d'A. Jones, eds., *Biographical Dictionary of American Mayors, 1820–1980: Big City Mayors*. Westport, Conn.: Greenwood Press, 1981.
Holt, James. *Congressional Insurgents and the Party System*. Cambridge, Mass.: Harvard University Press, 1967.
Hopkins, C. Edward. *The Rise of the Social Gospel in American Protestantism, 1865–1915*. New Haven: Yale University Press, 1967.
Hopkins, George B. "The New York Bureau of Municipal Research." *Annals of the American Academy of Political and Social Science* 41 (May 1912): 235–44.
Huff, Robert Arthur. "Frederic C. Howe, Progressive." Ph.D. diss., University of Rochester, 1967.
Humes, D. Joy. *Oswald Garrison Villard: Liberal of the 1920's*. Syracuse: Syracuse University Press, 1960.

Humphrey, Robert E. *Children of Fantasy: The First Rebels of Greenwich Village*. New York: John Wiley and Sons, 1978.
Hurst, Fannie. *Anatomy of Me: A Wonderer in Search of Herself*. Garden City, N.Y.: Doubleday, 1958.
Ions, Edmund. *James Bryce and American Democracy, 1870–1922*. London: Macmillan, 1968.
Irwin, Inez Haynes. "Adventures of Yesterday." Typescript, Schlesinger Library, Harvard University.
———. *Up Hill with Banners Flying: The Story of the Woman's Party*. Penobscot, Maine: Traversity Press, 1964. Reprint of *The Story of the Woman's Party*. New York: Harcourt, Brace, 1921.
Irwin, Will. *The Making of a Reporter*. New York: G. P. Putnam's Sons, 1942.
Jackson, Gardner. "The Reminiscences of Gardner Jackson." Columbia University Oral History Research Office Collection, May 1959.
Johannesen, Eric. *Cleveland Architecture, 1876–1976*. Cleveland: Western Reserve Historical Society, 1979.
Johnson, Donald. *The Challenge to American Freedoms: World War I and the Rise of the American Civil Liberties Union*. Lexington: University of Kentucky Press, 1963.
Johnson, James Weldon. *Along This Way: The Autobiography of James Weldon Johnson*. New York: Viking, 1933.
Johnson, Tom L. *My Story*. Edited by Elizabeth J. Hauser. New York: B. W. Huebsch, 1911.
Johnston, Robert D. *The Radical Middle Class: Populist Democracy and the Question of Capitalism in Progressive Era Portland, Oregon*. Princeton: Princeton University Press, 2003.
Joint Legislative Committee Investigating Seditious Activities. *Revolutionary Radicalism: Its History, Purpose and Tactics with an Exposition of the Steps Being Taken and Required to Curb It*. 4 vols. Albany: J. B. Lyon, 1920.
Josephson, Matthew. *Infidel in the Temple: A Memoir of the Nineteen-Thirties*. New York: Alfred A. Knopf, 1967.
Kantor, Harvey A. "Benjamin C. Marsh and the Fight over Population Congestion." In Krueckeberg, *American Planner*, 58–74.
Kaplan, Justin. *Lincoln Steffens: A Biography*. New York: Simon and Schuster, 1974.
Karnow, Stanley. *In Our Image: America's Empire in the Philippines*. New York: Random House, 1989.
Keating, Edward. *The Story of "Labor": Thirty-Three Years on Rail Workers' Fighting Front*. Washington, D.C.: Rufus H. Darby, 1953.
Kelly, Lawrence C. *The Assault on Assimilation: John Collier and the Origins of Indian Policy Reform*. Albuquerque: University of New Mexico Press, 1983.
Kempton, Murray. *Part of Our Times: Some Ruins and Monuments of the Thirties*. New York: Simon and Schuster, 1955.
Kennedy, David. *Over Here: The First World War and American Society*. New York: Oxford University Press, 1980.
Kerr, K. Austin. *American Railroad Politics, 1914–1920: Rates, Wages, and Efficiency*. Pittsburgh: University of Pittsburgh Press, 1968.
Kolko, Gabriel. *The Triumph of Conservatism: A Reinterpretation of American History, 1900–1916*. New York: Free Press, 1977.
Krueckeberg, Donald A., ed. *The American Planner: Biographies and Recollections*. New York: Methuen, 1983.

Kryder, LeeAnne Giannone, "Self-Assertion and Social Commitment: The Significance of Work to the Progressive Era's New Woman." *Journal of American Culture* 6 (1983): 25–30.

Kurth, Peter. *Isadora: A Sensational Life.* Boston: Little, Brown, 2001.

La Follette, Belle Case, and Fola La Follette. *Robert M. La Follette: June 14, 1855–June 18, 1925.* 2 vols. New York: Macmillan, 1953.

La Follette, Robert M. "The Beginning of a Great Movement." *La Follette's Weekly Magazine* 3 (February 4, 1911): 7–9, 12.

———. *La Follette's Autobiography: A Personal Narrative of Political Experiences.* Madison: University of Wisconsin Press, 1968.

Lamson, Peggy. *Roger Baldwin: Founder of the American Civil Liberties Union.* Boston: Houghton Mifflin, 1976.

Lane, Ann J. *To Herland and Beyond: The Life and Work of Charlotte Perkins Gilman.* New York: Pantheon Books, 1990.

Lane, Franklin K. *The Letters of Franklin K. Lane: Personal and Political.* Edited by Anne Wintermute Lane and Louise Herrick Wall. Boston: Houghton Mifflin, 1922.

Larsen, Charles. *The Good Fight: The Life and Times of Ben B. Lindsey.* Chicago: Quadrangle Books, 1972.

Lasch, Christopher. *The New Radicalism in America, 1889–1963: The Intellectual as a Social Type.* New York: Vintage, 1967.

Lash, Joseph P. *Dealers and Dreamers: A New Look at the New Deal.* New York: Doubleday, 1988.

Leonard, John William, ed. *Woman's Who's Who of America: A Biographical Dictionary of Contemporary Women of the United States and Canada, 1914–1915.* New York: American Commonwealth, 1914.

Lewinson, Edwin R. *John Purroy Mitchel: The Boy Mayor of New York.* New York: Astra Books, 1965.

Lichtman, Allan J. *Prejudice and the Old Politics: The Presidential Election of 1928.* Chapel Hill: University of North Carolina Press, 1979.

Link, Arthur, ed. *The Papers of Woodrow Wilson.* 69 vols. Princeton: Princeton University Press, 1966–94.

———. "What Happened to the Progressive Movement in the 1920's?" *American Historical Review* 54 (July 1959): 833–51.

———. *Wilson: Campaigns for Progressivism and Peace, 1916–1917.* Princeton: Princeton University Press, 1965.

———. *Wilson: The New Freedom.* Princeton: Princeton University Press, 1956.

———. *Woodrow Wilson and the Progressive Era, 1910–1917.* New York: Harper and Row, 1963.

Link, Arthur, and Richard L. McCormick, *Progressivism.* Arlington Heights, Ill.: Harlan Davidson, 1983.

Lippmann, Walter. "Trade and the Flag." *New Republic* 17 (February 26, 1916): 87.

Lombardi, John. *Labor's Voice in the Cabinet: A History of the Department of Labor from Its Origin to 1921.* New York: Columbia University Press, 1942.

Lord, Russell. *The Agrarian Revival.* New York: American Association for Adult Education, 1939.

———. *The Wallaces of Iowa.* Boston: Houghton Mifflin, 1947.

Lorenz, Carl. *Tom L. Johnson: Mayor of Cleveland.* New York: A. S. Barnes, 1911.

Louchheim, Katie, ed. *The Making of the New Deal: The Insiders Speak.* Cambridge: Harvard University Press, 1983.

Lovett, Robert Morss. "Candide's Progress." *New Republic* (December 9, 1925): 90–91.
Luhan, Mabel Dodge. *Movers and Shakers.* Vol. 3 of *Intimate Memories.* New York: Harcourt Brace, 1936.
Lunardini, Christine A. *From Equal Suffrage to Equal Rights: Alice Paul and the National Woman's Party, 1910–1928.* New York: New York University Press, 1986.
Lustig, R. Jeffrey. *Corporate Liberalism: The Origins of Modern American Political Theory, 1890–1920.* Berkeley: University of California Press, 1982.
Lynn, Kenneth, "The Rebels of Greenwich Village." In *Perspectives in American History*, edited by Donald Fleming and Bernard Bailyn, 8:335–77. Cambridge, Mass.: Charles Warren Center for Studies in American History, Harvard University, 1974.
MacKay, Kenneth Campbell. *The Progressive Movement of 1924.* New York: Columbia University Press, 1947.
MacMahon, Arthur W., and John D. Millett, *Federal Administrators: A Biographical Approach to the Problem of Departmental Management.* New York: Columbia University Press, 1939.
Mann, Arthur. *La Guardia: A Fighter Against His Times, 1882–1933.* Philadelphia: J. B. Lippincott, 1959.
———, ed. *The Progressive Era.* Hinsdale, Ill.: Dryden Press, 1975.
Marcaccio, Michael D. *The Hapgoods: Three Earnest Brothers.* Charlottesville: University Press of Virginia, 1977.
Marchand, C. Roland. *The American Peace Movement and Social Reform, 1898–1918.* Princeton: Princeton University Press, 1972.
Marriner, Gerald L. "A Victorian in the Modern World: The 'Liberated' Male's Adjustment to the New Woman and the New Morality." *South Atlantic Quarterly* 76 (Spring 1977): 190–203.
Marsh, Benjamin C. *Lobbyist for the People: A Record of Fifty Years.* Washington, D.C.: Public Affairs Press, 1953.
Masel-Walters, Lynne. "To Hustle with the Rowdies: The Organization and Functions of the American Woman Suffrage Press." *Journal of American Culture* 3 (Spring 1988): 167–83.
Mason, Alpheus Thomas. *Brandeis: A Free Man's Life.* New York: Viking, 1946.
Mattern, Edwin L. *Pi Chapter of Phi Gamma Delta: Seventy Years of Friendship, 1860–1930.* Cedar Rapids, Iowa: Torch Press, 1930.
Mattson, Kevin. *Creating a Democratic Public: The Struggle for Urban Participatory Democracy During the Progressive Era.* University Park: Pennsylvania State University Press, 1998.
Maxwell, Robert S., ed. *La Follette.* Englewood Cliffs, N.J.: Prentice-Hall, 1969.
———. *La Follette and the Rise of the Progressives in Wisconsin.* Madison: State Historical Society of Wisconsin, 1956.
May, Henry. *The End of American Innocence: A Study of the First Years of Our Own Time, 1912–1917.* New York: Alfred A. Knopf, 1959.
McCarthy, Charles. *The Wisconsin Idea.* New York: Macmillan, 1912.
McCarthy, Michael P. "'Suburban Power': A Footnote on Cleveland in the Tom Johnson Years." *Northwest Ohio Quarterly* 45, no. 1 (Winter 1972–73): 21–27.
McCartin, Joseph A. *Labor's Great War: The Struggle for Industrial Democracy and the Origins of Modern American Labor Relations, 1912–1921.* Chapel Hill: University of North Carolina Press, 1997.
McGeary, M. Nelson. *Gifford Pinchot: Forester, Politician.* Princeton: Princeton University Press, 1960.

McGerr, Michael E. *The Decline of Popular Politics: The American North, 1865–1928.* New York: Oxford University Press, 1986.

———. *A Fierce Discontent: The Rise and Fall of the Progressive Movement in America, 1870–1920.* New York: Free Press, 2003.

McKelvey, Blake. *The Urbanization of America, 1860–1915.* New Brunswick: Rutgers University Press, 1963.

Merz, Charles. *And Then Came Ford.* New York: Doubleday, Doran, 1929.

Middleton, George. *These Things Are Mine: The Autobiography of a Journeyman Playwright.* New York: Macmillan, 1947.

Miller, Spencer, Jr. "A Quarter Century of the People's Institute Founded by Charles Sprague-Smith." *Amherst Graduates' Quarterly* 13 (1924): 91–94.

Mitgang, Herbert, ed. *The Letters of Carl Sandburg.* New York: Harcourt, Brace and World, 1968.

Mock, James R. *Censorship, 1917.* Princeton: Princeton University Press, 1941.

Mock, James R., and Cedric Larson. *Words That Won the War: The Story of the Committee on Public Information, 1917–1919.* Princeton: Princeton University Press, 1939.

Moley, Raymond. *Twenty-seven Masters of Politics in a Personal Perspective.* New York: Funk and Wagnalls, 1949.

Mooney, Chase C., and Martha E. Lyman. "Some Phases of the Compulsory Military Training Movement, 1914–1920." *Mississippi Valley Historical Review* 38 (March 1952): 633–56.

Mooney, Rex Oliver. "Amos Pinchot and Atomistic Capitalism: A Study in Reform Ideas." Ph.D. diss., Louisiana State University, 1973.

Moore, Ernest Carroll. *How New York City Administers Its Schools.* Yonkers-on-Hudson: World Book, 1913.

Morgan, Kenneth O. "The Future at Work: Anglo-American Progressivism, 1890–1917." In Allen and Thompson, *Contrast and Connection,* 245–71.

Morison, Elting E. *Turmoil and Tradition: A Study of the Life and Times of Henry L. Stimson.* Boston: Houghton Mifflin, 1960.

Morris, Jan. *Manhattan.* New York: Oxford University Press, 1987.

Morris, Lloyd. *Incredible New York: High Life and Low Life of the Last Hundred Years.* New York: Random House, 1951.

Moses, Robert. *Working for the People: Promise and Performance in Public Service.* New York: Harper and Brothers, 1956.

Mowry, George E. *Theodore Roosevelt and the Progressive Movement.* New York: Hill and Wang, 1963.

Mulder, John M. *Woodrow Wilson: The Years of Preparation.* Princeton: Princeton University Press, 1978.

Munden, Kenneth W., ed. *The American Film Institute Catalog of Motion Pictures Produced in the United States: Feature Films, 1921–1930.* Vol. F2, pt. 1. New York: R. R. Bowker, 1971.

Murdock, Eugene C. "Life of Tom L. Johnson." Ph.D. diss., Columbia University, 1951.

Murray, Robert K. *Red Scare: A Study in National Hysteria, 1919–1920.* New York: McGraw-Hill, 1964.

Namorato, Michael Vincent, ed. *The Diary of Rexford G. Tugwell: The New Deal, 1932–1935.* Westport, Conn.: Greenwood, 1992.

———. *Rexford G. Tugwell: A Biography.* New York: Praeger, 1988.

National American Woman Suffrage Association. *Victory! How Women Won It: A Centennial Symposium, 1840–1940.* New York: H. W. Wilson, 1940.

Nevins, Allan, ed. *The Letters and Journals of Brand Whitlock.* 2 vols. New York: D. Appleton-Century, 1936.
New York: A Guide to the Empire State. New York: Oxford University Press, 1940.
New York City, Board of Estimate and Apportionment. *Report of Committee on School Inquiry.* Vol. 3. New York: City of New York, 1913.
Northshield, Jane, ed. *History of Croton-on-Hudson, New York.* Croton-on-Hudson: Croton-on-Hudson Historical Society and Bicentennial Celebration Committee, 1976.
Nourse, Edwin G., Joseph S. Davis, and John D. Black. *Three Years of the Agricultural Adjustment Administration.* Washington, D.C.: Brookings Institution, 1937.
Nye, Russel B. *Midwestern Progressive Politics: A Historical Study of Its Origins and Development, 1870–1958.* New York: Harper Torchbooks, 1965
Obituaries and Biographical Clippings of Residents of Syracuse, Onondaga County, and Adjacent Areas of Central New York from About 1860 to 1926. Syracuse Public Library Local History Department.
Ogg, Frederic A. "Robert M. La Follette in Retrospect." *Current History* 33 (February 1931): 685–91.
Olssen, Erik. "The Making of a Political Machine: The Railroad Unions Enter Politics." *Labor History* 19 (Summer 1978): 373–96.
O'Neill, William L. *Everyone Was Brave: The Rise and Fall of Feminism in America.* Chicago: Quadrangle Books, 1969.
———. *The Last Romantic: A Life of Max Eastman.* New York: Oxford University Press, 1978.
———. *The Progressive Years: America Comes of Age.* New York: Harper and Row, 1975.
O'Toole, Patricia. *When Trumpets Call: Theodore Roosevelt After the White House.* New York: Simon and Schuster, 2005.
Palmer, Frederick. *Newton D. Baker: America at War.* 2 vols. New York: Dodd, Mead, 1931.
The Paris Peace Conference, 1919. 13 vols. Papers Relating to the Foreign Relations of the United States. Washington, D.C.: Government Printing Office, 1942–47.
Parkhurst, Charles H. *Our Fight with Tammany.* New York: Charles Scribner's Sons, 1895.
Parrish, Michael E. *Felix Frankfurter and His Times: The Reform Years.* New York: Free Press, 1982.
Parsons, Elsie Clews. *The Family.* New York: G. P. Putnam's Sons, 1906.
Patton, Clifford W. *The Battle for Municipal Reform: Mobilization and Attack, 1875 to 1900.* Washington, D.C.: American Council on Public Affairs, 1940. Reprint, College Park: McGrath, 1969.
Paulson, Ross E. *Radicalism and Reform: The Vrooman Family and American Social Thought, 1837–1937.* Lexington: University of Kentucky Press, 1968.
Peck, Mary Gray. *Carrie Chapman Catt: A Biography.* New York: H. W. Wilson, 1944.
Peek, George N., with Samuel Crowther. *Why Quit Our Own.* New York: D. Van Nostrand, 1936.
Perkins, Van L. *Crisis in Agriculture: The Agricultural Adjustment Administration and the New Deal, 1933.* Berkeley: University of California Press, 1969.
Perlman, Selig, and Philip Taft. *Labor Movements.* Vol. 4 of *History of Labor in the United States, 1896–1932.* New York: Macmillan, 1935.
Perret, Geoffrey. *Old Soldiers Never Die: The Life of Douglas MacArthur.* New York: Random House, 1996.
Perry, Elizabeth Israels, "Training for Public Life: ER and Women's Political Networks in the 1920s." In Hoff-Wilson and Lightman, *Without Precedent,* 28–45.

Pinchot, Amos R. E. *History of the Progressive Party, 1912–1916*. Edited by Helene Maxwell Hooker. New York: New York University Press. Reprint, Westport, Conn.: Greenwood Press, 1978.

Pitkin, Thomas M. *Keepers of the Gate: A History of Ellis Island*. New York: New York University Press, 1975.

Plumb, Glenn E. *Labor's Plan for Government Ownership and Democracy in the Operation of the Railroads*. Washington, D.C.: Plumb Plan League, 1919.

The Policy and Standards of the National Board of Censorship of Motion Pictures. New York: National Board, 1915.

Post, Louis F. *The Deportations Delirium of Nineteen-Twenty: A Personal Narrative of an Historic Official Experience*. Chicago: Charles H. Kerr, 1923. Reprint, New York: Da Capo Press, 1970.

——. "Living a Long Life Over Again." Louis Freland Post Papers, Library of Congress.

Powers, Richard Gid. *Secrecy and Power: The Life of J. Edgar Hoover*. New York: Free Press, 1987.

Preston, William, Jr. *Aliens and Dissenters: Federal Suppression of Radicals, 1903–1933*. Cambridge, Mass.: Harvard University Press, 1963.

Pringle, Henry F. *Theodore Roosevelt: A Biography*. New York: Harcourt, Brace, 1931.

Rader, Benjamin G. *The Academic Mind and Reform: The Influence of Richard T. Ely in American Life*. Lexington: University of Kentucky Press, 1966.

Rarick, Holly M. *Progressive Vision: The Planning of Downtown Cleveland, 1903–1930*. Cleveland: Cleveland Museum of Art in cooperation with Indiana University Press, 1986.

Ratner, Sidney. *American Taxation: Its History as a Social Force in Democracy*. New York: W. W. Norton, 1942.

Richardson, James F. "Political Reform in Cleveland." In Van Tassel and Grabowski, *Cleveland*, 156–72.

Richardson, Reed C. *The Locomotive Engineer, 1863–1963: A Century of Railway Labor Relations and Work Rules*. Ann Arbor: University of Michigan Press, 1963.

Riis, Jacob A. "The People's Institute of New York: The Unique and Remarkable Work It Is Doing Among the Poor." *Century Magazine* 79 (April 1910): 850–63.

Riker, William H. *The Firing of Pat Jackson*. Syracuse: Inter-University Case Program, 1951.

Ritchie, Donald A. "The Gary Committee: Businessmen, Progressives and Unemployment in New York City, 1914–1915." *New York Historical Society Quarterly* 57 (October 1973): 327–47.

Roberts, George E. "Banking Fancies—and the Facts: An Answer to Frederic Howe's Outcry That Wall Street Controls the Banking System of the Country and That the Money Octopus Has Got Us in Its Clutches." *Nation's Business* (October 1920): 34, 36, 38.

Rochester, Stuart I. *American Liberal Disillusionment in the Wake of World War I*. University Park: Pennsylvania State University Press, 1977.

Rodgers, Daniel T. *Atlantic Crossings: Social Politics in a Progressive Age*. Cambridge, Mass.: Belknap Press, 1998.

Rose, William Ganson. *Cleveland: The Making of a City*. Cleveland: World, 1950.

Rosenbloom, Nancy J. "Between Reform and Regulation: The Struggle over Film Censorship in Progressive America, 1909–1922." *Film History* 1 (1987): 307–25.

——. "In Defense of the Moving Pictures: The People's Institute, the National Board of Censorship and the Problem of Leisure in Urban America." *American Studies* 33 (Fall 1992): 41–60.

Ross, Edward Alsworth. *Seventy Years of It: An Autobiography.* New York: Appleton-Century, 1936.
Rudnick, Lois Palken. *Mabel Dodge Luhan: New Woman, New Worlds.* Albuquerque: University of New Mexico Press, 1984.
Ryan, W. Carson. *Studies in Early Graduate Education: The Johns Hopkins, Clark University, University of Chicago.* Bulletin No. 30. New York: Carnegie Foundation for the Advancement of Teaching, 1939.
Rydell, Robert W. *All the World's a Fair: Visions of Empire at American International Expositions, 1876–1916.* Chicago: University of Chicago Press, 1984.
Sayre, Wallace S., and Herbert Kaufman. *Governing New York City: Politics in the Metropolis.* New York: W. W. Norton, 1965.
Schaffer, Ronald. *America in the Great War: The Rise of the War Welfare State.* New York: Oxford University Press, 1991.
———. "The New York City Woman Suffrage Party, 1909–1919." *New York History* 3 (July 1962): 267–87.
Scharf, Lois. "The Women's Movement in Cleveland from 1850." In Van Tassel and Grabowski, *Cleveland*, 67–90.
Schickel, Richard. *D. W. Griffith: An American Life.* New York: Simon and Schuster, 1984.
Schiesl, Martin J. *The Politics of Efficiency: Municipal Administration and Reform in America, 1880–1920.* Berkeley: University of California Press, 1977.
Schlesinger, Arthur M., Jr. *The Coming of the New Deal.* Boston: Houghton Mifflin, 1958.
———. *The Crisis of the Old Order, 1919–1933.* Boston: Houghton Mifflin, 1957.
———. *The Politics of Upheaval.* Boston: Houghton Mifflin, 1960.
Schneider, Dorothy, and Carl J. Schneider. *American Women in the Progressive Era, 1900–1920.* New York: Anchor Books, 1993.
Schwarz, Judith. *Radical Feminists of Heterodoxy: Greenwich Village, 1912–1940.* Lebanon, N.H.: New Victoria, 1982.
Sheean, Vincent. *Dorothy and Red.* Greenwich, Conn.: Fawcett, 1964.
Shotwell, James T. *At the Paris Peace Conference.* New York: Macmillan, 1937.
Sidlo, T. L. "Ohio's First Step in Tax Reform." *Yale Review* 18 (February 1910): 413–17.
Simon, James F. *Independent Journey: The Life of William O. Douglas.* New York: Harper and Row, 1980.
Smith, Charles Sprague. *Working with the People.* New York: A. Wessels, 1904.
Smith, Ernest Ashton. *Allegheny—A Century of Education, 1815–1915.* Meadville: Allegheny College History Company, 1916.
Smith-Rosenberg, Carroll. "The Female World of Love and Ritual: Relations Between Women in Nineteenth Century America." *Signs* 1 (Autumn 1975): 1–29.
Snyder, Charles E. "Unitarianism in Iowa." *Palimpsest* 30 (November 1949): 345–76.
Sochen, June. *The New Woman: Feminism in Greenwich Village, 1910–1920.* New York: Quadrangle Books, 1972.
Stansell, Christine. *American Moderns: Bohemian New York and the Creation of a New Century.* New York: Metropolitan Books, 2000.
Steel, Ronald. *Walter Lippmann and the American Century.* Boston: Little, Brown, 1980.
Steffens, Lincoln. *The Autobiography of Lincoln Steffens.* New York: Harcourt, Brace, 1931.
———. *Lincoln Steffens Speaking.* New York: Harcourt Brace, 1928.
———. "Ohio: A Tale of Two Cities." *McClure's Magazine* 25 (July 1905): 293–311.
———. *The Shame of the Cities.* New York: McClure, Phillips, 1904. Reprint, New York: Sagamore Press, 1957.
———. *The Struggle for Self-Government.* New York: McClure, Phillips, 1906. Reprint, New York: Johnson Reprint, 1968.

Steinson, Barbara J. *American Women's Activism in World War I*. New York: Garland, 1982.
Stevens, Doris. *Jailed for Freedom*. 1920. Freeport, N.Y.: Books for Libraries Press, 1971.
Strum, Philippa. *Louis D. Brandeis: Justice for the People*. Cambridge: Harvard University Press, 1984.
Suman, Michael W. "The Radical Urban Politics of the Progressive Era: An Analysis of the Political Transformation in Cleveland, Ohio, 1875–1909." 2 vols. Ph.D. diss., University of California, 1992.
Swanberg, W. A. *Dreiser*. New York: Charles Scribner's Sons, 1965.
Tannenbaum, Frank. *Osborne of Sing Sing*. Chapel Hill: University of North Carolina Press, 1933.
Tarbell, Ida M. *All in the Day's Work: An Autobiography*. New York: Macmillan, 1939.
Tarr, Joel Arthur. "From City to Suburb: The 'Moral' Influence of Transportation Technology." In *American Urban History*, 2nd ed., edited by Alexander B. Callow Jr., 202–12. New York: Oxford University Press, 1973.
Thompson, Jack M. "James R. Garfield: The Career of a Rooseveltian Progressive, 1895–1916." Ph.D. diss., University of South Carolina, 1958.
Thompson, John A. *Reformers and War: American Progressive Publicists and the First World War*. Cambridge: Cambridge University Press, 1987.
Thorburn, Neil. "A Progressive and the First World War: Frederic C. Howe." *Mid-America* 51 (April 1969): 108–18.
Tobin, Eugene M. *Organize or Perish: America's Independent Progressives, 1913–1933*. Westport, Conn.: Greenwood Press, 1986.
Toll, Seymour I. *Zoned American*. New York: Grossman, 1969.
Tucker, Cynthia Grant. *Prophetic Sisterhood: Liberal Women Ministers of the Frontier, 1880–1930*. Boston: Beacon Press, 1990.
——. *A Woman's Ministry: Mary Collson's Search for Reform as a Unitarian Minister, a Hull House Social Worker, and a Christian Science Practitioner*. Philadelphia: Temple University Press, 1984.
Tugwell, Rexford G. *The Democratic Roosevelt*. Baltimore: Penguin, 1969.
——. *Roosevelt's Revolution*. New York: Macmillan, 1977.
Turner, Florence. *At the Chelsea*. New York: Harcourt Brace Jovanovich, 1987.
United States Commission on Industrial Relations. *Final Report and Testimony*. Washington, D.C.: Government Printing Office, 1916.
United States Department of Agriculture, Agricultural Adjustment Administration. *Agricultural Adjustment: A Report of Administration of the Agricultural Adjustment Act May 1933 to February 1934*. Washington, D.C.: Government Printing Office, 1934.
United States Military Intelligence Reports: Surveillance of Radicals in the United States, 1917–1941. Frederick, Md.: University Publications of America, 1984.
Unofficial Observer [John Franklin Carter]. *The New Dealers*. New York: Literary Guild, 1934.
Urofsky, Melvin L., and David W. Levy, eds. *Letters of Louis D. Brandeis*. 5 vols. Albany: State University of New York Press, 1971–78.
Utlaut, Robert Louis. "The Role of the Chautauqua Movement in the Shaping of Progressive Thought in America at the End of the Nineteenth Century." Ph.D. diss., University of Minnesota, 1972.
Van Tassel, David D. "Introduction: Cleveland and Reform." In Van Tassel and Grabowski, *Cleveland*.

Van Tassel, David D., and John J. Grabowski, eds. *Cleveland: A Tradition of Reform.* Kent: Kent State University Press, 1986.
Vaughn, Stephen. *Holding Fast the Inner Lines: Democracy, Nationalism, and the Committee on Public Information.* Chapel Hill: University of North Carolina Press, 1980.
Villard, Oswald Garrison. *Fighting Years: Memoirs of a Liberal Editor.* New York: Harcourt, Brace, 1939.
Vincent, John Martin. "Herbert B. Adams." In *American Masters of Social Science,* edited by Howard D. Odum, 99–127. Washington, N.Y.: Kennikat Press, 1965.
Vorse, Mary Heaton. *A Footnote to Folly: Reminiscences of Mary Heaton Vorse.* New York: Farrar and Rinehart, 1935.
Vose, Pamela Daly. *The Masters School: 1877/1977: A Retrospective Portrait for the One-Hundredth Anniversary.* Dobbs Ferry, N.Y.: Masters School, 1977.
Walker, Samuel. *In Defense of American Liberties: A History of the ACLU.* New York: Oxford University Press, 1990.
Wallace, Henry Agard. "The Reminiscences of Henry Agard Wallace." Columbia University Oral History Research Office Collection, June 1951.
Walling, William English. "The German Paradise." *Masses* 8 (June 1916): 20.
Warner, Emily Smith, with Hawthorne Daniel. *The Happy Warrior: A Biography of My Father Alfred E. Smith.* Garden City, N.Y.: Doubleday, 1956.
Warner, Hoyt Landon. *Progressivism in Ohio, 1897–1917.* Columbus: Ohio State University Press for Ohio Historical Society, 1964.
Waterhouse, David L. *The Progressive Movement of 1924 and the Development of Interest Group Liberalism.* New York: Garland, 1991.
Weinstein, James. *The Corporate Ideal in the Liberal State: 1900–1918.* Boston: Beacon Press, 1968.
Welter, Rush. *Popular Education and Democratic Thought in America.* New York: Columbia University Press, 1962.
Werner, M. R. *Tammany Hall.* Garden City, N.Y.: Garden City, 1932.
Wesser, Robert F. *A Response to Progressivism: The Democratic Party and New York Politics, 1902–1918.* New York: New York University Press, 1986.
Wetzsteon, Ross. *Republic of Dreams: Greenwich Village, The American Bohemia, 1910–1960.* New York: Simon and Schuster, 2002.
"Where Are the Pre-war Radicals?" *Survey* 55 (February 1, 1926): 556–66.
Whipple, James Beaumont. "Cleveland in Conflict: A Study in Urban Adolescence, 1876–1900." Ph.D. diss., Western Reserve University, 1951.
Whipple, Leon. "A Pilgrim's Progress in Politics." *Survey* 55 (December 1, 1925): 313–14.
White, William Allen. *Masks in a Pageant.* New York: Macmillan, 1928.
Whitlock, Brand. *Forty Years of It.* New York: D. Appleton, 1914.
———. *The Letters and Journal of Brand Whitlock.* Edited by Allan Nevins. 2 vols. New York: D. Appleton-Century, 1936.
Whitman, Alden, ed. *American Reformers.* New York: H. W. Wilson, 1985.
Wiebe, Robert H. *The Search for Order, 1877–1920.* New York: Hill and Wang, 1967.
Williams, David. "The Bureau of Investigation and Its Critics, 1919–1921: The Origins of Federal Political Surveillance." *Journal of American History* 68 (December 1981): 560–79.
Winter, Ella. *And Not to Yield: An Autobiography.* New York: Harcourt, Brace and World, 1963.
Winter, Ella, and Granville Hicks, eds. *The Letters of Lincoln Steffens.* 2 vols. New York: Harcourt, Brace, 1938.

Wittenstein, Kate E. "The Heterodoxy Club and American Feminism, 1912–1930." Ph.D. diss., Boston University, 1989.
Wolfe, Allis Rosenberg. "Women, Consumerism, and the National Consumers League in the Progressive Era, 1900–1923." *Labor History* 16 (Summer 1975): 378–92.
Woolston, Florence Guy. "Marriage Customs and Taboo Among the Early Heterodites." Typescript, 7 pp., 1919. Inez Hays Irwin Papers, Schlesinger Library.
Young, Arthur Nichols. *The Single Tax Movement in the United States.* Princeton: Princeton University Press, 1916.
Young, Dallas M. *Twentieth-Century Experience in Urban Transit: A Study of the Cleveland System.* Cleveland: Press of Western Reserve University, 1960.
Zinn, Howard. *La Guardia in Congress.* New York: W. W. Norton, 1969.

INDEX

Page references in italic type indicate illustrations. Initials FCH refer to Frederic C. Howe and initials MJH refer to Marie Jenney Howe.

AAA. *See* Agricultural Adjustment
    Administration
absenteeism, 225, 226, 294, 298
Academy of Music, 6
Academy of Political Science, 310
ACLU (American Civil Liberties Union),
    304–5, 346n.27, 400
"Acres of Diamonds" (address), 6
Adams, Herbert Baxter
    advice on reform, 50–51
    business investment conversations, 94
    as influence, 28, 32, 101
    Shaw and, 23
    social service activities encouraged by, 54
    summer studies with, 18
    university faculty member, 19, 21
Adamson Act, 237
Addams, Jane, 89, 241, 248, 282, 290, 291
Adler, Felix, 242
adoption, 244–45, 367
AFL (American Federation of Labor), 311
African Americans, 233
Agricultural Adjustment Act, 380
Agricultural Adjustment Administration
    (AAA). *See also* consumers counsel office
    administrators, 381, 406
    consumers counsel role, views of, 387–89
    creation of, 381
    goals, 381, 406, 411–12
    internal conflicts and purge, 393–94, 406–11
agriculture. *See also* Agricultural Adjustment
    Administration (AAA); consumers
    counsel office
    farm labor issues, 406–7
    rural tenancy issues, 422, 423, 425
    socialization programs, 265–66, 273–75,
    312–13, 315, 416–18
Agriculture, Department of, 381, 393, 416, 422
Alden, Timothy, 7–8
All-American Farmer-Labor Co-Operative
    Commission, 313

Allegheny College, 7–16, 242, 421
Allegheny Literary Society, 11
Amalgamated Clothing Workers, 314
American Association for Agricultural Legis-
    lation, 289
American Civil Liberties Union (ACLU),
    304–5, 346n.27, 400
American Commission on Conditions in
    Ireland, 322–23
American Commission to Negotiate Peace, 283
American Committee Against Fascist
    Oppression, 383
American Committee on War Finance, 264
American Commonwealth, 22–23
American Economic Association, 76
American Economic Review reviews, 266–67,
    315–16n.25
American-European Travel Bureau, 377
American Federation of Labor (AFL), 311
American Historical Review reviews, 47
American Institute of Architects, 73
Americanism, 247–48, 305
Americanization Day, 215
Americanization movement, 215–16
American Journal of Sociology reviews, 239n.54,
    274n.75
American League for Civic Improvement
    conventions, 89
American Mercury reviews, 376
"The American Mind" (seminar), 337
American Political Science Review reviews,
    239n.55, 257n.33, 315–16n.25
American Sociological Society, 180
American Union Against Militarism (AUAM),
    248–49, 250, 304
Anglo-Irish War, 322
*Annals of the American Academy of Political
    and Social Science*
    articles, 32, 272, 348, 416
    book reviews, 144, 239n.54, 257n.33
Anthony, Susan B., 38, 95

Anti-Preparedness Committee, 248–49
anti-Semitism, 305n.4, 342
"An Anti-Suffrage Monologue" (MJH), 168–69
antiwar movements, 246–47, 248–52, 256
Appelbaum, Misha, 242
Appleby, Paul, 393, 423, 424, 429, 430
apprehensive nationalism, 215
The Arena, 111, 117, 121
artists colonies, 243
Assembly Herald, 18
assessments, tax, 134–36
Associated Charities of Cleveland, 130
Association for an Equitable Federal Income Tax, 236
Atlantic Monthly, 76, 104, 112n.57
AUAM (American Union Against Militarism), 248–49, 250, 304
autobiographies of FCH. See *The Confessions of a Reformer* (FCH)
automobiles, 81, 83, 140

Bacon, Peggy, 413
Baker, Newton
 as ambassador candidate, 228
 associates of, 46n.7
 background and career, 26, 57–58
 as city solicitor, 135
 Depression, correspondence during, 378, 416
 depression, correspondence on, 422
 FCH friendship with, 61, 91, 92, 164–65, 241, 420
 fraternity chapter memberships, 12–13
 Goodrich House residence, 58–59
 Howes' move to New York, 138–39
 Johnson's, Tom, relationship with, 80, 84n.45
 marriage, 61
 on MJH's health, 99n.25, 166n.7
 People's Institute recommendations, 83
 political involvement, 61
 presidential candidate choice (1912), 163
 during prosperity decade (1920s), 302
 railroad reforms, 269
 Stevenson accusations and response, 291
 Wilson administration lobbying correspondence to, 203
 Wilson presidential campaigns and appointments of, 203
Baker, Ray Stannard, 282, 356
Baldwin, Henry de Forest, 183, 184, 192, 211
Baldwin, Roger, 291, 304, 431, 444
Baldwin University Law School, 102
Baltimore American, 20

Banking for Service (FCH), 314
banks and banking
 cooperative, 313–14
 credit unions, 393, 420
 immigration reform and, 221
 wealth acquisition and, 93
 writings on, 316, 431
banned books, 290
Barrows, Alice, 402–3
Barton, Dante, 231, 232, 241, 252, 261
Barton, James L., 283–84
Baruch, Bernard, 247
Beacon Journal reviews, 392
Bean, Louis, 383, 388
Beer and Skittles Club, 49, 50
Beethoven Musical Society, 187
Belgium, 117, 118
Benedict XV, Pope, 278
Bennet, William S., 222–26
Berber, Henry Hervey, 38
"Bernard Shaw and *Back to Methuselah*" (seminar), 338
"Best Governed Community in the World" (FCH), 77n.27
Bethel Associated Charities (*later* Cleveland Associated Charities), 54, 59–61, 97
Big Consolidated (Big Con), 70
The Birth of a Nation (movie), 191–92
Black, Morris, 48–50, 57, 73
Black and Tans, 322
Blaisdell, Thomas C., Jr., 383, 384, 386, 388, 390, 412
Board of Education, 194–95
Board of Estimate, 193, 194, 196
Board of Motion Picture Censorship of New York, 188–89, 192
Board of Sinking Fund Trustees, 79
Boissevain, Eugene, 371
Bolsheviks, 277, 290, 295–96, 304
bombs, 293
Book and Thimble Club, 96
Bookman reviews, 239n.54, 257n.33, 266
books, banned, 290
Borglum, Gutzon, 210, 330, 342
bossism, 64, 82, 105, 106–7, 108, 141
Boston Transcript reviews, 374
Bourne, Jonathan, 150, 151, 153–54, 158
Bowman, Isaiah, 422
Boyce, Neith, 364
boycotts, 96
boys clubs, 56
Brailsford, H. N., 256
Brand, Charles J., 383, 389, 393, 394
Brandeis, Louis, 129, 154, 162–63, 232

bread prices, 389
"Breaking into the Human Race" (meeting theme), 169
bribery, 72–73, 82
Britain
  business trips to, 97
  city research, 24, 76–77, 114–16, 198–99, 238
  imperialism and, 276
  Ireland's independence, 321–24
  Middle East foreign policies, 283, 286
  municipal ownership research, 98
The British City (FCH), 114–16
British Labour Party, 316
The Brotherhood of Locomotive Engineers Co-operative National Bank of Cleveland, Ohio, 313
The Brotherhood of Railroad Trainmen, 311
Broun, Heywood, 337
Brown, Louise Fargo, 338
Brownell, William Crary, 105, 272–73
Bruere, Robert, 402, 403
Brunner, Arnold R., 74
Bryan, William Jennings, 50, 66, 80
Bryce, James, 22–23
Buck, Florence, 86
Bulletin (publication), 52, 53
Bulwinkle, Alfred L., 401
Bureau of Corporations, 100, 129
Bureau of Employment, 271
Bureau of Immigration, 212–13
Bureau of Municipal Research, 141
Bureau of Naturalization, 215
Burner, David, 327–28n.47
Burnham, Daniel H., 74
Burton, Theodore, 82
Byrns, Joseph M., 294

CAB (Consumer Advisory Board), 384, 399
Cadwallader, Starr, 56, 58
Calthrop, S. R., 38
Caminetti, Anthony, 212–13, 221, 292, 293, 297, 298, 299
Campus (newspaper), 11, 13, 14, 15
capital punishment, 196, 197
Carlsbad water cures, 98–99
Carnegie, Andrew, 182
Carnegie Hall public meetings, 159–60
Carranza, Venustiano, 227
Carrère, John M., 74
Carter, George, 146
Carter, John Franklin, 383
Caruso, Enrico, 214
Cary, George Lovell, 38
Casino, 335

Castle Garden immigration reception center, 140
Catholic World reviews, 199n.45
Catt, Carrie Chapman, 168, 179, 247, 277, 369
censorship, entertainment, 183, 187–89, 190–91
Century Association, 192–93
Century Magazine, 104
charitable organizations, 54, 59–61, 97, 130
Charity Organization Society, 54
Charles Scribner's Sons, 104, 105
Chase, Stuart, 356
Chautauqua Institution, 18, 28, 398
Chelsea Hotel, 164
Cheney and Baker Cups, 242
children
  adoption of, 244–45, 367
  crime and, 75, 108, 109, 114n.1
  education and recreation programs for, 186–87
  employment conditions, 96–97, 108, 130, 226–27
  hospital conditions, 97
  urban play areas for, 75
Children's Emancipation Day (pamphlet), 227
Childs, Marquis, 417
China, 228
Christensen, Parley, 321n.35
Christgau, Victor, 407, 408
Christian Century, 348
Christian Union, 20
Citizen's Municipal Committee, 195–96
Citizen's Union, 195
The City: The Hope for Democracy (FCH)
  articles supporting, 114
  The British City compared to, 116
  editor for, 105
  influences on, 24
  legacy, 443–44
  publisher for, 104
  railroads as monopolies, 267
  reform proposals in, 55n.29, 85, 105–11
  reviews, 111–12
  theory and audience development for, 77
The City (Ely), 103
City Club of New York, 180, 193, 195
city council positions, 49–50, 65–78, 78–79
"The City for the People" (FCH), 95
"The City of Cleveland in Relation to the Street Railway Question" (FCH), 52
City Vigilance League, 33
Civic Club of New York, 233, 251n.13, 306
civil liberties, 300–301, 304–5, 306
civil rights, 439
Civil Service reform movement, 217

Clark, Walter, 309
class structure, 82, 84, 106, 117, 142, 440–42. *See also* privilege
Clemens, Samuel L., 129
Clemson, John D., 4
Cleveland, Ohio
   charitable organizations, 54
   city council, 65–79
   description overview, 42
   ethnic demographics, 65
   homes in, 44, 56–57, 58–59, 91, 92
   industry and economic development, 43, 58, 65
   mayoral campaigns, 53, 66, 67–70, 78, 79, 82, 134, 135
   move to, 44
   natural monopolies and utilities issues, 52–53, 71–73, 133–34
   political reform leagues in, 51–54, 65
   population statistics, 43, 63, 65
   settlement houses, 54–59
   social clubs, 49
   social life, 48–49
   suffrage campaigns, 96n.19
   tax/land assessment boards, 134–36
   urban renewal and development programs, 73–75
"Cleveland—A City Finding Itself" (FCH), 77
Cleveland Associated Charities (*formerly* Bethel Associated Charities), 54, 59–61, 97
Cleveland Board of Public Service, 97
Cleveland City Railway Company, 52
Cleveland Council of Sociology, 59
Cleveland Electric Railway Company (ConCon), 52, 70, 82–83, 133–34
Cleveland Law School, 102–3
Cleveland-Marshall College of Law, 102
Cleveland News, 125–26
Cleveland Plain Dealer, 79, 91, 138, 144
C & O Canal, 397
Colby, Bainbridge, 235
Colcord, Lincoln, 295
College Corps of Cadets, 10
College of the City of New York, 204
Collier, John, 183, 188
Colliers (magazine), 172
Columbian Exposition, 73–74
Commerce and Labor, Department of, 100
Commissioner of Immigration. *See also* Ellis Island
   alien radical deportations, 297
   colleagues and supervisors, 212–13
   congressional investigation, 222–26
   detainment reforms, 213–14, 220
   duties of, 209, 217
   employee conditions and reforms, 216–17, 218
   enemy alien internment, 262–63, 291–92
   exclusion policies, 218–19
   food contractor controversies, 221–22
   goals of, 213
   government action and favors, 217
   labor union radicals, detention and deportation, 292–93
   political involvement of, 210
   portraits of, *208*
   position nomination and approval, 201–7
   reflections on job position, 209, 219
   removal proceedings, 294
   resignation, 297
   salary, 264n.49
   transportation reforms, 220–21
   wartime policies and, 249
   writing during, 237–41
Commissioner of Welfare campaign, 380
Commission on Industrial Relations, 229–30
Commission on Public Ownership of Public Utilities, 79–80
Committee for Federal Ownership of the Railroads, 237, 270
Committee for Immigrants in America, 215
Committee for the Nation, 401
Committee of Fifteen, 325
Committee of Forty-Eight, 318–21, 324
Committee of One Thousand of the National Committee for Constructive Immigration Legislation, 306n.7
Committee on Banking and Credit, 313
Committee on Industrial Relations, 215, 229–32, 316
Committee on Organization, 325
Committee on Public Information, 287–88
Committee on Unemployment and Relief, 233–34
Commons, John R., 59, 229, 230, 311
communists, 393. *See also* Red Scare
communist sympathizers, 340, 341, 344, 394, 399. *See also* Red Scare
concerts, 187
ConCon (Cleveland Electric Railway Company), 52, 70, 82–83, 133–34
Conference for Progressive Political Action (CPPA), 324–29, 333, 400
Conference on Democratic Control of the Railroads, 309, 310
The Confessions of a Monopolist (FCH), 5n1, 119–21
The Confessions of a Reformer (FCH)
   Bethel and Goodrich associations, 60–61

INDEX   471

crime and playgrounds, 75
dedication, 362, 371
disillusionment, 44–45
Flynn in, 92n.11
Ireland and Irish relationships, 322
marriage and wife, 362, 365–66
personal references in, 432
printings of, 1n.1
reviews, 351–55
writing of, overview, 348–51
confidentiality, correspondence, 372
congressional investigations, 222–26, 401–5
Congressional Union for Woman Suffrage, 170–71
Conklin, E. G., 338
Conneaut Water Works, 94
Conrad, David Eugene, 393, 411
Constitutional Amendments committee, 242
"The Constitution and Public Opinion" (FCH), 240
Consumer Advisory Board (CAB), 384, 399
consumers counsel office (Agricultural Adjustment Administration)
    AAA internal relationship issues, 393–94
    AAA purge and resignations, 408–12
    business sector attacks on, 399
    challenges, 413
    consumers counsel appointment, 382–83
    creation of, 381
    fair pricing issues, 389–90
    mission, 387
    post-purge operations, 412n.15
    public relations, 390–93
    staff, 384–86
    trade agreements division of, 386, 388–89
    writings for, 393
Consumers Guide (newspaper), 391–92, 412
Consumers League of Ohio, 56, 130
Conwell, Russell, 6
Cooke, Marjorie Benton, 175
Cooking Club, 37–38
Cooley, Harris R., 114
Coolidge, Calvin, 331
Cooperative Movement in Sweden (Childs), 417
cooperatives, 117, 119, 273–75, 312–15, 416–18, 438
corporate reform, 76, 100, 129
correspondence confidentiality, 372
corruption, 63, 68, 72–73, 82, 131–32
Cosmopolitan, 77, 104
Cosmos Club, 242, 384, 397
Costigan, Mabel, 325n.43
cotton contracts, 406–7
Couper, Mildred, 342–43

Coyle, David Cushman, 402
CPPA (Conference for Progressive Political Action), 324–29, 333, 400
Crane, Charles, 152, 277
Crane, Frank, 224
Crawford, Bill, 49
Crawford Democrat, 7
Creating a Democratic Public (Mattson), 441–42
credit, 313–14, 393, 420
Creel, George, 241–42, 259, 269, 281–82, 287–88
crime, 63, 75, 109
Croly, Herbert, 74, 112n.58
Croton-on-Hudson homes, 243–44
Crowell, T. Y., 46
Crowell Library of Economics and Politics (Ely, ed.), 46
Cummins-Esch bill, 311–12
Current History reviews, 418

dairy industry, 431
Dana, Harry W., 338
dancing clubs and parties, 165
Daniels, Cynthia, 370
Daniels, Josephus, 269
Davidson, Jo, 332–33
Davis, Chester, 394, 406, 407–8, 408–11, 412n.15
Davis, John, 331
death penalty, 196
debates, 295
Debs, Eugene, 321
decentralization, 108, 274
De Mille, Agnes, 175
De Mille, Anna George, 175
democracy
    cooperative movement as model of, 417–18
    European, 117–19
    imperialism vs., 229
    limitations of, 439–40
    single tax philosophies and, 122
    views of, 441–42
    Wisconsin idea of, 180
Democratic National Committee and Party, 378, 379–80
Democrats
    childhood view of, 6
    county platform program, 136–37
    platforms of, 123
    state senate effectiveness of, 133
    state senate organization of, 123–24, 129–30
Denmark
    agricultural models in, 265, 315, 416–18, 438
    city research, 117, 118, 119
    poverty extermination, 198

Denmark: A Cooperative Commonwealth (FCH), 315
Denmark: The Cooperative Way (FCH), 417
deportation
  of alien radicals, 291–92, 297, 298, 299, 306
  immigration exclusion policies and, 218–19
  of labor union radicals, 292–93
  wartime policies of, 218
Derber, Milton, 314n.24
Deshon, Florence, 166
Detroit, Michigan, 64
Dewey, John, 380
Dewey, Mrs. John, 170
Dial reviews, 47, 120, 239n.54, 274n.75
Dilling, Elizabeth, 399–401
direct primaries, 108n.46, 130, 134, 147
dissent as subversive behavior, 287–93
dissertations, 22, 27, 28, 46
divorce, 371
Dix, John A., Jr., 147
Dodge, Mabel, 165–66, 217, 363
Doherty, C. J., 282
Dorr, Rheta Childe, 174
Doty, Ed, 123, 133
Dreiser, Theodore, 165
Dressler, Marie, 169
Du Bois, W. E. B., *170*, 233, 439
Dunbar, Olivia Howard, 351
Duncan, Isadora, 217, 243
Duncan, Maria-Theresa, 343
Düsseldorf (Germany), 118

Easley, Ralph W., 79, 193–94, 230
Eastman, Crystal, 174, 247, 249
Eastman, Max, 166–67, 172, 174, 189–90, 363n.4
East Ohio Gas Company, 72
Edgemoor (home), 335
education, 182–87, 189, 194–95
Education Dramatic League, 187
Eisenhower, Dwight D., 424
electricity, 73, 359
Eliot, Thomas H., 386
Ellis Island. *See also* Commissioner of Immigration
  detention conditions and reforms, 213–14
  employees at, 216–17, 218
  food contractor controversies, 221–22
  as homeless/unemployment shelter, 216
  immigrant behavior comparisons on, 216
  immigrant statistics at, 213
  as immigration operations center, 140
  investigations at, 297–98
  as jail for convicts and illegal aliens, 219–20
  labor union radicals detained on, 292–93
  reputation, 213
  visits to, 206, 207
  wartime conditions and deportation restrictions, 218
  wartime enemy alien internments at, 262–63, 291
Elmira Reformatory, 20n.3
Ely, Richard T.
  agricultural legislation association membership invitation, 289–90
  books, 23, 46
  on FCH's post-graduate plans, 30
  FCH's relationship with, 23, 27, 28, 30, 32, 103
  social movement involvement of, 22, 54, 59
  as university faculty member, 18, 19, 21–22
  wartime positions and accusations, 288–89
employment issues
  charity and, 60
  child labor, 96–97, 108, 130, 226–27
  commissions/committees addressing, 229–34
  postwar expectations and reconstruction plans, 271–72
  unemployment, 131, 196–98, 216, 233–34
  women and, 96–97
  work day hours, 237
enemy aliens, 262–63, 292
Engineering News, 112n.58
Engineers, 313–14
England. *See* Britain
Espionage Act, 288
Ethical Culture Society, 242
"Eugene O'Neill and *The Hairy Ape*" (seminar), 338
European Cities at Work (FCH), 198–99
European research and writings, 115–19, 198–99, 238. *See also specific European countries*
European travels
  city research, 76, 119, 158
  Committee on Public Information appointment, 282
  Long Arm business trips, 97
  Nazi youth and antifascist movements, 383
  Paris homes, 369
  peace conferences, 282–83
  social reform research, 98
  university summer studies, 27
  water cures, 98–99
"Evenings" (Dodge entertainment gatherings), 165–66
Ezekiel, Mordecai, 381–82, 383

Fabian socialism, 118
Fairfax County home, Virginia, 397

Fairlie, John, 199
Fantastic Toe Club, 165
Farley, "Honest John," 53, 65
Farley, James, 378, 379, 380
Farm and Home Hour, 391
farm colonies, 265–66, 273–75
Farmer Labor Party, 325
farmers, as social class, 441, 442
farm issues and programs. *See* Agricultural Adjustment Administration; agriculture
Farm Tenancy Act, 423
fascism, 383, 417, 420
favoritism, 131
fear, referendums on, 240
Federal Credit Union Act, 393n.38
federal ownership, 237, 267–70, 303, 307–12
Federal Plan, 51
"The Federal Revenues and the Income Tax" (FCH), 32
Feisal, Prince of Iraq, 282
Fels, Joseph, 129, 179
Fels, Mary, 175, 179n.1
Fels Fund Commission, 179, 236, 269
feminism. *See also* suffrage, woman
  conspiracy theories, 364
  definition and components of, 173
  marriage views and, 38, 90–91, 166, 364–66
  mass meetings for, 169
  New York movement, 173–74
  women's clubs for, 174–78, 233n.42, 243, 367, 395, 396
feudalism, 142
A Fierce Discontent (McGerr), 440–41
The Fight (play), 189
"Fighting Twenty-fifth," 168
Finley, John H., 18, 26n.11, 102, 207, 420, 421
firehouses, 7
First Presbyterian (Old Stone) Church, 55
Fisher, Robert, 183, 184
Flynn, Elizabeth Gurley
  Dodge salon involvement, 166
  feminist women's clubs of, 174, 175, 177, 178
  Johnson and Howes meeting with, 80, 92
  as radical subversive, 298, 299, 400
  as social activist, 92
Folk, Joseph W., 77
food contractor controversies, 221–22
"Footlights" (theatrical group), 39
Foraker, Joseph Benson, 43
Foran, Martin, 58
For City and State, 149–50
Ford, Anne Paddock, 339
Ford, Henry Jones, 102, 249–50
foreign policy
  Mediterranean/Near East, 280, 281, 283–85

Mexico, 227–28, 250
Russia, 276–77, 283, 295–96
self-determination issues, 279–80, 283, 286, 321–22
war aims and peace settlements, 277–80, 282–83
wartime preparedness, 247–52, 256, 262
writings on, 241, 280
Fortas, Abe, 386
For the Music League, 187
Foster, William Z., 328
Fourteen Points address, 279, 286
France, 283, 285
franchises, 52, 67, 71, 82, 107, 120, 124–25
franchise taxes, 76, 124, 130
Frank, Jerome
  AAA internal conflict and, 393, 394
  as AAA legal counsel, 387
  AAA purge and dismissal of, 408
  on consumer counsel appointments and staffing, 382, 383, 384, 385
  Fairfax County visits, 397
  farm labor disputes, 407–8
  New Deal recruit, 386
Frankfurter, Felix, 146, 147
Franklin, Jay, 390
Frederic C. Howe (Liberty ship), 431n.58
"Frederic C. Howe: Gentleman" (Crane), 224
"Fredric W. Howe—Dead in 60th Year," poem based on, 421
freedom of press/speech, 189–90, 320
Freeman, Elizabeth, *170*
Freeman reviews, 315n.25
French Creek canal, 7
Fuchs, Adele, 367, 368, 369

Gaitlin, Flora, *170*
Gale, Zona, 329
"Galsworthy and *Strife*" (seminar), 338
Gardner, Gilson, 151, 162
Garfield, Garfield, Howe and Westenhaver, 46, 125–26
Garfield, Garfield and Howe, 45–46, 99
Garfield, Harry A.
  college presidency lobbying to, 204
  FCH's friendship with, 420
  at FCH wedding, 91
  Howes' friendship with, 241
  law firm of, 44–48, 50, 125–26
  loneliness and European travels correspondence to, 97
  manufacturing companies owned by, 93
  philosophy of life correspondence to, 101–2
  political reform leagues of, 51–52

Garfield, Harry A. (*continued*)
  presidential candidate choice (1912), 163
  as Princeton University professor of politics, 100–101, 102
  state senate race correspondence to, 123
  war and peace correspondence to, 431
  as Williams College president, 102
Garfield, James R.
  Cleveland's mayoral election, interest in, 82
  European correspondence to, 97
  FCH's Progressivism opinions shared with, 129
  Howes' friendship with, 241
  on immigration commissioner appointment, 207–8
  law firm of, 44–48, 49, 125–26
  MJH, correspondence about, 98
  political reform needs, 65
  presidential candidate choice (1912), 163
  as presidential candidate contender, 151
  1898 presidential election, 50n.20
  on public reaction to ordinance pamphlet, 52
  Roosevelt, Theodore, appointments, 99–100
Garfield, Lucretia, 111
Garfield and Garfield, 44–45
Gary, Elbert H. (Gary Committee), 233–34
gas companies, 72
Gaynor, William J., 141
General Federation of Women's Clubs, 390, 391
George, Henry, 22, 66, 69, 139, 398. *See also* Georgism
George, Henry, Jr., 129
George, Lloyd, 287, 324
George Sand: The Search for Love (MJH), 364, 370, 373–76
Georgism
  articles on, 399
  as Depression solution, 348
  foundations supporting, 399
  as social/political/economic remedy, 107, 143, 437, 438
  supporters of, 22, 66, 69, 121–22, 380
German enemy aliens, 262–63, 291
Germany
  antifascist oppression committees, 383
  Carlsbad visit and water cures, 98–99
  city studies, 117–19, 198–99, 238
  imperialism and, 276
  Nazi youth movement, 383
  postwar immigration and land reform articles, 289
  postwar pro-German accusations, 287–90
  submarine crisis, 227
  unemployment alternatives of, 198
  writings on, 253–55
Gilman, Charlotte Perkins, 88, 170, 174, 190, 247, 362
Gilman, Daniel Coit, 19
Gilman, George Houghton, 362
Giovannitti, Arturo, 170
Gitlow, Benjamin, 186
Glaspell, Susan, 174
Golden Rule Hall speech, 129
"Golden Rule" policy, 114n.1
Goldman, Emma, 80, 177, 298, 299, 400
Goldman, Eric, 302
Gompers, Samuel, 311
Goodnow, Frank, 194
Goodrich House, 54–59, 61, 79, 214
Gordon, Eleanor, 86
Gordon, Fred G. R., 340
Gorman, Herbert, 376
graft, 72, 132
Grand Chapter, 13
The Gray Dawn (film), 373
Great Depression, 348, 370, 377–78, 416
"Great Empire by the Lakes" (FCH), 77n.27, 104
Green, William, 325
Griffith, D. W., 191
Group Plan, 74, 110, 114
guilts, as lecture theme, 242

Hagedorn, Herman, 344
Hall, Bolton, 129, 179, 416
Hanna, Marcus Alonzo, 43, 51, 53, 70, 91, 99, 120
Hansen, Ole, 293
Hapgood, Hutchins, 363–65
Hard, William, 170
Harding, Warren G., 302
Hardwick, Thomas, 293
Harmon home, New York, 243–44, 377, 384, 395–96, 397
Harper's Weekly, 94, 104
Harriman, Florence, 230
Hart, Bushnell, 295
Haskins, Charles Homer, 26n.11
Hauser, Elizabeth, 95, 96n.19, 138, 139
Hays, Arthur Garfield, 319
Hazen, Charles D., 26n.11
HCL (high cost of living), 264–65
Hearst, William Randolph, 141, 195
Hebrew Orphan Asylum, 214
hecklers, 83
Heinz's pickles, 20

Henry Street group, 248, 249
Heterodoxy, 174–78, 233n.42, 243, 367, 395, 396
Hewitt, Abram S., 182
Hibbard, B. H., 266–67
Higham, John, 215
high cost of living (HCL), 264–65
The High Cost of Living (FCH), 264–67, 289
Hillman, Sidney, 325
Hillquit, Morris, 326
Hiram House, 55
Hiss, Alger, 386, 407, 408, 413
"A History of the Internal Revenue System" (FCH), 27
Hobson, J. A., 256
Hoffendahl, Julie Regula, 36
Hofstadter, Richard, 443
Holmes, John Haynes, 295
Home Missions Council, 214
home rule, 71, 85, 108, 122–23, 241
Homestead, Hot Springs, 48
Hoover, Calvin B., 390, 412n.15
Hoover, Herbert, 321
Hoover, J. Edgar, 305, 306, 320
Hopkins, John A. H., 172, 318–19
hospitals and sanitariums, 97
House, Edward M.
  Ford's peace ship and, 250
  foreign policy correspondence to, 281, 282–83, 283–85, 286
  immigration commissioner appointment, 207
  war aims and peace settlement groups, 278, 279
  as Wilson administration contact, 202, 204, 210
House Committee on Immigration and Naturalization, 224, 226, 244–45, 297–98
House Committee on Interstate and Foreign Commerce, 401
House Ways and Means Committee, 236
housing issues
  land values affecting, 109
  settlement movement and, 54–59, 61, 79, 214, 248
  urban conditions of, 63
Howe, Andrew Jackson, 4, 5n.1, 6–7, 48
Howe, Frederic C. *See also related topics*
  academic career, overview, 434–35
  aspirations, early, 17, 18, 30
  birth and childhood, 4–7
  career, overview, 433–35
  death and burial, 431
  education, 7–16, 18–29, 32, 35, 36, 41
  employment, early, 17–18, 20, 30–32
  estate, 431
  health, 419, 422, 433
  homes, list overview, 94
  honorary degrees, 242
  illustrated sketches of, *414*, *415*
  investments, 93–94, 264n.49
  legacy, overview, 1–3
  letters and papers, survival of, 432
  life introspection, 416
  life philosophies, 102, 435
  marriage (*see* marriage of FCH and MJH)
  personality descriptions, 132, 341, 344, 364, 371–72, 413–15, *414*, 444
  political career, overview, 434
  political philosophies, 226, 241, 307, 444
  portraits, 62, 68, *208*
  as radical subversive, description, 400
  reform philosophies, 1, 209, 357–48, 435–40
  religion, 5, 6, 242
  retirement plans, 431
  social life, overview, 432
  wealth acquisition philosophies, 92–93
  women's roles, views on, 39–40, 94–95
  writings, overview, 3, 416, 419
Howe, Gertrude Isabel, 4, 48
Howe, Jane (Clemson), 4, 5, 48
Howe, Josephine, 4
Howe, Louis, 378, 379, 382
Howe, Marian, 4
Howe, Marie Jenney
  as assistant editor to husband, 126
  on autobiography inclusion, 362
  background, 36
  career as reformer, overview, 3
  charitable organization board memberships, 54, 97
  Cleveland reform opportunities, 137
  Cleveland social life of, 92
  club leadership, 37–38
  death, 370, 371, 396
  description, 166–67, 364
  Des Moines trip, 97–98
  education, 37, 38, 86
  feminism and, 173–74
  in Hapgood autobiography, 364–65
  on Harmon life, 395
  health, 97, 98–99, 166, 177, 366, 368, 395–96
  husband's autobiography critique, 362
  on husband's personality, 371
  immigrant arrest cases, 220
  La Follette presidential campaign, 332
  letters, survival of, 396–97
  on letter writing confidentiality, 372
  marriage (*see* marriage of FCH and MJH)

Howe, Marie Jenney (*continued*)
   New York social life, 164–66, 243
   ordination and ministry work, 86–89, *87*, 90
   in Paris, 369
   political party memberships, 247
   as proof-reader, 272–73
   during prosperity decade (1920s), 368–69
   publications of, 89n.5
   radio censorship, 391
   Steffens's correspondence to, 353–54, 362, 372–73
   Steffens's friendship with, 165, 243, 368, 369, 371
   as subversive radical, 294, 305
   suffrage movement, 38, 89, 95–96, 167–73, *170*
   wartime activities, 247, 250
   on Washington, D. C., 384, 395
   women's club memberships, 174–78, 233n.42, 243, 367, 395, 396
   writings, 197, 364, 370, 372–74
"How the German City Cares for Its People" (FCH), 180
Hudgins and Dumas, 222
Huebsch, B. W., 346n.27
Huerta, Victoriano, 227
Hughes, Charles Evans, 171
Humanitarian (magazine), 243
Humanitarian Cult, 242
Hurst, Fannie, 172
Hylan, John F., 236
hyphenated Americans, 247, 252

Ickes, Harold, 157n.35, 378
immigrants
   Addams on urban art of, 89
   arrival statistics, 213
   assimilation and naturalization efforts, 214, 215
   attitudes toward, 213, 214–15, 218
   Cleveland demographics of, 65
   comparisons between, 216
   educational institutions assisting, 183, 209
   exclusion policies toward, 218–19
   FCH's assistance to family of, 244–45
   housing conditions of, 63
   New York City reception operations for, 140 (*see also* Commissioner of Immigration; Ellis Island)
   social settlement movement and, 54–55
   transportation conditions, 220–21
   wartime conditions and deportation restrictions, 218
   Wilson's wartime view of, 249
immigration. *See also* Commissioner of Immigration; Ellis Island; immigrants
   organizations supporting government reform, 306–7n.7
   transportation profits from, 220–21
   writings on, 241, 289, 306–7n.7
immigration laws, 218, 221
immigration reception centers, 140. *See also* Ellis Island
imperialism
   as cause of war, 255–57, 281, 287
   peace negotiations and, 286
   in Philippines, 429–30
   as presidential campaign issue, 229, 258, 331
Independent reviews, 239, 266
individualism, 117, 198, 238, 398
Industrial Defense Association, 305
Industrial Workers of the World (IWW), 292, 293, 304
industry. *See also* monopolies
   committees investigating, 215, 229–323, 316
   consumer advocacy *vs.*, 399
   corporate reform in, 76, 100, 129
   dairy, 431
   and economic development of Cleveland, 43, 58, 65
Information and Education Service, 272
inheritance taxes, 236
Inquiry, the, 278
Insurgents Club, 159–60
internal revenue system, 22, 27, 32, 46–47, 75–76, 204. *See also* taxation
International Lecture Association of Chicago, 94
"International Relations" (seminar), 337
Interstate Commerce Commission, 267, 308, 311
The Intimate Journal of George Sand (MJH), 370n.22, 376
investments, foreign, 348
Iowa Sisterhood [Sisters], 86, 89, 90, 363
Ireland, independence of, 321–24
Irish, East Side, 34–35
Irwin, Inez Haynes, 174, 175, 177–78, 371, 396
Irwin, Will, *170*, 172n.17
Isadora Duncan School of Dancing and Body Development, 343
IWW (Industrial Workers of the World), 292, 293, 304

Jackson, Gardner "Pat"
   on Blaisdell, 384
   consumers council appointment, 384–85, 386, 388

Davis's plans for consumer counsel, 406
farm labor disputes, 407, 408
FCH dismissal and resignation of, 409, 410–11
on FCH relationship with Taylor, 397
on FCH writing, 417, 418n.24
radicalism accusations, 393
Jacobi, Paula, 177
Jakobi, Paula, *170*
Japan, 228
Jenney, Alexander, 36
Jenney, Edwin, 37
Jenney, Edwin Sherman, 36
Jenney, Julie Regula, 36, 37
Jenney, Marie Hoffendahl. *See* Howe, Marie Jenney
Jenney, Marie Regula, 36–37
Jenney, William, 36
Jerry (bartender), 34
Jewish residents, and urban renewal controversies, 75n.22
Johns Hopkins University
  academic record, 27–28
  course load at, 21
  dissertations, 27
  evaluations of, 26, 28–29
  faculty, 19, 21–22
  financial difficulties and adjustment, 19–21
  graduate students at, 26
  mottos of, 26
  reputation and call statement, 18–19
  summer studies, 27, 28
  visiting lecturers, 22–26
Johnson, Albert, 298
Johnson, Grace, 175, 233n.43
Johnson, Hiram, 162, 321
Johnson, James Weldon, 175, 233
Johnson, Tom
  autobiography of, 95
  background, 66–67
  Baker appointments, 61
  brain trust associates of, 80
  as city council speaker, 59
  city planning and renewal efforts, 73–74
  congressional campaign strategies, 83
  death and burial, 139
  FCH's friendship with, 80, 84, 92
  FCH's political partnership with, 71, 77, 79–82, 83–85, 122, 136
  FCH's *The City* and, 111
  fictional characters modeled after, 119
  Flynn meeting, 92
  gubernatorial campaigns, 84
  Howes' move to New York, 138

La Follette meeting with, 148
marriage discussion in autobiography, 362
mayoral campaigns and platforms, 66, 67–70, 78, 79, 82, 134, 135
price of reform theories, 78. 70
senate bills, support of, 124, 130
single-tax commission member, 179
social life of, 80–81
street railway issues, 70–71, 134
suffrage views, 96
Johnston, Mercer, 358
Johnston, Robert D., 440, 443
Johnston, William H., 325, 329
Jones, Ellis O., *170*
Jones, Samuel "Golden Rule," 64, 76
Joseph Fels Fund Commission, 179, 236, 269
"Joseph W. Folk" (FCH), 77
Journal of Commerce, 411
Journal of the Gilded Age and Progressive Era, 440
judges, view of, 127
Juliette (prostitute), 223
Justice, Department of, 299, 300, 305, 307, 320
"Justice to Russia" (protest meeting), 295–96
juvenile justice, 75, 108, 109, 197

Kaldron (college annual), 11, 14, 15
Keating, Edward, 308n.10, 325
Keating-Owen child labor law, 226
Keller, Helen, 170, 204
Kellogg, Arthur, 342
Kellogg, Paul, 248, 348, 354–55, 391, 421, 444
Kent, William, 152, 153, 307
Kiefer, Daniel, 122, 179, 263, 437
Kinley, David, 26n.11
Kirchwey, Freda, 175, 178
Kitchin, Claude, 236, 264
Kneeland, Hildegard, 402, 403
Kohler, Fred, 114
Kolko, Gabriel, 143
Krock, Arthur, 404

labor. *See also* employment issues; labor unions
  commissions supporting reform, 215, 229–32, 316
  philosophies on, 436
  as social class, 442
Labor (newspaper), 308, 310, 311, 327
Labor, Department of, 212, 271–72
labor parties, 316–18
Labor Readjustment, 272
labor unions
  committees investigating, 229
  for cooperatives, 313–14

labor unions (continued)
  political parties of, 316
  progressives conference participation of, 324–25
  railroad ownership issues, 311
  strikes, 133, 237, 267
  subversive actions of, 292–93
"Labour and the New Social Order" (British Labour Party), 316
La Follette, Fola
  father's biography proposal, 418–19
  FCH correspondence from Philippines, 427, 430
  FCH's friendship with, 167, 241, 420, 421
  MJH book dedication to, 370n.22, 376
  MJH correspondence to, 268, 367, 372, 379, 384, 395–96
  MJH's friendship with, 148, 167, 241
  women's club memberships, 174
La Follette, Mary, 161
La Follette, Robert, Jr. "Bob," 329, 332, 420
La Follette, Robert, Sr. "Fighting Bob"
  background, 147–48
  FCH's relationship with, 148–49, 158–59, 162, 244
  on immigration commissioner appointment, 207
  income tax rates on wealthy, 236
  Plumb Plan support, 311–12
  as presidential candidate contender, 152, 159–63, 181, 321, 329–31, 350
  progressive organization affiliations, 149–52, 156–57, 158
  Progressives of Congress meetings, 328
  statues of, 332–33
  wartime accusations, 288
  wartime taxation positions, 264
  Why War and, 257–58
  Wilson administration lobbying correspondence to, 201–2
La Follette's Weekly Magazine, 148
La Guardia, Fiorello, 294
laissez-faire philosophy, 21–22, 263
La Marca, Giulietta, 224
The Land and the Soldier (FCH), 272–75
land policy
  democracy and peasant proprietorship, 117
  as election platform, 121
  farm colonies, 265–66, 273–75
  imperialism originating from land ownership, 255
  land monopolies, 265
  in Philippines, 428
  privilege and land ownership issues, 92–93, 142
  single tax philosophies as, 67, 110, 115, 116, 143
  tax assessments, 135–36
  writings on, 142, 347
Lane, Franklin K., 272n.68
Lansing, Robert, 250, 283, 285
Lasker, Bruno, 347n.31
law enforcement, 63, 114n.1
Lawrence of Arabia, 282
lawyers, views of, 127
League for Municipal Ownership and Operation, 193, 234
League for Small and Subject Nationalities, 279–80
League of Nations, 286–87
lecture appointments and tours, 102–3, 186, 263, 335, 337, 398–99
Legal Aid Society, 56, 130
Lehlbach, Frederick R., 403
Lehman, Herbert, 380
leisure time, proper use of, 195, 197
lesbian relationships, 370
Leslie, Frank, 369
Leslie Bureau of Suffrage Education, 369
Leslie Woman Suffrage Commission, 369
Le Sueur, Arthur, 317
Lewis, Sinclair, 345
libel lawsuits, 190
liberalism, 398, 444
liberals, term usage, 302
liberty, 398, 399
Lincoln Club, 56, 61, 79
Lindsey, Ben, 129, 163, 197
Link, Arthur S., 231, 434
Lippmann, Walter, 165, 241, 263, 279, 302, 309, 337
Literary Digest reviews, 112, 181, 199n.44, 257n.33
Literary Review reviews, 315–16n.25, 347n.31, 351
literature, subversive, 294
Little Consolidated (Little Con), 70
Liveright, Horace, 346n.27
Lodge, Henry Cabot, 247
Long Arm System Company, 93, 281
Lord, Russell, 409
Lovett, Robert Morss, 351, 383n.17
loyalty oaths, 304
Ludwig of Hesse-Darmstadt, Grand Duke, 346n.27
Lusitania (ship), 218, 248
Lusk, Clayton, 303–4
Lusk Committee, 303–4, 305, 400
luxury taxes, 32
"Lynch Law and the Immigrant Alien" (FCH), 306

MacArthur, Douglas, 423–24, 427–28, 429
MacKay, Kenneth, 331
MacKaye, Percy, 170
Macy, William F., 339–40
Magnes, Judah L., 295
Malone, Dudley Field, 172, 250
Manhattan Democratic organization, 141
Manila (Philippines), 422–30
Manila Hotel, 423, 429
Manly, Basil M., 230, 325, 378–79, 380
Mann Act, 219
Maria (housekeeper), 367
market agreements and codes, 386, 387–88, 406
Markham, Edwin, 170
Marlowe, Julia, 20
"Marriage Customs and Taboo Among the Early Heterodites" (Woolston), 175
marriage of FCH and MJH
  as autobiography subject, 362
  children, 244–45, 367
  commonalities, 372
  courtship, 36, 38–41, 61
  FCH reflection on, 167
  feminism and, 38, 90–91, 166, 364–65, 365–66, 366
  health issues, 366
  loneliness issues, 366–67
  MJH disappointment in, 363, 369
  overview, 432–33
  personality differences, 363, 364, 368, 371–72
  relationships outside, 369–70, 371
  wedding, 91
  women's traditional roles and, 39–40, 94–95
Marsh, Benjamin, 129, 234, 236, 237, 325, 412n.15
Martin, Everett Dean, 344
Marx, Karl, 398, 438
Masses (magazine), 190
Masters, Edgar Lee, 164n.1
Masters, Eliza B. (Lillie), 37
Mather, Flora Stone, 55
Mattson, Kevin, 441–42, 443
McAdoo, William Gibbs, 203–5, 210, 226, 258–59, 269, 270, 330
McAneny, George, 195
McCarthy, Charles, 153, 156–57, 158, 180
McCormick, Joseph Medill, 91, 162
McCormick, Richard L., 434
McCormick, Ruth (Hanna), 91
McCormick, Vance, 259
McCurdy, Allen, 320
McGerr, Michael, 440–41
McGugin, Harold, 402, 403
McKelway, A. J., 260, 261

McKinley, William, 43
McKinnon, W. S., 131
McKisson, Robert S., 43, 51, 53, 71
McNary-Haugen bill, 359
McNutt, Paul, 424
Meadville, Pennsylvania, 4, 5–6, 33. See also Allegheny College
Meadville Portfolio, 38
Meadville Theological School, 38, 86
Means, Gardiner, 384, 413
Mediterranean foreign policies, 280, 281, 283–85
Meeker, Royal, 242
Meiklejohn, Alexander, 242n.57, 344
men compared to women, as reformers, 174
Men's League for Woman Suffrage, 172
Methodist Church, 5, 6
Methodist Federation of Social Service, 324
Mexican Revolution, 227–28
Mexico, 227–28, 250
middle class, 440–41, 442–43
Middle East and Near Middle East, 281–85
Middleton, George, 148, 161, 167n.8
Milholland Boissevain, Inez, 96n.19, 190, 241
militarism, 247–48, 252, 256
Military Intelligence Division, 294–95, 320
Miller, Alice Duer, 175
Misses Masters' Boarding and Day School for Young Ladies and Children, 37
Mitchel, John Purroy, 193, 195–96, 195n.32, 234–35
Mitchell, John, 129
The Modern City and Its Problems (FCH), 237–39
Moley, Raymond, 382
monopolies. See also specific utilities and types of monopolies
  agricultural trade agreements legalizing, 388
  high cost of living due to, 265
  land, 265
  leading to corruption, 72–73, 120
  liberty vs., 107
  presidential campaign issue, 331
  public ownership of natural, 73, 85, 107
  Roosevelt, Franklin, administration and, 398
monotonists, 175
Montgomery, Donald, 385, 412n.15
morality, 25, 34
Morgan, J. P., 182
Morris, Jan, 192
Morris, Phillip, 341
Most, Johann, 22
Mother Earth (magazine), 298
mothers' pensions, 197

motion picture censorship, 183, 187–89, 190–91, 192
Mt. Airy Road, New York, 243
multiculturalism, 209
Municipal Association, 51–54, 65, 70, 78, 104, 123, 134
"The Municipal Character and Achievements of Chicago" (FCH), 77n.27
municipal government. *See also* municipal issues; municipal ownership
  class structure impacting, 82, 106
  corruption issues, 63, 68, 72–73, 82
  self-government issues, 71, 85, 108, 122–23, 241
  Shaw's lectures on, 24
  women in, 108
Municipal Government in Continental Europe (Shaw), 24
Municipal Government in Great Britain (Shaw), 24
municipal issues. *See also* municipal government; municipal ownership
  articles on, 52, 77, 95, 104, 180
  books on, 114–16, 198–99, 237–39 (see also *The City: The Hope for Democracy*)
  as campaign platform, 68
  Cleveland leagues promoting, 51–54, 65, 70, 78, 104, 123, 134
  crime and, 63, 75, 109
  European research and models, 76–77, 98, 115–19, 119, 158, 198–99, 238
  New York City leagues and societies promoting, 33
  population growth, 43, 63, 65, 140
  post-university interest in, 28
  premise of, 77–78
  publications about, 76–77, 104
  reasons for, overview, 63–64
  research bureaus for, 141
  strategies for, 64
  urban development and renewal, 63, 64, 73–75, 109, 110, 186
municipal ownership
  in Britain, 114–15
  criticism of, 115
  of natural monopolies and public utilities, 64, 70–71, 73, 81–82, 85, 107, 134
  in New York City, 193, 234
  writings on, 98, 104, 238
"Municipal Ownership in Great Britain" (FCH), 98
Municipal Traction Company, 82, 94, 133–34
Murdock, Marion E., 86

NAACP (National Association for the Advancement of Colored People), 191, 233, 400
Nantucket. *See* Sconset, Nantucket
Nation
  AAA purge editorial, 411
  articles, 306, 348
  book reviews, 112, 175, 181n.4, 199n.44, 239n.55, 257n.33, 274n.75, 418
  as subversive publication, 400
National Americanization [Day] Committee, 215–16
National American Suffrage Association (NAWSA), 89, 95, 119, 169, 170, 171, 172
National Association for the Advancement of Colored People (NAACP), 191, 233, 400
National Association Opposed to Women Suffrage, 169n.14
National Board of Censorship of Motion Pictures, 183, 190–91
National Civic Federation (NCF), 79, 193–94, 230, 339
National Civil Liberties Bureau raids, 291
National College Equal Suffrage League, 96n.19
National Consumers League, 96
National Home Library Foundation, 397n.53
National Labor Party, 321
National Municipal League, 129
National Municipal Review, 199n.45
National Popular Government League, 400
National Progressive League, 378–80
National Progressive League for Franklin D. Roosevelt, 420
National Progressive Republican League (NPRL), 150–58
National Recovery Administration (NRA), 384, 386, 389, 390, 399
The National Revenues (Adams, ed.), 23
National Security League (NSL), 247–48
National Single Tax League, 122, 236
National Woman's Party (NWP), 170–71
Nation's Business, 314
natural gas, 72
NAWSA (National American Suffrage Association), 89, 95, 119, 169, 170, 171, 172
NCF (National Civic Federation), 79, 193–94, 230, 339
Near East foreign policies, 280, 281, 283–85
Nearing, Scott, 295
"The Negro in New York" (committee), 233
Nestor, Agnes, 325
New Deal administration and agencies. *See also* consumers counsel office

administration employees, descriptions, 386
agricultural legislation and programs, 380–83
brain trust criticism and oppositionist propaganda, 398, 401–5
early blueprints for, 272
liberalism and, 398
progressives and presidential campaign, 378–80
as radical subversive, 400, 407
speeches on, 398–99
support of, 419, 440
New Dealers (term usage), 407
New Idea Woman's Magazine, 165
New Republic, 252–53, 277, 351, 400
New York City
  Chelsea area residence and residents, 164
  child welfare and social centers, 186–87
  description of growth, 140
  East Side/Irish neighborhoods, 34–35
  education reform, 181–86, 189, 194–95
  entertainment censorship, 187–92
  FCH's early years in, 30–35
  FCH's writing in, 179–81
  feminism movement in, 173–74
  Greenwich Village residence, 165
  Howes' move to, 136–39
  immigration reception centers in, 140 (*see also* Ellis Island)
  mayoral campaigns, 195–96, 234–36
  men's clubs of, 192–93
  municipal ownership issues, 193, 234
  population statistics (1910), 140
  social centers, 186–87
  social life in, 165–66, 241–43
  unemployment committees in, 233–34
New York Evening Post reviews, 374
New York Law School, 32
New York Peace Society, 262
New York Social Center Committee, 186
New York State, 140–41, 240–41
New York State Association of Motion Picture Exhibitors, 187
New York State Single Tax League, 236
New York State Woman Suffrage Association, 169
New York Times
  AAA purge editorials, 411
  articles, 289
  Bennet-Howe controversy editorials, 223–24
  book reviews: *The City*, 112; *The Confessions of a Monopolist*, 120–21; *The Confessions of a Reformer*, 352; *Denmark: A Cooperative Commonwealth*, 315–16n.25; *Denmark:*

The Cooperative Way, 418; *European Cities at Work*, 199n.44; *George Sand*, 375; *The High Cost of Living*, 267; *The Intimate Journal of George Sand*, 376; *The Modern City and Its Problems*, 239–40n.55; *The Only Possible Peace*, 280n.10; *Privilege and Democracy in America*, 144; *Revolution and Democracy*, 347–48n.31; *Wisconsin*, 180
  Carnegie Hall meetings reports, 160
  death penalty, letters on, 196
  FCH antiwar position editorials, 247, 251
  IWW detention reports, 292
  journalism employment with, 31
  obituaries, 396
  People's Institute editorials, 189
  prison system, letters on, 196
  Red Scare investigation defense interviews, 298–99
  Russian protest meeting reports and editorials, 295–96
  School of Opinion editorials, 338
  Wirt affair reports, 404
  women's peace parade reviews, 246
New York World's, 374
nickelodeons, 187
Nock, Albert Jay, 317
Non-Partisan League, 317, 318, 321, 324, 325, 347
Norris, George, 360, 378–79
North American Review, 200n45
NPRL (National Progressive Republican League), 150–58
NRA (National Recovery Administration), 384, 386, 389, 390, 399
NSL (National Security League), 247–48
NWP (National Woman's Party), 170

"Of Four Little Lawyers Only One Remains" (article), 125–26
O'Gorman, James, 205–6
Ohio Consumers League, 96–97
Ohio state, 43. *See also* Ohio state senate
Ohio state senate
  bills and legislation, 124–25, 130
  campaigns for, 84, 122–23, 133
  corruption investigations, 131–32
  Democrats of, organization and effectiveness, 123–24, 129–30, 133
  FCH's view of, 132–33
  nominations to, 84, 122, 137
  party affiliations, 123
Old and New (publication), 86, 89n.5
O'Mahoney, Joseph, 430
The Only Possible Peace (FCH), 280

Osborne, Thomas Mott, 197
Outlook, 117, 118, 188, 315n.25, 347–48n.31
Overman, Lee S., 291
Overman Committee, 291, 303, 305
Overstreet, Harry, 338

Paine, Thomas, 95
Palestine, 283
Palmer, A. Mitchell, 299
parades, peace, 246
Paris, France homes, 369
Paris Peace Conference, 277–80, 282–83
Parker, A. W., 299
Parker, A. Warner, 292
Parkhurst, Charles H., 33, 34
parks, 63, 75, 109
Parsons, Mary E., 48, 96
Paul, Alice, 170
pawnbroker interest rates, regulation of, 130–31
peace movements, 246–47, 248–52, 256
peace settlements and conferences, 277–80, 282–85
peace ship expeditions, 249–50
Peek, George, 381, 383, 386, 388–89, 393–94
Pennsylvania Tax Commission, 41
pensions, mothers', 197
People's Church, 183, 186
People's Forum, 182–83, 184, 186, 187, 197
People's Institute
  arts leagues, 187
  censorship boards, 187–89, 190–92
  controversies implicating, 189–90
  director appointments, 181, 183–84
  evaluation of director's position, 200
  founding of, 181–83
  immigrants and, 209
  lecture themes and speakers, 185–86
  organization and directional changes, 184–85
  prison reform supported by, 197
  resignation, 210–11
  social centers, development of, 186–87
  writings during, 197
People's Lobby, 129, 400
People's Music League, 187
Periodical Publishers Association, 161
Perkins, Maxwell, 105, 348, 416–17, 419, 431
Perkins, Van L., 412
Perlman, Selig, 314n.24
Permanent Organization committee, 242
Phi Beta Kappa, 242
Phi Gamma Delta, 11–13, 26, 242
Philippines, 422–30

Pinchot, Amos
  FCH's friendship with, 165, 420
  federal ownership of railroads, 237
  free speech/press speech, 190
  Howes' friendship with, 241
  immigration commissioner appointment, 207
  as industrial committee founding member, 231
  labor party development, 321
  at La Follette's Carnegie Hall meeting, 159, 160
  libel indictment bail, 190
  mayoral candidate endorsements, 235
  Mitchel as mayor, 234
  as presidential nominee contender, 151
  progressive national organization fund-raising contributions, 152
  Richberg correspondence on progressive movement, 360–61
  Roosevelt presidential nomination support, 159, 162
  Russian protest meetings, 295
  School of Opinion seminar speaker, 337
  at suffrage protest trial, 172
  taxation issues, 236
  wartime taxation, 264
  Wilson reelection organization, 259, 260, 261
Pinchot, Gifford
  at La Follette's Carnegie Hall meeting, 160
  as Pennsylvania governor, 327
  as presidential nominee contender, 151
  progressive national organization criticisms, 153–54, 155, 157
  progressive national organization fund-raising contributions, 152
  Roosevelt presidential nomination, 159, 162
Pingree, Hazen S., 64, 76
pink (communist sympathizers) accusations, 340, 341, 344, 394
Pittsburgh, Pennsylvania, 41
Plain Dealer, 79, 91, 138, 144
playgrounds, 63, 75
Plumb, Glenn E., 308
Plumb Plan League, 267–70, 303, 307–12
"The Political and Economic State" (seminar), 337
political parties, development of third, 316–17, 324–26, 328, 333
Political Science Quarterly reviews, 47
The Political Science Quarterly reviews, 144, 199n.44
population statistics, urban, 43, 63, 65, 140
Portland, Oregon, 440

Porto Rico secretarial appointments, 79n.33
Post, Louis F.
  alien arrests and deportation, 299–300
  autobiography reviews by, 351
  Caminetti and, 213
  Cosmos Club membership nominations by, 242
  directorship endorsements by, 183
  immigration commissioner appointments, 206, 207
  as labor department assistant secretary, 212
  as newspaper editor, 85, 129, 212
  reconstruction proposals, 271
Pound, Roscoe, 337
poverty. *See also* class structure
  charitable organizations, 54, 59–61, 97, 130
  slums and urban development, 64, 74, 109, 110
  solutions to, 182, 198
  unemployment and, 131, 196–98, 216, 233–34
"practical idealists," 55
preparedness movement, 247–53, 256, 262
Prescott, Anson W., 157
presidential campaigns
  1912, 151–53, 159–63
  1916, 229, 258–61
  1924, 321, 329–32, 330
  1928, 359–61
  1932, 378–80
  1936, 419–20
Pressman, Lee, 385, 386, 408
pricing, fair, 387, 389, 391
prison system, 109, 130, 196–97
privilege
  breakdown of, 119
  British cities and, 116
  categories of wealth, 92
  civilization as struggle between liberty and, 106
  definition of, 115
  economic *vs.* home comparisons, 167
  FCH's view of, 77, 115, 142–44
  Johnson's, Tom, view of, 77, 84
  keys to wealth, 92–93, 120
  solutions to, 67, 77, 143
  as Stimson's campaign platform, 146–47
  war contributing to, 253, 255–58
  writings on, 119–20, 142–44, 145–46, 159, 251, 346–47
Privilege and Democracy in America (FCH), 142–44, 145–46, 159, 251
probation officers, 75
Producers of Wealth Unite: Use Your Ballot for a Better America (FCH), 327n.46

professorships, 102
Progress and Poverty (George), 66, 69
Progressive National Executive Committee, 358
Progressive Party, 163, 195–96, 231–32, 321, 329–31
Progressivism, overview
  class distinctions and, 440–42
  FCH on, 129
  national organizations for Franklin D. Roosevelt, 420
  nonpartisan national organizations, 149–50, 159–60, 378–79
  political parties representing, 163, 195–96, 231–32, 321, 329–31
  Republican national organizations, 150–58
  Richberg on fear and, 360–61
  in 1920s, 302–3
prohibition, 240
The Promise of American Life (Croly), 112n.58
prostitutes, 219, 223, 298
protests, suffrage, 171–72
Provisional National Single Tax Commission, 236
P.S. 63, 186–87
The Public, 85, 129, 199n.44, 212, 268
public buildings, 73–74
public ownership. *See also* municipal ownership
  criticism of, 311
  federal, of railroads, 237, 267–70, 303, 307–12
  organizations supporting, 320
  overview, 438
public works programs, 131

Quarterly (fraternity journal), 12, 20
Quay, Matthew, 5–6
Quezon, Manuel, 422–23, 424–25, 427, 429
Quinlan, Patrick, 217

racial equity, 233, 439
Radical Division (Department of Justice), 305, 306, 320
radicalism, 287–91, 355–58. *See also* Red Scare
radio programs, 390–91
raids, 303–4
Railroad Administration, 270
railroad companies, 220–21, 237, 267–70, 303, 307–12
"The Railroads, the Public and Labor under the Plumb Plan" (FCH), 310
railways, street
  controversy over, as class struggle, 82
  fare box inventions, 81
  fares, 52, 67, 81–82, 133–34

railways, street (*continued*)
  holding companies for, 82, 83
  Municipal Association's pamphlet controversies, 52–53
  as natural monopoly, 64–65
  private *vs.* franchise ownership, 70–71, 81–82, 134
  urban growth and, 64
Raker, J. E., 298, 299
Rand, James H., Jr., 401
Rand School, 204, 295
Raskob, John J., 359
Rawleigh, W. T., 329, 361n.55
Ray, Frank P., 36
real estate assessment laws bills, 124
reconstruction, 270–72
Record, George, 236, 237
Red Devil (automobile), 83
Red Hill community, 243
The Red Network (Dilling), 399–401
Red Scare
  AAA internal conflicts and accusations, 388, 393–94
  alien arrests, detention and deportation, 291–92, 298, 299
  as betrayal of American freedom, 300–301
  books identifying radical subversives, 399–401
  consumer advocacy *vs.* industry accusations, 399
  dissent as disloyalty, 287–93
  government agency investigations, 305
  investigative committees and activities, 297–99, 303–4, 305
  labor unions as radical subversives, 292–93
  legislation supporting, 288, 304
  pro-Bolshevik accusations, 295–96
  School of Opinion criticism, 339–41, 344
  surveillance of subversive suspects, 294–95, 320
  Wirt affair, 401–5
"Reform, Leadership, and Christian Socialism" (MJH), 89
resistants, 175
retrenchment, 218
Retsforbundet (Justice Party), 121
Revenue Act, 236, 264
Review of Reviews reviews, 199
Revolution and Democracy (FCH), 346
Richberg, Donald, 360, 378, 404
Ridgway, E. J., 125
Ridgway's Weekly (magazine), 125, 126, 127–28
"The Right to Her Name" (meeting theme), 169

Roberts, George E., 314n.23
Robert Schalkenbach Foundation to Promote the Economics of Henry George, 399
Rockefeller, John D., 182
Rodgers, Daniel T., 444
Roe, Gilbert, 162, 190, 329
Roosevelt, Alice, 91
Roosevelt, Eleanor, 397, 419, 420, 423, 424, 429
Roosevelt, Franklin D. *See also* New Deal administration and agencies
  AAA internal relationships issues, 394
  FCH communications with, 397, 416, 419–20, 423
  presidential campaign and election, 378–80
  support of, 419
Roosevelt, Theodore
  at FCH/MJH wedding, 91
  Garfield, James, appointments, 99–100
  Garfield, James, as connection to, 129
  gubernatorial nominations of, 145, 146
  national progressive organization memberships, 151
  as presidential candidate contender, 151–52, 160–61, 162
  Republican state convention chairman, 144–45
  Wilson presidential endorsement, 258
  WWI preparedness movement, 247
Root, Elihu, 247, 277
Ross, Edward A., 26n.11, 30, 103, 111, 218
Rudolph, Max, 126
rural tenancy, 422, 425, 428
Russell, Charles Edward, 277
Russia, 276–77, 283, 290, 295–96, 346–47. *See also* Red Scare

Safford, Mary, 86, 88, 97, 372n.26
Sakdalista, 425
saloons, 33–34, 63
Sand, George, biographies about, 364, 369, 370, 370n.22, 373–76
Sanderson, Edward F., 211
Saturday Review of Literature reviews, 352
Saul, George F., 36
Schermerhorn, Elizabeth W., 375
Schlesinger, Arthur, Jr., 404
School Inquiry Committee, 194
School of Opinion
  discrimination incidents, 342
  editorials and reviews on, 338
  lectures and seminars, 337–39, 342, 343–45
  MJH's involvement at, 369
  music and dance programs, 342–43, 345
  proposal and development, 336

radicalism accusations, 339–41
student costs, 337
Schwarz, Judith, 175, 363
Sconset, Nantucket, properties. *See also* School of Opinion
  discrimination issues, 342
  foreclosure of, 377
  meeting and lecture halls at, 336, 342, 343
  property purchase and development, 335–226
  summer home at, 94, 99, 136, 138, 244
  town history and description, 335
Scott, Lester F., 183
Scribners, 94
Sedition Act, 288
self-determination, 279–80, 283, 286, 321–22
senate campaigns, 124–25, 130, 327
settlement houses, 54–59, 61, 79, 214, 248
The Seven Strings of the Lyre: The Romantic Life of George Sand (Schermerhorn), 375
Shadow Edge (Harmon home), 243–44, 377, 384, 395–96
"A Shameless Appointment" (Walsh), 400
sharecropper disputes, 406–7
Shaw, Albert, 23–24, 76, 324
Shea, Francis, 407, 408
shelters, homeless, 216
Sherman, Lawrence, 290
Shotwell, James T., 282, 285
Simkhovitch, Mary, 220
Singer, Caroline, 176
single-tax movement
  in Britain, 116
  conferences for, 179
  financial contributions to, 179
  land monopolies and, 265
  as municipal reform solution, 110
  organizations supporting, 236, 320
  overview, 436–38
  Philippines and, 428
  support for, 66, 69, 77, 85, 121–22, 129
  writings on, 122, 348
Sing Sing, 196–97
Six-Power Consortium, 228
Sixteenth Amendment, 236
Slivowitz punch, 49
slums, 64, 74, 109, 110
Smith, Alfred E., 304, 327, 359–60, 378
Smith, Charles Sprague, 182–83, 184–85, 186, 187–88
social centers, 186–87, 189
Social Gospel movement, 22, 54
socialism
  European models of, 117, 118, 253

MJH support of, 39, 89
  municipal, as criticism, 115
  public ownership as, 311
  schools denounced as experiments in, 339–40
  as solution for privilege, 143
  as subversive behavior, 290, 304
Socialist Party, 204, 324, 325, 328
Socialized Germany (FCH), 253, 290
Social Problems (George), 66
social problem study organizations, 59
Social Security Act, 386
social settlement movement, 54–59, 61, 79, 214, 248
social workers, and wartime activities, 248
Society for the Prevention of Crime, 33
Society to Recapture the Subway, 234
"Some Possible Reforms in State and Local Taxation" (FCH), 76n.25
Somers, W. A., 135
Spargo, John, 316–17
Springborn, William J., 70
St. Raphael Society for Italian Immigrants, 224
Stackpole, Edouard, 341, 343–45
steamship companies, 220–21
Stedman, Alfred D., 409
Steffens, Lincoln
  as ambassador candidate, 228
  at authors' suffrage meeting, 170
  autobiography of, 349n.35, 362, 368, 373
  death of, 422
  FCH as single-tax supporter, 437
  FCH correspondence to, 99, 136, 419
  FCH's autobiography review, 353–54, 362
  FCH's friendship with, 92, 165, 241, 420, 421–22
  free speech/press speaker, 190
  Johnson's, Tom, friendship with, 80–81, 83, 84n.43, 84n.45
  MJH correspondence to, 349n.35, 368, 373, 378, 391, 395
  MJH's friendship with, 165, 243, 368, 369, 371
  MJH's suffrage district, 168
  MJH's writing abilities, 372–73
  peace conference appointment, 282
  presidential elections, 332
  during prosperity decade (1920s), 302
  Red Scare, 301
  Russiam visit, 277
  Sconset plans, 336–37
  single-tax commission member, 179
  war aims and peace terms, 277
  watchdog group memberships, 129
Wirt affair, 404

Sterne, Maurice, 166
Stevens, Doris, 174
Stevenson, Adlai, 386
Stevenson, Archibald E., 290–91, 303, 400n.57
Stimson, Henry L., 145–47, 181
Stockwell bill, 124
Stone, Carlos M., 53
Stone, Warren, 313, 314–15n.24, 325
strikes, labor, 133, 237, 267
Strunsky, Simeon, 352
suburban growth, 64
subversives, radical, 287–91, 355–58. *See also* Red Scare
subway systems, 140, 193, 234
suffrage, woman. *See also* feminism
 authors' meetings for, 170
 bequeaths supporting, 369
 constitutional amendment fight, 170–71
 in Europe, 119
 FCH's views on, 108, 167, 172–73
 Johnson's, Tom, conversion, 96
 men's leagues and parades for, 172
 MJH's involvement, 38, 89, 95–96, 168–73, 366
 national organizations for, 89, 95, 119, 169, 170, 171, 172
 political parties for, 168–69
 state constitutional revisions on, 240
 state organizations for, 169
 White House protests and arrests, 171
Sullivan, Mark, 129
Supreme Court, 420
surveillance, government, 294–95, 320
Survey
 articles, 442
 book reviews, 181, 199n.44, 274n.75, 315–16n.25, 347, 354–55
 School of Opinion report, 338
 as subversive publication, 400
 symposiums, 355–58
Switzerland, 117, 118, 119
Symphony Orchestra of the Cloak and Suit Makers' Union, 187
Syria (Mediterranean territory), 283–85

Taft, Philip, 314n.24
Taft, William Howard, 82, 100, 133, 147, 151, 152–53, 229
Tammany Hall, 33, 141, 168, 210
Tarbell, Ida M.
 autobiographical references, 432
 books by, 5n.3
 career, 5, 18
 FCH friendship with, 18, 148

honorary degrees, 242n.57
peace conference attendance of, 282
prewar radicals symposium contributions, 356, 357
tariffs, 76
Tavern on the Moors, 336, 342, 343
taxation. *See also* single-tax movement
 constitutional amendments on, 236
 franchise taxes, 76, 124, 130
 inequity issues, 236
 internal revenue system publications, 22, 27, 32, 46–47, 75–76, 204
 land assessments and Somers system, 134–36
 in Philippines, 428
 wartime, 263–64
Taxation in the United States Under the Internal Revenue System (FCH), 46–47, 204
Tax Commission, 136
Taylor, Mary, 385, 386, 391, 397, 402, 412n.15
Taylor Hose Company No. 1, 7
Temporary National Economic Committee (TNEC), 430–31
"tennis cabinet," 100n.26
tent meetings, 83
textile pricing, 389–90
theater, 6–7, 20
Third National Conference on City Planning, 180
Thomas, Norman, 337, 378
Thomas Paine National Historical Association, 95
Thompson, Dorothy, 344–45
Time magazine, 404
Times Literary Supplement reviews, 375
Times-Press reviews, 392
TNEC (Temporary National Economic Committee), 430–31
Tobin, Eugene M., 2
Todd, Laurence, 402
Toledo, Ohio, 64
Town Hall Club, 243
Toynbee Hall, 54
Trading with the Enemy Act, 288
transportation, 63–64, 140, 193, 220–21, 234. *See also* railroad companies; railways, street
treaties, secret, 277, 283
Trevor, John B., 295
Tucker, Cynthia, 363, 372n.24, 372n.26
Tuckerman, Lawrence Bryant, 60
Tugwell, Grace, 397, 413
Tugwell, Rexford Guy
 AAA internal conflicts and, 389, 393, 406
 book review by, 352

consumers counsel, formation of, 381–82, 384, 385
  Fairfax County visits, 397
  on industry vs. consumer groups, 399
  New Deal appointment, 386
  special adviser reports written for, 416
  Wirt affair and, 402, 403, 404–5
Tumulty, Joseph P., 202, 203, 226, 270–71
Turner, Edward Raymond, 257n.33
Twain, Mark, 129
Tydings-McDuffie Act, 422

Uhl, Byron, 217, 292, 298
unemployment, 131, 196–98, 216, 233–34
Union League Club, 291, 303
Union of Russian Peasant Workers of America, 292
Unitarian church, 6
University of Wisconsin, 103, 288
upper classes, 441, 442
urban population statistics, 43, 63, 65, 140
urban reform. *See* municipal issues
urban spread, 63–64

Valera, Eamon de, 321
Varady, Roysi, 342
varietists, 175
A Victorian in the Modern World (Hapgood), 363–65
Vida (Irwin's sister), 371
Villa, Francisco "Pancho," 227
Villard, Oswald Garrison
  Fairfax County visits, 397
  FCH's friendship with, 421
  Irish self-determination committees of, 322, 324
  presidential candidate choice (1924), 329–30
  as seminar speaker, 337
  war preparedness proposals correspondence to, 252
Visiting Nurse Association, 75
Vorse, Mary Heaton, 174
voting pamphlets, 327n.46
voting rights. *See* suffrage, woman
Vrooman, Carl, 289

Wald, Lillian, 220, 247, 248
Walker, Francis, 47
Walker, Iris, 385
Wallace, Henry
  AAA administrator selection, 381
  AAA focus, views on, 406
  AAA internal conflicts and purge, 394, 409–10

consumers counsel appointment selection, 382–83
farm labor disputes, 408
Philippines correspondence to, 423, 424, 429
on Progressive League's success, 380n.9
Walsh, Francis Ralston, 400n.57
Walsh, Frank, 172, 215, 230–32, 252, 337, 359, 378–79
"The War Aims and Peace Terms It Suggests" (the Inquiry), 279
Warbasse, Agnes, 233–34
Ward, Lester, 107, 108n.45
Ware, Caroline, 386, 413
War Industries Board, 275
War Labor Policies Board, 272
Warner, Hoyt Landon, 114n.1
wartime policies. *See* World War I
Washington, D. C., 384, 395
Washington Post, 411
Watchorn, Robert, 226
water companies, 94
water cures, 98–99
Wayside (home), 243
wealth, 92–93, 115, 120. *See also* class structure; privilege
Westenhaver, David, 45–46, 126, 126n.30
Western Reserve University, 103
Westervelt, William I., 402, 403–4
"What Feminism Means to Me" (meeting theme), 169
What the Ballot Will Do for Women and for Men (FCH pamphlet), 172
Wheeler, Burton K., 329
Wheeler, David H., 14–15
"Where Are the Pre-War Radicals?" (article and symposium), 355–58, 442
"Where Are the Pre-War Radicals? A Rejoinder" (article), 442
Whipple, Leon, 352, 355
White, Henry, 285
White, William Allen, 151, 162, 282, 302, 309, 413
"White City," 73–74
White House, suffrage demonstrations at, 171
White labels, 96
White Lists, 96
White Slave Traffic Act, 219
Whitlock, Brand
  as ambassador candidate, 228
  on FCH as state senator, description, 132
  FCH's friendship with, 92
  marriage discussion in autobiography, 362
  presidential candidate choice (1912), 163
  privilege correspondence to, 119

Whitlock, Brand (*continued*)
  during Red Scare, 302
  as single-tax supporter, 129
  as Toledo mayor, 64
Whitman, Charles, 195
Why I Do Not Believe in Censorship of Motion Pictures (FCH pamphlet), 192
"Why I Want Woman Suffrage" (FCH), 172
Why War (FCH), 255–58, 290
"Why Women Do Not Vote" (MJH), 89
Wiebe, Robert, 3
Wilhelm II, Kaiser of Germany, 118n.11
William Palmer (fictional character), 119–20
Williams, Charles D., 231
Willoughby, Westel Woodbury, 26n.11, 27, 28
"Will the League of Nations Benefit Labor" (debate topic), 295
Wilson, William B., 205, 212, 220, 271, 292, 293, 299
Wilson, William L., 57
Wilson, Woodrow
  books dedicated to, 256
  Democratic platform proposal, 229
  farm colonies position, 275
  FCH relationship with, 25–26, 205, 225, 226
  foreign policies correspondence to, 281
  Fourteen Points address, 279, 286
  international policies, 227–28
  meetings with, descriptions, 286
  Mexican peace settlement appointments, 250–51
  as Moses, 282–83
  New York City mayoral race position, 235
  peacemaking foreign policies, 286–87
  personality and description, 25, 287
  presidential nomination and campaign, 162–63
  railroad reform, 268, 269–70
  reelection campaign, 258–61
  as role model, 25
  Russian commission, 277
  service lobbying and commissioner appointments, 201–3, 205–9
  suffrage amendment and opposition to, 171
  suffrage protester pardons, 172
  Supreme Court nominees, 232
  university appointments by, 100–101
  as university visiting lecturer, 24–25, 24–26
  wartime policies and programs, 246, 248–49, 258
Wilson Volunteers, 259–61
Winter, Ella
  antifascist committee secretary, 383n.17
  Hapgood autobiography, 363, 365
  on MJH and Steffens's mutual writing support, 373
  MJH correspondence to, 362, 368, 372
  Steffens's death, 422
Wirt, William A., 185, 401–5
Wisconsin: An Experiment in Democracy (FCH), 180–81
Wisconsin Loyalty League, 288
Wise, Stephen, 237, 259, 260
Witt, Nathan, 385
Witt, Peter, 59
Wittenstein, Kate E., 363
Wobblies (Industrial Workers of the World), 292, 293, 304
Woman Citizen (magazine), 369
Woman's Journal reviews, 375
Woman's Parade Committee, 246
Woman's Party's Committee of Contributing Editors, 370
Woman's Peace Party (WPP), 246–47
Woman Suffrage Party (WSP), 168–69
Women and Economics (Gilman), 88
"Women and Economics" (MJH), 88
women compared to men, as reformers, 174
Women's City Club, 243
women's issues. *See also* feminism; suffrage, woman
  antiwar/peace demonstrations, 246
  economic independence, 88
  employment conditions, 96
  in Europe, 119
  first female lawyers, 37
  hospital conditions, 97
  mothers' pensions, 197
  societal roles and expectations, 39–40, 94–95
  urban reform, 108
"Women's Municipal Vote" (MJH), 95
Wooblies (Industrial Workers of the World), 292
Wood, Leonard, 247
Woolley, Robert W., 259
Woolston, Florence Guy, 175
work, right to, 196–97
work day hours, 96–97, 237
working classes, 441
work week, 96–97
World's Fair (1904), 77
"World's Fair at St. Louis" (FCH), 77
World's Work, 76–77, 104
World War I
  antiwar *vs.* preparedness movements, 246–53, 256, 262
  causes of, 256, 276

dissent as disloyalty, 287–92
economic reform movements, 263
enemy alien internments, 262–63
immigrant during, 218, 249
personal finances affected by, 264n.49
promoting privilege, 255–58, 290
public information committee, 287–88
railroad crises and reforms, 267–70
reconstruction reforms, 270–75
taxation reform movements, 263–64

U.S. entry into, 262
war aims and peace settlements, 277–80
Wilson's policies during, 246, 248–49, 262

Yale Review reviews, 351
Young, Art, 190, 378
Young, Rose, 369–70

Zahn, Anita, 343, 345

www.ingramcontent.com/pod-product-compliance
Lightning Source LLC
Chambersburg PA
CBHW020300010526
44108CB00037B/171